Civil Religion

A Dialogue in the History of Political Philosophy

Civil Religion offers philosophical commentaries on more than twenty thinkers stretching from the sixteenth to the twentieth centuries. The book examines four important traditions within the history of modern political philosophy and delves into how each of them addresses the problem of religion. Two of these traditions pursue projects of domesticating religion. The civil-religion tradition, principally defined by Machiavelli, Hobbes, and Rousseau, seeks to domesticate religion by putting it solidly in the service of politics. The liberal tradition pursues an alternative strategy of domestication by seeking to put as much distance as possible between religion and politics. Modern theocracy is a militant reaction against liberalism, and it reverses the relationship of subordination asserted by civil religion: It puts politics directly in the service of religion. Finally, a fourth tradition is defined by Nietzsche and Heidegger. Aspects of their thought are not just modern but hypermodern, yet they manifest an often-hysterical reaction against liberalism that is fundamentally shared with the theocratic tradition. Together, these four traditions compose a vital dialogue that carries us to the heart of political philosophy itself.

Ronald Beiner is a professor of political science at the University of Toronto and a Fellow of the Royal Society of Canada. He has edited Hannah Arendt's *Lectures on Kant's Political Philosophy*; his other books include *Political Judgment*; *What's the Matter with Liberalism?* (winner of the Canadian Political Science Association's 1994 Macpherson Prize); *Philosophy in a Time of Lost Spirit*; and *Liberalism, Nationalism, Citizenship*.

D0770893

Civil Religion

A Dialogue in the History of Political Philosophy

RONALD BEINER
University of Toronto

CAMBRIDGE
UNIVERSITY PRESS

CAMBRIDGE UNIVERSITY PRESS
Cambridge, New York, Melbourne, Madrid, Cape Town, Singapore,
São Paulo, Delhi, Dubai, Tokyo, Mexico City

Cambridge University Press
32 Avenue of the Americas, New York, NY 10013-2473, USA

www.cambridge.org
Information on this title: www.cambridge.org/9780521738439

First published 2011

Printed in the United States of America

A catalog record for this publication is available from the British Library.

Library of Congress Cataloging in Publication data

Beiner, Ronald, 1953–
Civil religion : a dialogue in the history of political philosophy / Ronald Beiner.
    p. cm.
Includes bibliographical references and index.
ISBN 978-0-521-50636-6 (hardback) – ISBN 978-0-521-73843-9 (pbk.)
1. Political science – History.   2. Political science – Philosophy – History.   I. Title.
JA81.B35   2010
320.01 – dc22   2010015173

ISBN 978-0-521-50636-6 Hardback
ISBN 978-0-521-73843-9 Paperback

For Rebecca,
who reads these books quite differently

For it seems to him now that there are but a handful of stories in the world; and if the young are to be forbidden to prey upon the old then they must sit for ever in silence.

– J. M. Coetzee, Nobel Lecture ("He and his man")

Contents

Preface and Acknowledgments

[T]he style of dialogue and conversation ... carries us, in a manner, into company; and unites the two greatest and purest pleasures of human life, study and society.

– David Hume[1]

Texts that are inertly of their time stay there: those which brush up unstintingly against historical constraints are the ones we keep with us, generation after generation.

– Edward Said[2]

Great thinkers tend to be full of surprises. Marvelous surprises come to light as political philosophers in the Western tradition confront the political challenge of religion: Machiavelli celebrates St. Francis of Assisi. Hobbes, who places a more radical emphasis upon individual self-preservation than any other thinker, extols the practice of Christian martyrdom. Rousseau, the great champion of republican freedom, praises the politics of Islam. Nietzsche, who is famous for his pronouncement that "God is dead," is, according to the political structure of his argument, an emphatic theist. All of these thinkers, notwithstanding the fact that they have contributed to the radical secularization of modern politics, express not a little sympathy for some manner of theocracy.

The purpose of this book is to present a dialogue in the history of political philosophy. Political philosophy as a form of intellectual activity of course began historically with Socratic–Platonic dialogue. It can be argued that, for it to subsist as a living intellectual activity, political philosophy must continue to be a dialogical enterprise (and indeed, it is hard to imagine how political philosophy could be conceived otherwise). What is of interest to me here is

[1] David Hume, "Dialogues Concerning Natural Religion" in *Writings on Religion*, ed. Anthony Flew (La Salle, IL: Open Court, 1992), p. 186.
[2] Edward W. Said, *Freud and the Non-European* (London: Verso, 2003), pp. 26–27.

a dialogue between leading figures in the history of modern political philosophy concerning the relationship between politics and religion. In some cases, interlocutors in this dialogue are consciously aware of other interlocutors; in other cases, I have reconstructed the dialogue *as if* the interlocutors were consciously addressing each other's arguments. I start the dialogue in the middle, as it were, for reasons that are more or less evident. The term "civil religion" (*religion civile*) itself owes its prominence in the history of political philosophy to an immensely powerful thirty-five-paragraph chapter at the end of Rousseau's masterpiece, *Du Contrat Social*. I treat this chapter by Rousseau as the center of gravity of the ambitious set of debates between political philosophers on the topic of religion and politics, and I treat the civil-religion question itself as a gateway to political philosophy as a distinct and uniquely ambitious form of intellectual activity.

To present this study as participating in a continuing dialogue among leading thinkers in the Western tradition is already to take sides in methodological controversies about how to read and interpret the exemplary texts that compose this tradition. For a historicist–contextualist approach to these texts is in principle much less equipped to engage these texts in a directly dialogical way, for the simple reason that if historical context is decisive, then differences of historical context will block the possibility of Platonic-style dialogue *between* the thinkers who concern us, and the same will apply to the possibility of such dialogue between *us* and *them*.[3] To engage the problem of civil religion in a philosophical–dialogical way, one must treat the partners in this conversation (including ourselves) *as if* we were contemporaries living in the same time or living in some space of intellectual exchange beyond time. Perhaps this requires an act of intellectual abstraction, or maybe it requires a deliberately self-imposed historical naïveté, so to speak. Either way, one must believe that there exists some possibility of conducting an intellectual inquiry in a way that transcends differences of historical context to pursue the kind of dialogically motivated political philosophy proposed here.[4]

Richard Tuck gives us quite a sharp articulation of what is at issue between textualism and contextualism when he opens his little book on Hobbes with the following partisan statement on behalf of the contextualist view:

It is sometimes tempting to think that the heroes of the various histories of philosophy or ethics – men as different as St Thomas Aquinas, Machiavelli, Luther, Hobbes, Kant, or Hegel – were all in some sense engaged on a common enterprise, and would have recognized one another as fellow workers. But a moment's reflection reminds us that it is we who have made a unity of their task: from their own point of view, they belonged

[3] For some reflections in a similar vein, see Jeremy Waldron, *God, Locke, and Equality* (Cambridge: Cambridge University Press, 2002), chapter 1.

[4] Leo Strauss has captured the spirit of this enterprise in a characteristically memorable epigram: "The flight to immortality requires an extreme discretion in the selection of one's luggage." See Strauss, *Persecution and the Art of Writing* (Chicago: University of Chicago Press, 1988), p. 160.

to very different ways of living and had very different tasks to perform. They would have seen themselves as intellectually kin to men who do not figure in these lists – priests or scholars who had on the face of it no great philosophical interest.[5]

We can concede to Tuck that there may be a certain dogmatism in the notion that thinkers of Hobbes's stature are *only* interested in conversing with thinkers of equal stature across the ages. However, there is certainly no less dogmatism in Tuck's assurance that, "from their own point of view," such thinkers are only interested in conversing with their contemporaries. There is no lack of examples in the history of political philosophy of great thinkers who take themselves to be pursuing, among other things, a conversation with philosophers of other centuries (Machiavelli and Livy; Hobbes and Aristotle; Spinoza and Maimonides; Rousseau and Machiavelli; Nietzsche and Plato). The chapters that follow try to highlight some of these transhistorical conversations.[6]

Hobbes actually offers a nice illustration of the interplay of text (universalism) and context (historicism) in the practice of political theory. Hobbes took his principles of civil life to have universal validity, and he presented them as such; therefore one is only being faithful to the nature of Hobbes's enterprise as he understood it insofar as one considers these principles on the plane of universal validity (in competition with alternative theories throughout the history

---

[5] Richard Tuck, *Hobbes* (Oxford: Oxford University Press, 1989), p. 1. For a nice encapsulation of the "de-canonizing" (or canon-busting) impulse behind the Cambridge School, see Emile Perreau-Saussine, "Quentin Skinner in Context," *The Review of Politics* 69 (2007), pp. 106–111, particularly the story of the conversation between Peter Laslett and Quentin Skinner related on p. 107.

[6] I do not mean to deny that important insights can be obtained by means of a contextualist–historicist approach, nor is it necessary to deny this. I am simply making clear that in constructing this work as I have, I have embraced a strongly textualist approach to the political philosophy canon. It is quite possible to hold a kind of "dual legitimacy" view according to which both textualist and contextualist approaches can be sources of valuable insights into the relevant texts, notwithstanding their radically different methods of inquiry; that is, each can be an independent source of legitimate insights. J. G. A. Pocock argued along these lines in "The Historian and the Political Theorist," a lecture delivered at a conference on "Citizenship, Conscience and Political Education" on July 31, 2000, in Quebec City – an argument that struck me as quite persuasive. Pocock's suggestion is that "[t]heorist and historian ought not to be in an antagonistic relation, but in one where information and validation can be exchanged." There is considerable magnanimity in this hand of friendship extended by the historian to the theorist, and it is a gesture that the theorist has no reason not to reciprocate (cf., for instance, Waldron, *God, Locke, and Equality*, p. 11). See also Ian Ward, "Helping the Dead Speak: Leo Strauss, Quentin Skinner and the Arts of Interpretation in Political Thought," *Polity*, Vol. 41, Issue 2 (April 2009): 235–255, which argues – convincingly – for a division of labor between historicist and transhistorical approaches to the history of political thought. It should also be made clear that although Tuck is fully committed to a historicist reading of Hobbes, his approach to political theory is *not* through-and-through historicist – for Tuck believes that Hobbes's way of responding to moral skepticism remains importantly relevant to contemporary thinking. So although he privileges a contextualist interpretation over other interpretations, it is important to appreciate that it does not follow from Tuck's view that Hobbes's philosophy speaks only to Hobbes's own contemporaries. I pursue my challenge to Tuck in somewhat greater detail in a forthcoming essay entitled "'Textualism': An Anti-Methodology."

of political philosophy). However, there is no question that Hobbes's articulation of his civil vision was given the specific kind of urgency it had in relation to a crisis of political legitimacy in a particular time and place. It is surely no accident that the key works of Hobbes's political philosophy come to be unfolded between 1640 and 1651, and one should not be indifferent to this context in trying to understand his theoretical purposes. (Hobbes himself properly highlights this context when he writes, in the last paragraph of *Leviathan*, that his "[d]iscourse [was] occasioned by the disorders of the present time.") Many of the thinkers in this book, including Hobbes, wrote passionate responses to their contemporary critics, so they were obviously acutely attuned to the views of their contemporaries; but all of these thinkers were equally committed to philosophical dialogue with their interlocutors throughout the history of political philosophy, and therefore no less attuned to the questions of enduring validity that were at stake in these transhistorical debates. One should not attempt to persuade historians to become philosophers, nor attempt to persuade philosophers to become historians. Each should get on with his or her own job and contribute what they are able to contribute by way of illuminating works of political philosophy. Each of these approaches will be a source of essential insights, and neither should be slighted in favor of the other.

Therefore, although I do not intend to assert an intellectual monopoly for my own side of the debate, it should be clear that the approach adopted in this book is resolutely textualist – self-consciously and unapologetically so. That is, we find ourselves preoccupied with a more or less determinate set of privileged texts, and ask these questions: What's going on in these texts? What discursive games are they playing? What inner tensions and paradoxes do they exemplify? How do these texts engage and challenge *each other* – through implicit and explicit reciprocal dialogue? This last question is especially important, for without mutual dialogue between the texts, one would have manifestations of intellectual activity but not genuine political philosophy in the full sense. Political philosophy is dialogical in its essence, which is why the tradition of philosophical inquiry addressed in this book finds its origin in the dialogical work of Plato.[7] My way of doing political theory in this book is deliberately old-fashioned. In privileging certain texts, I am affirming that there is a canon of great thinkers, and that it is by inserting ourselves into the dialogue between these thinkers that we have the best chance of participating

---

[7] Much recent political theory has revolved around the axis of "deliberative" political theory versus "agonistic" political theory – that is, politics as dialogue versus politics as struggle. It can be freely conceded that there is an important agonistic dimension to the form of intellectual life that is political philosophy. In my view, the agonal process of political philosophy should be conducted in the spirit of a chess game: Yes, one wants to prevail intellectually over the other, but this does not exclude a form of real dialogue. The agon should be conducted in a way that is friendly, good spirited, and open to learning what the other has to teach. It is never a one-way street, never simply a matter of trouncing an opponent. In short, the agon that is political theory is always also dialogical.

in an aspired-to "conversation of [hu]mankind."[8] The classic articulation of the conception of theory practiced in this book is Machiavelli's description of his conversation with the ancients in his famous letter to Vettori of December 10, 1513,[9] and the chapters that follow presume that a conversation with the moderns (among whom Machiavelli himself is, of course, one of the most preeminent figures) is no less worthy of "regal and courtly garments" than Machiavelli's own conversation with the ancients.

"There are but a handful of stories in the world." That is, the great figures in the political philosophy tradition continually revolve around the same perennial issues and maintain among themselves a perennial mutual dialogue. If that is not a vindication of political philosophy as an intellectual discipline, then I do not know what is. The purpose of this book is to sketch a unified trajectory of philosophical reflection and debate from Machiavelli to John Rawls, via Bayle, Spinoza, Maistre, Tocqueville, and Schmitt. If, on one hand, political philosophy really exists as a coherent intellectual tradition, then it should in principle be possible to define shared problems and common concerns (although different and even radically opposed responses) within this tradition. On the other hand, perhaps the history of political philosophy is, in fact, a pseudo-tradition, offering only the appearance of meaningful dialogue, the reality of which it fails to vindicate. We cannot know which of these two propositions is true without actually gathering together the putative dialogue partners within this tradition and seeing what comes out of their arguments and counterarguments. That is what this book attempts to do.[10]

---

[8] The phrase was given currency by Oakeshott, but he borrowed it from Hobbes (*Leviathan*, chapter 15).

[9] Niccolò Machiavelli, *The Prince*, trans. Harvey C. Mansfield, 2nd ed. (Chicago: University of Chicago Press, 1998), pp. 109–110. Cf. the dream Machiavelli supposedly told on his deathbed according to which he would rather go to hell discussing politics with the likes of Plato, Plutarch, and Tacitus than go to paradise with Christian paupers. The dream is related in Roberto Ridolfi, *The Life of Niccolò Machiavelli*, trans. Cecil Grayson (London: Routledge & Kegan Paul, 1963), pp. 249–250. It should be added that Machiavelli's dream of a conversation in hell with Plato and Plutarch is itself a mirroring of Socrates' image of a philosophical conversation in Hades with the heroes and demigods of the past (*Apology* 41a–c). Rousseau's version of this perennial trope is a dialogue between Moses, Lycurgus, Solon, and Numa: See *The Collected Writings of Rousseau*, Vol. 4, ed. Roger D. Masters and Christopher Kelly (Lebanon, NH: University Press of New England, 1994), pp. 34–35. See also Hannah Arendt/Karl Jaspers, *Correspondence 1926–1969*, ed. Lotte Kohler and Hans Saner (New York: Harcourt Brace Jovanovich, 1992), p. 317.

[10] In putting together this inquiry in the very old-fashioned way I have, as a transhistorical dialogue about perennial issues concerning human existence, am I presuming that the canon from Plato onward gives us everything we need intellectually to think through our situation in the present? If so, is the presumption actually warranted? In "The Adequacy of the Canon," George Kateb makes a case that is worth considering that in certain essential ways, the canon fails us; Kateb, *Patriotism and Other Mistakes* (New Haven: Yale University Press, 2006), pp. 384–407. "The texts usually presume to speak timelessly" (p. 387), but on Kateb's account they do not suffice in enabling us to grasp the political horrors of the twentieth century.

It gives me great pleasure to acknowledge my large debt to cherished colleagues and former colleagues at the University of Toronto, who have taught me so much that helps inform reflection on the history of political philosophy, notably the following people: Edward Andrew, Ryan Balot, Alan Brudner, Joseph Carens, Simone Chambers, Frank Cunningham, Don Forbes, Ken Green, Gad Horowitz, Ryan Hurl, Duncan Ivison, Rebecca Kingston, Peggy Kohn, Nancy Kokaz, Alkis Kontos, Mark Lippincott, Jennifer Nedelsky, Clifford Orwin, Tom Pangle,[11] Melissa Williams, and Irving Zeitlin, as well as my Lockean friend at York University, Steve Newman. My largest debt, however, is to the many theses on topics relevant to this book written by Theory doctoral students in Political Science at the University of Toronto. In most cases, I served on their supervisory committees, but they did most of the teaching. Their theses have been for me a never-ending source of invaluable suggestions about books to read, texts to reread, and problems to ponder. The following is not a comprehensive list, but nonetheless conveys some indication of the scale of my debt: Richard Sigurdson, on Burckhardt and Nietzsche (1991); David Foster, on Locke's *First Treatise* (1991); James Alvey, on Adam Smith (1996); Judd Owen, on Rawls, Rorty, and Fish (1998); Mark Lloyd, on Shaftesbury and Locke (1999); Borys Kowalsky, on J. S. Mill (2000); Jeff Loucks, on Machiavelli and Montesquieu (2000); Simon Kow, on Hobbes and Milton (2001); Joshua Goldstein, on Hegel (2001); Nate McKune, on Carl Schmitt (2001); Daniel Pellerin, on Calvin (2002); Lee MacLean, on Rousseau (2002); Joe Hebert, on Tocqueville (2004); Marc Hanvelt, on Hume (2007); Robert Sparling, on J. G. Hamann (2008); Brent Cusher, on Plato and Rousseau (2009), and Gabriel Bartlett, on Thomas More (in progress). I am also grateful to another former student, Graeme Garrard, for helping to spur my interest in Maistre. Garrard in turn was prompted in this direction by his encounter at Oxford with Isaiah Berlin. Berlin clearly believed that the worst kind of liberal is a complacent liberal, and that the best way to avoid complacency is to engage in an intellectually serious and even intellectually respectful way with radical versions of illiberalism. I trust that this book is in keeping with the spirit of Berlin's liberalism in this regard.

Some chapters of this book draw freely upon work published elsewhere, notably "Machiavelli, Hobbes, and Rousseau on Civil Religion," *The Review of Politics*, Vol. 55, No. 4 (Fall 1993): 617–638; "Civil Religion," in *The Encyclopedia of Democracy*, ed. Seymour Martin Lipset (Washington, DC: Congressional Quarterly Books, 1995), Vol. 3, pp. 1052–1054; "George Grant,

---

[11] As regards my former colleague, Tom Pangle, my writing of this book clearly represents a tacit admission that with respect to one of the issues that he and I debated in my book, *Philosophy in a Time of Lost Spirit*, he was right and I was wrong: namely the issue concerning whether political philosophers are obliged to take up "the theological–political question." Given the tenacious staying power of religion and of its political claims, "coming to grips with God" turns out to be an ineliminable part of the business of political philosophy.

Nietzsche, and the Problem of a Post-Christian Theism," in *George Grant and the Subversion of Modernity*, ed. Arthur Davis (Toronto: University of Toronto Press, 1996), pp. 109–138; and "John Rawls's Genealogy of Liberalism," in *Reflections on Rawls: An Assessment of His Legacy*, ed. Shaun P. Young (Aldershot, UK: Ashgate, 2009), pp. 73–89. Finally, I should not omit to express my gratitude to the Social Science and Humanities Research Council of Canada for research funding throughout the years I have been writing this book. This generous funding from SSHRCC has paid for many things that have helped completion of the book, not the least of which has been Michael Gray's very helpful and efficient work on the index.

Introduction

[P]olitics . . . issues commands about everything in the state.

– Aristotle[1]

Civil religion: the appropriation of religion by politics for its own purposes. Why is this an important theme in the history of political philosophy? When religion asserts its *own* purposes, which are not those of politics, it poses an absolutely fundamental challenge to political authority, and politics cannot take lightly such a radical challenge to its authority. However, civil religion is itself quite a radical response to this predicament. This is why thinkers within the liberal tradition shy away from civil religion or try to come up with a less radical way of resolving the same predicament. This is the source of the profound three-way dialogue within the tradition of political philosophy – between religion, civil religion, and liberalism, which together offer a whole spectrum of possibilities of politicizing or depoliticizing religion.

Leszek Kolakowski offers his own succinct encapsulation of the idea of civil religion. He writes that "a kind of perverse theocracy . . . seemed to be encouraged even by the implacable Church-haters" – citing Marsilius of Padua, Machiavelli, Hobbes, Spinoza, and Montesquieu as exemplars of this intellectual tradition.[2] (In fact, Kolakowski could even have included Nietzsche in this,

---

[1] Aristotle, *Nicomachean Ethics*, trans. Martin Ostwald (Indianapolis: Bobbs-Merrill, 1962), p. 173. The context is a quick sketching of the issue of how the polis relates to the gods, which turns out to involve a reciprocal subordination: The gods are superior to the polis, but they are worshipped by the polis as the polis ordains. I would like to thank Crystal Cordell for alerting me to the significance of this text.

[2] Leszek Kolakowski, *Modernity on Endless Trial* (Chicago: University of Chicago Press, 1990), p. 179. A useful resource on the history of the idea of civil religion is Jeffrey R. Collins, *The Allegiance of Thomas Hobbes* (Oxford: Oxford University Press, 2005), chapter 1. For a very interesting account of the importance of the civil-religion idea in modern political thought from Machiavelli to Hegel via James Harrington, see Mark Goldie, "The Civil Religion of James Harrington," in *The Languages of Political Theory in Early-Modern Europe*, ed. Anthony

in his view dubious, tradition.)[3] Why would "church-haters" wish to embrace civil religion? If these thinkers perceive religion as politically subversive, or as posing a potential threat to political authority, then one evident theoretical strategy would be "to beat the religionists at their own game" – that is to say, to make politics itself the assertor of claims to authority that reach *beyond* politics or that transcend "merely" political authority.

What to do about religion? This is an inescapable problem of politics, and therefore it is a perennial question for political philosophy. The idea behind this book is a quite simple one, though its execution requires a complex work of interpretation and commentary. The idea is to situate John Rawls's account of religion in the Introduction to *Political Liberalism* in the centuries-long dialogue within the history of political philosophy in which it properly belongs. Rawls himself of course makes little effort to situate his account within a historical and still-continuing philosophical dialogue. On the contrary, he presents the theoretical outcome he endorses as a historical achievement, that is, as a given (namely liberalism's accomplished triumph as a fact of history). If these questions were once the subject matter of a living dialogue, then liberalism's solution to the political problem of religion has rendered continuation of the dialogue redundant (or so we may be led to believe).

Civil religion is the empowerment of religion, not for the sake of religion, but for the sake of enhanced citizenship – of making members of the political community better citizens, in accordance with whatever conception one holds of what constitutes being a good citizen. "Liberalism," with respect to this question, is the rejection of the idea of empowering religion *even for the sake of enhancing good citizenship*, and different theorists of liberalism offer different (but perhaps mutually reinforcing) arguments for rejecting the civil-religion idea. Presented in this way, civil religion and liberalism are opposing alternatives within the intellectual world of political philosophy, and the history of political philosophy can be cast (as it is cast in this book) as a continuing dialogue between these opposing alternatives.

This is a book written by someone with very little interest in religion as such. What deeply interests me is politics, and political philosophy as the articulation of far-reaching questions about the proper way to organize political

---

Pagden (Cambridge: Cambridge University Press, 1987), pp. 197–222. Goldie sees this as a principled intellectual tradition, and therefore as deserving of more intellectual sympathy than it gets from Kolakowski. As regards Harrington, he offers a particularly interesting case of what is a major theme in Part I of this book, namely the congruence between civil religion and vehement anticlericalism (and, arguably, Shaftesbury offers another important example of the same theme). An examination of these two intriguing thinkers, however, will have to await a sequel.

[3] Nietzsche is discussed in Part IV of this book. To anticipate our later argument about Nietzsche's affinities with the civil-religion tradition, let us just mention that for Nietzsche, in common with Machiavelli (*Discourses on Livy*, II.5), the highest politics consists in the founding of new religions. In fact, one might speculate that Nietzsche's sole aim in writing *Thus Spoke Zarathustra* was to prove that a single human being can sit down and invent a religion. What Moses and St. Paul did *can be done again.*

life. Nevertheless, even an interest in politics and political philosophy obliges one to be at least indirectly interested in religion. For even liberalism, in its various versions, construed as an attempt to domesticate or neutralize the impact upon political life of religious commitment, is for precisely that reason necessarily preoccupied with the problem of religion. It is to explore such questions that I have written this book.

With a project as large as this one, one should not be sparing with one's disclaimers. The selection of thinkers who figure in this dialogue (or series of dialogues) certainly does not exhaust the range of political philosophers who are relevant to the theme of civil religion, and the interpretation of any given thinker certainly does not exhaust what that thinker contributes to theorizing the relationship between religion and politics.

Any attempt to reflect on the theme of civil religion within the context of the history of political philosophy will of course start with Book IV, chapter 8 of Rousseau's *Social Contract*. Rousseau highlights in an especially sharp way the opposing demands of civic life on the one hand and those of religious, and especially Christian, commitments on the other. "Christian republic... these two words are mutually exclusive."[4] "[F]ar from attaching the citizens' hearts to the State, [the Christian religion] detaches them from it as from all worldly things."[5] The religion that dominates Western political communities is in radical tension with the needs of political authority, yet religious profession of some kind is indispensable for a sound political order: "[A] State has never been founded," Rousseau affirms, "without religion serving as its base."[6] Without question, Rousseau's chapter addresses with penetrating insight this basic problem; less clear is the extent to which it even comes close to resolving this problem – or was *meant* to resolve the problem. (Indeed, as I lay out in Part I, I am inclined to interpret the chapter as *intending* to show that the problem is in fact irresolvable, and in that respect it illuminates a dimension of political life more generally that is unresolvable.)[7]

---

4 Jean-Jacques Rousseau, *On the Social Contract*, ed. Roger D. Masters, trans. Judith R. Masters (New York: St. Martin's Press, 1978), p. 130.

5 Ibid., p. 128.

6 Ibid., p. 127.

7 If, according to my argument in Part I (and contrary to conventional readings of Rousseau), Rousseau ultimately recoils from articulating a "real" civil religion, what would a truly robust civil religion look like? One candidate might be John Toland's *Nazarenus*, ed. Justin Champion (Oxford: Voltaire Foundation, 1997). In Jonathan Israel's formulation, Toland's work constitutes an "astounding quasi-theological project... in which he seeks to dechristianize Christianity and remodel it as a republican civil religion." Israel, *Radical Enlightenment* (Oxford: Oxford University Press, 2001), p. 613. Trying to unravel the complicated discursive games being played in *Nazarenus* is too ambitious a task to be undertaken here. Roughly, Toland is involved in interpreting the original Jesus cult – through the medium of a spurious "fifth Gospel" – in a way that repositions it closer to Judaism and Islam, and farther away from St. Paul's version of Christianity. (He offers a "Christianisme Judaique et Mahometan," to cite the title of the original draft of the work.) In this sense, *Nazarenus* replicates (in Toland's own uniquely provocative way) some of the theoretical strategies explored in Part I of this book. But if Toland is to be

Political philosophy is generally a response to underlying crisis. Plato's *Republic* was a response to moral crisis in the Greek world. Aristotle's *Politics* was a response to a crisis with respect to the very existence of the Greek polis. The work of Pierre Bayle was provoked by the revocation of the Edict of Nantes. Rousseau's *Social Contract* was a response to the crisis of the monarchical order in Europe. Tocqueville's *Democracy in America* is a response to the collapse of aristocracy. And so on. *Liberalism*, above all, is a response to the crisis associated with the religious wars of the sixteenth and seventeenth centuries. This reverberates right through the whole liberal tradition, stretching right up to the most important work of the liberal tradition in recent times, John Rawls's *Political Liberalism*. Hobbes offered one kind of response to this challenge of religious sectarianism, and this context of religiously motivated civil war shapes his political vision in the most profound way. However, the most important work of political theory in response to the religious crisis of the sixteenth and seventeenth centuries is Locke's *Letter Concerning Toleration*. In my view it shapes his liberalism, and beyond that it defines the very meaning of the whole liberal tradition, in an even more profound way than his *Second Treatise of Government*. In a very far-reaching sense, liberalism as a political philosophy is a theoretical response to the challenge of the Protestant Reformation, and the religious–political wars that came out of the Reformation. Hobbes was certainly not a liberal in his politics, but his philosophical assumptions *are* liberal, and with respect to what each of them draws out of these shared liberal (egalitarian–individualist) philosophical assumptions, Hobbes and Locke represent two poles of the liberal tradition. As such, they represent two fundamentally opposing responses to the challenge of religion in relation to political community and political authority.

Has liberalism triumphed? What Montesquieu teaches (*Spirit of the Laws*, Book 25, chapter 12) is that the supreme measure by which one gauges whether the liberal regime has triumphed is the extent to which citizens quietly grow indifferent to religious preoccupations and have them supplanted by concerns about material comfort and commercial prosperity.[8] What is the

---

considered a theorist of civil religion, one would have to relate these themes in Toland back to similar themes in James Harrington and Henry Stubbe. On civil religion in Harrington, see Goldie, "The Civil Religion of James Harrington"; on Stubbe as a source for civil-religion theorizing, see James R. Jacob, *Henry Stubbe, Radical Protestantism, and the Early Enlightenment* (Cambridge: Cambridge University Press, 1983), chapter 8.

[8] Cf. Ian McEwan, *Saturday* (London: Jonathan Cape, 2005), p. 126: "It isn't rationalism that will overcome the religious zealots, but ordinary shopping and all that it entails . . . the promise of appetites sated in this world, not the next. Rather shop than pray." Straussians tend to interpret Montesquieu's suggestion about disarming religion by cultivating indifference rather than by confronting it head on as a kind of philosophers' conspiracy. Hence Thomas Pangle's claim that this text in *Spirit of the Laws*, 25:12, is "perhaps the most important single passage on religion in the entire *Spirit of the Laws*"; Pangle, *The Theological Basis of Liberal Modernity in Montesquieu's "Spirit of the Laws"* (Chicago: University of Chicago Press, 2010), p. 102. This may well be true, but rather than interpreting it as part of a secret conspiracy, it can be viewed, more prosaically, as just a matter of Montesquieu's acknowledging what he took to be the sociological realities of modern societies.

contemporary assessment according to this measure? Consider Iran, Algeria, the Sudan, Somalia, Nigeria, Ireland, Israel, Gaza, Lebanon, Pakistan, India, Turkey, Iraq, Afghanistan, Yemen.... The least that can be said is that the arrival of a liberal-bourgeois "end of history," implying the permanent eclipse of preliberal – including theocratic – possibilities, is by no means self-evident.[9] As a matter of fact, Fukuyama's end of history itself came to an end in 2001 – a mere twelve years after it began! – when radical Islam literally pulverized premature expectations of a permanent and universal reign of bourgeois liberalism. This book is premised on the view that *even if it ultimately turns out that some version of liberalism is our best means of containing the dangers of religion*, we will understand the liberal project better by locating it within a broader range of nonliberal and antiliberal theoretical projects.

Modern secularism nearly put an end to the dimension of theorizing expressed in the civil-religion tradition. In that sense, as theorists, we should perhaps be thankful to radical Islam (and perhaps also to evangelical Protestantism) for very robustly putting these questions back on the philosophical agenda. When one thinks of the first epigraph to chapter 30 – a view of Nietzsche articulated by Karl Löwith that I strongly endorse – one is astonished that a radical atheist like Nietzsche can *also*, simultaneously, be a radical adversary of the Enlightenment and its process of secularization (which is obviously continuing right up to our own day). If this continues to surprise and puzzle us, however, it simply means we have not understood the core of Nietzsche's theoretical challenge. For secularization expresses *precisely* the cultural trend toward flattening, homogenization, and cultural-spiritual atrophy that was of most urgent concern to him (and to Heidegger).[10] As I argue in my Nietzsche

9 For a good survey of possibilities of "desecularization," particularly in regard to Europe, see Peter J. Katzenstein and Timothy A. Byrnes, "Transnational Religion in an Expanding Europe," *Perspectives on Politics*, Vol. 4, No. 4 (December 2006): 679–694. See also Peter L. Berger, "The Desecularization of the World: A Global Overview," in *The Desecularization of the World: Resurgent Religion and World Politics*, ed. Berger (Grand Rapids, MI: Eerdmans, 1999), pp. 1–18. Among theorists, there is, at the moment, a good deal of fashionable talk about "postsecularism" as a, as it were, natural counterpart to postmodernism. Retracing the long and difficult process by which the Enlightenment made modern secularism possible, one should shudder (at least a little bit) at the facile notion of moving "beyond" secularism. One good reason for pursuing the kind of inquiry undertaken in Part II of this book is to make us a little more wary of postsecularism by providing some pertinent reminders about *presecularism*.

10 Nietzsche's great trope here is "unbending the bow," from the Preface to *Beyond Good and Evil* (also §§ 206 and 262, and *Genealogy of Morals* I.12). It is an image packed with paradox. As an enemy of Christianity, Nietzsche *ought* to be pro-Enlightenment, and in fact sometimes embraces strongly pro-Enlightenment rhetoric (e.g., *The Antichrist*, §§ 12–15; cf. *Beyond Good and Evil*, Preface: "Europe is breathing freely again," and "we" are the "heirs" of the fight against Plato's error). But "unbending the bow" is fundamentally an anti-Enlightenment image. If it is the "fight" against Platonism and Christianity that creates this "magnificent tension of the spirit," then the final winning of the fight – the triumph of the Enlightenment and the vanquishing of Platonism/Christianity – is a disaster. Which side is Nietzsche on? The side of Platonism and Christianity, which produced a civilizational "nightmare" but also thereby contributed to tensing the bow? Or the side of the Enlightenment, which destroys an unhealthy error but also unbends the bow?

interpretation, Nietzsche *blames* Christianity for its contribution to modern liberal secularization; hence he obviously does not see Christianity (especially Protestant Christianity) and secularization as philosophically opposed. A resurrection of illiberal possibilities strikes him as a sign of renewed vitality (and again the same is true of Heidegger).

Is civil religion still alive today as a theoretical possibility? One might say that civil religion has in some sense succumbed to the rationalism of the philosophical tradition per se. This actually goes all the way back to the beginnings of the tradition of political philosophy in Plato – namely Plato's argument against the poets at the end of *The Republic*, with its implied critique of the inadequacy and unreliability of a merely religious habituation to virtue, of "custom without philosophy."[11] Jürgen Habermas offers a contemporary expression of the same rationalist tradition when he proposes the possibility of "the social integrative powers of the religious tradition shaken by enlightenment" being supplanted by "the unifying, consensus-creating power of reason."[12] The assumption here is that we *can* find other ways in which to hold a political community together. For the whole rationalist tradition stretching from Plato to Habermas, only philosophy can ultimately accomplish the task assigned by the civil-religion tradition to mere religion (whether Homeric or Judeo-Christian), namely to draw citizens into a stable and coherent political community. Again, it is striking that thinkers as radically different as Machiavelli, Hobbes, Rousseau, and Nietzsche all agree in finding this rationalist assumption extremely dubious.[13]

[11] *The Republic*, Book 10: 619c–d; cf. *Phaedo*, 82b–c. For commentary, see Hans-Georg Gadamer, "Plato and the Poets," in *Dialogue and Dialectic*, trans. P. Christopher Smith (New Haven: Yale University Press, 1980), pp. 61–62, esp. n. 9. Let me add that in his challenges to Homer, Plato wasn't necessarily renouncing civil religion; more likely, what he wanted was to place responsibility for civil religion in the hands of philosophers rather than poets.

[12] *Habermas and Modernity*, ed. Richard J. Bernstein (Cambridge, MA: MIT Press, 1985), p. 197. More recently, however, Habermas has modified his views concerning religion; see, for instance, "A Conversation about God and the World," in Jürgen Habermas, *Religion and Rationality*, ed. Eduardo Mendieta (Cambridge: Polity, 2002), pp. 147–167; "Faith and Knowledge," in Habermas, *The Future of Human Nature*, trans. Hella Beister and William Rehg (Cambridge: Polity, 2003), pp. 101–115; and "Religion in the Public Sphere," in Habermas, *Between Naturalism and Religion*, trans. Ciaran Cronin (Cambridge: Polity, 2008), pp. 114–147. For a very interesting and helpful account of the Habermasian view expressed in such texts, see Simone Chambers, "How Religion Speaks to the Agnostic: Habermas on the Persistent Value of Religion," *Constellations*, Vol. 14, No. 2 (2007): 210–223. As Chambers does a good job of explaining, although it may in principle remain Habermas's purpose to make the moral insights of religion ultimately translatable into "profane philosophy," this process of secular translation is in practice more or less never ending. Hence Habermas is anxious that religion not be culturally (or politically) excluded while it is continuing to contribute moral meanings that still await secular translation.

[13] I will postpone a more definite verdict on the civil-religion tradition until the conclusion of this book. In the meantime, I want to discourage the inference that I am nostalgic about an age of theory when civil-religion theorizing was still possible. There are good reasons why civil religion has ceased to be a credible way to do political philosophy. Still, it is an important part of our tradition of political philosophy, and much can be learned by investigating not only why it is no longer possible but also what motivated this mode of theorizing in the first place.

If politics could be thoroughly secularized, or if religion could be thoroughly privatized, the problem of politics and religion might be soluble. Neither of these appears to be possible. It follows that religion will *always* pose challenges for political life – challenges for which mere theory cannot be expected to furnish solutions. Therefore, if solutions to the dilemmas of politics and religion are what we expect or hope for from the tradition of political philosophy, we are likely to find these hopes and expectations sorely disappointed. The motivation for seeking wisdom on these questions from canonical thinkers must then lie somewhere else. If contemporary Islam and contemporary evangelical theocratic (or theocracy-aspiring) politics challenge liberal citizenship in fundamental ways, then they raise anew the kinds of challenges to which the original civil-religion tradition attempted to respond. In that sense, some of the most sobering predicaments of contemporary politics can be liberating and enlivening for wide-horizoned theory.

PART I

MACHIAVELLI, HOBBES, ROUSSEAU

Three Versions of the Civil-Religion Project

I

Rousseau's Problem

Bayle has proved very well that fanaticism is more pernicious than atheism, and this is incontestable. But what he did not take care to say, and which is no less true, is that fanaticism, although sanguinary and cruel, is nevertheless a grand and strong passion which elevates the heart of man, makes him despise death, and gives him a prodigious energy that need only be better directed to produce the most sublime virtues.

– Jean-Jacques Rousseau[1]

The term *civil religion* comes from a particular text – Book IV, chapter 8 of Rousseau's *Social Contract*. Nevertheless, pursued with sufficient doggedness, radicality, and intellectual ambition, the idea of civil religion can open up to us not only the unique political thought-world of Rousseau's work as a whole but also the unique thought-worlds of *all* major figures in the tradition of modern political philosophy. More to the point, it can open up to us the dimension of full dialogue *between* these thinkers, and not just their own thought-worlds seen as singular wholes. It is in this sense that this book aims at the presentation of a dialogue, or of a set of dialogues. From the point of view of this dialogue within the history of political philosophy, one can say that when Rousseau composes his civil-religion chapter, he is already familiar with two possible solutions to the problem of adjudicating the uneasy relation between politics and religion offered by his predecessors in the tradition of modern political philosophy (to be explored in Chapters 2–5 of Part I); in that sense, the civil-religion chapter already inserts itself into a dialogue in progress. However, Rousseau rejects both of these possible solutions as undesirable. In the *Geneva Manuscript* he explores a possible solution of his own, but he jettisons this as well when he

---

[1] Jean-Jacques Rousseau, *Emile, or On Education*, ed. Allan Bloom (New York: Basic Books, 1979), p. 312, note. For a discussion of the tensions and paradoxes in *Emile* expressed in this astonishing footnote, see Chapter 17; cf. Rousseau's praise of Islamic fanaticism in "Essay on the Origin of Languages," in *The Collected Writings of Rousseau*, Vol. 7, ed. John T. Scott (Lebanon, NH: University Press of New England, 1998), p. 317.

comes to write the *Social Contract*. Hence, readers of Rousseau who believe the *Social Contract* should be interpreted as a determinate and realizable blueprint for an ideal political community need to think hard about the fact that the book concludes with the statement of a crucial political *problem* for which Rousseau is unable to propose any solution that he himself regards as acceptable.[2]

The *Social Contract* concludes with a stunning paradox. The key statement of Book IV, chapter 8 is that "a State has never been founded without religion serving as its base" (*"jamais État ne fut fondé que la religion ne lui servit de base"*).[3] This statement occurs in the context of a very penetrating analysis that lays out what one presumes to be an exhaustive survey of religious–political possibilities. There are two main alternatives: The first, to which Rousseau attaches the label "natural divine right," is strictly otherworldly in its focus and finds its purest embodiment in the Christianity of the Gospels; the second, which Rousseau refers to as "civil or positive divine right," embraces a variety of more worldly, theocratic regimes. These divide basically into two types: the fairly inclusive, local civil religion of Roman and other paganisms; and the more universalistic and therefore imperialistic theocracies of Islam and Judaism. All national religions will appear parochial relative to the universalism of Christianity, but as the contrast between Judaism/Islam and paganism shows, this parochialism can have either a (relatively) tolerant or aggressive cast. Rousseau also presents a third, hybrid, alternative – "mixed right" – which offers a kind of dual-sovereignty model, dividing authority between church and state. In practice, it means that the priests are tempted to usurp temporal authority for themselves, and to this extent undercut the established authority of the state. Rousseau calls it "the religion of the priest" and agrees with Hobbes in denying to this worldly–otherworldly religion any moral claim whatsoever. The most blatant target of this polemic is of course Catholicism, but as Rousseau concedes in the paragraph referring to Hobbes, this dividing of sovereignties is

---

[2] Terence Ball very helpfully assembles all the wild and misguided judgments made upon the civil-religion chapter by Rousseau scholars: See "Rousseau's Civil Religion Reconsidered," in Ball, *Reappraising Political Theory: Revisionist Studies in the History of Political Thought* (Oxford: Clarendon Press, 1995), pp. 107–130. Ball means to rescue Rousseau from his critics, but his own interpretation (the core of which is presented on pp. 125–128) is highly speculative, with not much in the text to support it. There are several problems here, one of which is that Ball takes the "totalitarian" readings of IV.8 too seriously. Another related problem is that he, like other readers, assumes he knows in advance the illiberal character of this teaching, and therefore fails to attend closely enough to the actual text and its complexities. An ambitious interpretation of Rousseau's civil religion is offered in Patrick J. Deneen, *Democratic Faith* (Princeton, NJ: Princeton University Press, 2005), chapter 5; but in my view the interpretation is skewed by Deneen's larger narrative according to which modern theorists like Rousseau seek to displace actual religions by embracing "transformative" secular religions that turn democracy itself into an object of faith. I accept elements of this interpretation. However, as will be clear throughout the argument of Part I, I do not see anything Promethean in Rousseau's civil religion; on the contrary, I interpret it as the chastening of Rousseau's civic republicanism.

[3] Jean-Jacques Rousseau, *On the Social Contract*, ed. Roger D. Masters, trans. Judith R. Masters (New York: St. Martin's Press, 1978), p. 127.

latent in the "spirit of Christianity" in general, not just the Catholic version of Christianity.[4]

Where does this leave us? Rousseau explicitly rules out the possibility of a sound politics in the absence of a civil religion. A religion that is neither strictly worldly nor strictly otherworldly (namely Catholicism) is vehemently rejected. A religion that is strictly otherworldly (non-Catholic versions of Christianity, including, especially, the authentic Christianity of the Gospels) is religiously true but, at best, politically useless. It fails to make available the civil religion that Rousseau insists is politically indispensable. The central paragraphs of the chapter (paragraphs 8–30) are devoted to showing that the project of reconciling Christianity with the requirements of politics is a hopeless one. One cannot speak of "a Christian republic," because "these two words are mutually exclusive."[5] This might suggest that Rousseau, as a partisan of republican politics, would be forced to embrace some species of theocracy, either of the pluralistic, pagan variety or of the imperialistic, monotheistic variety. Although Rousseau does voice significant sympathy for Roman religious practices and declares that "Mohammed had very sound views,"[6] this too is an option that he ultimately repudiates. Theocracies breed intolerance and intolerance is morally unacceptable. In this respect, Christian universalism embodies a moral truth that we cannot forgo. All good politics is parochial, and a religion that encouraged this parochialism, rather than helping us to transcend it (as true Christianity does), would diminish our humanity. Thus, although

---

4 Ibid.: "Hobbes...dared to propose the reunification of the two heads of the eagle, and the complete return to political unity, without which no State or government will ever be well constituted. But he ought to have seen that the dominating spirit of Christianity [*l'esprit dominateur du christianisme*] was incompatible with his system." The reference to "the spirit of Christianity" on p. 126 bears the same implication, viz., that it is Christianity in general, not Catholicism in particular, that tends to bifurcate sovereignty. Interestingly, Rousseau also criticizes the Shiite version of Islam because it too introduces a division of sovereignty between the state and the priests, creating political problems in non-Christian states such as Persia. Although the problem of divided sovereignty "is less apparent among the Mohammedans than among the Christians," it is nonetheless present as a problem in Islam as well; *Social Contract*, ed. Masters, p. 126. One may add that, with respect to the Shiite version of Islam, the problem is rooted historically in the claims to higher authority asserted by the Imams of Shiite tradition (Ali and his descendants); going back to the early centuries of Islam, this posed a persistent theocratic challenge to the de facto sovereignty of the caliphs. One could say that the regime would be a theocracy either way, but the point is that the special authority bestowed upon the Twelve Imams by Shiite tradition put a severe question mark over the theocratic credentials of the various caliphs. In any case, in light of Rousseau's reference here to theocratic tendencies in Shiite Islam, it is very striking that the notable case of a theocracy in current-day political life is precisely the Shiite regime in Iran.
5 Ibid., p. 130. Rousseau's statement that there is no such thing as a Christian republic is highly reminiscent of Locke's statement that "there is absolutely no such thing, under the Gospel, as a Christian Commonwealth"; John Locke, *A Letter Concerning Toleration*, ed. James Tully (Indianapolis: Hackett, 1983), p. 44. The two statements, however, are significantly different in their essential thrust. Rousseau's purpose is to assert that Christianity does not supply a basis for robust civic identity. Locke's purpose is to assert that Christianity is not a legitimate foundation for claims to political authority.
6 *Social Contract*, ed. Masters, p. 126.

Rousseau entirely accepts and restates Machiavelli's analysis of the antipolitical character of Christianity, he cannot follow Machiavelli in opting for some kind of anti-Christian politics. The Crusades show us what we get when we turn Christianity in a pagan direction,[7] and the Crusades were an abomination.[8] Even if, contrary to this argument, we could conceive a civil religion that was not subject to this criticism, that is, some kind of theocracy that remained politically attractive, Rousseau says that we would be seeking a possibility that is no longer attainable: The preservation or reestablishment of the ancient system is a futile endeavor. "The spirit of Christianity has won over everything."[9] In the last paragraph of the chapter he tells us that "there is no longer and can *never again be* [*il ne peut plus y avoir*] an exclusive national religion."[10] Thus we are left with the two unhappy alternatives of a morally true religion that is in its essence subversive of politics, and a sound civil religion that is both morally unattractive and, historically, an anachronism.

The standard reading of the *Social Contract* is of course that Rousseau *does* offer a civil religion. This comes in a quite distinct section of Book IV, chapter 8, confined to the last five paragraphs of a thirty-five-paragraph chapter,[11] and it is a real puzzle how the positive recommendations of these last five paragraphs manage to elude the powerful arguments Rousseau assembles in the thorough critical analysis of the first thirty paragraphs.[12] In the sentence that marks the transition between the critical first part of the chapter and the recommendatory second part, Rousseau writes, "setting political considerations aside, let us return to right and determine its principles."[13] But what does it mean to define principles of right in abstraction from "political considerations"? The passage seems almost to suggest that right stands in contradiction to politics, and that a political community that satisfied the principles of right (in particular, the moral imperative of tolerance, the theme of the final three paragraphs) would be incapable of political realization.

---

7 Ibid., p. 130.

8 Pierre Bayle, in § 140 of *Various Thoughts on the Occasion of a Comet*, calls the Crusades "the most frightful disorders ever heard of."

9 *Social Contract*, ed. Masters, p. 126. The text reads as follows: "Plusieurs peuples cependant, même dans l'Europe ou à son voisinage, ont voulu conserver ou rétablir l'ancien système, mais sans succès: l'esprit du christianisme a tout gagné."

10 Ibid., p. 131; emphasis added.

11 There is a parallel discussion in Rousseau's famous letter to Voltaire dated August 18, 1756: see *The Collected Writings of Rousseau*, Vol. 3, ed. Roger D. Masters and Christopher Kelly (Hanover, NH: University Press of New England, 1992), pp. 108–121, esp. 119–120. Rousseau, quite amazingly, tries to enlist Voltaire in his project of a civil profession of faith, urges Voltaire to "adorn it with your Poetry," and implores him to follow up his "Catechism of man" with a "Catechism of the Citizen" (p. 120; see also p. 196, n. 43).

12 Cf. Paul A. Rahe, *Soft Despotism, Democracy's Drift* (New Haven: Yale University Press, 2009), p. 136: "[Rousseau's] civil religion is what he calls 'a universal Religion.' As such, it is subject to certain of the objections that he leveled at Christianity."

13 *Social Contract*, ed. Masters, p. 130. The text reads as follows: "laissant à part les considérations politiques, revenons au droit, et fixons les principes."

When Rousseau says that "a State has never been founded without religion serving as its base," I assume that he has in mind a "real" religion[14] – a religion that could actually shape the motivations of citizens, thus fostering good citizenship and helping to consolidate the foundations of the state. What he offers in the last five paragraphs, however, is a highly attenuated "phantom" religion, an Enlightenment-style "religion of tolerance," one might say, in which liberal or negative tenets prevail over tenets that might positively build republican citizenship.[15] In embracing this rather watered-down quasi-religion, it is as if Rousseau bids farewell to his republican ideal, with the hearty parochialism and potential illiberalism that it implies. To such a "civil religion," it would be appropriate to respond with the challenge restated by Karl Löwith in his commentary on Jacob Burckhardt:

[A] Christianity reduced to morality and deprived of its supernatural and doctrinal foundations is no longer a religion. . . . [Burckhardt] felt keenly that a Christianity which is watered down to a humanitarianism in which the priest is "first of all a *Gebildeter*," a man of the educated classes, then a philosophizing theologian, and eventually a little

---

14 In an illuminating essay on "Civil Religion in America" in *Daedalus*, Vol. 96, No. 1 (Winter, 1967): 1–21, Robert N. Bellah argues that the American political tradition discloses a veritable civil religion that draws upon biblical symbols and imagery, but that invests them anew with a peculiarly political function. This civil religion represents a unique religious construction insofar as it subsumes and appropriates images of the Old Testament without being Jewish, and subsumes and appropriates symbolism of the New Testament without being Christian. Rather than being in any way sectarian, the American civil religion takes these materials given in the biblical tradition and forges from them the liturgical basis for a distinct religious community embracing the entire nation. (As Bellah points out, the French revolutionaries of 1789 also sought to forge a new civil cult, the latter involving a more militant break with Christian norms. One can add – with contemporary France in mind – that if republicanism requires a more robust subscription to shared principles of civic unity, then all republics need a civil religion, even if, paradoxically, this civil religion is constituted by shared commitment to *laïcité*.) One cannot rule out the possibility that Rousseau had something very much like this in mind with his own proposal of a civil religion. However, this still leaves unresolved why Rousseau, through most of the civil-religion chapter, treats various world religions as if they were real options, capable of directly constituting alternative political communities, rather than providing merely a pool of religious motifs that republican statesmen and legislators could draw upon for their own purposes. Cf. Richard John Neuhaus, "From Civil Religion to Public Philosophy," in *Civil Religion and Political Theology*, ed. Leroy S. Rouner (Notre Dame, IN: University of Notre Dame Press, 1986), p. 99: "[Unlike contemporary theorists of civil religion such as Bellah,] Rousseau bit the bullet. He made clear that what he meant by civil religion was a religion."

15 It is surely striking that Rousseau would end a book that otherwise presents itself as a militantly civic-republican critique of the liberal vision of politics with a "Lockean" conclusion (or, we could probably say with equal warrant, a "Spinozistic" conclusion). Who would imagine that Rousseau would end the *Social Contract* by aligning himself with *Locke*? (But see *Collected Writings of Rousseau*, Vol. 9, ed. Christopher Kelly and Eve Grace [Lebanon, NH: University Press of New England, 2001], p. 236, where Rousseau identifies his principles with those of Locke.) In particular, compare Rousseau's conclusion that intolerant religions cannot be tolerated with Locke's formulation of the same principle: *A Letter Concerning Toleration*, ed. James H. Tully (Indianapolis: Hackett, 1983), p. 50.

bit of a timid man – that such a Christianity cannot appeal to the secular world as an inspiring religion.[16]

In any case, nowhere in Book IV, chapter 8 does Rousseau explain how the anemic religion that he conjures up at the end can possibly satisfy the robust requirements that qualify a civil religion as a real civil religion, and it remains entirely mysterious how the liberalized religion to which he lowers his standard in the last five paragraphs of the chapter can elude the seemingly exhaustive framework of analysis laid out in the first thirty paragraphs. Rousseauian politics ends up with a paradox rather than a proposal.

Does Rousseau follow through on the brave-sounding challenge to Bayle quoted in the epigraph to this chapter? My conclusion is that he does not. One may recall Montesquieu's tacit suggestion that ancient citizenship, as grand as it is, is fatally impugned by the fact that republican virtue in its full rigor demands something equivalent to the fanaticism of self-abnegating monks (*Spirit of the Laws*, Book 5, chapter 2).[17] Reading Rousseau in the light of this Montesquieuian perspective, one can see Rousseau's profound ambivalence (which for him is accompanied by a philosophically acute aware- ness of why his sympathies lie on *both* sides of the fence). Montesquieu, too (here in accord not only with Rousseau but also with Machiavelli and Niet- zsche), accepted that moderns possess "small souls" in comparison with the ancients (*Spirit of the Laws*, Book 4, chapter 4), but he was willing to settle for small-souled modernity nonetheless. Again, the civil-religion chapter ultimately shows us that Rousseau's sympathies are on both sides while knowing they are contradictory.

[16] Karl Löwith, *Meaning in History* (Chicago: University of Chicago Press, 1949), p. 29. One may compare what Mark Lilla says about the impasse of Protestant and Jewish liberal theology in *The Stillborn God: Religion, Politics, and the Modern West* (New York: Knopf, 2007), p. 248; cf. pp. 301–302 and 308.

[17] It seems quite possible that Rousseau had this text from Montesquieu in mind when he wrote the following unforgettable lines in *The Government of Poland* that express his civic-republican vision in its most robust and least qualified version: "Proud, sacred liberty! If they but knew her, those wretched men; if they but understood the price at which she is won and held; if they but realized that her laws are as stern [*austères*] as the tyrant's yoke is never hard, their sickly souls, the slaves of passions that would have to be hauled out by the roots, would fear liberty a hundred times as much as they fear servitude. They would flee her in terror as they would a burden about to crush them." Jean-Jacques Rousseau, *The Government of Poland*, trans. Willmore Kendall (Indianapolis: Hackett, 1985), pp. 29–30. (Cf. Iris Murdoch's description of nuns in a monastic community: "these women lay upon themselves austerities from which you and I would shrink in terror"; Iris Murdoch, *The Bell*, London: Vintage, 2004.) It is as if Rousseau, in this hyper-republican text, is saying the following to Montesquieu: "Yes, it's true that republican virtue demands austerities comparable to those of self-abnegating monks. But that is the grandeur of republican virtue, not a reason to be repelled by it."

2

The Machiavellian Solution

Paganization of Christianity

[T]he law of gravitation of the state was discovered. The center of gravity of the state was found in the state itself... [Machiavelli and his successors] began considering the state from the human viewpoint and developed its natural laws from reason and experience. They did not proceed from theology any more than Copernicus let himself be influenced by Joshua's command that the sun stand still over Gideon and the moon over the valley of Ajalon.

– Karl Marx[1]

[W]e no longer understand that in spite of great disagreements among those thinkers, they were united by the fact that they all fought one and the same power – the kingdom of darkness, as Hobbes called it; that fight was more important to them than any merely political issue.

– Leo Strauss[2]

An examination of a few of the more "straightforward" possibilities that Rousseau knew and rejected may cast light on the dimensions of the quandary with which he presents us. In *Discourses on Livy*, Book I, chapters 11–15, Machiavelli makes even clearer than Rousseau does the standard by which a real civil religion is to be judged: That standard is the use to which paganism was put by the Roman republic.[3] Machiavelli provides ample lessons in these

[1] *Writings of the Young Marx on Philosophy and Society*, ed. and trans. Loyd D. Easton and Kurt H. Guddat (Garden City, NY: Anchor Books, 1967), p. 129.

[2] Leo Strauss, *Thoughts on Machiavelli* (Glencoe, IL: The Free Press, 1958), p. 231.

[3] These chapters focus on a discussion of Roman practices of oath taking, auguries, and (particularly) auspices in relation to military discipline; cf. the references to oaths, auspices, and deference to the gods in the concluding quotation from Livy in *Discourses*, Book III, chapter 36. There is a similar analysis in *Discourses* III.33, but here Machiavelli emphasizes that conformity with the auspices will be "of no avail" in the absence of "true virtue" (i.e., military virtuosity). This is accompanied by several references in the text to favorable auspices as "petty things" (*cose piccole*), "every least accident" (*ogni minimo accidente*), "things of little moment" (*cose di poco momento*), and "a vain thing" (*una cosa vana*). It would be easy to interpret these latter phrases as a deprecation of religiously inspired means of building confidence in the soldiers, relative to

five chapters of what it is to make prudent use of a religion, both politically and militarily, but "the Roman Church," failing to live up to its name, is incapable of doing this, and, like the Samnites in *Discourses* I.15, stirs up religious terror to no purpose. Machiavelli's criticism of the papacy is evident in the contrast he draws in Book I, chapter 14 between Papirius's shrewd manipulation of religious beliefs and Appius Pulcher's blatant disregard of those beliefs. The Roman court, because it is *blatantly* un-Christian, spreads contempt for its own religion, like Appius Pulcher, whereas it ought to be *using* Christian piety for political purposes, in emulation of the policy of Papirius.

Machiavelli makes perfectly clear throughout his discussions of religion in the *Discourses* that Christianity has tremendous civilizational resources at its disposal – to discipline its subjects, to carve "a beautiful statue... from coarse marble,"[4] but it has squandered these resources in the most appalling way. It has, as he argues in *Discourses* II.2, devalued honor and glorified passive martyrdom; has taught men to be humble, self-abnegating, and contemptuous of worldly things; has made the world effeminate and rendered heaven impotent. In sum, Christianity has celebrated slavishness and encouraged human beings to despise liberty, or the harsh politics required for the defense of liberty. Religion lies at the heart of Machiavellian politics, though this might not be immediately apparent to readers of *The Prince*. In a famous passage in *The Prince*, chapter 12, Machiavelli asserts the precedence of good arms over good laws because "where there are good arms there must be good laws."[5] But Machiavelli, in a parallel passage in *Discourses* I.11, continues his reasoning (as if in completion of a half-uttered thought): "where there is religion, arms can easily be introduced, and where there are arms and not religion, the latter can be introduced only with difficulty."[6] Just as arms take precedence over laws, religion takes precedence over arms. Hence Numa, founder of Rome's religion, takes precedence over Romulus: It was Numa who addressed himself to "things omitted" by Romulus and saw to it that "the orders of Romulus" were reordered in such a way that they would "suffice for such an empire."[7]

---

the indispensability of virtue. In general, Machiavelli's view is that although *pretended* piety is an invaluable political virtue, one should have no hesitation in, say, manipulating the auspices if that maximizes one's advantages (e.g., the story of the poultrymen told in *Discourses* I.14!). There are similar discussions in Bayle of prudent manipulation of auguries: See Pierre Bayle, *Various Thoughts on the Occasion of a Comet*, trans. Robert C. Bartlett (Albany, NY: SUNY Press, 2000), pp. 43, 69, and 99–100.

[4] Niccolò Machiavelli, *Discourses on Livy*, trans. Harvey C. Mansfield and Nathan Tarcov (Chicago: University of Chicago Press, 1996), p. 35.

[5] Niccolò Machiavelli, *The Prince*, 2nd ed., trans. Harvey C. Mansfield (Chicago: University of Chicago Press, 1998), p. 48.

[6] *Discourses on Livy*, trans. Mansfield and Tarcov, p. 35.

[7] Ibid., p. 34; cf. Rousseau, *The Government of Poland*, chapter 2: "Numa was the real founder of Rome." Machiavelli's praise of Numa in I.11 is somewhat misleading in the light of later chapters. Both in I.19 and in I.21, Machiavelli implies quite strong criticisms of Numa for neglecting the arts of war, thereby exposing the Romans to the danger of becoming "effeminate" (cf. Harvey Mansfield and Nathan Tarcov, "Introduction," pp. xxxiv–xxxv). Nevertheless, one

We see, then, that the business of founding states reposes on the more basic business of founding religions.

In stark contrast to the Roman religion, which ennobled and strengthened human beings, giving them a taste for liberty and a hunger for worldly glory, Christianity has educated humanity in the opposite direction, thereby weakening and enfeebling us. All of this, however, can be changed or reversed. As Machiavelli emphasizes in *Discourses* II.5, the founding of new religions is "from men," not "from heaven" – that is, it is subject to a kind of first-order politics. Just as paganism was able "to extinguish" [*estinguere*] its predecessor and was (nearly) extinguished in turn by Christianity, so presumably Christianity too is vulnerable to being supplanted by a post-Christian religion (or perhaps a resumption of paganism, or neopaganism).[8] This is what one might call the "civilizational" dimension of Machiavelli's politics. It comes to sight quite clearly in chapter 6 of *The Prince*. The "stars" of chapter 6 are four founder-princes, all of whom found something much more grand than mere states: Moses was the founder of the Hebrew civilization; Cyrus was the founder of the Persian civilization; Romulus was the founder of the Roman civilization; Theseus was the founder of the Greek civilization. To occupy *this* rank of prince, it would not suffice to found a state within a decrepit, late-Christian civilization; one would have to found a new religion.

Machiavelli suggests a more modest possibility in *Discourses* II.2, where he gives an extremely curious formulation to his critique of Christian civilization. He does not say that the world *has* become effeminate and heaven *is* disarmed, but that it "appears" as if this had become so owing to a *false interpretation* of Christian teaching. He says that, rightly interpreted, Christianity teaches that "the exaltation and defense of the fatherland" is permitted, that "it wishes us to love and honor it and to prepare ourselves to be such that we can defend it," and that if we thought otherwise, "it arises without doubt from the cowardice [*viltà*][9] of the men who have *interpreted* our religion according to idleness [*l'ozio*] and not according to virtue."[10] In other words, Christianity has had

---

can interpret the discussion in these latter two chapters of Numa's succession by Tullus as helping to elaborate Machiavelli's suggestion in I.11 that "where there is religion, arms can easily be introduced." See also Guicciardini's discussion of the ranking of Romulus and Numa in Francesco Guicciardini, "Considerations of the *Discourses* of Niccolò Machiavelli": *The Sweetness of Power: Machiavelli's Discourses and Guicciardini's Considerations*, trans. James B. Atkinson and David Sices (DeKalb, IL: Northern Illinois University Press, 2002), pp. 403–404.

8 *Discourses on Livy*, trans. Mansfield and Tarcov, pp. 138–139. For a powerful account of the dramatic upheavals by which new religions get established, see James Fitzjames Stephen, *Liberty, Equality, Fraternity*, ed. Stuart D. Warner (Indianapolis: Liberty Fund, 1993), p. 16.

9 Cf. Machiavelli's important reference to "*la viltà di Giovampagolo*" in *Discourses* I.27. *Viltà* can also mean that which is vile or base, so perhaps a better translation would be not just "cowardice" but "ignoble cowardice."

10 Ibid., pp. 131–132; emphasis added. Cf. the reference to "ambitious idleness" (*uno ambizioso ozio*: How can idleness be ambitious?) in the Preface to Book I, immediately after speaking of "the weakness into which the present religion has led the world" (*Discourses on Livy*,

the effects that it has had in the world on account of "false interpretations." As a serious attempt at a faithful rendering of Christian teaching, this is absolutely implausible, as Machiavelli himself surely knew perfectly well. What Machiavelli is saying to us is that it remains open to us as a civilization (or to some enterprising innovator within our civilization) to *reinterpret* Christianity in such a way that it secures the political advantages that the Romans were so adept at exploiting through a judicious manipulation of religious beliefs and practices. To blame the evils wrought by Christianity on a faulty interpretation is to invite a new interpretation, more consonant with the cultural demands of neopagan politics. Here Machiavelli states his program with unmistakable clarity: By speaking of the Christian quest for otherworldly salvation as if it were the product of a misinterpretation, Machiavelli indicates that Christianity can and ought to be reinterpreted as if it were not Christianity; specifically, as if it were a brand of paganism (i.e., a civil religion). Christianity has to be *paganized*.[11]

All of this suggests that the concept of "cultural warfare" is central to Machiavelli's vision of politics. The famous distinction between armed and unarmed prophets at the end of *The Prince*, chapter 6, is highly misleading in this respect, for it encourages us to think that warriors not priests, generals not philosophers, are the only ones capable of enacting any politics worth considering. However, a glance at *Discourses* III.1 suffices to convince us that this cannot be Machiavelli's real view. *Discourses* III.1 refers back to *Discourses* I.9, and *Discourses* I.9 refers backs to *The Prince*, chapter 6. Parallel to *The Prince*, chapter 6, the

---

trans. Mansfield and Tarcov, p. 6). These passages should be read in connection with parallel and equally important texts in *The Prince*, namely Machiavelli's warning about the perils of remaining "idle" [*ozioso*] at the end of chapter 14, and his denunciation of *ignavia* (indolence or laziness) in the last paragraph of chapter 24.

The theme of *l'ozio* also links up with Machiavelli's critique of the priesthood: See John T. Scott and Vickie B. Sullivan, "Patricide and the Plot of *The Prince*: Cesare Borgia and Machiavelli's Italy," *American Political Science Review*, Vol. 88, No. 4 (December 1994): 890, 895. Scott and Sullivan discuss how the Christian clergy, in Machiavelli's view, constitutes in effect a noble class that is doubly corrupt: because it is a noble class that is "disarmed," and because it lives a life of luxurious idleness (they cite *Discourses* I.12 and I.55).

[11] Instead of speaking of Machiavelli's "paganization" of Christianity in the title of this chapter, should I instead speak of his "Islamicization" of Christianity? Perhaps. After all, the most notable armed prophet in the history of religion is certainly Mohammed, as Machiavelli surely knows. Mohammed is never mentioned in chapter 6 of *The Prince*, but this discretion is no longer observed in Machiavelli's follower, Rousseau. A further reason for seeing Mohammed as an unspoken presence in chapter 6 of *The Prince* is that Mohammed may have conceived the deliberate project of setting himself up as an Arab Moses (the "exodus" of believers from Mecca, the establishment of an armed theocratic state in Medina, laws based on direct Revelation, and the triumph of believers and the scourging of unbelievers). According to Irving M. Zeitlin (drawing on the work of Richard Bell), Mohammed, precisely *qua* armed prophet, consciously modeled himself on Moses: See *The Historical Muhammad* (Cambridge: Polity, 2007), pp. 100–101, 105. Interestingly, Mohammed's actual career nicely fits Machiavelli's analysis: Mohammed as unarmed prophet (Mecca) fails; Mohammed as armed prophet (Medina) succeeds (cf. Zeitlin, pp. 119–120). In any case, there will be more discussion of this theme in Chapter 3.

theme of *Discourses* I.9 is "founding," while the theme of *Discourses* III.1 is "refounding" – how one restores a set of institutions to their original principles over against the inescapable process of decay and decrepitude to which earthly institutions are subject. The title of *Discourses* III.1 refers to religious institutions ("Sect") ahead of political institutions ("Republic"). Furthermore, the privileged example featured in that chapter recounts the restoration of Christianity by the religious orders, Franciscan and Dominican, at the beginning of the thirteenth century. Yet if St. Francis and St. Dominic were genuine *refounders* within the framework of Machiavelli's analysis, then Christ was a genuine founder.[12] The same point is confirmed even more decisively if we look at Machiavelli's commentary on Savonarola, not in *The Prince*, chapter 6, but at the end of *Discourses* I.11. Machiavelli says of Savonarola: "For his life, learning, and the subject he took up were sufficient to make [an infinite number of people] lend faith."[13] This directly contradicts the conclusion of *The Prince*, chapter 6, concerning unarmed prophets. One *can* persuade multitudes without being an armed prophet. "[T]he people of Florence... were persuaded by Friar Girolamo Savonarola."[14] Hence even the *failed* unarmed prophet shows that the example of a life and the vigor of one's teaching can in principle suffice to move a multitude. All the more is it the case that genuinely sincere Christians like St. Francis and St. Dominic can, by the living of an exemplary life, inject new vitality into what Christ founded. According to Machiavelli, St. Francis and St. Dominic did their work of refounding "with poverty and with the example of [i.e., exemplifying] the life of Christ."[15] If a refounding is the reenactment of originary virtue, then in the case of Christ too, the exemplification of a certain kind of life, a life of poverty and innocence, sufficed to found a large and durable civilization. Unarmed prophets do succeed. Hence the failure of Savonarola (highlighted in *The Prince*, chapter 6) was contingent, not necessary. "No one... should be terrified that he cannot carry out what has been carried out by others."[16] In other words, let no one despair of putting Christianity to political use. Christianity can be paganized.

This idea of paganizing Christianity provides invaluable aid in deciphering what would otherwise be an impenetrable riddle in *The Prince* – namely why Cesare Borgia looms as large as he does in the book, for on the face of it, it is by no means clear why Cesare merits the lavish attention that he receives. First of all, Cesare is a loser in a book that is supposed to be devoted to the celebration of winners. Machiavelli tells us repeatedly that Cesare is to be taken

---

[12] In the "Exhortation to Penitence," Machiavelli refers to Jesus as "our Emperor Jesus Christ" [*imperadore nostro Cristo Iesù*] – a paradoxical turn of phrase, to say the least! Machiavelli, *The Chief Works and Others*, Vol. 1, trans. Allan Gilbert (Durham, NC: Duke University Press, 1965), p. 173. Consider also Machiavelli's reference in *Discourses* I.12 to Jesus as one who "ordered" (i.e., founded) what can be construed as in effect a political order.

[13] *Discourses on Livy*, trans. Mansfield and Tarcov, p. 36.

[14] Ibid.

[15] Ibid., p. 211.

[16] Ibid., p. 36.

as exemplary ("I do not know what better teaching I could give to a new prince than the example of his actions"; "I shall never hesitate to cite Cesare Borgia and his actions").[17] Machiavelli even goes so far as to suggest that Cesare's politics are uncriticizable ("if I summed up all the actions of the duke, I would not know how to reproach him").[18] But this claim manifestly fails – from Machiavelli's own viewpoint – to survive even minimal scrutiny. In chapter 13, where Cesare is cited in support of the argument that it is always best to employ one's own troops, Cesare *first* tries mercenaries, *then* tries auxiliaries, and only then uses his own troops. If Cesare is so virtuous, why did he have to try three times before getting it right?

It might be argued that Cesare, despite his eventual failure, can be taken as exemplary by Machiavelli because only bad luck stood in the way of his achieving great success, and Machiavelli encourages precisely this view ("it was not his fault, because this arose from an extraordinary and extreme malignity of fortune").[19] Again, though, this thesis is completely untenable, as close attention to the text easily confirms. Although Machiavelli states repeatedly that Cesare was undone by fortune,[20] this is blatantly contradicted by the decisive final sentence of chapter 7. "[T]he duke erred," and *this* (not fortune) "was the cause of his ultimate ruin." [*Errò, adunque, el duca in questa elezione, e fu cagione dell' ultima ruina sua.*][21] Machiavelli believes that Cesare had it within his power to steer the College of Cardinals toward the election of a pope who would allow Cesare to proceed with his political enterprises, but instead he chose to go along with the selection of a pope he knew to be bitterly hostile to the Borgias, and he did so on account of a moment of credulity – a lapse hardly consistent with Machiavellian virtue.[22] Cesare's "ultimate ruin" was not the fault of fortune.

Machiavelli's standard of political judgment is clearly the contrast between virtue and fortune, and early on in chapter 7 Machiavelli cites two Italian princes, one of whom meets that standard and one of whom does not. Yet to the prince of virtue (Francesco Sforza) Machiavelli devotes no more than one

[17] *The Prince*, trans. Mansfield, pp. 27, 55. See also p. 33: "no fresher examples than the actions of that man."

[18] Ibid., p. 32.

[19] Ibid., p. 27.

[20] In addition to the statement cited in the preceding note, ibid.: "acquired his state through the fortune of his father and lost it through the same" (a summary of Cesare's career, which itself seems to underscore his lack of virtue). Cf. p. 102: "repulsed by fortune," discussed later in this chapter.

[21] Ibid., p. 33.

[22] Ibid.: "he made a bad choice." See *The Legations*, in Machiavelli, *The Chief Works*, Vol. 1, ed. Gilbert, p. 149: "he [Julius] has obligations to Duke Valentino [Cesare], having to a great extent to thank him for the papacy" (dispatch of November 11, 1503). There is further support for this judgment in the exclamation supposedly expressed by King Louis XII in reaction to the election of Pius III in September 1503: "That son of a whore [Cesare] has kept Rouen from the papacy!" *The Prince*, ed. Robert M. Adams (New York: Norton, 1977), p. 25, n. 5. Needless to say, if Rouen had been elected in September, Julius would not have been elected in November.

sentence, whereas to the prince of fortune (Cesare) he devotes the balance of the chapter, a space of about six or seven pages in a very short and compressed book (as well as other key passages in other parts of the book). The very title of the chapter devoted to Cesare – referring to "fortune" and "the arms of others," as opposed to the "virtue" and "one's own arms" of chapter 6's title – already indicates that Cesare was a second-rank prince, a player on what we might call the "B team" rather than the "A team."[23] Nonetheless, his exploits get a disproportionate amount of attention relative to princes who clearly rank higher according to the virtue–fortune schema. Why?

It is Burckhardt and Nietzsche who suggest the solution to this profound puzzle. Burckhardt writes,

He [Cesare], if anybody, could have secularized the States of the Church, and he would have been forced to do so in order to keep them. Unless we are much deceived, this is the real reason of the secret sympathy with which Machiavelli treats this great criminal; from Cesare, or from nobody, could it be hoped that he "would draw the steel from the wound," in other words, annihilate the Papacy – source of all foreign intervention and of all the divisions of Italy.[24]

In the same context, Burckhardt speculates about Cesare's more direct designs upon the papacy: "[I]n pursuing such a hypothesis [viz., Cesare's manipulation of his own election to the papacy!] the imagination loses itself in an abyss."[25] Nietzsche presumably picks this idea up from Burckhardt, and of course he embraces it with more relish than we would expect of Burckhardt:

I envisage a *possibility* of a perfectly supraterrestial magic and fascination of color: it seems to me that it glistens in all the tremors of subtle beauty, that an art is at work in

[23] Machiavelli's praise of Cesare Borgia is quite misleading. He writes, "[the duke] should be put forward, as I have done, to be imitated by *all those who have risen to empire through fortune and by the arms of others*" (*The Prince*, trans. Mansfield, p. 32; emphasis added). At first glance, this appears as unqualified praise. However, when one gives due attention to the part of the sentence I have italicized, it presents itself, in relation to the standard laid out in chapter 6, as extremely qualified praise.

[24] Jacob Burckhardt, *The Civilization of the Renaissance in Italy* (London: Phaidon Press, 1960), pp. 71–72. It is striking to reflect that as late as the Risorgimento (1862!), the Church is *still* the heart of opposition to Italian unification and the cause of foreign occupation. It is hard not to agree with Machiavelli on the seriousness of the problem when one considers that it took a further *three-and-a-half centuries* to solve the problem. Can one think of Machiavelli as the intellectual father of the Risorgimento?

[25] Burckhardt, *The Civilization of the Renaissance in Italy*, p. 73. It is worth noting that in Burckhardt's view, the health problems of Pope Alexander and his son during the critical period of August to November 1503 were due to poisoning (giving them a taste of their own medicine!), which would imply that Cesare's failure was less a matter of fortune and more a function of human agency. Ibid., pp. 70, 73, 277. More specifically, Burckhardt's thesis is that the two Borgias poisoned *themselves* by accidentally consuming a deadly powder they had prepared for a wealthy cardinal – which to an even higher degree attributes the death of Alexander and the near-death of Cesare to agency rather than fortune.

As Scott and Sullivan discuss, Burckhardt borrows this thesis of self-poisoning by the Borgias from Guicciardini: "Patricide and the Plot of *The Prince*," pp. 895–896 and 899 n. 16.

it, so divine, so devilishly divine that one searches millennia in vain for a second such
possibility; I envisage a spectacle so ingenious, so wonderfully paradoxical at the same
time, that all the deities on Olympus would have had occasion for immortal laughter:
Cesare Borgia as pope. Am I understood? Well then, that would have been the victory
which alone I crave today: with that, Christianity would have been *abolished*.[26]

As Burckhardt intimates, the key to unraveling the entire drama of *The Prince*
resides in the following passage in *Discourses* I.12:

[T]he church has kept and keeps this province divided. And truly no province has ever
been united or happy unless it has all come under obedience to one republic or to one
prince, as happened to France and to Spain. The cause that Italy is not in the same
condition and does not also have one republic or one prince to govern it is solely the
church.... [S]ince the church has not been powerful enough to be able to seize Italy,
nor permitted another to seize it, it has been the cause that [Italy] has not been able to
come under one head.[27]

Machiavelli's analysis in *Discourses* I.12 is quite clear. The worst alternative
is for the Church to steer a middle course, half-Christian, half-political (again,
exactly Rousseau's analysis). The papacy must either withdraw from politics
altogether and show that it is serious about practicing the religion it professes,[28]
or it must intervene in politics much more boldly and decisively. The latter is
the Cesarian policy. The very favorable treatment of Julius II throughout *The
Prince* teaches us that his conduct of the papacy certainly did not lack for
boldness, but it was a boldness animated by a crucially different intention,
as will be discussed shortly. As the story of Julius II in fact illustrates, a more
powerful papacy will be disastrous unless one goes *all the way* with the Cesarian
approach to ecclesiastical politics. The decisive question, then, is whether some
future pope (such as Leo X) will follow the lead of the Borgias. According
to this more radical alternative, Machiavelli's thought seems to be that if the

---

[26] *The Portable Nietzsche*, ed. Walter Kaufmann (New York: Viking Press, 1968), pp. 653–654
(*The Antichrist*, § 61). Nietzsche goes on to blame Luther for having spoiled "the tremendous
event that had happened [in Rome], the overcoming of Christianity in its very seat." Here, too,
Nietzsche is following Burckhardt. Cf. Nietzsche's letter to Georg Brandes of November 20,
1888: *Selected Letters of Friedrich Nietzsche*, ed. Christopher Middleton (Chicago: University
of Chicago Press, 1969), pp. 326–327. The Machiavelli–Burckhardt–Nietzsche triangle is also
discussed in Richard Sigurdson, *Jacob Burckhardt's Social and Political Thought* (Toronto:
University of Toronto Press, 2004), pp. 213–215. Sigurdson rightly points out that Nietzsche
loves Cesare whereas Burckhardt detests him; yet Cesare's "dream of destroying Christianity" arouses some degree of admiration in Burckhardt (p. 215). More generally, one can say
that Nietzsche's relationship to Burckhardt runs directly parallel to the relationship between
Machiavelli the radical and Guicciardini the conservative. For an eloquent characterization of
how Burckhardt's intellectual temperament differs from Nietzsche's, see Michael Oakeshott,
"The Detached Vision," *Encounter*, Vol. 2, No. 6 (June 1954): 69–74; but see also the critical
remarks by Perry Anderson in *Spectrum* (London: Verso, 2005), pp. 9–10.

[27] *Discourses on Livy*, trans. Mansfield and Tarcov, p. 38.

[28] Ibid., p. 37: "such religion...as was ordered by its giver" [*secondo che dal datore d'essa ne fu
ordinato*]. Leslie J. Walker's translation is "as was ordained for us by its founder."

Church is the chief *cause* of Italy's troubles, as he insists in *Discourses* I.12, then equally it ought to become the chief *cure* for Italy's troubles.

This project explains why Machiavelli concerns himself with the problem of "ecclesiastical principalities," and it is thus scarcely surprising that, once again, the career of Cesare occupies the center of *The Prince*, chapter 11. In fact, it would be reasonable to suppose that *The Prince* unfolds a hidden drama whose dramatic center is chapter 11. The underlying drama here is the founding of a Christian civil religion, that is, the possibility of unifying Italy through the agency of an ecclesiastical principality. The Cesarian project (or the Borgian project, to the extent that Cesare's father was privy to the full radius of his designs)[29] is the appropriation of the Church for pagan purposes, and it is *this* that sanctions Cesare's placement in such proximity to the heroes of chapter 6. If one accepts the (in my view inescapable) hypothesis that the unnamed redeemer in chapter 26 is Cesare, then Machiavelli is telling us that Cesare's designs were "ordered by God" – a phrase that refers us back to chapter 6, where Moses' initiatives were equally "ordered by God."[30] We thus find ourselves indeed raised within sight of the exalted plane of divine politics.

The year 1503 was clearly the critical one for this whole enterprise, and the events of that year were not favorable to Cesare's purposes, to put it mildly. Crucial to the drama of *The Prince* is the question of the transition from the Borgian papacy to the papacy of Julius. If Julius continues the Borgian policy of expanding the temporal power of the Church without altering the *character* of the Church, then Julius *aggravates* the problem set out in *Discourses* I.12 rather than helps to resolve it. By extension, if Julius fails to carry the Borgian project through to completion, then Cesare's efforts not only come to naught, they come to less than naught, for they serve to strengthen the Church without turning it toward trans-Christian purposes. All of this allows us to elucidate a corollary of the Cesare puzzle, which is why Cesare is in the spotlight rather than Julius, in spite of the fact that Julius is on the whole more virtuous than Cesare (taking virtue in a Machiavellian sense).[31] To explicate the underlying

---

29 As Scott and Sullivan point out, the reference in *The Prince*, chapter 11 to "Duke Valentino as [Alexander's] instrument" suggests that "Alexander, not Cesare, is the actor" ("Patricide and the Plot of *The Prince*," p. 896), and there are similar suggestions in chapter 7. Cf. *Discourses*, III.29, where Machiavelli speaks of the elimination of *signori* "by Pope Alexander VI" whereas in fact the pacification of the Romagna was carried out by Cesare (as he tells us in *The Prince*, chapters 7 and 17).

30 *The Prince*, ed. Mansfield, pp. 102 and 22.

31 This is borne out by some of Machiavelli's diplomatic dispatches, which suggest that he entertains more doubts about Cesare's abilities than *The Prince* would naturally lead us to assume. See, for instance, *The Legations*, in *The Chief Works*, Vol. 1, p. 128: "the government of this Lord since I have been here has rested only on his good fortune" (dispatch of October 23, 1502); p. 144: "the Duke lets himself be carried away by that rash confidence of his, and believes that the words of another man are going to be surer than his own have been" (dispatch of November 4, 1503); and in a dispatch of November 14, 1503, Machiavelli reports the judgment of two cardinals concerning Cesare's confusion and irresolution, one of whom declares the Duke "out of his mind" (pp. 150–151). This last dispatch refers to a point in Cesare's career when he was

drama of *The Prince*, one must discern the decisive contrast between the papacy as represented by Cesare (acting as the agent of Alexander VI) and the papacy of Julius II. Broadly speaking, Cesare was a loser and Julius was a winner, yet Machiavelli seems passionately interested in the fate of Cesare in a way that he simply is not with Julius, who ultimately outfoxed Cesare. The reason for Machiavelli's fascination with Cesare is that Cesare was devoted to expanding the temporal power of the Church within the larger project of "paganizing" the Church (i.e., making it the instrument of *his own* this-worldly purposes).[32] Julius, in contrast, sought to enlarge the temporal power of the papacy while *preserving* the papacy *as* the papacy.[33] Relative to this absolutely fundamental issue, it is for Machiavelli largely a matter of indifference that Julius was in fact a much more successful prince![34]

But if Julius did not see Cesare's project through to completion, perhaps some other "pagan Pope" will. Hence at critical points in the text the focus shifts to Leo X. Chapter 11 of *The Prince* ends with an appeal to the de' Medici pope to pursue the enterprise begun by his predecessors in the business of ecclesiastical politics, namely Cesare and Julius (but to do it in Cesare's spirit, not in Julius's). Chapter 26 again makes reference to Leo – as if he were saying to the de' Medici: Look what the Borgias had been able to do with the papacy, and follow their example! It is in the very same paragraph that Machiavelli recalls the unnamed savior-prince whose divine mission, "ordered by God for [Italy's] redemption," offered "a glimmer" of the highest possibilities, although "in the highest course of his actions, he was repulsed by fortune," and so Italy awaits the arrival of another.[35] In other words, the de' Medici must take up again the work of papal imperialism, and bring to completion the business

being shrewdly outplayed at his own Machiavellian game by Julius. One should not fail to note the important fact that it is precisely Julius II whom Machiavelli discusses immediately before the book's most famous passage (the "fortune is a woman" passage at the end of chapter 25).

[32] Robert Hughes has a lovely story about receiving "a catalogue from a mail-order cutlery firm, specializing in hunting and fishing knives [featuring] a stiletto concealed in a crucifix, made in Taiwan, and selling for $15.99"; see *Culture of Complaint: The Fraying of America* (New York: Warner Books, 1993), p. 159. As Hughes rightly observes, this "little weapon [was] worthy in conception, if not in craftsmanship, of the Borgias." His stiletto concealed in a crucifix in fact offers the perfect image of Cesare's (and Machiavelli's) enterprise.

[33] Cf. Burckhardt, *Civilization of the Renaissance*, p. 74: "in all essential respects [Julius II] was the saviour of the Papacy." Machiavelli in effect says the same thing: What the Borgias set in motion was by Julius "not only continued but increased," but *unlike them*, Julius "did everything for the increase of the Church" (*The Prince*, ed. Mansfield, p. 47). This is immediately followed by Machiavelli's usual bitter critique of the disastrous consequences of the power of the Christian papacy.

[34] Ridolfi also raises the question of whether Machiavelli's distaste for Julius is consistent with his enthusiasm for Cesare Borgia; see Roberto Ridolfi, *The Life of Niccolò Machiavelli*, trans. Cecil Grayson (London: Routledge & Kegan Paul, 1963), p. 118. Ridolfi rightly says that an important part of the explanation is that Machiavelli "hated the temporal power of the Church" (p. 119); but Cesare was *also* an agent of the Church's power, so Ridolfi's explanation only works if it is supplemented by the kind of interpretation I have offered.

[35] *The Prince*, ed. Mansfield, pp. 47, 102.

that Cesare left unfinished. One could say that the rhetorical climax of *The Prince* consists in what seems to be an appeal to the de' Medici in chapter 26 to resume the project of Cesare's that was derailed in 1503. Machiavelli writes that the de' Medici are "supported by God and by the Church *of which it is now prince.*"[36] He then stunningly adds, "nor was God more friendly to them [viz., founders such as Moses] than to you [viz., the de' Medici and Pope Leo X in particular]."[37] Machiavelli's purpose in this text is to sanctify "the piety of arms," and his privileged exemplar of this armed piety (on which Leo X is meant to model himself) is Moses as armed prophet.[38]

Although Machiavelli says at the beginning of *The Prince*, chapter 11, that "it would be the office of a presumptuous and foolhardy man to discourse on" ecclesiastical principalities,[39] ecclesiastical principalities – or at least one ecclesiastical principality in particular – are what he really cares about. The central drama of *The Prince* concerns the role of this ecclesiastical principality in obstructing national self-governance, and especially the doings of two popes and one pope's son in relation to this all-important drama.[40]

[I]f someone were to inquire of me how it came about that the Church has come to such greatness in temporal affairs despite the fact that, before Alexander, the Italian powers, and not only those that are called powers but every baron and lord, even the least, held her in low esteem in temporal affairs – and now a king of France trembles at her and she has been able to remove him from Italy and to ruin the Venetians – though this is known, it does not seem to me superfluous to recall a good part of it to memory.

Then Alexander VI arose.... And though his intent might not have been *to make the Church great, but rather the duke,* nonetheless what he did redounded to the greatness of the Church. After his death, the duke being eliminated, *the Church* fell heir to his labors. *Then came Pope Julius, and he found the Church great....* These things Julius not only continued but increased.... All these enterprises succeeded for him, and with

---

[36] Ibid., p. 102; emphasis added.

[37] Ibid., p. 103. On the divine favor shown to the de' Medici, cf. the text from *Discourse on Florentine Affairs after the Death of Lorenzo* quoted in Ridolfi, *The Life of Niccolò Machiavelli*, p. 184. Notable in this latter text is Machiavelli's appeal to Leo X to aim for worldly immortality and glory. Machiavelli's thought here and elsewhere is surely that because immortality and glory (and *not* otherworldly eternity) have become the de facto aims of the papacy – which has therefore become merely *nominally* Christian – its paganization ought to be accomplishable with very little real change. Compare also Machiavelli's reference to Pope Clement VII as an ineffectual "prince" in his famous letter to Vettori of April 16, 1525 (quoted in Ridolfi, p. 241).

[38] *The Prince*, ed. Mansfield, p. 103. The text is full of Mosaic imagery.

[39] Ibid., p. 45.

[40] Scott and Sullivan also argue that "*The Prince* has a plot" ("Patricide and the Plot of *The Prince*," p. 888). The plot they narrate overlaps to a great extent with the story I try to develop in this chapter. However, they add an extra spin to the story told here: that Cesare had available to him a ready expedient by which to end the papacy – namely to assassinate his own father and to wipe out the entire College of Cardinals. What Scott and Sullivan in effect propose is to read the whole of *The Prince* in the light of Giovampagolo Baglioni's missed opportunity to commit "papacide" in *Discourses* I.27 (as well as the "parricide" committed by Liverotto da Fermo in *The Prince*, chapter 8). I agree that it is tempting to interpret this as the final step in Machiavelli's line of reasoning about the problem of the papacy.

all the more praise, inasmuch as *he did everything for the increase of the Church and not of some private individual.*[41]

It is not hard to see why the final outcome of Cesare's career presents itself to Machiavelli as a top-to-bottom disaster: Not only do Cesare and his father decisively set in motion the process of accumulating vastly more power for the Church, but Cesare even helps to put in power a pope who redirects this accumulation of greater power for the Church so that it no longer serves the cause of making "some private individual" great but rather serves to make *the Church itself* great and powerful. What a fatal outcome! Once one grasps the true consequence of the worthy project undertaken by Alexander VI and his son Cesare, one sees that Cesare is not the *hero* of the book but on the contrary a bungler whose failed project has the most dire consequences. Cesare and his father set out to *use* the Church to make themselves extremely powerful. What they actually accomplished was to make *the Church* extremely powerful and Italy much weaker.[42]

---

[41] Ibid., pp. 45, 46–47; emphasis added. Arguably, the lines in which Machiavelli formulates his distinction between increasing Church power to secure the greatness of certain individuals (good) and doing so to secure the greatness of the Church (fatal!) are the most important in the whole book. Certainly, the Burckhardtian–Nietzschean reading we have offered suggests that this shift from the papacy as conceived by Alexander–Cesare and the papacy as conceived by Julius represents the central axis around which the book's main drama revolves.

[42] Leo Strauss also interprets Cesare not just as a failure but as *worse* than a failure because Cesare's actions bring about much greater power for the Church. See *Thoughts on Machiavelli*, p. 68 ("Cesare's successes ultimately benefited only the Church, and thus increased the obstacles to the conquest or liberation of Italy.... Cesare's failure was not accidental"); see also p. 308, n. 32 on the idea of "a new Cesare Borgia [who] might redeem Italy after having himself become Pope." According to Strauss, however, Machiavelli is not impressed by Leo X as a potential Cesare (ibid.).

3

Moses and Mohammed as Founder–Princes or Legislators

Islam is politics or it is nothing.

– Ayatollah Khomeini[1]

It is obviously not an accident that of the four instances of exemplary legislation discussed by Rousseau in Book II, chapter 7 of the *Social Contract*, no less than three of them are theocratic civic orders (namely those founded by Moses, Mohammed, and Calvin, Lycurgus's Sparta being the one exception)[2] – any more than it is an accident that Moses receives the privileged treatment that he does as a founder-prince in chapters 6 and 26 of *The Prince*.[3] This in itself

---

[1] Quoted in Bernard Lewis, *The Crisis of Islam: Holy War and Unholy Terror* (New York: Random House, 2003), p. 8.

[2] As regards Rousseau's appeal to Moses and Mohammed as exemplary legislators, see Masters's commentary: Jean-Jacques Rousseau, *On the Social Contract*, ed. Roger D. Masters (New York: St. Martin's Press, 1978), p. 142, n. 58. In the corresponding discussion in *The Government of Poland*, namely Chapter 2 ("The Spirit of Ancient Institutions"), the exemplary founders are Moses, Lycurgus, and Numa. Once again, two out of three are primarily legislators of religious institutions, with Lycurgus again being the lone exception. For an interesting comparison of Rousseau and Freud on the theme of Moses as founder, see Bonnie Honig, *Democracy and the Foreigner* (Princeton, NJ: Princeton University Press, 2001), chapter 2. For an account of why, from Rousseau's point of view, Moses is in fact emphatically *superior* to the other great legislators, see *The Collected Writings of Rousseau*, Vol. 4, ed. Roger D. Masters and Christopher Kelly (Lebanon, NH: University Press of New England, 1994), pp. 33–34.

[3] Cf. John T. Scott and Vickie B. Sullivan, "Patricide and the Plot of *The Prince*: Cesare Borgia and Machiavelli's Italy," *American Political Science Review*, Vol. 88, No. 4 (December 1994): 898 – "Moses is Machiavelli's most outstanding example of a prince who founds a state and orders a religion"; cf. p. 893. If founding both a religion and a state defines Machiavelli's highest standard, then obviously Mohammed too meets this highest standard. Scott and Sullivan also point out that Rousseau's "examples of legislators . . . are the same individuals Machiavelli cites" (p. 898, n. 3).

As Michael Walzer points out in *Interpretation and Social Criticism* (Cambridge, MA: Harvard University Press, 1987), p. 18, the very fact that Machiavelli refers to Moses as a "legislator" is already a blasphemy, a subversion of the biblical presentation of Moses. No doubt, the same

impresses upon us the urgency of the civil-religion concerns in Rousseau – and also of course in Machiavelli before him. What is more, Rousseau makes sure that the implicit lesson is not overlooked by the reader, for he concludes his chapter "On the Legislator" with an explicit insistence that the great and effective Legislator must see to it that the decisions of his own sublime reason are placed "in the mouth of the immortals in order to convince by divine authority those who cannot be moved by human prudence" (and then cites the authority of Machiavelli's civil-religion doctrine!).[4] Rousseau ends with the suggestion that Warburton is wrong to maintain "that politics and religion have a common object for us"; it is rather the case "that at the origin of nations, one serves as an instrument of the other" [*Il ne faut pas . . . conclure . . . que la politique et la religion aient parmi nous un objet commun, mais que, dans l'origine des nations, l'une sert d'instrument à l'autre.*].[5] This is *precisely* what defines civil religion.

So Rousseau cites Moses and Mohammed as founders of religions who were also great founder-legislators, whereas Machiavelli cites only Moses.[6] But is this really true? How does Mohammed figure in Machiavelli's analysis of founder-princes? To solve this crucial riddle, we need to look quite closely at *The Prince*'s famous invocation of "armed prophets." Machiavelli bestows upon Cesare Borgia the lavish attention that he does by virtue of Cesare's *ambition* to include himself in the class of founder-princes celebrated in chapter 6 of *The Prince*. He makes it into chapter 7 not on the strength of his actual achievements, but on account of the ambition that nearly gets him into chapter 6; he ends up on what I called in the last chapter the B team, but he has his eyes set on the A team. If Machiavelli had been writing *The Prince* in 1813 rather than 1513, it is clear that chapter 7 would have been devoted to another great loser, namely Napoleon – and for the same reason! Napoleon too, failure though he was, nonetheless had his eyes set on the right goal: the

applies to Rousseau. The same may also be said of Montesquieu, for as Clifford Orwin writes, "Montesquieu repeatedly casts the 'Law of Moses' as just that, the work of one human legislator among others for the use of one people among others" ("'For Which Human Nature Can Never Be Too Grateful': Montesquieu as the Heir of Christianity," in *Recovering Reason: Essays in Honor of Thomas L. Pangle*, ed. Timothy Burns, Lanham, MD: Lexington Books, 2010, p. 270).

4 *Social Contract*, ed. Masters, pp. 69–70.

5 Ibid., p. 70.

6 It is interesting to speculate about how Machiavelli would judge Rousseau's *third* exemplary theocratic founder-prince, namely Calvin. For a powerful account of the "politicalness" of Calvinism as a modern revolutionary "ideology," see Michael Walzer, *The Revolution of the Saints: A Study in the Origins of Radical Politics* (New York: Atheneum, 1976), chapter 2.

    We should, of course, also note in this context that the third theorist in the core civil-religion tradition that we're developing in Part I, namely Hobbes, *also* presents Mohammed as a "founder-prince": he includes Mohammed, alongside Numa, among "the first Founders, and Legislators of Common-wealths amongst the Gentiles." Thomas Hobbes, *Leviathan*. ed. C. B. Macpherson (London: Penguin, 1985), p. 177. One might say that if Hobbes *didn't* treat Mohammed in this way, then Hobbes wouldn't count as a theorist of civil religion (hence my argument in this chapter that Mohammed appears *tacitly* in Machiavelli's analysis, even if he does not appear explicitly).

paganization of Christianity, and the institution of a new world-historical civil religion. One of Napoleon's biographers writes in regard to Napoleon's library that "the Koran . . . is housed among the political works, beside the Bible and Montesquieu"; and he puts the following speech into Napoleon's mouth: "I became a good Catholic when I wanted to finish the war in Vendée; in Egypt, I was a Turk; when I wished to win over the Italians, I was an ultramontane. If I reigned over the Jews, I should rebuild Solomon's temple."[7] Nietzsche worships Napoleon for the same reason that Machiavelli waxes lyrical about Cesare, namely that they were at least *candidates* for the kind of higher politics practiced by a Moses or a Mohammed.[8]

As we saw in Chapter 2, Machiavelli offers in chapter 6 of *The Prince* a list of virtuous princes that suggests that the only truly exemplary political rulers are those who found world-historical civilizations. Conspicuously absent from this list are two prophets, one armed (Mohammed) and one unarmed (Jesus Christ). One might say that the two named prophets in chapter 6 – Moses (armed) and Savonarola (unarmed) – are as it were "stand-ins" for the two unnamed prophets. The grounds for this rhetorical strategy are obvious: It is politically respectable to celebrate Moses and criticize Savonarola, but it is not respectable to celebrate Mohammed and criticize Christ! Machiavelli's claim in chapter 6 that unarmed prophets fail is contradicted by *Discourses* III.1, as I argued in the previous chapter, and so it seems unlikely that the establishment of this claim is the real purpose of the comparison between Moses and Savonarola. Rather, it seems that Machiavelli's proper intention in offering this comparison is to state a preference: a preference for Mohammed over Christ.[9] The basis for this preference is laid out quite clearly in *Discourses* II.2: Unarmed prophets found

---

7 Emil Ludwig, *Napoleon*, trans. Eden and Cedar Paul (New York: Modern Library, 1933), pp. 117 and 589. For further information concerning Napoleon's civil religion, see pp. 119–120, 125, 179–181, 591–592, 599–600, 636, and 659–660.

8 In this connection, consider Nietzsche's high regard for Islam in *The Will to Power*, ed. Walter Kaufmann, trans. W. Kaufmann and R. J. Hollingdale (New York: Random House, 1967), pp. 92–93 (§§ 143–145); see also *The Antichrist*, §§ 59–60, esp. the last sentence of § 59: "Islam is a thousand times right in despising Christianity: Islam presupposes men." It goes without saying that Napoleon, in common with Nietzsche, much preferred the Old Testament to the New, and considered Moses to be a "man of mark" while Christ he judged a mere "fanatic" (Ludwig, p. 599). Cf. Rousseau: "The Jewish law, which is still in existence, and the law of the son of Ishmael, which has ruled half the world for ten centuries, still bear witness today to the great men who formulated them. And whereas proud philosophy or blind partisan spirit regards them merely as lucky impostors, the true political theorist [*le vrai politique*] admires in their institutions that great and powerful genius which presides over lasting institutions" (*Social Contract*, ed. Masters, p. 70). (Possible translations of *le vrai politique* include "the true statesman" or "the truly political person"; Frederick Watkins translates it as "the true student of politics.") As already noted, Rousseau, in a note earlier in the same chapter (Book II, chapter 7), praises Calvin in the same terms. Despite Rousseau's critical analysis of Christianity in his civil-religion chapter, and echoing his account of Protestantism in the *Geneva Manuscript*, this suggests that, for Rousseau, Protestant Christianity cannot be *immediately* discounted as a possible civil religion.

9 Cf. Leo Strauss, *Thoughts on Machiavelli* (Glencoe, IL: The Free Press, 1958), p. 84.

civilizations that render human beings weak and effeminate; armed prophets found civilizations that render human beings strong and glory-seeking.[10]

Can we *know* that Machiavelli had Mohammed in mind when he constructed his discussion of armed prophets? No. But the whole logic of Machiavelli's analysis points toward Mohammed as an archetypal armed prophet.[11]

---

[10] Cf. Leo Strauss, "Restatement on Xenophon's *Hiero*," in *On Tyranny*, ed. V. Gourevitch and M. S. Roth (New York: The Free Press, 1991), pp. 183–184. As Strauss points out, Machiavelli's idea of the armed prophet was anticipated by Maimonides in his "Letter on Astrology" (also known as the "Letter to Marseilles"): *Medieval Political Philosophy*, ed. Ralph Lerner and Muhsin Mahdi (Ithaca, NY: Cornell University Press, 1972), p. 229. According to Maimonides, the prophets denounced the people as fools because they dabbled in astrology instead of cultivating the arts of war and conquest. Judging from this passage, Maimonides read the Old Testament in the same way in which it was read by the modern civil-religion theorists from Machiavelli onward. (In a somewhat similar vein is Spinoza's suggestion at the end of chapter 3 of the *Theological–Political Treatise* that it was the effeminizing effect of the Jewish religion that was to blame for Israel's failure to regain its state.) For a modern version of the sentiments expressed in this Maimonidean text, see the discussion of the poems of J. L. Gordon in Elie Kedourie, *Nationalism*, 3rd ed. (London: Hutchinson, 1966), pp. 100–101. Also relevant here is Machiavelli's discussion of "today's mode of life" as shaped by Christianity and its devaluation of military training: See Niccolò Machiavelli, *Art of War*, trans. Christopher Lynch (Chicago: University of Chicago Press, 2003), pp. 59–61. As Paul A. Rahe helpfully discusses in connection with the text just cited, what is seen by Machiavelli as a dire problem for modernity is positively embraced by Montesquieu (and all other liberals) as a huge moral advantage of the modern condition: See Paul A. Rahe, "The Book that Never Was: Montesquieu's *Considerations on the Romans* in Historical Context," *History of Political Thought*, Vol. XXVI, No. 1 (Spring 2005): 61–63, 68. Montesquieu alludes to *Art of War*'s critique of Christianity, and responds to it, in *Spirit of the Laws*, Book 24, chapter 3: "we owe to Christianity ... a certain right of nations [*droit des gens*] in war, for which human nature can never be sufficiently grateful." Eric Voegelin offers an observation that illuminates very well what is at stake between Machiavelli and Montesquieu. See *The Collected Works of Eric Voegelin, Vol. 33: The Drama of Humanity and Other Miscellaneous Papers, 1939–1985*, ed. William Petropulos and Gilbert Weiss (Columbia, MO: University of Missouri Press, 2004), p. 375: "fratricidal wars ... are a political fact that must not be forgotten as the background of [Plato's] *Republic*. ... Plato suggests as a great improvement in the international law of war, that when one city is conquered by another, one shouldn't perhaps kill more than one-half of the population. So if you will be killing off less than one-half, then you are already a very progressive liberal, one would say, in the Platonic environment." This kind of reflection ought to take the luster off *all* ancient societies, but for Machiavelli it does not.

[11] The reason why Mohammed counts not only as one armed prophet among others but rather as *the* preeminent armed prophet is more or less self-evident. As Edward Luttwak writes, "Islam ... is the only major faith whose validity was historically affirmed by military victories; theologically, it still utterly depends on the promised martial superiority of its adherents." See Luttwak, "The Missing Dimension," in *Religion, The Missing Dimension of Statecraft*, ed. Douglas Johnston and Cynthia Sampson (Oxford: Oxford University Press, 1994), p. 16; cf. p. 18, n. 7.

It's a striking fact that, starting with Gentillet's influential *Contre-Machiavel* of 1576, it became an established trope among Machiavelli's harshest early critics to refer to Machiavelli's work as "*l'Alcoran des courtesans*": See Sydney Anglo, *Machiavelli – The First Century: Studies in Enthusiasm, Hostility, and Irrelevance* (Oxford: Oxford University Press, 2005), pp. 286, 340, 345, 360. Although this obviously does not prove anything, it nonetheless might say *something* about Machiavelli's affinities with Islam.

In this sense, it seems appropriate to read backward from Hobbes, Rousseau, and Nietzsche to grasp what the idea of an armed prophet really means.

I have conceded that Machiavelli's intention to present Mohammed as a model armed prophet is merely inferred – yet the fact that Machiavelli reflects seriously on the relation between Islam and *virtù* need not rely on inferences; there is clear textual evidence. In *Discourses* I.55, Machiavelli writes that "one sees [such goodness] remaining only in that province [viz., the free German cities and Swiss republics]."[12] Machiavelli expands on this statement in the Preface to Book II, where he refers to *five* nations subsequent to the Roman Empire that "lived virtuously": "the kingdom of the Franks, the kingdom of the Turks, that of the sultan, and the peoples of Germany today," as well as the "Saracen sect" that destroyed the Byzantine Empire.[13] According to James B. Atkinson and David Sices, *three* of the five regimes referred to in this text are Islamic: The kingdom of the Turks refers to the Ottoman Empire; the kingdom of the sultan refers to the Egyptian Mamelukes; and the Saracen sect is a generic reference to Islam.[14] Thus Islamic states clearly figure very prominently in this catalogue of "modern" virtue. In fact, Machiavelli goes out of his way to emphasize that the virtue that "is praised with true praise" is associated not just with nations or kingdoms but specifically with "sects," which again suggests that Islam ("which did so many great things and seized so much of the world after it destroyed the [Byzantine] Empire") provides a crucial exemplification of "living virtuously."[15] Furthermore, the reference to the "glory" being won by Selim I in *Discourses* I.19 again contradicts I.55's claim that only German or Swiss cities are sites of modern virtue.[16]

Joel Schwartz, in a commentary on Rousseau, writes that "[m]uch of the anti-Christian animus of the Enlightenment can be understood in terms of this [Machiavelli-inspired] equation" between Christianity and "the effeminacy of

---

[12] Niccolò Machiavelli, *Discourses on Livy*, trans. Harvey C. Mansfield and Nathan Tarcov (Chicago: University of Chicago Press, 1996), p. 111; cf. p. 129.

[13] Ibid., p. 124.

[14] *The Sweetness of Power: Machiavelli's Discourses and Guicciardini's Considerations*, trans. James B. Atkinson and David Sices (DeKalb, IL: Northern Illinois University Press, 2002), p. 159, n. 5.

[15] *Discourses on Livy*, trans. Mansfield and Tarcov, p. 124.

[16] Ibid., p. 53; cf. p. 67: "as the Turk does in our times" (*Discourses* I.30). There is a further important civil-religion-related dimension to Machiavelli's discussion of modern republics of virtue in the Preface to Book II. The main non-Islamic example is clearly Germany. Roughly contemporaneously with the composition of the *Discourses*, Germany became the center of the Lutheran revolt against the papacy. (Luther's challenge to the Church unfolded during the papacy of Leo X.) It is possible to interpret Machiavelli's emphasis on German virtue as a tacit endorsement (or at least approving anticipation) of the Reformation. In any case, the identification of what was soon to be Lutheran Germany as a special site of modern virtue surely heightens the singling-out of Catholic Christianity as the prime target of Machiavelli's critique of moral and political decadence. As Atkinson and Sices point out, the place in the text where Machiavelli in effect converges with Luther is the first sentence of *Discourses*, I.12: See *The Sweetness of Power*, p. 405, n. 1; see also p. 262, n. 3.

modern man."[17] Hume is a case in point. In an important chapter of his *Natural History of Religion* (Section X), Hume cites and reaffirms Machiavelli's teaching in *Discourses* II.2 that "the doctrines of the CHRISTIAN religion (meaning the catholic; for he knew no other) which recommended only passive courage and suffering, had subdued the spirit of mankind, and had fitted them for slavery and subjection."[18] According to Hume's own analysis, "theism" (i.e., Christianity) represents the deity as infinitely superior to mankind – a "belief [which is apt] to sink the human mind into the lowest submission and abasement, and [therefore] to represent the monkish virtue of mortification, penance, humility, and passive suffering, as the only qualities which are acceptable to [God]."[19] By contrast, "idolatry" [i.e., polytheistic religions] breeds "activity, spirit, courage, magnanimity, love of liberty, and all the virtues which aggrandize a people."[20] Accordingly, monks like "DOMINIC, FRANCIS, ANTHONY, and BENEDICT" displace heroes such as "HERCULES, THESEUS, HECTOR, ROMULUS," and "whippings and fastings, cowardice and humility, abject submission and slavish obedience" – rather than "the subduing of tyrants [and] the defence of our native country" – "are become the means of obtaining celestial honours among mankind."[21] Hume states that this whole comparison between Christianity and the pagan religions "with regard to courage [paganism] or abasement [Christianity]" serves to "confirm the vulgar observation that the corruption of the best things gives rise to the worst."[22] However, going back to Hume's source for this whole reflection, namely Machiavelli, forces us to ask whether the celebration of "monkish virtues" constitutes a "corruption" of Christian theism, or whether it carries us to the very *essence* of what that theism is supposed to be.

---

[17] Joel Schwartz, *The Sexual Politics of Jean-Jacques Rousseau* (Chicago: University of Chicago Press, 1984), p. 63; Schwartz's citation of Shaftesbury seems the most relevant one, though he also refers to Montesquieu. Consider also in connection with the theme of the effeminacy of Christianity one of John Aubrey's stories about Hobbes. Visiting John Selden at his deathbed in 1654, Hobbes apparently urged Selden to resist the attention of priests by asking him, "Will you that have wrote like a man, now dye like a woman?" Cited in Richard Tuck, *Hobbes* (Oxford: Oxford University Press, 1989), pp. 31–32.

[18] David Hume, *Writings on Religion*, ed. Anthony Flew (La Salle, IL: Open Court, 1992), p. 150.

[19] Ibid., p. 149. Of course, the profession of Christian humility can be merely professed, as Machiavelli would be the first to appreciate. Bentham has a wonderful story, entirely in the spirit of Machiavelli, about the relationship between humility and ambition. He tells of a pope (Sixtus IV – uncle of Julius II!) who, while he was still a mere cardinal, gave ostentatious displays of his humility. Having been the son of a fisherman, he used to place a fishing net on top of his dining table after dinner, supposedly so as not to forget his humble beginnings. After his election to the papacy he stopped doing this. He was asked why he discontinued the practice. His answer, as reported by Bentham, was as follows: "'Peace,' answered the Holy Father, 'when the fish is caught, there is no occasion for the net.'" See Jeremy Bentham, *A Fragment on Government*, ed. J. H. Burns and H. L. A. Hart (Cambridge: Cambridge University Press, 1988), pp. 80–81. For Machiavelli's praise of Sixtus IV, see *The Prince*, 2nd ed., trans. Harvey C. Mansfield (Chicago: University of Chicago Press, 1998), p. 46.

[20] Hume, *Writings on Religion*, ed. Flew, p. 149.

[21] Ibid.

[22] Ibid.

Machiavelli's project of paganizing Christianity as a neo-Roman civil religion does not necessarily mean that Machiavelli is insincere in celebrating St. Francis and St. Dominic as exemplars of a Christian life. In the same vein, he writes the following in *Discourses* I.12: "If such religion had been maintained by the princes of the Christian republic as was ordered by its giver [*secondo che dal datore d'essa ne fu ordinato*], the Christian states and republics would be more united, much happier than they are."²³ Machiavelli here seems to be pursuing the same line of thought as Rousseau's at the end of the *Social Contract,* namely that a strong case can be made on behalf of both "the religion of man" and "the religion of the citizen" (to use Rousseau's terms). Problems start when one attempts to "mix" them, producing a corrupted Christianity that is neither good religion nor good politics. Unfortunately, as both Rousseau and Machiavelli perceive very clearly, original Christianity sets the standard of a Christian life so transcendently high that the history of the Christian Church is bound to constitute a long series of such corruptions.²⁴

Hence, without impugning the sincerity of Machiavelli's celebratory treatment of St. Francis and St. Dominic, it should also be remembered that the same passage in which St. Francis and St. Dominic are hailed as refounders of the Christian religion ends by condemning the very religion they succeeded in revitalizing: It gives a free rein to evildoers, and it elevates prelates above worldly judgment.²⁵ The prospect of otherworldly punishments may intimidate the pious multitude, but it does nothing to restrain those who are most wicked (including prelates!).²⁶ This apparent contradiction (praising Christian saints, condemning Christianity) admits of being reconciled, however. To praise St. Francis and St. Dominic religiously is to condemn them politically, for Christ's religion is religiously admirable but politically disastrous (which,

---

²³ *Discourses on Livy,* trans. Mansfield and Tarcov, p. 37.

²⁴ Cf. Nietzsche: "Go through the moral demands exhibited in the documents of Christianity one by one and you will find that in every case they are exaggerated, so that man *could* not live up to them; the intention is not that he should *become* more moral, but that he should feel *as sinful as possible.*" Friedrich Nietzsche, *Human, All Too Human: A Book for Free Spirits,* trans. R. J. Hollingdale (Cambridge: Cambridge University Press, 1986), p. 77. See also John Aubrey, *Brief Lives,* ed. John Buchanan-Brown (London: Penguin, 2000), p. 138: "[Harrington] was wont to say … '[to live by nature's rules] is to live vertuously, but Divines will not have it so: and that when the Divines would have us be an inch above Vertue, we fall an ell belowe it.'" Also: Baron d'Holbach, *Christianity Unveiled,* trans. W. M. Johnson (New York: Gordon Press, 1974), p. 62: "Among human beings, human virtues are necessary; Christian virtues are not calculated on the scale of real life."

²⁵ *Discourses on Livy,* trans. Mansfield and Tarcov, pp. 211–212.

²⁶ Cf. the reference supplied by Mansfield and Tarcov; ibid., p. 212 n. 23. By the end of the paragraph devoted to St. Francis and St. Dominic, it is perfectly clear that in Machiavelli's view, the Franciscan and Dominican refounding of Christianity is, at least in its ultimate effects, more a reinvigoration of corruption than a reinvigoration of virtue.

There is an interesting parallel between what Machiavelli says about St. Francis and St. Dominic, and what Nietzsche says about the Reformation: In each case, Christianity was saved from succumbing to its own vices, but the ultimate effect, according to both analyses, was to preserve Christianity as what it essentially was, a source of moral decadence.

again, is *identical* to what later becomes Rousseau's civil-religion analysis). This is so *unless* – by more consistent observance of its precepts – Christianity can be politically neutralized. Consider Nietzsche's judgment on St. Francis: "Francis of Assisi, neurotic, epileptic, a visionary, like Jesus."[27] Machiavelli praises St. Francis in the *Discourses*, according to this reading, for the same reason that Nietzsche "praises" the Christianity of Jesus relative to the Christianity of St. Paul: If one has to have Christians, let them at least retreat into a remote private existence where they can do no harm.[28] Christianity became a plague only when Paul seized upon it as a way of giving a new direction to civilization as a whole. Christians are okay as irrelevant dreamers and kooks; the danger comes when they aspire to shape a whole civilization. Urging Christians to emulate St. Francis is therefore tantamount to urging them to get out of the political arena altogether, and to leave the business of politics to the pros. The general Machiavellian rhetoric not to do things by halves – for instance, not to be half-moral and half-immoral but rather to be wholly good or wholly evil – applies especially, one might say, to religion. Religion must be either 100% worldly (*entirely* at the service of civic purposes) or 100% unworldly (*entirely* divorced from political life). It is clear from this principle why Machiavelli saw the Renaissance papacy as such a disaster.

[27] *The Will to Power*, ed. Kaufmann, p. 129 (§ 221).

[28] For a similar suggestion about how, in Machiavelli's view, Christianity *benefits* politics by privatizing religion, see *Hannah Arendt: The Recovery of the Public World*, ed. Melvyn Hill (New York: St. Martin's Press, 1979), p. 311.

4

Refounding and "Filiacide"

Machiavelli's Debt to Christianity

> The New Testament is full of calls to leave or relativize solidarities of family, clan, and society and be part of the Kingdom.
>
> – Charles Taylor[1]

Machiavelli's revolutionary polemics against Christianity as a (corrupt) set of institutions and as an (effete) view of the world obscure his own very substantial debt to Christianity, which will be discussed briefly in this chapter. There is another dimension to Machiavelli's civil-religion theorizing that is much less obvious than his celebration of Roman paganism in *Discourses*, I: 11–15, but that is of considerable importance in grasping the full contours of his relationship to Christianity. This comes to light in his crucial discussion of refounding, which, as we saw in Chapter 2, he discusses in connection with the efforts of St. Francis and St. Dominic to refound Christianity itself. In order for refounding to work, there must be a profound, soul-shattering, "shock and awe" effect on the civic population. Christianity was able to provoke this kind of "shock and awe" effect in relation to Judaism, and Machiavelli hopes in effect to replicate this within the domain of secular politics. Machiavelli asks this: How can one replicate the kind of unqualified commitment that Christianity manages to elicit from its adherents, and redirect this commitment toward the political sphere? It would require in this sense a civil religion to displace Christianity and render it irrelevant to the same extent that Christianity displaced Judaism and paganism and rendered them irrelevant. (Is Islam a civil religion in this sense, and is that why Islam looks so attractive to later Machiavelli-inspired theorists such as Rousseau and Nietzsche?)

In *Discourses* III.1, Machiavelli writes, "it is a thing clearer than light that these bodies [republics and sects] do not last if they do not renew themselves. The mode of renewing them is . . . to lead them back toward their beginning." What does it mean to lead religions and republics back to the beginning? As

---

[1] Charles Taylor, *Modern Social Imaginaries* (Durham, NC: Duke University Press, 2004), p. 62.

Leo Strauss rightly says, "Machiavelli's return to the beginning means return to the terror inherent in man's situation, to man's essential unprotectedness. In the beginning there was terror."[2] Although the fundamental narrative of biblical religion is one of God's providence and loving (but also just) care for human beings, reflection on the examples of founding and refounding in the *Discourses* reminds us that there is also terror in the Bible.[3] The common thread running through the stories to which Machiavelli gives greatest emphasis in the chapters on founding and refounding (*Discourses* I.9, III.1, III.3, and III.22) links up in an important way with biblical narratives and, one might say, tries to replicate in the souls of citizens the effect that these biblical narratives have on the souls of believers. Machiavelli himself draws attention to the parallel between politics and religion by referring explicitly to religion in the title of *Discourses* III.1,[4] and by devoting an important section of the chapter to the monastic refounding of Christianity.[5] Following Augustine (*City of God*, XV.6),[6] Machiavelli, in I.9 of the *Discourses*, highlights the origins of civil life in the founder's crime, in particular, the crime of fratricide committed by Romulus: "[N]or will a wise understanding ever reprove anyone for any *extraordinary* action that he uses to order a kingdom or constitute a republic. It is very suitable that when the deed accuses him, the effect excuses him."[7] Machiavelli insists that Romulus's fratricide was not a tyrannical act because it was a necessary condition for the establishment of "a civil and free way of life."[8] Founders and refounders of civil and religious orders must resort to the

---

[2] Leo Strauss, *Thoughts on Machiavelli* (Glencoe, IL: The Free Press, 1958), p. 167.

[3] Cf. James Fitzjames Stephen, *Liberty, Equality, Fraternity*, ed. Stuart D. Warner (Indianapolis: Liberty Fund, 1993), p. 201: "[T]hough Christianity expresses the tender and charitable sentiments with passionate ardour, it has also a terrible side.... [T]he tenderness and the terrors mutually imply each other." Stephen's views are discussed later in Chapter 22.

[4] It is striking that "Sect" comes before "Republic" in this title.

[5] Cf. Francis Bacon, *The Advancement of Learning and New Atlantis*, ed. Arthur Johnston (Oxford: Oxford University Press, 1974), p. 85: "Is not the ground, which Machiavel wisely and largely discourseth concerning governments, that the way to establish and preserve them, is to reduce them *ad principia*, a rule *in religion* [emphasis added] and nature, as well as in civil administration?"

[6] In *City of God*, XV.6, Augustine traces Romulus's fratricide against Remus back to the "archetype" of the fratricide against Abel committed by Cain (whom he refers to as "the first founder of the earthly city"). See also III.6; and V.17, where Augustine refers to Rome as "that refuge of Romulus, where the offer of impunity for crimes of every kind collected a multitude which was to result in the foundation of the city" (cf. I.34). St. Augustine, *City of God*, trans. Henry Bettenson (Harmondsworth: Penguin, 1984), pp. 45, 93–94, 207, and 600–601.

[7] Niccolò Machiavelli, *Discourses on Livy*, trans. Harvey C. Mansfield and Nathan Tarcov (Chicago: University of Chicago Press, 1996), p. 29; emphasis added. "One could give infinite examples to sustain the things written above, such as Moses, Lycurgus, Solon, and other founders of kingdoms and republics who were able to form laws for the purpose of the common good because they had one authority attributed to them" (p. 30). There is another very important prince praised by Machiavelli for building a glorious empire (*Discourses* I.19) who also, like Romulus, founded his regime on fratricide, namely Selim I. See Suraiya Faroqhi, *The Ottoman Empire: A Short History*, trans. Shelley Frisch (Princeton, NJ: Markus Wiener, 2009), p. 60.

[8] *Discourses on Livy*, trans. Mansfield and Tarcov, p. 30.

extraordinary; reliance on ordinary laws or ordinary norms will not suffice.[9] The distinction between the *ordinary* (normal politics) and the *extraordinary* (the politics of founding and refounding) is amplified in the discussion of the contrast between Manlius Torquatus and Valerius Corvinus in *Discourses* III.22:

[T]o command strong things one must be strong; and he who is of this strength and who commands them cannot then make them observed with mildness. But whoever is not of this strength of spirit ought to guard himself from *extraordinary* commands [*imperi istraordinari*] and can use his humanity in *ordinary* ones, because ordinary punishments [*le punizioni ordinarie*] are imputed not to the prince but to the laws and to those orders. Thus one ought to believe that Manlius was constrained to proceed so rigidly by his extraordinary commands, to which his nature inclined him. They are useful in a republic because they return its orders toward their beginning and into its ancient virtue. As we said above, if a republic were so happy that it often had one who with his example might renew the laws, and not only restrain it from running to ruin but pull it back, it would be perpetual.[10]

As I mentioned earlier, there is a common thread to Machiavelli's discussion of founding and his discussion of refounding, and this common thread leads us to reflect on the crucial parallel between Machiavelli's project and the uncompromising demands made upon human beings by religion. Machiavelli's privileged examples in *Discourses* I.9, III.3, and III.22 teach us that just as the exemplary act of founding reposes on a fratricide, so the equally hard deed of refounding rests on violations of the family bond that are just as radical – *more* radical, in fact (for what will emerge as fairly obvious reasons). In his account of refounding in *Discourses* III.1, Machiavelli lists seven examples of exemplary events that serve to restore the republic to its original principles, and two of these examples get whole chapters devoted to them, namely the story of the execution of the sons of Brutus (*Discourses* III.3, referring back to an earlier discussion in I.16), and the story of the execution of the son of Manlius Torquatus. In I.16 he writes the following:

[A] state that is free and that newly emerges comes to have partisan enemies and not partisan friends. If one wishes to remedy these inconveniences, and the disorders that the difficulties written above might bring with them, there is no more remedy more powerful, nor more valid, more secure, and more necessary, than to kill the sons of Brutus.[11]

---

9 Cf. the discussion at the beginning of *Discourses* I.7 of the "ordinary" venting of humors (such as anger) in order to avoid "recourse to extraordinary modes that bring a whole republic to ruin." These "ordinary modes" are associated with what is provided for *within the laws*, as opposed to the "extraordinary modes," which are extralegal.

10 Ibid., p. 266; emphasis added. Machiavelli's conclusion here is jarring because it directly contradicts what he says at the end of *Discourses* III.17: "Because one cannot give a certain remedy for such disorders that arise in republics, it follows that it is impossible to order a perpetual republic, because its ruin is caused through a thousand unexpected ways."

11 *Discourses on Livy*, trans. Mansfield and Tarcov, p. 45.

This story is drawn from Livy, II.4–5:

[T]he traitors were condemned and punished, a spectacle made all the more conspicuous because the consulship imposed on the father the duty of carrying out the penalty on his sons: the man who should not even have witnessed the scene was the one fortune had chosen as executioner.... [The lictors] stripped, flogged, and beheaded the young men. During the whole time all were painfully aware of Brutus' eyes and expression, for as he fulfilled his duty as a public official the natural feelings of a father could be read in his face.[12]

Here is Machiavelli's own commentary on this episode (*Discourses* III.3):

Not less necessary than useful was the severity of Brutus in maintaining in Rome the freedom that he had acquired there. It is an example rare in all memories of things to see the father sit on the tribunals and not only condemn his sons to death but be present at their death. This will always be known by those who read of ancient things; that after a change of state, either from republic to tyranny or from tyranny to republic, a memorable execution against the enemies of present conditions is necessary. Whoever takes up a tyranny and does not kill Brutus, and whoever makes a free state and does not kill the sons of Brutus, maintains himself for little time.[13]

The decisive principle here is that it is not just tyrants who need to resort to terror in order to maintain their power. Leaders of republics, too, must employ tyrannical means if they are going to be able to sustain the requisite store of virtue needed to maintain liberty for a republican regime.[14]

The story of Manlius Torquatus's severity in regard to the execution of his son (Titus Manlius) in *Discourses* III.22 is actually far more shocking than the story of the sons of Brutus, as the relevant text in Livy (VIII.7–10) makes quite clear. Livy writes, "All were transfixed with horror by this dreadful command... [The spectators] stood rooted to the spot in silence, as if lost in amazement." Following the decapitation, "their voices broke out in agonized complaint so unrestrained that they spared neither laments nor curses," and

---

[12] Livy, *The Rise of Rome: Books 1–5*, trans. T. J. Luce (Oxford: Oxford University Press, 1998), pp. 75–76.

[13] *Discourses on Livy*, trans. Mansfield and Tarcov, p. 214. For Rousseau too, the story of Brutus and his sons provides an exemplary illustration of the stern requirements of republican virtue. See *Collected Writings of Rousseau*, Vol. 8, ed. Christopher Kelly (Lebanon, NH: University Press of New England, 2000), p. 267: "in order to do his duty [Brutus] lacerated his insides."

[14] Machiavelli might say that it is no accident that the phrase "Reign of Terror" is associated precisely with the founding of a republican regime. Needless to say, subsequent modern republics have also founded their new regimes on terror, so again, restoring these regimes to their original principles means resorting once again to the terror employed in their founding. Terror administered at regular intervals is a condition of (republican) virtue.

Edward Andrew has alerted me to a nice reference in the article on "Patrie" in the *Encyclopédie* to Brutus's decapitation of his sons: "this action would appear unnatural [*dénaturée*] only to feeble souls." This is just the kind of thing one can imagine Rousseau writing. One can reverse the logic here and say it is a good argument for having a feeble soul! In any case, Andrew, in an unpublished paper entitled "Rome as the Model Imperial Republic for the Eighteenth Century," offers good illustrations of how the killing of the sons of Brutus became an emphatic trope of Jacobin patriotism.

the subsequent cremation of the body was conducted "with all the honours that can attend any military funeral."[15] Unlike the sons of Brutus, who were after all conspirators against their own father, and therefore genuine objects of disgrace, Titus Manlius was punished for having fought and won a valiant duel with the Latin commander, Geminus Maecius, without the permission of the consul (his father).[16] Livy concedes that "the brutality of the punishment made the soldiers more obedient to their commander,"[17] and for Machiavelli, this suffices to vindicate Manlius: "[H]is severity in the death of his son made the army so obedient to the consul that it was the cause of the victory that the Roman people had against the Latins."[18] Manlius "killed his son" to secure "the obedience of the soldiers,"[19] and it worked; the consequence was indeed enhanced virtue necessary for victory.

These examples receive privileged treatment precisely because their unnaturalness fulfills the effect of dread and terror that Machiavelli associates with the hard business of restoring a republic to its original principles. Hence he writes this in III.1:

Because they were excessive and notable, such things made men draw back toward the mark whenever one of them arose; and when they began to be more rare, they also began to give more space to men to corrupt themselves and to behave with greater danger and more tumult. For one should not wish ten years at most to pass from one to another of such executions; for when this time is past, men begin to vary in their customs and to transgress the laws. Unless something arises by which punishment is brought back to their memory and fear is renewed in their spirits, soon so many delinquents join together that they can no longer be punished with danger. [The Medici rulers of Florence during the 15th century] used to say, to this purpose, that it was necessary to regain the state every five years; otherwise, it was difficult to maintain it. They called regaining the state putting that terror and that fear in men that had been put there in taking it, since at that time they had beaten down those who, according to that mode of life, had worked for ill. But as the memory of that beating is eliminated, men began to dare to try new things and to say evil; and so it is necessary to provide for it, drawing [the state] back toward its beginning.[20]

---

[15] Livy, *Rome and Italy*, trans. Betty Radice (Harmondsworth: Penguin, 1982), pp. 166–167.

[16] Cf. Spinoza, *Theological–Political Treatise*, chapter 19, where Spinoza praises Manlius Torquatus for his "pious act" in applying strict justice to his son. Therefore the issue for Spinoza is "justice" in not privileging family relations vis-à-vis the state, not "virtue" in Machiavelli's sense. There is a somewhat similar text in Hobbes: see *Leviathan*, ed. C. B. Macpherson (London: Penguin, 1985), p. 724, referring to *Deuteronomy*, 21.18–21. For Hobbes as for Spinoza, the point is that a father's execution of his son must be mediated by rule of law. The emphasis on rule of law is not entirely absent from Machiavelli's analysis, but clearly what he is most fixated on is the "memorableness" of something so jarring in relation to natural sentiment.

[17] Livy, *Rome and Italy*, p. 167.

[18] *Discourses on Livy*, trans. Mansfield and Tarcov, p. 267; cf. p. 160.

[19] Ibid., p. 265.

[20] Ibid., pp. 210–211.

The dominant metaphor in these passages is that of administering a beating [*battitura*]²¹ that will not soon be forgotten, and that must be administered precisely because enough time has elapsed for the last beating to be forgotten.

Now for the connection to biblical religion: In the light of Rousseau's interpretation of Judaism in terms of its being elevated from a merely "national" religion (ruled by one god among a plurality of gods) to an imperialistic (i.e., monotheistic) religion, we can think of Jewish monotheism as the seizure of tyrannical authority on the part of the Jewish God – as in effect the elimination of His brother-gods in order to found a civil order on the basis of singular authority.²² Furthermore, the whole of Christianity presents itself as a colossal refounding of biblical religion effected by the shocking event of that god's ordaining of the sacrifice of His only son.²³ Founding: fratricide; refounding:

---

²¹ Earlier in the same chapter (ibid., pp. 209–210), Machiavelli refers to the defeat of Rome by the Gauls also as a "beating" – but an "extrinsic" rather than "intrinsic" one (i.e., administered by forces from outside, rather than from within the polity itself). He states that such an "external beating" can have the same effect of restoring the republic to its original virtue.

²² It may seem very odd to conceive of Jewish monotheism as the product of a "fratricide." The idea might perhaps appear less odd if one follows Freud's speculations about how Mosaic Judaism had its roots in a form of Egyptian monotheism that rose up against the prevailing Egyptian polytheism, privileging the sun-god Aton and forcefully suppressing all the other gods. See Sigmund Freud, *Moses and Monotheism* (New York: Vintage, 1958). This interpretation allows Freud to encompass Jewish monotheism within his broader theory of totemism according to which all primitive religions replicate the same pattern: One god within a family of gods gradually rises to hierarchical supremacy over the others (henotheism), eventually becoming an all-powerful Father-God "not [suffering] any other gods beside him" (p. 171). (With respect to Judaism in particular, Freud later complicates the story by postulating a *second* Jewish monotheism, superimposed upon the first, this time derived from the volcano-god Jahve. But no matter: In either case one has a singular Jewish god rising to its status of absolute supremacy through what is in effect an autocratic seizure of divine monopoly.)

It is possible to speculate not only that the monotheism of the Israelites evolved from an "archaic polytheism" but also that traces of this polytheism were left in Elohim as a plural name. See Harold Bloom, *The American Religion* (New York: Simon & Schuster, 1992), pp. 111 and 113, and Donald Harman Akenson, *Some Family* (Montreal: McGill-Queen's University Press, 2007), p. 41. Both Bloom and Akenson note this in the context of discussing polytheistic aspects of Mormonism. Incidentally, Allah, the god of Islam, was *also* a god among other gods before *becoming* a monotheistic god: See Irving M. Zeitlin, *The Historical Muhammad* (Cambridge: Polity, 2007), pp. 54, 66–67, 99–100.

Freud never cites Machiavelli in his interpretation of the origins of Judaism, yet there are striking similarities between themes in Machiavelli's account of religion and those in Freud. Consider, for instance, *Moses and Monotheism*, p. 53, on extinction of the traces of former religions; pp. 57–58 and 140–141, on Mosaic "tyranny"; p. 136, on the capacity of singular human beings to create religions; and pp. 141–142, on the Jewish prophets as refounders of a fading religion. It goes without saying that Freud's theory, with its relentless emphasis on the family as a site of traumatic events – acts of imagined or symbolic murder – nicely complements the themes in Machiavelli that I have tried to highlight in this chapter.

²³ Freud presents Christianity not as a religion based on filiacide but rather as one based on patricide (murder of God the Father). On Freud's interpretation, the displacement of a father-religion by a son-religion reenacts the primeval drama of murder of the father by the son (see *Moses and Monotheism*, p. 175: "Originally a Father religion, Christianity became a Son religion"; also p. 111). Admittedly, this is a religion in which (according to Freud's account)

"filiacide." Nietzsche and Kierkegaard can help us appreciate the aspect of dread encountered in the unspeakably unnatural demands asserted by biblical religion and strangely replicated in Machiavelli's politics of founding and refounding. In *Beyond Good and Evil* (§ 46), Nietzsche tells us this:

From the start, the Christian faith is a sacrifice.... [I]t presupposes that the subjection of the spirit *hurts* indescribably; that the whole past and the habits of such a spirit resist the *absurdissimum* which "faith" represents to it. Modern men, obtuse to all Christian nomenclature, no longer feel the gruesome superlative that struck a classical taste in the paradoxical formula "god on the cross." Never yet and nowhere has there been an equal boldness in inversion, anything as horrible, questioning, and questionable as this formula: it promised a revaluation of all the values of antiquity.[24]

From within a radicalized Christian view, Kierkegaard's presentation of the Abraham and Isaac story in *Fear and Trembling* conveys a parallel message, for Kierkegaard offers a reading of the commanded filiacide as a kind of emblem of the unnaturalness of what is demanded by Christian faith.[25] (If, as

both father and son get murdered: With respect to the latter, Freud's story is that sacrifice of the son is required in order to atone for primeval patricide committed against the father. But whichever way one looks at this – whether from the perspective of patricide or that of filiacide – either way, Christianity owes its irresistible existential compellingness to a symbolic structure of *domestic murder.*

Two final remarks on this topic: There is an astonishing Hobbesian anticipation of Freud in Hobbes's identification of *Moses* as the "Father" in the Holy Trinity. See *Leviathan*, ed. Richard Tuck (Cambridge: Cambridge University Press, 1996), pp. 339–340 (chapter 42) and p. xli (Tuck's Introduction). One might also consider Machiavelli's theme of fathers and sons (e.g., King David and King Solomon) in *Discourses on Livy*, I.19: Machiavelli's argument is that one can only have good order under a peace-loving king if it is a sequel to rule by a war-loving king. Is it stretching imagination too far to think that this may be a subtle commentary on the relation between Judaism as a religion of the father and Christianity as a religion of the son? Machiavelli's emphasis on the unworkability of having two peace-loving regimes in succession may even be a gesture toward Islam as representing the need for a return to a more war-loving version of monotheism. (I am grateful to Jack Lucas for reminding me of this very interesting text.)

24 See also Thomas Paine, *The Age of Reason*, ed. Moncure Daniel Conway (Mineola, NY: Dover, 2004), p. 31: "The more unnatural anything is, the more is it capable of becoming the object of dismal admiration."

25 There are of course pagan versions of this – notably, the myth of Saturn devouring his children (as depicted in paintings by Rubens and Goya). However shocking the symbolism, though, there is no suggestion that Saturn was ever meant to be presented as a beneficent god. Cf. Sigmund Freud, *Interpreting Dreams*, trans. J. A. Underwood (London: Penguin, 2006), p. 270: "Cronus eats his children, rather as the boar eats the sow's litter." (This note derives from a suggestion made to me by Robert Eden many years ago.)

It is worth noting that Kierkegaard, too, addresses the question of the sons of Brutus, which supports the suggestion in this chapter that there is a general problem of filiacide that encompasses the Abraham and Isaac story in *Genesis*, the sacrifice of Jesus, and the Roman examples that concern Machiavelli. See Søren Kierkegaard, *Fear and Trembling*, ed. C. Stephen Evans and Sylvia Walsh (Cambridge: Cambridge University Press, 2006), p. 51. As the editors observe, Kierkegaard alludes to the parallel between Isaac and Jesus on p. 49 of *Fear and Trembling*.

Augustine highlights,[26] Romulus's fratricide points back to the archetype of Cain and Abel, then the Christian narrative of the sacrifice of God's son, Christ, can likewise be interpreted as pointing back to the archetype of Abraham and Isaac.) When Machiavelli argues that one can found or refound a civic community only by inspiring primal terror in citizens, thereby securing their unconditional obedience, he perhaps takes his cue from the radical inversion of the naturalness of family ties implicit in the Christian refounding of biblical religion.[27] Machiavelli himself draws attention to the refounding of religions, but his example – the monastic refounding of Christianity – looks extremely modest in relation to Christianity's "refounding" of monotheism (as well as the second refounding effected by Islam).

As Charles Taylor highlights in the epigraph to this chapter, Christianity in its founding document requires that the naturalness of the family be "trumped" by the supernatural demands of faith.[28] Texts in the *New Testament* that spell out this subordination of family ties include the following: *Matthew* 8:21–22, 10: 34–37, and 12:46–50; *Mark* 3:31–35 and 10:28–30; *Luke* 2:48–50, 8:19–21, 9:59–62, 11:27–28, 14:26, 14:33, and 18:28–30; *John* 1:12–13 and 3:3–8; and *Romans* 8:32 and 9:8.[29] All of these texts would be worth quotation and discussion, but let us content ourselves with letting the first represent all the others: the Apostle Matthew reports that one of Christ's disciples had "said unto him, Lord, suffer me first to go and bury my father. But Jesus said unto him, Follow me; and let the dead bury their dead." In other words, family obligations lose all moral force in the face of the trumping power of the Christian mission; the claims made upon us by our kin are dead to us in relation to what is truly living.[30] Machiavelli, too, demands a subordination of the family, but a subordination to politics, not a subordination to faith. This

---

[26] See note 6, this chapter.

[27] Cf. Harvey C. Mansfield and Nathan Tarcov, "Introduction" to *Discourses on Livy*, trans. Mansfield and Tarcov, p. xxxv: "It is no accident that the mode of renewing republics by the sensational execution (*D* III 1.3) bears a strange resemblance to the central mystery of the 'Christian sect.'"

[28] Cf. Joel Schwartz, *The Sexual Politics of Jean-Jacques Rousseau* (Chicago: University of Chicago Press, 1984), pp. 64–65, on Christianity's "devaluation of the family" from a Rousseauian perspective: "In the name of allegiance to the city of God, . . . Christianity is uncomfortable with both the republic and the family." On Calvin's reassertion of the radicalness with which the New Testament subverts family attachments, see Michael Walzer, *The Revolution of the Saints* (New York: Atheneum, 1976), p. 48; cf. pp. 197–198.

[29] J. M. Coetzee's story in *Elizabeth Costello* (London: Secker & Warburg, 2003), Lesson 5, about the two sisters, one a partisan of the ancient Greeks, the other a partisan of Christianity, could be read as a parable about Christianity's aspiration to trump familial bonds. This message is brought home most powerfully when Blanche says, with cruel coldness, to her sister: "You went for the wrong Greeks, Elizabeth" (p. 145).

[30] This text is of course famously cited by Karl Marx near the beginning of *The Eighteenth Brumaire of Louis Bonaparte*. Marx glosses the text as an absolute privileging of the future over the past. But a more immediate meaning of the text is an absolute privileging of the evangelical mission in relation to kin obligations. There is another version of Matthew's story near the end of *Luke*, chapter 9.

"trumping" of family obligation is, one might say, an index of the unnaturalness or inhumanity of the stern demands placed upon human beings by each of these totalizing commitments: religion in the one case, citizenship and patriotism in the other.[31]

Machiavelli's appeal to St. Francis and St. Dominic as exemplary refounders reminds one of Montesquieu's analogy between civic republicanism and monastic life more than two centuries later (*Spirit of the Laws*, Book 5, chapter 2). Both Machiavelli and Montesquieu understand that pure republican virtue, like pure Christian virtue, only works by asserting a single love, a single passion, and that there is something monumentally inhuman about focusing human energies in such a single-minded way. Machiavelli models his neorepublicanism on Christianity in this respect to exalt it as a new civilization-building (or rebuilding) project – a project worthy of celebration and unconditional human commitment: Anticipating Nietzsche, we can achieve our full humanity only by embracing with inhuman intensity a single-minded desire for what is superhuman.[32] Montesquieu, however, draws his analogy to suggest to his readers that one cannot fulfill one's humanity by focusing one's aim on one inhumanly abstracted passion.

---

[31] In *Discourses* III.22's contest between the severity of Manlius Torquatus and the mildness of Valerius Corvinus, severity wins, at least in regard to republics, because republics require absolute devotion to the public good, and Manlius's sacrifice of his son gives dramatic proof that he relinquished his private good in favor of the public good. *Discourses on Livy*, trans. Mansfield and Tarcov, p. 267. Machiavelli offers another vivid illustration of the human capacity for starkly unnatural negation of family ties in the story of Madonna Caterina in *Discourses* III.6 (Mansfield and Tarcov, pp. 231–232), but in this case the motivation is private vengeance rather than the public good. (One is also tempted to relate this theme to a similar theme in Plato's *Republic*: Once again, kin obligations must give way before obligations of a higher order.)

[32] Hence, for instance, Guicciardini's judgment that Machiavelli "always shows excessive fondness for extraordinary and violent measures"; *The Sweetness of Power: Machiavelli's Discourses and Guicciardini's Considerations*, trans. James B. Atkinson and David Sices (DeKalb, IL: Northern Illinois University Press, 2002), p. 412. Guicciardini may be overstating the point when he writes "always," but there is no question that there is a kind of cult of the extraordinary in Machiavelli (as there later is in Nietzsche); if one fails to see this, one misses a crucial dimension of Machiavelli's political philosophy. To appreciate the justice of Guicciardini's remark, it suffices to consider the chapter for which he is providing a commentary when he delivers this critical judgment, namely *Discourses*, Book I, chapter 26.

5

The Hobbesian Solution

Judaicization of Christianity

How we can have peace while this is our religion, I cannot tell.

– Thomas Hobbes[1]

Rousseau himself draws attention to Hobbes's contribution as a theorist of civil religion by addressing Hobbes's position in his own account of civil religion. Rousseau writes,

Of all Christian authors, the philosopher Hobbes is the only one who correctly saw the evil and the remedy, who dared to propose the reunification of the two heads of the eagle, and the complete return to political unity, without which no State or government will ever be well constituted. But he ought to have seen that the dominating spirit of Christianity was incompatible with his system, and that the interest of the priest would always be stronger than that of the State. It is not so much what is horrible and false in his political theory as what is correct and true that has made it odious.[2]

In a footnote elaborating on the last sentence of this quotation, Rousseau rebukes Grotius for having denied the Hobbesian principle that "it is the duty of each private individual to follow the religion approved in his homeland by the public authorities, if not adopting it in his heart, at least in professing it and submitting to it obediently."[3] My purpose in this chapter is to provide a sufficient elaboration of Hobbes's civil-religion doctrine to clarify what Rousseau

---

[1] Thomas Hobbes, *Behemoth, or The Long Parliament*, ed. Ferdinand Tönnies (Chicago: University of Chicago Press, 1990), p. 57. Citations of *Leviathan* in this chapter, unless otherwise indicated, refer to Thomas Hobbes, *Leviathan*, ed. C. B. Macpherson (London: Penguin, 1985).

[2] Ibid., p. 127. As Steven B. Smith has pointed out, the identification of Hobbes as a "Christian author" may well be a tacit reference to Spinoza as an alternative source of similar truths: See *Spinoza, Liberalism and the Question of Jewish Identity* (New Haven: Yale University Press, 1997), p. 117.

[3] Jean-Jacques Rousseau, *On the Social Contract*, ed. Roger D. Masters (New York: St. Martin's Press, 1978), p. 127, note, and p. 153 n. 134. The quotation is from a letter by Grotius, cited by Rousseau, dated April 11, 1643, in which Grotius describes to his brother his response to reading Hobbes's *De Cive*.

(in this highly compressed passage) sees as true in Hobbes, and whether Hobbes is in fact subject to the criticism Rousseau presents concerning the Hobbesian doctrine.

The idea of Hobbes as a civil-religion theorist is hardly a novel suggestion.[4] Certainly, all that Hobbes has to say on the subject of religion in *De Cive* and *Leviathan* gives one every impression that Hobbes is a theorist for whom the specifics of Christian doctrine count for very little, and for whom the imperatives of political authority count for almost everything (or rather, for whom the specifics of Christian doctrine matter *insofar as* they affect the fate of political authority).[5] One's first impulse is to say that Hobbes's main purpose is to ensure maximum discretion for the sovereign in the determination

[4] Cf. Eric Voegelin, *The New Science of Politics* (Chicago: University of Chicago Press, 1952), p. 155, referring to "Hobbes's intention of establishing Christianity (understood as identical in substance with the law of nature) as an English *theologia civilis* in the Varronic sense." More recently, see Jeffrey R. Collins, *The Allegiance of Thomas Hobbes* (Oxford: Oxford University Press, 2005), chapter 1. Collins points out that Rousseau may have adapted his term "civil religion" from Hobbes's term "Civill worship" (p. 46; cf. pp. 47 and 56). For a good encapsulation of the essential purpose of Hobbes's theology, see John C. Higgins-Biddle's "Introduction" to John Locke, *The Reasonableness of Christianity*, ed. Higgins-Biddle (Oxford: Clarendon Press, 1999), pp. lxxviii–lxxx.

[5] Consider *Behemoth*, p. 45: When *A* defines good or evil actions and habits according to "their causes and usefulness in reference to the commonwealth," *B* complains that *A* has omitted "the greatest of all virtues, religion" – to which *A* responds that he *has not* omitted it. That is to say, giving a suitable account of the needs of civil authority already subsumes the moral relevance of religion. The idea of religion as a site of moral virtue in its own right is superfluous.

This is not to say that there are not Hobbes scholars who take Hobbes's professions of piety very seriously. For two examples, see Herbert W. Schneider, "The Piety of Hobbes," and Paul J. Johnson, "Hobbes's Anglican Doctrine of Salvation," in *Thomas Hobbes in His Time*, ed. Ralph Ross, Herbert W. Schneider, and Theodore Waldman (Minneapolis: University of Minnesota Press, 1974), pp. 84–101 and 102–125. Classic accounts of Hobbes as committed to his own quite robust version of Christian theology are to be found in J. G. A. Pocock, *Politics, Language, and Time* (Chicago: University of Chicago Press, 1989), chapter 5; and Eldon J. Eisenach, *Two Worlds of Liberalism* (Chicago: University of Chicago Press, 1981), Part I. More recently, Michael Allen Gillespie has made an ambitious attempt to take Hobbes seriously as a Christian theologian: See Gillespie, *The Theological Origins of Modernity* (Chicago: University of Chicago Press, 2008), chapter 7. Edwin Curley, in "'I Durst Not Write So Boldly,' or How to Read Hobbes' Theological–Political Treatise" (available at http://sitemaker.umich.edu/emcurley/spinoza), gives very thorough consideration to a wide range of such views, and Curley ultimately rejects them. An argument parallel to Curley's is also to be found in the critique of the Pocock–Eisenach interpretation of Hobbes in David Johnston, *The Rhetoric of Leviathan* (Princeton, NJ: Princeton University Press, 1986), chapters 5–7.

Is it possible for a thinker moved by genuine Anglican piety to propose the summary execution of all priests, as Hobbes does in *Behemoth*? It was certainly possible to be a *Christian* in seventeenth-century England and to want all priests banished, but it was not possible to be an *Anglican* (which is what Hobbes claimed to be) and want this. (Hobbes may have left us a final clue with respect to his rejection of religion, namely his self-composed tombstone inscription: See Richard Tuck, *Hobbes*, Oxford: Oxford University Press, 1989, p. 39. It is also worth noting that Hume, who certainly knew about such matters, considered Hobbes "an enemy to religion": Ibid., p. 95.) In chapter 46 of *Leviathan*, Hobbes makes the striking claim that Aristotle dissembled his true beliefs to avoid "the fate of Socrates." Although many scholars think otherwise, readers of Hobbes have always suspected that what he here accuses Aristotle of really applies to Hobbes

of cultic requirements, and that it would be unwise to risk limiting this discretion by inquiring too closely into the desirable contents of a state religion. This is a true but insufficient response. It is insufficient because it fails to explain why Hobbes in fact devotes such monumental time and energy to problems of scriptural exegesis. The answer to this puzzle is that Hobbes came to the same insight grasped by Machiavelli before him and Rousseau after him, namely that genuinely Christian aspirations are so radically otherworldly that they subvert the authority of temporal power; and so Hobbes, in common with Machiavelli and Rousseau, must search for a way to neutralize the threat to the requirements of secular politics posed by Christianity.[6] To summarize the civil-religion strategies of these three political philosophers, one could say the following: Rousseau's "solution" is to offer a minimalist civic creed that abstracts as much as possible from specifically Christian content – although this is not really a solution to the paradoxes and contradictions that Rousseau brilliantly highlights in his civil-religion chapter; Machiavelli's solution is to paganize Christianity through the heroic figure of Cesare Borgia, who embodies the will to "draw the steel from the wound" by undoing the political power of the papacy[7]; and Hobbes's solution is to "Judaicize" Christianity by reinterpreting Christian Scripture according to a pre-Christian understanding of a political messiah.[8]

To define Hobbes's place within the civil-religion tradition, it will be necessary to offer a reading of the much-neglected Parts III and IV of *Leviathan*; but let us begin by turning to *De Cive*, which emphasizes the first of the two aspects of Hobbes's doctrine referred to previously, namely the urge to accord to the sovereign maximal latitude in shaping a religious code for a particular political community. Rousseau, in his civil-religion chapter of the *Social Contract*, presents Judaism as a theocratic teaching, and as such, he both appreciates its

---

himself (cf. the end of Curley's essay). See also the reference to "secret thoughts" in *Leviathan*, p. 137.

[6] Cf. Stephen Holmes's parallel account of civil religion in Hobbes, "Introduction" to *Behemoth*, pp. xliv–xlvii; e.g., p. xliv: "[A] prudent sovereign will attempt to monopolize the pretense of spiritual power along with the reality of physical force. He will attempt to become the Pope, or the head of the Church, in his own lands.... Remember that the colossus on the frontispiece of *Leviathan*, bestowing his protection on a peaceful city, holds the secular sword in one hand and a bishop's crosier in the other. There is no question here of any separation between Church and State. On the contrary, Hobbes's main intellectual target is 'that seditious *distinction* and *division* between the power *spiritual* and *civil*.' In a way, his life's work was a sustained attempt to obliterate this distinction, to erect a commonwealth that would be, as he explained in the subtitle to *Leviathan*, simultaneously ecclesiastical and civil." See also p. xlviii: "Hobbes hopes to confiscate the intangible power of religious fraud from dangerous clergy and bestow it safely on the King." For a fuller discussion of the church–state duality of the imagery on *Leviathan*'s frontispiece, see Carl Schmitt, *The Leviathan in the State Theory of Thomas Hobbes: Meaning and Failure of a Political Symbol*, trans. George Schwab and Erna Hilfstein (Chicago: University of Chicago Press, 2008), p. 18.

[7] Jacob Burckhardt, *The Civilization of the Renaissance in Italy* (London: Phaidon Press, 1960), pp. 71–72.

[8] One should probably leave open the question of whether Jesus himself adhered to this "pre-Christian" understanding: See the last paragraph of note 40, this chapter.

political advantages and ultimately criticizes it politically (for theocracies are either universalistic and therefore imperialistic, or they are simply parochial and therefore blind to the universalistic truths eventually made available by Christianity). Hobbes, by contrast, attempts to draw from the Old Testament a *critique* of theocracy. For Hobbes, the Old Testament tells the story of an alternation between the "maistry" (i.e., mastery) of kings accompanied by the "ministry" of priests, on the one hand, and, on the other hand, the maistry of priests accompanied by the rival authority of prophets.[9] Monarchy is the only way to curtail the threat of anarchy associated with Hebrew theocracy. The fundamental problem is that the Israelites are "a people greedy of prophets."[10] Kingship is the only sure way of coping with this problem. The Hebrew people themselves recognize this, and therefore *demand* a king,[11] to which God then "consents."[12] Another way of expressing this greediness for prophets (subverters of priestly or theocratic authority) is to say that the Hebrews were "the greatest enemy to human subjection," resistant to a kingly authority that would be for them all too reminiscent of that under which they had suffered under the Pharaohs.[13] The only solution to this problem (summed up in Hobbes's phrase "private zeal"[14]) is to reserve to kings the authority to decide who is and who is not a true prophet. The text from *1 Sam.* viii.7 ("Hearken unto the voice of the people in all that they say unto thee") is crucial for Hobbes because it proves that the people themselves came to realize this.[15] As Hobbes

[9] The terms "maistry" and "ministry," and the question of whether at any given point in time the priests are one or the other (sovereign or subordinate), are presented in *De Cive*, chapter 16, paragraph 16: *Man and Citizen*, ed. Bernard Gert (Garden City, NY: Anchor Books, 1972), p. 327. The English translation of *De Cive* offered in Gert's edition is a text entitled *Philosophical Rudiments Concerning Governing and Society*, which has long been assumed to be Hobbes's own translation of *De Cive* (Gert makes this assumption). Richard Tuck, however, has strongly challenged the presumption that Hobbes composed, or even approved, the *Philosophical Rudiments* translation. For discussion of the evidence that Hobbes never authorized the publication of *Philosophical Rudiments*, see Thomas Hobbes, *On the Citizen*, ed. Richard Tuck and Michael Silverthorne (Cambridge: Cambridge University Press, 1998), pp. xxxiv–xxxvii. The Silverthorne translation renders the ministry–maistry distinction as a distinction between ministry and magistracy: ibid., p. 201. Cf. *Leviathan*, p. 531: "Preachers... have not Magisteriall, but Ministeriall power."

[10] *Man and Citizen*, p. 323. Cf. *Leviathan*, pp. 506–507: Following Joshua and Eleazar there was no clear authority among the Hebrews. Rather than simply obeying authority, the people "looked for a sign," that is, were always on the lookout for new prophets.

[11] *Man and Citizen*, pp. 315, 323, 324–325.

[12] Ibid., pp. 323, 324.

[13] Ibid., pp. 314–315.

[14] Ibid., p. 323. On the theme of private zeal, cf. *Leviathan*, pp. 723–725.

[15] *Man and Citizen*, pp. 315, 323. Harrington picks up this text from Hobbes and, as one would expect, gives it a republican-slanted reading: "[P]aradoxically, the establishment of the Israelite monarchy confirms the unique legitimacy God accords popular government." See James Harrington, *The Commonwealth of Oceana and A System of Politics*, ed. J. G. A. Pocock (Cambridge: Cambridge University Press, 1992), p. 107; and Gary Remer, "After Machiavelli and Hobbes: James Harrington's Commonwealth of Israel," in *Political Hebraism*, ed. Gordon Schochet, Fania Oz-Salzberger, and Meirav Jones (Jerusalem: Shalem Press, 2008), p. 222.

interprets the text, the Hebrews are demanding a *genuine* king, in preference to Samuel as a quasi-king with authority undermined by theocratic elements of his regime. Hence this scriptural text: "And the Lord said unto Samuel, Hearken unto the voice of the people . . . for they have not rejected *thee* [viz., Samuel, to the extent that he represents kingly power], but they have rejected *me* [God, as symbolizing theocratic complications in Samuel's regime], that *I* [i.e., the priests] should not reign over them."[16] Hobbes makes clear that God is to be identified with priestly rule when he writes, "they cast off God's government, that is to say, that of the *priest*, by whom God ruled."[17] For Hobbes, *1 Sam.* viii.7 refers to a "Lockean" revolution against the theocratic rule of the priests; "the people themselves" deposed the priests.[18]

The key issue in *De Cive*, chapter 16 is the transition from "judges" to "kings" (Samuel to Saul), and the question of why this transition was necessary. One may contrast this with Locke's account in the *Second Treatise of Government*, paragraph 109: For Locke, "judges" and "kings" mean the same thing, namely generals or "captains in war." Locke finds the distinction between Samuel as "judge" and Saul as "king" irrelevant because what is salient for him is what is common to both epochs, namely absolutist authority. As he says, *both* eras belong to "the infancies of common-wealths" (paragraph 110); that is, they precede the age in which "men found it necessary to examine more carefully the original and rights of government; and to find out ways to restrain the exorbitances, and prevent the abuses of that power" (paragraph 111). Because Hobbes, in contrast, endorses rather than opposes absolutist authority, the distinction between judges and kings *is* relevant. For Hobbes the question is this: *Who controls* that authority, priests or kings? According to Hobbes, what the Hebrews had prior to King Saul was a *de jure* theocracy ("the *kingdom* was by covenant *priestly*, that is to say, God's government by priests"), with sovereignty in the hands of the high priest,[19] but a de facto anarchy "by reason of the great esteem they [the Israelites] had of prophecies."[20] Hobbes's analysis is that theocracy is inherently unstable because priests lack the authority to settle the question of who is or is not a true prophet. What Moses founded was a theocracy *as opposed to* a monarchy, that is to say, "*a priestly* kingdom, a government most free, in which [the Hebrews] were to be subject to no human power."[21] In other words, the rule of priests is a recipe for political chaos. Only *kings* can stabilize the political community by reserving to

---

[16] *Man and Citizen*, p. 323; emphasis added. In 2003, Mohammed Dahlan, the former head of the Palestinian preventive security forces in Gaza, used language highly reminiscent of Hobbes when he made this remark, apropos the very limited Palestinian Authority presence in Gaza at that time: "Right now, only God [i.e., Hamas] is in charge." *Globe & Mail*, March 10, 2003, p. A8.

[17] *Man and Citizen*, p. 324; Hobbes's italics.

[18] Ibid., pp. 322–323.

[19] Ibid., p. 322.

[20] Ibid., p. 323.

[21] Ibid., p. 338; Hobbes's italics.

themselves authority concerning true and false prophets. Therefore, Hobbes's affirmation of undivided temporal authority is, as he sees it, merely a philosophical appropriation of a truth already contained within the narrative of the Old Testament.

On Hobbes's interpretation, this whole set of problems is one that did not apply to the original Mosaic regime, for Moses united in his own person ultimate ecclesiastical and civil authority (and this was the greatness of Moses, as all civil-religion theorists would agree). "[T]his power [of interpreting God's word], during the life of Moses, was entirely in himself"[22]; "Moses alone was the interpreter of God's word."[23] The problem began with his successor, Joshua. Under Moses, Aaron the High Priest was entirely subject to Moses' ultimate authority (and of course political rule was *not* passed on to Aaron), whereas under Joshua there was a dual sovereignty, with real sovereignty (the sovereignty that really counted in this theocratic regime) vested in Eleazar, Joshua's high priest: "Eleazar the priest had not only the priesthood, but also the sovereignty"; "Joshua had not a power equal with that which Moses had."[24] Note that "judges" signifies the rule of high priests as opposed to rule by a king (or at least *de jure* rule of priests, challenged by de facto rule of prophets – freelancers!). The source of this whole problem, in Hobbes's view, is the refusal of the Hebrews to accept the rule of civil authority (again, their greediness of prophets), bringing with it the inevitable consequence of an anarchic rule by "private zeal." Thus the whole purpose of *De Cive*, chapter 16 (as well as *Leviathan*, chapter 40) is to show that *theocracy does not work* (or at least theocracy in the Old Testament sense, i.e., the rule of priests, does not work). It might be possible to sum up Hobbes's political reading of the New Testament in Part III of *Leviathan* by saying that only a resurrected Christ, ruling *eternally*, could make Jewish theocracy work.

In *De Cive*, chapter 13, Hobbes presents a "query," namely, "whether it be the duty of kings to provide for the salvation of their subjects' souls, as they [the kings] shall judge best according to their own consciences."[25] Having posed the query, Hobbes says merely that "we will leave this difficulty in suspense."[26] In fact, the whole of Part III of *De Cive* is intended as a comprehensive answer to this question posed but not answered in chapter 13, paragraph 5, namely whether it is right for kings to intervene in what concerns the salvation of their subjects' souls. The whole thrust of Part III is to answer in the affirmative. The establishment of a civil religion is part and parcel of what it is to exercise kingly authority. Hobbes's civil religion as laid out in *De Cive*, Part III, can be summed up as follows. The Christian prince must affirm God's existence, must not set up idols, and must affirm that Jesus is the Christ. Beyond that, the

---

[22] Ibid., p. 319.
[23] Ibid., p. 321.
[24] Ibid., p. 322.
[25] Ibid., p. 257.
[26] Ibid., p. 260.

Christian prince can institute any articles of faith and any rites that he cares to, and Christian subjects are fully bound by these dogmas and rites. As for rule by *non*-Christian princes, Christian subjects must bear allegiance to these princes in all that concerns temporal matters. If the non-Christian prince's conduct of spiritual matters forces the Christian subjects to betray their faith, the latter must be prepared to suffer martyrdom on behalf of their faith, rather than resist civil authority. Failing that, they show themselves to be less than wholehearted in their commitment to Christian faith.[27] It goes without saying that the civil religion of non-Christian princes is fully binding upon non-Christian subjects. This "theology" is through and through political. It is not the theology of someone primarily concerned with the salvation of the soul, but the theology of someone primarily concerned that the pursuit of salvation of the soul not interfere with the requirements of political order.

A decisively important aspect of Hobbes's "political theology" is highlighted in the title of chapter 14 of *De Cive*: "Of Laws and Trespasses" (or "Of laws and sins," as it is listed in "The Index" [the table of contents] of the *Philosophical Rudiments* version of *De Cive*).[28] The very distinction between laws and trespasses suggests two realms, subject to two kinds of authority. For precisely that reason, it is essential to Hobbes's project of subordinating church to state that he collapse the distinction between "sin" or "trespass" (sacred, eternal) and "law" (secular, temporal). *Both* must be rendered equally subject to civil authority, for the alternative is to convey to the citizens that kings are less powerful than priests. Hence Hobbes writes, "if each pastor had an authority granted him to remit and retain sins in this manner, all awe of princes and civil magistrates, together with all kind of civil government would be utterly destroyed. For Christ hath said . . . that 'we should not fear them who slay the body, but cannot kill the soul; but rather fear him, who can cast both soul and body into hell' (*Matthew* 10:28). Neither is any man so mad, as not to choose to yield obedience rather to them who can remit and retain their sins, than to the powerfulest kings."[29] In *Leviathan*, chapter 29, Hobbes drives home the essential point, which is that if there rises up within the commonwealth a "Ghostly Power" that claims jurisdiction over sin, "it challengeth by consequence to declare what is Law, (*Sinne being nothing but the transgression of the Law*)."[30] As soon as one asserts a notion of sin subject

[27] Cf. *Leviathan*, pp. 674–675.
[28] *Man and Citizen*, pp. 107, 271. In the Latin text, the same title – *De Legibus et Peccatis* – occurs in both places. The Silverthorne translation (*On the Citizen*, pp. 17, 153) eliminates the discrepancy, rendering *peccatis* as "sins" in both places.
[29] *Man and Citizen*, p. 357. For some forceful counterarguments (with respect to whether oth- erworldly punishments necessarily trump this-worldly sanctions), see John Stuart Mill, *Three Essays on Religion*, 3rd ed. (London: Longmans, Green and Co., 1923), pp. 89–90.
[30] *Leviathan*, p. 371; emphasis added. Cf. Spinoza, *Theological–Political Treatise*, chapter 19: "[W]e could not conceive sin [*peccatum*] to exist in a state of nature." Also relevant is Spinoza's suggestion in chapter 4 that it would be a "contradiction in terms" to say that Adam sinned in the Garden of Eden, because he *could not* violate divine (i.e., natural) laws to which he

to spiritual jurisdiction distinct from legal jurisdiction, one gets the unavoidable result: "two Kingdomes, and every Subject . . . subject to two Masters."[31] "[I]t followeth . . . there must needs be two Common-wealths, of one & the same Subjects; which is a Kingdome divided in it selfe, and cannot stand"[32] – which is precisely the problem of the diremption of the two heads of the eagle concerning which Rousseau claimed that Hobbes possessed correct insight into "the evil and the remedy [*le mal et le remède*]."

De Cive, as we have seen, serves a primarily negative purpose, namely to shelter civil authority against the political presumptions of the priests, to knock down these priestly ambitions, and to fend off the theocratic challenge. Part III of *Leviathan*, by contrast, tells a rather different story and points in the direction of a much more ambitious Hobbesian project.[33] *De Cive* leaves the content of Hobbes's civil religion (in common with the Rousseauian civil religion at the end of the *Social Contract*) pretty much open to the discretion of the sovereign. In *Leviathan*, however, that is not so (and it is for Rousseauian reasons that it isn't so!). Let us, then, turn now to the *Leviathan*'s discussion of religion.

In *Leviathan*, Part III, we learn that the drama told in *De Cive*, chapter 16, concerning the Hebrews' overthrowing of the theocracy as founded by Moses tells us only half a tale. The whole story can be summarized as follows: First, Moses founds a theocracy, that is, a regime ruled by those who claim to rule in the name of God. The problem with this theocratic regime is that it spawns people who claim prophetic powers, and this makes it impossible to assert any singular civil authority. As Hobbes sums up the problem, "the Jewes . . . called mad-men Prophets."[34] The analysis at the end of chapter 40,[35] as I understand it, is that there was a continual crisis of political authority among the Jews because political authority rested upon theocratic credentials. By right, civil and religious authority were united in the high priest; in practice, there was anarchy, with every self-professed prophet posing a threat to the authoritativeness of the Mosaic regime. To sustain itself, a theocracy requires

---

was necessarily subject. See also Spinoza, *Political Treatise*, trans. Samuel Shirley (Indianapolis: Hackett, 2000), p. 45: "[I]n a state of nature there is no sin. . . . [S]in cannot be conceived except in a state, that is, where what is good and bad is decided by the common law of the entire state." For Spinoza as for Hobbes, it is only in the context of sovereign-legislated law that the notion of sin begins to make sense. In fact, Spinoza offers a more radical version of the Hobbesian doctrine because he denies even in principle the idea of natural law as a transcendent standard vis-à-vis civil law.

31 *Leviathan*, p. 370.

32 Ibid.

33 Cf. Richard Tuck: "[T]he principal reason for the writing of *Leviathan* [was] to argue for a new religious order introduced by the sovereign" (*On the Citizen*, p. xxxiii). In fact, Tuck claims that it was the much more radical civil-religion teaching of *Leviathan*, relative to the rather modest civil-religion teaching of *De Cive*, that accounts for Hobbes's unwillingness "to sanction an English translation of *De Cive*" (p. xxxi).

34 *Leviathan*, p. 143.

35 Ibid., pp. 509–512.

the "charismatic authority" of a figure like Moses (or Ayatollah Khomeini). Without such a figure, theocratic authority splinters or fragments in succeeding generations. But this crisis of political authority was never really resolved, even after official sovereignty was shifted from high priests to kings. The monopoly of authority was always precarious. Hobbes's conclusion seems therefore to be that the Mosaic regime, even in its monarchical phase, is inherently unstable. A regime where the people are led to expect authority to emanate from the divine inspiration of prophets does not work. (Of course, one may speculate about whether the same analysis applies to theocratic regimes in our own day.)

When the Israelites themselves came to realize the nature of their political problem, we reach Stage 2 of the story, namely that the people demand "a King, after the manner of their neighbour nations," which signifies that they "cast off God's yoke" (i.e., ended the theocracy).[36] Hence the drama of Samuel and Saul related in *De Cive*, chapter 16, and retold in *Leviathan*, chapter 40: [T]he people revolt, and the priests agree to relinquish authority; "with the consent of God himselfe" signifies that the high priests accept the people's verdict, and agree to forfeit their sovereignty without a struggle.[37] However, there is a further act in this drama, which is Stage 3: Christ "restores" the Kingdom of God (i.e., reinstitutes the theocracy).[38] In other words, Christ's mission is to reestablish the earthly theocracy founded by Moses and interrupted by Saul and his successors. Hobbes asserts that the claim to be "Christ" means claiming to be "King of the Jews," quite literally, and this is precisely what Jesus claimed for himself (viz., to be the Jewish Messiah, *as the Jews conceived* the idea of the Messiah).[39] Crucial to this whole enterprise of reasserting the Judaic meaning of the Messiah is Hobbes's insistence that the biblical phrase "Kingdom of God" refers to a real rather than metaphorical kingdom.[40] He points out that the metaphorical rather than literal meaning has prevailed in Christian writing and preaching because the literal meaning "gives too much

---

[36] Ibid., p. 424; cf. pp. 368, 445–447.

[37] Ibid., pp. 507–508.

[38] Ibid., pp. 424, 447, 448, 515.

[39] Ibid., pp. 413, 447, 517.

[40] Ibid., pp. 442, 447, 488–489, 491–494. It is worth noting that, among Christian and quasi-Christian denominations, at least one was committed, as late as the end of the nineteenth century, to this Hobbesian notion of an *earthly* "Kingdom of God" – namely Mormonism. See Donald Harman Akenson, *Some Family* (Montreal: McGill-Queen's University Press, 2007), chapter 3, and Harold Bloom, *The American Religion* (New York: Simon & Schuster, 1992), chapter 4.

Admittedly, Hobbes's account of Christianity may appear jarring simply because St. Paul's interpretation of Christianity has been so dominant within the history of Christianity. Hobbes in effect anticipates the "Ebionite" view offered in John Toland's *Nazarenus*. For a recent argument that the Ebionite–Tolandite view in fact corresponds to the self-understanding of Jesus himself and those immediately around him (prior to the "hijacking" of Christianity by St. Paul), see Barrie Wilson, *How Jesus Became Christian* (Toronto: Random House, 2008). If Toland's Ebionite view is correct, then Hobbes is simply steering Christianity back to the (pre-Pauline) self-understanding of Jesus and his immediate followers.

light to Christian Kings to see their right of Ecclesiasticall Government."[41] In other words, the "Kingdom of God" is not an otherworldly destination, but the site of a this-worldly power struggle between kings and priests. With this utterly bizarre interpretation of the New Testament,[42] the *Leviathan* thus picks up and pursues the political drama narrated in chapter 16 of *De Cive*.

What Hobbes is in effect saying here is what Machiavelli said in *Discourses* I.12, that if the spirit of religion "had been kept up by the rulers of the Christian commonwealth as was ordained for us by its founder, Christian states and republics would have been much more united and much more happy than they are," *provided that* the religion founded by Christ is interpreted as if it were the religion of the Old Testament, and Christ himself is interpreted as if he were Moses.[43] (The shock value of this reduction of Christ to Moses is enhanced when one bears in mind John Aubrey's report that Hobbes shared the Machiavellian view of Moses as an armed prophet.[44]) It seems reasonable to say that Hobbes's civil religion consists in "Judaicizing" Christianity parallel to the way in which Machiavelli's civil religion, as we have argued, consists in paganizing Christianity. What it means to Judaicize Christianity is that the Christian religion ceases to assert any otherworldly claims whatsoever, and limits itself to this-worldly claims on behalf of Christ's eventual reclamation of temporal power.[45] However, as the theocratic monarchy only commences

[41] *Leviathan*, p. 447.

[42] Cf. the judgment by a contemporary (Henry Hammond), cited by Patricia Springborg, that what *Leviathan* offered was "a farrago of all the maddest divinity that ever was read"; as well as the judgment by another contemporary (Brian Duppa), cited by Noel Malcolm, that "as in the man, so there are strange mixtures in the book; many things said so well that I could embrace him for it, and many things so wildly and unchristianly, that I can scarce have so much charity for him, as to think he was ever Christian." Springborg, "Hobbes on Religion," and Malcolm, "A Summary Biography of Hobbes," both in *The Cambridge Companion to Hobbes*, ed. Tom Sorell (Cambridge: Cambridge University Press, 1996), p. 347 and p. 34.

[43] *Leviathan*, pp. 480–481, 512, 515, 518, 520.

[44] See *Aubrey's Brief Lives*, ed. Oliver Lawson Dick (Harmondsworth: Penguin, 1972), p. 317: "Thomas Hobbs said that if it were not for the gallowes, some men are of so cruell a nature as to take a delight in killing men more than I should to kill a bird. I have heard him inveigh much against the Crueltie of Moyses for putting so many thousands to the Sword for Bowing to the Golden Calf." Cf. Niccolò Machiavelli, *Discourses on Livy*, trans. Harvey C. Mansfield and Nathan Tarcov (Chicago: University of Chicago Press, 1996), p. 280. Another very interesting dimension to Hobbes's condemnation of the cruelty of Moses as reported by Aubrey is suggested by something pointed out by Michael Walzer, namely that *Exodus*, chapter 32, was a favorite scriptural text for regicidal English Puritans. Needless to say, that would give Hobbes special reason to despise that text. See Walzer, *The Revolution of the Saints* (New York: Atheneum, 1976), p. 109, n.126; cf. p. 296. (However, in *Leviathan*, p. 723, Hobbes presents Moses' atrocity against the worshippers of the golden calf not as an extrajudicial slaughter but rather as a legal execution. His point here, perhaps, is that modeling oneself on the righteous wrath of Moses presumes a legal authority that Moses himself possessed but that his modern aspiring emulators conspicuously lack.)

[45] Similar lines of interpretation are developed in David Johnston, *The Rhetoric of Leviathan* (Princeton, NJ: Princeton University Press, 1986), chapter 7. Johnston argues that Hobbes's emphasis on a kingdom of God *to come* is meant to respond to Presbyterian claims on behalf of a supposedly already-existing Calvinist theocracy.

with the Second Coming, and Christ is not (yet) around to reassume rulership of the Jewish theocracy, full authority, both civil and ecclesiastical, can be exercised by the existing temporal power *until* Christ comes again to reclaim his rightful throne.[46] ("He [Christ] taught all men to obey in the mean time them that sate in Moses seat."[47]) Hobbes insists that Christ will return to earth to assume permanent rule over a reestablished Mosaic theocracy. But if so, what was the point of the First Coming? Hobbes gives this answer: "to restore unto God, by a New Covenant, the Kingdome, which being his by the Old Covenant, had been cut off by the rebellion of the Israelites in the election of Saul."[48] On this account, there is no real difference between the covenant of the Old Testament and the covenant of the New Testament; both are concerned with the securing of political authority.[49] God sacrificed Christ, Hobbes writes, "for the reduction of his elect to their former covenanted obedience."[50] This means that one gets all the advantages of theocracy while avoiding the palpable disadvantages of theocracy. Hobbes's proposal is in effect to "restore" the old Jewish theocracy, but to improve it by bestowing a monopoly of prophetic authority in the person of Christ, thus ensuring that the established sovereign can rule without suffering the nuisance of other prophets who rise up with

[46] *Leviathan*, pp. 512, 514, 517.

[47] Ibid., p. 516. Hobbes does say here that Christ posed no threat to the civil authorities of his time because "[t]he Kingdome hee claimed was to bee in another world," which seems to suggest an otherworldly interpretation of Christianity; but to render this text consistent with what Hobbes says elsewhere about Christ's kingdom, I think one has to interpret "another world" as "another time."

   According to Pocock, the prophetic status of Moses entails that "Moses becomes the lieutenant of God in a way in which the civil sovereign can never be" (*Politics, Language, and Time*, p. 170). The notion of "sitting in Moses's seat" pending Christ's return suggests that Pocock's claim cannot be sustained. The scriptural text that Hobbes cites, *Matthew* 23: 2–3, refers to "scribes and Pharisees," which leaves open a bit of ambiguity between Moses' civil authority and his ecclesiastical authority. Yet this trope of "obeying them that sat in Moses's seat" (or "in Moses' chair") is repeated twice by Hobbes on p. 516, and both times it is clear that Hobbes sees "*the Magistrates*" ("their then Civill Government") as occupants of this seat; cf. the citation of the same scriptural text in *Behemoth*, pp. 50–51, as well as the reference to the King as "God's lieutenant" on p. 51. Clifford Orwin's encapsulation of Hobbes – "divine right shorn of... its divinity" – seems a reasonable characterization of the kind of theocratic authority being appealed to by Hobbes in these and related texts; see Orwin, "On the Sovereign Authorization," *Political Theory*, Vol. 4, No. 1 (February 1975): 39.

[48] *Leviathan*, p. 515.

[49] Emile Perreau-Saussine points out interestingly that similar strategies were employed by Bossuet on behalf of the Gallicanism of Louis XIV. Both Hobbes and Bossuet turned to images of Hebrew theocracy to vindicate the monarch as "God's lieutenant." See "French Catholic Political Thought from the Deconfessionalisation of the State to the Recognition of Religious Freedom," in *Secularisation Revisited*, ed. Ira Katznelson and Gareth Stedman-Jones (Cambridge: Cambridge University Press, forthcoming). Cf. Schmitt, *The Leviathan in the State Theory of Thomas Hobbes*, p. 82 (and Tracy B. Strong, "Foreword," p. xv), on "lieutenant of God" as a venerably established Catholic trope; and Orwin, "On the Sovereign Authorization," p. 43, n. 46, on the Erastianism implicit in divine right of kings theory. In *Leviathan*, p. 705 (cf. p. 712), Hobbes acknowledges that the doctrine of a "Lieutenant amongst us, by whom we are to be told what are [Christ's] Commandments," is a Papist doctrine.

[50] *Leviathan*, p. 516.

rival claims to authority. A Christian theocracy (concentrated in the person of the sovereign) offers the advantages of Jewish (Mosaic) theocracy without the political drawback of Jewish prophets.

Hobbes thinks that it was for good reasons that the Hebrews overthrew their theocracy, but dethéocratizing the regime does not necessarily offer a sufficient cure for the problem of political authority with which they were grappling. A better solution, he thinks, is to reintroduce theocracy, but to ensure that the sovereign is the supreme and unchallengeable arbiter (as Moses was) of religious truth. The key here (as in *De Cive*) is to monopolize judgment concerning true and false prophets.[51] The safest way of securing this monopoly of judgment (as exercised by Moses in the matter of the seventy prophets)[52] is for the sovereign to claim for himself an exclusive title to being "God's Prophet" or "God's Lieutenant."[53] Hobbes wants ultimately to retheocratize politics rather than to dethéocratize it because only through (nominally Christian) theocratic politics can the sovereign claim sufficient authority to strip Christianity of the otherworldly teachings that threaten temporal authority.[54] (Thus Hobbes would no doubt argue against Rousseau's civil religion that it is not theocratically ambitious enough.[55])

In *De Cive*, Hobbes confers upon the sovereign virtually unchecked authority to shape theological doctrine according to his own purposes; in *Leviathan*, Hobbes in effect urges the sovereign to seize upon this latitude he has been granted to reshape Christianity in the image of the Old Testament. Because a Hobbesian monarch possesses the power to decide theological questions by the sheer exercise of political authority, Hobbes wants this theocratic authority to be exercised in imposing a "Judaic" reading of Christianity upon the Church. This intention can be seen most clearly in Hobbes's suggestions about how to reinterpret Christian doctrines of heaven and hell on the basis of the Old

[51] As we shall see in Chapter 9, the problem of true vs. false prophets is also a crucial theme for Spinoza. One of the decisive criteria specified by Hobbes for identification of true prophets is "the not teaching any other Religion than that which is already established" (*Leviathan*, p. 412). It would appear to follow from this criterion that no prophet of a *new* revelation (Moses, Jesus, Mohammed) can be a true prophet!

[52] *Leviathan*, pp. 464–465.

[53] Ibid., pp. 462, 466, 468–469, 476–478.

[54] Cf. Carl Schmitt's analogy between Hobbes's depiction of Christ and "the domestication of Christ" by Dostoyevsky's Grand Inquisitor: [T]he purpose is "to neutralize the effect of Christ in the social and political sphere; to de-anarchize Christianity, while leaving it at the same time as a kind of legitimating effect.... A clever tactician gives up nothing as long as it is not completely useless." This is quoted in Tracy Strong, "Foreword," p. xxiv. Schmitt's phrase "to de-anarchize Christianity" strikes me as particularly apt. Strong, on pp. xxv–xxvi, gives a very helpful account (parallel to my own) of how Hobbes and Schmitt pursue their strategies of deanarchizing Christianity.

[55] There is no question that Hobbes would be perfectly happy with the fully secular state that is an accomplishment of contemporary political life. Nevertheless, Hobbes was convinced – as were other profoundly anticlerical types like Spinoza and Hume – that religion was too deeply entrenched in the psyche of ordinary human beings to be banished in any glimpsable future. Hence, in Hobbes's view, the next best thing is to appropriate the power of religion on behalf of the authority of the state.

Testament. He insists that the eternal life forfeited by Adam will be, once we recover it through Christ, a life lived *on earth* (rather than drawing men up to heaven, Christ returns to *earth* as an eternal governor), and Hobbes similarly appeals to the Old Testament to debunk the Christian ideas of hell[56] and the devil[57]: The "Devil" refers to worldly enemies of the Hebrews, such as the Canaanites; "Hellfire" refers to the Jerusalem garbage dump![58] Moreover, according to Hobbes, Christ himself rests his claim to being the Messiah on the authority of the *Old* Testament: "And of the Old Testament, our Saviour himselfe saith to the Jews (*John* 5.39) *Search the Scriptures.... If* hee had not meant they should Interpret them [i.e., base their understanding of Christ's messiahdom on the *Old* Testament], hee would not have bidden them *take thence* [my italics] the proof of his being the Christ."[59] It is to be inferred, then, that Christ interprets his own mission in Old Testament terms. A nontheocratic politics would not give the sovereign sufficient discretion to reinterpret Christian teaching in such a way as to render it politically harmless, and this would defeat Hobbes's ultimate purpose. As Rousseau says, Hobbes's aim is to "reunify the two heads of the eagle," and Hobbes realizes that only through a kind of theocratic politics can they be fully reunified.[60] Hobbes's object is not to divorce theology and politics, but rather, as he puts it, to substitute "a Priesthood of Kings" for "a Kingdome of Priests."[61]

---

[56] *Leviathan*, pp. 480–481, 485ff. See the interesting discussion of Hobbes's asymmetrical treatment of heaven and hell by Richard Tuck: *Leviathan*, ed. Tuck (Cambridge: Cambridge University Press, 1996), "Introduction," pp. xli–xliii. Tuck describes Hobbesian civil religion "as part of the grand Hobbesian enterprise of liberating men from terror," and also states that there is something "utopian" in the aspiration to design "a new religion . . . seen as a necessary part of reconstructing society" (p. xliii).

[57] *Leviathan*, pp. 488–489.

[58] As various commentators have observed, Hobbes *must* debunk the doctrine of otherworldly damnation because unless he is able to do this, his project to found political order on fear of this-worldly death as the most abysmal fear necessarily fails. Cf. Leo Strauss, *Natural Right and History* (Chicago: University of Chicago Press, 1953), p. 198. See also the précis of the *Leviathan* quoted by Pierre Bayle on pp. 87–88 of Bayle, *Political Writings*, ed. Sally L. Jenkinson (Cambridge: Cambridge University Press, 2000), which very forcefully highlights the centrality of this issue.

[59] *Leviathan*, p. 544; cf. p. 617: "*Search the Scriptures . . . they are they that testifie of mee.* Our Saviour here speaketh of the Scriptures onely of the Old Testament; for the Jews at that time could not search the Scriptures of the New Testament, which were not written."

[60] Hobbes's resolve to keep the two heads of the eagle united helps to explain why he insists that Eleazar the High Priest, not Joshua, was civil sovereign of Israel following Moses, for this allows him to argue in chapter 42 that Cardinal Bellarmine's appeals to the high priest on behalf of papal sovereignty really refer to the high priest *qua* civil sovereign and not the high priest *qua* high priest (ibid., pp. 547, 566, 572, 585, 587, 597). The same motivation may also explain why Hobbes makes the surprising claim, stated repeatedly in chapter 40, that Aaron inherited the Mosaic sovereignty (pp. 501, 502, 506): If the regime Moses founded was a strict theocracy, then sovereignty had to be handed down from high priest to high priest.

[61] Ibid., p. 447. This crucial distinction parallels *De Cive*'s distinction (see note 9, this chapter): maistry of kings (ministry of priests) vs. maistry of priests (ministry of kings). The key to Hobbes's theocratic politics is his opposition between *kingly theocracy* ("a Christian common-wealth") and *priestly theocracy* (the story of the Old Testament). Rousseau, as we

The strongest confirmation of Hobbes's authentic place within the Machiavellian–Rousseauian civil-religion tradition is Hobbes's discussion of the fall of old religions and the founding of new religions. According to Hobbes, old religions die on account of the corruption of priests: Not only are they corrupt but they are perceived to be corrupt; and new religions arise as a consequence of "the faith which a multitude hath in some one person."[62] The Protestant Reformation offered of course a powerful reminder of how this process works. However, once it is recognized that, as Machiavelli pointed out, new religions are "from men" rather than "from heaven,"[63] that innovations in and transformations of religious belief and practice are legitimate objects of statecraft,[64] then the way is clear for Hobbes's project of a reinterpreted Christianity made serviceable for politics.[65]

have already seen, is skeptical of this distinction and suspects that priestly theocracy will inevitably subvert kingly theocracy (as he claims has in fact happened in the kingly theocracies of England and Russia). It should also be noted that Rousseau's alternatives of "masters" and "ministers" (*maîtres–ministres*) is directly based on Hobbes: *On the Social Contract*, pp. 126–127.

For a somewhat similar set of juxtapositions, see "Considerations upon the Reputation, Loyalty, Manners, and Religion of Thomas Hobbes" (1662), in *The English Works of Thomas Hobbes*, ed. Sir William Molesworth (London: John Bohn, 1839–1845), Vol. IV, p. 433: "Nor can he [Hobbes] be made to believe that the safety of a state depends upon the safety of the Church, I mean of the clergy. For neither is a clergy essential to a commonwealth.... He believes rather that the safety of the Church depends on the safety of the King... and that the King is no part of the flock of any minister or bishop, no more than the shepherd is of his sheep,... and all the clergy, as well as the people, the King's flock." As with the trope of masters and ministers, the question here is this: Who is the shepherd and who is the flock?

[62] *Leviathan*, pp. 181–183, 179.

[63] *Discourses on Livy*, ed. Mansfield and Tarcov, p. 139.

[64] Echoing Machiavelli, Hobbes speaks of "how the Religion of the Gentiles was a part of their Policy": *Leviathan*, pp. 173–178. On p. 177, Hobbes classifies Mohammed among "the first Founders, and Legislators of Common-wealths among the Gentiles," as if Islam were merely a variant of paganism. Richard Tuck informs us that at least in the case of one of Hobbes's disciples, namely Henry Stubbe, the Hobbesian interpretation of religion as civil religion had the effect of suggesting the political superiority of Islam to Christianity. See *Hobbes*, p. 89. As noted elsewhere in this book, this partiality for Islam seems to be an enduring pattern within the civil-religion tradition (for reasons made explicit by Rousseau). The project to "Islamicize" Christianity also looms large in Toland's *Nazarenus*. For interesting discussions of the relation between Stubbe and Toland, see James R. Jacob, *Henry Stubbe, Radical Protestantism, and the Early Enlightenment* (Cambridge: Cambridge University Press, 1983), chapter 8, and Justin A. I. Champion, "Legislators, Impostors, and the Politic Origins of Religion: English Theories of 'Imposture' from Stubbe to Toland," in *Heterodoxy, Spinozism, and Free Thought in Early-Eighteenth-Century Europe*, ed. Silvia Berti et al. (Dordrecht: Kluwer, 1996), pp. 333–356. See also the editor's "Introduction" to John Toland, *Nazarenus*, ed. Justin Champion (Oxford: Voltaire Foundation, 1999), p. 86. Needless to say, both Stubbe and Toland directly anticipate Rousseau's claim in *Social Contract* IV.8 that "Mohammed had very sound views" (i.e., Islam is better equipped than Christianity is to serve republican purposes). One further interesting extension of this post-Hobbesian tradition is John Edwards's claim that *The Reasonableness of Christianity* borrows its theology from the *Koran*: See *John Locke and Christianity*, ed. Victor Nuovo (Bristol: Thoemmes Press, 1997), pp. 218–219.

[65] Pocock, in his well-known essay on "Time, History and Eschatology," makes the point that it is implausible that Hobbes would have devoted fully half the text of *Leviathan* to problems of

To conclude, let us return to Rousseau's challenge to Hobbes, namely that "he ought to have seen that the dominating spirit of Christianity was incompatible with his system." Here Rousseau betrays a fundamental misunderstanding of Hobbes's teaching on civil religion, for Hobbes *did* see that the spirit of Christianity was incompatible with his system, and hence he devoted a tremendous effort to the reinterpretation of Christianity so that it would cease to be incompatible with Hobbesian politics.[66]

scriptural interpretation if, in Hobbes's own view, theology constituted a form of "insignificant speech" (*Politics, Language, and Time*, pp. 160–162). The appropriate response to Pocock, in my view, is that the project of reinventing Christianity is an ambitious project, and there is no reason not to expect that Hobbes would have judged that project worthy of the most stupendous intellectual energies.

[66] Cf. Holmes, "Introduction" to *Behemoth*, p. xxxv: "The Bible is [in Hobbes's view] an anarchy-provoking work...because no one can tell with certainty what it means" (cf. *Behemoth*, pp. 9, 10, 51–52). This is precisely why, according to Hobbes's perspective, it is a crucial political responsibility to *dictate* or *stipulate* the meaning of the Bible.

6

Behemoth

Hobbesian "Theocracy" versus the Real Thing[1]

> Neither is any man so mad, as not to choose to yield obedience rather to them who can remit and retain their sins, than to the powerfulest kings.
>
> – Thomas Hobbes[2]

> [Religion] may speak about the bliss of the next world, but it wants power in this one.
>
> – Christopher Hitchens[3]

There is an extensive analysis of policy toward religion in *Behemoth*, and therefore we should not omit this important work from our discussion of Hobbesian civil religion.[4] What Hobbes was fundamentally concerned with in this book was *theocracy* in the proper (i.e., non-Hobbesian) sense as a historical regime. Civil religion is acceptable and even desirable from a Hobbesian point of view because it is a mode of theocracy ruled by the sovereign and subordinated to

---

[1] What is implied in the title of this chapter about Hobbes's relationship to the English Saints and their Puritan Revolution is brought out very well in Tracy B. Strong's Foreword to Carl Schmitt, *The Leviathan in the State Theory of Thomas Hobbes* (Chicago: University of Chicago Press, 2008), p. xxv: "Hobbes and Schmitt think the leviathan (as mortal God, hence as Christ/Messiah) *holds back* the kingdom of God on this earth or at least makes no move to bring it about. This is why this is political theology and not theological politics." To put it in Strong's categories, "theological politics" is precisely what was being pursued by the regicidal Saints (which is why Hobbes conjures up a symbolic opposition between the *Book of Job*'s two mythical monsters – Leviathan as a force of order and Behemoth as a force of disorder).

[2] Thomas Hobbes, *Man and Citizen*, ed. Bernard Gert (Garden City, NY: Anchor Books, 1972), p. 357.

[3] Christopher Hitchens, *God is Not Great: How Religion Poisons Everything* (Toronto: McClelland & Stewart, 2007), p. 17.

[4] Thomas Hobbes, *Behemoth, or The Long Parliament*, ed. Ferdinand Tönnies (Chicago: University of Chicago Press, 1990). *Behemoth* is a dialogue between two unnamed interlocutors, A and B. A clearly speaks for Hobbes because at certain crucial points in the text (e.g., the exchange at the bottom of p. 180), B expresses views that Hobbes without question rejects.

political–nonreligious concerns for civic order. Puritan theocracy – that is, *real* theocracy – is *not* acceptable because it is a subordination of political concerns to religious imperatives. As we saw in the previous discussion, Hobbes offers his own version of a theocratic politics to preclude a usurpation of political authority on the part of authentically religious claimants. As Stephen Holmes nicely puts the point, Hobbes "rhetorically divinizes the state" in the hope of diverting "religious piety away from Puritan sects, Presbyterian ministers, Anglican bishops, and, of course, the Pope."[5] But *genuine* theocracy, as witnessed in the English Civil War, thus runs directly contrary to the Hobbesian version of theocracy. For that reason, a ferocious root-and-branch anticlericalism occupies the very center of Hobbes's vision of politics, accounting for what Holmes calls Hobbes's "obsession with religion."[6]

Strangely, Hobbes begins with a critique of Papism – strange because this was surely peripheral to the problems of Charles I (it was *anti*-Papists, not Papists, who were challenging Charles's authority).[7] This allows Hobbes to pose very sharply and very directly what we already know to be the central preoccupation of his civil-religion theorizing (viz., the threat of divided sovereignty):

---

[5] Stephen Holmes, "Introduction," in Hobbes, *Behemoth*, p. xlv. Holmes's characterization here of the Hobbesian project is particularly helpful in indicating that the scope of Hobbes's critical enterprise comprehends the *whole* of existing Christendom (not just Catholicism and extremist Protestant sects). Cf. p. xxxiv: "Christianity [i.e., Christianity per se] is especially dangerous."

[6] Ibid., p. xi; cf. p. xlix. Hobbes lists seven sets of enemies of the sovereign authority of Charles I, of which the *first three* are religious – first, Presbyterian ministers; second, Papists; and third, Independents (*Behemoth*, pp. 2–4). However, he chooses to zero in on the Papists as his primary critical target (p. 20: "one of the distempers of the state of England in the time of our late King Charles"). The critique of "Papist pretense" extends from p. 5 to p. 21, at which point Hobbes takes up the issue of "that other distemper," "the power of the Presbyterians" (pp. 21, 22). Holmes's hypothesis as to why "Presbyterian ministers" are given the privileged attention that they get from Hobbes is that they, unlike the Puritans, are still an active force in the 1660s; hence Hobbes's polemics against *them* are likely to have more immediate political effect: Holmes, "Introduction," p. xxxv, n. 62.

[7] Cf. Alan Ryan, "Hobbes, Toleration, and the Inner Life," in *The Nature of Political Theory*, ed. David Miller and Larry Siedentop (Oxford: Clarendon Press, 1983), p. 201: "it is rather puzzling that Hobbes should have been so alarmed by the Papacy's contribution to the Kingdome of Darknesse as late as 1651," noting (n. 14) that the same puzzle applies to *Behemoth*. One of the particularly odd features of Hobbes's decision to give primacy to Catholicism as a polemical target is that it has the seeming consequence of aligning Hobbes with the challengers of royal authority. For of course what largely defined Puritan fanaticism was fanatical anti-Catholicism, and one of the chief Puritan grievances against Charles I and his regime was his alleged closet sympathy for Catholicism, and the perceived tendencies on the part of Charles's so-to-speak high priest, William Laud (Bishop of London, subsequently promoted by Charles to Archbishop of Canterbury), to move the established church back in a Papist direction. The accusation of "popery" was constantly being leveled against Charles and the bishops (cf. *Behemoth*, p. 24), so it is in that respect strange that Hobbes would give so much emphasis to the evils of Papism. Hume, in his analysis of Laud's imprudence, gives a very helpful account of why Puritan radicals were able to see in Laud's policies signs of a reembrace of Catholicism: See David Hume, *The History of Great Britain: The Reigns of James I and Charles I*, ed. Duncan Forbes (Harmondsworth: Penguin, 1970), pp. 331–337.

This [Papist] power of absolving subjects of their obedience . . . is as absolute a sovereignty as is possible to be; and consequently there must be two kingdoms in one and the same nation, and no man be able to know which of his masters he must obey.[8]

Papism impugns the temporal authority of all earthly sovereigns (Hobbes's phrase is, "by pretence of his power spiritual, [the Pope encroaches] upon the temporal rights of all other princes of the west"[9]) by means of the argument that because Christ is "King of all the world," and the Pope is Christ's vicar, therefore "what Christ could give, his vicar might give," that is, political title to worldly domains.[10] Hobbes implies quite clearly that Christian kings fail to recognize what fatal injury they do to their own sovereignty when they include the words "by the gift of God" (i.e., by the gift of the priests) in their titles, and when they allow bishops to confer upon them their crown and scepter.[11] Papal innovations extending beyond Scripture are presented by Hobbes as a set of conspiracies intended to weaken kingly authority: The celibacy of priests had the effect of barring kings (who are necessarily concerned with the possibility of heirs) from the aura of the priesthood; the practice of confession instituted a network of "spies" listening in on the secret thoughts of the subjects of the state (and increased still further the priest's privileged aura); and the dispatching of a mobile unit of "preaching friars" was an additional device for the propagation of sermons that would inevitably play up ecclesiastical authority and diminish the authority of the civil power.[12] Even the founding of universities, on Hobbes's view, was originally just another papal conspiracy designed to ensure that the ideology of the Church remained firmly in control.[13] These are presented as radical criticisms of Catholic Christianity in particular. But the fact that Hobbes, in the context of this critique of Catholicism, switches in one key sentence (a sentence so daring that Hobbes felt compelled to erase it from the original manuscript of *Behemoth*!) from "his [the Pope's] bishops" to "bishops" in a generic sense, gives a fairly clear indication that Hobbes

---

[8] *Behemoth*, p. 8.

[9] Ibid., pp. 11–12.

[10] Ibid., p. 12.

[11] Ibid. Hume makes a strikingly similar observation, citing the example of the modification inserted by Laud in the coronation service for Charles I, the effect of which was to insinuate that the King was beholden to the *Church* for his civil authority: See *The History of Great Britain*, pp. 336–337.

[12] *Behemoth*, pp. 13–16; cf. Holmes, "Introduction," p. xxxvii. As regards the last of these three papal-conspiratorial devices, see *Behemoth*, p. 16: "Only in Christendom" is it permitted for private men to make orations "without first making the state acquainted." "The heathen Kings foresaw, that a few such orators would be able to make a great sedition."

[13] *Behemoth*, pp. 17–18. Hobbes expands on his critique of the universities on pp. 39ff.: Universities spawned preachers, and preachers spawned popular disregard of the needs of civil authority. The universities (originally in the service of the Pope) taught doctrines of disobedience rather than of the duty of the multitude. As a result, the universities were not what they ought to have been, a place for the dissemination of "the science of *just* and *unjust*" (namely Hobbes's own science), but rather a "Trojan horse" for theocratic subversion of monarchical authority (pp. 39–40).

intended his attack on Papism as a bridgehead for a more general assault upon clericalism per se.[14]

There was an easy solution to the political shenanigans of the Pope: Every king of Europe had merely to do what Henry VIII did, *and to do it in concert –* "made themselves every one, as Henry VIII did, head of the Church within their own respective dominions."[15] However, the various kings counted on the Pope to be useful to themselves in the overall power equation, and as a result, the Pope remained more powerful than he ought to have been. Hence, even after Henry disempowered "the Romish religion" in England, the Pope continued to dispatch "Jesuits and other emissaries of the Roman Church" to stir up trouble.[16] So much for the contribution of Catholicism to the anarchy of 1640. Hobbes now shifts to the Presbyterian contribution.

It is not for nothing that Hobbes refers, in his account of the denouement of English Catholicism, to the "rebellion of the Presbyterians and other democrat-ical men."[17] For the Reformation as such launched a democratic revolution of staggering proportions. By opening up such a huge controversy concerning the meaning of Scripture, it required vernacular translation of the Bible – so that "every man, to the best of his power, [could] examine by the Scriptures, which of them was in the right."[18] This overturned what was in this respect genuine wisdom on the part of the old Church: "[T]he Pope did concerning the Scrip-tures the same that Moses did concerning Mount Sinai. Moses suffered no man to go up to it to hear God speak or gaze upon him, but such as he himself took with him" (to which *B* rejoins: "Certainly Moses did therein very wisely.").[19] The inevitable (and from a Hobbesian perspective much-to-be-lamented) con-sequence of this abrogation of Papal–Mosaic wisdom was that "every man became a judge of religion and an interpreter of the Scriptures to himself."[20] For all of Hobbes's animus against Papism, he is on this by no means trivial issue on the side of the Pope.[21]

---

[14] Ibid., p. 6. The relevant sentence is placed within square brackets by Tönnies; the crucial phrase begins, "but most bishops." Another very significant erased (but restored) passage is on p. 89, where Hobbes makes clear to what extent he blames the Anglican bishops in their vanity and arrogance for their own downfall (thereby contributing to the downfall of the commonwealth as a whole). On p. 95 Hobbes again erases an anti-Anglican text. The clear pattern, then, is for Hobbes to erase passages that are most hostile to Anglicanism. It goes without saying that Tönnies is owed thanks for restoring these important erased passages.

[15] Ibid., p. 21; cf. Holmes, "Introduction," p. xxxvi, n. 64: Hobbes "wants an Erastian 'subordi-nation of the Church to the civil state.'"

[16] *Behemoth*, p. 20; cf. pp. 43–44: "since we broke out of their [the Catholic Church's] net in the time of Henry VIII, they have continually endeavoured to recover."

[17] Ibid; cf. p. 193: "the Presbyterians and men of democratical principles."

[18] Ibid., p. 21.

[19] Ibid.

[20] Ibid., p. 22.

[21] Ibid.: "this license of interpreting the Scripture was the cause of so many several sects [resulting in] the disturbance of the commonwealth." However, as Holmes remarks ("Introduction'" p. xlvi), Hobbes is nevertheless able to discern eventual political advantages in being able to

In any case, Hobbes goes on to argue that Protestants driven into exile during Queen Mary's attempt to restore Catholicism were mightily impressed by the (for Hobbes, woeful) example provided by Calvinist theocracy in Geneva ("for want of better statesmen"), and were inspired to seek something similar in England when the ascension of Queen Elizabeth allowed them to return.[22] Thus it was European Calvinism in its theocratic incarnation that laid the seeds for a theocratic revolution in England (spurred in large part by Scottish Calvinism). This ecclesiastical democratism in turn gave tremendous impetus to a radical, antimonarchical love of democracy in the political sphere.[23] What is worse, from Hobbes's point of view: papal "pretense," or Calvinist theocratic democracy?[24]

It is a striking irony of Hobbes's account that precisely Hobbesian theocratic theory turned out to be the source of disaster in practice.[25] Hobbes argues that the process of the dissolution of kingly authority began in 1637 with the King's misguided decision to impose the Anglican prayer book upon the Presbyterians

school the subjects of the realm in vernacular versions of the Bible. These political advantages can be reaped only if Hobbes (or a king suitably educated by Hobbes) can teach the common subject the most politically salutary "true" reading of the Bible. If not, then Reformation implies unbounded anarchy.

[22] *Behemoth*, p. 22; cf. p. 136. Cf. Hume, *The History of Great Britain*, p. 73: "[T]he persecutions of Mary . . . chased abroad all the most obstinate reformers [who] had leisure to imbibe a stronger tincture of the enthusiastic genius; and when they returned, upon the accession of Elizabeth, they imported it, in its full force and virulence, into their native country."

[23] *Behemoth*, p. 23; cf. p. 26. Again, cf. Hume, *The History of Great Britain*, p. 74.

[24] Holmes highlights the interesting puzzle raised by the text in the Epistle Dedicatory to *Leviathan* where "Hobbes claims to advocate a middle way between 'too great Liberty' and 'too much Authority.' How can there be too much authority for Hobbes?" ("Introduction," p. xlii). *Behemoth*'s account of the opposing religious tyrannies of Papism and Calvinism might suggest a different solution than the one Holmes proposes. Could Hobbes's thought have been that in comparison with papal tyranny on the one side (*Behemoth*, pp. 21, 172) and Presbyterian tyranny, or anarchy-cum-tyranny, on the other side (p. 169), even absolutist monarchy – with its more modest claims on the souls of its subjects – presents itself as a moderate compromise between liberty and authority?

[25] The *theory* is laid out in *De Cive*, chapter 15, and *Leviathan*, chapter 31. For the key statement of what the theory requires, see Thomas Hobbes, *Leviathan*, ed. C. B. Macpherson (London: Penguin, 1985), p. 405: "But seeing a Common-wealth is but one Person, it ought also to exhibite to God but one Worship; which then it doth, when it commandeth it to be exhibited by Private men, Publiquely. And this is Publique Worship; the property whereof, is to be *Uniforme*: For those actions that are done differently, by different men, cannot be said to be a Publique Worship. And therefore, where many sorts of Worship be allowed, proceeding from the different Religions of Private men, it cannot be said there is any Publique Worship, nor that the Common-wealth is of any Religion at all." For an interesting discussion (although one that in my view puts too much emphasis on the idea of pleasing God and not enough emphasis on the strictly political imperative of unifying the commonwealth), see Jeremy Waldron, "Hobbes on Public Worship," in *Toleration and Its Limits*, ed. M. S. Williams and J. Waldron (New York: New York University Press, 2008), pp. 31–53. In any case, if Hobbes believes that practice must in all cases abide by theory, then his narrative in *Behemoth* would have to be significantly different than it is.

of Scotland.[26] The King's inability to enforce this policy had a catastrophic effect on his long-term authority, and subsequent concessions to the Presbyterians altered the whole balance of power between Anglicans and Presbyterians in the realm as a whole. If the King had not attempted to "anglicanize" Scottish Presbyterianism in the first place, he would not have set in motion the whole course of events that led to the undoing, in the end, of his very authority.[27] In effect, Hobbes holds that the misguidedness of the King's policy consisted in failing to respect religious pluralism within the King's realm, and instead insisting upon an imposition of (Hobbesian–theocratic) religious uniformity. It is therefore an entailment of Hobbes's own argument that the King would have been much better advised to respect a Lockean–Montesquieuian pluralism of religions than to enforce (or try to enforce) a Hobbesian political dictation of religious conformity. There is in Hobbes's political thought as expressed in *Behemoth*, as Holmes emphasizes in his Introduction, a dimension of prudential awareness of the possibility of counterproductive overreaching on the part of kings that is overlooked in usual accounts of the Hobbesian theory of sovereignty.[28]

On p. 47, after a great deal of heated polemics against Catholics and Presbyterians, Hobbes finally turns to the Anglican clergy. Although "their life and conversation, is for the most part very good, and of very good example," their doctrine is not in principle so far removed from the more blatantly subversive divisions of Christendom: "[I]f they [the Anglican clergy] had number and strength, . . . they would attempt to obtain that power [to subordinate civil authority to their own presumed moral authority], as the others have done."[29] If the bishops of the Anglican Church reserve to themselves the right to interpret Scripture, as of course they do,[30] and if Scripture is presumed to be the source of absolute moral judgment, then the problem of the subversive potential of religion is in principle posed no less by Anglican clergy (even if in a contingent case they happen to remain loyal) than by their Catholic and Presbyterian counterparts. As we saw in Chapter 5, the problem is solved only if the *state* (the sovereign) reserves to itself privileged interpretation of Scripture.

B is clearly taken aback by *A*'s argument that there is less difference in principle between loyal Anglicans and rebellious Presbyterians than the former are likely to assume.[31] The bottom line, for Anglican theology no less than

---

[26] *Behemoth*, p. 28.

[27] The larger subnarrative here (the undermining of monarchical authority in the course of skirmishes with the Scottish) stretches from p. 28 ("that unlucky business") to p. 35. On pp. 30–31, Hobbes clearly implies that it was a mistake for the King to negotiate peace with the Scots: Threats to whip them into line followed by complete capitulation on the issue of bishops in Scotland were bound to do gross damage to the king's authority.

[28] See, for instance, Holmes's commentary on the prayer-book affair: "Introduction," p. xli ("royal misgovernment . . . led to the breakdown of authority").

[29] *Behemoth*, p. 47. Hobbes says that the speech and practice of the Anglican clergy are "much better than their writings" (which are still implicitly subversive).

[30] Ibid., p. 48.

[31] Ibid., pp. 48–49.

for other forms of Christian theology, is this: "[W]e are . . . to obey God rather than men,"[32] and this is in essence a subversive doctrine. If it is the commands of God rather than the commands of man that are ultimately to be obeyed, *and* if the priest not the King remains "judge of the meaning of Scripture," then "it is impossible that the life of any King, or the peace of any Christian kingdom, can be long secure."[33] *A* in the end convinces *B* that the supposed loyalists (*qua* Christians) pose in principle the very same challenge to kingly authority as was mounted in practice by the rebels; Presbyterian sedition, judged according to Anglican doctrine, can absolve itself just as easily as it can according to its own doctrine.[34]

The discussion in Dialogue 1 finally circles back to the problem of the accessibility of scripture in vernacular languages, which remains a key question. The core of *A*'s position (identical to Hobbes's position) is that Scriptural interpretation must reside strictly in the hands of the appointees of the sovereign.[35] *B* reasonably responds to this: "I understand not to what end they were translated into English."[36] Why would the common subjects of the Crown be "not only permitted, but also exhorted, to read" the Scriptures if the necessary consequence of this is an anarchy of interpretations? In his reply, *A* claims that he is not persuaded that it is "hurtful to have the Scriptures in English,"[37] but whether it is hurtful or profitable clearly depends on who has ultimate authority to direct readers to which biblical texts (either passages in Scripture that are civil-authority promoting or those that are civil-authority undermining). If the vernacular reading of Scripture were purely "profitable," as *A* tries to suggest at the end of his reply, then it is impossible to see why

---

[32] Ibid., p. 49; cf. Holmes, "Introduction," p. xxxviii, n. 67. Hobbes takes as his source here Richard Allestree's *The Whole Duty of Man*.

[33] *Behemoth*, p. 50.

[34] Ibid. Cf. Hume: "All the doctrines, which the Romish church had borrowed from some of the early fathers, and which free'd the spiritual from subordination to the civil power, were now adopted by the church of England" (*The History of Great Britain*, p. 336).

[35] *A* makes this statement: "Whatsoever is necessary for [the plainer sort] to know, is so easy, as not to need interpretation" (*Behemoth*, p. 55). However, this seems to be an incredibly naïve view (and there is nothing naïve about *A*). *There is always an interpretation* (championed either by partisans of civil authority or by ax-grinding ecclesiastics or by metaphysical-hair-splitting theologians).

At this point in the text, *A* appeals to the humble understanding of "the plainer sort of men" in order to puncture the destructive pride of "wise men" – a deliberate replication of a standard *biblical* trope (as noted by Holmes, "Introduction," p. xlvi). Hobbes makes clear a few pages later (p. 60), however, what he really thinks of the ordinary judgment of ordinary human beings when he states that the people lack "judgment enough" to assess the truth or falsity of Catholicism relative to Protestantism. More blatant still is *A*'s reference, on p. 68, to "the ignorant multitude." See also p. 144: "Common people know nothing of right or wrong by their own meditation"; and Hobbes's account, on pp. 158–159, of the insufficiency of "good natural wit" for the understanding of a man's duty.

[36] Ibid., p. 52.

[37] Ibid., p. 53. Framing his reply in this way suggests that anxiety about a vernacular Bible is strictly *B*'s view, whereas the truth, surely, is that *B* is merely articulating what is implicit in *A*'s own understanding of the relationship between the King, the clergy, and the Bible.

it has been so easy for ministers of different theological persuasions to draw anarchical and seditious teachings from the Bible. In that sense, *B*'s challenge remains unrefuted: Vernacular access to the Bible is only harmless if one maintains strict (civil-religious) control over its interpretation (in which case it is indeed puzzling why one should permit popular access to Scripture in the first place).

The idea of independent access to the Bible is a fiction; access to it is always and necessarily determined by a political context governed by civil authority. If people are able to read the Bible, they can do so only by the grace of the sovereign: "[T]he Scripture itself was ... received but by the authority of Kings and States."[38] That is to say, all religion is at bottom civil religion – it has the right to institutional status within the state only with the sanction of the sovereign power, or because the state suffers it to exist.[39] The King is "God's lieutenant,"[40] and as "head of the Church," ought to hold standing as "chief judge of the rectitude of all interpretations of the Scripture."[41] Therefore his interpretation trumps rival interpretations; "to obey the King's laws ... is ... to obey God."[42]

Dialogue 1 concludes with the argument that Henry VIII's liberation of England from the grip of the Pope (as welcome as it was) ultimately failed to solve the fundamental problem. For Anglican clergy picked up right where the Catholic Church left off, laying claim to the same "divine right" formerly "pretended to" by the Pope.[43] Even after listening to *A*'s arguments in the course of the first dialogue, *B* takes it for granted that the Presbyterians are the real problem.[44] One does not have to scratch too far below the surface of *A*'s discussion, however, to see that he is essentially as anti-Anglican as he is anti-Presbyterian.[45]

---

[38] Ibid.

[39] Cf. p. 90: "[R]eligion in itself admits no controversy. It is a law of the kingdom."

[40] Ibid., p. 51.

[41] Ibid., p. 53.

[42] Ibid., p. 53; cf. p. 58: "[T]he civil laws are God's laws, as they that make them are by God appointed to make them."

[43] Ibid., p. 57; cf. *Leviathan*, ed. Macpherson, p. 715: "For it is not the Romane Clergy onely, that pretends the Kingdome of God to be of this World, and thereby to have a Power therein, distinct from that of the Civill State." In "Considerations upon the Reputation, Loyalty, Manners, and Religion of Thomas Hobbes," written about six years before *Behemoth*, Hobbes wrote that the Anglican bishops' embrace of "that seditious distinction and division between the power spiritual and civil" is best interpreted as "a relic still remaining of the venom of popish ambition." See *The English Works of Thomas Hobbes*, ed. Sir William Molesworth (London: John Bohn, 1839–1845), Vol. IV, p. 432. Hobbes even has the *chutzpah* to say in the same breath (referring to the bishops): "Nor ever spake he [Hobbes himself] ill of any of them"!

[44] *Behemoth*, p. 57.

[45] Holmes rightly refers to "Hobbes's attack on Anglicanism" ("Introduction," p. xxxviii). Alan Ryan speaks of Hobbes's "fierce hostility to the power of the Anglican Church": See "A More Tolerant Hobbes?" in *Justifying Toleration*, ed. Susan Mendus (Cambridge: Cambridge University Press, 1988), p. 39. The anti-Anglican thrust of Hobbes's argument is underscored in a letter from John Aubrey to John Locke: "[T]he King has read and likes [*Behemoth*] extremely, but tells [Hobbes] there is so much truth in it he dares not license for feare of displeasing the

What does one actually do when irresponsible ministers get carried away with petty theological disputes, and start to tear apart the commonwealth by getting citizens to join in the war of theology? This question comes up at the beginning of Dialogue 2. *B*'s view is that it was a mistake for the Archbishop of Canterbury (as a quasi-government official) to intervene in the controversy concerning free will, and that the appropriate policy would have been to suppress the whole controversy ("put them both to silence").[46] *A* basically agrees with *B*'s point that it was a terrible mistake for Archbishop Laud to try to impose his own view on the Presbyterians, but he expresses this position in a way that gives it what is (for Hobbes) a surprisingly liberal ring: "Suppression of doctrine does but unite and exasperate, that is, increase both the malice and power of them that have already believed them." The state should rest satisfied with "constraining obedience" and not allow itself to be drawn into the perilous swamp of people's beliefs.[47] Again, as we saw earlier, a prudential respect for religious pluralism should, in practice, prevail over what one might have expected to be, in theory, Hobbes's preference for (imposed) religious uniformity.

To what extent are the problems that are of concern to Hobbes in this work unique to Christianity? In Dialogue 2, *B* states that it is a unique fact about Christianity that civil authority is pulled hither and thither by theologians (i.e., priests with philosophical pretensions); "I think it was never seen in the world, before the power of popes was set up, that philosophy [i.e., philosophy in the service of theology] was much conducing to power in a commonwealth."[48] *A* disagrees: Many ancient commonwealths experienced analogous problems with philosopher-priests.[49] Although there is much in *Behemoth* to suggest that priestly subversion of kingly authority is a peculiarly Christian problem (or at least a preeminently Christian problem), the story of the Ethiopian priests, drawn from Diodorus Siculus,[50] offers dramatic proof that the same problem arises in pre-Christian religions. The story concludes with a harsh but effective method of "rectifying the kingdom": King Ergamenes simply massacres all the priests.[51] As Hobbes makes explicit in *A*'s next set of remarks, he is quite willing to contemplate a similar remedy for "seditious ministers" in the kingdom of Charles I.[52]

Bishops." Quoted by Richard Tuck in "Hobbes and Locke on Toleration," in *Thomas Hobbes and Political Theory*, ed. Mary G. Dietz (Lawrence: University Press of Kansas, 1990), p. 154.

[46] *Behemoth*, p. 62.

[47] Ibid. Cf. p. 73, where Hobbes again harshly criticizes Laud for needlessly dragging contentious theology into "affairs of State." Paul J. Johnson presents Laud as committed to an Erastianism very much like Hobbes's: See "Hobbes's Anglican Doctrine of Salvation," in *Thomas Hobbes in his Time*, ed. R. Ross, H. W. Schneider, and T. Waldman (Minneapolis: University of Minnesota Press, 1974), pp. 113–114; but Johnson makes no reference to Hobbes's severe critique of Laud in *Behemoth*.

[48] *Behemoth*, p. 90.

[49] Ibid. In the text, *A*'s reply is attributed to *B*, but this is plainly a typographical error.

[50] Ibid., pp. 93–94.

[51] Ibid., p. 94.

[52] Ibid., p. 95. Holmes aptly calls this "Machiavellian advice" ("Introduction," p. xl, n. 73).

The narrative in Dialogues 3 and 4 gradually shifts from the story of the Long Parliament's triumph over the King to the story of the mounting ambitions of Oliver Cromwell. As Hobbes tells these stories, both have an implied religious dimension: Just as Hobbes associates the Long Parliament with the seditious teachings of the Presbyterians, so he associates Cromwell's army (and the Rump Parliament) with "the Independents."[53] Therefore, so to speak, the political-military story is replicated on a religious plane: Just as the Long Parliament's sedition against the King was repaid with their own authority being challenged by Cromwell's army, so the Presbyterian rebellion against the bishops was likewise repaid with challenge to *their* authority by more radical sects. Hobbes refers, very sharply, to the latter as "this brood of their [the Presbyterians'] own hatching"[54] (making quite clear that in Hobbes's view, the first set of greedy rascals got exactly what they deserved in being shoved aside by the second set of greedy rascals). The Long Parliament was the political vehicle of Presbyterian sedition vis-à-vis the King (and Anglicanism), and the army became the political vehicle of the sedition of Independents vis-à-vis the Long Parliament. Hence, whether one reads the story in a political register or in a religious one, in either case we have a gang of rebels (viz., Parliamentarians/Presbyterians) who are forced to swallow their own bitter medicine.

In a famous passage in chapter 47 of *Leviathan*, Hobbes speaks of three "knots upon [Christian] liberty," and of how these three knots were in turn "dissolved" in England from Elizabeth to the English Civil War.[55] Knot 1 is the power of excommunication imposed as a quasi-political punishment for disobedience. Knot 2 is episcopal hierarchy. Knot 3 is the papacy. Elizabeth dissolved the third knot. The Presbyterian revolt in the early stages of the English Civil War dissolved the second knot. The triumph of the Independents over the Presbyterians dissolved the first knot. This leaves the impression (which Hobbes more or less asserts explicitly) that the outcome as of 1651, with Independents in charge of the regime, is a vindication of Christian liberty – one that Hobbes himself pretty much endorses. The question is this: Is there a fourth knot that has yet to be dissolved? Does Independency represent the final triumph of Christian liberty, or is it too part of the problem?[56]

---

[53] *Behemoth*, p. 142. Notice that this is Hobbes's characterization of the *army*; Cromwell himself is repeatedly described by Hobbes as just a religious opportunist – see, e.g., p. 136: In matters of religion, Cromwell was "nothing certain, but applying himself always to the faction which was strongest, and was of a colour like it." Cf. p. 195: The Long Parliament was composed of a Presbyterian faction (seditious but not regicidal) and an Independent faction (regicidal); the Independent faction became the Rump.

[54] Ibid., p. 136.

[55] Hobbes's presentation of himself here as a defender of "Christian Liberty" may seem highly paradoxical (although it is not the only place in his work where he presents himself in this way – see note 24). It is one of many indications that Hobbes is playing a very complicated game, and that one should be on one's guard against taking his seemingly simple doctrines at face value.

[56] My own view basically coincides with that expressed by James Farr in "Atomes of Scripture: Hobbes and the Politics of Biblical Interpretation," in *Thomas Hobbes and Political Theory*, ed.

Although it is not at all obvious from Hobbes's general narrative that religious controversies were the main thing driving the ambitions of the Long Parliament, his suggestion in Dialogue 2 (following the story of Ergamenes the Ethiopian king) that murdering 1,000 clerics would have sufficed to spare 100,000 who perished in the civil war surely implies that religion was indeed decisive in this whole conflict.[57] Hobbes makes this fully explicit in Dialogue 4: "The mischief proceeded *wholly* [my italics] from the Presbyterian preachers, who, by a long practiced histrionic faculty, preached up the rebellion powerfully."[58] "To what end?" asks *B*. Hobbes has *A* affirm that it was the desire for theocracy: A democratic revolution in the state would lead to democratic rule within the Church, "and by consequence (as they thought) seeing politics are subservient to religion, they might govern."[59] In short, all this havoc was set off by theocratic ambition.[60] Theocracy was indeed the outcome, but as we have seen, it was not a Presbyterian theocracy.[61]

Dietz, pp. 189–190. Independency "*if it be without contention* . . . is perhaps the best." But is the qualification satisfied? Was there any lack of contention among the sectaries of the 1640s? Cf. Pocock's reference to the "Erastian realization that the struggle against sectaries was a second front of the war against papists." J. G. A. Pocock, *Politics, Language, and Time* (Chicago: University of Chicago Press, 1989), p. 181; see also pp. 187, 192–192, and 197. One could say that the fourth knot consists in religionists thinking that their opinions are not subject to the larger imperatives of political order and civil authority. One cannot enjoy Christian liberty if the society is in a state of civil contention, and one cannot avoid civil contention if the rights of conscience are being abused by radical sects. Consider also the brilliant summary of the core teaching of the *Leviathan* quoted by Pierre Bayle on pp. 87–88 of Bayle, *Political Writings*, ed. Sally L. Jenkinson (Cambridge: Cambridge University Press, 2000); it would certainly be hard to square a doctrine of religious liberty with Hobbes's teaching as thus encapsulated.

[57] For similar judgments by Locke, see *Political Writings*, ed. David Wootton (Indianapolis: Hackett, 2003), pp. 144–145, 147–149, and 153. Cf. Adam Smith, *The Theory of the Moral Sentiments*, ed. D. D. Raphael and A. L. Macfie (Indianapolis: Liberty Fund, 1982), p. 318: "It was the avowed intention of Mr. Hobbes . . . to subject the consciences of men immediately to the civil, and not to the ecclesiastical powers, whose turbulence and ambition, he had been taught, by the example of his own times, to regard as the principal source of the disorders of society."

[58] Ibid., p. 159; cf. Hume's reference to the pulpit as "that dangerous tribunal" (*The History of Great Britain*, p. 599).

[59] *Behemoth*, p. 159. The phrase "politics are subservient to religion" would, I assume, be rendered in contemporary English as "statesmen are subservient to religion."

[60] Cf. *B*'s comment on the general predisposition toward theocracy on the part of Presbyterians: "[T]hey would fain be absolute governors of all they converse with," presuming "that where they reign it is God that reigns, and nowhere else" (p. 167); as well as the exchange between *A* and *B* a few pages later (p. 172) concerning the rejection by the Scots of the Rump's demand for a united commonwealth, on the grounds that "it drew with it a subordination of the Church to the civil state in the things of Christ." According to *B*, this position constituted "a downright declaration to all kings and commonwealths in general: that a Presbyterian minister will be a true subject to none of them in the things of Christ; which things what they are, they will be judges themselves." What this amounts to, *B* adds, is an abrogation of "our deliverance from the Pope's tyranny" – i.e., the replacement of one theocracy with another.

[61] It is easy to assume that full theocracy is to be associated with the Puritans, but Hume offers strong reasons to doubt that, *qua* theocrats in the strict sense, the Independents were more

In *Behemoth*, Hobbes is of course very free with anti-Papist rhetoric, but it would be farfetched to deduce from this that there is anything especially Protestant about Hobbes's civil-religious vision. On the contrary, Hobbes's unremittingly harsh account, throughout the book, of the treacherous and destructive politics of Presbyterian preachers, Independent "fanatics," and even Anglican bishops gives us ample reason to think that, from a Hobbesian perspective, the post-Reformation splintering of Christianity was bound to make the problem of undivided civil authority *more* intractable. Holmes writes,

Hobbes fears religious anarchy so much that he praises the Pope's no-translation policy, states that the King should monopolize communication with God, and denounces the priesthood of all believers. He dislikes a situation in which "every man became a judge of religion, and an interpreter of the Scriptures to himself" for the simple reason that private interpretation is "the cause of so many sects." He wants an Erastian "subordination of the Church to the civil state in the things of Christ" to guarantee that the commands of God never conflict with the commands of the sovereign. Toleration spells chaos, a religious state of nature wherein individuals are "assured of their salvation by the testimony of their own private spirit."[62]

As Holmes goes on to add, however, Protestantism is not the core problem: "The anarchical strain in Christianity ... long predated the Reformation."[63] The problem is Christianity per se.[64]

---

radical than the Presbyterians: See *The History of Great Britain*, pp. 615–617 (cf. p. 656), for an important discussion of their respective positions toward toleration, use of powers of excommunication, and the status of civil authority vis-à-vis clerical authority. Hume forcefully makes the point that because they embraced toleration toward all Protestant sects and "pretended not [i.e., did not assert a claim] to erect themselves into a national church," the Independents were in that sense less theocratic in principle than *either* the Presbyterians *or* the Anglicans.

[62] Holmes, "Introduction," p. xxxvi, n. 64. The fact that Holmes refers to Hobbes as supporting a no-translation policy shows that Holmes does not buy *A*'s line on p. 53 that vernacular access to the Bible is profitable rather than hurtful. Concerning Hobbes's "ambivalence" on this issue, cf. Ryan, "A More Tolerant Hobbes?" p. 49.

[63] Holmes, "Introduction," p. xxxvi.

[64] For a summary by Hobbes of the subversive tendencies of *all* the branches of English Christendom (including the Anglican bishops), see *Behemoth*, pp. 135–136. In fact, he basically sees them all – popes claiming divine right, Anglican bishops claiming the same thing, Presbyterian theocrats claiming divine inspiration, and finally, the other sects, "all commonly called by the name of fanatics" and "out-doing the Reformation ... both of Luther and Calvin" – as in effect in competition with each other to see which holds the title of being more subversive than all the others! See also *Man and Citizen*, ed. Gert, p. 180, note, where Hobbes portrays the subversion of political authority (a chronic "root of civil war") as something common to the various branches of Christianity; as well as John Dewey's commentary on this text in "The Motivation of Hobbes's Political Philosophy," in *Thomas Hobbes in his Time*, ed. Ross, Schneider, and Waldman, pp. 15–16.

7

Geneva Manuscript

The Apparent Availability of a Rousseauian Solution

> Public instruction no longer exists and can no longer exist, because where there is no longer fatherland, there can no longer be citizens. These two words, *fatherland* and *citizen*, should be effaced from modern languages. I know well the reason why this is so, but I do not want to tell it.
>
> – Jean-Jacques Rousseau[1]

In Chapter 1, we saw that in the first thirty paragraphs of the *Social Contract*'s penultimate chapter, Rousseau offers the following analysis of politically relevant religious possibilities:

1. There may be politics without a civil religion, which he rejects.
2. There may be "pure" Christianity, which he religiously accepts but politically rejects.
3. There may be corrupted Christianity, which contests the sovereign's claim to undivided political authority – which is very forcefully rejected. (The chief instance is Catholicism, but Rousseau refers also to Shintoism[2] and Tibetan Buddhism.)

---

[1] Jean-Jacques Rousseau, *Emile*, trans. Allan Bloom (New York: Basic Books, 1979), p. 40. As Bloom intimates on p. 482, n. 8, Rousseau does spell out this reason in the civil-religion chapter of the *Social Contract*. The discussion of the *Geneva Manuscript* that follows was originally prompted by an astute challenge from Joe Carens.

[2] For an interesting discussion of Shinto as a deliberately intended civil religion, see Ian Buruma and Avishai Margalit, *Occidentalism: A Short History of Anti-Westernism* (London: Atlantic Books, 2005), pp. 7 and 63. This, however, was a nineteenth-century development.

4. There may be monotheistic theocracy, which is either (a) conquering and proselytizing (Islam),[3] or (b) simply conquering, or genocidal (Judaism)[4] – both of which are rejected.

---

[3] Although Rousseau writes that "Mohammed had very sound views" (Jean-Jacques Rousseau, *On the Social Contract*, ed. Roger D. Masters, trans. Judith R. Masters, New York: St. Martin's Press, 1978, p. 126), given Rousseau's resolute anti-imperialism it is hard to believe that he had as much sympathy for Islam as this suggests. More likely, it is simply the aspect of "reuniting the two heads of the eagle" that appeals to Rousseau, particularly relative to Christianity. Napoleon's affinity toward Islam was, no doubt, much more thoroughgoing!

On the theme of the relation between monotheism and imperialism, it is worth noting Freud's emphasis on monotheism (which he traces back to Egypt) as "an ancillary effect of [Egyptian] imperialism." Sigmund Freud, *Moses and Monotheism* (New York: Vintage, 1958), p. 80; cf. pp. 108 and 137. Cf. Nietzsche's correlation between monotheism and imperialism in *Genealogy of Morals*, Second Essay, § 20. Reflection on the relationship between monotheism and empire forces us to pose the civil-religion question (which must have occurred to Machiavelli even if he never stated it explicitly): *Would the Arabic tribes of the Arabian Peninsula ever have conquered a world empire but for Mohammed's invention of Islam as a civil religion?*

[4] This is the implication of Rousseau's statement that only with the Jewish god (i.e., the first monotheistic religion) does one shift from the pagan idea of national gods among the gods of other nations, to the imperialistic idea of a *jealous god* (*Social Contract*, ed. Masters, p. 125). Rousseau states that in relation to the Ammonites, the Jewish god was merely a pagan god, so to speak (cf. *Lessing's Theological Writings*, ed. Henry Chadwick, London: Adam & Charles Black, 1956, pp. 89–90, on Jehovah as a premonotheistic "national deity"); but in relation to the Canaanites (and presumably other peoples as well) the god of Israel was a "jealous god" (i.e., a god who sanctioned genocide: *peuples proscrits voués à la destruction* – proscribed peoples slated for destruction). This gave rise to holy wars, or wars of religion, which, according to Rousseau, is a strictly monotheistic concept; cf. "Letter to Beaumont," *Collected Writings of Rousseau*, Vol. 9, ed. Christopher Kelly and Eve Grace (Lebanon, NH: University Press of New England, 2001), p. 54. Simone Weil's views concerning the Old Testament are relevant here: "Practically the only thing the Hebrews did was to exterminate." This is quoted by Iris Murdoch, but Murdoch makes clear her own disapproval: "[T]he only city over which [Weil] does not lament is Jerusalem." Iris Murdoch, *Existentialists and Mystics: Writings on Philosophy and Literature* (London: Chatto & Windus, 1997), p. 160. On the theme of genocidal war in the Old Testament, cf. Machiavelli, *Discourses on Livy*, Book II, chapter 8. See also Baron d'Holbach, *Christianity Unveiled*, trans. W. M. Johnson (New York: Gordon Press, 1974), pp. 15, 23, 24, and 68; Voltaire, *Philosophical Letters: Or, Letters Regarding the English Nation*, ed. John Leigh, trans. Prudence L. Steiner (Indianapolis: Hackett, 2007), p. 114; and Thomas Paine, *The Age of Reason*, ed. Moncure Daniel Conway (Mineola, NY: Dover, 2004), pp. 90, 96, 99, 102–103, 106, 112, 114–115, 150, 185, and 197–199. Finally, the theme of genocide in the Old Testament is very powerfully ventilated in the BBC–PBS coproduction, *God on Trial*.

However, there is a further aspect to Rousseau's analysis that somewhat takes the edge off the harsh reading sketched herein. Although the concept of holy wars originates with Judaic monotheism, Rousseau emphasizes that the Jews tend to be the victims rather than the oppressors in such wars. Having been vanquished, they refuse obstinately to recognize the gods of their masters, and their monotheistic claims render them objects of persecution (as is later true for the Christians as well). Thus, it might be said, part of Rousseau's story is that the Hebrews introduce wars of religion negatively, by inviting other peoples to enforce submission to rival gods, and not just positively, by striving to expand the dominion of the Hebrew god.

5. There may be what one might call "benign theocracy," or a fairly tolerant national religion,[5] namely paganism, especially Roman paganism, for which Rousseau feels evident sympathy but which he nonetheless rejects (perhaps with regret!) as historically anachronistic.

Finally, Rousseau switches in the final five paragraphs of the chapter to a very different possibility – a predominantly *liberal* civil religion that, as we saw in Chapter 1, somehow simply floats above this analytic framework. (One may rightly observe how strange it is that Rousseau chooses to offer such a liberal conclusion to a rather illiberal book.) Yet in the *Geneva Manuscript* (an earlier version of the *Social Contract*), Rousseau flirted with an additional possibility, tacitly dropped in the definitive version of his treatise on politics, which we might call a distinctively *Protestant* civil religion. Rousseau writes, "Experience teaches that of all the Christian sects, Protestantism, as the wisest and gentlest, is also the most peaceful and social. It is the only one in which the laws can maintain their dominion and the leaders their authority."[6] Here Rousseau refers to Protestant Christianity as a "social" sect, whereas in the definitive version of his teaching on civil religion, he devotes the central analysis of the chapter to demonstrating that it is of the very essence of Christianity to be "contrary to the social spirit" ["*Je ne connais rien de plus contraire à l'esprit social.*"].[7] Why is the Protestant option dropped? Now of course it may have been the case that Rousseau, as a Swiss Protestant, was (and for good reason) deeply fearful of

---

[5] Cf. Hume's *Natural History of Religion*: "[I]dolatry . . . naturally admits the gods of other sects and nations to a share of divinity, and renders all the various deities, as well as rites, ceremonies, or traditions, compatible with each other" (David Hume, *Writings on Religion*, ed. Anthony Flew, La Salle, IL: Open Court, 1992, p. 145). Hume goes on (pp. 145–148) to discuss how monotheistic religions, by contrast, although they have a much more worthy conception of deity, are at the same time much less tolerant (p. 146: "The intolerance of almost all religions, which have maintained the unity of God"). See also Voltaire, *Treatise on Tolerance*, ed. Simon Harvey (Cambridge: Cambridge University Press, 2000), pp. 29–35. It is possible that, on this topic, all three of these thinkers – Voltaire, Rousseau, and Hume – took their cue from Shaftesbury: *Characteristics of Men, Manners, Opinions, Times*, ed. Lawrence E. Klein (Cambridge: Cambridge University Press, 1999), pp. 11 and 373. See also Hobbes, *Leviathan*, ed. C. B. Macpherson (London: Penguin, 1985), p. 178; John Locke, *Political Writings*, ed. David Wootton (Indianapolis: Hackett, 2003), p. 138 ("the authority of antiquity"); Montesquieu, "Dissertation sur la politique des Romains dans la religion" ("cet esprit de tolerance et de douceur qui régnait dans le monde païen"); Montesquieu, *Persian Letters*, Letter 85; Montesquieu as cited in Thomas L. Pangle, *The Theological Basis of Liberal Modernity in Montesquieu's "Spirit of the Laws"* (Chicago: University of Chicago Press, 2010), p. 171, n. 14; Nietzsche, *Beyond Good and Evil*, § 46; Freud, *Moses and Monotheism*, p. 21 (on Amenhotep IV's founding of monotheism in 1375 BC: "religious intolerance, which was foreign to antiquity before this and for long after, was inevitably born with the belief in one God"); Bertrand Russell, *Why I am Not a Christian*, ed. Paul Edwards (New York: Simon & Schuster, 1957), p. 36; Ernest Gellner, *Postmodernism, Reason and Religion* (London: Routledge, 1992), p. 92; and last but not least, John Rawls, *Political Liberalism* (New York: Columbia University Press, 1996), pp. xxiii and xxv.

[6] *Social Contract*, ed. Masters, p. 201.

[7] Ibid., p. 128.

French Catholicism, and that the "purely civil profession of faith," the name-less (and rather anemic) religion described at the end of the chapter, is the only politically viable way of plumping for Protestantism in the midst of a religiously intolerant Catholic culture. This is certainly a possible way of reading what Rousseau is up to in the concluding paragraphs of the *Social Contract*. I, how-ever, do not think this interpretation does full justice to the deep philosophical tensions that are at work in Rousseau's thinking.[8] As Roger Masters's acute observation in an editorial note makes clear, Rousseau's political philosophy is incompatible with the Christian idea of universal benevolence.[9] As a Christian, Rousseau ought to have embraced the sort of secularized Christian universal-ism exemplified by Diderot, but Rousseau's political principles (in opposition to Diderot) steer him in a decidedly particularist ("pagan") direction.[10] In fact, as Masters rightly points out, Rousseau takes himself to have refuted what he refers to, in Book 1, chapter 2 of the *Geneva Manuscript*, as "the gentle laws of brotherhood," rejecting them as placing unrealistic expectations on human nature.[11] Because universal brotherhood is not to be hoped for, the best politics would strive to enlarge individual self-concern into a kind of collective selfish-ness ("my interest" becomes fused with "the interest of the polis"), and in a way it is precisely this at which the Rousseauian general will aims.[12] Exactly in the spirit of Edmund Burke, Rousseau condemns that phony cosmopolitanism that allows individuals to "boast of loving everyone in order to have the right to love no one."[13] On the other hand, Rousseau, unlike Machiavelli, has by

---

[8] A further problem with this "Protestant" interpretation is that the polemic against Catholicism is blatant enough in the *Social Contract* that Rousseau would have aroused Catholic wrath in any case.

[9] *Social Contract*, ed. Masters, p. 154, n. 137. See also p. 203, n. 3.

[10] Rousseau's debate with Diderot's cosmopolitanism in the *Geneva Manuscript*, Book 1, chapter 2 suggests that it may have been Diderot whom Rousseau had in mind when he referred in the *Second Discourse* to "great cosmopolitan souls, who surmount the imaginary barriers that sep-arate peoples and who, following the example of the sovereign Being who created them, include the whole human race in their benevolence": *The First and Second Discourses*, ed. Roger D. Masters, trans. R. D. Masters and J. R. Masters (New York: St. Martin's Press, 1964), pp. 160–161. This text makes explicit that monotheistic religion is what inspires cosmopolitan political principles; cf. *Geneva Manuscript*: "[I]t was only Christianity that generalized [cosmopolitan ideas] sufficiently" (*Social Contract*, ed. Masters, p. 162). On Rousseau's relation to Diderot, see Masters's discussion: *Social Contract*, ed. Masters, pp. 15–16; for the text to which Rousseau was responding in the *Geneva Manuscript*, see Denis Diderot, *Political Writings*, ed. John Hope Mason and Robert Wokler (Cambridge: Cambridge University Press, 1992), pp. 17–21.

[11] *Social Contract*, ed. Masters, p. 160.

[12] Cf. Francesco Guicciardini, "Considerations of the *Discourses* of Niccolò Machiavelli," in *The Sweetness of Power: Machiavelli's Discourses and Guicciardini's Considerations*, trans. James B. Atkinson and David Sices (DeKalb, IL: Northern Illinois University Press, 2002), p. 404: "[I]t is the custom of republics not to share the fruits of their freedom and power with any but their own citizens."

[13] *Social Contract*, ed. Masters, p. 162 (*Geneva Manuscript*); see also *Emile*, p. 39. Cf. Burke's polemical opposition between "kind" and "kindred" in "Letter to a Member of the National Assembly," in *The Works of Edmund Burke*, Vol. 4 (London: Oxford University Press, 1934), p. 300. Ironically, the prime target of Burke's critique in this context is Rousseau himself! (Part

no means broken with the Christian spirit of universal human brotherhood, as his sharp attack on the "national religions" in the civil-religion chapter makes perfectly evident.[14] We are left with an unbridgeable tension between Christian universalism and pagan parochialism. If Rousseau is alive to this tension, as he certainly is in the *Social Contract*, then Protestantism (contrary to what Rousseau had seemed to suggest at the end of the *Geneva Manuscript*) cannot be a sustainable civic option.

of what Burke intended was surely a gibe at Rousseau's notorious abandonment of his own children.)

[14] In the *Geneva Manuscript* (*Social Contract*, ed. Masters, pp. 160–161), Rousseau goes further, claiming that *all* religions naturally lend themselves to political abuse, leading to "the furies of fanaticism" and untold bloodshed.

8

Social Contract

The Ultimate Unavailability of a Rousseauian Solution

> The general opinion [concerning Rousseau] indeed, was, that he had too much philosophy to be very devout, and had too much devotion to have much philosophy.[1]

In *Meaning in History*, Karl Löwith writes the following (in the context of a discussion of Vico):

> Rousseau's alternative that the political religions of antiquity were useful but false, while Christianity is true but socially useless, did not occur to [Vico]. Hence he could also be unconcerned about Rousseau's attempt at a synthesis between the universal (Christian) religion of "man" and that of the "citizen" in a new kind of Christian "civil religion."[2]

Indeed, in the *Geneva Manuscript* Rousseau does claim of his projected civil religion that "the advantages of the religion of man and the citizen will be combined. The State will have its cult and will not be the enemy of anyone else's."[3] The *Social Contract*, however, claims no such thing, and if our reading of Rousseau presented here has been a faithful one, then Rousseau was entirely right to retract the *Geneva Manuscript*'s overly ambitious promise of a synthesis of Christianity and paganism. Of our three authors in Part I, the only one who really wanted a synthesis of "the religion of man" and "the religion of the citizen" was surely Hobbes, in the sense that Hobbes genuinely abhorred the pagan politics that tempted both Machiavelli and Rousseau, and therefore sought to temper the harshness of that politics with what both Machiavelli and Rousseau saw as the "slavishness" of Christianity. (To confirm this point, one need merely imagine how Hobbes would react to Machiavelli's and Rousseau's celebrations of Rome.)

---

[1] David Hume, *A Concise and Genuine Account of the Dispute between Mr. Hume and Mr. Rousseau* (London: T. Becket and P. A. De Hondt, 1766), p. 43 (translator's note).

[2] Karl Löwith, *Meaning in History* (Chicago: University of Chicago Press, 1949), p. 130.

[3] Jean-Jacques Rousseau, *On the Social Contract*, ed. Roger D. Masters, trans. Judith R. Masters (New York: St. Martin's Press, 1978), p. 200.

Let us now see if we can get in a clearer focus Rousseau's relation to the two predecessors in whose shadow the discussion of civil religion is conducted.[4] First, Machiavelli: As Lionel McKenzie helpfully points out, Rousseau, in *Social Contract*, Book II, chapter 7, offers a veiled criticism of Machiavelli's blatantly cynical version of civil religion in, for instance, *Discourses* I.14.[5] Rousseau wants a legislator who not merely hoodwinks the people with pagan tricks, but who embodies a "wisdom" that genuinely bespeaks "divine authority." "The legislator's great soul is the true miracle that should prove his mission."[6] Yet the final sentence of *Social Contract* II.7 shows that the larger enterprise remains Machiavellian: "One must not conclude from all this, as Warburton does, that politics and religion have a common object for us, but rather that at the origin of nations, one serves as an instrument of the other."[7] I think McKenzie misses the real meaning of Rousseau's correction of Machiavelli. What's really going on in *Social Contract* II.7 is that Rousseau realizes that Machiavelli *undermines* his own civil-religion enterprise by being so explicit about the con worked by religion.[8] Thus Rousseau is obliged to keep alive the civil-religion project

---

[4] Focusing on Rousseau's relationship to Machiavelli and Hobbes may be misleading insofar as it suggests that Rousseau's only sources in thinking about civil religion were modern sources. The political philosophers he cites in *Social Contract* IV.8 are Machiavelli, Hobbes, and Bayle, but I suspect that his relationship to Plato is also relevant to his interest in civil religion. For a discussion of the seriousness of Rousseau's engagement with Plato, see Michael J. Silverthorne, "Rousseau's Plato," *Studies on Voltaire and the Eighteenth Century*, Vol. 116 (1973): 235–249; and for a discussion of civil religion in Plato's *Laws*, see Thomas L. Pangle, "The Political Psychology of Religion in Plato's *Laws*," *American Political Science Review*, Vol. 70, No. 4 (1976): 1059–1077 and Pangle, "Politics and Religion in Plato's *Laws*: Some Preliminary Reflections," *Essays in Arts and Sciences*, Vol. 3 (1974): 19–28. In the latter article, on p. 23 and pp. 26–27, respectively, Pangle highlights both similarities and contrasts between civil religion in Rousseau and civil religion in *The Laws*. See also Catherine and Michael Zuckert, *The Truth about Leo Strauss* (Chicago: University of Chicago Press, 2006), p. 126. My hunch is that, although Rousseau cites only modern political philosophers in *Social Contract* IV.8, his intention in taking up the theme of civil religion was actually to bridge or straddle ancient and modern political philosophy.

[5] See Lionel A. McKenzie, "Rousseau's Debate with Machiavelli in the *Social Contract*," *Journal of the History of Ideas*, Vol. 43 (1982): 223–224. McKenzie quotes the passage in *Social Contract* II.7 where Rousseau criticizes forms of civil religion as manipulative as the resort to "engrav[ing] stone tablets, buy[ing] an oracle, pretend[ing] to have a secret relationship with some divinity, train[ing] a bird to talk in his ear" (ed. Masters, p. 70), and McKenzie then notes the similarity of these examples to the kinds of religious charlatanry typically praised by Machiavelli. But of course these conjuring tricks are not limited to paganism. At the end of *Discourses* I.11, Machiavelli refers to Savonarola's claims to divine favor and strongly implies that these are just as dubious as the shenanigans of Roman poultrymen. (And note that engraving stone tablets is an Old Testament example!)

[6] *Social Contract*, ed. Masters, p. 70.

[7] Ibid.

[8] For some helpful thoughts on the problem indicated here (namely the self-undermining effect of Machiavelli's cynicism about religion), see Patrick J. Deneen, *Democratic Faith* (Princeton, NJ: Princeton University Press, 2005), pp. 57–58. However, when Rousseau speaks, in the very same text in *Social Contract* II.7, of "the fathers of nations... [attributing] their own wisdom to the Gods," and of legislators placing the decisions of sublime reason "in the mouth of the immortals," he runs into the very same problem from which he is trying to extricate Machiavelli! (It goes without saying that similar problems arise for Nietzsche.)

by undoing Machiavelli's cold cynicism. However, whether the civil-religion project is ultimately salvageable is the question raised by the discussion that follows.

When Rousseau says that "there is no longer and can never again be an exclusive national religion,"[9] he is in effect giving up on his preferred vision of politics, a robust civil religion, and satisfies himself with a feeble second best: religious toleration to minimize social divisions. However, this is well short of the religiously enforced social unity required for true political health. In switching from "political considerations" to "principles of political right," Rousseau abandons the maximalist goal of a true civil religion and opts for a minimalist goal – something more than anti-political Christianity but much less than the "national religion" of the pagans. He agrees with Machiavelli on the political superiority of paganism to Christianity, but he is not willing to pay the price Machiavelli is willing to pay for a restored paganism. In that sense, it is Rousseau's Christian morality that prompts him to back away from the full-blooded civil religion offered by Machiavelli.[10]

As for Hobbes, he and Rousseau diverge precisely because Hobbes is still in pursuit of that synthesis of "man" and "citizen" that Rousseau has given up for impossible. Hobbes's solution is a Christian civil religion that is no less "political" than the national religions, but that can nonetheless claim the sanction of Christianity by emphasizing (implausibly!) the continuity between the New Testament and the Old Testament. As Rousseau says, however, "the Gospel is not a civil religion," unless one is prepared to paganize Christianity by

---

[9] *Social Contract*, ed. Masters, p. 131. Cf. Rousseau, *The Government of Poland*, trans. Willmoore Kendall (Indianapolis: Hackett, 1985), p. 8: "If [modern men] assemble, it is in churches, for the sake of a cult which is in no sense national, which never in any way reminds them of their fatherland." However, one cannot help wondering (and the whole purpose of this interpretation has been to work through this puzzle) why a cult is so much to be commended by being *national* if the ancient national religions, as Rousseau presents them in *Social Contract* IV.8 – which generate both "heroes" and "fanatics" in the words of the *Geneva Manuscript* (*Social Contract*, ed. Masters, p. 197) – are ultimately inhuman in their particularism, and if the truth of Christianity reposes upon its universalism.

As we saw in the passage from *Emile* that served as our epigraph for Chapter 1 of this book, Rousseau was even capable of defending fanaticism as a way of pursuing his challenge to bourgeois civilization. However, as the passage just cited from the *Geneva Manuscript* confirms, one can equally find in Rousseau acute Montesquieuian insights into the moral limits of the fanatical *Übermenschen* of antiquity whom Rousseau otherwise worshipped. This Montesquieuian moment in Rousseau, it should by now be clear, is the core of our reading of Rousseau's civil religion.

[10] Hence he writes in the *Geneva Manuscript* that it "is not permissible to strengthen the bond of a particular society at the expense of the rest of the human race" (*Social Contract*, ed. Masters, p. 196). (Cf. Chapter 7, note 10.) This moral universalism is strongly qualified, though not entirely abandoned, when Rousseau formulates the more thoroughgoing particularist vision of the *Social Contract*. The text cited in this note provides a telling example: In the final version (p. 128), Rousseau deletes the reference to the human race and substitutes an appeal to the security of the state ("*sa propre sûreté*").

sending its subjects out on Crusades[11] (something that Hobbes himself is hardly likely to view with favor). Rousseau certainly sympathizes with Hobbes's desire to subordinate priests to temporal authority, but he thinks Hobbes grossly underestimates the degree of difficulty that this involves; hence Rousseau points out that even English kings, who in principle combine spiritual and temporal authority, in fact remained ministers to the priests, not, as Hobbes thought, masters over the priests.[12] Overall, Rousseau sets out to show the impossibility of any synthesis such as is undertaken by Hobbes by analyzing the synthesis into its parts and proving that the parts are incombinable. Let us again review the alternatives: The Christianity of the Gospels is religiously true but politically subversive. Pre-Christian theocracy is, in its pagan versions, war mongering and bloodthirsty, and, in its Jewish version, intolerant and imperialistic (and the same is true of post-Christian theocracy, viz., Islam). Catholicism, with its combination of worldliness and unworldliness, offers the worst of both worlds. If this indeed exhausts the options, then a Hobbesian synthesis is simply unavailable. (Once again, Protestantism is offered in the *Geneva Manuscript* as a supplementary option and is recommended as superior to the alternatives previously rejected. It "binds the citizens to the State by weaker and gentler ties," turning away from the society of "heroes and fanatics" that engenders pagan zealotry.[13] It offers a religion of tolerance, forgoing pagan virtues to avoid pagan vices. If it were in fact possible to describe this as a proper civil religion – "splitting the difference" between Christianity and Machiavelli, as it were – then there would indeed be a Rousseauian solution. The linchpin of my whole interpretation is the presumption that when Rousseau came to pen the *Social Contract* in its definitive version, he thought through this possibility much more fully and deliberately renounced it.)

Rousseau says that Hobbes "ought to have seen that the dominating spirit of Christianity was incompatible with his system." As I argued in Chapter 5, Hobbes *does* see this, and hence – like Machiavelli – reinterprets Christianity so that it is no longer Christianity. (Leo Strauss zeroes in on the crucial problem: "Christianity, owing to the circumstances of its origin, offers much stronger support for the dualism of spiritual and temporal power, and therewith for perpetual civil discord, than the Old Testament teaching."[14] Interpreting the New Testament as if it were the Old Testament is meant to solve the problem.) It should be clear enough by now what Rousseau would say in answer to the Machiavellian and Hobbesian solutions. He would say that Christianity is antipolitical *in its very essence*; that it cannot be paganized or Judaicized. Again, "the Gospel is not a civil religion" – or at least, it could be turned

---

[11] *Social Contract*, ed. Masters, p. 198; cf. p. 130.
[12] Ibid., pp. 126–127. Rousseau and Hobbes clearly share a dim view of what Rousseau calls "the religion of the priest" (p. 128).
[13] Ibid., p. 197.
[14] Leo Strauss, *Persecution and the Art of Writing* (Chicago: University of Chicago Press, 1988), p. 175.

into a civil religion only at a morally unacceptable price. Perhaps another way of putting this would be to say that Rousseau is resistant to the idea of de-Christianizing Christianity because he is more of a Christian than either Machiavelli or Hobbes.[15]

As we saw in Chapter 7, Rousseau's thought fluctuates between two opposed and contradictory standpoints, the standpoint of cosmopolitan brotherhood and the standpoint of national particularism,[16] and the idea of civil religion seems to get caught in the interstices of this tension.[17] We come back in the end to Rousseau's odd distinction between "political considerations" and "principles of right." In paragraph 17 of the civil-religion chapter Rousseau states that, "considered politically," the three kinds of religion he analyzes (this-worldly, otherworldly, and a this-worldly–otherworldly hybrid) are, all three of them, flawed ("*elles ont toutes leurs défauts*"). Then, proceeding to explain why each of these possibilities is undesirable (devoting most of the subsequent paragraphs to a demonstration of why Christianity is unsuitable as a civil religion), Rousseau suddenly switches gears in paragraph 30, saying that he is putting to one side the political standpoint and returning to questions of right. If, however,

[15] As we saw in the epigraph to this chapter, the translator of Hume's account of his quarrel with Rousseau presents it as a "general opinion" of Rousseau that his thought is situated in some indefinable location between philosophy and piety. It turns out that Hume himself had a similar view. During Rousseau's time in London being looked after by Hume, Lord Charlemont, an acquaintance of Hume, bumped into him in the park and suggested to Hume that "He must be perfectly happy in his new Friend, as their sentiments [viz., sentiments on the subject of religion] were, I believed, nearly similar – 'Why no, Man,' said He, 'in that you are mistaken. Rousseau is not what you think him. He is indeed a very sensible, and wonderfully ingenious Man, but our Opinions are by no mean the Same. He has a hankering after the Bible, and is indeed little better than a Christian in a Way of his own.'" This story is quoted in Ernest Campbell Mossner, *The Life of David Hume*, 2nd ed. (Oxford: Oxford University Press, 2001) p. 523; the source is Lord Charlemont's "Anecdotes of Hume" (manuscript deposited in the Royal Irish Academy, Dublin).

[16] As if to prove my point, the very thinkers who are condemned in the *Geneva Manuscript* for their cosmopolitanism are praised by Rousseau in the *Second Discourse* as "great cosmopolitan souls, who surmount the imaginary barriers that separate peoples"! *The First and Second Discourses*, ed. Roger D. Masters (New York: St. Martin's Press, 1964), p. 160.

[17] Patrick Deneen rightly highlights the puzzle posed by Rousseau's claim in the *Confessions* (end of Book I) that if he had never been thrust out of Geneva, he might have been both "a good Christian" and a "good citizen": See *Democratic Faith*, p. 151 and p. 329, n. 17. (Indeed, one can ask, in connection with Geneva, if Christianity and politics are as deeply in tension as Rousseau declares, why does Rousseau present Calvin as an exemplary Mosaic-style legislator in *Social Contract* II.7?)

Joshua Mitchell, in his interpretation of the civil-religion chapter, presents civil religion as a "mode of atonement" – that is, a means of healing a rupture in the soul: *Not by Reason Alone: Religion, History, and Identity in Early Modern Political Thought* (Chicago: University of Chicago Press, 1993), pp. 116–117. To fulfill this purpose, a viable civil religion would have to repair the breach between "the Cross" and "the Eagle" – a breach introduced by Christianity ("the diremption wrought by Christianity"). However, Mitchell concedes that such a notion represents no more than a pious hope on the part of Rousseau: Considering how critical Rousseau is both of Christianity and of civil society, it seems highly improbable that the breach is capable of being repaired.

Rousseau's proposals for a civil-religion abstract from politics, in what sense do his reflections on matters of principle provide any practical guidance for the actual reorganization of social and political life? The very distinction invoked here between political and moral analysis seems quite strongly to suggest that the two types of analysis yield contradictory prescriptions: Theocracy "works" as a civil religion but violates political right, whereas Christianity satisfies principles of moral legitimacy but does not "work" as a basis for politics. Good politics presupposes a false and inhuman religion; a true religion breeds bad politics. Hence each serves merely to cancel the practical validity of the other. If the problem of civil religion presents as much of an aporia as our reading has suggested, then one is required to reread the whole of the *Social Contract* in the light of this impasse with which the book concludes. True politics is particularistic and true religion is universalistic, and so "civil religion" does not name a genuine synthesis of religion and politics but rather identifies their necessary contradiction.[18]

Rousseau has been the greatest champion of the idea of citizenship during the past few centuries. Nonetheless, Rousseau himself was already able to see that one can only go so far with the idea of citizenship in the modern world. The civil-religion chapter, with its rejection of national religions (that is, robustly civic and illiberal civil religions) and its embrace of a Lockean doctrine of toleration, expresses precisely this insight. Thus, the civil-religion chapter, read perennially by critics of Rousseau as showing his incompatibility with liberalism, is not the proof of Rousseau's antiliberalism but rather the proof of his liberal hesitations about his own civic-republican utopia. Perhaps *this* is the ultimate solution to the puzzle of why Rousseau opts for *religion civile* rather than *religion civique*.[19]

---

[18] One might mention, however, an interesting counterexample discussed by Voltaire, namely Pennsylvania, with William Penn as a wise legislator and Quakerism as a civil religion. The account given by Voltaire suggests at least one case in which the circle was squared. See *Philosophical Letters: Or, Letters Regarding the English Nation*, ed. John Leigh, trans. Prudence L. Steiner (Indianapolis: Hackett, 2007), pp. 12–13.

[19] Generally speaking, *civil* is a "liberal" word and *civic* is a "republican" word. In that sense, the very term *civil religion* already signals a retreat back to liberalism.

PART II

RESPONSES TO (AND PARTIAL INCORPORATIONS OF) CIVIL RELIGION WITHIN THE LIBERAL TRADITION

9

Baruch Spinoza

From Civil Religion to Liberalism

He [Hobbes] told me he [Spinoza] had cut through him a barre's length, for he durst not write so boldly.

– John Aubrey[1]

We see that nearly all men parade their own ideas as God's Word, their chief aim being to compel others to think as they do, while using religion as a pretext.

– Baruch Spinoza[2]

Spinoza was writing the *Theological–Political Treatise* at around the same time that Hobbes was composing *Behemoth*. What the experience of the English Civil War had taught Hobbes was that it was time to put the churches out of business, at least with respect to their political ambitions. But *Behemoth*, for all the stridency of its anticlericalism, was a rather tame contribution to reflection on the relationship between religion and politics compared with the explosiveness of Spinoza's challenge to biblical religion. Hobbes (and later Locke) completely deferred to Scripture as an absolutely authoritative text, with an authority equal to that of reason.[3] For Spinoza, by contrast, this

[1] John Aubrey, *Brief Lives*, ed. John Buchanan-Brown (London: Penguin, 2000), p. 441. In "'I Durst Not Write So Boldly,' or How to Read Hobbes' Theological–Political Treatise" (available at http://sitemaker.umich.edu/emcurley/spinoza), Edwin Curley points out that there is an alternative reading of Aubrey's manuscript according to which "had cut through him a barre's length" ought to read "had outthrowne him a bar's length." The latter refers to an ancient weight-throwing game, and, according to Curley, makes better sense of the text.

[2] Baruch Spinoza, *Theological–Political Treatise*, 2nd ed., trans. Samuel Shirley (Indianapolis: Hackett, 2001), p. 86.

[3] When Spinoza uses a phrase such as "I should like to confirm by Scriptural authority" (ibid., p. 76), this suggests that texts in Scripture have the same trumping authority for Spinoza as they have for Hobbes and Locke (and indeed for all orthodox Jews and Christians). This is highly misleading. As we will see, Spinoza's conflation of knowledge of God and "the natural light of reason" has the decisive consequence that there is no intellectual space left for Scripture to assert anything that supplements or surpasses the natural light of reason. This is the momentous claim

authority is entirely subject to the superior authority of reason, and it does not stand up well to rational scrutiny.[4]

Spinoza's core insight is that, although Hobbes's determination to subordinate religious authority to the domain of civil authority was a move in the right direction, the theocratic conception of political life had to be challenged much more radically than Hobbes was able to grasp. That is, liberalism, not civil religion, is the appropriate response to theocracy.[5] (Arguably, the doctrine of right = power in the early chapters of the *Political Treatise* is incompatible with any coherent version of liberalism. Rather than attempt to find a way around this hugely difficult problem in Spinoza's political philosophy, in what follows I will largely ignore this central teaching of the *Political Treatise* – even though aspects of the problem are present in the *Theological–Political Treatise* as well.[6])

The purpose of the *Theological–Political Treatise*, Spinoza writes in the Preface, is to show the compatibility between "piety and the peace of the commonwealth" on the one hand and freedom on the other. There is a false piety that presents these as incompatible, and it seeks to usurp "the right of civil authorities...under the guise of religion." This false piety must be defeated and replaced by a true piety that recognizes the benign character of – indeed, embraces as indispensable – "the citizen's free judgment."[7]

---

relative to which all parallel intellectual revolutions in Hobbes and Locke look extremely tame. Curley argues that, in the case of Hobbes at least, Scripture was accorded equal authority with reason, not because Hobbes truly believed this but because it provided "a useful cover" (p. 33) for Hobbes's actual commitment to the primacy of reason. It is also important to mention that although Hobbes does not swing a sledgehammer at Scriptural authority the way Spinoza does, it *is* true that aspects of the Spinozistic enterprise of biblical criticism are strongly anticipated in chapter 33 of *Leviathan*; so, for instance, in questioning the Mosaic authorship of the Pentateuch, Spinoza was pursuing leads first sketched by Hobbes (cf. notes 90 and 98 later in this chapter).

[4] Cf. *Theological–Political Treatise*, p. 166: "[A]s long as we are simply concerned with the meaning of the text and the prophets' intention, Scripture should be explained through Scripture; but having extracted the true meaning, we must necessarily resort to judgment and reason before we can assent thereto"; and p. 167: "I am utterly astonished that men can bring themselves to make reason, the greatest of all gifts and a light divine, subservient to letters that are dead, and may have been corrupted by human malice [, thereby denigrating] the mind, the true handwriting of God's word." As we will see later in this chapter, the theme of "corruption by malice" is very important in shaping Spinoza's reading of Scripture.

[5] Although basically true, the formulation here will be very heavily qualified in Chapter 10, and even more so in Chapter 11. Perhaps a better formulation would be to say that Spinoza is torn between what draws Hobbes to civil religion and what eventually draws Locke and other liberals to liberalism (though liberalism ultimately prevails for Spinoza).

[6] The problem here is nicely summed up by Edwin Curley's formulation that "Spinoza is sometimes more Hobbesian than Hobbes himself [and] more Machiavellian than Machiavelli himself." See "Kissinger, Spinoza, and Genghis Khan," in *The Cambridge Companion to Spinoza*, ed. Don Garrett (Cambridge: Cambridge University Press, 1996), p. 328. The only response I can offer (not dissimilar to Curley's) is one of puzzlement: How can a thinker who so powerfully anticipates the spirit of liberalism embrace such a doctrine? One could speculate that the equation of right and power is an idiosyncratic metaphysical gesture that tells us nothing about the content of Spinoza's politics, but does this suffice to save the coherence of Spinoza's protoliberalism?

[7] *Theological–Political Treatise*, p. 3.

Chapter 1 of the *Theological–Political Treatise* offers a series of challenges to Maimonides's conception of prophecy as the product of "a perfect and accomplished human intellect" – a case of "overflow of the intellect," "through the intermediation of the Active Intellect," whose bounty reaches not only the rational faculty but also the imaginative faculty.[8] Hence, on the Maimonidean view, prophecy is fundamentally cognitive – indeed, the perfection of cognition. Prophets are not merely philosophers; the notion of the intellectual overflow into the imaginative faculty tries to capture the extra perfection embodied in prophets but not in philosophers. With respect to their *rational* and *intellectual* capacities, however, prophets lack nothing in relation to philosophers. Spinoza denies this. Interestingly, he continues to refer to prophecy as "prophetic knowledge" – as opposed to "natural knowledge."[9] Nevertheless, Spinoza's critique of Maimonides (exclusively emphasizing the imaginative faculty of prophets and eliminating any reference to their share in the rational faculty) forces one to wonder what is cognitive about prophetic knowledge – that is, in what respect prophetic knowledge constitutes knowledge.

This puzzle is given much greater impetus by a stunning claim made by Spinoza near the end of chapter 1. He writes that "since Nature's power is nothing but the power of God, it is beyond doubt that ignorance of natural causes is the measure of our ignorance of the power of God."[10] This is of course closely related to the central and most radical idea in Spinoza's philosophy, namely that God and nature are indistinguishable.[11] The clear suggestion

---

[8] Moses Maimonides, *The Guide of the Perplexed*, trans. Shlomo Pines (Chicago: University of Chicago Press, 1963), Vol. 2, pp. 371, 374, 369. Maimonides's account of prophecy is presented in *Guide of the Perplexed*, Part II, chapters 32–48. Leo Strauss develops a far more extensive dialogue between Spinoza and Maimonides than is immediately suggested by Spinoza's own explicit criticisms of Maimonides; see *Spinoza's Critique of Religion* (New York: Schocken Books, 1965), chapter 6. In particular, what emerges from this dialogue is much more shared ground between Spinoza and Maimonides than is apparent from Spinoza's own characterization of the relationship to Maimonides – to the extent that Strauss refers to Spinoza as a "disciple" of Maimonides (p. 251).

[9] *Theological–Political Treatise*, pp. 9, 19.

[10] Ibid., p. 19. One way of interpreting this statement would be to say what Christopher Hitchens says about the relation between science and religion: that "the findings of science are far more awe-inspiring than the rantings of the godly." *God is Not Great: How Religion Poisons Everything* (Toronto: McClelland & Stewart, 2007), p. 57; cf. p. 71 and the first quotation from Albert Einstein on p. 271. To have access to (modern) natural science is to know God, whereas to claim divine knowledge in the absence of (real) knowledge of natural causes is merely to *think* one knows God. Cf. Thomas Paine, *The Age of Reason*, ed. Moncure Daniel Conway (Mineola, NY: Dover, 2004), p. 50: "natural philosophy... is the true theology"; cf. p. 128.

[11] Cf. Steven Nadler, *Spinoza: A Life* (Cambridge: Cambridge University Press, 1999), p. 190. It follows from Spinoza's equation of God and nature that there can be no miracles, as Spinoza elaborates in chapter 6. For miracles are supposed to be divine intercessions in the order of nature; so in suspending the operation of natural laws, God would be contravening his own nature, which is contradictory. Spinoza concludes, therefore, that the doctrine of miracles in the Bible is a misunderstanding of the nature of God. (*Theological–Political Treatise*, p. 72: "[I]f anything were to happen in Nature contrary to her universal laws, it would be necessarily contrary to the decree, intellect and nature of God. Or if anyone were to maintain that God

in this statement is that the *true* prophets are the scientists and philosophers who have revolutionized our understanding of the world by penetrating the real character of natural causes.[12] Spinoza has already dismissed Maimonides' attempt to champion the perfection of the intellect or of the rational faculty of the prophets. Furthermore, there is no question that Spinoza has a less than elevated view of imagination relative to reason (which is clearly expressed when he talks of what prophets are able to perceive "*merely* through their imagination," for the lack of "assured rational principles").[13] Spinoza has up until this point in the chapter insisted that prophetic knowledge is a mode of divine knowledge, just as natural knowledge is.[14] If, however, the prophets lacked genuine knowledge of natural causes, then on what basis were they in a position to convey knowledge of God? Again, we are compelled to ask this question (and ask it more emphatically than before): Where is the knowledge in prophetic knowledge? One also wonders about the significance of the fact that prophetic knowledge is now an obsolete mode of knowledge, as Spinoza highlights when he draws attention to the fact that "there are no prophets among us today."[15] Why would one form of divine knowledge vanish from the human scene whereas the other form of divine knowledge (the true form?) is flourishing as never before among Spinoza's own contemporaries in

performs some act contrary to the laws of Nature, he would at the same time have to maintain that God acts contrary to his own nature – of which nothing could be more absurd.")

[12] One would not have to rank prophets and natural scientists if imagination and reason were of equal status. Clearly, however, this is not Spinoza's view. Hence he writes on p. 21 (chapter 2): "Those with a more powerful imagination are less fitted for purely intellectual activity, while those who devote themselves to the cultivation of their more powerful intellect, keep their imagination under greater control and restraint, and they hold it in rein, as it were, so that it should not invade the province of intellect." The clear implication is that reason and imagination are not complementary human capacities, but rather in antagonistic relation to each other – so that as our appreciation for the achievements of reason ascends, our respect for the prophetic imagination declines. For the explicit assertion that "prophecy is inferior to natural knowledge," see p. 22.

[13] *Theological–Political Treatise*, p. 20; emphasis added. According to the account offered in Abraham Anderson, "Descartes the Impostor, Bayle, and the Hidden Origins of Enlightenment," in Anderson, *The Treatise of the Three Impostors and the Problem of Enlightenment* (Lanham, MD: Rowman & Littlefield, 1997), pp. 129–162, these conceptions regarding prophecy and philosophy, imagination and reason, are already present in Descartes, and are in turn traceable from Descartes back to Averroes; see esp. pp. 134 and 141. The three-way relationship between Averroism, Cartesianism, and Spinozism (as well as the convoluted puzzle of Pierre Bayle's relation to all three traditions) is an important topic that I will not attempt to pursue. However, see Paul A. Rahe, *Against Throne and Altar* (Cambridge: Cambridge University Press, 2008), chapters 2 and 4, for speculations about how Averroism might have quietly rippled through modern European political thought.

[14] In fact, there is some suggestion that prophetic knowledge is in some respects superior to natural knowledge when Spinoza concedes that the prophets "may doubtless have perceived much that is beyond the limits of intellect" (*Theological–Political Treatise*, p. 20). That suggestion, however, runs counter to the basic thrust of the chapter, which is that "natural knowledge . . . is in no way inferior to prophetic knowledge" (ibid., p. 9).

[15] Ibid., p. 10; cf. Hobbes, *Leviathan*, ed. C. B. Macpherson (London: Penguin, 1985), p. 414.

seventeenth-century Europe?[16] What does this say about the status of prophetic "knowledge" relative to natural knowledge? (Spinoza presumes that we live in a postprophetic world: a world where the prophecies have dried up and the miracles have ceased.[17] It may well be that most religious believers in the contemporary world would concede that this is so – but many would not. Try telling Mormons that our world is a postprophetic world; try telling adherents of Pentecostalism that the miracles have ceased. The process of disenchantment catalyzed by the intellectual revolution of the seventeenth century has had a very widespread, but by no means universal, effect.)

The divine knowledge of the prophets is further impugned when Spinoza writes that in biblical times, in a context where "men did not know the causes of prophetic knowledge," they "referred it like all other portents to God, *and were wont to call it divine knowledge.*"[18] Again: How can divine knowledge be based on ignorance? "Ignorance of natural causes is the measure of our ignorance of the power of God," so claims to divine knowledge in a context where knowledge of natural causes was impossible must be ill founded. If to be ignorant of natural causes is to be ignorant of God, then only knowledge founded on "assured rational principles" constitutes real knowledge of God.[19]

It is true that Spinoza makes special allowance for the status of Moses among the Hebrew prophets (on this issue he seems to be in agreement with Maimonides),[20] and he makes similar special allowance for Jesus.[21] In these

---

[16] Consider what Spinoza says on p. 21 (chapter 2) about "the demands of our age" vs. "the rantings of superstition."

[17] As discussed at length and with great insight by Curley (as I cited earlier in note 1), there are strikingly similar issues in Hobbes: See, for instance, Hobbes, *Man and Citizen*, ed. Bernard Gert (Garden City, NY: Anchor Books, 1972), p. 72; also, the last paragraph of *Leviathan*, chapter 32. See also David Johnston, *The Rhetoric of Leviathan* (Princeton, NJ: Princeton University Press, 1986), pp. 162, 181, and 182. For a very different reading of the same issue, see A. P. Martinich, *Hobbes: A Biography* (Cambridge: Cambridge University Press, 1999), p. 242.

[18] *Theological–Political Treatise*, p. 19; emphasis added.

[19] This account of the prophets seems to have found a direct echo in Bayle: "The popular mind being incapable of rising to the sublimity of the sovereignly perfect Being, the prophets had to lower God to the level of men and to make him babble to us as a wet-nurse babbles to an infant she is nursing." Quoted by Robert C. Bartlett from the *Historical and Critical Dictionary* (article on "Rimini, Gregoire de") in Pierre Bayle, *Various Thoughts on the Occasion of a Comet*, ed. Bartlett (Albany, NY: SUNY Press, 2000), p. 15, n. 16.

[20] *Theological–Political Treatise*, p. 11; cf. *The Guide of the Perplexed*, Part II, chapter 35. The fact that Moses is categorically privileged in relation to the other prophets does *not* mean, for Spinoza, that Moses had a sublime or worthy conception of God. This is brought out very clearly in chapter 2, where *Solomon* is presented as having a far more philosophical conception of God than that of Moses (p. 31).

[21] Spinoza's statement about Christ's attainment of "a degree of perfection surpassing all others" (*Theological–Political Treatise*, p. 14) suggests that Christ is superior to Moses in respect to divine knowledge. The same implication seems to follow from Spinoza's juxtaposition of their respective relations to God: In Moses' case, "face to face" (p. 13); in Christ's case, "mind to mind" (p. 14). It is worth pointing out that in the light of Spinoza's doctrine (p. 52) that to know anything about God is to connect with "God's intellect" (in effect, to think what God thinks),

two unique cases, we seem to be presented with a possibility of direct access to God that was denied to "run-of-the-mill" prophets. However, even if Spinoza exempts Moses and Christ from the diminished status that prophets have for him relative to their status in Maimonides, Spinoza's general demotion of prophets – on account of their perceiving divine knowledge "merely through their imagination" – and his privileging of natural knowledge over prophetic knowledge nonetheless seem unmistakable.

Chapter 2 highlights the scientific ignorance of the prophets, and the manifold ways in which both the form and content of their prophecies reflect not God's will but the limitations of their own personalities, life horizon, and belief structures. Soldiers draw on military imagery for their prophecies; farmers draw on imagery of the countryside. Angry prophets deliver wrathful prophecies; kindly prophets are the vehicle of merciful divine communications. Prophets whose understanding of nature presumes the movement of the sun around the earth will obviously be a source of prophetic visions that reflect that belief. As Spinoza points out, the text of *1 Kings* 7:23 (elaborating the revelation to Solomon of the divine blueprint for construction of the Temple) offers clear evidence of mathematical ignorance on the part of the recipient of God's revelation.[22] Noah could believe that a single flood could exterminate the entire planet only on the basis of the historically intelligible belief that "the world beyond Palestine was uninhabited."[23] The problem here is clearly not one of God's mathematical or geographical ignorance (which makes no sense) but rather the ignorance of men of antiquity whose prophetic visions are founded on imagination rather than on reliable intellect. (Spinoza's preferred formulation, given clear emphasis in this chapter, is that the kind of certainty made available by biblical prophets "was not a mathematical certainty, but only a moral certainty."[24])

[T]he view we are maintaining implies no impiety. Solomon, Isaiah, Joshua and the others were indeed prophets; but they were also men, subject to human limitations.... [Matters of the highest importance] could have been, and in fact were, beyond the knowledge of the prophets without prejudice to their piety.... [T]hey won such praise and repute not so much for sublimity and pre-eminence of intellect as for piety and faithfulness.[25]

In short, Spinoza thinks that we can defer to the prophets *morally* without deferring to them *intellectually*. (They can be held up as our moral superiors at the same time that they are our unquestionable intellectual inferiors.)

it has to be said that Spinoza presumes to have the same relation to God that he attributes on p. 14 to Christ – namely "mind to mind." (That, by the way, puts Spinoza closer to God than Moses!)

[22] Ibid., p. 27.
[23] Ibid.
[24] Ibid., p. 22; cf. p. 23.
[25] Ibid., pp. 27–28.

No one in the seventeenth century is going to *announce* his lack of piety. Knowing that this is the case, none of Spinoza's contemporaries (not even Hobbes!) was prepared to take at face value Spinoza's insistence that his debunking of the intellectual credentials of the Bible's leading moral exemplars – figures who *defined* biblical righteousness – was unproblematically consistent with authentic piety. Spinoza's claim is that it does not damage piety to acknowledge the unavoidable deficiency of natural knowledge in the age of the prophets: Their ignorance as human beings situated in a particular time and place is no objection to God, and it does not blunt the moral power of the prophets as exemplars of righteousness. We can see Spinoza's point, but at the same time we can see why Spinoza's critics were incredulous that he could expect to demonstrate the emphatically *human* character of the content of biblical texts while leaving the authority of Scripture unaffected.[26]

When Spinoza, near the end of chapter 2, formulates his thesis according to the notion that *"God* adapted his revelations to the understanding and beliefs of the prophets,"[27] he tries to make the argument sound as if a more or less traditional conception of God is still presumed,[28] and as if Spinoza's demonstration of the human limitations of the prophets in no way detracts from the status of the Hebrew Bible *as revelation.*[29] But how many readers of the *Theological–Political Treatise* (apart from those who see it as merely the machinations of a heretic) will be able to sustain their commitment to the Bible as revelation in the face of Spinoza's debunking of the content of the various "revelations"? One can *say* that it is a matter of God "adapting his revelations to the understanding and beliefs of the prophets," but a much more straightforward inference from Spinoza's line of argument is that these revelations mirror prescientific ways of thinking because those were the beliefs held by the *human authors* of a human, all-too-human text.[30]

Up to this point in the book, Spinoza's line is that however deficient the understanding of those who receive divine revelation, the moral truth of the Hebrew Bible is completely unimpugned. What the Bible says *morally* retains philosophical validity even if what it says with respect to the understanding of nature falls far short of philosophical validity. (But if God is nature, how can

---

[26] On p. 27 Spinoza warns that if biblical exegetes have the hermeneutical latitude to explain away the ill-founded science he shows to be in the texts, then that will necessarily "impair the authority of Scripture." The clear implication is that his own interpretive efforts *do not* impair the authority of Scripture.

[27] Ibid., p. 32; emphasis added.

[28] In other words, this conception is of God as volitional agent rather than God as Nature defined by fixed but intelligible laws – and therefore determined outcomes; cf. ibid., p. 36.

[29] The Old Testament is the main target of chapter 2, but Spinoza's brief remarks at the end of the chapter (pp. 33–34) make clear that the same principles apply to the New Testament.

[30] On p. 32, Spinoza writes that *God* "adapted his revelations to the understanding and beliefs" of the recipients; in chapter 3 (p. 36), Spinoza writes that *"Moses* was speaking to the understanding of the Hebrews" (emphasis added). In the first formulation, God makes a judgment about what the ancient Hebrews are capable of understanding; in the second formulation, it is *Moses* who makes this judgment.

one misunderstand nature while – morally speaking – having a true understanding of God?[31] Let us leave that question to one side.) Nevertheless, Spinoza now shifts to an issue that submits precisely the *moral* teaching of the Hebrew Bible to an impugning rational scrutiny. As he did in the previous chapter, Spinoza again insists that this is a case of "speaking merely according to the understanding of" the recipients of revelation.[32] It is far more difficult, though, to uphold that line in the current context, for here what is at issue are not peripheral questions of whether particular prophets comprehend mathematics or astronomy but something that goes to the core of the moral vision expressed in the Old Testament. Rousseau would say that a "national religion," whatever its benefits for the life of proper citizens, *cannot* coincide with the "true religion," for the true religion – "the religion of man" (*la religion de l'homme*) – is necessarily a *universal* religion. However, the religion of the Old Testament is emphatically not a universal religion but the national religion of a particular people. Spinoza says exactly what Rousseau says: The doctrine of chosenness as a core pillar of the religion of the Hebrews impugns the *moral* validity of their religion. What gets impugned *now* is not the knowledge of the world of the recipients of revelation but the moral exemplariness of the kind of deity that the Old Testament presents. For Spinoza expressly concedes that "God ordained those laws in the Pentateuch for them [the Hebrews] alone, . . . that he spoke only to them, . . . that the Hebrews witnessed marvels such [as] have never befallen any other nation."[33] How is this morally legitimate?

Miracles would have displayed God's power no less if they had been wrought for other nations as well, and the Hebrews would have been no less in duty bound to worship God if God had bestowed all these gifts equally upon all men.[34]

The target of criticism here seems to be *God* (not just His prophets) for bestowing gifts unequally and working miracles only for the benefit of a particular nation. This has the appearance of such a direct philosophical challenge to the moral wisdom of the Old Testament that Spinoza enters into a complicated account of the unique (but ultimately not-so-unique) "vocation of the Hebrews" that somewhat blunts (or at least renders more oblique) the force of this moral critique.

Again, the problem that Spinoza is wrestling with in this chapter relates to the question I have already posed: If Spinoza's challenges to the (epistemic) wisdom of the prophets are not supposed to impugn the *moral wisdom* of the Hebrew Bible, why is it not the case that this core moral wisdom *is* impugned by the doctrine of the chosenness of the Hebrew nation? Spinoza's solution to this

---

[31] Ibid., p. 50: "[W]e acquire a greater and more perfect knowledge of God as we gain more knowledge of natural phenomena. . . . [T]he greater our knowledge of natural phenomena, the more perfect is our knowledge of God's essence." Cf. p. 75: "[W]e get to know God and God's will all the better as we gain better knowledge of natural phenomena and understand more clearly . . . how they operate in accordance with Nature's eternal laws."

[32] Ibid., p. 35.

[33] Ibid., p. 36.

[34] Ibid., p. 35.

dilemma, both very odd and quite surprising, is to reinterpret the meaning of "chosenness" in a way that conforms to his (radically unbiblical or antibiblical) philosophy. Spinoza argues that it is a major challenge for any society to organize itself in such a way that it can survive the perils of the world and win security for its people. Some nations are successful and some are unsuccessful. What determines success for some and failure for others is by definition a matter of God's "favor" because there are clearly principles of nature in play, and Spinoza (as we have seen) does not distinguish between natural laws and "divine laws." That which follows from "the predetermined order of Nature" is at the same time unfolding "God's eternal direction and decree."[35] If these natural laws/divine laws work to the "good fortune" of the Hebrews, with respect to "the material success and prosperity of their state,"[36] then that constitutes "election" or chosenness in Spinoza's sense. In precisely this sense, one would have to say that the American nation was a divinely chosen people in the twentieth century, just as the Chinese nation looks to be a divinely chosen people in the twenty-first century!

It follows from Spinoza's account of what rendered the Hebrews a chosen people that what *he* associates with their chosenness has absolutely nothing in common with what the Jews themselves typically understand by their status as chosen. The law code of the Hebrews was a unique and parochial system of laws for a particular nation, and insofar as faithful adherence to those laws accomplished security for their state, one could say that "God's" "special" provision for their welfare was realized. However, other successful states *also* received "special" divine provision in the same way: Contrary to what the notion of chosenness *seems* to imply, the Jews were *not* the recipients of blessings denied to other nations.[37] Spinoza uses this reinterpretation of chosenness

---

[35] Ibid., pp. 36–37.

[36] Ibid., p. 38. One can speak colloquially of "good *fortune*" on the part of an individual or a people, but the aspect of contingency that this expression seems to suggest is misleading, for of course, strictly speaking, according to Spinoza's philosophy, there is *no* contingency in any natural (= divine) outcome. Spinoza makes this point very clearly on p. 37, where he defines "fortune" as the direction of human affairs by God–nature "through causes that are external and unforeseen" (but *not* undetermined).

[37] Ibid., pp. 39–40. At this stage in the argument, the "monotheistic" religion of the Hebrews appears very much like one civil religion amidst a plurality of similar civil religions. Spinoza somewhat qualifies this thought – at least momentarily – when he remarks that he "cannot be sure" whether other civil religions included the kind of prophetic revelations recorded in the Old Testament (p. 39). Here, clearly, the emphasis is on Judaism as a "commonplace" (p. 38) rather than unique religion. I write "at least momentarily" because just a page after expressing doubt whether Gentile religions had prophets comparable to those of the Hebrews, Spinoza affirms without reservation "that all nations possess prophets and that the gift of prophecy was not peculiar to the Jews" (p. 40). Cf. p. 41: "Therefore there is no doubt that other nations, like the Jews, also had their prophets"; also pp. 42, 45.

For passages quoted from Scripture that suggest that the theism of the Old Testament is not thoroughgoingly monotheistic, cf. p. 29! There is a very similar observation concerning the qualified monotheism of the Hebrews in Rousseau's account of Moses and the Israelites in *Social Contract* IV.8: See *On the Social Contract*, ed. R. D. Masters, trans. J. R. Masters (New York: St. Martin's Press, 1978), p. 125.

to read more universalism into the Old Testament than appears at first glance to be consistent with the doctrine of chosenness.[38] So, at the end of this discussion, is Spinoza a critic of the Hebrew Bible's parochialism or a defender of its universalism? I think he actually wants to play both hands. With respect to those who may be open to a more universalistic reading of the Old Testament, he wants to give encouragement to that moral universalism. However, with respect to those who insist on adhering to a more conventional understanding of the Hebrews' chosenness, he wants to be able to criticize as fundamentally flawed (because it is nonuniversalistic) the moral vision of a religion so construed.[39]

It follows from Spinoza's whole account of chosenness in chapter 3 that the Jews' status as chosen *lapses* as soon as their "good fortune" (with respect to prosperity and national independence) comes to an end. At the end of chapter 3 Spinoza addresses this according to the theme of whether the election of the Hebrews is an "eternal" election. His emphatic claim is that it is not. "Not eternal" means that "the election of the Jews was . . . a temporal matter, concerned only with their commonwealth."[40] That is, election of the Jews is associated with a secure, prosperous, and flourishing state. If the state ceases to flourish, and even more so, if the commonwealth of the Jews *ceases to exist*, that by itself proves that the Jews are no longer chosen (no longer favored by God or by nature). As elsewhere, Spinoza chooses to phrase this in a quite provocative way. There was a time, he claims, when the Canaanites were chosen (favored) by God – that is, blessed with material advantages – no less than the Hebrews were. However, "God *rejected* them"[41] – allowed the material advantages associated with independent statehood to succumb to their "folly" and their "dissolute living."[42] Precisely the same principle applies to the Jews: Election by God is no guarantee that this will not be followed by rejection by God (especially because there are naturally explicable processes of moral

---

[38] Cf. editor's note: *Theological–Political Treatise*, p. 40, n. 4.

[39] This insistence on a particularistic interpretation of Judaism is what Spinoza on p. 42 labels "Pharisaism"; cf. p. 44. The provocative question Spinoza raises here is whether Judaism per se is a form of Pharisaism, or whether a more universalistic reading of the Old Testament can be redeemed (cf. editor's note: p. 42, n. 6). As already suggested, it seems that this question, for Spinoza, is not fully decided.

It may be that in using "Pharisees" as a term of abuse, Spinoza was affirming his intellectual affinity with the notorious heretic, Uriel da Costa, who was excommunicated by the Amsterdam Jewish community 33 years prior to Spinoza's own excommunication. For a discussion of Da Costa touching on his polemical employment of the term "Pharisees," see Nadler, *Spinoza: A Life*, pp. 66–73. For discussion of some relevant themes in Da Costa, see Strauss, *Spinoza's Critique of Religion*, pp. 53–63. Strauss usefully highlights the rootedness of the critique of religion shared by Da Costa and Spinoza in the *Reformation* view that "[a]ll later teachings or laws are, as contrasted with the original revelation, no more than falsifying additions, fictions, untruth and the work of men" – a process of adulteration whereby the power lust and greed of priests "have corrupted and befouled the pure doctrine" (p. 55).

[40] *Theological–Political Treatise*, p. 44.

[41] Ibid.; emphasis added.

[42] Ibid., p. 45.

and political corruption[43]). If the Canaanites could lose their chosenness by frittering away their moral and political virtue, there is certainly no reason why the same cannot happen to the Jews. A people that loses its state has no way to secure its "material welfare,"[44] and this by definition (viz., Spinoza's definition) means that they are not chosen – in other words, no longer chosen.[45] (In short, it comes about that their chosenness *lapses*.) The only "eternal" election is reserved for the rare human beings who satisfy *universal* criteria of true virtue, not members of a particular tribe (whether virtuous or not).

If the chosenness of the Jews lapses, why do the Jews still exist as a people whereas other ancient peoples have disappeared without a trace? Spinoza has an answer to this question: They stubbornly clung to customs such as circumcision specifically for the purpose of keeping themselves separate from host nations.[46] Spinoza blames the Jews themselves for the failure to assimilate, and this failure of assimilation has resulted in the collective survival of the Jews far beyond that of contemporaneous peoples. As Bonnie Honig aptly highlights (though she does not refer to Spinoza), the Mosaic particularism (the "unassimilatability") that Spinoza condemns is precisely what Rousseau finds *attractive* in Moses' lawgiving.[47] Honig's discussion alludes to the important discussion of Moses in *The Government of Poland*, chapter 2, that directly parallels – but directly opposes – Spinoza's discussion. Rousseau writes *in praise of Moses* that "he put countless prohibitions upon [the Hebrews], all calculated to ... make them, with respect to the rest of mankind, outsiders forever. Each fraternal bond that he established among the individual members of his republic became a further barrier, separating them from their neighbors and keeping them from becoming one with those neighbors."[48] Spinoza could have written the same

---

[43] Cf. what Spinoza says on p. 46 about the enfeeblement of the spirit of the Tatars.

[44] Ibid., p. 47.

[45] It is perhaps going too far to present Spinoza as a prophet of modern Zionism – as Ben-Gurion apparently did (editor's note: p. 46, n. 8) – but Spinoza did not rule out the possibility of the Jews' resuming an independent commonwealth, and in that strict sense resuming their chosenness; see p. 46. *Today* they are once again a Chosen People, but prior to 1948 they were not.

[46] This answer is sketched out on pp. 45–46. See also *Theological–Political Treatise*, pp. 197–198.

[47] Bonnie Honig, *Democracy and the Foreigner* (Princeton, NJ: Princeton University Press, 2001), p. 138, n. 35.

[48] Jean-Jacques Rousseau, *The Government of Poland*, trans. Willmoore Kendall (Indianapolis: Hackett, 1985), p. 6. In one of Rousseau's "Political Fragments," he is even more emphatic about the achievements of the Mosaic laws: "The laws of Solon, of Numa, of Lycurgus are dead; those of Moses, far more ancient, are still alive. Athens, Sparta, Rome have perished, and have no longer left any children on the earth. Zion, destroyed, did not lose hers.... How strong must a legislation be to be capable of producing such marvels[?]" Rousseau goes on to write that such a "unique marvel ... deserve[s] the study and admiration of wise men in preference to all that Greece and Rome offer that is admirable in political institutions and human establishments." *The Collected Writings of Rousseau*, Vol. 4, ed. Roger D. Masters and Christopher Kelly (Lebanon, NH: University Press of New England, 1994), p. 34. For a strikingly similar argument by John Toland, see *Nazarenus*, ed. Justin Champion (Oxford: Voltaire Foundation, 1999), pp. 237 and 239. For Kant's intervention in this debate between

passage – with the crucial difference that for *him* there would be nothing to praise here.

As he does at the end of chapter 2, Spinoza, at the end of chapter 3, again turns from the Old Testament to the New Testament. His purpose this time is to present the image of a biblical religion that is uncontroversially universalist, and where the moral-religious universalism is not subverted by "Pharisees" wedded to the idea that Revelation is intended only for one privileged nation. One cannot help but be struck by how powerfully Spinoza aligns himself with Christianity at the end of chapter 3. On page 43 of the Hackett edition he writes that "his [Paul's] doctrine is the same as ours"; and on page 44 he writes that "Paul's teaching coincides exactly with ours." The reason is clear. Because the moral universalism of the Old Testament is (at best) theologically controversial, and because the moral universalism of the New Testament is unambiguous, the most reliable way for Spinoza to defeat parochialist interpretations of Judaism is to side ultimately with the New Testament.[49] "True virtue," as Spinoza repeatedly emphasizes, is universal.[50] Hence a religion that bases its notion of election or chosenness on anything other than true virtue must either be reinterpreted in a vigorously universalistic direction (Spinoza's non-Pharisaical version of Judaism) or rejected (entailing Spinoza's embrace of Christianity).

Chapter 4 offers an account of the nature of law that raises profound questions about the respects in which the Torah is to be subsumed under Divine Law, versus the respects in which it is to be subsumed under human law. Spinoza claims that there is a "natural Divine Law" that articulates the supreme good or highest blessedness inscribed in human nature. This supreme good consists in "philosophic thinking," "pure activity of mind," and "intellectual cognition of God"[51] – all of which are identical in nature. All other laws pertaining to the correct regulation of human conduct are merely "human laws."[52] Where does the Law of Moses fit within this fundamental schema? "Natural Divine Law," as Spinoza conceives it, "is of universal application, or common to all mankind. . . . [I]t does not demand belief in historical narratives of any kind whatsoever"[53] – hence the import of qualifying this kind of

Spinoza and Rousseau (very much on the side of Spinoza), see *Religion within the Boundaries of Mere Reason*, ed. Allen Wood and George di Giovanni (Cambridge: Cambridge University Press, 1998), note on pp. 139–140.

[49] Hence Spinoza is, philosophically speaking, committed to Christianity in a way that Hobbes patently is not. As J. G. A. Pocock nicely phrases it, if Christ's mission was merely to resume the Mosaic theocracy (as both Hobbes and Harrington claim), then it is reasonable to ask "whether the Son added anything to the Father": See the "Introduction" to James Harrington, *"The Commonwealth of Oceana" and "A System of Politics,"* ed. J. G. A. Pocock (Cambridge: Cambridge University Press, 1992), p. xxii. One might say that Spinoza took up the challenge of responding to this Hobbesian view, and of doing so on the basis of philosophical rather than religious or theological standards.

[50] *Theological–Political Treatise*, pp. 43, 45, 47.

[51] Ibid., pp. 51, 50.

[52] Ibid., p. 51.

[53] Ibid.

law as "natural." This law also "does not enjoin ceremonial rites,"[54] and it offers no reward other than "the law itself" – namely the experience of "true freedom."[55] "The natural light of reason" is our true compass, and relative to that, "authority and tradition... are mere shadows."[56] It follows that religious ceremony is trashed; appeals to otherworldly rewards and punishments are trashed; and the authority of any particular historical narrative (whether in one Testament or the other) is dramatically devalued. What status can be salvaged for Scripture (particularly with respect to its status as law) in the face of this absolute elevation of the natural light of reason and absolute depreciation of authority and tradition?[57]

The uncircumventable question that chapter 4 raises is this: Is the category of nonnatural Divine Law (to which the Law of Moses belongs) really a viable category? Is not the distinction between *natural* Divine Law and human law really an exhaustive disjunction, so that a kind of ostensible law that belongs to neither one category nor the other fails to meet the conditions of the only two types of law that are actually legitimate? We can restate Spinoza's answer to this fundamental question as follows: Moses' "Law of God" was a civil religion – namely a religion intended to allow "the people of Israel [to] be united in a particular territory," thereby "form[ing] a political union or state," and "constrain[ing that people] to obedience."[58] But a civil religion is not religion (or at least not a philosophically respectable religion); and a Law of God employed for the purposes aimed at by Moses is not a legitimate Divine

---

54 Ibid.

55 Ibid., p. 52.

56 Ibid.

57 The "natural" in natural Divine Law refers not only to the nature–convention distinction (p. 60: *ex natura/ex solo instituto*), but also, and crucially, as Spinoza signals on p. 58, the natural–supernatural distinction (*lumine naturali/lumine supra naturali*); cf. the discussion of "natural light" vs. "supernatural light" on pp. 99–101 and 103–104 (chapter 7). It follows that natural Divine Law is closer to "the natural light of reason" than it is to the supernatural doctrines of the Bible, whether Old Testament or New Testament.

On p. 51, Spinoza claims that the Law of Moses, even though it fails the test of universality (being addressed *qua* law to "one particular people"), nonetheless counts as "the Law of God, or Divine law" (though not *natural* Divine Law) because "we believe it to have been sanctioned by prophetic insight." One has every reason to regard this as a provisional conception, later to be questioned and undermined. This is made explicit as early as the first paragraph of chapter 5, where Spinoza writes that the "ceremonial observances [legislated by Moses] do not pertain to the Divine Law, and therefore do not contribute to blessedness and virtue" (p. 59). On p. 51, Spinoza had written that "the *natural* Divine Law does not enjoin ceremonial rites" (emphasis added); but by the beginning of chapter 5, this principle has been amended to Divine Law per se. (That is to say, there is *no* Divine Law that is not natural Divine Law.)

58 Ibid., p. 53; cf. p. 64, on Moses' introduction of (according to Shirley's rendering) "a state religion" [*religionem in Rempublicam introduxit*]. This text makes the point that Moses' civil religion allowed him to "encourage" soldiers to achieve military success "rather than [terrorize them] by threats of punishment"; and "to make the people do their duty from devotion rather than fear." This formulation abstracts from the Machiavellian insight (which Spinoza elsewhere seems to share – see, for instance, note 72, this chapter) that civil religion of the Mosaic variety can offer a *higher-order* terrorization of soldiers and the populace.

Law. The Mosaic code may have been successful (at least during the time that the Israelites retained their own state) in satisfying the purposes that Moses established for the law. However, does that make Moses' law a Divine Law in any sense remotely comparable to the sense in which the natural Divine Law is a Divine Law? No. Although Spinoza does not express his point in exactly these terms, I think the argument of chapter 4 can be reprised in a fairly accurate way by saying that Spinoza rejects Judaism precisely because it was intended by Moses as a civil religion and nothing but a civil religion.

For the third chapter in a row, as Spinoza approaches the end of the chapter he turns from the Old Testament to the New Testament. As before, what sets Christ's teaching apart from the laws and prophecies of the Hebrew Bible is its sublime *universality*:

Christ was sent to teach not only the Jews but the entire human race. Thus it was not enough for him to have a mind adapted to the beliefs of the Jews alone; his mind had to be adapted to the beliefs and doctrines held in common by all mankind, that is, to those axioms that are universally true.[59]

Unlike the Old Testament prophets (including Moses), Christ mediated the divine truth in a mode of "pure thought."[60] Insofar as Christ, too, proclaimed certain aspects of his teaching in the form of law, "he did so because of the people's ignorance and obstinacy"[61] – implying that "the [Hebrew] prophets who laid down laws in God's name"[62] (again including Moses) did *not* do so merely to instruct the ignorant but *also* because they themselves possessed a deficient understanding of divine law. Whether the common people were capable of appreciating this or not, discerning recipients of Christ's teaching received it in the mode of "eternal truth, not of prescribed laws."[63] The reference to "pure thought" clearly aligns Christ with *philosophy* as Spinoza understands and practices it, and the subtle but unmistakable implication is that Christ's contribution, consisting in freeing people "from bondage to the [Mosaic] law,"[64] was an essential condition on the road to true philosophy. Christ and Paul are presented as proto-Spinozistic philosophers: Like Moses, they are still compelled to convey images of divine law that are accessible to the multitude, but unlike Moses, they grasp the more transcendent conception of divinity *beyond* these popular images, and thereby anticipate true philosophy.[65] One could say

---

59 Ibid., p. 54.
60 Ibid.
61 Ibid.
62 Ibid., pp. 53–54.
63 Ibid., p. 55.
64 Ibid.
65 It is important to appreciate in this context that St. Paul (not Jesus) was the one who tore Christianity away from the Mosaic law. When Spinoza gives such strong philosophical support to Paul in particular, it is difficult to interpret this otherwise than as a philosophical endorsement of the abolition of Judaism.

that Christ and Paul stand midway between Moses, with his civil religion, and Spinoza, with his purer, more strictly transcendent understanding of God as Pure Intellect.

The chapter ends with a fairly lengthy celebration of Solomon, the nonprophet[66] ("who is commended in the Scriptures not so much for prophecy and piety as for prudence and wisdom"[67]). If there are still aspects of Mosaic civil religion in Christ and Paul (that is, Divine Law that is not natural Divine Law), then it is Solomon, in the Bible, who comes closest to Spinoza's image of the true philosopher.[68] The wisdom of Solomon (which is also Spinoza's wisdom) pertains to doctrines of punishment. The wisdom here – close in spirit to aspects of ancient Greek wisdom[69] – is that the virtuous are rewarded by their virtue and the foolish and wicked are punished by their folly and wickedness.[70] The former have tranquil souls and the latter have agitated souls.[71] The Mosaic view, by contrast, is that the wicked are punished by worldly and otherworldly punishments, as laid out in (nonnatural) Divine Law.[72] Christ and Paul represent a very substantial progress beyond the Mosaic conception (in the direction of the philosophic conception), but they do not rise up to the full height of a properly philosophic view.[73] Natural Divine Law (as articulated by Spinoza) states that one should do what is right *for the sake of what is right*, and not to escape humanly or divinely legislated sanctions.[74] To rise to this insight is to

[66] *Theological–Political Treatise*, pp. 56–58.

[67] Ibid., p. 56. However, see also p. 77, where Solomon's understanding of nature (and therefore understanding of God) is severely impugned.

[68] Why is *Solomon* associated with a properly philosophic view? Spinoza answers this question on p. 215 (cf. p. 213): Solomon understood that the only source of justice is *human* justice ("indications of divine justice are to be found only where just men reign"). The idea of a Divine Judge as a guarantee of ultimate justice is pure superstition. Cf. Strauss's reference to "the fatalism of the Book of Ecclesiastes": *Spinoza's Critique of Religion*, p. 257.

[69] Given these affinities, it is odd that Spinoza polemicizes against the Greek philosophers: see p. 153; cf. p. 5. See also Spinoza's disparaging comment on the ancient philosophers in Letter 56: Spinoza, *The Letters*, trans. Samuel Shirley (Indianapolis: Hackett, 1995), p. 279. Naturally, Hobbes's work is full of such polemics, but aspects of Spinoza's philosophy are far closer to the Greeks (especially Plato) than anything one finds in Hobbes.

[70] Solomon's view (the philosophic view) is best encapsulated in *Proverbs* 16: 22: "The punishment of fools is their folly," quoted by Spinoza on pp. 56 and 58 of the *Theological-Political Treatise*.

[71] Ibid., pp. 56–57; cf. p. 172: "[T]he Holy Spirit itself is nothing other than the peace of mind that results from good actions."

[72] On the face of it, this theme of the (from a philosophical standpoint) unsavory punitiveness of the Old Testament seems to be in tension with Spinoza's suggestion on p. 92 that Moses' intention "to found a good commonwealth" required him to establish norms of severe punishment.

[73] Cf. p. 78: Only *philosophy* can teach that "God cares equally for all."

[74] Ibid., pp. 55–56; cf. p. 52. The account of doctrines of punishment at the end of chapter 4 links up directly with Spinoza's focus on p. 162 on the doctrine of forgiveness as the ultimate tenet of faith – in the absence of which, as he rightly emphasizes, it is hard to make sense of the idea of God's mercifulness. (However, on p. 55 he characterizes the notion of God as merciful as a concession to "the understanding of the multitude and the defectiveness of their thought"!)

escape bondage and achieve freedom, and the proper name for this liberating insight is "philosophy."[75]

It is well known what the Mosaic law code requires of its adherents. What, however, is "commanded" by natural Divine Law? Basically, its injunctions are as follows: Be good. Do the right thing. Live virtuously – and live a virtuous life not to escape the wrath of the law, applying the coercive hand of punitive sanctions (a life of bondage), but to acquire a quiet and untroubled soul – a soul in repose (a life of freedom).[76] Virtue is its own reward, and folly is its own punishment. The Christianity of the New Testament is closer to Spinoza's conception than is the Judaism of the Old Testament (because it puts less emphasis on conformity to a specific law code); yet one readily suspects that even in the case of Christianity, appeals to crass rewards and crude punishments are not absent.[77] A notable difference between the first (coercive) kind of "Divine Law"[78] and the second (based on freedom) is that the first can, in various circumstances, place its adherents in tension with the established laws and norms of the civil society in which they live, whereas the second cannot.[79] Living virtuously and doing the right thing cannot pose a threat to the established civil order, whereas parochial customs and positive laws mandated by a holy text *can* disrupt the civil order. (When Steven Smith notices that Rousseau's reference to Hobbes as the only one among the "*Christian* authors" to anticipate Rousseau's theme may be an oblique reference to similar insights in Spinoza,

[75] Cf. *The Letters*, Letter 43 (p. 238) for an important discussion of the "slavishness" of a conception of religion founded on punishment. The fact that the addressee of this letter is a Christian is relevant to my discussion in note 77.

[76] As has been suggested to me by Ryan Balot, Spinoza's idea of "blessedness as repose" (*beatitudo = tranquillitas*) likely has its philosophical roots in Epicureanism. One might say that the object of the philosophic life, for Spinoza no less than for the Epicureans, is imperturbability, or a life of sublime equanimity. Cf. Rousseau's idea of "the serenity of the just man" [*la sérénité du juste*] in the "Profession of Faith" (*Emile*, trans. Allan Bloom, New York: Basic Books, 1979, p. 288).

[77] On p. 62, Spinoza claims that in the case of the *New* Testament (in contrast with the thoroughly material and mundane rewards promised in the Old), "the promised reward is the Kingdom of Heaven" (with the implication that this is to be interpreted metaphorically). This suggests that with respect to punishments as well, those conjured up by the New Testament are merely spiritual and metaphorical. Maybe this really is Spinoza's view; maybe it is not. Even on the assumption that it *is* Spinoza's view, however, one can ask this: What are the chances that Spinoza would be able to persuade Nietzsche (and those of us schooled by Nietzsche) that there is nothing grossly punitive in Pauline Christianity?

[78] Cf. p. 60: The "aim [of the law of Moses] was to coerce the Hebrews rather than instruct them."

[79] On p. 62, Spinoza remarks that the Jews in Egypt "were bound by no law other than the natural law, and doubtless the law of the state in which they dwelt, insofar as that was not opposed to the natural Divine Law." The final phrase of this sentence makes it sound as if in principle it is possible for there to be a conflict between natural Divine Law and the law of the (host) state – and that in such situations of conflict, natural Divine Law must have supremacy. Given Spinoza's elaboration of the meaning of natural Divine Law (which is identical to universal natural law), it is difficult to see where such conflict might arise – unless one were living in, say, a Nazi state where murder became the law of the land.

this is the kind of point that Smith likely has in mind.[80]) It is because of this potential tension between the religious laws and the norms established in the civil order that Spinoza goes out of his way to emphasize in chapter 5 that all requirements to perform ceremonial observances *lapse* as soon as the Jewish exile commences.[81] This has the same force as a contemporary Muslim insisting that Muslims are under no obligation to perform Koranic observances when they live in non-Islamic societies, and as Seymour Feldman points out, this claim by itself would have constituted ample grounds (from the perspective of the orthodox) for Spinoza's excommunication in 1656.[82]

The ease with which Spinoza's kind of universalistic Divine Law can be accommodated within different political orders is best highlighted when he refers, in chapter 5, to the prohibition of Christian rituals in Japan. Even with the external rites of Christianity rigorously forbidden, it is possible to "live a blessed life."[83] Clearly, then, it is possible to be faithful to the injunctions of the Divine Law as Spinoza understands it (which is the *condition* of living a blessed life) without running afoul of the civic requirements of a non-Christian state – whereas the practice of culturally specific external rites *does*, at least in the view of the Japanese state, run afoul of the political order. The choice of a Christian example makes clear that the problem that concerns Spinoza here is not restricted to *Jewish* ceremonial practices. Different cultic customs divide human beings, whereas the embrace of a *philosopher's* religion, which is what the Spinozistic Divine Law is, draws us toward the foundation of a true universalism for all human beings.

Chapter 5 spells out the shockingly subversive doctrines that Scripture, with its merely "empirical" religion, is only for "the common people," who are

---

[80] See Chapter 5, note 2. Rousseau never refers to Spinoza in the *Social Contract*, which is curious given the discernibly Spinozistic character of the conclusion of Book IV, chapter 8 (to say nothing of the Spinozistic character of the theological teaching in Book 4 of *Emile*); cf. Jonathan Israel, *Radical Enlightenment* (Oxford: Oxford University Press, 2001), pp. 266 and 269. It is also important to note that Rousseau's appeal to the "true religion" (*la religion véritable*) in *Social Contract* IV.8 invokes a key Spinozistic term of art. Near the end of the *First Discourse*, Rousseau refers to the "dangerous reveries of the likes of Hobbes and Spinoza" (specifically, he laments that the invention of the printing press makes these dangerous reveries available to humankind in perpetuity). It seems clear, in the light of this passage in the *First Discourse*, that whatever intellectual affinity Rousseau might have felt for Hobbes and Spinoza, he had reason to want to keep them expressly at arm's length.

[81] Sometimes Spinoza states that the Mosaic law is valid "only while their state existed" (p. 59); sometimes he emphasizes that it is valid only when they possess an "*independent* state" (p. 62; emphasis added). It follows from the second formulation that the Jews are under no obligation to follow ceremonial laws not only under conditions of exile but also during the time they reside in their own land but are subject to Roman rule.

[82] Ibid., p. 61, n. 1; cf. p. x. On p. 62, Spinoza makes the astonishing claim that the Jews, after the loss of their independent state, retained their rites in order "to oppose the Christians rather than to please God." One cannot imagine a clearer statement that for Spinoza there was no real piety in what, from the point of view of the Jewish elders of Amsterdam, precisely *defined* their piety.

[83] Ibid., p. 65.

incapable of appreciating "logical thinking"; that true philosophers have no need of Scripture; and that there is a purer form of piety – philosophic piety – that is categorically superior to popular piety.[84] Spinoza distinguishes between the stories in the Bible (from which the common people "take pleasure") and "the doctrine implicit in the narratives" (which can be grasped by philosophers). If one is capable of grasping "the doctrine implicit in the narratives," one can also grasp the doctrine *without* the narratives. Moreover, the common people need priests "to instruct them" in the meaning of the narratives; the philosophers clearly do not.[85] On the one hand, one can have people who have absolute faith in the narratives but live lives that fall short of being blessed because the doctrine implicit in the narratives eludes them; on the other hand, one can have people (e.g., a diligent follower of Aristotle's ethics[86]) who are "totally unacquainted with the Biblical narratives" and yet live lives that are "absolutely blessed."[87] Following through the line of thought implied by this contrast persuades Spinoza not just that philosophic piety is as pious (judged according to works[88]) as popular piety, but that it is *superior to* (i.e., more rationally grounded than) popular piety.[89] What is the conclusion to be drawn

---

[84] Ibid., pp. 66–67. There is a great paradox here that comes to light in considering Leo Strauss's critique of the Enlightenment. On the one hand, Spinoza is clearly a decisive – perhaps *the* most decisive – inspirer of the Enlightenment; on the other hand, we see from texts like these that Spinoza has a strong commitment to precisely the views that rendered Strauss a root-and-branch opponent of the Enlightenment (hence Strauss's appreciation for Spinoza as a practitioner of esotericism). Yirmiyahu Yovel puts the point this way: "Although Spinoza's theory of reason was potentially modern and democratic, his view of the sage and the multitude was still medieval." *Spinoza and Other Heretics, Vol. 1: The Marrano of Reason* (Princeton, NJ: Princeton University Press, 1989), p. 31. According to Strauss (*Spinoza's Critique of Religion*, p. 101), Hobbes is in this respect more revolutionary than Spinoza: On account of Hobbes's doctrine of the reasonableness of all men, the distinction between the wise men and the vulgar becomes irrelevant, and *"[b]ecause* that distinction [loses its salience], there is no necessity for recourse to religion" in grounding political allegiance. By contrast, Spinoza, strikingly less radical than Hobbes, remains an "Averroist." (There are reasons to see this text as expressing the very essence of Strauss's political philosophy.)

   Why does Strauss, who presents himself as committed to the view that the Enlightenment was a colossal error, in effect develop his political philosophy under a Spinozistic banner (the "theologico-political" problem)? One can say that from Strauss's perspective, there are fundamentally two kinds of political philosophies – those according to which (at least exoterically) reason and revelation can be harmonized (Maimonidean political philosophies); and those according to which reason and revelation are essentially and necessarily in tension (Spinozistic political philosophies). For the former, there is in principle no theologico-political problem; for the latter, there obviously is. Waving the banner of "the theologico-political problem" was Strauss's way of signaling to his readers that his political philosophy was in this decisive sense Spinozistic, not Maimonidean. Cf. Catherine and Michael Zuckert, *The Truth about Leo Strauss* (Chicago: University of Chicago Press, 2006), p. 154.

[85] *Theological–Political Treatise*, p. 68.

[86] Ibid., p. 69.

[87] Ibid., p. 68.

[88] Ibid., p. 70.

[89] It is possible to see this as a modern reenactment of Plato's critique of the "ungrounded" *paideia* offered by poets like Homer. Gadamer thematizes this Platonic critique in his essay on

from this argument? If all human beings were philosophers, one could discard the Scriptures without any cost to piety!

After the debunking of miracles in chapter 6, Spinoza devotes chapters 7–10 to the work of biblical criticism that has made the *Theological–Political Treatise* so famous and so influential within modern Western culture.[90] I do not propose to enter into a detailed account of Spinoza's biblical philology. Nonetheless, there are some important statements in chapter 7 that bear highlighting because they relate to the larger philosophical purpose of the work. He begins chapter 7 with the theme of "innovations in religion"[91] – meaning basically deliberate adulteration of the meaning of Scripture motivated by clerical self-interest – suggesting that one can (with the help of his scientific principles of Scriptural interpretation) disentangle "Scripture itself" from the "inventions" and "fabrications" of those who appropriate it for their own purposes.[92] The *divinity* of Scripture resides in the truth of its moral doctrines.[93] In that sense one could say that philosophy remains the arbiter of the divinity of Scripture, for philosophy determines what constitutes true moral doctrines according to demonstrable axioms,[94] and it is therefore in a unique position to establish the truth of the moral doctrines expressed in Scripture. One could put this point a little more strongly by saying that an understanding of what is divine in Scripture (as opposed to what has been superimposed upon Scripture by means of the inventions and fabrications of theologians and other charlatans) is parasitic upon philosophy's insight into the true nature of morality. There are true prophets in the Bible, but the truth of their prophecy resides in their intellectual grasp of what is "right and good."[95] We do not start with faith in the prophets. Rather, we start with rationally "evident" insight into their moral rectitude (their teaching of "true virtue"), and we derive our faith in them from that.[96] This is clearly an assertion of the primacy of reason – presented as a

---

"Plato and the Poets": See Hans-Georg Gadamer, *Dialogue and Dialectic*, trans. P. C. Smith (New Haven: Yale University Press, 1980), pp. 39–72, esp. the discussion of "custom without philosophy" (*Republic*, Book 10) on pp. 61–62. For more specific reference to Platonic texts, see my Introduction, note 11.

90 It is important to emphasize that Spinoza applies his philological methods *only* to the Old Testament. Chapter 11 is not a philological chapter. Rather, it offers a philosophical account of where to situate the New Testament in the balance between reason and Revelation. (However, Spinoza does gesture in the direction of a parallel philological inquiry applied to the New Testament on p. 150.)

This whole enterprise of Old Testament biblical criticism was anticipated in chapter 33 of *Leviathan*. As Curley points out in "'I Durst Not Write So Boldly,'" p. 53, it was the (not unreasonable) view of Leibniz that Hobbes had "sown the seeds" for this Spinozistic intellectual and cultural revolution. See also Martinich, *Hobbes: A Biography*, pp. 247–249.

91 *Theological–Political Treatise*, p. 86; cf. p. 105 (beginning of chapter 8): "the addition of new ideas of their own devising"; and p. 110: "fashion a new Scripture of one's own devising."

92 Ibid., pp. 86, 87.

93 Ibid., pp. 87–88.

94 Ibid., p. 87.

95 Ibid., p. 88.

96 Ibid.

resolute commitment to a principle of utter fidelity to the authentic (as opposed to the fabricated or adulterated) text of Scripture[97] – and the primacy of reason *means* the secondariness, or derived character, of faith.

Needless to say, it is difficult to continue to think of the Bible as the same kind of book one previously thought it was once one is disabused of the false belief that it is a single, seamless, sacred text and one learns, on the basis of Spinoza's principles of philological study, that it is in fact a collection of texts written by different authors, in different times and places, for different audiences, and for different purposes.[98] However, one should not necessarily infer from this that the philological exercise is strictly a debunking exercise. Spinoza states that the essential purpose here is to distinguish "teachings of eternal significance" from "those which are of only temporary significance or directed only to the benefit of a few,"[99] and there is no reason not to take this statement at face value. This is perfectly consistent with the doctrine previously laid out that there is indeed something authentically divine contained in Scripture – namely "true virtue"[100] as articulated or exemplified by true prophets, which represents an essential point of convergence between Scripture and reason or philosophy. It is important, however, to emphasize that this is not a convergence between Scripture and reason that accords symmetrical weight to each. As previously argued, it is a convergence according to the judgment of reason, and it seems clear that the "teachings of eternal significance" that Spinoza is seeking to locate in Scripture in the midst of so much that is merely contingent would *also*

---

[97] Cf. p. 136: "I am doing a service to Scripture by preventing its clear and uncontaminated passages from being made to fit with faulty passages, and thus being corrupted." See also p. 135: "[T]hey contaminate what is sound with what is corrupt."

[98] Ibid., p. 90; cf. pp. 158 and 167. Is there a Divine Author of the Bible? If so, it's hard to make sense of Spinoza's philological enterprise, the core of which is to endeavor to distinguish the *particular* authors who compose the various biblical books. Interestingly, at the bottom of p. 96 Spinoza pointedly hesitates to employ the term "authors." Is this his way of acknowledging that the assumption of human authors challenges the notion of a Divine Author? Perhaps – or maybe it is merely intended to register his awareness that the main job of these so-called authors likely consisted in "simply transcribing" preexisting texts (p. 132; cf. pp. 135–136). In any case, Spinoza has zero doubt that the Bible is a compilation of the writings and chronicles of a considerable variety of human authors. In chapter 8 Spinoza develops the view that the first twelve books of the Hebrew Bible were written by a single author who he consistently refers to as "the historian" (*Historicus*); on p. 113 (cf. Supplementary Note 16, top of p. 235) he states his firm opinion that this single author was Ezra. This coincides with Hobbes's view: See *Leviathan*, ed. Macpherson, pp. 422–423, on Esdras (i.e., Ezra). In *Theological–Political Treatise*, chapter 10 (p. 132), Spinoza also commits himself to the thesis that another single historian composed the Books of Daniel, Ezra, Esther, and Nehemiah, although he does not have a clue who this latter historian was.

See Hitchens, *God is Not Great*, pp. 161–168, for a sobering reflection on the human vs. divine authorship of a more recent supposedly revealed text (namely the Book of Mormon) – and by extension, revealed scriptures in general. For a more detailed account of the Mormon "revelation," see Donald Harman Akenson, *Some Family: The Mormons and How Humanity Keeps Track of Itself* (Montreal: McGill-Queen's University Press, 2007), chapter 2.

[99] *Theological–Political Treatise*, p. 90.

[100] Ibid., p. 91.

in principle be accessible to philosophy even if the different texts by different authors in different times for different audiences that collectively compose Scripture never came into existence.

Spinoza's appeal to "teachings of eternal significance" revealed in Scripture suggests a fully positive relationship to the Bible as an authoritative text. However, Spinoza also has a much darker story to tell in regard to Scripture, which chapter 7 also sketches or at least gestures toward. As was obvious to Hobbes among Spinoza's immediate predecessors, a text that is "universally regarded as sacred"[101] is a source of immense social and political power for those who hold monopolistic authority with respect to its interpretation.[102] This power associated with authoritative interpretation of the sacred text engages the interests of the clerical or rabbinical class who exercise this power. As Spinoza writes,

a language is preserved by the learned and unlearned alike, whereas books and the meaning of their contents are preserved only by the learned. Therefore we can readily conceive that the learned may have altered or corrupted the meaning of some passage in a rare book which they had in their possession.[103]

There is no presumption of trustworthiness on the part of the clerical class; on the contrary, there is, for Spinoza, every presumption that this form of power, like other forms of power, corrupts those who possess and exercise it[104] – in Spinoza's view a great temptation to alteration or manipulation of the sacred text for the self-seeking ends of the priestly class.[105] Hence the restoration of textual authenticity requires that the text be submitted to rigorous scrutiny by a disinterested and scientifically disciplined agent of "quality control." Spinoza's philology constitutes this agency of disinterestedness and scientific discipline.

---

[101] Ibid., p. 90.

[102] On pp. 95–96, Spinoza offers a quite interesting discussion of the much later vowelization of the (vowel-less) ancient Hebrew text. In effect he is saying this: Imagine how much power lay in the hands of the later interpreters who inserted these vowel-ascribing accents! (Hitchens refers to parallel aspects of the editing of a canonized Koran – including its vowelization – in *God is Not Great*, pp. 130–131.)

[103] *Theological-Political Treatise*, p. 93.

[104] Cf. p. 129, where Spinoza expresses particularly sharply his judgment of the untrustworthiness of the rabbis who made the key decisions about the scriptural canon ("It is indeed a matter of deep regret that decisions of high and sacred import rested with these men. . . . I cannot help doubting their good faith"). For Spinoza's forceful discussion of the process of choosing a scriptural canon, see pp. 136–137.

[105] Spinoza's reference on p. 99 to "malice" (*malitia*) tells us that self-interest is not necessarily the worst part of the story. It is as if the actual text of Scripture has inscribed in it all the vices lurking in those who had power over its transmission.

Spinoza's deep suspicion of privileged priestly interpreters directly hooks up with the issue, cited earlier, of reliance only on "the natural light of reason" vs. appeal to a (by definition) mysterious "supernatural light" – a theme that Spinoza picks up again at the end of chapter 7. These two themes are directly linked because the appeal to supernatural light asserts the monopolistic authority of ecclesiastical elites, whereas the reliance only on natural light affirms the competence of all rational individuals to interpret Scripture for themselves. This is a very important theme in the closing pages of chapter 7.

Everything in Spinoza's philology contributes to undermining belief in the unity and seamlessness of the Bible as a sacred text. He identifies particularly decisive evidence of this lack of seamlessness when he (in chapter 10) gets to the Book of Daniel, part of which was actually "written in Chaldaic [and therefore probably] taken from the chronicles of the Chaldeans."[106] This non-Hebrew text, once incorporated, becomes, astonishingly, "as sacred as the rest of the Bible."[107] (As Spinoza highlights in the immediately preceding discussion, there are also reasons to believe that the Book of Job may have derived from non-Hebrew sources, but this thesis, he concedes, is more conjectural.[108]) As Spinoza explicitly points out, this incorporation in the Hebrew Scripture of non-Hebrew fragments represents a tremendous vindication of Spinoza's universalism:

[The thesis of the incorporation in the Book of Daniel, of texts from the chronicles of the Chaldeans, if clearly established] would afford striking evidence to prove that Scripture is sacred only insofar as we understand through it the matters therein signified, and not insofar as we understand merely the words or the language and sentences whereby these matters are conveyed. It would further prove that books that teach and tell of the highest things are equally sacred, in whatever language and by whatever nation they were written.[109]

That is, the demystification of what is *thought* to be sacred in Scripture helps to disclose what is *truly* sacred – namely (in the most elevated aspects of Scripture) the content of its morality, a morality that in principle can be located, and when located is no less sacred, in *all* cultures.

At the end of his treatment of the Old Testament, Spinoza insists that his enterprise involves no blasphemy or subversion of Scripture because "no book is ever free from faults."[110] But is the Bible to be regarded as a book like other books? Are errors of grammar or errors of transcription from preexisting chronicles consistent with the understanding of the Bible as a product of Divine Revelation? These questions obviously were not lost on Spinoza's critics. Spinoza thinks he has an answer to such questions, an answer laid out in chapter 12, but as he makes clear at the beginning of chapter 12, he is fully aware of the "outcry" that his philological inquiry will arouse.

The first sentence of chapter 11 affirms the prophetic status of Christ's Apostles; but every other sentence in the chapter has the purpose of developing a distinction between prophecy and teaching, the net effect of which is to present Christianity basically as a religion that has cast off prophecy (which is a both crucial and salutary transformation of its predecessor-religion).[111]

---

[106] Ibid., p. 131.
[107] Ibid., p. 132.
[108] Ibid., p. 131.
[109] Ibid.
[110] Ibid., p. 136.
[111] To cast off prophecy is to cast off Revelation. This is a supremely sensitive topic, so Spinoza treads carefully, and the argument of the chapter does not exactly go in a straight line. The

Prophecy is "authoritative," contains "dogma and decrees," and expresses an absoluteness that reflects "the absolute power of [God's] nature."[112] New Testament teaching, on the other hand, is tentative, argumentative, appeals to reasons, and engages the judgment of its listeners or readers.[113] As authors of the Epistles, the Apostles are not prophets "express[ing] God's decrees" or "God's command" but teachers and philosophers or quasi-philosophers relying on "their own natural faculty of judgment."[114] It obviously serves Spinoza's project of a liberalization/rationalization of Judeo-Christian religion for him to present the Epistles that compose the New Testament[115] almost as a mode of philosophy, or as leaning a little bit more to the reason side of the reason–Revelation dichotomy. This has the clear consequence of attenuating the New Testament's claim to be a Revealed text, but Spinoza has no reason not to be willing to embrace this consequence.[116]

In contrasting the teachings of the New Testament as the product of the Apostles' own "natural faculty of judgment" with the Old Testament based on a much more traditional (impeccably orthodox, we could say) conception of Revelation, Spinoza seems to forget his own understanding of God as Nature. For in this account, he appeals to a notion of Moses and the other prophets receiving explicit marching orders from a *personal* God conceived very much in the way that the disdained "Pharisees" surely conceive the relation between God and His prophets – that is, God revealing Himself to the prophets in such a way that His will is immediately and indubitably made known to them.[117] Does

---

essential thrust of it, however, is that the New Testament, as compared with the Old Testament, represents decisive movement between the poles of Revelation and reason.

[112] *Theological–Political Treatise*, pp. 138, 139.

[113] Ibid., p. 139.

[114] Ibid., p. 140. The idea of the Apostles as (mere) teachers is also an important theme in chapter 42 of *Leviathan*. The key point for Hobbes is that "power ecclesiasticall" could not be traced back to the Apostles because "there was then no government by Coercion, but only by Doctrine, and Perswading."

[115] One can quite properly ask why the Epistles receive all the attention in chapter 11 and the Gospels get no attention. The answer readily suggests itself: Spinoza's purpose here is to rest the distinction between the Old Testament and the New Testament on the distinction between prophecy and teaching; and the Epistles obviously express better than the Gospels Spinoza's conception of the Apostles as teachers. (He affirms, from the first sentence of the chapter onward, that they are *also* prophets, but unless the Epistles allow us to see them *primarily* in a different guise, Spinoza would not be able to make the decisive differentiation between the two Testaments that the core idea of the *Theological–Political Treatise* requires him to make.)

[116] *Theological–Political Treatise*, p. 140: "the modes of expression and discussion employed by the Apostles in the Epistles clearly show that *these originated not from revelation and God's command* but from their own natural faculty of judgment, and contain nothing but brotherly admonitions mingled with courteous expressions (very different, indeed, from prophetic authoritativeness)"; emphasis added.

[117] On p. 141, Spinoza links this whole contrast to the parochialism–particularism of "the prophets of old" vs. the universalism of the Apostles. The old prophets needed more specific marching orders because their prophetic mandate was tied to particular nations, whereas this *is not* necessary in the case of the Apostles because *their* mandate is a more open-ended (universalistic) pedagogic mission. (However, as Spinoza acknowledges in the closing sentences of the

Spinoza himself think that this is the correct way to conceive God? Emphatically not. However, reembracing the orthodox image of Old Testament prophecy helps to reinforce Spinoza's rhetoric of the New Testament as a new, more *rational*, more philosophic, version of religion.[118]

Prophecy embodies the obligation or imperative to transmit God's commands, whereas teaching rests on a capacity to exercise discretion in getting the message received. In other words, teaching on the basis of reasons and arguments opens up a space of human freedom that is denied to the prophet (and also denied to the subjects of God who receive these commands via the prophets).[119] Spinoza acknowledges that part of what defines the Apostles is their prophetic capacity to receive God's revelation, but he deliberately downplays this aspect of the mission of the Apostles and emphatically plays up the pedagogic side of their mission precisely in order to give effect to his construal of the New Testament as the expression of a new experience of freedom within the monotheistic tradition.

chapter – and as the editor rightly highlights in n. 2 on p. 144 – it was really only Paul among the various Apostles who was a cosmopolitan preacher. I suppose, though, that one could rephrase Spinoza's claim as follows: *In principle*, the New Testament was a universalistic teaching, even if in practice the primary addressee of the Gospel remained the Jews.)

[118] Ibid., p. 142: "[T]he Epistles of the Apostles were dictated solely by the natural light." By contrast, "it was not by virtue of the natural light – that is, the exercise of reason – that the prophets perceived what was revealed to them" (p. 139). Nonetheless, one should also mention that in the same paragraph in which Spinoza states that the Epistles were dictated solely by the natural light, he also does some significant backtracking: The Apostles *qua* prophets *were* recipients of revelation; and "although religion as preached by the Apostles... does not come within the scope of reason, yet its substance... can be readily grasped by everyone by the natural light of reason." It is on account of these equivocations (the Apostles *qua* prophets participate in the supernatural light but dispense with this access to supernatural light in disseminating their teachings in the Epistles) that I spoke earlier of Spinoza presenting the New Testament as "leaning a bit more to the reason side" rather than falling straightforwardly on the reason side.

Who was the founder of the Enlightenment? How did it acquire this particular name? Does it have some relation to Spinoza's appropriation of the Cartesian trope of "the natural light" as his preferred term for reason? One can perhaps trace the beginnings of the rhetoric of "*lumière*" back to Bayle: See Pierre Bayle, *Various Thoughts on the Occasion of a Comet*, trans. Robert C. Bartlett (Albany, NY: SUNY Press, 2000), pp. 37, 41, 60, 71, 212, 276, and 315. Perhaps one can go further back, to Hobbes: As David Johnston highlights in *The Rhetoric of Leviathan*, chapter 5, Hobbes's polemic against "the Kingdome of Darknesse" in Part 4 of *Leviathan* presupposes a kingdom of light (founded on "the Light of Nature") that one can reasonably associate with what became the Enlightenment. In any case, the conception of Spinoza as the decisive founder of the Enlightenment is the central thesis of Jonathan Israel's book, *Radical Enlightenment: Philosophy and the Making of Modernity 1650–1750*. However, if one thinks that the emancipatory power of Spinoza is limited to readers in the seventeenth and eighteenth centuries, consider Ayaan Hirsi Ali, *Infidel* (New York: The Free Press, 2007), pp. 281–282.

[119] Ibid., p. 143: Paul's "freedom to exhort." In addition (same page), the Apostles, in common with all other teachers, "always prefer to instruct those who are beginners and have never studied under any other master." The implication is that there is one and only one master in the domain of prophecy–Revelation. Hence, again, an essential freedom belongs to the teacher (and the students), juxtaposed to a lack of freedom in the prophets (and in the subjects of God to whom the prophecies are addressed).

The theme of chapter 12 is what is corrupt and what is incorruptible in Scripture. This is an inescapable question in the light of Spinoza's philological inquiry, for much of that inquiry consists precisely in exposing corruptions in the text and, by implication, corruptions in the souls of the rabbinical guardians of the text who contributed to those very textual corruptions.[120] Let me pose again the questions I posed earlier: In what sense is either the Old Testament or the New Testament a product of Revelation? Chapters 7–10 teach us that the Old Testament is primarily the outcome of ancient scribes transcribing (accurately or with multiple errors of transcription) even more ancient manuscripts, yielding texts that are then edited or corrupted by unreliable medieval rabbis.[121] Chapter 11 teaches us that the New Testament is primarily the outcome of teachers' exercising their own highly personal freedom of pedagogy – a freedom to craft Jesus' teaching reflecting their own judgments about how to maximize its appeal to potential adherents. To say that Holy Scripture is shot through with human contingency would be an enormous understatement.[122]

At the end of my discussion of chapter 10, I stated that Spinoza thought he had an answer to those critics who were not only worried that his philological researches would fatally subvert the authority of the Bible but were also absolutely outraged at the prospect. His answer is quite a simple one. It is that one should not "fetishize" the Bible as the repository of God's Word, and that one should be able to see that what is religiously true in the Bible transcends the particular words and phrases of a text that, in common with all other books, is highly exposed to the contingencies of publication and transmission. In fact, true piety demands that one not fall prey to the kind of superstition that reveres Scripture as an idol-like fetish: To fetishize the Bible is "to worship paper and ink" – a version of the sin of worshipping "likenesses and images."[123] The prophets are true prophets[124] and the Word of God is authentically divine, but that does not mean that the text is available to us through some kind of immaculate conception. The core of Spinoza's response consists in an appeal

---

[120] Strauss closes his Spinoza book with an interesting suggestion about what Spinoza thought was the ultimate object of the conspiracy by the "Pharisees" to tamper with the text of the Hebrew Bible: See *Spinoza's Critique of Religion*, p. 268. The article on "Book of Ecclesiastes" in *JewishEncyclopedia.com* mentions, with respect to the canonicity of *Ecclesiastes*, that "endeavours were made to render it apocryphal [on account of its perceived tendency] toward heresy – that is, Epicureanism."

[121] This theme of how later religious authorities exercise responsibility for the editing of prophecies is interestingly illustrated by the history of Mormonism. See the discussion in Akenson cited earlier in note 98.

[122] Cf. *Theological–Political Treatise*, p. 149: "They were the fortuitous work of certain men."

[123] Ibid., p. 146.

[124] On p. 170, Spinoza appeals to Moses' authority in elaborating the distinction between true prophets and false prophets. The appeal to reliable "signs and wonders" (i.e., miracles) looms large within this Mosaic account (cf. pp. 181, 182). Of course, though, Spinoza has already thoroughly debunked miracles in chapter 6, which makes it very hard to take at face value Spinoza's endorsement of the Mosaic doctrine of the true prophet. There are parallel discussions in Hobbes: See *Leviathan*, chapters 32 and 36; cf. Johnston, *The Rhetoric of Leviathan*, pp. 162–163, who also highlights the problem of how one is supposed to sustain a notion of the true prophet once miracles have been thoroughly debunked.

to the words of St. Paul: The true epistle is "written not with ink, but with the Spirit. . . . not in tables of stone, but in fleshy tables of the heart" (2 *Corinthians* 3:3); and the essence of Spinoza's philosophical religion coincides with St. Paul's central challenge to the Old Testament – that the "spirit" and not the "letter" is what defines true religion and true piety. "[T]he Word of God . . . is true religion,"[125] and because the corruptions of the text are not sufficient to deprive us of knowledge of true religion, it follows that neither are they sufficient to deprive us of the Word of God.

Spinoza ends the chapter with a distinction between the words of Scripture, which indeed admit of being corrupted, and the essential *meaning* of Scripture, which is impervious to corruption.[126] After all the sinister suggestions in earlier chapters about the radical unreliability of the crucial transmitters of Scripture (the rabbis who selected the canon, the rabbis who inserted the missing vowels, and so on), Spinoza now goes out of his way to reassure his readers that these corruptions "take nothing away from the divinity of Scripture,"[127] for the Divine Law's essential message (love of God, love of one's neighbor as oneself) shines through incorruptibly.

[125] Ibid., p. 149.
[126] Ibid., p. 150.
[127] Ibid., p. 151.

10

Philosophy and Piety

Problems in Spinoza's Case for Liberalism (Owing to a Partial Reversion to Civil Religion)

[I]t is only in concession to the understanding of the multitude and the defective-ness of their thought that God is described as a lawgiver or ruler, and is called just, merciful, and so on.

– Spinoza[1]

[A]s to the question of what God . . . really is, . . . this is irrelevant to faith.

– Spinoza[2]

[T]he truth of a philosophy exists in its effects. . . . [I]f you would understand Spinoza, look to his critics. Of what did they accuse him? What in his philosophy did they find most objectionable? How strong was their reaction? What legal and coercive measures did his work provoke?

– Warren Montag[3]

Gradually the ordinary people are enlightened.

– Thomas Hobbes[4]

As Spinoza states very clearly in the subtitle of the *Theological–Political Treatise*, the central purpose of the book is to demonstrate the unqualified

---

[1] Baruch Spinoza, *Theological–Political Treatise*, 2nd ed., trans. Samuel Shirley (Indianapolis: Hackett, 2001), p. 55; cf. Spinoza, *The Letters*, trans. Samuel Shirley (Indianapolis: Hackett, 1995), p. 348 (Letter 78).

[2] *Theological–Political Treatise*, p. 162.

[3] Warren Montag, *Bodies, Masses, Power: Spinoza and His Contemporaries* (London: Verso, 1999), p. xiv. Montag intends this as an encapsulation of the Althusserian approach to Spinoza.

[4] Thomas Hobbes, *De Homine*, chapter 14, Paragraph 13 (translation by Edwin Curley). Cf. J. Judd Owen, "The Tolerant Leviathan," *Polity*, Vol. 37, No. 1 (January 2005): 142. (Owen's translation is "The multitude is educated little by little.")

compatibility between piety and "freedom of philosophizing."[5] A liberal society requires a protected space for intellectual freedom. The foundations of this project are laid at the end of chapter 13 with the argument that "the intellectual knowledge of God which contemplates his nature as it really is in itself... has no bearing on the practice of a true way of life, on faith, and on revealed religion."[6] What defines religion rightly conceived is the *practical* obligation to practice justice and charity on the assumption that one is thereby imitating God's justice and charity. Philosophers can think what they please because religion is not a matter of having an intellectual grasp of propositions about the nature of God. Investigations in the realm of metaphysical truth (including metaphysical inquiry into the nature of God) can be safely left in the hands of scientists and philosophers without any cause for worry that these investigations will impinge upon the authority of religion: Understanding that religion is a matter of practice, not theory, makes clear that the full intellectual freedom exercised by philosophers like Spinoza in a liberal society can do no harm to (again, "has no bearing on") the practice of religious faith and piety. Moral *practice*, and that alone, is the test of piety or impiety, which means that there can be no impiety in philosophical inquiry per se,[7] however much it pushes the boundaries of intellectual freedom. There is no moral obligation to hold correct beliefs (and given "the limited intelligence of the common people,"[8]

---

[5] Cf. *The Letters*, pp. 185–186 (Letter 30), stating the three essential objectives of the work: to remove the prejudices of theologians; to refute the accusation of atheism applied to Spinoza by "the common people"; and "to vindicate completely" the freedom to philosophize.

[6] *Theological–Political Treatise*, pp. 156–157.

[7] Ibid., p. 160: "[O]nly by works can we judge anyone to be a believer or an unbeliever." It is easy to see how this definition of piety functions as a refutation of anyone accusing Spinoza of impiety. If Spinoza lives a morally good life (and no one has ever been able to claim otherwise), then by definition (i.e., by his definition), he is pious. If "only by works can we judge anyone to be a believer or an unbeliever," then nothing in the content of Spinoza's philosophy can convict him of impiety. When Spinoza writes that "the true enemies of Christ are those who persecute the righteous and the lovers of justice" (ibid.), it follows from this that the orthodox who set themselves up as enemies of Spinoza (a lover of justice) prove themselves to be *by that very fact* "enemies of Christ."

[8] Ibid., p. 157; cf. p. 158: "Scripture is adapted to the intellectual level... of the unstable and fickle Jewish multitude." Did Spinoza really think that the argument in the *Theological–Political Treatise* would succeed in disarming popular hostility toward philosophers, and popular hostility toward himself in particular? The point is often made (for instance, by Feldman in the Introduction) that Spinoza, in publishing the book in Latin, sought to keep it out of the hands of "the multitude" (hence his efforts to head off its publication in the Dutch vernacular). However, the very fact that there was immediate pressure to publish a Dutch translation shows very clearly that the project of insulating the multitude from arguments being exchanged among the learned was bound to be hopeless – particularly if Spinoza's larger liberal project turned out to be successful (which it did). As for the *reason* Spinoza sought to head off a vernacular edition of the book, the fate of his friend Adriaan Koerbagh supplies an obvious answer (cf. Steven Nadler, *Spinoza: A Life*, Cambridge: Cambridge University Press, 1999, pp. 297–298). One may assume that the Dutch Republic, *relative to the other European states of the time*, was tolerant and liberal. Consider, though, what one of Amsterdam's magistrates thought to be an appropriate

this would in any case be a moral obligation that it would be impossible to make good on); conversely, the philosophizing of philosophers is a completely independent enterprise, so that, once again, what results *intellectually* from philosophers philosophizing is of no relevance to the demands of piety. Hence, in the words of Letter 30, liberalism is "vindicated." (That is, the intellectual freedom that is at the core of a liberal society receives moral certification not for the positive reason that it advances moral and religious welfare – though Spinoza is clearly committed to that view as well – but primarily for the negative reason that it leaves piety untouched.)

One could say that there is a "civil religion" aspect to this view of religion.[9] What is decisive in biblical religion as Spinoza presents it is that the faithful act with justice and charity because they are convinced that, in so acting, they are modeling themselves on God's justice and charity. Furthermore, Spinoza says repeatedly that they are right to think in this way about their relation to God. Nevertheless, he states very clearly in chapter 4 that "it is only in concession to the understanding of the multitude and the defectiveness of their thought that God is described as a lawgiver or ruler, and is called just, merciful, and so on."[10] The purpose of Scripture is to inculcate obedience,[11] and the falsity of the beliefs on the basis of which the obedience is inculcated is no valid objection against Scripture. The question, however, can be put to Spinoza, as it can be put to other civil-religion theorists[12]: Once it is announced in the pages of the *Theological–Political Treatise* that the notion of a just and merciful God is a conception pandering to the defective intellect of the multitude, and has no philosophical validity whatsoever, will the inculcation of pious obedience be left unaffected? Instead of vindicating Spinoza's view of the *separation* of piety

---

punishment for Koerbagh's crime of publishing Spinozistic views: "that his right thumb be cut off, that his tongue have a hole bored through it with a red-hot iron, and that he be imprisoned for thirty years, with all of his possessions confiscated and all of his books burned" (Nadler, p. 269). As Nadler highlights (p. 286), Spinoza's own presentation of Amsterdam as a paragon of liberal toleration (*Theological–Political Treatise*, p. 228) is rhetorical rather than descriptive.

[9] Cf. *Theological–Political Treatise*, n. 3 on pp. 162–163 (editor's note).

[10] Ibid., p. 55. One can raise the same question about obedience as one raises about justice or charity as the imitation of God's justice or mercy. If God as ruler or lawgiver is once again merely a concession to popular misconceptions, in what sense is "obedience" the right way to characterize the relation of human beings to God? When Spinoza writes that Scripture's core teaching is that "there is a Supreme Being who loves justice and charity, whom all must obey in order to be saved" (pp. 161–162), the second part of this statement (the need to obey God) seems as philosophically misleading as the first part (God's love of justice and charity). For a similar set of observations by Strauss, see *Spinoza's Critique of Religion* (New York: Schocken Books, 1965), p. 119.

[11] Ibid., p. 159: "[B]oth the Testaments are simply a training for obedience."

[12] Cf. Chapter 8, note 8. Spinoza's closest point of convergence with the idea of civil religion occurs when he states on p. 171 that one of the important reasons for granting moral authority to Scriptural religion is that doing so is "of considerable advantage to the state." If Spinoza really believes this, however, then why does so much of the *Theological–Political Treatise* have the effect of undermining confidence in the reliability of Scripture on the part of its adherents?

and philosophy,[13] does it not once again vindicate Plato's view that "custom without philosophy" is ultimately unsustainable?

These issues figure prominently in the quite interesting debate between Spinoza and Lambert de Velthuysen (conducted via Jacob Ostens).[14] Velthuysen zeroes in on the decisive fact that Spinoza's account of philosophy and piety has the direct consequence that all truth claims in Scripture are categorically dismissed: As encapsulated by Velthuysen, Spinoza's doctrine entails (and it does not bother Spinoza that this is what it entails) "that the prophets and the holy teachers – and so God himself, who spoke to men through their mouths – employed arguments which, if their nature be considered, are in themselves false," and hence "that Holy Scripture is not intended to teach truth."[15] Specifically, how can Spinoza recommend Scripture as a route to virtue insofar as it enjoins its adherents to imitate God's justice and mercy at the very same time that he publicizes the fact that images of God as just and merciful express an entirely false idea of the divine nature?[16] Does not Spinoza here fall into the typical trap of the civil-religion theorists who embrace religion on account of its moral-civil benefits while simultaneously announcing in a public medium that that is what they are doing, which thereby has the effect of *undermining* the

---

[13] *Theological–Political Treatise*, p. 169: "[E]ach has its own domain. The domain of reason . . . is truth and wisdom, the domain of theology is piety and obedience." On p. 159, Spinoza states that the distinction between faith and philosophy constitutes "the main object of this entire treatise." Cf. p. 164: "[B]etween faith and theology on the one side and philosophy on the other there is no relation and no affinity. . . . [T]hese two faculties . . . are as far apart as can be. The aim of philosophy is, quite simply, truth, while the aim of faith . . . is nothing other than obedience and piety." In the last paragraph of chapter 14, Spinoza states that this distinction between truth and piety represents "the most important part of the subject of this treatise."

[14] *The Letters*, trans. Shirley, Letters 42 and 43 (pp. 225–242). Letter 69 (pp. 323–324) is a letter sent directly to Velthuysen seeking his permission for publication of their debate (or a suitably revised version of it). The fact that Spinoza wanted a new version of the *Theological–Political Treatise* to include his exchange with Velthuysen serves to privilege Velthuysen among Spinoza's many critics. Cf. Nadler, *Spinoza: A Life*, pp. 323–324.

[15] *The Letters*, p. 227.

[16] Ibid., p. 226: In Spinoza's view, "the ignorance of the multitude has given rise to modes of speech whereby emotions are ascribed to God" (quote from Velthuysen). Velthuysen is alluding to the passage on p. 55 of the *Theological–Political Treatise* quoted as the first epigraph to this chapter. Consider also p. 53: "[Moses] imagined God as a ruler, lawgiver, king, merciful, just and so forth; whereas these are all merely attributes of human nature, and not at all applicable to the divine nature." Cf. *The Letters*, p. 348 (Letter 78); p. 269 (Letter 54); and esp. p. 277 (Letter 56): "[A] triangle, if it could speak would . . . say that God is eminently triangular, and a circle that God's nature is eminently circular," suggesting that the anthropocentric character of human conceptions of God ought to be interpreted in the same light. All of this is in blatant contradiction with *Theological–Political Treatise*, chapter 13, when Spinoza suggests, for instance, "that the knowledge which God through the medium of his prophets has required of all men universally . . . is no other than the knowledge of his divine justice and charity" (p. 154); "that God is supremely just and supremely merciful, that is, the one perfect pattern of the true life" (p. 156); and "that God has asked no other knowledge from men but knowledge of his divine justice and charity" (p. 157).

actual truth-claims of religion?[17] (We can call it the civil-religion paradox.[18])
One can well ask this: Is it a surprise that Spinoza was unable to convince his
critics that his philosophic piety was the true piety, and that he was not the
subverter but the servant of the Divine Law inscribed in Scripture?[19] Velthuysen was not a partisan of Neanderthal orthodoxy but rather a fellow liberal.[20]
Spinoza met him in Utrecht in 1673 and clearly thought well of him.[21] If
Spinoza could not convince someone like Velthuysen of his piety, he certainly
did not have the slightest chance of making headway with the truly orthodox
types (as indeed he did not). Leo Strauss is right that the many contradictions
in the *Theological–Political Treatise* suggest some effort on the part of Spinoza
to sow confusion about just how radical his most radical ideas are.[22] Still,
when one considers the reaction to his book among his contemporaries, one
is again forced to ask who exactly Spinoza thought he was fooling with his
"esotericism."

Here is Velthuysen's summary of Spinoza's stance toward biblical religion:
"[T]he doctrine of the political-theologian... banishes and thoroughly subverts all worship and religion, prompts atheism by stealth, or envisages such
a God as can not move men to reverence for his divinity, since he himself is

---

[17] Cf. Menachem Lorberbaum, "Spinoza's Theological–Political Problem," *Hebraic Political Studies*, Vol. 1, No. 2 (Winter 2006): 207. According to Lorberbaum's formulation of the paradox,
what Spinoza is struggling to do is to discredit institutionalized religion (which in significant
measure involves discrediting its sacred texts) while salvaging enough of the content of biblical
religion to make "political theology" (i.e., civil religion) a viable project. Spinoza is moved to
do this because he is not persuaded that religion is eliminable from human affairs and because,
like Hobbes, he thinks religion is more safely deposited in the hands of the civil sovereign than
in the hands of priests.

[18] The fact that, for instance, Spinoza can so thoroughly debunk "signs and wonders" and yet
still refer to them as the mark of true prophets shows very clearly that there are still civil-
religion vestiges in Spinoza's liberalism (cf. note 124 of Chapter 9). The question raised by the
civil-religion paradox is this: Who exactly is this supposed to fool?

It has been helpfully pointed out to me by Emile Perreau-Saussine that this challenge to
what I am calling the civil-religion paradox corresponds very well to Augustine's rejection of
civil theology in his critique of Varro.

[19] *Theological–Political Treatise*, p. 146: "I have said nothing that is impious or that smacks
of impiety"; p. 136: "I am doing a service to Scripture." What would Spinoza's orthodox
contemporaries assume to be his real attitude toward religion? It is easy to draw an answer to
this question from the infamous clandestine text, *Traité des Trois Imposteurs*, which offers a
crudely popularized no-holds-barred version of Spinozism. For a translation and commentary,
see Abraham Anderson, *The Treatise of the Three Impostors and the Problem of Enlightenment*
(Lanham, MD: Rowman & Littlefield, 1997). For a helpful discussion of the (uncertain) dating
and authorship of the *Traité*, see Jonathan Israel, *Radical Enlightenment* (Oxford: Oxford
University Press, 2001), pp. 694–700.

[20] See *The Letters*, pp. 35–36 (Introduction), and p. 225, n. 213. Cf. Nadler, *Spinoza: A Life*,
pp. 307 and 317. On pp. 307–311, Nadler offers a helpful account of the broader political
situation that helps to explain why a Cartesian like Velthuysen would be so anxious to condemn
Spinoza.

[21] Nadler, *Spinoza: A Life*, pp. 317, 323–324; *The Letters*, p. 324, n. 344.

[22] Leo Strauss, "How to Study Spinoza's *Theologico-Political Treatise*," in Strauss, *Persecution
and the Art of Writing* (Chicago: University of Chicago Press, 1988), pp. 142–201.

subject to fate; no room is left for divine governance and providence, and the assignment of punishment and reward is entirely abolished."[23] Spinoza is of course annoyed at the imputation of atheism, because one of the main objects of writing the *Theological–Political Treatise*, according to Letter 30, had been precisely to fend off such accusations. Velthuysen, however, might have been willing to accede to Spinoza's protestations that he was not an outright atheist and to allow that Spinoza was merely a deist.[24] Either way, the rest of Velthuysen's summary seems pretty much on the mark.[25]

There is a central tension in Spinoza's argument: He wants to reassure the faithful that philosophy and other forms of free intellectual life are innocuous because they do not impinge upon the function of Scripture in inculcating obedience. However, his strong reservations about biblical doctrines of punishment and reward, for instance,[26] prove that he is far from comfortable with the modes of inculcating obedience that are typical of Scripture. Spinoza claimed to be at a loss to understand why his views were received as so subversive, but writing in the midst of a culture utterly fixated on notions of damnation, Spinoza (a) upheld a doctrine of necessity according to which divine punishment would be flatly unjust; and (b) promulgated a view of God according to which the idea of God's retribution against the sinful makes no sense. What is there to be surprised about? It is fine to say that the kind of piety encouraged in the New Testament (free obedience–free piety) is morally superior to the piety enforced in the Old Testament (coerced obedience–coerced piety),[27] but this

---

[23] *The Letters*, p. 236.

[24] Ibid., p. 225: "I think he has renounced all religion. At any rate, he does not rise above the religion of the Deists."

[25] Not only does Spinoza utterly reject the imputations of atheism but he strenuously denies Velthuysen's claim that, in Spinoza's view, "God's precepts and law" cease to be what ultimately upholds virtue (Velthuysen: *The Letters*, pp. 227, 236; Spinoza's reply: pp. 239–240). It is true that there is no lack of appeals to divine law in the *Treatise*, but it is hard to credit the idea of God as a source of "decrees" if there is no *personal* God. Of course, Spinoza himself also makes it explicit in the first epigraph to this chapter that the image of "God as lawgiver" is merely a concession to the vulgar. As for the weighty issues raised by Velthuysen's implied criticism of the Spinozistic view that "the purpose of the prophet's mission was . . . not to teach any truth" (*The Letters*, pp. 227–228), Spinoza offers no reply. Cf. Bayle's complaint about the evasiveness of Spinoza's letters: Pierre Bayle, *Historical and Critical Dictionary*, ed. Richard H. Popkin (Indianapolis: Bobbs-Merrill, 1965), p. 301, note *n*.

[26] In Letter 42, Velthuysen rightly zeroes in on this issue (pp. 226–227, 236). As noted in Chapter 9, note 75, Spinoza's reply in Letter 43 reiterates in the clearest terms that the Bible's doctrine of otherworldly rewards and (particularly) punishments is resolutely rejected. The implications of Spinoza's philosophy for doctrines of punishment also constitute a crucial theme in the correspondence between Spinoza and Oldenburg in Letters 74–75 and 77–79. As Robert Sparling has drawn to my attention, Hobbes offers a doctrine of naturalized "divine punishment" that is very similar in effect to Spinoza's: See *Leviathan*, ed. C. B. Macpherson (London: Penguin, 1968), pp. 406–407. See also Pierre Bayle, *Various Thoughts on the Occasion of a Comet*, end of § 231.

[27] Incidentally, Spinoza, in his reply to Velthuysen via the letter to Ostens (*The Letters*, Letter 43, p. 241), makes very explicit that he regards Islam as, in effect, a case of "backsliding" to the more primitive coercive or slavish piety of the Old Testament: "Mahomet was an impostor,

hardly leaves piety per se untouched by philosophy per se. Even in advancing a moral-intellectual preference for the New Testament over the Old Testament, philosophy thereby *intervenes* in the realm of piety, and this in turn undermines Spinoza's case that intellectual life "has no bearing on . . . revealed religion."

Is it not true, however, that for Spinoza, even the New Testament falls considerably short of the most sublime sort of piety? The ultimate teaching of chapter 15, and by extension the ultimate teaching of the work as a whole, is that there are two completely distinct modes of salvation for human beings. There is the *free* salvation conferred by philosophy that permits "only a few"[28] to do good for its own sake and practice virtue on account of (in Velthuysen's words) "the beauty of virtue" and nothing else.[29] Alternatively, there is for the majority of human beings who are "less gifted with intelligence"[30]

---

since he completely abolishes the freedom which is granted by that universal religion revealed by the natural and prophetic light." (Cf. *Theological–Political Treatise*, p. 3, and *The Letters*, p. 343.) However, one might ask this: If this is the basis on which one judges Mohammed to be an impostor or false prophet, does not Moses appear also as a false prophet on the same basis? This question has even more force when we link it to the discussion on p. 170 of the *Theological–Political Treatise* according to which, *in Moses' own view*, false prophets are "those who preach false gods" – considered in the light of Spinoza's demonstration throughout the book of how far removed the Old Testament's images of God are from a true conception of divinity. Yet Spinoza, notwithstanding the seeming hostility to Islam expressed in this passage in Letter 43, in fact does not contradict his commitment to the shared moral truth in all religions, for in the next paragraph he affirms that whether Mohammed is a true prophet or a false prophet is irrelevant to what really matters, morally and religiously, with respect to Islam: "[T]he Turks and the other Gentiles, if they worship God by the exercise of justice and by love of their neighbour, . . . possess the Spirit of Christ and are saved."

28 *Theological–Political Treatise*, p. 172.

29 *The Letters*, p. 227. Bayle, in note E of the article on Spinoza in *Historical and Critical Dictionary*, also very strongly emphasizes this theme of a civil religion enforced by otherworldly sanctions vs. the idea of virtue sought for its own excellence. Bayle associates the latter with Epicurean doctrine, but he very puzzlingly claims that the Epicurean doctrine is what "Spinoza would have put forth if he had dared to dogmatize publicly." Because Spinoza *does* publicly enunciate this doctrine, is this Bayle's way of hinting at the doctrines *Bayle himself* would have embraced "if he had dared to dogmatize publicly"? (My thanks to Miguel Morgado for drawing my attention back to this important text.) Cf. Bayle, *Various Thoughts on the Occasion of a Comet*, § 178. See also *Lessing's Theological Writings*, ed. Henry Chadwick (London: Adam & Charles Black, 1956), p. 96.

30 *Theological–Political Treatise*, p. 171; cf. p. 153: Scriptural doctrine conveys "very simple matters able to be understood by *the most sluggish mind*" (emphasis added). To repeat a point I made in Chapter 9, if all human beings were philosophers, then biblical religion would be redundant. "Revelation" is necessary because of the contingent fact that philosophers constitute a tiny minority, and the rest, the ordinary types who make up humanity's vast majority, need to practice obedience to be virtuous. (*Theological–Political Treatise*, p. 172: "I wish to emphasise in express terms . . . the importance and the necessity of the role that I assign to Scripture, or revelation. . . . For all men without exception [i.e., including those less gifted with intelligence] are capable of obedience, while there are only a few – in proportion to the whole of humanity – who acquire a virtuous disposition under the guidance of reason alone. Thus [without Scripture, relying only on philosophy], the salvation of nearly all men would be in doubt.") Again, Spinoza here verges on a civil-religion teaching.

another route to blessedness or salvation, namely misconceiving God as a law-giver issuing decrees (via the prophets) and obtaining "very great comfort" by knowing themselves to be obedient to those decrees.[31] Both paths, Spinoza insists, are equally legitimate ways to salvation. Who, however, can fail to see that given Spinoza's emphatic distinction between the *freedom* of the universal true religion and the slavishness of any other conception of religion,[32] Scriptural religion is being impugned at the very same time as it is receiving his ostensible endorsement and support? Spinoza's account of philosophy and piety thus tends in the direction of suggesting that what is *true* in religion corresponds to philosophy. All else is superstition (either superstition pure and simple, or superstition employed as a mode of enforcing virtuous conduct upon those who lack the intellectual capacity to derive it from reason alone).

Is there for Spinoza the possibility of a process of enlightenment capable of renegotiating this static relationship between philosophy and religion (or between the few and the many)? If religion is associated politically with the "obedience-state" and philosophy is associated politically with the "liberty-state," there are evident political reasons why Spinoza would not be satisfied with a static and unchangeable relation between philosophy and religion. In particular, one wonders whether Spinoza's depiction of the New Testament Apostles as free-minded *teachers* is not ultimately intended as a way of suggesting a less static image of the relationship between philosophy and religion – or even as an anticipation of an Enlightenment still to come.[33]

---

[31] Ibid., p. 172.

[32] In other words (just to spell it out), the true purpose of the distinction between slavish religion and free religion is not to draw a boundary between the Old Testament and New Testament, but rather to draw a boundary between biblical religion and philosophy. If the essential function of Revelation is to enforce obedience, then the Old and New Testaments have far more in common with each other than either does with philosophy. As Spinoza puts it on p. 178, "only he is free who lives whole-heartedly under the sole guidance of reason."

[33] A conception of this kind (that is, of Revelation as a vehicle of eventual enlightenment) seems to be what Lessing drew from the *Theological–Political Treatise*: See "The Education of the Human Race," in *Lessing's Theological Writings*, ed. Chadwick, pp. 82–98. Cf. Steven B. Smith, *Spinoza, Liberalism, and the Question of Jewish Identity* (New Haven: Yale University Press, 1997), p. 180.

Spinoza's Interpretation of the Commonwealth of the Hebrews, and Why Civil Religion Is a Continuing Presence in His Version of Liberalism

[E]veryone is by absolute natural right the master of his own thoughts.

– Spinoza[1]

[W]hat no monarch could achieve by fire and sword, churchmen succeeded in doing by pen alone.

– Spinoza[2]

How far does Spinoza actually go with his liberalism? Starting in chapter 16 of his *Theological–Political Treatise*, Spinoza tries to answer this question by defining what properly belongs to the judgment of the public magistrate and what belongs to the conscientious judgment of the free individual, and by building up the basic structure of a modern political philosophy. Like Kant more than 100 years later, Spinoza seeks to combine a defense of freedom of thought and expression with an account of obedience to the state.

"[C]onsidered as solely under the dominion of Nature,"[3] human beings operate strictly according to the necessities of appetite, and they are fully within their rights to do so. Just as for Hobbes, though, the imperative to transcend fear and anxiety prompts natural individuals to trade in the unlimited self-seeking of *natural right* for the moral reciprocity of *reason*. Nevertheless, reason is an insufficient lever for getting individuals to quit the state of nature and embrace "this highest good, the preservation of the state."[4] The solution is a contract or covenant, motivated by "hope of greater good or [especially] fear

---

[1] Baruch Spinoza, *Theological–Political Treatise*, 2nd ed., trans. Samuel Shirley (Indianapolis: Hackett, 2001), p. 223.
[2] Ibid., p. 218 (i.e., whereas German emperors were powerless to dislodge the "ascendancy" of the Pope, Luther and Calvin *were* able to undo this ascendancy through purely intellectual means).
[3] Ibid., p. 174.
[4] Ibid., p. 176.

of greater evil,"[5] whereby all natural rights are transferred to the state.[6] With the overwhelming power thereby concentrated in its hands, the state is in a formidable position to enforce compliance, if need be "through fear of the ultimate penalty."[7] Spinoza departs from Hobbes in calling this "a democracy,"[8] but it is clear that the basic structure of the argument is hugely indebted to Hobbes. Having put together a Leviathan constructed fundamentally on the basis of Hobbesian principles, how does Spinoza then secure a space for liberty and conscientious judgment?[9]

Subjects have to obey the sovereign power, but provided they do so not merely to serve the sovereign's own interests, being a subject is different from being a slave,[10] and obedience to the state is compatible with being the free citizen of a free commonwealth. If we are not attuned to the need for a monopoly of rightful power and authority in the hands of the state, we fall back into the destructive anarchy of the state of nature; but if we are not attuned to the need for the liberty of law-abiding citizens of the commonwealth, then membership in the state becomes a mode of servitude (which is intolerable). Therefore, the basic challenge of constructing a viable political order depends on striking the right balance between obedience and liberty.

Is there a suitable balance between obedience and liberty in the political theory stated in chapter 16? One has no reason to doubt Spinoza when he emphasizes that an elaboration of "the benefits of freedom in a commonwealth" constitutes the "main purpose" of his analysis.[11] Still, as between

---

[5] Ibid., p. 177.

[6] This theory of the "transfer" of rights appears to be limited to the *Theological–Political Treatise*. Both in the *Political Treatise* and in the brief discussion of Hobbes in Letter 50, Spinoza's view is that natural rights are *not* transferred to the sovereign. Instead, we are presented with the doctrine that right equals power: The power of the sovereign exceeds that of individual citizens, so the sovereign's right simply trumps (rather than absorbs) the rights of individual citizens. The conclusion is often drawn that the basic theory of the *Political Treatise* is therefore not a contractarian theory. As I noted in Chapter 9, this idea of right equals power is a very odd view for a liberal or protoliberal like Spinoza to be embracing. According to Lewis Samuel Feuer, Spinoza lost most of his faith in democracy and republican self-government in the wake of the political crisis of 1672; *Spinoza and the Rise of Liberalism* (Boston: Beacon Press, 1958). If this is true, then it might help account for why the theoretical foundation of the *Political Treatise* is so hard edged.

[7] *Theological–Political Treatise*, p. 177.

[8] Ibid. Democracy, as Spinoza points out, appears as "the most natural form of state, approaching most closely to that freedom which nature grants to every man. For in a democratic state nobody transfers his natural right to another so completely that thereafter he is not to be consulted; he transfers it to the majority of the entire community of which he is part. In this way all men remain equal, as they were before in a state of nature" (p. 179). This *is* certainly a major departure from Hobbes, as is Spinoza's preoccupation with "the benefits of freedom in a commonwealth" (ibid.).

[9] On p. 178, Spinoza makes the point, parallel to a similar argument in Hobbes, that rulers undermine their own interests insofar as they abuse their power. However, one would have to be completely innocent of knowledge of human history to find this a reassuring argument.

[10] Ibid.

[11] Ibid., p. 179.

the Hobbesian and Lockean poles of Spinoza's vision of politics,[12] his political theory (at least in chapter 16) seems strongly biased toward Hobbes. In
Spinoza's account, sovereign powers judge what will serve the common good,
and subjects, in complying with these judgments, serve not only the sovereign's
interests but also their own (thereby proving that they are not mere slaves of
the state).[13] Perhaps the scope of the civic judgment exercised by the ordinary
citizen is not nothing in this account, but the scope is certainly minimized. The
fundamental relation between state and subject is that the sovereign renders
judgments and the subject obeys.[14] So what becomes of reason and judgment
("the benefits of freedom")?

Spinoza does not fail to apply his Hobbesian principles to the problem of
politics and religion, as the last pages of chapter 16 make clear, and it is
surely not too much of a surprise that he draws directly Hobbesian conclusions. Where there is a conflict between the sovereign's command and God's
command, which has precedence? Suppose "a prophet expressly sent by God
and proving his mission by indisputable signs" arrived to challenge the state's
decrees. Even *then*, the sovereign power would be answerable only to God
(which is Hobbes's line) – that is, if the sovereign insists on defying what seems
clearly to be ordained by divine law, "he may do so to his own peril and hurt
without any violation of right, civil or natural."[15] "Divine command" would
trump "human command" only in a case where "a sure and indubitable revelation" presented itself, and given that Spinoza has already given a rebuff to
the prophets themselves, what would count as satisfying this condition?[16] If
exceptions were made to the bindingness of state authority related to claims of
conscientious religious commitment, the whole authority of the state would fall

---

[12] For purposes of this argument, I will leave to one side questions about whether there are in
Hobbes significant anticipations of Lockean liberalism (I explore some aspects of the issue
in an article entitled "Three Versions of the Politics of Conscience: Hobbes, Spinoza, Locke"
forthcoming in the *San Diego Law Review*). Richard Tuck in particular has offered a forceful
presentation of Hobbes as a proto-Lockean theorist of toleration: Tuck, "Hobbes and Locke on
Toleration," in *Thomas Hobbes and Political Theory*, ed. Mary G. Dietz (Lawrence: University
Press of Kansas, 1990), pp. 153–171. Tuck argues that in the late 1660s, Hobbes became, and
was understood by his contemporaries to have become, "a radical tolerationist" (p. 167). James
Farr, in the same volume, argues that Tuck overstates the theme of toleration in Hobbes. See
Farr, "Atomes of Scripture," pp. 188–190 and p. 195, nn. 91 and 92. This is an important and
interesting debate, and there are illuminating insights on both sides.

[13] *Theological–Political Treatise*, p. 179.

[14] Ibid., p. 181: "[S]ince the state must be preserved and governed *solely by the policy of the
sovereign power* and it is covenanted that *this right belongs absolutely to it alone*, if anyone
embarks on some undertaking of public concern on his own initiative and without the knowledge of the supreme council, he has violated the right of the sovereign power and is guilty of
treason and is rightly and properly condemned" (emphasis added). The least that one can say
about this passage is that it is not liberalism as Locke, Montesquieu, Tocqueville, and J. S. Mill
understood liberalism!

[15] Ibid., p. 182.

[16] Ibid.

to pieces, as Spinoza states very clearly[17] – for appeals to religion would easily supply a "pretext [by which] everyone could assume unrestricted freedom to do as he pleases."[18] "[I]t belongs completely to the sovereign power ... to make what decisions it thinks fit concerning religion,"[19] and Spinoza's Hobbesian theory of wholesale forfeiture of rights held in the state of nature guarantees that no one has even a minimal normative basis for challenging this state authority. The fact that chapter 16 ends with these themes cannot help but arouse the suspicion that Spinoza develops the argument in this chapter in such a way as to exalt the Leviathan to near-Hobbesian proportions precisely to repel any challenges to the state's authority emanating from the realm of religion.

As already stated, the decisive question, still unanswered, is this: What becomes of individual reason and judgment, given Spinoza's Hobbes-like affirmation of near-absolute state sovereignty in chapter 16? Before Spinoza answers this question, though, he veers into a long and puzzling detour addressing the nature of the ancient Hebrew commonwealth. In chapter 16, Spinoza had already started formulating his own political philosophy, so why does he revert back to an analysis of the ancient Hebrews? Chapter 16 is Spinoza's civil-religion (Hobbesian) chapter, and chapter 20 is his liberal (Lockean) chapter. Why is the intellectual movement from civil religion to liberalism mediated by a reflection on the Hebrew commonwealth? As various scholars have pointed out, there are contextual reasons why Spinoza might have felt it reasonable to give privileged attention to the Hebrew commonwealth.[20] I am not fully convinced, however, that these contextual considerations tell the whole story. Why

---

[17] Here's a contemporary example: In August, 2007, the state of Israel ordered the army to evacuate a tiny illegal Jewish settlement in Hebron. Twelve Orthodox Jews serving in the army were ordered by rabbis not to participate, and they obeyed the command of their rabbis rather than the command of the state. The head of the IDF's Central Command stated that in disobeying orders, the twelve soldiers were "threaten[ing] the foundations of the Israeli Defense Forces" and ordered them court-martialed (*Globe & Mail*, August 7, 2007, p. A11). This example illustrates the continuing contemporary relevance (which is perhaps too obvious to require illustration) of Spinoza's point that, in cases like this, the exercise of conscientious judgment shaped by religious commitments indeed poses a severe challenge to the authority of the state.

[18] *Theological–Political Treatise*, p. 183.

[19] Ibid. What if the sovereign power in question is a "heathen"? Here, too, Spinoza follows Hobbes's lead. Why should the theory of the transfer of natural rights vest any less authority in heathen sovereign powers than it does in Jewish and Christian sovereign powers? Relinquishing one's right to defend oneself to the sovereign power at the same time involves (for the same reason) relinquishing one's right to defend one's religion (ibid.; cf. p. 214). Spinoza once again tosses in the red herring of exceptions in cases of "sure revelation," but this has just as little force as it did in the preceding discussion.

Of possible relevance to this whole analysis was the Sabbatean episode of the 1660s, the conclusion of which was Sabbatai Zevi's coerced conversion to Islam enforced by the Ottoman sultan. See the interesting discussion in Steven Nadler, *Spinoza: A Life* (Cambridge: Cambridge University Press, 1999), pp. 249–254.

[20] See Seymour Feldman's Introduction to the *Theological–Political Treatise*, p. xviii: "To many Dutch Protestants, especially those following John Calvin, the ancient Israelite polity led by

not? The problem Spinoza is addressing (as is true as well for all the political philosophers considered in this book) is not just the particular theocratic ambitions of a specific group of Dutch Calvinists, but rather the challenge posed to *all* forms of civil authority by *all* appeals to theocratic authority. Addressing theocracy in its archetypal form (the Mosaic regime) is a way of responding to the problem of civil religion per se.

Even though Spinoza emphasizes that "there is no absurdity in conceiving men whose beliefs, love, hatred, contempt and every single emotion is under the sole control of the governing power,"[21] clearly one is straining the boundaries of human nature in aiming at this kind of tyrannical authority. What, then, is the appropriate way in which to maintain civic stability while respecting the

Moses is the model for the Christian political regime"; cf. pp. xxx and xliii. In other words, it is still relevant to debunk ancient Israelite-style theocracy because theocracy (in the guise of Calvinism) remains a live possibility – except that Spinoza's actual account in chapter 17 is far more sympathetic than what one would associate with this kind of debunking operation. See also Nadler, *Spinoza: A Life*, pp. 14 and 357, n. 28, on how Protestant Dutch culture, perhaps particularly among orthodox Calvinist Counter-Remonstrants, was preoccupied with what was seen as the continuing religious relevance of the Old Testament. In fact, interest in seeking political models in the Old Testament was not limited to orthodox Counter-Remonstrants: for a good treatment of how both Remonstrant and Counter-Remonstrant factions were drawn to an Hebraic self-image, see Miriam Bodian, "The Biblical 'Jewish Republic' and the Dutch 'New Israel' in Seventeenth-Century Dutch Thought," *Hebraic Political Studies*, Vol. 1, No. 2 (Winter 2006): 186–202. In pursuing this topic, a good starting point (although it does not mention Spinoza) is Simon Schama, *The Embarrassment of Riches* (New York: Knopf, 1987), chapter 2.

Perhaps the best account of how Spinoza's narrative concerning the Hebrews relates to the contemporary Dutch context is to be found in Michael A. Rosenthal, "Why Spinoza Chose the Hebrews: The Exemplary Function of Prophecy in the *Theological–Political Treatise*," *History of Political Thought*, Vol. 18, No. 2 (Summer 1997): 207–241, esp. pp. 231–240. A rather different account is offered in Lea Campos Boralevi, "Classical Foundational Myths of European Republicanism: The Jewish Commonwealth," in *Republicanism: A Shared European Heritage*, ed. Martin van Gelderen and Quentin Skinner (Cambridge: Cambridge University Press, 2002), Vol. 1, pp. 247–261. On p. 261, Campos Boralevi makes the interesting suggestion that there had already been, long before Spinoza, a well-established intellectual tradition of appealing to "the Jewish Commonwealth" (the *respublica Hebraeorum*) as a "foundational myth" of Dutch republicanism. According to her thesis (which she promises to develop in a forthcoming book), it was Spinoza's deliberate intention to address and "overthrow" this tradition. Campos Boralevi's suggestion also provides a possible solution to the puzzle, to be discussed later in this chapter, of why chapters 17 and 18 of the *Theological–Political Treatise* offer such contrasting analyses of the Jewish commonwealth, namely that Spinoza may have been responding to the fact that the ancient Hebrew commonwealth was a source of inspiration for *both* Dutch theocracy *and* Dutch republicanism. Thus Spinoza (on this theory) was torn between sympathy for the Hebrew model (*qua* republican) and the impulse to criticize it (*qua* theocratic). Consider in particular Campos Boralevi's reference to Petrus Cunaeus's interest in "the agrarian laws, which provided for equality in the Hebraic model" (p. 259). It is very striking that for Spinoza as well, as I comment on later, this is a highly appealing aspect of the Hebrew commonwealth. Unfortunately, Campos Boralevi does not spell out in any detail what Spinoza retained and what he rejected in relation to the Dutch republican tradition that interests her.

[21] *Theological–Political Treatise*, p. 186.

natural distinction between things pertaining to "outward act[s]" and those pertaining to "internal act[s] of the mind"?[22] Spinoza does not explain why an account of Moses and the Hebrews is the best way to tackle this question, but the implication is that if we could resolve the issue with respect to theocracy in the strict sense, we would be properly equipped to resolve the question for all states.

Given "the fickleness of the masses," the fact that "the masses are governed solely by their emotions, not by reason," and the rule of selfishness, vanity, envy, and a hundred other vices, the establishment of stable political authority poses a formidable challenge.[23] An extreme solution to this problem is for kings to present themselves as descendants of immortal gods.[24] However, Spinoza vehemently rejects such appeals to theocratic authority (supposedly "established by God, not by the votes and consent of men"): "[O]nly utter barbarians allow themselves to be so blatantly deceived and to become slaves instead of subjects, with no interests of their own."[25] How does the Mosaic theocracy fare in relation to this severe antitheocratic judgment? The account Spinoza gives (at least initially) is surprisingly positive. First of all, the liberation from Egyptian bondage placed the Hebrews in an archetypal contractualist situation: The Hebrews "regained their natural right over everything that lay within their power, and every man could decide afresh whether to retain it or to surrender it and transfer it to another."[26] Hence the rule of Moses arose from a classic social contract constructed by free individuals in a "state of nature."[27] Moreover, it was not really *Moses* who was the recipient of this transfer of natural right but rather *God* insofar as the covenant affirmed only that "law [proclaimed] as prophetic revelation": a "transference of right to God." "It was God alone . . . who held sovereignty over the Hebrews."[28] In other words, what we have here is a classic social contract issuing in a classic theocracy. Spinoza goes out of his way to insist that unlike the Roman and Macedonian princes cited in the preceding discussion, this theocracy was *not* founded on deceit – it was a product of free consent, a surrender of natural

---

[22] Ibid.
[23] Ibid., p. 187.
[24] Ibid., p. 188.
[25] Ibid.
[26] Ibid., p. 189.
[27] Ibid. Richard H. Popkin offers a strikingly different interpretation of this reversion to a state of nature subsequent to the exodus from Egypt. See Popkin's Foreword to *Heterodoxy, Spinozism, and Free Thought in Early-Eighteenth-Century Europe*, ed. Silvia Berti et al. (Dordrecht: Kluwer, 1996), p. xv: "Moses pretended to have divine authority in order to save the Israelites who had relapsed into the state of nature after their escape from Egypt and were disintegrating as a social group." My view is that Spinoza sees the reversion to the state of nature not as mere anarchy but rather with respect to its potential in constituting a genuinely archetypal contractualist situation. That is, Popkin sees it in its Hobbesian aspect; I see it in its Lockean aspect.
[28] *Theological–Political Treatise*, p. 189.

right "by express covenant and oath."[29] Moses was not the Hebrew king; *God*
was king.[30] To oppose the state, either as an external enemy or as an internal traitor, meant opposing oneself to God. This was a state that in principle
dissolves any "difference... between civil law and religion"[31] – a theocratic
form of government in the strictest sense. But then, in a remarkable reversal,
Spinoza claims that the theocratic nature of the state applied only *in theory*,
not *in reality*,[32] for the *de jure* theocracy embodied in the Hebrew state was a
de facto democracy!

Nevertheless, Spinoza immediately goes on to explain that democracy is *not*
what the Hebrew state was *under Moses*. According to the terms of the initial
covenant, where the surrender of right was to God and not to any other man,
"this covenant left them all completely equal," "as in a democracy."[33] All of
this changed, however, when the Hebrews turned to Moses as an authoritative
mediator with God; in effect, Spinoza says, the Hebrews lost their nerve, and
preferred to rely on Moses as interpreter of God's will rather than attempt
to deal directly with God as sovereign. At this point, "the first covenant"
(one can call it the theocratic–democratic covenant) gets "abrogated," and it
is replaced with what is in effect a *monarchical* (Hobbesian) covenant. Moses
becomes "the divine oracle," and all the absolute rights of sovereignty formally
reposing in God now flow to Moses: "the right to consult God alone in his
tent, ... the authority to make and repeal laws, to make decisions on war and
peace, to send envoys, to appoint judges, to choose a successor."[34] At *this* stage
of the narrative, Moses' theocracy looks indistinguishable from the deceitful
theocracies of Augustus and Alexander.

What transpires *after* the reign of Moses? Because Moses opted not to
appoint a successor with the same absolute powers that he exercised himself, what arose was a decisive *division* of sovereignty between the high priest
(Aaron, followed by Eleazar) vested with "the right to interpret the laws and
to promulgate God's answers" and a commander-in-chief (Joshua) charged
with "the right and power to govern the state in accordance with laws thus
expounded."[35] Given that Spinoza insists that this is a theocracy, the function
of the high priest is clearly central to the emanation of political power, and

---

[29] Ibid.; cf. p. 222: "Moses had gained the strongest of holds on the minds of his people not by
deception but by his divine virtue." However, Spinoza immediately acknowledges that, genuine
prophet or not, Moses "was not exempt from [the people's] murmurings and criticisms." In
other words, the Mosaic regime displayed *both* elements of "free consent" *and* elements of
monarchical heavy-handedness.

[30] Needless to say, it is very hard to know what to make of such expressions (which run throughout
the chapter) when articulated by a philosopher who is on record as holding that any moves to
anthropomorphize God are no more than concessions to popular ignorance.

[31] *Theological–Political Treatise*, p. 189.

[32] Ibid., pp. 189–190.

[33] Ibid., p. 190.

[34] Ibid., pp. 190–191.

[35] Ibid., p. 191.

hence the new regime (or modification of the regime) amounts to a "Montesquieuian" constitutionalism founded on separation of powers. Given the theocratic character of the regime, one might well assume that the high priest would hold the upper hand (which is what Hobbes emphatically asserts in his interpretation of the same regime),[36] but Spinoza makes clear that this is not the case.[37] The regime is now organized according to what one might call a "joint-sovereignty" arrangement: The division of labor between two cosovereigns, one interpreting God's will and the other drawing implications for law and command, has the effect of rendering each side of the arrangement dependent on (and therefore restrained by) the other.

Spinoza thereby contests Hobbes's claim in chapter 40 of *Leviathan* that the transition from Moses to his immediate successors was *not* marked by a splitting up of sovereignty but rather the *retention* of undivided sovereignty in the person of the high priest.[38] Spinoza's analysis of crucial differences between the Mosaic and post-Mosaic regimes clearly gains far more significance theoretically once it is related to Spinoza's philosophical dialogue with Hobbes. In fact, looming over the disagreement between Spinoza and Hobbes on a point of scriptural exegesis is the theoretically decisive question of how to interpret the founding of the Mosaic regime as the Hebrew Bible's representation of the archetypal social-contract or covenantal situation.[39]

Indeed (following Hobbes's suggestion), it seems odd that Aaron would inherit Moses' function as "the divine oracle"[40] *without* also inheriting Moses' monarchical authority. Spinoza's characterizations of ultimate authority in this

---

[36] See *Leviathan*, ed. C. B. Macpherson (Harmondsworth: Penguin, 1968), p. 547: "Moses, and Aaron, and the succeeding High Priests were the Civill Soveraigne"; p. 587: "the High Priest ... was the Civill Soveraign"; p. 597: "Before the People of Israel had (by the commandment of God to Samuel) set over themselves a King, after the manner of other Nations, the High Priest had the Civill Government."

[37] On the contrary, there are indications that the theocratic elements of the regime are *subordinate*: Spinoza points out (p. 191) that the Levites, notwithstanding their formally superior status as the priestly tribe, were in fact civically inferior because they lacked a territorial stake comparable to that of the other tribes, and therefore were, by Moses' decree, materially dependent for their livelihood on the rest of the people. Consider also Spinoza's powerful claim that the "second state" of the Hebrews (i.e., the state associated with the Second Temple) was significantly weaker than the original (Mosaic) state ("a mere shadow of the first") because "the priests [had] usurped the right to govern" (p. 198; cf. p. 203). This too highlights a certain sense in which the original Mosaic regime was *not* a full theocracy (i.e., in the first regime someone was doing the governing other than the class of priests). Cf. notes 87, 89, 93, and 94, this chapter.

[38] See my discussion in Chapter 5, note 60.

[39] As Spinoza puts it in the conclusion of chapter 17 (*Theological–Political Treatise*, p. 204), "the divine right, or the right of religion, originates in a contract, without which there is no right but natural right." In other words, the Hebrew Bible and secular political philosophy *agree* in presenting the social contract as the foundation of political right. However, if this is so, was Hobbes correct in presenting absolute monarchy as the natural outcome of such a contract? If Hobbes is right that the Mosaic regime was in principle a monarchy, then the answer (at least as far as the Bible is concerned) is yes. If Spinoza is right that this regime in principle *was not* a monarchy, then the answer is no.

[40] *Theological–Political Treatise*, p. 191.

regime are equivocal, and they are clearly meant to reflect the equivocality of the post-Mosaic regime itself: "[Joshua] alone had the right in emergencies to consult God," but he was (unlike Moses) obliged to do so "through the mediation of the high priest."[41] The same applies to the promulgation of God's commands: "Joshua alone had the authority to do so," but the content of these commands came from the high priest. Who was really in charge? "[T]he complete control of war was in [Joshua's] hands alone,"[42] yet his authority still fell far short of Moses'. When *Moses* transmitted the words of God, these utterances immediately constituted binding "decrees," but after Moses it required Joshua and Aaron–Eleazar working together to generate "commands and decrees."[43] Spinoza presents this ambiguity with respect to true sovereignty within the post-Mosaic regime as a deliberate design on the part of Moses himself: Moses appointed "ministers, not masters of the state."[44] This whole discussion is highly reminiscent of Machiavelli's theme of autocratic princes who lay the foundations for republican regimes (in *Discourses on Livy*, Book 1, chapter 9).[45] Furthermore, just as Joshua's authority was constrained by having to consult God through the mediation of Eleazar, so no less was it the case that Eleazar's authority was constrained insofar as he could deliver his oracles "only when requested by the commander-in-chief or the supreme council or similar authorities, and not whenever he wished, like Moses."[46] The army "swore allegiance not to the commander-in-chief nor to the high priest, but to their religion and to God."[47] The point is that *no one* – neither the commander-in-chief nor the high priest – possessed Moses' singular authority "to make and repeal laws, to decide on war and peace, and to choose men for religious and secular office, all these being the prerogative of a sovereign."[48] The theocratic character of the regime turns out to be in a certain sense a distraction: The true change in the character of the regime was from an absolute monarchy to a republic. The solution to the familiar puzzle of why Spinoza is more sympathetic to the Old Testament Hebrews in chapter 17 than he was in earlier chapters is easy: Spinoza is far more sympathetic to Moses' achievements as a *legislator* than he is to the content of Mosaic *religion*.[49]

---

[41] Ibid., p. 192.

[42] Ibid.

[43] Ibid., p. 193.

[44] Ibid., p. 192.

[45] This Machiavellian theme of the autocrat who founds a republic is not without relevance to twentieth-century politics. Consider, for instance, Anne Norton, *Leo Strauss and the Politics of American Empire* (New Haven: Yale University Press, 2004), p. 135: "Atatürk regarded himself as shepherding Turkey from the sultanate to more democratic forms of rule. He was a dictator, he declared, so that Turkey might never have another."

[46] *Theological–Political Treatise*, pp. 192–193.

[47] Ibid., p. 192.

[48] Ibid.; cf. p. 205: Moses as "an absolute ruler in all matters."

[49] Cf. Menachem Lorberbaum, "Spinoza's Theological–Political Problem," *Hebraic Political Studies*, Vol. 1, No. 2 (Winter 2006): 222: "[T]he TTP develops two readings of the Bible. . . . The former [chapters 1–5] views Moses primarily as a theologian, the latter [chapters 17–18],

Notwithstanding Spinoza's confusing (though telling) suggestion about the Mosaic or post-Mosaic state being a virtual "democracy,"[50] he repeatedly insists that it was "neither a democracy nor an aristocracy nor a monarchy, but a theocracy."[51] What are the attractions of a theocratic regime so understood? To answer this question, we need to consider where things stand, in Spinoza's view, subsequent to Joshua. Each tribe composed in effect its own state on its own territory (joined only by a common religion bound to the Temple), and the captains of the various tribes regulated their own affairs, without need of a commander-in-chief. The Hebrew Commonwealth was now an alliance of confederated states.[52] At this stage one had a dispersion of powers, and eventual conflict among the tribes. Overall, one had a well-functioning theocratic regime that restrained both rulers and ruled in such a way that the ruled were prevented from rebelling and the rulers were prevented from becoming tyrants.[53] There were two main restraints on the rulers: first, the need to appeal to the Levites for interpretation of the laws (making clear that they did not monopolize sovereignty); second, the fact that armies drew upon "the whole citizen body" rather than mercenaries.[54] Echoing a point emphasized earlier in the narrative, these soldiers owed their ultimate allegiance to God, not to any particular captain,[55] and this imposed a significant check on the ambitions of the captains. A further check on the captains implicit in a theocratic regime of this kind was the possibility of prophets' rising up to crystallize popular unrest.[56] The captains could stifle these challenges to their authority aroused by self-proclaimed prophets, but only if the captains were doing a good job of running their states.

---

primarily as a statesman and founder of a polity." See also the account of Moses as an exemplary legislator (and the priestly undoing of the Mosaic project) in Rosenthal, "Why Spinoza Chose the Hebrews," pp. 225–231. One cannot avoid thinking of Rousseau's praise of Calvin in *Social Contract* II.7. Does appreciation for Calvin's contribution as a legislator require Rousseau to admire Calvinist *religion*? The answer is obvious.

[50] Ibid., p. 190.

[51] Ibid., p. 191; cf. pp. 194–195 (where Spinoza repeats the same formula but reverses the order of the conventional regimes). According to the interpretation I am trying to develop in this chapter, the key question for Spinoza (with Hobbes in mind) is not how the theocratic regime founded by Moses differs from a democracy but how it differs from a monarchy.

[52] See note 61, this chapter. In "Spinoza and Harrington: An Exercise in Comparison," *Bijdragenen Mededelingen Betreffende de Geschiedenis der Nerderlanden*, Vol. 102, No. 3 (1987): 435–449, J. G. A. Pocock presents Spinoza as a theorist of sovereignty pure and simple, very much like Hobbes; but Pocock considers only the *Political Treatise* and gives no attention to the complexities of the *Theological–Political Treatise*.

[53] Ibid., p. 195.

[54] Ibid., p. 196.

[55] Ibid., pp. 192, 196.

[56] The parallel discussion in Hobbes focuses on prophets as a source of anarchy – as I discussed in Chapter 5 in my interpretation of *De Cive*, chapter 16, and *Leviathan*, chapter 40. Significantly, Spinoza sees them (at least at this stage of the argument) as a source of liberty. One finds a similar view in J. S. Mill, *Utilitarianism, On Liberty, and Considerations on Representative Government*, ed. H. B. Acton (London: Dent, 1972), pp. 200–201.

Spinoza mentions two other advantages of this theocratic political order: its reliance on meritocratic principles in the selection of captains (i.e., it was not an aristocracy); and its bias in favor of peace over war because the army, being in effect a citizen militia, put decisions about war and peace in the hands of the people who would be required to fight such wars. With respect to the regime's effect on the people (rather than the captains), Spinoza again adopts a surprisingly favorable view of the theocracy. Here Spinoza focuses on the theocratic character of the regime as a spur to "ardent patriotism," a virtue twinned to the vice of disdain for other peoples. In the view of the Hebrews, "they alone were God's children," which inevitably cast non-Hebrews as "God's enemies."[57] Devotion to God and devotion to the state were inseparable, so patriotism and piety were no less inseparable.[58] This section is a dramatic anticipation of Rousseau's account of the Mosaic regime in chapter 2 of *The Government of Poland*, as well as Rousseau's account of Mosaic religion as a *national* religion in the civil-religion chapter of the *Social Contract*.[59] Spinoza is in fact a treasure house of civil-religion reflection precisely because the themes of all of the great figures in the tradition of theory elicited by the problem of civil religion – of Machiavelli, Hobbes, Locke, and Rousseau – intersect and are brought into (sometimes unresolved) dialogue in the pages of the *Theological–Political Treatise*. This discussion is "Rousseauian" because Spinoza not only condemns the Mosaic customs for stoking up mutual hatred between the Hebrews and other peoples (for "hatred that ha[s] its source in strong devotion or piety . . . is the bitterest and most persistent of all kinds of hatred"), but he also *appreciates* the power of these same customs to inspire the Hebrews with a capacity for civic action manifesting "unexampled steadfastness and valour."[60]

Even more impressive from Spinoza's point of view is the fact that the theocratic regime was designed in such a way that these religious bases of patriotism were backed up by a set of institutions giving citizens a compelling *material* stake in devotion to their state: a highly egalitarian distribution of property[61];

---

[57] *Theological–Political Treatise*, p. 197.

[58] Ibid.

[59] Ibid., pp. 197–198: "[T]he patriotism of the Hebrews . . . was so fostered and nourished in their daily ritual that it inevitably became part of their nature. . . . [The effect was to render them] altogether unique and completely distinct from other peoples." This is precisely the basis upon which Rousseau extols Moses as an exemplary founder in *The Government of Poland*.

[60] *Theological–Political Treatise*, p. 198. One is tempted to draw an analogy with contemporary Islam. Consider the following statement by Fatah al-Islam spokesman Abu Salim Taha, quoted in the *Globe & Mail*, May 24, 2007, p. A15: "We are ready to face the Lebanese army. A small number of believers can fight a large number of atheists and Crusaders and win." This is an appeal to "virtue" that would certainly be appreciated by Rousseau, and Spinoza shows that he is capable of appreciating it as well.

[61] Spinoza likely borrowed both the theme of Hebrew egalitarianism and that of Hebrew federalism from Petrus Cunaeus. There is now a very active group of scholars centered around the journal *Hebraic Political Studies*, including Arthur Eyffinger, Guido Bartolucci, Fania Oz-Salzberger, Eric Nelson, and Lea Campos Boralevi, devoted to exploring these themes starting

sturdy provisions for charitable assistance, again backed up by religious sanction; and the "training in obedience" provided by laws that regulated daily life
so rigidly.[62] Up to this point in the narrative of chapter 17, the overwhelming
impression is of a well-ordered and basically admirable regime.[63] Does Spinoza
endorse such a theocracy? Before answering this question, let me summarize my
analysis by schematizing the narrative – which may help to highlight complexities of this regime that are barely captured in Spinoza's deliberately simplifying
classification of the regime as a theocracy.

Stage 1 (first covenant) consists in the rule of God, which corresponds to
authentic theocracy, de facto democracy.

Stage 2 (second covenant) consists in the rule of Moses, which is a theocratic
monarchy, which one can encapsulate as formal theocracy, de facto absolute
monarchy.[64]

Stage 3 consists in the joint-sovereignty regime shared between Joshua and
Aaron–Eleazar. For the regime still to count as a theocracy in the full sense, the
high priest really ought to control ultimate sovereignty (which is what *Hobbes*
asserts with respect to this stage of the regime); but Spinoza emphatically and
decisively rejects this.

Stage 4 consists in the confederation of tribes, with power dispersed
among distinct captains, none of whom retains anything approaching absolute (Mosaic) sovereignty. Is this still a theocracy? Surely it was, for one has
to assume that there is a basic continuity with the original theocratic regime;
otherwise, it would not make sense to evaluate the civic advantages of the
theocracy by considering the structure of the post-Joshua regime. The final

---

with Grotius and Cunaeus and defining a tradition of seventeenth-century "neo-Hebraic republicanism." How Spinoza relates to this interesting tradition is clearly an important question. See
Petrus Cunaeus, *The Hebrew Republic* (Jerusalem: Shalem Press, 2006); and for helpful intro-
ductions to this new scholarly movement, see the essays by Meirav Jones and Kalman Neuman
in *Political Hebraism: Judaic Sources in Early Modern Political Thought*, ed. Gordon Schochet,
Fania Oz-Salzberger, and Meirav Jones (Jerusalem: Shalem Press, 2008). Harrington was a contemporary of Spinoza's who may have drawn the same lesson from Cunaeus's account of the
Hebrew agrarian laws: See Gary Remer, "After Machiavelli and Hobbes: James Harrington's
Commonwealth of Israel," in *Political Hebraism*, pp. 212 and 220. See also Rousseau, *Emile*,
trans. Allan Bloom (New York: Basic Books, 1979), p. 313, note. A comprehensive treatment
of this theme is offered in Eric Nelson, "'For the Land is Mine': The Hebrew Commonwealth
and the Rise of Redistribution," a paper delivered at the "Political Hebraism" conference held
at Princeton University in September, 2008.

[62] *Theological–Political Treatise*, pp. 198–200.

[63] At this point in the narrative (namely the top of p. 200), one could legitimately ask this:
Why is this ancient theocracy *not* "a model to be imitated" (p. 204; Feldman, Introduction,
Theological–Political Treatise, pp. xviii, xxx, xliii)? This is not a question one would be able
to ask four or five pages later.

[64] It goes without saying that it is extremely problematic (not least from Spinoza's own point of
view!) to distinguish temporally between a "stage" at which the theocracy is ruled by God and
a "stage" at which it is ruled by Moses. That, however, is precisely what Spinoza's narrative
suggests. The point, clearly, is that Moses' absolute monarchy is not the primordial outcome
of the Hebrew social contract; it was preceded by a form of democratic republicanism.

stage (prior to conflict and dissolution) maps onto the Dutch republicanism of the 1660s associated with Johan de Witt, as Spinoza himself makes explicit in the course of the narrative.[65]

So what is going on in this strange and unexpected analysis? Spinoza's narrative suggests that a founding of political community originating from a free covenant by naturally free individuals ought not to terminate in absolute monarchy. Mosaic absolute monarchy (the apparently Hobbesian outcome of the state of nature created by the liberation from Egyptian bondage) is not what it appears to be. In principle, Mosaic theocracy is a democracy, or at least a republic. That is, with Spinoza having closely aligned himself with Hobbes in chapter 16, the biblical narrative in chapter 17 represents the beginning of the theoretical movement whereby Spinoza disengages himself from Hobbes.[66] Very much in the same way that Machiavelli conceptualizes the founding of republics by tyrants (e.g., the founding of Rome by Romulus), Moses is a Machiavellian prince who founds a republic (or what ought to have been a republic, if it had been possible to stabilize it in an enduring way).[67] In other words, the whole sequence of suggestions in the biblical narrative of chapter 17 starts to make sense when translated into the categories of political philosophy: Spinoza in effect employs a Machiavellian motif (the founding of republics by princes)[68] to ensure that a Hobbesian state of nature issues in something other than Hobbesian absolute sovereignty. I am inclined toward the hypothesis that the purpose lying behind this whole exercise in scriptural exegesis is simply to

---

[65] Ibid., p. 193. For an account of De Witt's confederated republicanism, see Nadler, *Spinoza: A Life*, pp. 254–259. As Nadler discusses, in moving from republicanism to democracy, Spinoza went substantially further than was acceptable to De Witt (Nadler, pp. 256 and 267).

[66] Cf. Edwin Curley, "Kissinger, Spinoza, and Genghis Khan," in *The Cambridge Companion to Spinoza*, ed. Don Garrett (Cambridge: Cambridge University Press, 1996), pp. 330–332. Curley is right that after defending a version of Hobbesian theory in chapter 16, "we find Spinoza . . . taking much of it back" in chapter 17 (p. 330); and he is also right (as I will discuss later in this interpretation) that "there is a similar movement of thought [namely an embrace of Hobbes followed by a rejection of Hobbes] in the final two chapters" (p. 331). It may be helpful to think of Spinoza's argument in chapters 16–20 in the image of a pendulum swinging back and forth between contradictory positions.

[67] I have discussed the warm embrace of Moses by Machiavelli and Rousseau elsewhere in this book, but for an interesting example of how Moses figures in republican mythology, see the illustration on p. 155 of D. N. DeLuna, "Topical Satire Read back into Pocock's Neo-Harringtonian Moment," in *The Political Imagination in History: Essays Concerning J. G. A. Pocock*, ed. DeLuna (Baltimore: Owlworks, 2006), along with DeLuna's commentary on p. 154. This is a frontispiece to a 1700 edition of the works of Harrington edited by John Toland, and Moses is depicted in a pantheon alongside other heroes of the republican tradition (Solon, Lycurgus, Numa – and Confucius!). Cf. Toland's celebration of the "respublica Mosaica" in Appendix I of *Nazarenus*. See also Jonathan I. Israel, *Radical Enlightenment* (Oxford: Oxford University Press, 2001), p. 611.

[68] Maistre, looking at things from the antirepublican side, makes the same point: See Joseph de Maistre, *Against Rousseau*, ed. Richard A. Lebrun (Montreal: McGill-Queen's University Press, 1996), p. 68 ("even nations destined to be republics have been constituted by kings").

give "theocratic credentials" to an alternative account of the social contract – that is, a more republican–democratic account than *Hobbes*'s monarchical account.[69] Hobbes is the starting point in this sequence of chapters, and appeal to scripture helps Spinoza shift Hobbes's contractarianism in a quite different direction.[70]

After this catalogue of the *advantages* of a well-ordered theocratic state, Spinoza owes us an account of the corresponding *perils* of such a regime. Contrary to what the positive narrative suggests, the Hebrew state is far from being a stable political order, and Spinoza closes the chapter with an account of the seeds of its instability and ultimate collapse. Thus the theme now shifts to the *defects* of the regime – the aspects of the regime that would have had to have been different if it had been designed "to be of longer duration."[71] Indeed, Spinoza goes so far as to refer to the construction of the theocratic order as an expression of divine anger and vengeance – an anger that can be traced all the way back to the original foundation of the Mosaic legislation. Spinoza quotes both Ezekiel ("I polluted them in their gifts") and Tacitus ("God's concern was not for their security, but for vengeance") to this effect.[72] This is an astounding reversal: It switches from a presentation of the regime as a well-ordered system for generating devotion and patriotism to a presentation of the regime as a means of inflicting divine punishment upon the sinful! Here the focus is on the Levites as the priestly class, and on the deep tensions between them and the rest of the people. The Levites only acquired the job of administering the sacred rites after "the firstborn [originally intended for this ministry] were rejected as defiled" as a consequence of their worship of the golden calf.[73] As

---

[69] Spinoza's purpose here is nicely illuminated by an argument posed by Maistre: "Everything that nations have told us of their origins proves that they are agreed in regarding sovereignty as divine in its essence; otherwise they would all have told us very different tales. Never do they speak to us of a *primordial contract*, of voluntary association, of popular deliberation. No historian cites the *primary assemblies* of Memphis or Babylon" (ibid., p. 59). Spinoza, in effect, is suggesting that in *Exodus* we *are* told a tale of political community originating in voluntary association and popular deliberation.

[70] Strong textual evidence for this thesis occurs on p. 213, where Spinoza writes that the Hebrew covenant "is an exact parallel to what we have shown to be the development of a democracy, where all by common consent resolve to live only by the dictates of reason." The Hebrew democracy was unique insofar as it led to the Hebrews' "transferring their right to God," but "this transference was notional rather than practical; for in reality they [at least initially] retained their sovereignty absolutely" (p. 214).

[71] *Theological–Political Treatise*, p. 200.

[72] Ibid.

[73] Ibid. In *the most* puzzling sentence of a generally puzzling chapter, Spinoza writes that "the state might have lasted indefinitely if the just anger of the lawgiver had allowed it to continue in its original form." Ibid., p. 203, cf. p. 204: "its lasting qualities," and p. 205 (first sentence of chapter 18): "might have lasted indefinitely." (As discussed in my interpretation of *Discourses* III.22 in Chapter 4, this image of the indefinitely enduring regime was first conjured up by Machiavelli, perhaps as a way of marking his sharp repudiation of the ancient political philosophers who insisted that all regimes, even the best, inevitably perish. Spinoza alludes to *Discourses* III.22 in his reference to Manlius Torquatus in *Theological–Political Treatise*,

Spinoza had discussed earlier (but without referring to the resentments this had aroused), the Levites, like other priestly classes, were handed a free lunch by the nonpriestly tribes. Spinoza speaks of them as having been "maintained in idleness."[74] Moreover, the rulers, resenting their own dependence on the priests, were only too happy to stoke up the people's "alienat[ion] from the high priest." Worst of all, the other tribes were all too aware that they were providing unearned subsistence for a class of priests who were not their kin precisely as a "penalty" – as a deliberate reminder of God's wrath when the state was first established. What had previously been depicted as a well-functioning and basically admirable system of obedience and civic pride is now shown to be a simmering cauldron of felt humiliation and resentment. It turns out that resentment toward the Levite priests is what initiated the process of fragmentation among all the tribes: The various tribes would "have remained far more closely united" if there had been equal access to the sacred offices among all the tribes.[75] God's purpose here was precisely to bring "desolation" down upon the Hebrews [*ut eos vastarem*] by using the election of the Levites as a continual and stinging reminder of His original wrath.[76]

This widespread popular resentment rebounded on Moses himself,[77] for the people, even during the years of wandering in the desert, seized on the election of the Levites as "a reason for believing that Moses was acting not by divine decree, but at his own pleasure, in that he had chosen his own tribe before all others and had bestowed on his own brother the office of high priest in perpetuity."[78] Having previously set out reasons why the theocratic system was designed in such a way as to ensure that rulers would not become

p. 215.) What the sentence *seems* to suggest is, first, that the episode of the golden calf caused such grief either to Moses or to God (the sentence is unclear about who counts as the relevant "lawgiver") that it prompted introduction of *the* fatal flaw of the whole regime – the appointment of the Levite tribe as a permanent and exclusive priestly class; and second, that if this particular flaw had been avoided (i.e., if the regime had not been founded on righteous anger), the theocracy might have been what it had the promise to be – a perfect and possibly eternal political order. Does Spinoza really believe this?

74 *Theological–Political Treatise*, p. 201.

75 Ibid. It is also relevant to consider whether the resentment against the Levites was rooted in the fact that the Levites were the agents of Moses' slaughter of the sinning Israelites: See *Exodus* 32: 26–28.

76 *Theological–Political Treatise*, pp. 200, 202.

77 This theme of the Israelites' resentment against Moses is, as is much else in Spinoza, proto-Freudian. Cf. Feuer, *Spinoza and the Rise of Liberalism*, p. 299, n. 49. (According to Freud's version of the story, the resentment of the Israelites against Moses and the Levites was related to the fact that *both* Moses *and* the Levites were foreigners, Egyptians.)

78 *Theological–Political Treatise*, p. 202. One cannot help wondering why Aaron's direct involvement in the business of the golden calf does not disqualify him from being the beneficiary of this Mosaic nepotism. This, however, is a puzzle about the biblical narrative, not a puzzle about Spinoza. For a fascinating discussion of how Aaron became, for the Dutch, a symbol of the need for clerical submission to the authority of the state, see Rosenthal, "Why Spinoza Chose the Hebrews," pp. 207–208 and 235–236; cf. Schama, *The Embarrassment of Riches*, pp. 116–121.

tyrants and the ruled would not rebel,[79] Spinoza now presents it precisely as a system whose (deliberate) defects naturally summon up rebellion. As he had emphasized right at the start of this discussion, if being "stiff-necked" and rebellious (as the Israelites were described in God's conversation with Moses at the time of the golden calf episode) turns out to be a continuing trait of the Hebrew nation, this is not a matter of contingent flaws of character but rather points to problems of institutional design in the Mosaic regime.[80]

The overall depiction is of a regime that is both attractive and deeply flawed with respect to its capacity for eliciting civic commitment and either inhibiting or giving cause for rebellion. If basic aspects of the regime, as constructed in the first place, serve not to secure the welfare of the citizens but rather to inflict desolation upon the Hebrews so as to satisfy God's (or Moses') vengeance, then theocracy is certainly not a model for any contemporary state: Hence chapter 18's highlighting of just how misguided a regime the Hebrew theocracy would turn out to be (especially when further debased by the transition to monarchy). Eventually, the problems that had their root in the original construction of the theocracy became so severe that the people abandoned "divine rule" and opted for ordinary monarchy.[81] Of course, this did not solve the fundamental problem – which was rooted in the theocratic division of sovereignty. The kings, being kings, desired "absolute sovereignty," which certainly was not available to them "as long as control over the laws was exercised not by them but by the high priest, who guarded the laws in the sanctuary and interpreted them to the people."[82] All of this was naturally perceived by the kings (rightly so) as a rival "dominion within their dominion," "an empire within their empire," and as "rule by sufferance."[83] Whereas in the earlier narrative, while the regime was being portrayed in a positive light, the sharing of sovereignty was seen as an attractive feature of the regime, Spinoza has now seemingly come round to a Hobbesian analysis according to which split sovereignty is fatal to political order. By the same token, the resort to prophets, seen in Spinoza's earlier analysis as a check on licentious power, is now seen in a Hobbesian light, as a force for anarchy.[84] It is as if all the aspects of the regime that had contributed to Spinoza's positive account of theocracy come to be seen as having an effect precisely opposite to what had previously been claimed. The promise of theocracy was to forestall tyranny by the ruler and rebellion by the people by employing appeals to priestly authority to check the ruler's power; nonetheless,

---

[79] *Theological–Political Treatise*, p. 195.

[80] Ibid., p. 200: "[I]f God had willed their state to be of longer duration, he would ... have given them laws and ordinances of a different kind and would have established a different mode of government."

[81] Ibid., p. 202. As discussed in Chapter 5, Hobbes tells the same story in *Leviathan*, chapter 40 – namely the revolt against theocratic rule, and continuing theocratic subversion of the new regime after institution of the Hebrew monarchy.

[82] *Theological–Political Treatise*, pp. 202–203.

[83] Ibid., pp. 202, 203.

[84] Spinoza is also quite critical of the prophets on p. 207, for reasons akin to Hobbes's reasons.

the end result of this system of split sovereignty was precisely popular rebellion and kingly tyranny.[85] No attempted solution worked: One could only solve the problem by scrapping "the whole constitution."[86] Although the positive narrative developed by Spinoza through most of the chapter is a concerted challenge to Hobbes's account of the same regime, the negative narrative presented at the end of the chapter is a *vindication* of Hobbes. Spinoza in the end was no less convinced than Hobbes was that the Jewish theocracy was an unworkable regime.[87]

In chapter 18 Spinoza borrows the rhetorical trick of chapter 11 of *The Prince*, where Machiavelli says he would not presume to discourse concerning ecclesiastical principalities and then proceeds to devote a whole chapter to this topic: Similarly, Spinoza, at the end of chapter 17, states that he has no desire to discuss the rule of priests in the "second state," but then he goes on to make this the principal theme of chapter 18.[88] In chapter 18, Spinoza pursues a topic that was hinted at in chapter 17 but not developed thematically: the change in the character of the regime from the "first state" (in important respects a kind of democracy)[89] to the "second state" (a full theocracy, with effective sovereignty "usurped" by the class of priests[90]). Religiously, this meant a degeneration into superstition (because the priests were free to promulgate any nonsense they wished), and politically it meant a descent into sectarian strife (because theocracy naturally spawns warfare between sects[91]).

As we saw in the discussion of chapter 17, Hobbes may have been vindicated in his view of the ultimate unworkability of a theocratic regime, but Spinoza certainly has no desire to offer a more general vindication of Hobbes, and, in particular, he has no desire to make any concessions to Hobbes's prescription concerning a suitable cure for theocratic temptations (namely absolute monarchical authority).[92] In this respect, chapter 18 considerably clarifies why so

---

[85] See the discussion on p. 202 of the people naturally tending toward rebellion and the discussion on p. 203 of the monarchy naturally tending toward tyranny.

[86] Ibid., p. 203.

[87] If the "first state" was unworkable *qua* partial theocracy, the "second state" was far worse by virtue of being what Hobbes claimed the first state was, namely a state where absolute sovereignty was held by the priests. A regime that is an absolute theocracy in this sense is so abhorrent to Spinoza that he does not even attempt to analyze it: See p. 204.

[88] Chapter 18 is also shaped by the characteristic Machiavellian trope of an original religion that was pristine and genuinely virtue promoting, and a later priestly religion that was corrupt and morally debilitating. Cf. Spinoza's allusion to religious corruption in his reference to "impious churchmen" on p. 219.

[89] Consider the phrase "as long as the people was sovereign" on p. 207, followed in the next sentence by the phrase "after the people . . . changed the original form of their state to a monarchy." See also p. 209: "[T]hese laws . . . were instituted for a people, or a council, which regarded itself as sovereign."

[90] *Theological–Political Treatise*, p. 206: "usurping the government."

[91] Ibid., p. 206: "For when men begin to dispute with superstitious fervour, and the civil authority favours one side or the other, they cannot be reconciled and inevitably split into sects."

[92] Spinoza's rejection of Hobbes is particularly highlighted on p. 210 in the discussion of Cromwell's displacement of Charles I as merely an alternation between one tyrant and another.

much hangs on Spinoza's earlier dispute with Hobbes: If the high priest *qua* high priest held full sovereignty right from the start, one could not condemn the Second Temple's absolute theocracy as a *corruption* (a "usurpation") of the original regime. For the priests to take control of lawmaking and the issuing of decrees[93] (and even issues of legal judgment and excommunication! – not a neutral topic for Spinoza[94]) represented a dramatic departure from their original and constitutional function of performing sacred rites and merely interpreting what God intended with His laws. One could say that for Spinoza, the corruption of the priests went hand in hand with the corruptions of a monarchical regime (which is not what the Mosaic regime originally was). During the premonarchical period, wars were fought to secure the noble ends of "peace and freedom," whereas with the change to a monarchical regime, war became the instrument of a politics of "glory."[95] Hobbes's great mistake, Spinoza implies, is his failure to appreciate the impossibility of kings' respecting "the ancient rights of the people," for respecting these rights renders a king the people's "servant rather than its master," and this is intolerable for kings as kings.[96] The import of *Hobbes's* version of the Mosaic founding is that (at least in the biblical story) there *were* no such "ancient rights," and so it becomes one of Spinoza's leading purposes in chapter 17 to supply an alternative version of the Mosaic founding.

In chapter 17, very surprisingly, Spinoza had made substantial concessions to the civic attractions of a Mosaic regime. Yet notwithstanding Spinoza's efforts in that chapter to appreciate the potential advantages of such a regime, it is clear by the end of chapter 18 that a Mosaic regime is completely irrelevant to the challenges of regulating political order in non-Mosaic states, and that a Mosaic theocracy can in no way offer what the Dutch Calvinists conceived it to be – "a model to be imitated."[97] This, of course, does not mean that there

---

It is true that Spinoza refers to Charles as a "lawful king" and presents Cromwell as a worse tyrant than his predecessor, but the theme that Spinoza is illustrating here is precisely the equivalence of monarchy and tyranny.

[93] *Theological–Political Treatise*, p. 206: Under the original constitution, the high priests "had no right to issue decrees, only the right to give God's answers when requested by the captains or the councils."

[94] Ibid., p. 205: According to the original constitution of the polity, "it was not for [the priests] to judge citizens or to excommunicate anyone." See also p. 218: "No one has the right and power...to excommunicate...except by the authority and permission of the sovereign." Apparently, as is pointed out in Jan W. Wojcik, "'Behold the fear of the Lord,'" in *Heterodoxy, Spinozism, and Free Thought*, ed. Berti et al., p. 357, note, this issue of rightful powers of excommunication goes to the core of what defines Erastianism: "In the narrow sense of the term, an 'Erastian' is...one who believes that the Church has no power to excommunicate [as opposed to] the broader sense in which it is used today to refer to one who believes that the State, and not the Church, has supremacy in ecclesiastical affairs." See also Johann P. Somerville, *Thomas Hobbes: Political Ideas in Historical Context* (New York: St. Martin's Press, 1992), pp. 127–134.

[95] *Theological-Political Treatise*, p. 207.

[96] Ibid., p. 209.

[97] Ibid., p. 204. See note 20, this chapter.

are not crucial lessons for contemporary politics to be drawn from the story of the Hebrews. The moral of chapter 18 is not that the theocratic experience of the ancient Hebrews is irrelevant, but *on the contrary*, that the effects of their theocracy are *all too relevant* to contemporary politics: Theocracy (especially in the context of a fully monarchical regime) is a recipe for civil war and endless bloodletting. In fact, there is a double lesson: If one wants to see the laws corrupted, one should transfer sovereignty vested in the people over to a king[98]; and if one wants to see the whole civic order corrupted, one should hand unlimited power to the priests. If the combination of republicanism and democracy yields peace and freedom, then the combination of monarchy and theocratic rule yields the quest for "glory," "fatal ambition,"[99] and rivers of blood.

Spinoza returns to the rhetoric of "Pharisees" employed earlier in the *Treatise*. This allows him to draw a direct line between "the anger of the Pharisees" that resulted in crucifixion of the innocent Christ and the iniquity of *contemporary* Pharisees who solicit the tyrannical "anger of the mob" in targeting victims no less innocent (including Koerbagh and later De Witt).[100] This is the stage at which violent sectarianism is let loose, and "the authority of sectarian leaders" displaces "the authority of [civil] magistrates."[101] At this point in the narrative, Spinoza allows himself to make explicit that this is a direct commentary on the contemporary situation – with its deference to power-hungry priests,[102] its persecution of "heretics," and its imminent purging of republican leaders[103] – to the extent that this was not already obvious to his readers. (Nadler puts it nicely: "It would have taken a particularly dim wit for a contemporary *predikant* not to recognize himself in Spinoza's depiction of the Jewish high priests."[104]) Just as the Hebrew commonwealth was originally founded on "the ancient rights of the people"[105] and fell into desolation when monarchy and priestly rule took over, so the original constitution of Holland

---

[98] *Theological–Political Treatise*, p. 208: "[A]s long as the people held the reins of governments, the laws remained uncorrupted and were observed with greater constancy."

[99] Ibid.

[100] Ibid. See Nadler, *Spinoza: A Life*, chapters 10 and 11. Rosenthal's article cited in note 20 gives a particularly good account of what, from Spinoza's point of view, was at stake in these contemporary Dutch events. Cf. Spinoza's reference in chapter 20 to that "corrupted" kind of state "where superstitious and ambitious men who cannot tolerate men of integrity have gained such a great reputation that the common people pay more heed to them than to the sovereign" (*Theological–Political Treatise*, p. 225). See also p. 227: Illiberal laws "pander to . . . the anger of those who cannot endure enlightened minds." Spinoza's references to "the frenzied anger of the mob" (ibid.) read almost like a premonition of the terrible fate meted out to De Witt.

[101] *Theological–Political Treatise*, p. 209.

[102] Cf. p. 228, where he speaks of "the real schismatics" and their "lust for supremacy."

[103] Johan de Witt was savagely murdered by an Orangist mob just two years after the publication of the *Theological–Political Treatise*.

[104] Nadler, *Spinoza: A Life*, p. 284.

[105] *Theological–Political Treatise*, p. 209.

was also not a monarchical one but rather allowed the people to retain ultimate sovereignty.[106] The revolt against Philip II was merely a reassertion of the "original sovereignty" of the Estates when confronted with a monarchical usurper.[107] The transformation of the Hebrew commonwealth from a state founded on the sovereignty of the people to one based on monarchical (i.e., tyrannical) principles – especially one dominated by priests – was a recipe for "utter ruin,"[108] and Spinoza ends the chapter by suggesting that exactly the same analysis applies to Holland.

Finally, after the long detour of chapters 17–18, we get the ultimate Spinozistic argument for (a) the exclusion of ecclesiastical authority from the domain of civil-state authority and (b) the rights of "individual free judgment."[109] These are both core liberal principles: Chapter 19 is devoted to articulating the first, and chapter 20 is devoted to articulating the second. What we have in chapters 16–20 is a steady *oscillation* between the Hobbesian and Lockean poles of Spinoza's political thought. Chapter 19 is again a decidedly Hobbesian chapter, that is, a reassertion of the full power of the state to ordain authoritatively what counts as piety and what religious duty requires. Nadler offers a helpful distinction between outer piety and "inner piety": The former is subject to the sovereign's decree whereas the latter "is a matter of inalienable, private right [which] cannot be legislated, not even by the sovereign."[110] Notwithstanding Spinoza's commitment to liberal ideas of individual freedom and conscientious judgment, Spinoza is *not* a liberal when it comes to defining the relationship between religion and the state. The liberal idea is the idea of *separating* the realm of religion and that of politics; the civil-religion idea is the idea of empowering the state to legislate religious norms according to what is dictated by the state's own purpose and responsibilities. Characterized thus, Spinoza is clearly on the civil-religion side.[111] We are back to the question that has run through all these chapters: How do we reconcile Spinoza's liberalism with

---

[106] Ibid., p. 211: "[S]overeign right was always vested in the Estates."

[107] Ibid.

[108] Ibid. For some related references, see Mark Goldie, "The Civil Religion of James Harrington," in *The Languages of Political Theory in Early-Modern Europe*, ed. Anthony Pagden (Cambridge: Cambridge University Press, 1987), p. 210, n. 32.

[109] *Theological–Political Treatise*, p. 209.

[110] Nadler, *Spinoza: A Life*, p. 284. Spinoza's version of this distinction (*Theological–Political Treatise*, p. 212) is "*acts* of piety" ("the outward forms of religion") vs. "piety itself" ("the inward worship of God").

[111] This is enunciated most explicitly on p. 217: "As for the arguments by which *my opponents seek to separate religious right from civil right*, maintaining that only the latter is vested in the sovereign while the former is vested in the universal church, these are of no account, being so trivial as not even to merit refutation" (emphasis added). As I put it in the next paragraph, Spinoza wants a *one-way* firewall between clerical authority and state power. Nothing in the domain of religious right is in principle off limits vis-à-vis civil right, apart from the right of individuals to think what they will in the privacy of their own minds (expressed publicly to some degree in the "freedom of philosophizing" *qua* free speech). The problems start when the *priests* define what is and is not religiously acceptable, which then leads to blasphemy laws, identification of heretics, and so on.

his commitment to a Hobbes-style civil religion where the *state* is in charge of religious norms and practices?

Spinoza wants to erect a firewall between the authority of priests and the power of the state, but this is meant to be a firewall that operates in one direction only. The point is not to prevent the state from legislating in regard to matters of religion but rather to prevent clerics and theologians from infringing on the right of civil magistrates to decide matters of "state business" – including who to punish and who to excommunicate.[112] What we have here is still in effect a civil religion *à la* Hobbes: "[I]t is... the duty of the sovereign alone to decide what form piety towards one's neighbor should take.... the sovereign is the interpreter of religion.... no one can rightly obey God unless [in his practice of piety] he obeys all the decrees of the sovereign."[113] The sphere within which individuals can think freely and judge conscientiously (the space of liberalism) can be secured only when religious authority has been severely constrained, and *that* is only possible when the state is empowered to trump the authority of the various sects. This is, once again, a strongly Hobbesian line of thought.

"Those who hold the sovereign power... must be both interpreters and guardians" not only of civil law *but also of religious law*.[114] Whereas Spinoza in chapter 17 seemed to suggest that it was politically advantageous to have sovereignty split between captains and high priests, he now insists that "a division of the sovereignty" is wholly unacceptable, and because sovereignty cannot straddle the civil–ecclesiastical divide, it must repose totally on the civil side (encompassing matters pertaining to the regulation of religion). Because sovereignty is indivisible, "God has no special kingdom over men except through the medium of temporal rulers."[115] Piety is identical to whatever serves the welfare of the commonwealth,[116] and therefore the temporal ruler who genuinely cares about securing the common welfare thereby satisfies (in fact defines) the highest standard of piety. "[I]n modern times religion... belongs solely to the right of the sovereign."[117]

[A]nyone who seeks to deprive the sovereign of [the authority to decide matters of religion] is attempting to divide the sovereignty; and as a result, as happened long ago

---

[112] *Theological–Political Treatise*, pp. 208, 205–206; cf. p. 216, where he speaks of "the sovereign, to whom alone it belongs to transact public business."

[113] Ibid., pp. 215–216.

[114] Ibid., p. 212.

[115] Spinoza has a very simple syllogism to "prove" the validity of this proposition. There was no possible idea of justice in the state of nature. Justice is a product of political order. However, at the same time "God's kingdom" consists in nothing other than "the rule of justice and charity." Therefore the kingdom of God and the kingdom of the civil sovereign are coterminous. This proof, Spinoza adds, has equal force whether one comes to true religion via prophetic means or via rational means. See *Theological–Political Treatise*, p. 213. Spinoza also has a second proof: Because it involves a false conception of God for God to be "conceived as a ruler or lawgiver" (cf. the first epigraph to Chapter 10 of this book), the only possible source for *legislation* of religious laws is the temporal sovereign (p. 214).

[116] Ibid., p. 215.

[117] Ibid., pp. 217–218.

in the case of the kings and priests of the Hebrews, there will inevitably arise strife and dissensions that can never be allayed. Indeed, he who seeks to deprive the sovereign of this authority is paving the way to his own ascendancy.... For what decisions can be taken by sovereigns if this right is denied them?[118]

As in chapter 16, this is a straightforwardly Hobbesian position.

In the context of rebutting those who assert the independent authority of clerics, Spinoza returns to the issue that divides him from Hobbes: Was the high priest, subsequent to Moses, the true sovereign? No, "the authority to carry out... priestly duties" was *derivative* of the *civil* sovereignty reposing in Moses, and therefore the high priest was neither the locus of unified sovereignty nor even a freestanding holder of partial sovereignty; the high priest was merely one who fulfilled certain offices conferred upon him by the civil magistrate (which is what Moses first and foremost was).[119] Still, this "quibble" between Spinoza and Hobbes (related to their opposing views concerning monarchy and republicanism) does not detract from their much more fundamental agreement: Religion must be rigorously subordinated to the absolute trumping authority of the civil state. It is true that during the *second* commonwealth, the priests commanded total sovereignty,[120] but central to Spinoza's account is the insistence that this was a case of improper "usurpation" of rule as established according to the original covenant.

So why is it so hard to persuade Christians that it is better for the peace of the commonwealth *and for religion itself* for the determination of suitable expressions of piety to be relegated to a *state* religion presided over by a temporal sovereign? Answering this question requires an understanding of the crucial difference between the origins of Judaism and the origins of Christianity – a difference that from a political point of view strongly favors Judaism. Moses' religion *was* a state religion – a religion legislated by the state's founder, Moses himself. By the same token, it was two kings, David and David's son Solomon, who conceived and built the Temple and organized all the details of worship within it.[121] Christianity, by contrast, originated as a set of teachings promulgated by "men of private station... long accustomed to address[ing] private religious assemblies... without any regard to the state."[122] In addition, the

---

[118] Ibid., p. 218. Why is the division of sovereignty now presented as a fatal flaw of the Hebrew constitution when it was presented in (much of) chapter 17 as decidedly a political advantage? This is a key puzzle in the group of chapters we are interpreting in this chapter, and my reference to the oscillation between Hobbesian and Lockean poles of Spinoza's political thought is a proposed solution to this puzzle: When Spinoza wants to accord theoretical privilege to republicanism over monarchy, he plays up the theoretical advantages of divided sovereignty, and when he wants to emphasize the dangers of theocratic challenges to temporal authority, he presents divided sovereignty as an intractable problem *à la* Hobbes. It is helpful to think of Spinoza's interpretation of the Hebrew commonwealth as a kind of theoretical tightrope-wire act.

[119] Ibid., p. 217.

[120] Ibid.

[121] Ibid., pp. 220–221. Strictly speaking, David designed the Temple and Solomon built it. *I Chronicles*, chapter 28, explains why Solomon rather than David actually built the Temple.

[122] *Theological–Political Treatise*, pp. 219–220.

clerics who presided over this church through the centuries were absolutely determined not to yield the autonomous authority that originally defined the religion. A key device in maintaining this authority was to envelop religion in convoluted theological doctrines and obscure metaphysics,[123] and Spinoza's advice to "sovereigns of our times" is to make sure that they do not let themselves fall into this trap of "theologized" religion.[124]

Having in chapter 19 conferred upon the civil state full sovereignty with respect to legislation of "*acts* of piety," that is, "*outward* forms of religion,"[125] Spinoza now makes emphatically clear that this right of legislation does *not* apply to "beliefs." "All these are matters belonging to individual right, which no man can surrender even if he should so wish."[126] Part of Spinoza's argument rests on the notion that if a sovereign is in fact powerless to achieve X, legislation of X cannot be a legitimate right of the sovereign. ("[T]he right of sovereigns is determined by their power."[127]) One way of formulating the Spinozistic principle here is to say that if it requires a wholesale contravention of human nature to uphold a certain right of the sovereign, that right is nonexistent.[128] It is a natural human trait for human beings to form their own opinions, and having formed them, to communicate them to others. Therefore it is a misguided interpretation of the rights of sovereignty to get into the (totalitarian) business of legislating beliefs.[129] It follows from the foundation of the state in a social contract that its whole rationale consists in *security* for the citizens (the security they lacked in the precivil state of nature). Therefore, any

---

[123] Ibid., pp. 220. Another key device was the trick of requiring clerical celibacy because no king, by definition, would be willing to pay this price for merging monarchical authority and the authority associated with being "the supreme interpreter of religion."

[124] Ibid., p. 221; cf. p. 229: "[L]aws enacted concerning speculative matters are quite useless."

[125] Ibid., p. 212.

[126] Ibid., p. 222.

[127] Ibid., p. 223. This statement forms a bridge between the contractarian theory of the *Theological–Political Treatise* and the right equals power doctrine of the *Political Treatise*. Needless to say, it is bizarre to offer a statement like this on the same page on which Spinoza writes that "the purpose of the state is, in reality, freedom" (cf. note 6, this chapter, as well as Chapter 9, note 6).

[128] Cf. *Theological–Political Treatise*, p. 227: One should opt for that system of government that "is in closest accord with human nature." According to Spinoza, this principle favors democracy because a democratic form of government "comes closest to the natural state" (p. 228).

[129] This is of course an anachronism. Spinoza speaks of how "the most tyrannical government" would aspire to shape its citizens (p. 223). However, our contemporary vocabulary of totalitarianism helps quite a bit to convey Spinoza's argument.

Obviously, not every tyranny is "totalitarian," but arguably the Spanish and Portuguese Inquisition *was*. It is hardly surprising that someone coming out of a Marrano background would be particularly sensitive to the notion that the state should content itself with enforcing conformity of outward behavior and not seek to police inner conviction as well. Spinoza never refers to what the Inquisition inflicted upon Jews and Muslims, but this historical-biographical experience is implicitly inscribed in Spinoza's text. For an interesting attempt to trace patterns in Spinoza's life and thought back to Marrano "patterns of experience," see Yirmiyahu Yovel, *Spinoza and Other Heretics, Vol. 1: The Marrano of Reason* (Princeton, NJ: Princeton University Press, 1989).

attempt to terrorize members of the state (which is what would be necessary to dictate their beliefs) contradicts the very nature of the state in regard to its normative foundations. A state constructed on contractarian principles cannot trample on our most inviolable natural rights, and that is exactly what would be entailed in the state denying people the right to believe what they believe and to think what they think. In short, "the purpose of the state is, in reality, freedom."[130]

Spinoza acknowledges that speech is located somewhere *between* (free) thought and (legitimately legislated) outward conduct – "words can be treasonable as well as deeds" – and therefore specifying the appropriate normative principle is a little more complicated than it would be if thought and conduct were an exhaustive disjunction.[131] "[T]here is a considerable diversity in the free judgment of men.... it is impossible that all should think alike and speak with one voice."[132] Although Rawls never refers to Spinoza in any of his works,[133] Spinoza here anticipates what Rawls calls "the burdens of judgment": namely the idea that individuals left to judge matters according to their own lights will spontaneously generate a wide diversity of distinct opinions.[134] If one gives ten individuals liberty to form their own judgments on a particular matter, one should expect to be confronted with ten interestingly different points of view. The decrees of the sovereign must be obeyed, but to challenge a misguided law by "submit[ting one's] opinion to the judgment of the sovereign power" is to "act as a good citizen."[135] The idea here is that to challenge existing laws by an appeal to the passions amounts to sedition, whereas to offer one's opinions in a spirit of dispassionate reason is a form of responsible citizenship[136] and should be perceived as such even by the sovereign who is the source of binding decrees. Spinoza thereby stretches the boundaries of free thought, and he makes the case that if we have an inalienable "right to reason and judge," this right extends also to speaking – provided it is not emotive or rhetorical speaking but speaking in the mode of "rational

---

[130] *Theological–Political Treatise*, p. 223.

[131] Ibid. On p. 229, Spinoza says that if the sovereign limits itself to regulating "men's actions," it follows that each individual should have liberty "to think what he will and to say what he thinks." This clearly presumes that speech belongs on the side of thought rather than action – even though this is put in question by Spinoza's admission that one can commit treason through speech.

[132] Ibid., p. 224; cf. p. 228, where he states that "all men cannot think alike."

[133] This fact is actually very odd, considering that Spinoza is one of the key figures in the intellectual tradition that Rawls makes his own – namely the contractarian tradition.

[134] Good evidence of this view in Spinoza is offered in Letter 76, where Spinoza claims that Islam has constructed the most formidable machinery of any religion for "controlling men's minds" because "no schisms have arisen in their Church." Spinoza, *The Letters*, trans. Samuel Shirley (Indianapolis: Hackett, 1995), p. 343. The claim itself is completely wrong because it takes no account of the three branches of Islam (Sunni, Shi'a, and Kharijite), but the point is that human beings will spontaneously form a diversity of opinions unless there exists an all-powerful ecclesiastical authority whose purpose is to impose uniformity.

[135] *Theological–Political Treatise*, p. 224.

[136] Ibid.

conviction."[137] Naturally, Spinoza is aware that an argument for free speech is (politically) far more ambitious than an argument for free thought. Nonetheless, he insists that one cannot really respect freedom of thought without making considerable allowance for freedom of speech as well.

By analogy with religion, loyalty to the state is properly judged by *works*; therefore one should err on the side of allowing maximum liberty of opinion. The wise legislator will know better than to try to police every vice: "He who seeks to regulate everything by law will aggravate vices rather than correct them."[138] Driving too firm a wedge between free thought (which cannot be policed) and free speech (which can) will result in a citizenry of sycophants and plotters. Precisely the best and most pious citizens will be the most resentful, and this in itself will constitute a corruption of the state. The policing of beliefs will tend to target not the "villains" but the "men of good character,"[139] and the net effect will be to breed just the kind of vicious sectarianism analyzed in chapter 18.[140]

Chapter 20 is the consummated statement of Spinoza's liberalism. If we have relinquished to the sovereign power our natural rights of self-defense, and even our right to "defend our religion," we have *not* relinquished (nor can we relinquish) our natural right to think freely. If political life is a balance between obedience and liberty, then chapter 16 is an articulation of the imperatives of obedience whereas chapter 20 is an articulation of the unadulterated claims of liberty. Having in chapter 16 come up with a social-contract theory that puts most of the weight on absolute state sovereignty (intended, according to our reading, to put a severe clamp on the political claims of religion), Spinoza, in chapter 20, swings to the other side of the balance and puts all his emphasis on liberty and conscientious judgment. As even Hobbes had to some extent anticipated, obedience pertains to outward conduct, whereas liberty pertains to inner conviction.[141]

One should note how chapter 20's distinction between obedience and liberty maps onto the piety–philosophy distinction developed in chapters 13–15: As we saw in the previous chapter of this book, a crucial move in Spinoza's case for liberalism is his endeavor to drive a substantial wedge between the pursuit of

---

[137] Ibid.: *Acting* "against the sovereign's decree is definitely an infringement of his right, [but] this is not the case with thinking, judging, *and consequently with speaking too*, provided one does no more than express or communicate one's opinion, defending it through rational conviction alone" (emphasis added).

[138] Ibid., p. 225.

[139] Ibid., p. 226.

[140] Spinoza explicitly harks back to "the lessons learnt from the history of the Hebrews" (ibid., p. 227). On p. 228, Spinoza refers to the Remonstrant–Counter-Remonstrant strife as if it belonged to the remote past, but as noted in Chapter 10, note 8, Spinoza is surely aware that this kind of nasty sectarianism was still very much alive in Amsterdam in his own time.

[141] As we will subsequently see in Part III, Carl Schmitt interprets the Spinoza–Hobbes relationship as a case in which Spinoza exploits a *possibility* of liberalism in Hobbes's thought that is indeed present in Hobbes, but that constitutes no more than a germ of later liberalism. This is, to be sure, a reasonable interpretation, but Schmitt manages to cast it within a larger theoretical framework that is both morally and intellectually ugly.

truth and the practice of (conventional) piety. Religion enforces obedience, but this is done according to the superintending regulation of the state; it is in both cases crucial to see the extent to which Spinoza, very tellingly, identifies freedom with philosophy. Religion is the sphere within which people who do not have the capacity to reason freely for themselves are provided with guidance about how to live virtuously. However, in pursuing this mission, the agencies of religion are, as they are for Hobbes, themselves submitted to guidance by the state:

[G]overnments are the guardians and interpreters of religious law as well as civil law, and they alone have the right to decide what is just and unjust, what is pious and impious.[142]

Nevertheless, this is compatible with the most important liberties, for these same governments "can best retain this right and preserve the state in safety only by granting to the individual citizen the right to have his own opinions and to say what he thinks."[143]

There are similar tensions in the final chapters of the *Theological–Political Treatise* to those I discussed in the previous two chapters. Spinoza is involved in a delicate balancing act: On one hand he is trying to open up more space for individual liberty; on the other hand, he is trying to prevent priests and religious authorities from exploiting this freedom in the interests of trumping state authority. Giving the state unlimited authority to legislate religion corresponds to civil religion *à la* Hobbes. That, at least, is where the conclusion of chapter 16 (as well as much of chapter 19) tends. It may seem paradoxical for a liberal like Spinoza to go in this direction, but if we have correctly penetrated Spinoza's intentions, then he is driven by the same theoretical imperatives that drove Hobbes's civil religion.

What is unique about Spinoza's political philosophy is that it maintains *both* Hobbesian civil religion *and* the beginnings of a properly liberal politics in an uneasy (and highly unstable) balance. Notwithstanding the Hobbesian moments in his political thought, Spinoza was the one who launched the crusade for liberalism. This long struggle had the outcome Spinoza intended. How do we know this? Because Freud's *Future of an Illusion*, unlike Hobbes's *Behemoth* and Spinoza's *Ethics*, was not published posthumously.[144]

---

[142] *Theological–Political Treatise*, p. 7.
[143] Ibid.
[144] It should be obvious that this "triumph of liberalism" remains even today no more than a very partial and qualified one. As noted elsewhere in this book, religion remains formidably strong in the contemporary world, and the versions of religion that are strongest are often highly illiberal ones.

I am very grateful to Eric Nelson, Ofir Haivry, and the late Emile Perreau-Saussine for valuable suggestions in response to this interpretation of Spinoza when I presented it to a conference on "Political Hebraism" held at Princeton University in September 2008.

12

John Locke

The Liberal Paradigm

[T]here ought to be no Power over the Consciences of men.

— Thomas Hobbes[1]

I have often wondered that men who make a boast of professing the Christian religion, which is a religion of love, joy, peace, temperance and honest dealing with all men, should quarrel so fiercely and display the bitterest hatred towards one another day by day, so that these latter characteristics make known a man's creed more readily than the former.

— Baruch Spinoza[2]

[Y]ou know how easy it is under pretense of spiritual jurisdiction to hook in all secular affairs.

— John Locke[3]

The idea that religion and politics don't mix was invented by the Devil to keep Christians from running their own country.

— Rev. Jerry Falwell[4]

Unfortunately, there is no coherent philosophical defense of moderation as moderation, or what might be called "good-natured and liberal muddling through." This is because philosophy is by nature immoderate.

— Stanley Rosen[5]

---

[1] Thomas Hobbes, *Leviathan*, ed. C. B. Macpherson (London: Penguin, 1968), p. 711.
[2] Baruch Spinoza, *Theological-Political Treatise*, 2nd ed., trans. Samuel Shirley (Indianapolis: Hackett, 2001), p. 4.
[3] John Locke, *Political Writings*, ed. David Wootton (Indianapolis: Hackett, 2003), p. 138.
[4] Sermon, July 4, 1976.
[5] Stanley Rosen, *Hermeneutics as Politics* (New York: Oxford University Press, 1987), p. 138.

Is it true that there is no coherent philosophical defense of moderation as moderation? Not all philosophers are Platonists or Nietzscheans. In fact, there is a substantial liberal subtradition within the history of political philosophy whose purpose is precisely to demonstrate that not all philosophy is immoderate. Clearly, John Locke is one of the founders of this tradition of liberal political philosophy, and taking liberalism seriously as a philosophy of moderation entails taking Locke seriously.

Hobbes, as quoted in the epigraph to Chapter 5, asked, How can we have peace while Christianity is our religion? Locke believed that he had an answer to this question (namely mutual toleration between Christian sects). It is apparent, then, that Hobbes is the representative of the civil-religion tradition with whom Locke is most immediately in dialogue (whether by intention or not).[6] If liberalism as a theoretical tradition is partly defined by its rejection of (or uneasiness about) the civil-religion project, then Locke's debate with Hobbes will clearly constitute an important chapter in the dialogue about civil religion within the history of political philosophy.[7] So let us start with a restatement of Hobbes. As with so much else in their political philosophies, Hobbes addresses the same fundamental problem that Locke addresses, though their ultimate solutions may be radically different.[8] This is certainly the case with respect to

---

[6] Of course, insofar as the early ("pre-Lockean") Locke embraced a Hobbesian commitment to "the need for an absolute state authority to impose religious orthodoxy" (David Wootton, Introduction to Locke, *Political Writings*, ed. Wootton, p. 28), this intended or implicit dialogue with Hobbes also constitutes a dialogue with his own earlier self. Cf. Richard Vernon, *The Career of Toleration: John Locke, Jonas Proast, and after* (Montreal: McGill-Queen's University Press, 1997), p. 25.

[7] Mark Goldie has made the suggestion that even in Locke, there is a significant civil-religion dimension. He writes that because Locke excludes Catholics from his regime of toleration on the grounds that they are not reliable patriots, it follows that "Locke does not advocate just the liberal privatization of religion, but has a doctrine of civil religion." Mark Goldie, "The Civil Religion of James Harrington," in *The Languages of Political Theory in Early-Modern Europe*, ed. Anthony Pagden (Cambridge: Cambridge University Press, 1987), p. 202. This is an interesting suggestion: One could indeed say that Locke's refusal to extend toleration to Catholics has the aspect of a civil religion because, as for Hobbes before him and Rousseau after him, Catholicism presents itself to Locke as the most toxic version of the view that religionists are subject to *two* authorities, with in this case the civil authority subordinate to papal authority (cf. the anti-Catholic arguments in *Political Writings*, ed. Wootton, pp. 138–139 and 202–203). Obviously, there are much less sympathetic ways to interpret Locke's policy toward Catholics (see, e.g., Edward G. Andrew, *Patrons of Enlightenment*, Toronto: University of Toronto, 2006, chapter 4 for an argument upholding Bayle's superiority to Locke as a theorist of toleration). It should also be noted that at least one important Locke scholar, namely Jeremy Waldron, is skeptical that Locke (in his mature political thought) is opposed to toleration of Catholics; Waldron's revisionist argument is presented in *God, Locke, and Equality* (Cambridge: Cambridge University Press, 2002), pp. 218–223. In an earlier article, however ("Locke: Toleration and the Rationality of Persecution," in *Justifying Toleration*, ed. Susan Mendus, Cambridge: Cambridge University Press, 1988, p. 73), Waldron adheres to the standard view rather than his later revisionist view.

[8] Cf. Mark Lilla, *The Stillborn God, Religion, Politics, and the Modern West* (New York: Knopf, 2007), p. 298: "Hobbes thought that his science proved the need for an absolute sovereign exercising absolute control over public worship. But those who followed his lead soon saw that

their distinctive approaches to the problem of politics and religion. As always, we can take our cue from Rousseau's encapsulation of Hobbes's view:

[T]he philosopher Hobbes is the only one who clearly saw the evil and its remedy, who dared to suggest reuniting the two heads of the eagle, and fully restoring that political unity without which no state or government will ever be well-constituted.

Rousseau, like Hobbes, was preoccupied with the problem of *sovereignty*, that is, the need for a robust unity within the political community to sustain political order. Rousseau and Hobbes had radically different ideas about how to secure political sovereignty (or the "one-ness" of political authority), but they were agreed in seeing that religion, with its implication of a "two-ness," a duality, of ultimate authority, posed a radical threat to the idea of sovereignty, of undivided authority. As Rousseau says, the Hobbesian solution is a "reuniting [of] the two heads of the eagle": the clear subordination of religious authority to *civil* (i.e., political) authority. Hobbes puts it this way in *Leviathan*, chapter 31:

[T]here be [many] that think there may be . . . more Soveraigns than one, in a Commonwealth; and set up a *Supremacy* against the *Soveraignty*; *Canons* against *Lawes*; and a *Ghostly Authority* against the *Civill*. . . . Now seeing it is manifest, that the Civill Power, and the Power of the Common-wealth is the same thing; and that Supremacy, and the Power of making Canons, and granting Faculties, implyeth a Common-wealth; it followeth, that where one is Soveraign, another Supreme; where one can make Lawes, and another make Canons; there must needs be two Common-wealths, of one & the same Subjects; which is a Kingdome divided in it selfe, and cannot stand.[9]

As Hobbes forcefully expresses here, there is an intrinsic problem of religious authority in relation to civil authority. All religions assert an authority of their own said to be sanctioned by *divine* authority. The obligations asserted by a civil magistrate, enshrined in the laws of the commonwealth, are bound to look quite paltry in relation to claims to authority asserting divine sanction. As Hobbes sees clearly, there is no easy way to separate these implicitly opposing claims to authority. What is at stake, fundamentally, is a clash of sovereignty: "[T]hey are . . . two Kingdomes, and every Subject is subject to two Masters."[10] It follows from the very idea of sovereignty, as Hobbes understands it (and again, Rousseau agrees), that this is an intolerable situation. Hobbes's ultimate theoretical response is to propose a kind of "theocracy" in which theological–ecclesiastical authority is appropriated by the civil sovereign himself, to ensure that no competing claims to authority are asserted by churches or by priests. If our most urgent need as citizens is to inhabit a *single* community of civic authority, then the intrinsic threat to this singularity of political sovereignty emanating from religions must be neutralized through the (political) imposition

---

religious variety and toleration might attain the same basic end of making political life peaceful, prosperous, and reasonable."

[9] *Leviathan*, ed. Macpherson, p. 370.
[10] Ibid.

of a single shared civic religion. Rousseau is right that Hobbes anticipates his civil-religion idea, for reasons that are basically the same as those that motivate Rousseau's own formulation of the civil-religion notion. A political community that is not joined together under the same laws and the same ultimate authority is not really a political community at all, but merely a confederation of sects waiting to resume war against rival sects.[11]

That can suffice as a restatement of Hobbes and Rousseau. Now let us look at Locke, who formulates a completely different solution to the problem of different religions inhabiting the same political space. Is there some way of respecting the claims that these religious communities make upon their own members while neutralizing the potential threat that they pose to the shared civic community embodied in the state? Locke's *A Letter Concerning Toleration* is intended to provide his answer to this question.[12]

Locke is the first one to offer a thoroughgoing philosophical account of what later comes to be called "the separation of church and state." The enterprise here is exactly the one that Hobbes declared to be an impossible task – namely to draw a boundary between the proper authority of churches and the proper authority of the state.[13] Locke writes,

I esteem it above all things necessary to distinguish exactly the Business of Civil Government from that of Religion, and to settle the just Bounds that lie between the one and the other. If this be not done, there can be no end put to the Controversies that will be always arising, between those that have, or at least pretend to have, on the one

---

[11] For a strong statement of this principle (that "a Common-wealth is but one Person"), see ibid., p. 405. However, if Hobbes and Rousseau emphasize the *unity* of the civic cult, why does Rousseau end his civil-religion chapter with an appeal for religious toleration, which implies a plurality of religions? (One can pose the same question in relation to what one can discern in Hobbes as an embryonic doctrine of toleration.) Part of the answer is that Rousseau and Hobbes seek not only to shift religious authority from church to state but also to diminish the scope of religion itself, allowing more space for doctrinal and ritual differences. Moreover, this is also part of the reason why civil religion presents itself, paradoxically, as a theoretical tradition oriented toward *liberalizing* religion at the same time as it appears focused on the assertion of a unitary state religion.

[12] John Locke, *A Letter Concerning Toleration*, ed. James Tully (Indianapolis: Hackett, 1983). The text used in this edition is the original 1689 translation by William Popple. All parenthetical page references in this chapter refer to this edition. For very helpful suggestions about how to defend Locke against his (seventeenth- and twentieth-century) critics, see Vernon, *The Career of Toleration*.

[13] Although it is easy to assume that a Lockean separation of church and state is directly opposed to a Hobbesian denial of such separation, one should not rule out the possibility of there being more common ground than appears at first glance. J. Judd Owen makes the interesting point that the doctrine of a separation between church and state is more skewed to the state side of the equation than is generally recognized. "The separation of church and state in the American case is first and foremost a Constitutional (i.e., civil) matter, the ultimate court of appeal for which is the Supreme Court of the state. The American solution thus satisfies the core requirement of Hobbes's statist absolutism, which politically subordinates spiritual authority to the temporal authority." Owen, "The Tolerant Leviathan," *Polity*, Vol. 37, No. 1 (January 2005): 142, n. 44.

side, a Concernment for the Interest of Mens Souls, and on the other side, a Care of the Commonwealth. (p. 26)

In his letter to Henry Stubbe of 1659, Locke had written, concerning the relationship between the spiritual and secular domains, "in a commonwealth wholly Christian it is no small difficulty to set limits to each and to define exactly where one begins and the other ends."[14] Determining "exactly where one begins and the other ends" is precisely the project that Locke sets for himself in the *Letter Concerning Toleration*. Unlike Hobbes, Locke thinks that a clear line can be drawn between the two because each has its own proper concern, its own "Business," completely distinct from the proper business of the other:

The Commonwealth seems to me to be a Society of Men constituted only for the procuring, preserving, and advancing of their own *Civil Interests*. *Civil Interests* I call Life, Liberty, Health, and Indolency of Body; and the Possession of outward things, such as Money, Lands, Houses, Furniture, and the like. (p. 26)

The theoretical strategy laid out in this passage is to establish a clear and definite *division of labor* between church and state: It is the function of the state to look after the needs of the body (including our basic need for physical security and so on), whereas it is the function of churches to care for the needs of the soul. For each to trespass on the rightful concerns of the other is illegitimate; each must stick rigorously to its concerns, its own business:

[T]the whole Jurisdiction of the Magistrate reaches only to these Civil Concernments; and . . . all Civil Power, Right and Dominion, is bounded and confined to the only care of promoting these things; and that it neither can nor ought in any manner to be extended to the Salvation of Souls. (ibid.)

This radical split between the world of "outward things" (presided over by a civil government) and an inner world of the soul and its need for salvation (in respect of which different churches contend for the allegiance of different individuals in charge of their own belief) is entailed, for Locke, by a true understanding of the nature of religion. Religion is only a meaningful sphere of human experience to the extent that individuals outwardly embrace forms of religious life that authentically reflect their genuine inner beliefs. "The Care of Souls is not committed to the Civil Magistrate" (ibid.) because "All the Life and Power of true Religion consists in the inward and full perswasion of the mind; and Faith is not Faith without believing" (ibid.), and this is something that no outward civil power can touch. Governments can pass laws forcing its citizens to conform to "outward Worship," but this is a distortion of genuine religious faith, because religion concerns the achievement of salvation, and we can attain salvation only by embracing forms of religious practice that reflect our actual inner conviction. "True and saving Religion consists in the inward perswasion of the Mind" (p. 27), whereas the Power of the Civil Magistrate "consists only

[14] Locke, *Political Writings*, p. 138.

in outward force." Hobbes was much less interested in inner conviction than in outward profession on the part of citizens of the commonwealth, but from Locke's perspective this just proves that Hobbes is not really interested in the actual purpose of religion, which is to help its believers achieve salvation of their souls.[15] As soon as the coercive hand of the state intrudes into the domain of religion, the very purpose of religion in the lives of individuals is negated. Locke allows the state to engage in *persuasion* on behalf of a preferred church, but *coercion* is ruled out: "[I]t is one thing to perswade, another to command; one thing to press with Arguments, another with Penalties" (ibid.). Even if the state happened to align itself with the true religion, it would not advance the prospects of salvation for those it coerced into belief, for without the inner conviction, *real* belief one might say, salvation would still be denied to them. It is essential, then, that the state leave individuals within its jurisdiction space in which to decide their own convictions – that is, pursue salvation according to their own lights.

Here Locke makes a distinction between what he calls "charitable Care, which consists in teaching, admonishing, and persuading" (p. 35), which is legitimate, and what he calls "Magisterial Care" or "prescribing by Laws, and compelling by Punishments" (ibid.), which is entirely illegitimate as a way for the state to influence people's religious commitments. "The Care therefore of every man's Soul belongs unto himself, and is to be left unto himself" (ibid.). What if this means that individuals neglect the care of their souls? Locke gives the following answer: "What if he neglect the Care of his Health, or of his Estate, which things are nearlier related to the Government of the Magistrate than the other?" (ibid.). That is, all individuals have an obligation to look after their own need for salvation, and if they neglect this obligation, it is not the job of the state to force them to attend to it[16] (nor, given what has already been argued in Locke's *Letter*, will coercion by the state actually help them secure the salvation they would otherwise miss out on). "It is in vain for an Unbeliever to take up the outward shew of another mans Profession. Faith only, and inward Sincerity, are the things that procure acceptance with God" (p. 38). Therefore, "when all is done, they must be left to their own Consciences" (ibid.).

It constitutes an important aspect of this vision that Locke conceives *churches* in a way similar to the way he conceives *states* – that is, in

---

[15] Notwithstanding the striking similarities between the published theologies of Hobbes and Locke, these theologies serve essentially different (indeed opposed) political purposes; for a good account, see John C. Higgins-Biddle's Introduction to Locke, *The Reasonableness of Christianity*, ed. Higgins-Biddle (Oxford: Clarendon Press, 1999), pp. lxxviii–cxv.

[16] Wootton argues that in two of the sequels to Locke's *Letter*, namely the *Second Letter* and the *Third Letter*, Locke "retreats" from the radicalness of this view: See Introduction to *Political Writings*, p. 106. Wootton's hypothesis is that Locke, in these texts, was seeking to forge a strategic alliance with Anglican latitudinarians. This involved conceding the legitimacy in principle of a state religion, and this in turn undermined the strictness of Locke's previous separation between the state as the enforcer solely of secular interests and religion as the preserve of spiritual interests.

individualist–contractualist categories. The bedrock of Locke's liberalism (as is true of any thoroughgoing liberalism – which explains why Hobbes is ultimately not a liberal, notwithstanding the fact that aspects of his thought point cautiously in that direction[17]) is the notion of the conscientious individual given space to come to his or her own conscientious judgments. This is true of religious life no less than it is true of civil–political life. "A Church [is] a voluntary Society of Men, joining themselves together of their own accord"; "it is a free and voluntary Society" (p. 28). Just as the state would negate the very meaning of religion if it coerced or pressured citizens into some particular church, so too churches themselves would violate the purposes of religion if they bound adherents against the volition of those adherents. Thus the purpose of this theory is not just to liberate citizens from threats posed by the coercive powers of the state but also to liberate believers from the coercive powers of their own churches. Individuals should be at liberty freely to enter or freely to exit from religious communities in accordance with their own genuine inner conviction. We should not, for instance, be bound by the religions of our parents – individuals should be able to decide freely, by their own individual lights, which religious commitment merits their allegiance. The state is ultimately (with respect to its philosophical grounding) a voluntary association composed of freely contracting individuals, and the same thing is true – or ought to be true – of churches: They too are by right voluntary associations composed of freely consenting individuals. We may today take all of this for granted, but in seventeenth-century England, this was of course a revolutionary doctrine, and Locke articulated it with a theoretical power that continues to inform and animate current-day liberalism.

Of course, there is a *dual* purpose underlying this whole argument. On the one hand, Locke wants to prohibit the state from meddling in the affairs of salvation and of religious conscience. Here the purpose is to insulate religion from the coercive hand of the state. On the other hand, and equally importantly, Locke wants to prohibit churches from using the instrumentality of politics to enforce their creeds – that is, to insulate politics from the imperialistic impulses of the churches. As Locke puts it, "there is absolutely no such thing, under the Gospel, as a Christian Commonwealth" (p. 44). (Saying this already makes explicit Locke's very direct and very deliberate repudiation of Hobbes's political vision![18]) If we are to avoid the utter corruption of both church and state, then church must remain purely church (concerned only with inner

---

[17] Cf. the first epigraph to this chapter.

[18] Cf. Higgins-Biddle, Introduction, p. lxxxviii. Saying that "there is absolutely no such thing, under the Gospel, as a Christian Commonwealth" suggests clearly that any attempt to politicize Christianity involves a fairly basic violation of what Christianity is supposed to be about. (Rousseau says the same thing, except that for him this counts as a decisive political *critique* of Christianity.) In Chapter 13, I offer an interpretation of *The Reasonableness of Christianity* according to which depoliticizing the idea of the Messiah is crucial to Locke's differentiation between the Old Covenant and the New Covenant. This is in a subtle but important way related to his denial of the notion of a Christian commonwealth.

conviction and the salvation of souls), and the commonwealth must remain purely commonwealth (concerned strictly with "bodies" and their material goods). In other words, all Christian sects must categorically resist what we can call the "theocratic temptation" in any form. From this point of view, Hobbes's flirtation with a kind of theocratic politics threatened to corrupt both the rightful purposes of the commonwealth and the rightful purpose of churches, and any theocratic impulse arising from within Christianity itself is likewise a corruption of Christianity and also a corruption of politics.

One might say that the theocratic temptation is implicit in the very nature of religion. Every religion, by its very nature, takes its own beliefs and practices to be true and those of rival faiths to be mistaken. That is to say, from a sect's own point of view, toleration means allowing the adherents of every other faith to tumble into perdition. Would it not be better to extend the charity of one's own faith by coming to the rescue of these otherwise lost souls? Locke, however, knows all too well that this is the perfect recipe for precisely the horrific wars of religion that Locke's philosophy of toleration is intended to avert. Locke insists that each of us distance ourselves from our own religious commitments sufficiently to recognize that *"every* Church is Orthodox to it self" (p. 32; emphasis added)[19] – that is, each takes itself to be the only source of salvation and takes every other one to be a route to damnation. If each takes upon itself the mission of securing through politically coercive means the salvation of all the others, then an unavoidable dynamic sets in that leads straight to endless religious war. The only way of avoiding this inescapable dynamic is for each creed and each sect to deliberately abstain from political (coercive) as opposed to persuasive (noncoercive) routes to salvation: "Arguments ... [are] the only right Method of propagating Truth" (p. 33). When Locke says that "every Church is Orthodox to it self," this is more or less an acknowledgment that the theocratic temptation is latent in every form of religion (i.e., simply by virtue of its own beliefs and its own commitments, it is incapable of seeing other religions as possible sources of salvation). Indeed, this is precisely why the theocratic temptation must be resisted so unyieldingly. In Locke's view, the only sure way of resisting the temptation to meddle in the salvation of adherents of other faiths is to recognize an unbreachable boundary between religion and politics:

[T]he Church it self is a thing absolutely separate and distinct from the Commonwealth. The Boundaries on both sides are fixed and immovable. He jumbles Heaven and Earth

---

[19] This text is the centerpiece of Stanley Fish's brilliant deconstruction of the *Letter Concerning Toleration*: See Fish, "Mission Impossible: Settling the Just Bounds Between Church and State," *Columbia Law Review*, Vol. 97, No. 8 (December 1997): 2255–2333. Fish's point is that Locke's dictum applies to liberalism as a kind of secular religion as much as it applies to any properly religious sect, and therefore the presumption of most liberals that they have ascended to a unique sort of impartiality lacks foundation. It makes sense that Fish would build his critique of contemporary liberalism on a subversive reading of Locke's *Letter*, for the *Letter Concerning Toleration* has a strong claim to being considered the founding text of the philosophy of liberalism that Fish (gadfly that he is) has put so much energy into challenging.

together, the things most remote and opposite, who mixes these two Societies; which are in their Original, End, Business, and in every thing, perfectly distinct, and infinitely different from each other. (p. 33)

The core purpose of the *Letter Concerning Toleration* is to supply a principled basis upon which to distinguish the purposes of government ("Life, Liberty, Health, and Indolency of Body; and the Possession of outward things, such as Money, Lands, Houses, Furniture, and the like") from the purposes of religion (salvation, or "the care of Souls"), such that one can legitimately enforce a *categorical* separation between what magistrates do and what churches do. Hence the decisive alternative posed by Locke's political philosophy is the liberal *separation* of religion and politics versus the theocratic (or civil-religious)[20] *union* of religion and politics.

Locke asserts that there is a single exception to his categorical separation between the sphere of politics and the sphere of religion, namely "the Commonwealth of the *Jews*, [which] different in that from all others, was an absolute Theocracy" (p. 44). The claim is that "[t]he Laws established there concerning the Worship of One Invisible Deity, were the Civil Laws of that People, and a part of their Political Government; in which God himself was the Legislator," hence in this unique case there was not, nor could there be, "any difference between that Commonwealth and the Church." For this reason, the magistrates of that particular theocratic state had no choice but to punish "Idolaters" who committed apostasy against "the *Mosaical* Rites." Locke goes on: "Now if any one can shew me where there is a Commonwealth, at this time, constituted upon that Foundation, I will acknowledge that the Ecclesiastical Laws do there unavoidably become a part of the Civil; and that the Subjects of that Government both may, and ought to be kept in strict conformity with that Church, by the Civil Power." Locke himself, however, a mere two pages previously (pp. 42–43), had in fact specified a contemporary parallel case, namely the Calvinist theocracy in Geneva, and there is certainly no suggestion by Locke in his discussion of Geneva that a modern state claiming a theocratic constitution for itself can be rightly exempted from the liberal principles articulated in the *Letter Concerning Toleration*.

---

[20] If theocracy is excluded because it violates the principle of a settling of just bounds between magistrate and church, then civil religion is ruled out for exactly the same reason.

"The Gods of the Philosophers" I

Locke and John Toland

> That there is a God, and what that God is, nothing can discover to us, nor judge in us, but natural reason.
>
> – John Locke[1]

> [T]he pillars of revelation are shaken by those men who preserve the name of religion without the substance of religion.
>
> – Edward Gibbon[2]

> It is amusing to hear the modern Christian telling you how mild and rationalistic Christianity really is and ignoring the fact that all its mildness and rationalism is due to the teaching of men who in their own day were persecuted by all orthodox Christians.
>
> – Bertrand Russell[3]

> The Gods of Moses, Mahomet, and Saint Paul (Jesus is perhaps an exception) do not sound like liberals.
>
> – Brian Barry[4]

One could say that Locke pursues two strategies for domesticating religion without resorting to a civil religion.[5] The first strategy is the one pursued in the

---

[1] John Locke, *Political Writings*, ed. David Wootton (Indianapolis: Hackett, 2003), p. 238. Cf. the *First Treatise*'s appeal to reason as "[Man's] only Star and compass" (*Two Treatises of Government*, ed. Peter Laslett, Cambridge: Cambridge University Press, 1988, p. 182).

[2] Edward Gibbon, *The History of the Decline and Fall of the Roman Empire*, ed. David Womersley (London: Allen Lane, 1994), Vol. 3, p. 439.

[3] Bertrand Russell, *Why I Am Not a Christian*, ed. Paul Edwards (New York: Simon & Schuster, 1957), pp. 36–37.

[4] Brian Barry, "John Rawls and the Search for Stability," *Ethics*, Vol. 105 (July 1995): 909.

[5] As pointed out in Chapter 12, Mark Goldie suggests that the strictures against Catholics and atheists in the *Letter Concerning Toleration* represent a kind of residual civil religion in Locke: See Mark Goldie, "The Civil Religion of James Harrington," in *The Languages of Political*

Letter Concerning Toleration – namely a privatization of religion as well as the opening up of space for a multiplicity of sects that will help ensure against the dominance or excessive power of any one sect. The second strategy is that pursued in *The Reasonableness of Christianity* – that is, the strategy of bending religion toward the rationalism of philosophy, a strategy initiated by Spinoza's *Theological–Political Treatise* and pursued further by a later sequence of towering thinkers (notably, Rousseau, Kant, and Hegel).[6] The basic idea here is that of philosophy taking religion by the hand and leading it toward a less superstitious, less dogmatic, and more intellectually and morally respectable version of itself.

It may seem quite odd to think of it this way, but it is almost possible to see Pascal, with his famous contrast between *"Dieu d'Abraham, Dieu d'Isaac, Dieu de Jacob"* and *"Dieu des philosophes et savants,"* as having been the one to enunciate the project of a philosophical or rationalizing religion intended to provide a substitute for biblical religion.[7] No less paradoxical is the fact that it was Hume, the great religious skeptic, who posed the most severe challenge to this philosophical enterprise with his argument (which I discuss in Chapter 18) that no *philosopher's* religion – whether that of Spinoza or Locke or Rousseau – can answer to the existential longings or psychological needs that elicit conventional religions. Mere reason cannot satisfy longings that have a basis in a sphere other than that of reason. To be sure, Kant and Hegel continued the enterprise of philosopher's religions beyond Hume, but, arguably, they

---

Theory in Early-Modern Europe, ed. Anthony Pagden (Cambridge: Cambridge University Press, 1987), p. 202. I think this suggestion goes too far in extending the meaning of the idea of civil religion. As I flag later in this chapter, Straussians interpret *The Reasonableness of Christianity* as a civil religion because, on their reading, Locke presents his theology for purely civil rather than for philosophical reasons. However, even if one were persuaded by the Straussians that Locke is more skeptical about Christianity than most Locke scholars believe him to be, given Locke's strenuous separation between religion and politics, it is difficult to see how the *Reasonableness* could count as a civil religion.

6 On rationalized religion as one Enlightenment strategy among others, cf. Steven B. Smith, *Spinoza, Liberalism, and the Question of Jewish Identity* (New Haven: Yale University Press, 1997), pp. 2–4. It should be clear that *both* liberal strategies, the toleration strategy and the strategy to rationalize religion, relate back to the *Theological–Political Treatise* and indeed shape the entire agenda of that work. The key difference, of course, is that there remains, as I sought to highlight in Chapters 9–11, a substantial civil-religion dimension to the political philosophy of Spinoza. It may seem implausible to see Locke as in any sense a Spinozist, but see Douglas J. Den Uyl and Stuart D. Warner, "Liberalism and Hobbes and Spinoza," *Studia Spinozana*, Vol. 3 (1987): 279: "Feuer argues that Spinoza influenced Locke and that the tenets Locke drew up for the creed of the 'society of Pacific Christians' correspond exactly to Spinoza's tenets for a universal religion" (citing Lewis Samuel Feuer, *Spinoza and the Rise of Liberalism*, Boston: Beacon Press, 1958), pp. 257–258).

7 Blaise Pascal, *Pensées et Opuscules*, ed. Léon Brunschvicg (Paris: Classiques Hachette, 1963), p. 142; for an English translation of Pascal's "Memorial," see *Pensées*, ed. A. J. Krailsheimer (London: Penguin, 1966), pp. 309–310. Needless to say, Pascal's "Memorial" (1654) preceded the efforts by Spinoza, Locke, and later philosophers to turn the articulation of a *"Dieu des philosophes"* into a systematic philosophical program.

confirmed rather than refuted Hume's challenges.[8] One of the chief purposes of Spinoza's *Theological–Political Treatise* was to define a new agenda for political philosophy: to appropriate what is morally attractive in Judeo-Christian religion while jettisoning what is not morally attractive by substituting a *rationalizing* or *philosophical* religion for the actual substance of biblical religion. This agenda was robustly taken up by a group of key thinkers who would not dare acknowledge it as a *Spinozistic* philosophical project. Arguably, the leading attempts to pursue this philosophical agenda can be found in Locke's *Reasonableness of Christianity*, Book 4 of Rousseau's *Emile*, and Kant's *Religion within the Boundaries of Mere Reason* (although another top candidate would be the philosophy of Hegel).[9] In this chapter I want to begin sketching the outlines of this shared project, with the aim of eventually judging these efforts by Locke, Rousseau, and Kant in relation to the original Spinozistic agenda.[10]

In *The Reasonableness of Christianity*, Locke aimed at articulating a theology that was faithfully Christian rather than a form of deism, but his contemporaries tended to read it – and we can still read it today – as starting down a slippery slope toward more radically subversive theologies that were willing to go further than Locke himself in diluting Christian orthodoxy.[11] Let us trace the main themes of this Lockean theology.

---

[8] For an account of Moses Mendelssohn, Lessing, Kant, and Hegel as heirs of Spinoza, see Smith, *Spinoza, Liberalism, and the Question of Jewish Identity*, chapter 7. For a good discussion of late-nineteenth- and early-twentieth-century attempts to rationalize religion, and the ineffectuality of those attempts, see Mark Lilla, *The Stillborn God: Religion, Politics, and the Modern West* (New York: Knopf, 2007), chapter 5. Consider also in this connection the story related by Steven B. Smith of Hermann Cohen's weeping when he realized that his reduction of God to "a concept or an idea" left out "the God of creation (*Borei olam*)": See Smith, "How to Commemorate the 350th Anniversary of Spinoza's Expulsion," *Hebraic Political Studies*, Vol. 3, No. 2 (Spring 2008): 171.

[9] Arguably, one could add Shaftesbury to this list; cf. Stanley Grean, *Shaftesbury's Philosophy of Religion and Ethics* (Athens, OH: Ohio University Press, 1967), p. xi: "Shaftesbury's religious theories laid the groundwork for later attempts to formulate a religion 'within the limits of reason alone.'" One could also add Thomas Paine, whose *The Age of Reason* (completed in 1795 – exactly 100 years after *The Reasonableness of Christianity*) constituted another major landmark on the way toward fulfilling the deist project of founding religion on reason rather than revelation.

[10] Because Bayle constitutes a decisive intermediary between Spinoza and Rousseau, the narrative begun in this chapter will be resumed following the discussion of Bayle in Chapters 14–16.

[11] John Locke, *The Reasonableness of Christianity as Delivered in the Scriptures*, ed. John C. Higgins-Biddle (Oxford: Clarendon Press, 1999); hereafter *Reasonableness of Christianity*. I will not attempt to enter into standard debates concerning Locke's suspected Socinianism in any detail, but Wootton seems to me to make a good case that Locke *was* sincerely committed to Socinian views: See Introduction to *Political Works*, pp. 66–72. As Wootton highlights, if Locke was a Socinian, then *both* Dunn (Locke as a Calvinist) *and* Strauss (Locke as a surreptitious anti-Christian) are mistaken. In particular, Wootton makes a persuasive argument that proving that Locke was not an orthodox Christian does not constitute a proof that he was not a Christian. (See p. 71: "Straussians are right . . . to claim that something strange is going on when Locke appeals to the Bible, but wrong to conclude that Locke's intention is to undermine faith. In fact, he is trying to insinuate a rationalist, Socinian reading of the Bible.") More broadly, one may start to suspect that seventeenth-century contemporaries tended to get

Christianity as a "Doctrine of Redemption" requires above all clarification of "*Adam*'s Fall": "To understand . . . what we are restored to by Jesus Christ, we must first consider what the Scripture shews we lost by *Adam*."[12] Calvinists, on one hand, "would have all *Adam*'s Posterity doomed to Eternal Infinite Punishment for Adam's sin." Deists, on the other hand, find this conception so repugnant to the idea of divine justice that they move to the opposite extreme – denying the doctrine of redemption altogether. Locke's claim is that Adam and his posterity did indeed pay a price for the original transgression, but this price was the imposition of *mortality* upon the human race, not the imposition of eternal damnation. The orthodox Calvinist interpretation, says Locke, "seems a strange way of understanding a Law, which requires the plainest and directest words, that by *Death* should be meant Eternal Life in Misery."[13] When Adam was expelled from "the Tranquility and Bliss of Paradise,"[14] his posterity were expelled as well; but expulsion from paradise does not constitute being thrust into hell. There is indeed a "Redemption by Jesus Christ,"[15] but it is a redemption from the condition of mortality, not a redemption from damnation.

Why is it just for God to impose a penalty not only on Adam but also on Adam's posterity? Locke's answer is that no one has a *right* to eternal life; therefore, mortality in itself is not a punishment.[16] This does not mean that punishment is not part of the divine scheme, but when human beings are punished, they are punished for their own moral failings, not some original sin traceable back to Adam.[17] Still, even if "this estate of death" is not a punishment, properly speaking, liberation from it is a positive good, and this is

---

these things right: Spinoza was a heretic, Hobbes an atheist, Bayle less pious than he let on, and Locke a committed Socinian. However, Victor Nuovo, in his Introduction to Locke, *The Reasonableness of Christianity as Delivered in the Scriptures* (Bristol: Thoemmes Press, 1997), pp. v–xxx, resists the notion that Locke's theology was Socinian; cf. Nuovo's Introduction to *John Locke and Christianity*, ed. Nuovo (Bristol: Thoemmes Press, 1997), pp. ix–xxvi. Nuovo's view is that Locke had, in his own mind, succeeded in identifying a genuine *via media* between orthodox and Socinian theology. Indeed, Locke himself presents his project on the very first page of the *Reasonableness* as an attempt to mediate between "two Extreams . . . [a Calvinist extreme which] shook the Foundations of all Religion [and an opposing extreme which] made Christianity almost nothing" (*Reasonableness of Christianity*, p. 5); but this text is more plausibly read as a repudiation of deism than as a repudiation of Socinianism. Furthermore, given Locke's denial of original sin and his emphasis on Jesus as (merely?) the Messiah rather than part of the Divinity, it is easy to understand why his contemporaries were keen to denounce him as a Socinian. For an exceptionally thorough assessment of the forms of guilt by association applied to Locke by his contemporaries, see Higgins-Biddle's Introduction to *Reasonableness of Christianity*, pp. xv–cxv; Higgins-Biddle, like Nuovo, argues that Locke has his own unique theological position and is therefore neither a deist nor a Socinian nor a Hobbist.

[12] *Reasonableness of Christianity*, p. 5.
[13] Ibid., p. 7.
[14] Ibid., p. 8.
[15] Ibid.
[16] Ibid., p. 10.
[17] Ibid., p. 11.

just what Jesus promises – that is, the "restor[ation of] all mankind to Life."[18]
There are indeed "wages of sin," but they apply to individuals on account of
their own transgressions (their own "unrighteousness") rather than by virtue
of being posterity of Adam.[19] In sum, the human condition is not an inherited
"state of Guilt"[20]; whether the individual is punished or returns to a condition
of eternal life will be judged "according to his deeds."[21]

Locke certainly does not rule out the notion of all human beings as sinners,
for *Romans* 3:23 asserts specifically that all have sinned – but this is a function
of individual transgressions of the Law of Reason or Law of Nature, not of
original sin.[22] If all are sinners, how can anyone expect salvation? To answer
this question, Locke in chapter 3 introduces the key distinction between the
"Law of Works" and the "Law of Faith" that allows even sinners to hope for
salvation. With respect to the Law of Works, there is either perfect obedience
or transgression, either righteousness or unrighteousness. The Law of Faith,
however, opens up the option of God "counting their Faith for Righteousness,
i.e. for a compleat performance of the Law."[23] That is, "Faith is allowed
to supply the defect of full Obedience; and so the Believers are admitted to
Life and Immortality *as if* they were Righteous."[24] The Law of Works as
disclosed in the Mosaic dispensation consisted of "God's positive Injunction"
binding on the Hebrews in particular (the "Civil and Ritual part of the Law
delivered by Moses") as well as a "Moral part of the Law of *Moses*" that
applies universally.[25] It is this "Moral part" corresponding to "the Moral Law,
(which is every where the same, the Eternal Rule of Right)"[26] that concerns
Locke. This is the law that all human beings transgress, but whose transgression
can be forgiven if faith in God's word can be accepted as a substitute for
righteousness.[27] If human beings chronically fall short of what is required of
them under the Law of Works, and if faith is then our sole hope of averting
the punishment to which our transgression otherwise exposes us, what are the
beliefs that define this saving faith? "We must therefore examine and see what
God requires us to believe now [as opposed to during the Mosaic dispensation]

---

[18] Ibid. The notion of Jesus as Redeemer implies that there is something in respect of which human
beings stand in need of redemption. Hence John Edwards's challenge in *Socinianism Unmask'd*:
"For I ask, what was the end of his being sent? Was it not to Help Mankind, to rescue and
deliver them from some Evil?" (*John Locke and Christianity*, p. 212). However, Locke clearly
believes that he has this problem covered without having to embrace the idea of original sin.
[19] *Reasonableness of Christianity*, p. 12.
[20] Ibid., p. 7.
[21] Ibid., p. 11, quoting *Romans* 2:6.
[22] *Reasonableness of Christianity*, p. 13.
[23] Ibid., p. 21.
[24] Ibid., p. 19; emphasis added.
[25] Ibid., pp. 19, 20.
[26] Ibid., p. 20.
[27] Ibid., p. 21: "*God imputeth righteousness without works, i.e.* without a full measure of Works,
which is exact Obedience," quoting *Romans* 4:6.

under the Revelation of the Gospel"[28] – an examination that Locke undertakes beginning in chapter 4.

The next several chapters unleash a blizzard of Scriptural texts, all of which boil down to "this single Truth, that *Jesus* was the *Messiah*; that Salvation or Perdition depends upon believing or rejecting this one Proposition."[29] Jesus' Resurrection from the dead must also be believed, because no one could believe Jesus to be the Messiah while believing him to be mortal[30]; and accepting Jesus' status as the promised Messiah means resting on him one's hopes for "remission of sins."[31] This is indeed "a minimalist creed"[32] – one that is highly reminiscent of the similarly minimalist creed formulated by Hobbes.[33] Locke's principal strategy for minimizing the Christian creed – as was emphatically seized upon by his leading critic, John Edwards – was to give strong primacy to the Gospels (as well as *Acts*) over the Epistles.[34] What was clear to both Locke

---

[28] *Reasonableness of Christianity*, p. 22.

[29] Ibid., p. 31. Locke flags both here and at the very end of chapter 5 that "there is something more required to salvation." What comprises this "something more" is "Repentance," which is discussed in chapters 11 and 12. According to the elaboration on p. 111, repentance involves "not only a sorrow for sins past, but . . . a turning from them, into a new and contrary Life"; and on p. 112, that "Repentance is an hearty sorrow for our past misdeeds, and a sincere Resolution and Endeavour, to the utmost of our power, to conform all our Actions to the Law of God." As comes out in his discussion of "Devils" on p. 110, sinners who believe in the messiahship of Jesus but do not repent their sins in this sense are not saved.

[30] Ibid., p. 26.

[31] Ibid., pp. 28 and 33, quoting *Acts* 10:43. Cf. *Matthew* 1:21: "[H]e shall save his people from their sins," quoted in *Reasonableness of Christianity*, p. 36. In this text, Locke states clearly that "his people [and] their sins" refers to "the Jewish nation."

[32] Nuovo, Introduction to the Thoemmes Press edition of the *Reasonableness*, p. xxv, summarizing the challenges put to Locke by John Edwards.

[33] The charge against Locke of being a disciple of Hobbes ("he took *Hobbes's Leviathan* for the *New Testament*, and the *Philosopher of Malmesbury* for our *Saviour* and the *Apostles*") was one of Edwards's most inflammatory accusations: See Higgins-Biddle, Introduction to *Reasonableness of Christianity*, p. lxxvi. Higgins-Biddle is committed to absolving Locke of the charge of being a Hobbist, but the fact remains (as Higgins-Biddle does not hesitate to concede: p. lxxvi) that the theological "innovation" on which Locke most prided himself, namely the reduction of the doctrinal content of Christianity to the single proposition of Jesus' messiahship, seems identical to Hobbes; on p. lxxxviii, Higgins-Biddle calls this "their common thesis." (Cf. the judgment of a contemporary critic, Richard Willis, cited by Higgins-Biddle: p. lxxv. For Locke's reply to Willis, see the Thoemmes Press edition of the *Reasonableness*, pp. 420–421.)

[34] Locke's main defense of this hermeneutic policy in *Reasonableness of Christianity* is laid out in chapter 15. Rousseau, in the "Letters Written from the Mountain," also insists that Christianity is defined by the Gospels, not by St. Paul: See *Collected Writings of Rousseau*, Vol. 9, ed. Christopher Kelly and Eve Grace (Lebanon, NH: University Press of New England, 2001), pp. 186–187. It is noteworthy that in demoting the status of the Epistles within the Scriptures, Locke employs a recognizable Spinozistic trope: namely that the Epistles are written "by proper Accommodations to the Apprehensions of those they were writ to" (p. 166). One should also point out that this whole argument implicitly anticipates the argument explicitly mounted by John Toland in *Nazarenus*, namely that Christianity as articulated by St. Paul was a different (and theologically more ambitious) creed than the simple faith revealed by Jesus. Locke concludes the *Reasonableness* by urging that if salvation requires mastery of sophisticated theological doctrines, Christianity could not be what it was intended to be, namely a doctrine of salvation capable of being comprehended by the "poor, ignorant, illiterate" (p. 170; cf. the

and Edwards was that most of the theologically controversial doctrines that
spawned opposing Christian sects were located in the Epistles[35]; and therefore
marginalizing the Epistles relative to the Gospels would not only lower the
threshold for inclusion in the Christian fellowship but also (as a consequence)
promote Locke's project of toleration. As Locke puts it in his first *Vindication*,
what is needed above all is "the reconciling of differences in the christian
church, which has been so cruelly torn, about the articles of the christian faith,
to the great reproach of christian charity, and scandal of our true religion," and
one is far more likely to attain this purpose by referring back to the original
"apostles creed" than by acceding to Edwards's "enlarged" version of Christian
orthodoxy.[36]

Locke affirms repeatedly in these chapters "that *Messiah* and *Son of God*
were Synonymous terms, at that time, among the Jews,"[37] which conveys
clearly that there was nothing in the nature of Jesus that exceeded the Jewish
conception of the Messiah (again, a seeming flashback to Hobbes) and surely
fueled suspicions about Locke's anti-Trinitarianism. Of course, the Jewish conception of the Messiah was that of a political liberator, and Locke explicitly
affirms these aspects of messiahship as realized in Jesus: What was expected of
the Messiah was "deliverance . . . in a Kingdom, he was to set up"; "an extraordinary Man [sent to] work their Deliverance" from "Foreign Dominion."[38]

reference on p. 91 to the "Learning" of St. Paul). Exactly the same rhetoric is employed by
Toland throughout *Christianity not Mysterious*, and by Rousseau in *Emile*, trans. Allan Bloom
(New York: Basic Books, 1979), p. 299, note, and p. 310.

[35] See *Reasonableness of Christianity*, p. 168 ("the contending Parties").

[36] Thoemmes Press edition of the *Reasonableness*, p. 169. For a powerful statement of this key
constitutive purpose shaping Locke's motivation both in the *Letter Concerning Toleration* and
in the *Reasonableness of Christianity*, see *Political Writings*, ed. Wootton, pp. 144–145.

[37] *Reasonableness of Christianity*, p. 34.

[38] Ibid., p. 36; cf. p. 38: "[A] Kingdom was that which the Jews most looked after, and wished
for"; that the Messiah, when he came, would be "*the RULER in Israel*," quoting *Micah* 5:2.
See also p. 44, where he speaks of Jesus as "the King whom the Jews expected"; p. 47, where he
discusses "the whole Nation of the Jews expecting at this time their *Messiah*, and deliverance
by him from the Subjection they were in to a Foreign Yoke"; p. 58, "the King and Deliverer
that was promised them"; p. 121, "*King of Israel*"; and p. 139, "a Prince, and a Saviour to
his People." The interpretation of the Messiah on p. 72 as a liberator from Roman hegemony
helps to explain what motivated the hostility of the chief priests and Pharisees (which Locke in
other places puts down to envy), namely fear that the prospect of a nationalist revolution, so to
speak, "[would] draw the Roman Arms upon us, to the Destruction of us and our Country."
All of this suggests, and Locke clearly implies that it suggests (see p. 38), that the phrases
"Kingdom of God" and "Kingdom of Heaven" refer strictly to a refounded theocratic political
commonwealth of the Israelites. Hobbes at least spells out that Jesus will return to complete
his political mission of assuming kingship of a renewed theocracy; Locke, by contrast, never
attempts to address the central puzzle associated with the claim that Jesus was the Messiah
for whom the Hebrews had yearned. See also Immanuel Kant, *Religion within the Boundaries
of Mere Reason*, ed. Allen Wood and George di Giovanni (Cambridge: Cambridge University
Press, 1998), p. 96, which suggests the idea of Christ as the fomenter of an abortive nationalist
revolt, although Kant also suggests (p. 96, note) that Christ's *real* intended mission was an
anticlerical revolution.

This is what the Jews awaited "according to their Ancient Prophecies,"[39] and Jesus was the fulfillment of these prophecies. Did Jesus provide political liberation for the Jews? Did he refound their independent kingdom? Locke never says that he did, nor does he explain how Jesus' failure to do this was consistent with the validity of his status as Jewish Messiah.[40] All he says is that the Messiah was expected to perform miracles and Jesus indeed performed miracles.

Chapter 8 pursues a lengthy discussion of Jesus' persecution by the Sanhedrin, his fear of premature execution (before he had completed his mission), his exile from Jerusalem, and his anxiety about revealing his identity as Messiah. All of this may well remind us of Locke's own story: of persecution, of fear of execution, of exile in Holland, and of reticence about announcing his authorship of this and other important works of theory.[41] The purpose of chapter 8 is to explain why someone who *was* the awaited Messiah would exert himself to obscure this very status and mission. Nevertheless, Locke's account surely raises more puzzles than it resolves: Jesus had to avoid "caus[ing] any disturbance in Civil Societies and the Governments of the World" to prove himself innocent of accusations of being a political threat; he had to avoid arousing "Tumult and Sedition" among the multitude who yearned for their Messiah; consequently, he had to disavow being the "Deliverer" of the Jews even though being Messiah meant precisely that.[42] How could Jesus be the Messiah awaited by the Jews if he was unwilling to provoke the political upheaval that would be

---

[39] *Reasonableness of Christianity*, p. 36.

[40] On p. 40, Locke asserts that Jesus lived a life "every way conformable to the Prophesies of him." How could this be true if the core of the Jewish prophecies of a Messiah prophesied a political liberator? On p. 45, Locke highlights the fact that from the perspective of "the Magistrats of the World," once Jesus had been executed "and appeared no longer any where," it was hard to take seriously "the talk of a King." In other words, it was reasonable to fear Jesus as a possible Messiah (in the Jewish sense) while he was alive, but difficult to credit this claim once he had been executed. (Furthermore, even *before* he was executed, he appeared to Pilate as "a King of no consequence"; see p. 46.) Cf. Michael S. Rabieh, "The Reasonableness of Locke, or the Questionableness of Christianity," *Journal of Politics*, Vol. 53, No. 4 (1991); 950, n. 14. As Rabieh implies, one of the big puzzles of the *Reasonableness of Christianity* is why Locke does not feel obliged to make greater acknowledgment of the reasonableness of the Jewish rejection of Jesus on account of his "not conform[ing] to prior prophecies about the Messiah" (Rabieh, p. 950). Similar questions are raised by Baron d'Holbach in *Christianity Unveiled*, trans. W. M. Johnson (New York: Gordon Press, 1974), p. 35 and p. 37, note.

[41] See in particular Locke's reference to Jesus' "wonted and necessary caution," and his eventual willingness to "appear amongst them openly" (*Reasonableness of Christianity*, p. 44). Similarly, Locke's discussion on p. 67 of Jesus' "owning...himself to be him," that his true identity as Messiah "should be afterwards fully understood...when he had left the World," brings to mind the fact that Locke himself let go of his anonymity only posthumously. It is no more than speculation, but still tempting to speculate, that this whole drama narrated by Locke in chapters 8–9 of Jesus' reluctance to reveal his identity and mission is, among other things, a subtle commentary on Locke's own experience of the necessity of hiding his identity as a political philosopher and a theologian.

[42] Ibid., pp. 50–51; cf. p. 52, where he states "that this was He, of whom the Scripture spoke, who was to be their Deliverer."

inseparable from the Messiah's mission of founding a new Jewish kingdom?[43] Locke in these chapters insists that the core of Christian belief is defined by the acknowledgment that Jesus is the Messiah prophesied by the Hebrew Scriptures ("we no where in the Gospel hear of any thing else had been proposed to be believed by [Christian believers]"[44]); yet on Locke's own account, Jesus goes out of his way to avoid and disavow precisely the political mission of establishing a new theocratic order that, as Locke himself highlights, was what the Jews associated with their Messiah.

The first suggestion of the inadequacy of the Old Testament interpretation of the Messiah occurs in chapter 9 (p. 62): In the sermon at Capernaum (*John* 6: 22–69), Jesus expounds his messianic vocation in parables ("in obscure and Mystical terms") to discourage the insurrectional tendencies of "those who looked for nothing but the Grandeur of a Temporal Kingdom in this World, and the Protection and Prosperity they had promised themselves under it." Jesus was their Messiah, but he offered a conception of the awaited Kingdom that "plainly baulk'd their Expectation."[45] The Hebrews received a different kind of messiah than the one they had been led to expect.[46] Again, this is the first intimation by Locke that an important part of Jesus' task as Messiah is to reconceive what it means to be the Messiah.

Locke returns to this all-important theme on p. 89: "The *Jews* had no other thoughts of their *Messiah*, but of a Mighty Temporal Prince, that should raise their Nation into an higher degree of Power, Dominion, and Prosperity than ever it had enjoyed. They were filled with the expectation of a Glorious Earthly

---

[43] Cf. p. 53: It was safe for Jesus to announce his identity as the Messiah to the Samarian woman in *John* 4:26 because here there was no threat of Jews "mak[ing] an Insurrection to set a *Jew* up for their King." Again, was this not what it meant to yearn for a Messiah?

[44] *Reasonableness of Christianity*, p. 54; cf. p. 58: "This was all the Doctrine they proposed to be believed. For what [the Apostles] taught, as well as our Saviour, contained a great deal more; but that concerned Practice, and not Belief."

[45] Ibid., p. 62.

[46] It is particularly striking that *even in the case of the Apostles*, Jesus' idea that his messianic mission was fundamentally nonpolitical (and required his martyrdom) was not "suited to their expectation of the Messiah" (p. 65). See also p. 73: "[T]heir [the Apostles'] Notion of the *Messiah* was the same with that which was entertained by the rest of the Jews; (*viz.*) That he should be a Temporal Prince and Deliverer"; p. 89: "though they with others expected a Temporal Kingdom on Earth"; and p. 102: "A *Messiah*, and not a King, you [Apostles] could not understand. . . . And had I told you in plain words that I was the *Messiah*, and given you a direct Commission to Preach to others that I professedly owned my self to be the *Messiah*, you and they would have been ready to have made a Commotion, to have set me upon the Throne of my Father *David*." Even *after* the Resurrection, the Apostles still have not readjusted their Old Covenant conception of the Messiah, as we see on p. 105 when Locke quotes the Apostles (*Acts* 1:6) as they ask the resurrected Jesus, "Lord, wilt thou at this time restore again the Kingdom to *Israel*"; and when he quotes *Luke* 24:21: "[W]e trusted that it had been He which should have redeemed *Israel*; i.e. [Locke's gloss:] We believed that he was the *Messiah*, come to deliver the Nation of the *Jews*." So, astonishingly, what was true during the life of Jesus remained true when the Apostles reencountered him after his Resurrection, namely that "their Notion of the *Messiah* was the same with that which was entertained by the rest of the Jews" (p. 73).

Kingdom." If this is what it meant to be the Messiah, then Jesus could hardly have been the Jews' long-awaited Messiah (at least as they conceived him). Similarly, on p. 101: "They were yet so full of a Temporal Kingdom, that they could not bear the discovery of what a kind of Kingdom his was, nor what a King he was to be." Clearly, this whole theme is closely tied to the fact that Jesus at some point evolves from being a *national* messiah to being a universal messiah. This transformation is anticipated on pp. 53–54 when Locke cites the story of the Samaritan woman who led her compatriots to the knowledge that Jesus was (not just the Jewish Messiah but) "the Saviour of the World."[47] On pp. 78 and 79, Locke presents Jesus' new role as Messiah of a *Gentile* Kingdom as a punishment to the Jews for failing to recognize him as the Messiah that he was.[48] This account, however, is extremely puzzling: As Locke himself makes clear, the Jewish multitude would quite readily have received Jesus as the liberator and new king for whom they yearned if Jesus did not exert himself powerfully to discourage this yearning for a political revolt. Jesus was indeed rejected by the Jewish leadership, concerned as they were to stay in the good graces of the Roman authorities; but Locke emphasizes that the Jewish masses were entirely ready to accept Jesus as "their King and Deliverer."[49]

In short, Jesus found himself in the midst of a complicated political drama, and he worked hard not to set off the political conflagration that was already waiting to ignite. It does not make sense, then, to say that Jesus went from being a national messiah to being a universal savior to punish the Jews for their failure to acknowledge him. The Jesus that Locke presents is a man like himself: cautious, prudent, sensitive to the political context in which he finds himself, and, above all, determined not to jeopardize his all-important mission by taking unnecessary risks.[50] Why *would* the Jews associate such a man with the liberator who had been promised them? What is particularly hard to make out in Locke's account – and perhaps in the biblical narrative itself – is how a supposed messiah bearing the Davidic royal lineage[51] and therefore seemingly born for political responsibilities can be so determined to avoid implication in the political aspirations of his nation. A promised overturner of the existing order who dreads being thought a revolutionary? Is the real story here one

---

47 The biblical text is *John* 4: 42; cf. Locke's reference to Jesus as a Messiah "promised by God to the World" (and not merely to the Jews) on p. 120. See also p. 169, where Locke explains that Jesus was "declared to all Mankind"; "constituted the Lord and Judge of all Men, to be their King and Ruler." Locke never clarifies how the Messiah went from being the deliverer of one particular nation to being the savior of all mankind.

48 Cf. Kant, *Religion within the Boundaries of Mere Reason*, ed. Wood and di Giovanni, p. 140, note.

49 *Reasonableness of Christianity*, p. 80: "[T]he Opinion that was spread amongst the People [was] that he was the *Messiah*."

50 A typical Lockean formulation is "the Prudent and wary carriage of our Saviour...that he might not incur Death with the least suspicion of a Malefactor" (p. 99). All of this is referred to by Paine (in implicit response to Locke?) as "pusillanimity": See Thomas Paine, *The Age of Reason*, ed. Moncure Daniel Conway (Mineola, NY: Dover, 2004), p. 40.

51 *Reasonableness of Christianity*, p. 92.

that speaks more directly to Locke's own context – namely how the need for political order trumps the yearning for revolution?

This brings us to chapter 10. Here (p. 95) we are presented with the startling suggestion that Jesus is no longer the redeemer of the Jewish nation but rather one who will take vengeance upon the Jewish nation,[52] one who has come to "put an end to their Church, Worship, and Commonwealth."[53] He "fore-tell[s] the Destruction of [the Temple]," "the Destruction of *Jerusalem*."[54] He is now the terminator of the Mosaic dispensation. Locke's interpretation of *John* 16: 8–14 is that "the *Jews* sinned in not believing me to be the *Messiah*."[55] The Jews sinned because they expected a political messiah and were presented instead with a nonpolitical or antipolitical messiah? Because they were presented with a messiah too reticent (or cautious) to announce himself to be the Messiah? I am not competent to judge whether *The Reasonableness of Christianity* offers a theology that is or is not coherent, but it is hard to see how the story that Locke draws from the four *Gospels* can yield something coherent, a story that in its essentials runs as follows: First, Jesus' identity is decisively defined by his being the Messiah promised by the ancient Hebrew prophecies. Second, Jesus, for reasons of not wanting to provoke "Tumult" and "Sedition,"[56] obscures this identity. Third, the Jews are deserving of "destruction" of their religion and of their political aspirations because the Messiah delivered by the New Covenant does not coincide with the Messiah promised by the Old Covenant.

What hypothesis can we come up with to make some sense of the paradoxes that suffuse *The Reasonableness of Christianity*? As was intimated on p. 103 ("it hath not been yet fully discovered to you, what kind of Kingdom it shall be"), and is now spelled out a little more explicitly on p. 111, the Messiah as King is King in a transformed sense: Somehow, "Kingdom" in the literal (political) sense has come to take on a metaphorical meaning[57] – the kingdom of believers represented in "The Church" (also described as a "Kingdom in Heaven," a "Heavenly [or otherworldly] Kingdom"[58]). If, as was argued in

---

[52] Cf. p. 70, where Locke discusses "his coming to execute Vengeance on the Jews."

[53] The suggestion about ending the Jewish *commonwealth* is the one that is truly shocking, for all the messianic yearnings associated with the awaited Messiah had to do with *restoring* the (independent) Jewish commonwealth. In that sense, the New Covenant directly inverts the meaning of the Old Covenant (even according to the *Apostles'* understanding of the meaning of a Messiah!).

[54] *Reasonableness of Christianity*, pp. 94, 95.

[55] Ibid., p. 100. Rousseau offers a similar narrative in *Collected Writings of Rousseau*, Vol. 8, ed. Christopher Kelly (Lebanon, NH: University Press of New England, 2000), pp. 269–270: Christ's initial project was to liberate the Jews, but because the Jews proved themselves to be unworthy of this liberation, Christ took up a different, more universal, project.

[56] *Reasonableness of Christianity*, pp. 92, 100.

[57] The image of Jesus as lawgiver is similarly metaphorical (see p. 120) – at least if one considers the sense of moral lawgiver as metaphorical in relation to political lawgiver as literal. Locke elaborates on p. 151 on the meaning of Jesus as moral lawgiver vis-à-vis the moral counsels of various ancient sages whose prescriptions were advisory rather than commanded.

[58] Ibid., p. 117.

the *Letter Concerning Toleration*, there is a fundamental principled boundary between the sphere of legitimate political concerns and the sphere of salvation, then not only must the understanding of Christianity be purged of controversial theological doctrines – which believers are free to embrace or not embrace according to their own conscientious convictions rather than being subject to coercion by clerical authorities[59] – but it must also be thoroughly purged of any political dimension. It is impossible for the Old Covenant to remain the Old Covenant in the absence of a political dimension (including yearnings for political redemption of a particular nation[60]); hence there must be a (depoliticized) New Covenant. Being a Christian requires believing in Jesus as a nonpolitical messiah[61] and living a good life as a private moral agent.[62] Punishing the Jews for remaining faithful to their Old Covenant seems harsh, but it may be that Locke could conceive no other reason for accepting Jesus as the promised Messiah even though he fulfilled none of the messianic expectations that the Jews associated with messiahship. In any case, depoliticizing biblical faith demanded the sharpest possible break with the Old Covenant.[63]

The theme of chapters 12–15 is Christianity as a (strictly) moral creed. If one acknowledges Jesus as Messiah then one will defer to him as "King" and therefore submit with unconditional obedience to his "laws," and these laws turn out to be the laws of moral life. Spinoza had vacillated between a political and a moral interpretation of biblical religion; Locke's interpretation is through-and-through moral. The Old Covenant articulated a creed that was both political and moral; the New Covenant, as Locke highlights emphatically, is exclusively moral. The core theological doctrine is "REPENT...for the Remission of Sins" (*Acts* 2:38),[64] but the content of this doctrine is determined by an understanding of those moral laws that define repentance.[65] As for Spinoza, theology is subsumed by morality.[66]

---

[59] Ibid., p. 109.

[60] This is in clear contrast to the universalism of Christ's kingdom; see p. 117. In chapter 14, Locke appeals to universal reason in grounding the universalism of Christianity.

[61] By way of contrast, see Paine, *The Age of Reason*, p. 28.

[62] As I pointed out in note 29, Locke makes repentance a necessary condition of being a Christian, and as he specifies on p. 112, repentance means "[living] a good life."

[63] Although Hobbes and Locke seem agreed on reducing Christianity to the bare formula of Christ's messiahship, Hobbes's insistence on the unity of religion and politics prompts him to interpret Christianity in close proximity to the Old Testament, whereas Locke's determination to separate politics and religion necessitates a sharp break between the Old and New Covenants. Judged according to the interpretations I have offered, this is the key difference between them.

[64] *Reasonableness of Christianity*, p. 131.

[65] Consider esp. p. 133: "None are Sentenced or Punished for Unbelief; but only for their Misdeeds"; and p. 134, where he states, "every where the Sentence follows, doing or not doing; without any mention of believing, or not believing." Faith contributes to remission of sins, but divine punishment is punishment for immorality, not for unbelief (or for doctrinal heresy). In that sense, moral practice trumps belief or doctrine.

[66] This certainly does not mean that Spinoza is as much of a Christian as Locke is. Locke is committed to an otherworldly doctrine of salvation. Spinoza, by contrast, is committed to the Epicurean doctrine that virtue is its own reward. The main thematic discussion of the afterlife

Where does this leave us with respect to the relationship between reason and revelation? It is the task of chapters 14 and 15 to answer this question. There must be independent rational access to the laws of morality because human beings existed before Revelation, and it would be unjust to deny them the possibility of salvation simply because they did not affirm a faith that was not available to them.[67] Hence Locke, in chapter 13, specifies that God's bounty is revealed "either by the light of Nature, or particular Promises."[68] This suggestion is elaborated on in chapter 14 in response to what is an even more severe version of the same problem, namely the following: What can be required of those with access neither to the actual Messiah of the New Covenant nor to the promised Messiah of the Old Covenant?[69] Again, "God had, by the Light of Reason, revealed to *all* Mankind . . . that he was Good and Merciful."[70] According to Locke, the order of obedience, frailty, repentance, and divine forgiveness is revealed by "the Light of Nature."[71] Hence those who lived prior to Revelation were done no injustice. However, if "the Light of Reason" or "the Light of Nature" has already revealed what is required in order to be judged righteous, is Revelation then redundant? It is obvious that Locke will give a negative answer to this question.

"[I]t was not without need," Locke declares, "that [Jesus the Messiah] was sent into the World."[72] Jesus appeared in a world dominated by priestly superstition, a world where reason had been excluded from religion.[73] The Israelites were a nation of light relative to heathen darkness,[74] but even they made little progress in communicating the truth of monotheism to other nations.[75] It was

---

in *Reasonableness of Christianity* is on pp. 161–163. Central to that discussion is an account of why the Christian appeal to the afterlife is more effective in promoting virtue than the ancient pagan philosophers' appeal to the idea of virtue for its own sake ("that she [virtue] is her self a Reward"). A second important difference, somewhat related to the first, is that there is far more punitiveness in Locke's interpretation of Christianity than there is in Spinoza's. Hell is very much a part of Locke's "moral" version of Christianity. (As Rabieh points out ["The Reasonableness of Locke," p. 954, n. 16], because the New Covenant introduces both a heaven and a hell that did not exist between Adam and Jesus, many will be far worse off under the New Covenant than they were under the Old. In this respect, the New Covenant presents itself as a highly problematical proof of God's "mercy.") Higgins-Biddle (Introduction, p. lxxii) points out that Locke's final view was that there is punishment in an afterlife but not *eternal* punishment (hell but not eternal hell).

[67] *Reasonableness of Christianity*, p. 135. As Locke discusses on p. 138, the Old Testament recounts righteous individuals (Abel, Noah, Sarah) who obviously were not in a position to embrace Jesus as Messiah. This seems clear proof, even from a Christian point of view (because it is confirmed by St. Paul), that non-Christians can obtain salvation.

[68] Ibid., p. 137; cf. p. 138.

[69] Ibid., p. 139.

[70] Ibid.; emphasis added.

[71] Ibid., pp. 140–141.

[72] Ibid., p. 142.

[73] Ibid., p. 143.

[74] Ibid., p. 144.

[75] Ibid., pp. 145–146.

the Christian Revelation alone that represented the decisive turning point in the universal propagation of the truth of monotheism.[76] This was the first purpose of Christ being sent; the second purpose, equally important, was to teach the laws of morality that "Natural Reason" proved insufficient to convey.[77] "Natural Religion" and Revelation teach the same truths,[78] but Revelation seems able to teach them with an efficacy that Natural Reason never achieves.[79] "'Tis true there is a *Law of Nature*. But who is there that ever did, or undertook to give it us all entire, as a Law[?]"[80] Hence Locke is very far from asserting that whatever we have from Revelation is independently and sufficiently available from reason. ("[S]ome parts of [the moral] Truth lye too deep for our Natural Powers easily to reach, and make plain and visible to mankind, without some Light from above to direct them."[81]) There is no subordination of revelation to reason in Locke, as there is in the deists (or in Spinoza). Still, Locke's theology represented an important step on the way toward a form of religion in which dogma counted for very little and morality, almost everything.[82]

Is Christianity ultimately strengthened or weakened by Locke's strategy of "rationalizing" it by paring away doctrines such as original sin and the divinity of Christ[83]? Was he fundamentally a savior of Christianity or a subverter of Christianity? This seems an open question. Obviously, from the point of view of John Edwards, Locke's leading contemporary accuser, Locke was no Christian at all,[84] and the Edwards view is still alive today among Straussian interpreters

---

[76] Ibid.

[77] Ibid., p. 148.

[78] Cf. p. 149: The truths of Revelation "as soon as they are heard and considered . . . are found to be agreeable to Reason; and such as can by no means be contradicted." See also p. 153, where Locke discusses "a full and sufficient Rule for our direction . . . conformable to that of Reason"; p. 156: "'Tis no diminishing to Revelation, that Reason gives its suffrage too to the Truths Revelation has discovered"; and p. 169: God's "Law . . . could not be otherwise than what Reason should dictate."

[79] Ibid., p. 149: "Experience shews that the knowledge of Morality, by meer natural light, (how agreeable soever it be to it) makes but slow progress, and little advance in the World."

[80] Ibid., p. 153.

[81] Ibid., p. 155. Higgins-Biddle, in his editorial notes (p. 149, n. 1, p. 155, n. 1, and p. 156, n. 2), interprets this section of the *Reasonableness* as an antideist argument.

[82] Cf. Charles Blount's encapsulation of the deist creed: "The Morality in Religion is above the Mystery in it. . . . [T]he credulous Christian that believes Orthodoxly, but lives ill, is not safe" (*John Locke and Christianity*, p. 151).

[83] Denial of the divinity of Jesus seems most directly implied in the discussion on pp. 113–114 of the equal status of Adam and Jesus as "Sons of God." Locke's critics were quick to pounce on this telltale sign of Socinianism.

[84] For a nineteenth-century critique of Locke no less harsh than Edwards's seventeenth-century critique, consider Joseph de Maistre, *St. Petersburg Dialogues*, ed. R. A. Lebrun (Montreal: McGill-Queen's University Press, 1993), p. 189: "A dreadful sect was beginning to organize itself [and in Locke's *The Reasonableness of Christianity*] it was its good luck to come upon a book . . . where all the germs of the most abject and detestable philosophy were found covered by a meritorious reputation, enveloped by wise forms, and even flanked as needed by some texts of Holy Scripture."

of Locke.[85] However, one might equally consider Eldon Eisenach's suggestion that in the eighteenth-century context of the dual crisis of Anglicanism and Puritanism, a Lockean-rationalist strategy was the only way to keep Christianity in business.[86] It is beyond the scope of my study to attempt to resolve this issue, but obviously the same question poses itself throughout the whole long tradition of attempts to liberalize Christian theology (and presumably the process of liberalizing other religious traditions as well).

How far does the *Reasonableness* actually go in liberalizing Christianity? In a journal entry dated April 3, 1681, Locke wrote, "the miracles were to be judged by [the rationality of] the doctrine, and not the doctrine by the miracles"; the text as a whole basically asserts the subordination of revelation to reason.[87] The *Reasonableness*, with its appeal to Jesus' performance of miracles and its presentation of reason as requiring revelation as its natural supplement, comes nowhere near the radicalness of this journal entry.[88] However, a work

---

[85] See esp. Rabieh, "The Reasonableness of Locke." For a review of broader methodological issues raised by a Straussian reading of Locke, see Michael Zuckert, "Of Wary Physicians and Weary Readers: The Debates on Locke's Way of Writing," *The Independent Journal of Philosophy*, Vol. 2 (1978): 55–66.

[86] Eldon J. Eisenach, "Mill and Liberal Christianity," in *Mill and the Moral Character of Liberalism*, ed. Eisenach (University Park: Pennsylvania State University Press, 1998), pp. 213–215. Cf. p. 221: "Were all those urging that the Christianity of the future should center on ethical teachings and social justice subverting Christianity, or were they earnestly seeking to keep it alive in the modern world?" As Eisenach highlights, questions of this kind rendered issues of religious identity necessarily "contested ground" from Locke all the way up to Victorian England. Eisenach argues that the process whereby "Locke, the Socinian heretic, [became] the mainstay of Christian apologetics in the Church of England in the next century" (p. 222) established a pattern replicated by Mill's Protestant-rationalist contemporaries.

[87] *Political Writings*, ed. Wootton, pp. 238–240; the quotation is from p. 240. Cf. the first epigraph to this chapter, which is drawn from the same text. Locke's phrase, "submission . . . of our *reason* to *faith*," suggesting the ultimate trumping power of divine revelation (*An Essay Concerning Human Understanding*, ed. Roger Woolhouse, London: Penguin, 1997, p. 613), seems directly opposed to the 1681 text and is one that could never have been uttered by a deist. Cf. the phrase "the dominion of faith" (ibid.). In those matters where "our mind, by its natural faculties and notions, cannot judge," reason must defer to revelation. Nevertheless, "whether it be a divine revelation, or no, *reason* must judge." Hence the authority that Locke concedes to revelation is part of a supremely delicate balancing act between the authority of revelation and the authority of reason.

[88] Relative to what came later, there may be more theological liberalism in the title of Locke's book than there is in the book itself. Cf. Jeremy Waldron, *God, Locke, and Equality* (Cambridge: Cambridge University Press, 2002), p. 104, n. 54 and pp. 207–208, n. 53. The title of Locke's book indeed suggests something much closer to deism than what one encounters in the substance of his theology. Cf. Rabieh, p. 939: "Since Christianity rests its claim to truthfulness on supernatural revelation, the very phrase 'reasonableness of Christianity' seems paradoxical. If Christianity is perfectly reasonable, then it is accessible to natural reason and hence not in need of revelation." If Locke saw the matter thus, he would be a deist, but as we have already seen, there are good reasons to think that Locke in fact saw himself as a *critic* of deism, starting with his formulation of what he took his project to be on the very first page of the *Reasonableness*. (Locke claims in the *Second Vindication* that "my book was chiefly designed for deists" [to convert them back to Christianity?]: See Thoemmes Press edition of the *Reasonableness*, p. 375; cf.

roughly contemporaneous with the *Reasonableness* that *did* follow through on the subordination of revelation to reason intimated in Locke's journal entry was John Toland's *Christianity not Mysterious* – referred to by I. T. Ramsey as "the sequel to Locke."[89] Here we seemingly have what Locke's theology merely gestured toward: a full-blown religion of reason. In the *Reasonableness*, Locke refers to the "mysteries of Salvation"; Toland, by contrast, declares already in his title that there are no such mysteries.[90] Furthermore, Book 4, chapter 18 of the *Essay Concerning Human Understanding* affirms that "things above reason" indeed exist, whereas Toland's title again directly denies this.[91] All the tensions and ambiguities that haunt Locke's account of the relation between reason and revelation now seem to be cast aside.[92] Whereas Locke is determined

p. 265, and Higgins-Biddle, Introduction to *Reasonableness of Christianity*, p. xxvii.) Higgins-Biddle (p. xxxviii) interprets the title of *Reasonableness of Christianity* not as protodeist but as antideist.

[89] Editor's Introduction to Locke, *The Reasonableness of Christianity* (Stanford, CA: Stanford University Press, 1958), p. 17; cf. Higgins-Biddle, Introduction, p. xxviii. I have used the Kessinger Publishing reprint of *Christianity not Mysterious* (London, 1702). Toland's book was first published in 1696 – one year after the original publication of the *Reasonableness*. The full title of Toland's book is *Christianity not Mysterious: Or a Treatise Shewing that there is nothing in the Gospel Contrary to Reason, Nor Above: And that no Christian Doctrine can be properly call'd a Mystery*. It is obviously no coincidence that three of the four books treated in the discussion straddling this chapter and Chapter 17 refer to reason in their titles. The titles of the books by Locke, Toland, and Kant all announce the same project, but Toland's announces it with the greatest boldness. (Locke's *Reasonableness* was denounced; Kant's *Religion* was censored; but Toland's book, like Rousseau's *Emile*, was actually *burned*.)

[90] *Reasonableness of Christianity*, p. 109; cf. *Christianity not Mysterious*, p. 5 (for what seems like a tacit criticism of Locke). For a helpful discussion of the reception of *Christianity not Mysterious*, see Justin Champion, *Republican Learning* (Manchester: Manchester University Press, 2003), chapter 3, esp. pp. 73–76 and 78–80 on the (both personal and intellectual) relationship between Locke and Toland. Higgins-Biddle, in his Introduction to *Reasonableness of Christianity*, pp. xxxi–xxxvii, also discusses the relationship between Locke and Toland. On p. xlix, Higgins-Biddle mentions that judicial proceedings were initiated jointly against the two books in 1697 (cf. Champion, pp. 70–71). On pp. xxxi and xxxv, Higgins-Biddle considers the intriguing possibility that Locke had access to a partial draft of Toland's book before he had completed the *Reasonableness*, so that what Locke may have meant by his later claim that his book was written "for deists" was that in 1695 he was already responding to Toland's 1696 book! According to this interpretive thesis, *Christianity not Mysterious* was actually the intended *target* of, rather than the sequel to, the *Reasonableness*.

[91] Hence Toland's subtitle ("nothing in the Gospel Contrary to Reason, Nor Above") positions him both with and against Locke: The "nothing contrary to reason" is faithfully Lockean; the "nothing above reason" is anti-Lockean. Nonetheless, it should be emphasized that as Toland presents the issue, it is not a matter of revelation being *submitted* to the judgment of reason, but something more like a reciprocity of reason and revelation; hence his Locke-like insistence that "*Reason* is not less from God than *Revelation*" (p. 140). Cf. "An Apology for Mr. Toland" (included in the same Kessinger Publishing reprint), p. 8.

[92] Those tensions and ambiguities are on vivid display in the *Essay Concerning Human Understanding*, pp. 607–614. For instance, the fact that "traditional revelation" is, by definition, mediated by tradition would seem to impugn its reliability – a potentially subversive suggestion capable of being exploited by later deists (although Toland's challenges to revelation are barely more radical than Locke's). Nevertheless, the radicalism of this suggestion does not stop Locke

to prevent his rationalism from sliding into deism,[93] Toland's title gives the appearance of throwing caution to the winds in pushing Locke's tentative rationalism as far as it will go. As Locke himself perhaps anticipated (especially if Higgins-Biddle's thesis about Locke's access to a draft of *Christianity not Mysterious* is correct),[94] Toland's radicalization of Locke, as announced in his title, made the *Reasonableness* look a lot more subversive than Locke intended it to be.[95] The irony, though, is that in the end, leaving aside the seeming subversiveness of the title, there is nothing terribly radical about Toland's text. Toland and Locke are not Spinoza, and apart from the mantra-like slogan of reason in place of mystery, deist rhetoric is barely more conspicuous in Toland than in Locke. *Christianity not Mysterious* represents a mere baby step in the direction of the kind of no-holds-barred assault upon revelation offered in a later deist work like Paine's *Age of Reason.*[96]

In contrast to Locke, it did not take Toland very long to summon up the boldness to place his name on the title page of his treatise.[97] (Indeed, one wonders whether his reference to "he [who is] forced . . . to propose his Sentiments to the World, by way of Paradox, under a borrow'd or fictitious Name [or anonymously – R.B.]" – in contrast to those "who have the Courage to act more above-board" – is a subtle dig at Locke.[98]) In the Preface, Toland presents himself, like Locke, as a defender of "reveal'd Religion," "the Verity of Divine Revelation," and "the Divinity of the New Testament."[99] Rather than *subverting* Christianity by purging it of all mysteries elevated above reason, Toland declares himself to be *vindicating* Christianity by showing it to be

from asserting the superiority of revelation to reason in those concerns constituting "the proper matter of faith."

[93] Higgins-Biddle does a particularly good job of explaining how Locke's project of refuting the deists puts a major strain on his commitment to natural law (as well as natural religion): See Introduction, pp. ci–cviii. Locke realizes that, on one hand, if he puts too much emphasis on the sufficiency of natural reason then he encourages a slide into deism; on the other hand, if he puts too much of a damper on the sufficiency of natural reason then it looks as if he has lost faith in natural law. It seems like an unwinnable position.

[94] See note 90.

[95] Hence the initiation of judicial proceedings against both books cited in note 90. If Locke's "for the deists" meant Toland in particular, it would surely have struck Locke as a huge (and not amusing) irony that his efforts ended with his book being indicted alongside Toland's.

[96] There is a huge difference between asserting, as both Locke and Toland do, that revealed religion is itself rational, and asserting, as Paine does, that Revelation is "fabulous," i.e., a combination of "fable and imposture" (*Age of Reason*, p. 153). Biblical religion is referred to as fabulous in Paine's subtitle ("An Examination of True and Fabulous Theology").

[97] See Champion, *Republican Learning*, p. 70.

[98] *Christianity not Mysterious*, pp. iv–v. Cf. *Collected Writings of Rousseau*, Vol. 9, pp. 48 and 219–220. See also Toland's reference (p. ix) to a kind of writing that, "as it falls out very ordinarily," aims at more than it declares (in contrast to writing with "Sincerity and Simplicity"). Again, this could conceivably be read as a reference to Locke's cageyness.

[99] *Christianity not Mysterious*, p. xxiv ("I demonstrate the Verity of Divine Revelation against Atheists, and all Enemies of reveal'd Religion"). On p. 173, Toland implicitly but unmistakably denies that he is a deist. For an explicit denial of deism, see "An Apology for Mr. Toland," p. 19.

through-and-through a religion of reason.[100] However, whereas Locke struggled to maintain a finely balanced equilibrium between reason and revelation, in Toland the balance tilts decidedly toward reason.[101] Whereas Locke intimates that "traditional revelation" is epistemologically problematical without actually asserting that it is,[102] Toland pushes this Lockean suggestion in a more directly Spinozistic direction.[103] Whereas Locke is silent about the doctrine of the Trinity, Toland says just enough to make known his skepticism.[104] Whereas Locke attempts to mitigate the harshness of the doctrine of hell (without actually renouncing this doctrine), Toland gives at least some indication of joining Hobbes and Spinoza in repudiating this cruel punitiveness of Christian orthodoxy.[105]

Those on the lookout for evidence of heterodoxy in Toland would no doubt have been attentive to these passing hints in Section 2 of *Christianity not Mysterious*, but overall one has to say that as was the case with Locke's *Reasonableness*, there is far more radicalism in the title of Toland's treatise than in the book itself. What does it mean to say that there is nothing mysterious, nothing above reason, in revealed religion? Depending on the authority of the Church to vouch for the divinity of Scripture is circular, because the Church's own authority *derives* from Scripture; hence the divinity of Scripture must be grounded upon reason if it is to have any foundation at all: "[Scripture] has in itself, I grant, the brightest Characters of *Divinity*: But 'tis *Reason* finds them out, examines them, and by its Principles approves and pronounces them sufficient."[106] Of course, reviewing the aspects of religion that Toland

---

[100] See "An Apology for Mr. Toland," p. 24. Champion, who interprets *Christianity not Mysterious* as being every bit as subversive as Toland's contemporary critics took it to be, refers to Toland's profession of adherence to Christianity as a "masquerade" (*Republican Learning*, p. 70).

[101] For instance, *Christianity not Mysterious*, p. 37, where he states that "to believe the Divinity of *Scripture* . . . without rational Proofs . . . is a blameable Credulity."

[102] See note 92.

[103] Hence Toland's statement on p. 18 of *Christianity not Mysterious* that "as we are extreamly subject to Deception, we may [often take] Humane Impostures for *Divine Revelation*." Cf. p. 42, where he speaks of "the Impostures and Traditions of Men." How can one be unconditionally committed to "the Verity of Divine Revelation" if (as Hobbes began to intimate and as Spinoza announced through a bullhorn) the received text of Revelation was the object of likely manipulation? On p. 43, Toland states that whereas "the Revelation of Man" may always involve deception, God's Revelation "*is always true*." "*God [is not] capable to deceive me, as Man is*." However, with hints already dropped about the possibility of "Impostures," how can we be sure that human deceptions have not already entered into "what God is pleas'd to discover to me"? On pp. 111–112, Toland, in strong criticism of arbitration over the meaning of Scripture by the early Church Fathers, protests against the idea that "Truth and Falshood should be determin'd by a Majority of Voices." As Paine, though, powerfully highlights (*Age of Reason*, pp. 32–33, 171–172, 173 note, 181, 196, and 204), *the very text of Scripture* was decided by identical means.

[104] *Christianity not Mysterious*, p. 27.

[105] Ibid., p. 29. On p. 134, however, he seems to allow that the doctrine of damnation for nonbelievers is an essential part of Christianity.

[106] Ibid., p. 33.

considers rationally intelligible helps to fill in the picture of what defines his understanding of Christianity. There is no mystery in the notion of eternity.[107] There is no mystery in the notion of infinity.[108] The soul is no mystery because "its Properties are more immediately known to us" than the properties of material bodies.[109] The attributes of God are not a mystery to us because the idea of "his Goodness," "his Mercy," "his Justice," and "his Wisdom and Power" does not exceed our understanding.[110]

What, then, of the nature of Jesus Christ and his divine mission? Toland provides little that is specific on this score; he tends to presume that the content of the Gospel teaching is more or less obvious. "[T]he Coming of *Christ* [and] the *Resurrection* of the Body [are] Matter[s] of Fact... deliver'd in the Gospel"; matters of "historical Fact communicable by God alone."[111] What are mysteries *before* God offers His revelation (i.e., the revelation of the New Testament) cease to be mysteries afterward, such as the puzzle of why the just seem damned no less than the unjust.[112] Toland actually goes further than Locke in accepting the doctrine of original sin.[113] Toland quotes from *Romans* 16: 25–26 to the effect that with the preaching of Jesus Christ, "the MYSTERY which was kept secret since the World began... now is made MANIFEST."[114] This pretty much suggests that revelation as such means the turning of mystery into nonmystery. If so, it certainly seems to drain all possible subversiveness from what one may initially have associated with Toland's title. Why Toland sees no mystery in doctrines such as the Resurrection, the rising of the dead, and the redemption of otherwise-damned sinners is itself a not trivial mystery.[115]

This leaves the crucial issue of miracles, and their relation to a Christian religion of reason. If we take Paine's *Age of Reason* as setting the ultimate standard of pure deism, Paine's position is indeed a radical one: Mystery and miracle "are incompatible with true religion."[116] Toland's view seems nondeist, judged by this standard; the miracles reported in the Gospels (and the Old Testament) are rational rather than transrational. This problem is addressed in Section 3, chapter 5. Because Toland rules out (pretty much by definition) the possibility of anything being contrary to or beyond reason, the existence of miracles (which he does not deny) must be compatible with reason. Hence "[t]he

---

[107] Ibid., p. 80.

[108] Ibid., p. 81.

[109] Ibid., p. 86.

[110] Ibid., pp. 86–87.

[111] Ibid., p. 90.

[112] Ibid., pp. 89, 91.

[113] Ibid., p. 92. Another respect in which Toland appears more orthodox than Locke is in his not marginalizing the Epistles (though Toland does exclude the *Book of Revelation* from the Gospel; see p. 106).

[114] Ibid., p. 94.

[115] On p. 127, Toland states that God "wants [not] Ability to inform [his Creatures] rightly." Is it really true that there was no more rationally accessible way for God to instruct His creatures concerning His purposes than the delivered text of the Bible?

[116] Paine, *Age of Reason*, p. 75.

miraculous Action...must be something in itself intelligible and possible, tho the manner of doing it be extraordinary."[117] If a physician cures an ailment, this is by the ordinary operation of the laws of nature. If such a cure is "the immediate Effect of supernatural Power," then it falls within the domain of the miraculous.[118] Both are equally graspable by human reason. "No *Miracle* then is contrary to Reason, for the Action must be intelligible, and the Performance of it appear most easy to the Author of *Nature*, who may command all its Principles at his Pleasure."[119] Miracles do not exactly violate the laws of nature but rather lend "supernatural assistance" to these laws to achieve purposes equal in intelligibility to those served by "its ordinary Operations."[120] It is hard to avoid the judgment that Toland here simply eludes the problem by opting for an excessively facile reconciliation between reason and what is above reason.

Even if Toland aspired to offer a version of Christianity that was more reasonable than Locke's *Reasonableness of Christianity*, we can see from his appeals to "the Verity of Revelation" and his vindication of the rationality of miracles that there is absolutely no comparison between the rationalism of Toland's deism and, say, that of Paine (so much closer to the spirit of Spinoza) a century later. Hence, writing from a twenty-first-century vantage point, it is hard to make out why *Christianity not Mysterious* was received as such a revolutionary text (certainly as compared with Spinoza's *Theological–Political Treatise*, with its head-on challenges to revealed religion), except that if the larger cultural context was one of the hegemonic order starting to succumb to deist challenges, even baby steps would put one that much closer to the edge of the slippery slope toward a post-Christian culture.[121]

---

[117] *Christianity not Mysterious*, p. 145.

[118] Ibid.

[119] Ibid., p. 146; cf. p. 132, on the faith of Abraham as defined by *reasonable* trust in divine miracles.

[120] Ibid., p. 150. To be sure, Toland polemicizes against miracles associated with the credulity of "papists" and others in the grip of priestly superstition (pp. 147–149), but he takes at face value all the miracles reported in the Bible.

[121] Cf. p. 110, where Toland sketches the sense of waning control on the part of church authorities.

14

Bayle's Republic of Atheists

[R]eligion . . . is one of the greatest instruments of morality and civilization which God ever decided to employ.

– Alexis de Tocqueville[1]

If I spoke badly . . . about the devout, it is only because I am revolted every day when I see petty people in their gossipy circles with their foolish affairs who are capable of every sort of despicable and violent action talking devoutly of their *holy religion*. I am always tempted to shout at them: "Rather than be Christians of this kind, be pagans with pure conduct, proud of your soul and with clean hands!"

– Alexis de Tocqueville[2]

[I]t is certain that the greatest part of the peoples of the earth are still plunged in the frightful shadows of infidelity.

– Pierre Bayle[3]

One enters into disputes concerning dogma, and one in no way practices morality. Why? Because practicing morality is difficult and pursuing disputes concerning dogma is very easy.

– Montesquieu[4]

---

[1] Alexis de Tocqueville, *The European Revolution and Correspondence with Gobineau*, ed. and trans. John Lukacs (Garden City, NY: Doubleday Anchor Books, 1959), p. 304.

[2] Ibid., p. 306.

[3] Pierre Bayle, *Various Thoughts on the Occasion of a Comet*, trans. Robert C. Bartlett (Albany, NY: SUNY Press, 2000), p. 90.

[4] Montesquieu, *Œuvres completes*, ed. Daniel Oster (Paris: Du Seuil, 1964), p. 1074 (*Mes pensées*, no. 2112). Cf. *Collected Writings of Rousseau*, Vol. 9, ed. Christopher Kelly and Eve Grace (Lebanon, NH: University Press of New England, 2001), p. 56.

I saw that there were professions of faith, doctrines, forms of worship that were followed without belief, and that, since nothing of all that penetrated either heart or reason, it influenced conduct very little.

– Jean-Jacques Rousseau[5]

The civil-religion theorists were not oriented toward the possibility of secular politics. As Joshua Mitchell writes, for Hobbes the "alternatives are either a 'Christian Commonwealth' (Part III [of *Leviathan*]) or a 'Kingdom of Darkness' (Part IV [of *Leviathan*]). *A secularized world is not a genuine possibility*; the attempt to deny religion its due leads not to a world enlightened by autonomous reason, but rather, ironically, one dominated by superstition and steeped in the kingdom of darkness!"[6] A secularized world first becomes a possibility in Bayle (and of course Rousseau is explicit in his rejection of Bayle). Hence one could say that Pierre Bayle is the first thoroughgoing anti-civil-religion theorist in the Western tradition.[7] In fact, Sally Jenkinson argues that Bayle was unique among early modern political philosophers in his rejection of civil religion:

[It was] accepted by natural law philosophers such as Grotius, Hobbes, Selden, Spinoza, Harrington and Locke, no less than by Gallican Catholics such as Richelieu and Bossuet . . . that a civil religion, whose clergy was subordinate to the secular authority, was a requisite part of the internal process of orderly government. All parties would agree, though for subtly different reasons, that society itself was cemented through holding in common certain [religious] beliefs, [and that the clergy] should form a *corps* of civilizing educators. The notion that a religion so understood was vital to the public good was so generally insisted upon that in contesting it Bayle would find himself confronting all parties – Catholics and Protestants, lay men and clergy.[8]

---

[5] *Collected Writings of Rousseau*, Vol. 9, p. 53.

[6] Joshua Mitchell, *Not by Reason Alone: Religion, History, and Identity in Early Modern Political Thought* (Chicago: University of Chicago Press, 1993), pp. 228–229, n. 6; emphasis added.

[7] Arguably, this rejection of civil religion is stated as a principle in *Various Thoughts*, § 90, where it is argued that "pious frauds" are wrong even if it is true that these falsehoods "aid piety." Cf. the end of § 91, referring to the debate between Augustine and Varro. See Augustine, *The City of God against the Pagans*, ed. R. W. Dyson (Cambridge: Cambridge University Press, 1998), p. 182. Bayle concedes that "there are scarcely any statesmen, or people of the church" who are not of Varro's view that truth must sometimes be sacrificed to the needs of civil theology. (Augustine says the same thing.) See also the discussion of civil religion in § 131. In that text, Bayle insists that idolatrous religions are inefficacious in improving the morality of human beings but concedes that they *are* efficacious in bolstering the attachment of citizens to their republics. Therefore, ironically, although Bayle is a target of Rousseau's civil-religion chapter, Bayle and Rousseau agree that "from the point of view of politics," civil religion is serviceable "in regard to the strengthening of the republic" (*Various Thoughts*, p. 162). Bayle rejects civil religion for moral reasons, not for political reasons.

[8] Sally L. Jenkinson, "Two Concepts of Tolerance: Or Why Bayle is Not Locke," *The Journal of Political Philosophy*, Vol. 4, No. 4 (1996): 306–307. Cf. a suggestion put to me by Edward Andrew that "popular Hobbesianism where the state assumes control over a national church was espoused by Mandeville, Voltaire, Hume, Diderot, Rousseau, and most of the leading lights of the Enlightenment" (personal communication). It would seem that Bayle offers an exception (or qualified exception – see note 12) to this general tendency of Enlightenment thought.

What Bayle offers, according to Jenkinson, is "a general critique of post-Reformation [E]rastian theory,"⁹ and all the predecessors or contemporaries of Bayle cited in the preceding quotation count as various kinds of Erastian, that is, civil-religion, theorists. One might add that Rousseau represents the culmination of this Erastian tradition, because he sums up the underlying notion with the very conception of a "civil religion."¹⁰

The rejection of Erastianism does not mean that Bayle shares nothing in common with Hobbes, or that Hobbes's concerns about rebalancing the relationship between politics and religion are not Bayle's concern as well. As Elisabeth Labrousse highlights in her recounting of Bayle's politics, Bayle's appeal to the absolute authority of the civil sovereign is no less unconditional than Hobbes', and for very similar reasons:

Following Hobbes..., Bayle sees absolute monarchy as signifying the supremacy of the civil power and its independence from religious authorities, specifically the national clergy and the Vatican. Only an authoritarian, absolute monarchy in France can be powerful enough to keep the tribe of ecclesiastics in their place.... [W]hat [Bayle] categorically rejects is the validity of clerical authority in secular and political matters, for example in civil legislation.... [I]n Bayle's view, [absolutist prerogatives of the monarch] are the only way to make the supremacy of the civil power secure against powerful clerical adversaries.¹¹

So again, rejection of Erastianism does not mean that there is not much in common between Bayle and Hobbes; but it does mean that Bayle departs from Hobbes in seeing the need for an assertion of *religious–theological* monopoly on the part of the sovereign.¹²

⁹ Jenkinson, "Two Concepts of Tolrance," p. 310.
¹⁰ Cf. ibid., p. 311: "Locke's theory of toleration, no less than [the later theories] of Montesquieu or Rousseau, seems to fall squarely within the earlier tradition of [Erastian–civil-religion theory]"; and Jenkinson, "Nourishing Men's Anger and Inflaming the Fires of Hatred: Bayle on Religious Violence and the 'Novus Ordo Saeclorum,'" *Terrorism and Political Violence*, Vol. 10, No. 4 (Winter 1998): 69. See also Jenkinson's Introduction to Bayle, *Political Writings* (Cambridge: Cambridge University Press, 2000), p. xxxiv (Bayle "attempts to re-construct a religiously impartial opposition to the 'baroque' and Erastian state"). See Bayle's discussion of civil religion (including Islamic civil religion) in *Various Thoughts*, § 111.
¹¹ Elisabeth Labrousse, *Bayle*, trans. Denys Potts (Oxford: Oxford University Press, 1983), pp. 76–77. Labrousse denies that Bayle's advocacy of absolutism contradicts his commitment to toleration; as Bayle sees it, Louis XIV's Revocation of the Edict of Nantes "was the action of a bigot under the thumb of his confessor, not that of a king making his own decisions" (p. 78).
¹² Ibid., p. 80: "[T]he political authorities have no need, and for that matter no right, to assume the direction of a nation's religious convictions." However, one can well ask how it is possible to embrace a Hobbesian understanding of sovereignty while rejecting Erastianism, for Erastianism is pretty much inseparable from Hobbesian sovereignty. Hence Edward Andrew's suggestion that Bayle "thought that the cause of toleration was perhaps best secured by Hobbesian Erastianism – 'better Leviathan than Torquemada.'" Andrew, *Patrons of Enlightenment* (Toronto: University of Toronto Press, 2006), p. 87 (quoting Labrousse). It seems that what Bayle offers is a curious synthesis of Hobbes and Locke (which is also the case in Spinoza, or so I argued in Chapter 11).

I cannot enter here into the controversy concerning the sincerity or insincerity of Bayle's professed piety.[13] For our purposes, it is more important to explore the argument concerning the moral-civic innocuousness of atheism to which Montesquieu and Rousseau felt they needed to respond. As Robert Bartlett puts it, Bayle's argument that "a decent society of atheists is possible in principle" was a view that was "unique to him in the history of political thought until then" – that is, until the articulation of this view in Bayle's *Various Thoughts on the Occasion of a Comet*.[14] Bayle starts to develop this argument in Letter 7. The argument is a response to the view that God must make extraordinary interventions to deter atheism because atheism would inevitably lead to "the ruin of human society."[15] He argues in §§ 102–113 that atheism

---

[13] See Michael Heyd, "A Disguised Atheist or a Sincere Christian? The Enigma of Pierre Bayle," *Bibliothèque d'Humanisme et Renaissance*, Vol. 39, No. 1 (1977): 157–165. In *Bayle*, Elisabeth Labrousse presents Bayle as a committed fideistic Calvinist. She cites Bayle's deathbed profession: "I die a Christian philosopher" (*Bayle*, p. 47). However, not only is there, as Labrousse notes, in this deathbed profession an echo of Averroistic unbelief, but, more seriously, Labrousse herself argues throughout her book that the very notion of "Christian philosopher" is for Bayle a flat-out oxymoron. Cf. Jonathan Israel, *Radical Enlightenment* (Oxford: Oxford University Press, 2001), pp. 331–341, which raises many doubts about Labrousse's fideist reading of Bayle. See also the editor's Introduction to Bayle, *Various Thoughts*, trans. Bartlett. Bartlett makes a good case for interpreting the *Various Thoughts* in a Spinozistic light. See in particular pp. xxxvii–xxxix; the argument here is that "general providence," as opposed to "particular providence," is a euphemism for no providence at all (see *Various Thoughts*, p. 104). What this ultimately means is that Bayle's God is not the biblical God but rather Spinoza's "*Natura sive Deus.*" (In *Various Thoughts*, § 91, Bayle associates the view that "nature is nothing other than God himself acting . . . according to certain laws" with "sound philosophy" [*bonne Philosophie*].) Rousseau, in his letter to Voltaire of August 18, 1756, appeals to the very same conception of universal versus particular providence, after having joined Voltaire in admiring Bayle's "wisdom and caution in matters of opinion": See *The Collected Writings of Rousseau*, Vol. 3, ed. Roger D. Masters and Christopher Kelly (Lebanon, NH: University Press of New England, 1992), pp. 116 and 114.

Consider also the following sweeping statement of Bayle's skepticism: "It is more likely that the opinions established in the mind of the majority of men are false than it is that they are true" (*Various Thoughts*, pp. 39–40; cf. p. 28: "[I]n things where there is no more reason on one side than on the other, the error is always more on the side of those who affirm than on the side of those who suspend their judgment"). To be sure, Bayle hastens to qualify this generalization by saying that he "exempt[s] . . . matters of faith" (p. 39), but he fails to explain *why* he exempts matters of faith. Indeed, if we consider the context defined by the entirety of the *Various Thoughts*, it seems obvious that it is *particularly* with respect to matters of faith that Bayle's skepticism is applicable. Cf. Maistre's quite cutting comment on Bayle in *Œuvres*, ed. Pierre Glaudes (Paris: Robert Laffont, 2007), pp. 311–312. Finally, I add that puzzles of the sort that apply to Bayle can also be traced back to earlier generations of the fideist tradition, as can be attested by chapter 5 of Richard H. Popkin, *The History of Scepticism*, rev. ed. (New York: Harper & Row, 1964).

[14] Bartlett, "Introduction," p. xxiii. Leo Strauss, by contrast, sees Bayle's argument as having its intellectual point of departure in Hobbes: See Strauss, *Natural Right and History* (Chicago: University of Chicago Press, 1953), p. 198.

[15] *Various Thoughts*, p. 134; cf. p. 139: "It has been recognized in all times that religion was one of the bonds of society."

is not a threat because human beings are naturally fearful and therefore naturally superstitious. Philosophers such as Anaxagoras, Socrates, and Epicurus[16] can see that everything is explicable according to natural causes, which might *seem* to present the threat of a general subversion of religion. Again, though, owing to the ubiquity of fear and hence of superstition, this is no threat at all; it simply renders philosophers the targets of persecution by the society at large (§ 110; cf. § 200).[17] Twice within this sequence of chapters, Bayle introduces an arresting analogy between the Bible's jealous God and what one would expect of a jealous husband. The husband can cope with a wife who loves neither him nor anyone else; what the husband *cannot* abide is the wife sharing her favors with other lovers. The same is true of God. God is less offended by human beings who are indifferent to gods per se (atheism) than by those who share their affections with rival gods (idolatry).[18] In § 113, Bayle makes the point that this analogy is not something he has conjured up on his own – it is suggested by the Bible itself: "Scripture speaks of idolatry as adultery committed against the glory of a jealous God."[19] Finally, Bayle makes the point that "the Devil" ("*le Diable*," "*le Demon*") prefers idolatry to atheism; hence it follows that God must prefer atheism to idolatry.

The next stage of the argument is one that the author of the *Various Thoughts* (even as an anonymous author!) does not dare to state in his own voice. As Bayle repeatedly indicates,[20] this supposedly merely *reported* discourse on atheism and idolatry runs through the balance of Letter 7, and the whole of Letters 8 and 9. In effect, Bayle takes upon himself a *double* anonymity in delivering his teaching on the relative virtue, or at least relative nonviciousness, of atheism. Bayle's argument for the moral neutrality of atheism centers on the moral inefficacy of religion. The core of the argument is presented in § 131. The argument is based on what one could call the superficiality of

---

[16] Ibid., pp. 141, 142, and 134.

[17] One has to observe that Bayle's own intended project in the *Various Thoughts* necessarily undermines this aspect of his argument. If the book succeeds in persuading its readers to throw off superstition, then the appeal here to humanity's perennial credulity and need for superstition would no longer be valid. The capacity of philosophers to trace natural phenomena to natural causes would be universalized, and atheism would then indeed become a threat. I add that, unlike the works of Spinoza, Bayle's work is written in a vernacular language rather than the language of the clerical or scholarly elite and is therefore in principle available to all literate citizens.

[18] See *Various Thoughts*, p. 145 (paraphrasing Plutarch): "[O]ne does more wrong to the divinity by believing it to be such as the superstitious represent it to themselves than by believing that it is nothing." Idolatry rather than atheism is the true impiety. Cf. p. 164, as well as the quotation from Arnobius on p. 240. Rousseau adopts exactly the same line, using the same quotation from Plutarch but without citing Bayle; see *Emile*, ed. Allan Bloom (New York: Basic Books, 1979), p. 259; cf. p. 277. D'Holbach places an epigraph from Seneca that makes a very similar point on the title page of *Christianity Unveiled*.

[19] *Various Thoughts*, p. 144.

[20] See § 124, the end of § 128, the end of § 132, the beginning § 133, the beginning and end of § 192, and the beginning and end of § 193. Cf. Bartlett, "Introduction," p. xxx.

religious practices in relation to the depth of the moral corruption of human beings.[21] Concupiscence is "the source of all crimes." Idolatrous religions do not get at the root of this moral corruption because they restrict themselves to "external exercises." "The vague and confused knowledge of providence" offered by idolatrous religions is no match for the moral criminality of human nature: Neither atheists nor idolaters could form societies in the absence of "a brake [*un frein*] stronger than that of religion – namely human laws."[22] Is the situation different, though, in the case of the Christian religion? The principle of the moral inefficacy of religion seems to apply whether one considers idolatrous religions or nonidolatrous religions, for Bayle immediately proceeds to the judgment that human vice is so widespread that "if human laws did not impose order, all societies *of Christians* would soon be destroyed."[23] In § 130, in the midst of a thorough catalogue of pagan iniquities, Bayle tellingly mentions that "Christians . . . commit these same crimes."[24] "The true religion" and "the false religions"[25] are equally impotent in the face of the moral depravity of human beings.

Letter 8 develops a related yet broader and deeper line of argument. If it is true, as Letter 7 had suggested, that Christians are in general no more virtuous than pagans, one is compelled to ask how this can be, given the sublimity (as well as the actual *validity*, the truth) of the moral and theological doctrines of

---

[21] One certainly does not find in Bayle the kind of challenges put to the doctrine of original sin that one encounters in Hobbes and Spinoza. Bayle himself tacitly highlights this disagreement between him on the one side and Hobbes and Spinoza on the other when he writes, at the end of § 160, that "we scarcely see a freethinker [*Esprit fort*] who is willing to agree to the corruption of man." Cf. p. 219, where Bayle invokes the authority of Pascal on the doctrine of original sin; see also § 192.

[22] *Various Thoughts*, p. 162; cf. p. 161: Religion "is too weak a barrier [*une trop faible barrière*] to restrain the passions of man"; p. 180, where he speaks of "the brake that represses the malignity of the heart"; and p. 204: "[R]eligion is not a brake capable of restraining our passions." Rousseau uses exactly the same image (*Emile*, p. 312), although his conclusion is the opposite of Bayle's; for Rousseau's fullest response to Bayle, see the accompanying footnote on pp. 312–314. As Bayle points out at the end of § 137, it is hard to judge whether religious sanctions (including hell) have any independent weight in restraining various moral transgressions when "fairly terrible temporal penalties" are the more obvious means of discouraging these crimes. In fact, it is very clearly his view that the temporal sanctions are doing all the real work in inhibiting human vice.

[23] *Various Thoughts*, p. 162; emphasis added.

[24] Ibid., p. 160; cf. p. 169: Christians no less than pagans live "in the greatest and most vicious dissoluteness."

[25] Ibid., p. 162. The true religion is defined fundamentally by the project of combating the passions and promoting virtue. That is, the distinction between false religions and the true religion rests on the *moral* qualities of the latter. As Rousseau was later to emphasize, the pagan religions were oriented much more toward the civil-religion function of preserving the polity and bolstering citizens' attachment to their republic. The ultimate test of the true religion resides in its service to morality. But does Christianity make good on its promise to improve morality? With respect to "the greatest number" of human beings, the answer is a clear no. Christianity "is not successful" in improving upon the moral record of paganism (ibid.).

Christianity. Letter 8 proposes an answer to this puzzle. We can call it a theory of the superficiality of religious belief in relation to the actual springs of moral practice or moral agency.[26] In § 131 Bayle spoke of "the vague and confused knowledge of providence" embodied in idolatrous religions. However, even if one had a religion ("the true religion") that arrived at a precise and accurate idea of Providence, would this religion, by virtue of its doctrines, be effective in reshaping moral agency? That is the question that Letter 8 pursues. Human beings are more consistently moved by "the dominant passion of the heart," "the inclination of the temperament," "the force of adopted habits," and "the taste for or sensitivity to certain objects"[27] than by "general knowledge . . . of what [one] should do."[28] This is clearly a version of Aristotle's doctrine of *akrasia*: Human beings may know what is required in order to act well, but this moral knowledge in no way guarantees ethical conduct. In other words, human beings are intrinsically hypocritical creatures, and the principles they profess are no guide to their actual behavior. In § 140, Bayle offers an especially powerful example of this human capacity to turn a blind eye to our own principles, namely the Crusades: The fact that they were "an enterprise of devotion" [*une enterprise de devotion*] did not preclude the Crusaders from committing "the most frightful disorders ever heard of."[29] At the level of principles, no religion is more gentle and peace loving than Christianity. Nevertheless, Christian nations have outdone all other nations in forging armies that are formidable engines of "greed, shamelessness, insolence, and cruelty."[30] They have achieved perfection in the art of war "without the knowledge of the Gospel crossing the path of this cruel design in the least."[31] What better proof of Bayle's argument that moral and religious principles exist only to be sacrificed to human passions? One could say that with respect to the moral principles that define the religion, Christianity ought to have brought about a tremendous improvement in the quality of moral life in relation to paganism. Clearly, Bayle's judgment is that this promise of moral improvement was a miserable failure,[32] and moreover that this abysmal failure tells us something essential about the relation between religion and morality.

The flip side of the argument that sincere religious belief is compatible with abominable vice is the argument that there can be such a thing as virtuous

---

[26] A particularly good encapsulation of Bayle's view of the disjunction between belief and conduct is offered in § 176.

[27] *Various Thoughts*, p. 168.

[28] Ibid., p. 167.

[29] Ibid., p. 173.

[30] Ibid., p. 175 (§ 141).

[31] Ibid.

[32] In § 160, Bayle speaks of "the distressing depravity of morals that has descended upon the whole of Christianity for a thousand years." If this is indeed the moral record of Christianity, it seems an astonishing mystery that Christianity has not completely discredited itself, given that it took itself to be the embodiment of an infinitely higher morality than that embodied in the pagan world. Bayle thereby basically implies that "those who doubt our mysteries" are being reasonable in so doubting.

atheists, and this is precisely the argument that Bayle offers starting in § 145. If virtue is not founded on piety, what *is* it founded on? Bayle answers, "a certain disposition of the temperament, fortified by education, by personal interest, by the desire to be praised, by the instinct of reason, or by similar motives that are met with in an atheist as well as in other men."[33] In § 146, Bayle goes so far as to claim that his argument that atheists are not disqualified from the practice of virtue is consistent with "the theology of St. Augustine"! The line of thought goes roughly as follows: Paganism is theologically so corrupt that if pagans are ever virtuous, pagan virtue must owe nothing at all to religious belief. Therefore, if it is possible for virtue to exist among pagans, it must equally be possible for it to exist among atheists.

The next phase of Bayle's argument (Letter 9) is concerned with offering speculations concerning the moral life of a society of atheists. Bayle immediately returns to the theme of the necessity of severe laws in *all* human societies (pagan, Christian, or atheist). If original sin maintains the kind of iron grip on human nature that Bayle claims it does throughout the book, there is only one solution, and it has little to do with religiosity: *Human justice* [*la Justice humaine*] will enforce virtue, and wherever it relaxes its check [*lâche la bride*] on vice, vice will flourish (§ 161). Where "the justice of the state" fails to legislate, vice runs rampant (§ 162).[34] Starting in § 174, however, Bayle switches to an entirely different issue. The issue now is not whether a "society of atheists" would be as virtuous as (or no more vicious than) a pagan society or a Christian society. The issue now is whether there can exist virtuous atheist individuals. In §§ 174–175, Bayle lays out a character study of the archetypical philosophical atheist who lives a morally exemplary life, and whose virtues include frugality, sobriety, austerity, gravity, asceticism, and devotion to abstract thought.[35] Where does Spinoza stand in relation to this account of atheist virtue? Bayle ends § 181 with a moral criticism of Spinoza. Spinoza's great vice, according to § 181, is a prideful "constancy" [*la constance*] in standing by his principles, which is more

---

[33] *Various Thoughts*, p. 180.

[34] As Bayle discusses in §§ 162–164, "the harsh law of honor" offers a useful supplement (at least in the case of "shamelessness") to the laws of the state. With respect to the vice of shamelessness, Bayle on p. 224 asserts the superiority of pagan virtue to Christian virtue (even though pagan religion propagated images of the shamelessness of the gods), owing to the efficacy of the principle of honor. Nevertheless, honor, although it is helpful in restraining shamelessness, is at best a mixed blessing. On p. 212, Bayle speaks of Christians exhibiting an "idolatrous" devotion toward rules of honor.

[35] Compare this list of attributes to the adjectives applied to "the true religion" on p. 231! See Bartlett's Introduction, pp. xlii–xliii, for a consideration of the possibility that this depiction of the virtuous atheist is meant as a self-description. On p. 215, Bayle corrects the mistaken common assumption that because Epicureanism articulated a version of philosophical hedonism, its adherents must have departed from these virtues. On the contrary, Epicurus himself and his true followers exemplify very well Bayle's portrait of the philosophical individual who denies essential articles of faith such as providence and the immortality of the soul yet lives a life of exemplary moral austerity. Cf. Bayle's celebration of Epicurus in § 178 (where Bayle gives more emphasis to the piety of Epicurus while expressing doubt about its sincerity).

than a little odd, given that the overwhelming criticism of Christians ventilated throughout the *Various Thoughts* is their seeming incapacity to remain faithful to their principles.[36]

As Robert Bartlett points out, the core argument of the *Various Thoughts* relentlessly draws attention to "the fundamental similarity between pagan idolatry and biblical faith,"[37] for if idolatrous superstitions were limited to pagan religions, it would be redundant and pointless for Bayle to be making his argument against the superstitious fear of what comets portend ("people [today] do not fail to be as prostituted in the most extravagant and criminal idolatries as in ancient times"[38]). The superstitious dread of comets serves as a demonstration of the *continuity* between pagan superstition and Jewish or Christian superstition. In addition, this has manifest implications as well for the argument in Letters 7–9, for if atheism is morally superior to "idolatry" then it is also morally superior to Christianity with respect to what paganism and Christianity share *qua* forms of popular credulity and superstition. In this sense, the term "idolatry" is ambiguous: In its narrower signification it refers strictly to the varieties of pagan culture, but it can just as well be interpreted more broadly to encompass *all* forms of superstition, whether pagan or Christian.[39] In the passage from which I have drawn the third epigraph to this chapter, Bayle states that *"most men remain idolaters* or have become Mohammedans."[40] Bayle himself encourages us to read this passage as referring to the various non-Christian religions (such as Hinduism,[41] which, unlike Islam, is a polytheistic

---

[36] The title of § 181 is telling: "New Remark to Show That Men Do Not Live According to Their Principles." Spinoza, however, *did* live according to his principles. Bayle offers an even more powerful example of the moral constancy of atheists in his account of Vanini in the following section (§ 182), discussed in note 44. See also *Political Writings*, ed. Jenkinson, pp. 312–320.

[37] Bartlett, "Introduction," p. xxx; see Bartlett's elaboration on p. xlv, n. 14.

[38] *Various Thoughts*, p. 90.

[39] On p. 89 he writes, "nothing is more abominable to [God] than the worship of idols." The Jews erred in worshipping the golden calf, thereby bringing down upon themselves "the deadliest of all punishments," namely exile and captivity. Could one not say, however, in the spirit of Spinoza, that subscribing to an unworthy conception of God constitutes a form of idolatry? If so, would it not follow that embracing polytheistic practices represents only one way among others of becoming idolatrous? It is in precisely this spirit that Bayle writes that those modern Christians who see God as troubling Himself to make His will known through prodigies have fallen into an attribution "unworthy of the wisdom and holiness of God" (*Various Thoughts*, p. 92; cf. p. 126: "attribut[ing] to [God] a conduct unworthy of his wisdom"; p. 131: "unworthy of the goodness and wisdom of God"; and p. 261). They, no less than the ancient pagans, can be legitimately spoken of as "idolaters." Cf. p. 148: "To worship what one falsely imagines to be God is an act of idolatry." Bayle offers a particularly good representation of what is unworthy about the images of God implied in talk of prodigies in the citation from Maximus Tyrius quoted in note *d* of § 101 (the roadside prophet who hawks his bargain prophecies to chance passersby).

[40] *Various Thoughts*, p. 90; emphasis added.

[41] Cf. *Various Thoughts*, p. 91.

religion). One may well suspect, though, that Bayle's real view is that the "most men remain idolaters" claim includes the forms of superstition propagated by Christianity. In § 73, Bayle refers to India, China, and Japan as idolatrous nations, but if idolatry is associated with "a blind and raging superstition," why would Bayle not classify, say, Catholic France as an idolatrous nation?[42] As Bayle puts it in § 79, "Christians are as much afflicted as other men by the malady of making presages for themselves out of everything." That is, Christians are no less superstitious ("idolatrous" in the broader sense) than pagans are.[43] If the Christian dread of comets is as idolatrous as the pagan dread of comets (and one would be hard put, from Bayle's point of view, to explain why it *is not* idolatrous), then the moral vindication of atheism in Letters 7–9 also vindicates atheism *in relation to Christianity*.

Finally, one has to ask this: Why does Bayle feel he needs to take on the project of vindicating the virtue of atheists at all?[44] Why is *this* taken to be

---

[42] Furthermore, if one assumes that superstition among the Christians is limited to *Catholics*, Bayle, on p. 118, goes out of his way to emphasize that Calvinists and Lutherans are in the grip of the same superstitions. See also Bayle's important reference on p. 306 to the "excess of zeal" associated with early Protestantism as "a religion still hot from the forge."

[43] Cf. *Various Thoughts*, p. 105: "Christians have the same prejudice, . . . they give in to the same weaknesses as the pagans"; and p. 118, where he states that "the character of the people of today is altogether similar to that of the ancients." Consider also the dictum by St. Eligius cited on p. 113, that to be a superstitious Christian "is to be in part a pagan."

On p. 162, Bayle distinguishes between "the true religion" and "the false religions." As I discussed earlier, however, it turns out that the true religion is no more efficacious in making human beings virtuous than the idolatrous religions are. The problem is particularly acute when one considers that it is Bayle's view (like Spinoza's) that religion is fundamentally judged on *moral* grounds – on whether it can secure the soundness of moral practice (see pp. 184–185: "[T]here cannot be true devotion . . . in a soul that does not love God *and that does not obey God*" [emphasis added]; and pp. 186–187: "[T]he true faith [consists in] the disposition of the heart that leads us to renounce all that we know to be contrary to the will of God"). *No morality, no religion.* How then can Christianity be judged superior to paganism if both are equally impotent in the face of human vice? This is a key move in weakening the distinction between idolatrous religion and nonidolatrous religion.

[44] The theme of the moral vindication of atheists is developed most powerfully (albeit obliquely) in the striking account of Vanini's martyrdom in § 182. If atheism were really associated with cynical immoralism, then the sensible thing for Vanini to have done would have been to work "to make the world devout" to take advantage of other people's credulity. Instead, he fearlessly preached atheism. Bayle can conceive only two possible explanations: Either Vanini sought glory, in which case he transcended a narrow hedonism, or he disinterestedly sought to liberate human beings from the fear of hell, which Bayle calls "a false idea of generosity." It is hard not to conclude that what is exemplified here is the ancient and noble idea of virtue practiced for its own sake – that is, realization of the higher standard of justice disclosed in the story of Gyges that is beyond the reach of most Christians (see p. 222, notes *a* and *e*; cf. the story of the woman with the flame and the water on p. 221). Christians know that God will see through their hypocrisies, yet they still practice hypocrisy. Vanini, in contrast, does not believe in an all-seeing divine spectator, yet he nonetheless pays the highest price in refusing to betray the cause of decency. Hence Vanini's supposedly "false idea of generosity" is in fact a higher morality.

essential to the achievement of Bayle's philosophical purposes? Why does an argument intended to promote toleration – most immediately, the toleration of Huguenots by Catholics and the toleration of Catholics by Huguenots – seem to be focused on the moral capacities of atheists? Here is one possible answer. As long as people think that religious belief is a necessary condition of sound morality and sound politics, they will have an incentive to be what Bayle refers to as "zealot[s] for divine worship" [zelé pour le service divin].[45] They will insist on the unique truth of their own dogmas and ceremonies and regard competing beliefs as enemies of morality and patriotism.[46] In note b of § 131, there is a quotation from Juvenal's Satires that captures the idea here very well: "On both sides there is the greatest fury on account of their neighbors' gods, and each place hates the other."[47] This note is attached to a critique of Jerome Cardan (a sixteenth-century Italian mathematician who challenged the moral benefits of belief in personal immortality) that concedes "some reason" to Cardan's view "that the belief in the immortality of the soul has caused great disorders in the world through wars of religion that it has excited in all times."[48] Wars of religion are not a phenomenon unique to the conflict between Catholics and Reformers; they are coeval with religious belief per se. If Bayle can convince his readers that ethical conduct will be (at worst) neither better nor worse in the absence of religion – that "belief in the immortality of

---

[45] Ibid., p. 168; cf. p. 194, where he refers to "great zealots" [grand Zelateurs]. Zealotry is what joins wicked and superstitious pagans to wicked and superstitious Christians. See also p. 243: "It would be a thousand times better . . . to be indifferent to all the sects of the Christian religion than to have, in favor of the true one, so impious a zeal."

[46] Cf. p. 178: "[F]aith in a religion . . . is often apt to excite in the soul anger against those who are of a different sentiment." The theme of the "implacable hatred" between one sect and another is also pursued in §§ 139 and 155–156.

[47] Cf. the theme of religiously motivated "fury" [la fureur] at the end of § 139, as well as § 140's account of Christian-inspired "disorders" and "ravages" in the case of the Crusades. In the next section (§ 141), Bayle takes up the challenge asserted by the Machiavellian view (reasserted later by Rousseau) that the spirit of Christianity is too passive and pacific to undergird the rigors of citizenship. Bayle makes important concessions to the Machiavellian view but then concludes that "there are not on earth nations more bellicose than those that profess Christianity" (p. 174).

[48] Ibid., p. 162; emphasis added. Bayle elaborates the basis of his critique of Cardan in § 141: In principle, Christian faith ought to render its adherents courageous in war and capable of "heroic patience" in enduring persecution. These could be resources for superior citizenship and would refute Cardan's view that otherworldly beliefs always make us worse citizens in this world. The problem, of course, is that Christian courage eventually gets put in the service of cruelty and violence to the extent that (as quoted in the previous note), notwithstanding the peace-loving "spirit of our holy religion," "there are not on earth nations more bellicose than those that profess Christianity" (p. 174). Once we reach this point in the argument, Bayle seems to have swung round to a vindication of Cardan rather than a refutation of him. (On p. 173, Bayle had cited the same statement about Christian bellicosity but tried to resist it "because it serves only to show that Christians do not live according to their principles." Yet in the course of §140, we see that Christians not living according to their principles is precisely Bayle's point.)

the soul" can be suspended without setting in motion a necessary moral and political catastrophe – then the stakes of religious belief will be dramatically diminished, and it might be possible, for the first time in human history, to live *without* wars of religion.[49]

To be sure, this is a much grimmer view than the one expressed later by Hume, Voltaire, and Rousseau, namely that pagan societies were religiously tolerant and that wars of religion are associated *only* with monotheistic religions.[50] Bayle's grimmer view gives one more reason to look favorably upon the colossal experiment of shelving religion altogether. As Bayle puts it in §129, we have "no annals of any atheistic nation."[51] A society without religion would be an experiment without precedent, and it would be impossible to know, in advance of experiencing such a thing, whether the "disorders in the world" would be less in such a postreligious world. What we *do* know is how vicious and conflict ridden have been the universally religious societies that have hitherto defined human history. (Relevant here is Bayle's characterization of religion as a "great machine that is customarily used to stir peoples" [*la grande machine avec laquelle on a de coûtume de remuer les Peuples*].[52]) What would we have to lose by venturing such an experiment? If, as Bayle declares in §136, "Jew and Mohammedan, Turk and Moor, Christian and Infidel, Indian and Tatar" are universally and in equal measure subject to the corruptions of "ambition, avarice, envy, the desire to avenge oneself, shamelessness, and all the crimes that can satisfy these passions," what further harm would we be exposing ourselves to by experimenting with a form of society that rested upon none of these faiths?[53] Is it perhaps Bayle's thought that an

---

[49] Of course, the main argument of Letters 7–9 is that religion fails to be efficacious in promoting *virtue*. The suggestion here, by contrast, is that there are positive *vices* proper to religion as such. If that suggestion is correct, Bayle is obviously impugning religion much more severely than the surface structure of the argument lets on.

[50] In §221 Bayle cites some examples that contradict what later became the Hume–Voltaire–Rousseau thesis that pagan religion was intrinsically open ended and therefore tolerant. In his next section (§222), Bayle suggests that although the principle of "the zeal of each people for its [uncontaminatedly ancestral] religion" sometimes waned in the pagan world, it was always capable of being "rekindled." Interestingly, in §244 Bayle presents Islam as a model of religious toleration. In §243, Bayle had argued that designs for large-scale conquest are obstructed by simultaneously pursuing religious persecution, and in §244 Bayle seizes upon Mohammed and his immediate successors as an illustration of this principle. Bayle's suggestion is that Mohammed's commitment to toleration of Christians, such as it was, was motivated more than anything by the notion that it would facilitate his expansionary designs, which is consistent with the argument of §243. Still, it has the effect of presenting Mohammed and the Caliphs as more enlightened than many or most Christian princes.

[51] Cf. p. 180.

[52] Ibid., p. 294.

[53] See esp. p. 194: "If the court of France had been atheistic, it could never have maintained such conduct." The conduct to which Bayle refers is persecution, massacre, and the incitement of civil war on the part of the French monarchy. No other line in the *Various Thoughts* offers a more severe condemnation of religion and its impact on politics.

atheist regime would have a better chance than a Christian regime of realizing the moral aspirations of Christianity, because Christians find it just as difficult to extricate themselves from prejudice and superstition as pagans do, and this gets in the way of fulfilling the higher morality that ought to define Christianity?

15

Montesquieu's Pluralized Civil Religion

> Christianity . . . did not establish entirely new virtues; but it changed their relative position. Certain rude and half-savage virtues had been on the top of the list; Christianity put them on the bottom. The milder virtues (such as neighborly love, pity, leniency, the forgetfulness even of injuries) had been on the bottom of the antique list; Christianity placed them above all others.
>
> – Alexis de Tocqueville[1]

Montesquieu begins Book 29 of *The Spirit of the Laws* with the claim that his book's purpose is to prove that the legislator must embody the spirit of moderation: Political good, he says, is always to be located between two extremes. This Aristotelian idea of virtue as a mean between extremes points us back to the beginning of Book 25, where Montesquieu highlights two extremes in the experience of religion: piety and atheism. Applying the Montesquieuian rule yields the notion that the legislator should aim at splitting the difference between piety and atheism. Piety is defined here as love of religion; atheism is defined as fear of religion. The wise legislator should neither love nor fear religion but should be guided by a third principle, namely the possible *utility* of religion. Or rather, attending to the utility of religion should combine an appreciation of the advantages that can come with a loving respect for a particular religion established within a given society, with fear of the evils that can arise from the reign of religion at its worst. The prudent legislator is concerned with how to *use* both the pious man's love for religion and the atheist's fear of religion to secure good political purposes. However, it goes without saying that someone who can think about religion *both* from the pious person's perspective (surveying the goods of religion) and the atheist's perspective (surveying the evils of religion) can truly inhabit neither perspective, neither that of atheism nor that of piety.

---

[1] Alexis de Tocqueville, *The European Revolution and Correspondence with Gobineau*, ed. John Lukacs (Garden City, NY: Doubleday Anchor Books, 1959), p. 191.

Given how the Rousseauian interpretation of civil religion functions as a hub for the whole of this book, one can hardly avoid relating Montesquieu to the corresponding views in Rousseau.[2] Let us recall the interpretation presented in Part I. The standard reading of *Social Contract* IV.8 is that Rousseau gives consummate expression to his illiberal politics by ending the book with the highly illiberal project of positing a state religion. Rousseau seems to point in this illiberal direction by radically contrasting the antipolitical character of modern Christianity with the politicizing function of ancient paganism. This, however, is a false impression: Although Rousseau does his utmost to highlight the political deficiencies of Christianity by playing up the civic character of paganism, he ultimately rejects the latter, saying that the "religion of the citizen" leads eventually to cruel intolerance and theocratic imperialism. The "civil religion" that Rousseau lays out at the end of the chapter falls well short of civic religion on the Roman model: Rousseau insists that "there is no longer and can never again be an exclusive national religion." Rather, Rousseau, no less than Locke, places *tolerance* at the center of his teaching on the relation between church and state. I do not think it would be an overstatement to say that Rousseau concludes a supposedly antiliberal theory of politics with a celebration of liberalism.

It immediately becomes evident that the way in which Rousseau sets up the problem is (as is everything in Rousseau) thoroughly shaped by Montesquieu. Consider the crucial passage in which Rousseau defines his own position in relation to the alternatives of piety and atheism. He refers to "the opposing sentiments of Bayle and Warburton, one of whom claims that no religion is useful to the body politic, the other of whom maintains, to the contrary, that Christianity is its firmest support." This, it seems clear, is Rousseau's reply to Montesquieu's critique of Pierre Bayle in chapters 2 and 6 of Book 24. Stated thus, Rousseau's position is perfectly clear: The state needs a civil religion, but Christianity (though it may be theologically true) must be excluded as a candidate for the required civil religion. (In other words, he accepts Montesquieu's critique of Bayle's "civil atheism" in Book 24, chapter 2, but he categorically rejects Montesquieu's defense of Christianity in Book 24, chapter 6.) Montesquieu's position, as we shall see, is much more complicated.

---

[2] For an attempt to sketch affinities between Rousseau and Montesquieu in regard to the theme of civil religion, see Sergey Zanin, "Rousseau, Montesquieu et la 'religion civile,'" in *Montesquieu, l'état et la religion* (Sofia: Éditions Iztok-Zapad, 2007), pp. 186–212. Civil religion is the main theme of Montesquieu's early work, "Dissertation sure la politique des Romains dans la religion" (*Œuvres completes*, ed. Daniel Oster, Paris: Du Seuil, 1964, pp. 39–43). On p. 41, Montesquieu cites St. Augustine's surprising concession, in *City of God*, Book 4, chapter 31, that Varro's affirmation of the expediency of veiling many truths and getting the people to embrace many falsehoods serves to disclose "the whole policy of the supposedly wise men by whom cities and peoples are ruled." This is in effect an admission by Augustine that politics as practiced historically is virtually inseparable from civil religion. In common with the other versions of civil religion surveyed in this book, Montesquieu's text certainly does not lack for anticlericalism: It is easy to interpret his harsh critique of the greed, idleness, and anticivic character of the Egyptian priests (p. 42) as a thinly veiled commentary on the Catholic priesthood.

What strikes one immediately at the start of Book 24 is how the non-Christian religions are pushed to the foreground, and Christianity is pushed to the background. Montesquieu begins with the "false religions."[3] The fact that these religions are false (i.e., that they are incapable of "leading men to the felicities of the next life") is irrelevant to the question of their possible contribution to human happiness in this life, that is, their public utility. The same principle is applied to Christianity and to the non-Christian religions, namely their contribution to political good, and Christianity's theological superiority is beside the point in this context: Montesquieu writes only as an "écrivain political," one who proceeds strictly according to a "human way of thinking" (as opposed to being concerned with "des vérités plus sublimes").[4] The last sentence of the first chapter is breathtaking in its implications, once one thinks through what it actually means. What he says is this: "The Christian religion...no doubt wants the best political laws and the best civil laws for each people" – that is to say, "for each people," whether that people is *Christian* or *non-Christian* (because many of the "peoples" referred to in this sentence will of course be non-Christian).[5] If it is true (as Montesquieu certainly believes) that those laws are rendered better than they would otherwise be by the fact of their dependence on those non-Christian religions, then – according to Montesquieu – Christianity itself affirms the role of those religions in constituting the social-political life of those non-Christian societies. The only consequence one can draw from this discussion is that the privileged status of Christianity is radically challenged (notwithstanding its theological superiority – again, irrelevant here), implying a huge expansion of the theoretical interest to be accorded to the contribution to human good on the part of the *non-Christian* religions.[6] This impression is very strongly reinforced with the first challenge to Bayle, in chapter 2, where Montesquieu challenges Bayle's critique of pagan religions. That is, Montesquieu first defends non-Christian religions; it is only in chapter 6 that he gets to defending Christianity against Bayle. Montesquieu reaffirms the traditional (pre-Bayle) idea of atheism: Without religion, men are wild animals, and they require religious restraint to hold their passions in check (especially for the princes; religion is "the only bridle that can hold those who fear no human laws").[7] This is the case whether the religions that perform this function are Christian or pre-Christian.

---

3 Montesquieu, *The Spirit of the Laws*, ed. Anne Cohler, Basia Miller, and Harold Stone (Cambridge: Cambridge University Press, 1989), p. 459.

4 Ibid.

5 Ibid.

6 In *Letters Written from the Mountain*, Rousseau highlights this shocking aspect of Montesquieu's teaching to make *his own* views appear less anti-Christian by comparison: See *Collected Writings of Rousseau*, Vol. 9, ed. Christopher Kelly and Eve Grace (Lebanon, NH: University Press of New England, 2001), p. 149.

7 *Spirit of the Laws*, p. 460. As I mentioned in Chapter 14, Bayle himself uses the "bridle" metaphor in § 161 of *Various Thoughts*.

In chapters 3 and 4, Montesquieu begins to consider the specific advantages of Christianity, but these are considered not in general or in the abstract but specifically in contrast to the vices of Islam, which is presented as the natural religion of despotism. Relative to Islam as a warrior-religion, and even relative to the pagan religions of antiquity, Montesquieu stresses that one has reason to be grateful for the civilizing effects of Christianity. The decisive standard in deciding between Christianity and Islam is which is more effective in "softening the mores of human beings" [*adoucir les mœurs des hommes*], and there is no question but that Christianity wins the contest according to this standard.[8] In fact, he states that this vindication of Christianity, on political grounds, is more convincing than its vindication on theological grounds: "[I]t is much more evident to us that a religion should soften the mores of men than it is that a religion is true."[9] Montesquieu is more sure about the political attractions of Christianity than he is about its truth!

It is striking that Montesquieu commences his defense of Christianity by juxtaposing it to Islam. One cannot help but think of this in relation to Machiavelli's critique of Christianity. One thinks, in particular, of the famous chapter 6 of *The Prince*, which in Part I we read as an implicit vindication of *Islam relative to Christianity*. Though Machiavelli does not explicitly say so, Islam is (paradigmatically) a religion of armed prophets, whereas Christianity is (paradigmatically) a religion of unarmed prophets. Machiavelli's vehement celebration of armed prophets and vehement denunciation of unarmed prophets is therefore an (implicit) exalting of Islam over Christianity. Montesquieu's first real account of the political advantages of Christianity is a deliberate inversion of Machiavelli's judgment. Machiavelli's consistent view is that Christianity has fatally "softened the mores of men," relative to what they were under

---

[8] *Spirit of the Laws*, p. 462 (Book 24, chapter 4); cf. Book 24, chapter 3: "[L]a douceur...si recommandée dans l'Évangile"; as well as Rousseau, *Emile*, trans. Allan Bloom (New York: Basic Books, 1979), p. 313, note ("La religion mieux connue, écartant le fanatisme, a donné plus de douceur aux mœurs chrétiennes"). See also Montesquieu, *Œuvres completes*, ed. Oster, p. 1079 (*Mes pensées*, no. 2172): "While it is true enough that the Christian religion has not made many princes virtuous, it has nonetheless softened human nature [*adouci la nature humaine*]: it has caused the Tiberiuses, the Caligulas, the Neros, the Domitians, the Commoduses, and the Elagabaluses to disappear." However, in the "Dissertation sur la politique des Romains dans la religion" (*Œuvres completes*, ed. Oster, p. 41), Montesquieu highlights precisely the "esprit de douceur" of Roman paganism. Montesquieu's idea that Christianity (i.e., Christianity per se, if such a thing exists) contributes decisively to the softening of mores is certainly not borne out in the case of Puritan politics, for instance. Michael Walzer highlights the centrality of warfare and rigorously disciplined soldiering as privileged images of a properly Christian life as conceived within Calvinist radicalism: See *The Revolution of the Saints* (New York: Atheneum, 1976), chapter 8. On pp. 289–290, Walzer explicitly challenges Machiavelli's analysis of Christianity (implicitly shared by Montesquieu) on the basis of Puritan militancy and its unique brand of warrior ethic. Another version of such a challenge is of course presented in Bayle's *Various Thoughts*, §§ 140–141; Montesquieu does not respond to this aspect of Bayle's critique of Christianity (although Montesquieu's own account of the Spanish conquest of Mexico, discussed later in this chapter, is a tacit acceptance of Bayle's critique).

[9] *Spirit of the Laws*, p. 462.

pagan regimes, and is to be categorically rejected on precisely this ground. Montesquieu asserts, counter to Machiavelli, that Christianity's outstanding virtue is its softening effect (provided that it remains faithful to "the gentleness so recommended in the gospel"[10]), and that it is to be politically affirmed on precisely this ground. For Montesquieu, directly contrary to Machiavelli, the great challenge of modern politics is to make human beings *less* warlike, not *more* warlike.

We come now to the second confrontation with Bayle, this time concerned not with the aspersions Bayle casts upon the pagan religions but with the aspersions he casts upon Christianity: Christians are by nature anarchists, and a Christian state is a contradiction in terms.[11] Here Rousseau sides decisively with Bayle, and Montesquieu's critique of Bayle is at the same time a critique, by anticipation, of Rousseau. Montesquieu insists, contrary to Bayle and contrary to Rousseau, that there is no reason why Christianity cannot serve as a civil religion – making people better citizens, attaching them to the laws, making them more devoted to the homeland; in short, doing all the things Rousseau says a civil religion must do but that Christianity cannot do. Montesquieu in effect says that a look at the historical record of avowedly Christian states proves Bayle (and Rousseau) wrong. If certain otherworldly teachings of the gospel seem to rule out this capacity of Christianity to serve a civil-religion function, the mistake here (Bayle's mistake) is to interpret these not as *counsels*, addressed to the (remote) possibility of human perfection, but instead as *laws*, which of course must be modified in deference to an imperfect world. A critic of Montesquieu might suggest that this is itself a dubious interpretation of the otherworldly perfectionism of Christianity in its original purity (but then Montesquieu is not concerned with getting Christianity right on the level of theology but with interpreting it in a way that maximizes its political attractions).[12]

So much for Montesquieu's defense of Christianity: This, however, cannot be the whole story. The religion Christ founded is a religion focused upon *poverty*, *chastity*, and *self-abnegation*. Montesquieu's preferred regime is a regime with a bustling population, a vibrant commercial economy, and a healthy regard for material self-interest. There cannot help but be a certain tension between Christianity as it originally defined itself and the political vision vindicated in

---

[10] Ibid., p. 461.

[11] *Spirit of the Laws*, Book 24, chapter 6; cf. *Œuvres completes*, ed. Oster, p. 1036 (*Mes pensées*, no. 1812). Montesquieu does not cite any texts but he may be alluding to *Various Thoughts*, § 141. In this section Bayle takes up the ancient pagan critique of Christianity according to which Christian principles "enervate courage" and is a religion "suited only to create cowards." Bayle does not present himself as the originator of this critique, but he makes large concessions to such pagan critics. The theme of this section of *Various Thoughts* is directly related to Machiavelli's critique of Christianity in *Discourses* II.2 and directly anticipates Rousseau's critique of Christianity in *Social Contract* IV.8.

[12] Cf. Thomas L. Pangle, *Montesquieu's Philosophy of Liberalism* (Chicago: University of Chicago Press, 1973), pp. 253–254.

The Spirit of the Laws. One sees this for instance in Book 24, chapter 11, when Montesquieu writes that "religion should not give [men] an overly contemplative life."[13] He proceeds to focus on Islam as his example of a religion that is excessively contemplative – he also refers to "Foë" (Buddhism) and "Laockium" (Taoism) – but given what he had said earlier of Islam as a religion that "speaks only with a sword,"[14] and given Montesquieu's criticisms of (Christian) monastic life throughout the book, it would seem that Christianity exceeds Islam in its reproachable otherworldliness.[15] Pangle probably overstates the point when he writes that "Montesquieu's project cannot succeed unless he can show the way to a destruction or emasculating transformation of Christianity. The endorsement and promotion of commerce leads inevitably to a confrontation with Christianity."[16] This is an overstatement because there is nothing in the text to indicate that Montesquieu aims at a "destruction" of Christianity; "emasculating transformation" seems closer to the mark. In fact, in certain crucial respects that concern Montesquieu, Protestant Christianity represents an "emasculating transformation" of original Christianity and one that Montesquieu entirely welcomes and affirms. We see this quite strikingly in the chapter immediately following the one in which Montesquieu introduces his precept–counsel distinction. The principle summarized at the beginning of Book 24, chapter 7 – "Human laws made to speak to the spirit should give precepts and no counsels at all; religion, made to speak to the heart, should give many counsels and few precepts"[17] – is illustrated by Montesquieu with what is for him a crucial aspect of the Christian legacy: the interpretation, in the course of the history of Christianity, of celibacy as a "law" binding upon the priestly class rather than as a "counsel."[18] The fact that the Protestant Reformation restored celibacy to its rightful status as a mere "counsel" must surely be, for Montesquieu, a major consideration in weighing up the relative attractions of Protestant Christianity and Catholic Christianity. This is a further indication of Montesquieu's partiality for Protestantism that had already been intimated in his association of Protestantism with "the spirit of liberty" in Book 24, chapter 5.

Let us now recap the three positions sketched in this chapter, that is, those of Bayle, Montesquieu, and Rousseau:

1. For Bayle, civil religion is unnecessary. There is no guarantee that a society socialized to a false religion will be more moral than a society of atheists. "True religion" fares no better, because Christianity is

---

[13] *Spirit of the Laws*, p. 466.
[14] Ibid., p. 462.
[15] Hume and Adam Smith clearly picked up this theme from Montesquieu; see Chapter 19, notes 52 and 53.
[16] Pangle, *Montesquieu's Philosophy of Liberalism*, p. 248.
[17] *Spirit of the Laws*, p. 464.
[18] Ibid.

incapable of furnishing a civil religion.[19] In any case, theological truth is no guarantee of moral practice, because most human beings (including Christians) are very poor at putting their principles into practice.[20]

2. For Rousseau, civil religion *is* necessary. Paganism worked very well as a civil religion for the ancient republics but is no longer acceptable and no longer viable: "The spirit of Christianity has won over everything." Rousseau agrees with Bayle that Christianity is hopeless as a civil religion. This is obviously a big problem for someone who thinks republics need a civil religion yet has ruled out alternatives to Christianity, and it is by no means clear that Rousseau has located a solution to this problem.

3. Montesquieu agrees with Rousseau on the need for civil religion but does not accept the position shared by Bayle and Rousseau that a *Christian* civil religion is a nonstarter.

I should now clarify what I said earlier about Montesquieu's teaching on civil religion being a more complicated position than Rousseau's. There are certainly intriguing complexities in Rousseau's civil-religion doctrine, but his position is uncomplicated at least in the sense that he straightforwardly rejects Christianity (whether in its Catholic or Protestant versions) as a possible civil religion. Here Montesquieu's teaching is indeed less clear. He certainly affirms the possibility of a Christian civil religion, but at the same time he sees enormous drawbacks (not necessarily the same as those that concern Rousseau) attached to the historical legacy of Christianity. To put it simply, the problem of Christian otherworldliness that was to preoccupy Rousseau is also a problem for Montesquieu. Christianity is not to be ruled out as a possible civil religion, but neither is it advantageous in every respect.

The core of Montesquieu's civil-religion teaching is this: Stick with what you have got. Montesquieu is convinced that there are explicable reasons why

---

[19] Unlike Rousseau, Bayle never states this as a principle, but as I pointed out in note 11 of this chapter, this view, more or less attributed to Bayle by Montesquieu, is a plausible interpretation of *Various Thoughts*, § 141.

[20] Bayle presents himself as rejecting Spinoza, and Montesquieu and Rousseau present themselves as rejecting Bayle, but all four thinkers (and Locke and Kant as well) are 100 percent in agreement with respect to what is truly essential – namely the view that religion, including Christianity, does far less to improve morality than it promises, and that to provide a remedy one must put much less emphasis on fine points of theology and much more emphasis on the performance of moral duties. See in particular the epigraphs from Montesquieu and Rousseau cited in Chapter 14, both of which capture Bayle's main thesis in the *Various Thoughts*; see also *Collected Writings of Rousseau*, Vol. 8, ed. Christopher Kelly (Lebanon, NH: University Press of New England, 2000), p. 262: "I think that everyone will be judged not concerning what he has believed, but concerning what he has done." As regards Kant's participation in this philosophical consensus, see *Religion within the Boundaries of Mere Reason*, ed. Allen Wood and George di Giovanni (Cambridge: Cambridge University Press, 1998), p. 134: "[The] history [of Christianity], so far as the beneficial effect which we rightly expect from a moral religion is concerned, has nothing in any way to recommend it" (in this connection, Kant even goes so far as to cite Lucretius – p. 135); See also p. 191, where Kant endorses "the complaint . . . that religion still contributes all too little to the improvement of human beings."

each society has the particular religion that it does. What he most fears is reckless religious revisionism, or worse, religious imperialism.²¹ I think that the criticism he would make of Rousseau's account of civil religion is very similar to the criticism he makes of the preceding tradition of political philosophy in general at the end of Book 29. Like Plato, Aristotle, Machiavelli, Harrington, More, and others, Rousseau is searching for *the* one best regime. Therefore Christianity is held up to a standard of philosophical perfection that no actual religion can satisfy. I think that Montesquieu would criticize Rousseau for failing to be sufficiently appreciative of the terrific variety of possible civil religions, each with their unique strengths and weaknesses, as rooted in the distinctive geography, climate, national temper, and historical specificity of different societies. Consider the following story reported in 1995:

Some time soon in Tibet, a 200-year-old golden urn containing three balls of dough will be given a good shaking in front of a large statue of Buddha. Stuffed inside the balls will be slips of paper, each with the name of a different six-year-old Tibetan boy written on it. Once two balls have fallen out of the urn, the remaining ball will be pried open, and the name slip read out. Thus will end a six-year search for the reincarnation of the Panchen Lama, second only to the exiled Dalai Lama in the hierarchy of Tibetan holiness. Or, at least, so the Communist leaders of China hope. . . . [China's leadership] has insisted that the arcane "drawing-of-the-lots" ritual must be followed to the letter to select the new Panchen Lama.²²

It strikes me that Montesquieu would absolutely relish the fact that, according to this account, the officially atheist political leadership in China has been compelled to defer to the religious opinions of the Tibetans. He would see this as bearing out his conviction that religion is not a matter of some theoretical construction, but rather a sociologically embodied product of history and circumstance that one tampers with at one's peril. To this extent, Rousseau falls into the trap typical of the tradition of political philosophy from Plato onward, and Montesquieu would say that, notwithstanding his own severe misgivings about the social–political adequacy of Christianity, Rousseau's dismissal of Christianity's claims to serving a civil-religion function evinces Rousseau's typical theorist's failure to respect Christianity's sociological reality.²³

---

²¹ Montesquieu's opposition to the idea of religious imperialism is admirably liberal. However, the flip side of this view, which is a prescription that the state, if possible, close its doors to the introduction of new religions (*Spirit of the Laws*, Book 25, chapter 10), is considerably less liberal. Both the liberal and antiliberal sides of Montesquieu's position anticipate Rousseau.

²² Rod Mickleburgh, "Chinese insist on rite to pick new lama," *The Globe & Mail*, November 15, 1995, pp. A1 and A16.

²³ As I consider in Chapter 20, Tocqueville is Montesquieu's genuine nineteenth-century heir. Montesquieu would say the following in response to Rousseau's civil-religion chapter (and Tocqueville would say the same thing): What matters, civically speaking, is not what is in the Gospel but rather how churches and adherents who call themselves Christian function in and contribute toward an actual civic order. Bayle and Rousseau may be right that the Gospel is an anarchist creed, but sociology counts for more than theology. In any case, Scripture can mean just about whatever interpreters want it to mean: For evidence of the unlimited elasticity of

Notwithstanding the important disagreements between Montesquieu and Rousseau, there is one crucial issue on which they are in absolutely full agreement. For both of them, any morally defensible civil religion must embody tolerance toward alternative religions.[24] This comes out in Book 24, chapter 8, where Montesquieu offers the example of the religion of the people of Pegu (in Burma). Montesquieu writes that the people of Pegu "believe that one will be saved in any religion whatever," and this is the mark of their gentleness and compassion.[25] Montesquieu emphasizes that this is a *false* religion (the people of Pegu suffer "the misfortune of having a religion not given by god"), inviting us to raise the question of whether the true religion, the one given by God, is up to the same moral standard. If the belief that people can achieve salvation "in any religion whatever" is the condition of true gentleness, then this casts Christianity in a morally problematical light, for the historical record of Christianity is of course far from reassuring in this regard. (Compare the last paragraph of *Social Contract*, IV.8.)

The problem of Christianity for Montesquieu is that it can be a source of gentleness *or* harshness. This dual possibility is illustrated in chapters 3 and 4 of Book 10. In chapter 3, Montesquieu discusses different approaches to the right of conquest. The gentlest way is simply to extend the conqueror's laws to a new jurisdiction; the harshest approach consists in wholesale extermination. Montesquieu suggests that Roman practice corresponds to the pole of utmost harshness, whereas that which "we follow at present" is situated at the pole of gentleness. Therefore "homage must be paid to our modern times," including "the religion of the present day."[26] If this were unqualifiedly true, Christianity would be demonstrated to be absolutely superior to ancient paganism. However, Montesquieu reminds us very forcefully in the very next chapter that it is not true. First, we all know perfectly well that it was not the Roman norm to exterminate the peoples it conquered; rather, the Roman Empire spread by extending the jurisdiction of Roman law and expanding the membership of Roman citizenship. However, neither is it the case that Christianity has enlightened the modern world about the evils of genocide (as it *ought* to have done if historical Christianity had remained faithful to the teachings of the Gospel). In Book 10, chapter 4, Montesquieu quite deliberately brings up the example of the Spanish conquest of Mexico[27] – thereby contradicting his teaching in the previous chapter concerning the gentleness of Christian modernity (and also

---

the Christian Gospel, see Thomas Linehan, "'On the Side of Christ': Fascist Clerics in 1930s Britain," *Totalitarian Movements and Political Religion*, Vol. 8, No. 2 (June 2007): 287–301.

[24] For an instructive account of Montesquieu's contribution to the discourse of toleration that was starting to make headway in the eighteenth century, see Rebecca E. Kingston, "Montesquieu on Religion and on the Question of Toleration," in *Montesquieu's Science of Politics*, ed. D. W. Carrithers, M. A. Mosher, and Paul A. Rahe (Lanham, MD: Rowman & Littlefield, 2001), pp. 375–408.

[25] *Spirit of the Laws*, p. 465.

[26] Ibid., p. 139.

[27] Ibid., p. 142.

clearly calling into question the homage he says must be paid to our modern times: In chapter 3 Montesquieu says pointedly that he will "leave others to judge how much better we have become"; by the next chapter, his readers are in a position to make this judgment). The Spanish *could have* taught the Mexicans a more gentle religion than their own, but this was not the kind of Christianity that they brought with them to Mexico. The Christianity of the Spaniards was a "raging superstition"[28] and it legitimized extermination of the Mexicans. The Christian gentleness celebrated by Montesquieu in Book 10, chapter 3 is indeed a potentiality, but one that real Christianity sometimes realizes and sometimes fails to realize. Christianity certainly contains a potentiality for gentleness, and all the good consequences that this gentleness brings, but Christianity also contains a potentiality for harshness and evil, and the student of human affairs must be fully aware of this dual potentiality in "the religion of the present day."[29]

---

[28] Ibid.

[29] In Book 4, chapter 6 of *Spirit of the Laws*, Montesquieu refers to "the pillages of the Spaniards" as "one of the greatest wounds mankind has yet received." This certainly raises questions about the claim that Christianity elevated humanity to a higher moral plane by "softening human nature" relative to what it was under paganism. Cf. Judith N. Shklar, *Montesquieu* (Oxford: Oxford University Press, 1987), p. 61: "Christianity did not even make the later Romans less cruel"; and Rebecca Kingston, *Montesquieu and the Parlement of Bordeaux* (Geneva: Droz, 1996), p. 146: "The Spanish conquistadores [conducted] a massive attack on essentially peaceful nations which posed no threat to Spain. Montesquieu expresses his particular dismay [with respect to] how theological arguments were consistently invoked to legitimize such cruelty." More generally, see Shklar, p. 84: "[Montesquieu] was convinced that religion added much to human fears and misery"; and Montesquieu as quoted in Thomas L. Pangle, *The Theological Basis of Liberal Modernity in Montesquieu's "Spirit of the Laws"* (Chicago: University of Chicago Press, 2010), p. 171, n. 14: "Only a pen dipped in blood or tears could describe the terrible effects of [Christian and Islamic] zeal." One should also compare Locke's expression of indignation at the abuse of Christianity in the context of imperial domination of indigenous cultures: "unless these innocent Pagans . . . will forsake their ancient Religion, and embrace a new and strange one, they are to be turned out of the Lands and Possessions of their Forefathers, and perhaps deprived of Life it self. Then at last it appears what Zeal for the Church, joined with the desire of Dominion, is capable to produce; and how easily the pretence of Religion, and of the care of Souls, serves for a Cloak to Covetousness, Rapine, and Ambition" (John Locke, *A Letter Concerning Toleration*, ed. James H. Tully, Indianapolis: Hackett, 1983, p. 43).

16

The Straussian Rejection of the Enlightenment
as Applied to Bayle and Montesquieu

> [T]he *libertin érudit* stance has a natural tendency to undo itself, to speak the truth which it is always hinting at and denying.
>
> – Abraham Anderson[1]

> There is no secret that is wholly secret.
>
> – Anne Norton[2]

In *The Idea of Enlightenment*, Robert C. Bartlett offers an interesting account of Montesquieu's "quarrel" with Bayle, the purpose of which is to show that Bayle and Montesquieu really agree on the end (to defang religion) and differ only on the question of means, or on strategies to realize the goal.[3] Bartlett's larger

---

[1] Abraham Anderson, "Sallengre, La Monnoye, and the *Traité des trios Imposteurs*," in Anderson, *The Treatise of the Three Impostors and the Problem of Enlightenment* (Lanham, MD: Rowman & Littlefield, 1997), p. 105. Cf. p. 103: "[T]he result of the [post-Cartesian] new philosophy is that... questions of literary erudition or secret traditions... are dissipated by the light of the modern day, in which what matters is not old traditions but rational argument and public truth." In a similar vein Anderson writes, "In the end, the obscurantism of the *libertins érudits* – their attempt to distinguish a private sphere of scholarly truth-telling and philosophical lucidity from a public sphere of religious illusion and shared belief – collapses into rationalist Enlightenment."

[2] Anne Norton, *Leo Strauss and the Politics of American Empire* (New Haven: Yale University Press, 2004), p. 96.

[3] Robert C. Bartlett, *The Idea of Enlightenment: A Post-Mortem Study* (Toronto: University of Toronto Press, 2001), chapter 2. See, esp., p. 30: Montesquieu and Bayle "do not have fundamentally different ends in mind... they disagree only over the best strategy to attain that end: both philosophers envisage a day when, to the very great benefit of politics, the concern for religion and the questions it raises would fall into desuetude, the lives of citizens being taken up with other, more mundane, and more strictly speaking natural concerns"; p. 37: Montesquieu and Bayle "are at one on the fundamental questions. Both agree that religion is responsible for greater ills than benefits... and that it can safely be demoted if the task of politics becomes the pursuit of such goods (e.g., liberty understood as security) as can clearly be traced to natural passions"; and p. 38: "If Montesquieu refused to go quite as far as Bayle in toying with the possibility of a simply atheistic politics, this refusal stems only from his greater moderation or prudence, not from a disagreement over principle." Cf. Thomas L. Pangle, *Montesquieu's*

thesis – that modern rationalism, as exemplified by Bayle and Montesquieu, is doomed to ultimate failure – is very puzzling though, for the domestication of religion and humbling of theocratic politics sought by Bayle and Montesquieu have largely come to pass in modern societies. Bartlett's adverse judgment on modern rationalism is founded on a complicated Straussian argument about modern philosophy as a betrayal of the existential supremacy of philosophy itself. This too is very puzzling, for the Enlightenment was a cultural battle between philosophy and religion, the outcome of which was an unconditional triumph for philosophy.[4]

How can philosophy not be vindicated by winning a cultural victory of such proportions? I suppose it is possible to think that it was the actual victory of philosophy over religious orthodoxy that diminished philosophy as a comprehensive engagement with the most important alternatives. (That is, ancient political philosophy is existentially superior because it still grapples with civic piety as a genuine alternative, whereas modern political philosophy tends to operate on a less grand plane precisely to the extent that religion is assumed to have been defeated as a rival basis for human self-understanding.)[5] Another possibility is the view that philosophy was diminished insofar as its victory over orthodoxy "piggybacked" on natural science.[6] In any case, it seems paradoxical to interpret what was historically a colossal cultural victory for philosophy as a defeat for philosophy.[7]

Philosophy of Liberalism (Chicago: University of Chicago Press, 1973), p. 253: Montesquieu's "method of answering [doubts about Christianity raised by Bayle] shows his essential agreement with them."

[4] As I flagged earlier in Chapter 9, note 84, Strauss and Spinoza *shared* the view that the nonphilosophical multitude were irrational, required hand-holding by priest-dominated religion, and bore a natural hostility to philosophers. Nevertheless, they were in deep disagreement about how to respond to this situation. One possibility, of course, is for philosophers to feign conventional piety. The other strategy (the Enlightenment strategy) is for philosophers to undertake to reform the broader society in a fundamental way so as to abate the conflict between philosophers and nonphilosophers. Obviously, only a tremendous loosening of the hold of religion on ordinary members of the society could satisfy this purpose. Again, it is a puzzle that Strauss (privileging as he did the "class interests" of philosophers) did not have more appreciation of the advantages (precisely for philosophers!) of the more radical Enlightenment strategy.

[5] *The Idea of Enlightenment*, pp. 68, 120, 187–193.

[6] Nietzsche offers suggestions along this line in *Beyond Good and Evil*, Part Six, §§ 204–207.

[7] The *reason* the Enlightenment is interpreted as a defeat for philosophy is as follows. In this view (that is, Bartlett's view, derived from Strauss and Pangle), the Enlightenment, in triumphing over orthodox religion ("the Cave"), simultaneously triumphs over ancient political philosophy, which is impossible without the continued existence of the cave. However, ancient political philosophy constitutes *real* philosophy. Therefore, the triumph over ancient political philosophy means the defeat of philosophy. (According to Bartlett, *The Idea of Enlightenment*, pp. 122–123, 157–163, 185, 187–188, and 190, ancient political philosophers are no less atheistic than are modern political philosophers. If, however, philosophy consists in liberation from the cave *for philosophers*, then care must be taken to shield nonphilosophers from the philosophers' own atheism. This, and this alone, is what distinguishes ancient political philosophy from modern political philosophy.)

The Straussian theme that we have just sketched is not unique to Bartlett; rather, it is characteristic of certain Straussians (Pangle is a notable example[8]) that modern political philosophy's challenge to religion is thought to require a defense of religion, not on account of religion itself, but on account of what is conceived to be ancient political philosophy's stake in the outcome of this battle. It is not that religion as such is viewed as sacred but rather that ancient political philosophy is seen as sacred, and the respective concerns of each are thought to be sufficiently overlapping (for instance, with respect to the need to respond to the problem of mortality[9]) that an assault on the former is treated as tantamount to an assault on the latter. One can even go so far as to say that the heart of Straussian political philosophy is discernible in the interpretation of Bayle and Montesquieu offered by Bartlett. (What I have in mind in speaking of the heart of Straussianism is Strauss's rejection of the Enlightenment's rejection of religion without actually disagreeing with the Enlightenment's view of religion – supposedly in the interests of the entire club of philosophers.[10]) Strauss partly writes as if the Enlightenment never happened, and partly writes as if, insofar as the Enlightenment did happen, it ought not to have happened. This is a very odd stance for a thinker who both privileges the class interests of philosophers and thinks that philosophers are naturally exposed to persecution by nonphilosophers. Whatever benefits might have accrued to nonphilosophers on account of the Enlightenment (and they

---

[8] See Thomas L. Pangle, *The Theological Basis of Liberal Modernity in Montesquieu's "Spirit of the Laws"* (Chicago: University of Chicago Press, 2010). As with all of Pangle's work, this new Montesquieu book is meticulously researched and seeks to convey the grandeur of Montesquieu's challenge to a Christian-dominated Europe. However, the rhetoric of the book also has a certain aspect of resuming the interrogation of *The Spirit of the Laws* by Montesquieu's theological persecutors. What is certainly jarring here is the implied suggestion that the project of reassessing the Enlightenment's critique of religion entails a willingness to make a philosopher like Montesquieu once again answerable to trial by religious orthodoxy (so that, for instance, Bossuet becomes the standard for judging Montesquieu). Surely not even Strauss himself wanted to go this far. Pangle's interpretation is full of insights into the more subversive side of Montesquieu's stance toward Christianity and provides abundant illustration of how irony functions as a weapon of subversion in a great Enlightenment thinker such as Montesquieu. Why, however, would anyone other than an eighteenth-century Catholic cleric be as shocked and horrified by Montesquieu's subtle literary thrusts as Pangle sometimes professes to be? Leo Strauss, for one, was *not* shocked and horrified, as we can see very clearly from Strauss's letter to Karl Löwith of November 26, 1946, *Independent Journal of Philosophy*, Vol. 4, p. 115. However, I do not want to suggest that all Straussian interpreters of Montesquieu read Montesquieu as Pangle reads him. For one interpretation that, at least by implication, offers a strong challenge to Pangle's way of reading Montesquieu, see Clifford Orwin, "'For Which Human Nature Can Never Be Too Grateful': Montesquieu as the Heir of Christianity," in *Recovering Reason: Essays in Honor of Thomas L. Pangle*, ed. Timothy Burns (Lanham, MD: Lexington Books, 2010), pp. 269–282.

[9] The issue is framed thus in Pangle, *The Theological Basis of Liberal Modernity*, pp. 136-137.

[10] The best account of Strauss's "strategic" approach to revealed religion that I know of is Laurence Lampert, "Strauss's Recovery of Esotericism," in *The Cambridge Companion to Leo Strauss*, ed. Steven B. Smith (Cambridge: Cambridge University Press, 2009), pp. 63–92.

are not trivial!), the Enlightenment certainly made life far safer and far more hospitable for philosophers and other intellectuals.

How, then, do we go about making sense of this major paradox of Strauss's thought? Stephen Holmes helps us to make sense of it when he zeroes in on the problem of religion as defining the core Straussian understanding of the human condition. On the Straussian view, Enlightenment per se is a misguided enterprise because it violates the most essential "natural" distinction between human beings who can face the terrors of life without the consolations of religion (philosophers) and those who cannot (all other human beings) – that is, those who are uniquely capable of liberating their minds outside of the cave versus those who require the existential security of the cave and who would be utterly crushed by the mental liberation that defines true philosophers. The meaning of philosophy resides in the existence of "only a few exceptional souls [who] can go eyeball to eyeball with the fundamental structures of human existence, including death, without blinking."[11] Holmes cites Allan Bloom to this effect: "[T]he uncompromisable difference that separates the philosophers from all others concerns death and dying. No way of life other than the philosophic can digest the truth about death."[12] What is this truth? Holmes offers the following stark but accurate image: "Life is like falling off Chicago's 110-story Sears Tower"[13] – a "bleak fate" from which there is no possible escape. The unyielding pavement awaits us, come what may. Philosophers are those heroic beings who face the "existential terror" without the consolations of religion; the rest of humanity requires mythologies to mask this horrifying reality. Furthermore, the project of Enlightenment misguidedly treats the second group (the herd of ordinary mortals) as if they belonged to the first group (those superhuman beings who live the philosophic life). Enlightenment illegitimately crosses the inviolable natural divide between those who are intended for captivity in the cave and those who are intended for breathing the free sunlit air outside the cave.[14]

---

[11] Stephen Holmes, *The Anatomy of Antiliberalism* (Cambridge, MA: Harvard University Press, 1993), p. 76; cf. pp. 64, "look[ing] at these steep truths without squinting," and 65, "capacity to look savage reality in the face and not blink." Cf. Perry Anderson, *Spectrum* (London: Verso, 2005), p. 9, on (according to Strauss) philosophy's unfaltering penetration of the "terrible realities of cosmic disorder" and the incapacity of the many to "endure" the truth glimpsed by the few.

[12] Holmes, p. 65; the text quoted is from Allan Bloom, *The Closing of the American Mind* (New York: Simon & Schuster, 1987), p. 285.

[13] Holmes, pp. 64–65.

[14] At a conference on "Hermeneutics and Structuralism: Merging Horizons" at York University in Toronto (November 23, 1978), Bloom and Hans-Georg Gadamer debated these issues. (The debate can be viewed on a DVD entitled *Voegelin in Toronto*.) Gadamer argued that a major part of what shaped Socratic–Platonic philosophy was the need to face up to the challenge posed by "the Greek Enlightenment" (i.e., the challenge of the sophists), and that Socratic–Platonic philosophy was joined in common cause with ordinary Greek piety in responding to this challenge. Bloom countered that there was never such a thing as a "Greek Enlightenment," because none of the ancient Greek thinkers – neither Plato nor Gorgias – proposed to liberate the common citizenry from the cave.

This is a bracing picture of what is at stake in political philosophy's relation to society at large. Is it persuasive? No – for three reasons. *First*, esotericism as a way of practicing philosophy is dead.[15] A large portion of Strauss's hermeneutic practice consists in explaining what is exoteric and what is esoteric in leading works of political philosophy, something he would obviously not be doing if esotericism were still a living practice or a living possibility within the tradition of political philosophy. Even if everything Strauss says about the esotericism of Plato and the esotericism of Alfarabi were entirely correct, Strauss himself, as a post-Enlightenment philosopher, is disabled from continuing the tradition of esoteric philosophy simply by virtue of drawing attention to esotericism as a philosophical practice.[16] Pangle, Bloom, and Strauss do theory as if esotericism continued to be the hallmark of genuine philosophy, whereas in fact the public articulation of these themes (the cave, the natural chasm between the philosopher and the multitude, the perils of enlightenment) is itself a tacit acknowledgment that the days of esotericism as a coherent practice are over.[17]

[15] Esoterically, Strauss held Montesquieu in high esteem, precisely *qua* critic of religion; see the letter to Löwith cited earlier in note 8, esp. the admiring reference to Montesquieu as "completely anti-Christian." Presumably, though, this is not an opinion Strauss can broadcast publicly consistent with his views of the relation between philosophers in their intellectual autonomy and nonphilosophers in their need of the myths of the cave; one is limited to whispering this opinion in the ear of a trusted friend. Nevertheless, the post-Enlightenment reality is that even private letters of philosophers get published in fairly accessible public places available to be read, in principle, by all members of a liberal society (or in the case of the Internet, by a *global* electronic community of readers). So much for esotericism. (One could say that Strauss succumbs to what I called, in Chapter 10, the civil-religion paradox.)

[16] It is self-evident that a pious fraud cannot work if it is announced to be a pious fraud. As we saw in Part I (Chapter 8, note 8), this is a problem common to Machiavelli, Rousseau, and Nietzsche: They simultaneously want to put religion into service for political ends and *say* that is what they want. It is an esotericism that cannot possibly work. One finds a similar problem in Friedrich von Hayek, at least according to the reading of Hayek provided by Perry Anderson; see *Spectrum*, pp. 16–17. According to Anderson, Hayek aims at an instrumentalization of religion for political purposes (for instance, the need to span the breach between the presumption on the part of economic actors that market outcomes reflect principles of desert, and the reality that in fact they do not). However, if one *announces* that religion is to be instrumentalized for these purposes, the project of instrumentalization is hardly likely to be a success. Anderson cites the following text: *The Collected Works of F. A. Hayek, Volume 1: The Fatal Conceit: The Errors of Socialism*, ed. W. W. Bartley III (Chicago: University of Chicago Press, 1989), chapter 9 and Appendix G. However, it is not entirely clear from this text whether in Hayek's view this is merely a function served by religion in the past or whether pious frauds of this kind will continue to be required as a mode of legitimizing economic life even in the more disenchanted epoch we currently inhabit.

[17] To thematize (i.e., make explicit) the esoteric–exoteric distinction, as Strauss did throughout his career as a political philosopher, is fundamentally antiesoteric and hence subverts – and ultimately destroys – esotericism as a practice of philosophy (which in turn destroys philosophy in Strauss's own account of the perennial nature of philosophy). Cf. Stanley Rosen, *Hermeneutics as Politics* (New York: Oxford University Press, 1987), pp. 109 and 112. In addition, for a very helpful and illuminating discussion of this massive problem in the work of Strauss, see Catherine and Michael Zuckert, *The Truth about Leo Strauss: Political Philosophy and American Democracy* (Chicago: University of Chicago Press, 2006), chapter 4. As the Zuckerts admit, Strauss's strategy of exposing esotericism rather than attempting to reinstate it was,

(Indeed, one may also ask oneself how effectively even Socrates practiced his esotericism if his challenges to civic piety were overt enough to cost him his life.) In any case, there is no conceivable advantage to be gained, either civic or intellectual, in whispering one's truths in a post-Enlightenment context where the universal norm is for intellectuals to speak and write exactly what they think.

Second, we live in a world where many millions of people live their lives without the consolations of either philosophy or religion, and they seem to be none the worse for it. *Third*, we live in a world where the greatest dangers to peace, freedom, and possibilities of a decent existence appear to emanate from religion, not from the efforts of secularizing intellectuals.[18] It seems an irrefutable deduction from the second and third points that Bayle's political philosophy is more compelling than Strauss's.[19]

from the point of view of Strauss's own conception of philosophy, "a problematic strategy indeed" (p. 133; cf. p. 144). Moreover, the Zuckerts are right to claim that what the doctrine of esotericism was, above all, for Strauss was a beguiling rhetoric intended "to lure students to the philosophic life" (p. 289, n. 57; cf. pp. 135 and 140). The problem is that the intellectual disadvantages of making esotericism so central to philosophy far outweigh its rhetorical or pedagogic attractions. Stephen Holmes rightly raised this challenge: "What Strauss underestimated... was the irreparable damage done to philosophy by its need to play hide and seek"; Holmes, *The Anatomy of Antiliberalism*, p. 86. Thus we are left with what strike me as two unanswerable challenges: Strauss himself, in making esotericism an explicit theme of philosophy, acknowledges that it is no longer relevant to the practice of philosophy; and insofar as one thinks it *is* still relevant, we get drawn into an endless labyrinth that is actually very bad for philosophy.

[18] Cf. Peter L. Berger, "The Desecularization of the World: A Global Overview," in *The Desecularization of the World: Resurgent Religion and World Politics*, ed. Berger (Grand Rapids, MI: Eerdmans, 1999), pp. 15–16: "It would be nice to be able to say that religion is everywhere a force for peace. Unfortunately, it is not. Very probably religion in the modern world more often fosters war, both between and within nations. Religious institutions and movements are fanning wars and civil wars on the Indian subcontinent, in the Balkans, in the Middle East, and in Africa, to mention only the most obvious cases." If it is indeed true that religion is a chronic source of civil and international conflict, insofar as it was the aim of various Enlightenment thinkers to weaken the grip of religion, then it is difficult not to see this as a reasonable project.

[19] This is not to deny that there is an esotericist dimension to Bayle. As I discussed in my chapter on Bayle, he wrote very much in the shadow of the fate of Vanini. (Consider the maxim cited in § 247 of *Various Thoughts*: "When he conceals himself, he prepares thunderbolts." This maxim is immediately followed by the suggestion that the best policy is to temper Machiavellian audacity with prudence.) Nevertheless, Bayle's response to this situation was to try to advance the movement of Enlightenment, whereas Strauss writes (whether he believed this or not) as if the Enlightenment were merely a project to diminish the status of philosophy. Stanley Rosen (see note 17, this chapter) is very good on the paradoxes of Strauss's relationship to the Enlightenment. What is the fundamental problem with the Enlightenment from Strauss's point of view? In diminishing the peril that philosophers are likely to suffer at the hands of nonphilosophers, the Enlightenment also rendered the distinction between philosophers and nonphilosophers less salient. *It made philosophers seem like ordinary human beings*, even in their own eyes. The question Strauss wants to raise is whether this basic trade-off is ultimately to the advantage of philosophers.

17

"The Gods of the Philosophers" II

Rousseau and Kant

> As soon as peoples took it into their heads to make God speak, each made Him speak in its own way and made Him say what it wanted. If one had listened only to what God says to the heart of man, there would never have been more than one religion on earth.
>
> – Jean-Jacques Rousseau[1]

> [T]he "Profession of Faith of the Savoyard Vicar" . . . may one day make a revolution among men.
>
> – Jean-Jacques Rousseau[2]

> Our age is, in especial degree, the age of *Kritik*, and to *Kritik* everything must submit. Religion through its sanctity, and law-giving through its majesty, may seek to exempt themselves from it. But they then awaken just suspicion, and cannot claim the sincere respect which reason accords only to that which has been able to sustain the test of free and open examination.
>
> – Immanuel Kant[3]

In Chapter 13 I began a survey of leading attempts to replace revealed religion with versions of natural religion as conceived by philosophers, not prophets – a theoretical enterprise that arose in the seventeenth century and culminated in the nineteenth. I now resume that narrative.

The next major work in this tradition (that is, the tradition of those who attempted to use philosophy as a lever by which to pry religion away from dogma, intolerance, and theocratic orthodoxy) is Rousseau's *Emile*. One of the main reasons Rousseau's work is so intriguing is that he is both a severe critic of the liberal philosophy of politics and life and himself a part of the liberal tradition; he is both a critic of Enlightenment and himself an Enlightener. He is

[1] Jean-Jacques Rousseau, *Emile*, trans. Allan Bloom (New York: Basic Books, 1979), p. 295.
[2] *Collected Writings of Rousseau* [henceforth *Collected Writings*], Vol. 8, ed. Christopher Kelly (Lebanon, NH: University Press of New England, 2000), p. 23.
[3] Immanuel Kant, *Critique of Pure Reason* (London: Macmillan, 1980), p. 9, note.

both the author of the vehement critique of modernity in the *Discourse on the Sciences and Arts* and the author of the liberal theology in Book 4 of *Emile*. Rousseau was the author not of a single coherent political philosophy but of several mutually incompatible political philosophies. The key line in his work is this: "Common readers, pardon me my paradoxes. When one reflects, they are necessary."[4] That is, life itself is paradoxical, and the chief vocation of the theorist is to give expression to this paradoxicality. As he put it in his letter to Voltaire of August 18, 1756 ("Letter on Providence"),[5] life does not admit of a single existential catechism. There are at least two – the catechism of man and the catechism of the citizen – and it is impossible to live one's life simultaneously according to both catechisms. In Part I of this book we pursued a dialogue with his catechism of the citizen; now let us look briefly at his catechism of man.

As is well known, the main purpose of the version of deism developed in *Emile* is to articulate a generic religion of reason focused very concertedly on the interiority of the inner voice audible to all moral beings. Rousseau was much less interested in Christianity per se than either Locke or Toland (hence he was much more of a Spinozist than either of them). It follows that Rousseau's theology represented far more of a threat to the hegemony of Christian culture in Europe – a fact that escaped none of his critics and persecutors.

The theology of the "Profession of Faith" is a very simple one. It is a teaching that, first of all, is equally distrustful of subtle theological doctrines and of never-ending philosophical disputes. It tries to cut through all these by an appeal to the simplicity of the heart and the simplicity of the inner voice of conscience[6]: "Let us consult the inner light."[7] The "Profession of Faith" founds its epistemology on "the sincerity of [the Vicar's] heart."[8] Knowledge of the truth of divinity is drawn not from Revelation but from reflection on basic facts of human experience: "[M]y glance must first be turned toward myself."[9] We perceive a material universe that moves only when motion is imparted to it by external causes, whereas we have immediate experience of the spontaneity of our own will. Hence we possess an immediate grasp of the fundamental difference between material bodies that must be set in motion and willing entities (of which we are one) that set themselves in motion. With respect to the material universe, this points to an ultimate cause, for without this the universe would remain forever inert and motionless. The passivity

---

4 *Emile*, ed. Bloom, p. 93.
5 *Collected Writings*, Vol. 3, ed. Roger D. Masters and Christopher Kelly (Lebanon, NH: University Press of New England, 1992), p. 120. For a helpful discussion of affinities between Rousseau's deism and the deism of Voltaire, see Ronald Ian Boss, "Rousseau's Civil Religion and the Meaning of Belief: An Answer to Bayle's Paradox," *Studies on Voltaire in the Eighteenth Century*, Vol. 84 (1971): 123–193. According to Boss, despite the bitter personal enmity between them, Rousseau and Voltaire "were really allies" (p. 131; cf. pp. 154–156 and 185–186).
6 *Emile*, p. 280: Materialists are "deaf to the inner voice."
7 Ibid., p. 269.
8 Ibid., p. 270.
9 Ibid.

of matter, and therefore its dependence on a spontaneous will, points to the refutation of all materialism. This yields what the Vicar calls his "first dogma," namely that "a will moves the universe and animates nature."[10] If matter in motion proves a will, then matter moving "according to certain laws" proves an intelligent will. This is the Vicar's second article of faith, namely "that the world is governed by a powerful and wise will."[11]

God is powerful and wise because He imparts motion to the material universe as an ordered whole. Beyond that, the nature of God is completely inaccessible to us.[12] Hence conventional theology is a waste of time. Rousseau, however, gives us a new kind of theology, one focused not on the attributes of God but on the moral experience of human beings (which is entirely accessible to us). Morality is only possible if human beings can freely will (i.e., are not determined by an undivided nexus of material causality), and therefore freedom of the will is the Vicar's third article of faith.[13] The Vicar states that he will leave the narrator (Rousseau) to "deduce" the remaining articles of faith "without [his] continuing to count them out."[14] Clearly a fourth article of faith is that all evil flows from human beings and their wicked passions; no evil can be blamed on God. This theodicy coincides with the theodicy offered in the "Letter on Providence," and the version in *Emile* is no more persuasive than the one presented to Voltaire. Pain is a "warning" of bodily dysfunction for which we should be grateful; death is a "remedy" for self-inflicted evil.[15] If we lived a life of natural simplicity, the ills that we have brought on ourselves by offending nature would immediately vanish.[16] Man, not God, is the author of evil. Evil is a product of disorder, and man, not nature, is the source of disorder.[17]

[10] Ibid., p. 273. Interpreters who question whether the Vicar's arguments really reflect Rousseau's own views should consult the "Letter to Franquières," *Collected Writings*, Vol. 8, pp. 259–270, which makes clear beyond question that the Vicar's theology is also Rousseau's theology.

[11] *Emile*, p. 276. It goes without saying that what seemed to Rousseau like knockdown arguments for the truth of deism were utterly demolished by Darwin, as one sees very clearly from reading pp. 275–276. Without question, the "abject souls" jeered at on p. 278 won the argument in the end.

[12] Ibid., p. 277.

[13] Ibid., p. 281.

[14] Ibid.

[15] Ibid.

[16] Ibid., pp. 281–282.

[17] Ibid., p. 282. Similar arguments are stated by Rousseau in his own name in the "Letter to Franquières," *Collected Writings*, Vol. 8, pp. 265–266. Voltaire let pass without a substantive reply Rousseau's "Letter on Providence," but he clearly was not moved by Rousseau's appeal to an absolutely harmonious universe: "[W]hat harmony [*concert*] – floods, earthquakes, abysses [*gouffres*]?" (Voltaire's marginalia on the section of the "Profession of Faith" that we are currently discussing, quoted by Boss, "Rousseau's Civil Religion," p. 154, n. 10). In the "Letter on Providence," Rousseau notoriously goes so far as to blame the destruction wrought by the Lisbon earthquake on human city-building practices. One can see why Voltaire did not think this was worthy of a reply. James Wood, "Between God and a Hard Place," *New York Times*, Jan. 24, 2010, p. WK 11, suggests that not that much has changed between 1755 and 2010

The fifth article of faith is otherworldly justice for the virtuous (and less confidently, for the wicked). Virtue clearly is not rewarded in *this* life: "[T]he wicked man prospers, and the just man remains oppressed."[18] If this were the whole story, conscience would be outraged and moral life would be shaken to its core. Virtue must be rewarded with happiness, and this requires an afterlife where the just can be happy. It is for this moral reason that the Vicar affirms the immortality of the soul. If the virtuous truly received no reward, this would constitute a shocking "dissonance in the universal harmony,"[19] and because the Vicar is already committed to the thesis of cosmic harmony by the second article of faith, there *must* exist an afterlife. The just are rewarded; what about the punishment of the unjust? Rousseau's doctrine in the "Profession of Faith" is that the latter are punished by remorse: The virtuous (when reborn) remember their good deeds and those who are evil remember their crimes; hence, "the felicity of the good and the torment of the wicked."[20] The voice of conscience will have infinitely more power in the afterlife than it had in this life, and this will amply reward the virtuous and punish the vicious. This, to be sure, is a version of the doctrine of damnation, even if it seems a relatively mild version.[21] Rousseau affirms that the wicked will suffer "torment" [*le tourment des méchants*], even if they are tormented only by their own feelings of guilt, but he hedges on the question of whether the torments will be eternal. Even if one hesitates to call it a doctrine of "hell," there seems little question that divine punishment forms part of Rousseau's theological scheme.[22]

with respect to the issue of theodicy raised by the Rousseau–Voltaire debate. Read in the light of these two theodicies (the one in the "Letter on Providence" and that in *Emile*), one can see quite clearly that the *Second Discourse* is also in effect a theodicy. The *Second Discourse*'s account of how human vices arise from human institutions is a vindication of nature, which is simultaneously a vindication of nature's Maker. Thus this fourth article of faith is built directly on the social theory laid out in the *Second Discourse*.

[18] *Emile*, p. 282; cf. Rousseau's reference to the ring of Gyges story in Plato's *Republic* on p. 307. Similar arguments about the insufficiency of virtue for virtue's sake and therefore the need for religion to bolster virtue in the face of worldly temptation are presented in the "Letter to Franquières," *Collected Writings*, Vol. 8, pp. 266–268; on p. 268 Rousseau insists that Glaucon's challenge in the ring of Gyges story cannot be answered without resort to religious conceptions (namely the idea of a divine onlooker in the absence of human onlookers).

[19] *Emile*, p. 283.

[20] Ibid.

[21] At the end of the lengthy footnote on pp. 312–314 responding to Bayle, Rousseau insists that philosophers must supply a substitute for doctrines of hell such as the Persian conception of Poul-Serrho (which Bayle, for instance, does not). This suggests that Rousseau himself *has* provided such a substitute (that is, as in Locke, moral laws backed up by otherworldly sanctions). Here, however, Rousseau seems to be handing the orthodox a mallet with which to beat him, for his own version of Poul-Serrho is pretty pale and does not seem to carry much conviction.

[22] Cf. pp. 258–259, which also suggests a commitment to damnation of unbelievers; these statements are made in the voice of the narrator of *Emile*, not the Savoyard Vicar. Admittedly, children and those whose cultural circumstances give them no access to knowledge of God will not be denied the "presence [of God] in the other life." Willful believers, however, will indeed be punished, for those whose "blindness" is voluntary must be brought "before the bar of eternal

Having laid out the articles of faith that define his theology, the Vicar then proceeds to elaborate on the morality of pure conscience that goes hand in hand with this theology: The rules of moral conduct are to be found "written by nature with ineffaceable characters in the depth of my heart."[23] The core of Rousseau's moralizing–subjectivizing philosophical anthropology is expressed in the following key passage:

Conscience, conscience! Divine instinct, immortal and celestial voice, certain guide of a being that is ignorant and limited but intelligent and free; infallible judge of good and bad which makes man like unto God; it is you who make the excellence of his nature and the morality of his actions. Without you I sense nothing in me that raises me above the beasts, other than the sad privilege of leading myself astray from error to error with the aid of an understanding without rule and a reason without principle.[24]

This passage gives the impression that Rousseau's celebration of sentiment is meant as a renunciation of reason, but this would be to infer more of an opposition between sentiment and reason than Rousseau actually intends: "[M]y rule of yielding to sentiment more than to reason is confirmed by reason itself."[25] Nevertheless, for all of Rousseau's appeals to the natural light of reason, there is also, and paradoxically, a fideistic dimension to his theology. In a letter to the Abbé de Carondelet of November 11, 1764, Rousseau wrote, "I do not believe, but I want to believe and I want it with all my heart."[26] This comes extremely

---

justice." This is as close as Rousseau ever comes to affirming that his version of deism allows for both heaven and hell. Of course, "the happiness of the just, the punishment of the wicked" is on Rousseau's list of "dogmas of the civil religion" in *Social Contract* IV.8. Nevertheless, see the "Letter on Providence," *Collected Writings*, Vol. 3, p. 117: "[T]he eternity of punishments [is a doctrine] which neither you nor I, nor ever a man thinking well of God, will ever believe." If one puts the main emphasis in this sentence on the word "eternity," then the letter to Voltaire is indeed compatible with the doctrine in *Emile*. However, it seems jarring (to put it mildly) that Rousseau could have been so emphatic in declaring that no one who thought well of God could believe in an eternity of punishment, while simultaneously maintaining that mere "torment of the wicked" was perfectly consistent with the notion of a benevolent deist God.

[23] *Emile*, p. 286.

[24] Ibid., p. 290.

[25] Ibid., p. 272. See also the union of mind and heart encapsulated on p. 295 ("serving God according to the understanding He gives to my mind and the sentiments He inspires in my heart"). It is also telling that, in the dialogue constructed by the Vicar on pp. 300–301, the Vicar (and Rousseau) are on the side of "the reasoner."

[26] Quoted in Boss, "Rousseau's Civil Religion," p. 175, n. 11. It must be admitted, though, that "not believing but wanting passionately to believe" is hardly a confident assertion of faith. Cf. the "Letter on Providence," *Collected Writings*, Vol. 3, p. 121: "All the subtleties of Metaphysics will not make one doubt for a moment the immortality of the soul, and a beneficent Providence. I feel it, I believe it, I wish it, I hope it, I shall defend it until my last breath." On p. 117 he concedes that he is indeed subject to "wavering" (at least when he remains strictly on the level of reason and the balanced "equilibrium" of reason's deliberations). Rousseau opts for faith not because he is spared doubts but because "the state of doubt is a state too violent for my soul." (The latter phrase is copied verbatim in the "Profession of Faith," *Emile*, p. 268.) See also a reported conversation with Rousseau (Francis Waterhouse, "An Interview with Jean Jacques Rousseau," *PMLA*, Vol. 37, [1922]: 116) in which he avows the same tension between

close to saying that if Rousseau must choose between philosophy and faith, he will choose faith. One might say that Rousseau offers a theology that speaks to all tastes: to fideists who distrust reason, to theological rationalists like Locke and Toland, and to those who seek an antitheological theology.

It should be clear from this account that Rousseau's theology does not lack for aspects of orthodoxy. He remains committed to doctrines of the world as an ordered creation, the justice and goodness of the Creator, what is in effect a doctrine of human sinfulness,[27] and an uncompromising theodicy. Rousseau even offers his own reconceptualization of heaven and hell (even if his version of hell is a bit too gentle for orthodox tastes). Where, then, is the heterodoxy sufficient to warrant branding Rousseau a shameless anti-Christian and persecuting him accordingly? Conspicuously (certainly relative to Locke and Toland), Rousseau's theology is unfolded with only a single reference to Scripture prior to commencing his critique of revealed religion.[28] As the Vicar puts

---

(sentimental) belief and (rational) skepticism. Cf. "Letter to Beaumont," *Collected Writings*, Vol. 9, ed. Christopher Kelly and Eve Grace (Lebanon, NH: University Press of New England, 2001), pp. 49 and 74. On pp. 75–76, Rousseau insists that the Vicar's doubts apply only to revealed religion and not at all to natural religion (and the same is true for Rousseau himself, as the "Letter to Franquières" makes perfectly clear).

[27] It is true that for Rousseau natural man is innocent, which rules out the idea that "man is naturally wicked" (*Emile*, p. 287); not surprisingly, the very first point that Beaumont raises in his condemnation of *Emile* is Rousseau's rejection of original sin ("Pastoral Letter," *Collected Writings*, Vol. 9, p. 4; see pp. 29–31 for Rousseau's reply). "There is no original perversity in the human heart" ("Pastoral Letter," p. 4, quoting *Emile*, p. 92); but at the same time, it seems that for Rousseau human passions cannot help but become corrupted, and human institutions cannot help but become unnatural. In that sense the natural innocence of man seems no more relevant to the quasi-natural fact of human corruption than (in the orthodox view) the original innocence of Adam is to the fact of original sin. Rousseau himself seems to make this very point in "Letter to Beaumont," *Collected Writings*, Vol. 9, p. 31. Both on the biblical account and on Rousseau's own account, man is originally good and becomes chronically wicked. Rousseau claims that his account simply gives a better explanation of this riddle. For anecdotal evidence of Rousseau's strong conviction concerning human wickedness, see Waterhouse, "An Interview with Jean Jacques Rousseau," p. 115.

Admittedly, this emphasis on human depravity is in tension with Rousseau's account of innate moral sentiment in the middle section of the "Profession of Faith," but Rousseau would not be Rousseau without philosophical tensions! (There are three sections to the "Profession of Faith": first, the deist theology proper; second, the morality of conscience that accompanies this theology; and third, the critique of revelation.) Cf. *Emile*, p. 291: "If [conscience] speaks to all hearts, then why are there so few of them who hear it? Well, this is because it speaks to us in nature's language, which everything has made us forget"; and p. 293, where he states that "all our first inclinations are legitimate,... all our vices come to us from ourselves." Hence the doctrine of original sin is both true *and* false: false because natural man is innocent; true because human beings are inexorably driven to corrupt nature.

[28] *Emile*, p. 284, note (citing Psalm 115). Jeffrey Macy, "'God Helps Those Who Help Themselves': New Light on the Theological–Political Teaching in Rousseau's Profession of Faith of the Savoyard Vicar," *Polity*, Vol. 24, No. 4 (Summer 1992): 615–632, makes this (inaccurate, as it turns out) scriptural reference the focus of his interpretation of the "Profession of Faith." The broader argument is that Rousseau uses his footnotes to intimate his own skepticism about central tenets of the Vicar's natural religion. Just as Straussian interpreters of Locke see him as

it, his theological system is developed "according to my natural lights"[29] – that is, without the benefit (or disadvantage) of revelation. Where does this leave the existing religions of the world (not least, Christianity)? As a natural religion, Rousseau's theology implies (and often asserts) the redundancy of those (historical, that is, nonnatural) religions. "I adore the supreme power. . . . I do not need to be taught this worship; it is dictated to me by nature itself."[30] The Vicar makes the seemingly hubristic claim that he can "derive . . . from the good use of [his] faculties" whatever truths are needed concerning religion.[31] "The greatest ideas of the divinity come to us from reason alone."[32] Without doubt, this is far bolder than anything we got from Locke or Toland in Chapter 13. Furthermore, revealed religions are not only redundant; more than this, they are positively harmful: They stoke up human pride, intolerance, and cruelty.[33] Scripture consists of *men's* revelations, not God's revelation.[34] As Paine was to put it before the end of the eighteenth century, *nature* is God's only revelation.[35]

more of a religious skeptic than seems credible to mainstream Locke scholars, so Macy interprets *Emile* more as a matter of the utility of religion than of its truth. Christopher Kelly and Eve Grace, in their Introduction to *Collected Writings*, Vol. 9, raise similar doubts about Rousseau's theological commitments in the light of the "Letter to Beaumont" and "Letters Written from the Mountain." If Macy's interpretation were correct, it would certainly be puzzling why Rousseau does not do more to cushion (or even suppress) his challenges to revealed religion. Why go to the trouble of developing a deist theology if the necessary myths are already available in existing religions? I can repeat the comment by Wootton that I quoted in the context of my discussion of Locke in Chapter 13: Rejection of orthodox Christianity does not entail rejection of Christianity per se, and (in the case of Rousseau) rejection of Christianity does not entail rejection of religion per se.

29 *Emile*, p. 286.
30 Ibid., p. 278. This redundancy is made fully explicit on p. 295: "You see in my exposition only natural religion. It is very strange that any other is needed!" This statement by the Vicar is a response to the narrator's observation on p. 294 that the Vicar's natural religion is precisely what strikes Christians as nothing but atheism. See also pp. 313–314: The narrator says that the Vicar's speech provides "an example of the way one can reason with one's pupil. . . . So long as one concedes nothing to the authority of men or to the prejudices of the country in which one was born, the light of reason alone cannot, in the education founded by nature, lead us any farther than natural religion. This is what I limit myself to with my Emile." Much as Christians perceive it to be atheism, Rousseau has embraced deism as the only religion worth teaching.
31 Ibid, p. 295; cf. pp. 297 and 307.
32 Ibid., p. 295.
33 Ibid. They do this not only by making human beings care passionately about particular dogmas that divide adherents of different religions but also, not uncommonly, by propagating images of "a god who is angry, jealous, vengeful, partisan" (p. 299, note).
34 Ibid., p. 295; cf. p. 297. See also Rousseau's quotation from Pierre Charron: "Religions are, whatever is said, gotten from human hands and by human means" (p. 296, note); and p. 303 ("Were not all books written by men?").
35 Thomas Paine, *The Age of Reason*, Part I, chapter 9. Cf. *Emile*, p. 306: "I . . . closed all the books. There is one open to all eyes: it is the book of nature." This hostility toward books on the part of Rousseau the famous author (cf. Waterhouse, "An Interview with Jean Jacques Rousseau," p. 114) nicely illustrates Rousseau's view, discussed at the start of this chapter, concerning the necessity of paradoxes.

The Vicar then, upping the ante, turns to the theme of the human contingency of revealed religions. In particular, they are subject to the contingency of geography; choice of a particular creed "is the effect of chance," a consequence of "being born in this or that country."[36] Believers born in Paris will be Catholics; believers born in Constantinople will be Muslims. The implication is that neither has any more intrinsic validity than the other. The revelation of each appears to the other as pure superstition.[37] Therefore, one must concede nothing "to the authority of men or to the prejudices of the country in which one was born."[38] One who sought to base his religion on rational foundations rather than mere prejudice would say, "I must . . . examine everything for myself"; "no one has a right to rely on the judgment of others."[39] Notwithstanding Rousseau's polemics against the Enlightenment in his other works, it is his deployment of the language of "prejudices" [*préjugés*] that shows him to be in fact a true son of the Enlightenment. If the historical (non-natural) religions win the allegiance of their adherents on account of paltry accidents of time and geography, then these religions (including Christianity) are exposed as mere prejudices, and Rousseau is no less of an Enlightener than Voltaire by virtue of promoting liberation from these prejudices.[40] Rousseau adds to all of this an aggressively Spinozistic account of the implausibility of miracles, and he asserts the unlikelihood that God would allow the truth of the true religion to hang on people's credulity.[41] So it is in this third section of the "Profession of Faith" that Rousseau's heterodoxy is on full display.

Nonetheless, just when Rousseau's view of religion appears to be verging on militant Spinozism, he pulls back. Having suggested that none of the supposed revelations of the various religions is any more authoritative than any of the others, he now affirms that the Christian Gospel offers a morality of such purity that it is reasonable to conceive of Jesus as a god.[42] At this stage of the argument,

---

[36] *Emile*, pp. 258 and 297.

[37] Ibid., pp. 258 and 303–304.

[38] Ibid., p. 313.

[39] Ibid., pp. 305, 306.

[40] This is part of what Boss means in saying that Voltaire was able to recognize Rousseau as a cultural ally, even when Rousseau was exerting himself to abuse and denounce his fellow *philosophes*. In *Collected Writings*, Vol. 9, p. 84, Rousseau observes bitterly that Voltaire received honors such as being elected into the Académie français for holding the same views that earned Rousseau arrest warrants and the burning of *Emile*. Voltaire, too, saw the injustice: "He has been persecuted for sentiments which are mine" (quoted by Boss, "Rousseau's Civil Religion," p. 155).

[41] *Emile*, p. 298; cf. p. 301. Rousseau also uses the inflammatory language of "impostors" [*imposteurs, fourbe*] (pp. 299, 300). An acquaintance of Rousseau's, Antoine Sabatier de Castres (see note 53), claims that Rousseau's critique of miracles was thoroughly indebted to Spinoza's *Theological–Political Treatise*.

[42] *Emile*, pp. 307–308; cf. *Collected Writings*, Vol. 8, pp. 269–270. In "Letters Written from the Mountain," (*Collected Writings*, Vol. 9, pp. 198–199), Rousseau goes so far as to present himself as merely a commentator on the Christian Gospel. Rousseau's most direct affirmation of his fidelity to Christianity is "Letter to Beaumont," *Collected Writings*, Vol. 9, pp. 47–48. This greatly displeased Voltaire: "[Y]ou adhere formally to the pure and holy religion of deism

Rousseau embraces the Montesquieuian inclusive or pluralized approach to religion that I discussed in Chapter 15. Because it is legitimate for the state to "prescribe in each country a uniform manner of honouring God by public worship," and because what truly matters in the domain of religion is good moral conduct rather than particular dogmas, one can be (as Montesquieu was) accepting of whatever religious practices suit "the climate, the government, the genius" of particular nations (provided they meet the inviolable test of religious tolerance).[43] People should be faithful to the religion to which they are born: Islam for the Turks, Catholicism for the French, Calvinism for the Swiss.[44] The fact that morality forms the core of all true religion, and that all religions share this moral core, permits a salutary relativization of religious practices. Hence the sum of the Vicar's criticisms of revealed religion in no way precludes him from being a faithful minister of the Catholic rituals.[45] Making a truly impartial survey of the various religions to weigh up their relative strengths and weaknesses is a task too daunting for any mortal human being: It is better simply to appreciate the universal true religion as instantiated in one's own native (mainly false) religion.[46] Thus the rhetoric deployed at the close of the "Profession of Faith" is not one of Spinozistic defiance but rather Montesquieuian wisdom: "[L]et us not disturb the worship [that the laws] prescribe."[47] "Go back to your country, return to the religion of your fathers,"[48] even if the religion of your fathers is the residuum of accumulated

---

yet you pretend to be a Christian" (Boss, "Rousseau's Civil Religion," p. 186, quoting from Voltaire's marginalia on the "Letter to Beaumont"). Cf. Voltaire's complaint about Rousseau penned even before the publication of *Emile*: Boss, p. 155, n. 11.

[43] *Emile*, p. 308.

[44] Paradoxically, the argument of the third section of the "Profession of Faith" goes around in a complete circle. The section started with a delegitimization of revealed religions because they reflect no more than the accidents of birth of their adherents. By the end of the section, the Vicar is insisting that "it is an inexcusable presumption to profess a religion other than that in which we were born" (p. 311), because *choosing* error is in God's eyes more culpable than *inheriting* error.

[45] Ibid., pp. 308–309.

[46] Through most of the third section of the "Profession of Faith," the Vicar presents himself as impartial vis-à-vis the various existing religions, but on p. 311 he declares that the Calvinism into which Rousseau was born in Geneva is "of all the religions on earth...the one which has the purest morality and which is most satisfactory to reason." Needless to say, this is a surprising endorsement coming from a Catholic clergyman! Doubts about the Vicar's statement are raised by Rousseau's own note on p. 313, which suggests that Islamic religious principles are both more charitable and more tolerant than those of Christianity.

[47] Ibid., p. 310. In *Collected Writings*, Vol. 9, p. 149, Rousseau seems to criticize Montesquieu for a relativization of religion: Montesquieu's challenge to Christianity "went further" than Rousseau's because Montesquieu "said the Muslim religion was best for Asiatic countries." The Vicar's principle that ultimately people should keep faith with the religion of their fathers surely implies the same relativization.

[48] *Emile*, p. 311. The Vicar's ultimate view that it is best to keep faith with one's inherited religion seems somewhat in tension with a view of religion that puts so much emphasis on conscience – and also in tension with his forceful efforts to relativize and challenge inherited religions in relation to a deist religion that is more rational because he has spun it out of his own rational faculties.

prejudices. The Vicar ends his speech by presenting himself as a mediator between the Christian *dévots* and the atheistic *philosophes*.[49] This presentation points back to Montesquieu's conception, which I discussed in Chapter 15, of political virtue as a mean between piety and atheism.[50]

Is the "Profession of Faith," either on its own or as transposed into the civil creed at the end of the *Social Contract*, a civil religion?[51] It is in the sense that Rousseau intended it as a necessary bulwark for moral and social life, in an age when revealed religion was subject to increasingly robust challenges.[52] However, in offering a deistic religion of the heart stripped of the narrative resources of revealed religion, he placed himself in a predicament not that different from Spinoza's. The reaction from orthodox Christians would be the same for Rousseau as it had been for Spinoza: not gratitude for defending religion in light of its social utility, but hatred and contempt for what was perceived as a shameless debunking of revelation.[53] The outcome of the "Profession of Faith" in *Emile* replicates that in the civil-religion chapter of the

---

[49] *Emile*, p. 313. Does *les philosophes* refer to contemporaries such as Voltaire and Diderot, or does it refer to an earlier generation of philosophers such as Spinoza and Bayle? As I pointed out in Chapter 14, the phrase "brake on the passions" in the previous paragraph (to which Rousseau's long anti-Bayle footnote is attached) is a tacit citation of Bayle, which makes me incline toward the second of these two possible interpretations.

[50] Boss suggests that Voltaire shared the same project, which is also part of the reason why Voltaire saw himself as intellectually closer to Rousseau than one would infer from the personal animosity between them. For a sampling of the atheist pole of the antinomy that Rousseau is trying to mediate, see Baron d'Holbach, *Christianity Unveiled*, trans. W. M. Johnson (New York: Gordon Press, 1974). The book was originally published in 1766 (according to David Holohan, editor of a recent edition of the book), but d'Holbach was able to conceal his authorship of it during his lifetime. As Rousseau elaborates his doctrine of otherworldly punishments in "Letter to Beaumont," it is precisely the *philosophes* who have the knowledge to apprehend God but willfully refuse to do so who will be punished for their pride, whereas ignorant savages (and ignorant masses in developed societies) must be judged innocent: *Collected Writings*, Vol. 9, pp. 40–41. It may be added that it is unsurprising that Rousseau, as a self-appointed mediator, suffers a fate fairly typical of those assuming such a role: The orthodox are struck by how much Rousseau shares with an infidel like d'Holbach, whereas the *philosophes* are struck by how much Rousseau shares with the pious.

[51] Just as Straussian interpreters of Locke read *The Reasonableness of Christianity* as a civil religion, so Macy reads the "Profession of Faith" as a civil religion.

[52] Cf. Boss, "Rousseau's Civil Religion," *passim*. On p. 310, Rousseau says that generally speaking, "one must not disturb peaceful souls or alarm the faith of simple people." However, Rousseau's times are not ordinary times; "everything is shaken" because the Enlightenment has provoked a unique crisis in the status of religion. Hence one must take extraordinary measures to "preserve the trunk at the expense of the branches." Deism is the trunk and revealed religions are the discarded branches. In other words, Rousseau articulates a heterodox theology as an emergency response to a preexisting cultural crisis. If this has the effect of unsettling the faith of simple people, this is not Rousseau's doing. For an important elaboration, see "Letters Written from the Mountain," Fifth Letter: *Collected Writings*, Vol. 9, p. 227.

[53] For evidence that Rousseau himself appreciated the parallel with Spinoza, see his reported statement that Spinoza's *Theological–Political Treatise* "is the one book among all modern works which has been most denounced by the priests, though it is just the one from which they might have drawn the greatest number of arguments in favour of Christianity." Quoted from Antoine Sabatier de Castres, *Apologie de Spinoza et du Spinosisme* (1805) in Walter Eckstein, "Rousseau and Spinoza: Their Political Theories and Their Conception of Ethical

Social Contract: Once the range of historical religions have been excluded on account of their violence, their cruelty, and their intolerance, one is left with a minimalist creed that, as Hume was right to observe, would have limited potential in seizing people's religious imaginations in the way that the jettisoned historical religions had.[54] Hume's point was that it would be unrealistic to expect a merely rational or philosophical religion (a natural religion rather than a revealed religion) to gain a purchase on the souls of ordinary human beings. Insofar as religion is believed to be necessary to serve essential socializing and moralizing purposes (as Rousseau evidently did), it is not clear that one can subtract those aspects of religion that lead to superstition, fanaticism, and human conflict and still have a religion robust enough to serve these socializing and moralizing purposes.[55]

In Part I of this book, I expressed my skepticism that the deist creed formulated at the end of the *Social Contract* counts as a real civil religion, not least as judged by Rousseau's own standards of a real civil religion. My view remains the same in the present context.[56] As Rousseau himself intimates in the examples that animate his discussions in the *Social Contract* and *The Government of Poland* (Moses, Lycurgus, Numa, Mohammed, and Calvin),[57] a real civil religion requires something considerably more robust (and considerably more divisive) than the deism of *Emile*.[58] Even if Rousseau shared with Voltaire and D'Alembert the "desperate hope" that some version of deism could serve as a

Freedom," *Journal of the History of Ideas*, Vol. 5, No. 3 (June 1944): 269; according to Sabatier, Rousseau made the statement in a direct conversation between the two of them concerning the *Theological–Political Treatise*. (I owe this reference to Larissa Atkison.) This is not to suggest that Rousseau sees himself as an ally of Spinoza: The critique of monist metaphysics on p. 279 of *Emile* seems to be, at least in part, a (vehement) critical response to Spinoza. In the "Letter to Beaumont," Rousseau complains bitterly that "the Atheist Spinoza" enjoyed princely treatment compared with the hounding and victimization he himself suffered: See *Collected Writings*, Vol. 9, p. 24.

54 See Chapter 18.

55 Cf. Boss, "Rousseau's Civil Religion," p. 141: The project (on the part of Voltaire and D'Alembert) to institutionalize deism as a public cult, to replace existing religions, "was a desperate hope." One can apply the same judgment to Rousseau.

56 Cf. Paul A. Rahe, *Soft Despotism, Democracy's Drift* (New Haven: Yale University Press, 2009), p. 136: (a) Rousseau's civil-religion enterprise "is an attempt to square the circle"; and (b) "Rousseau knew it." As the reader knows by now, I think Rahe is right on both counts.

57 Rousseau, *The Government of Poland*, trans. Willmoore Kendall (Indianapolis: Hackett, 1985), p. 8: "All three [Moses, Lycurgus, and Numa] found what they were looking for in distinctive usages, in religious ceremonies that invariably were in essence exclusive and national." Rousseau wants "a cult which is . . . national" and that enforces the cultural differences between human beings, but he also wants a generic deism that promotes toleration and gives human beings an appreciation of the universality of a shared human religiosity. That is, he both wants and does not want a civil religion!

58 It is very telling that the kind of national particularism celebrated in *The Government of Poland* is directly criticized in *Emile*: "[Wanting] an exclusive form of worship [and wanting] God to have said to me [or said to my people – R.B.] what He had not said to others" represents a deeply flawed conception of divinity (*Emile*, p. 296). In *Emile*, Rousseau is an Enlightened debunker of "the prejudices of the country in which one was born" (p. 313); in his political works, he enthusiastically endorses them.

public cult, the reality is that a mere philosopher's religion could never be a viable civil religion.[59]

We turn finally to Kant's *Religion within the Boundaries of Mere Reason*.[60] The fundamental purpose of Kant's *Religion within the Boundaries* is to specify, within the sphere of religion, what is humanly required of those who are to live up to the vision of moral autonomy articulated within Kant's practical philosophy. The problem for Kant is how to conceive a form of religion that itself fully embodies human autonomy, as opposed to the many instantiations of religious belief and practice that are merely heteronomous.[61] This can furnish a standard for judging religions as more autonomous or less autonomous: Whereas Judaism is the pure type of a religion of heteronomy,[62] Protestant

---

[59] In the Introduction to this book, I suggested the possibility that although Rousseau did not offer a workable civil religion, John Toland, in his *Nazarenus*, did. Why is that? One answer could go as follows: To take the civil-religion idea seriously would involve designing a new religion (or at least reassembling the materials of existing religions in radically new ways). In fact, there are in the history of political philosophy examples of such a project. As we explored in Part I, there are suggestions of such a project in Machiavelli and Hobbes. Another example is provided by Nietzsche's *Thus Spoke Zarathustra*. Rousseau never does this. To be sure, there is a liberal tradition in Spinoza and the successors of Spinoza considered in this chapter (including Rousseau) aimed at refashioning Judeo-Christian religion in ways that satisfy philosophical standards. However, these are not civil religions because they share the fundamental intention to substitute a universalist, rationalist, and secularizing quasi-religion for real religions. (The first epigraph to this chapter makes clear how much the religion of *Emile* shares with Spinoza, and how remote it is from any real Revelation-based religion.) Perhaps Toland too belongs in this post-Spinoza category, for he too intends to loosen the boundaries of religions sufficiently to include everyone. On one hand, it is at least *possible* that Toland intended to contrive a hybrid of Judaism, Christianity, and Islam that would be serviceable for civic-republican purposes (as has been hypothesized by James R. Jacob, Justin Champion, and Jonathan Israel). On the other hand, it may just be the case that Toland was presenting what he took to be a more accurate account of the founding texts of Christianity. (Cf. Thomas Paine, *The Age of Reason*, ed. M. D. Conway, Mineola, NY: Dover, 2004], p. 173, note.) For articulations of the Jacob–Champion–Israel thesis concerning *Nazarenus*, see James R. Jacob, *Henry Stubbe, Radical Protestantism, and the Early Enlightenment* (Cambridge: Cambridge University Press, 1983), chapter 8; Justin A. I. Champion, "Legislators, Impostors, and the Politic Origins of Religion: English Theories of 'Imposture' from Stubbe to Toland," in *Heterodoxy, Spinozism, and Free Thought in Early-Eighteenth-Century Europe*, ed. Silvia Berti et al. (Dordrecht: Kluwer, 1996), pp. 333–356; and Jonathan I. Israel, *Radical Enlightenment* (Oxford: Oxford University Press, 2001), pp. 609–614. For a recent work offering historical arguments directly parallel to Toland's, see Barrie Wilson, *How Jesus Became Christian* (Toronto: Random House, 2008).

[60] Immanuel Kant, *Religion within the Boundaries of Mere Reason*, ed. Allen Wood and George di Giovanni (Cambridge: Cambridge University Press, 1998); hereafter, *Religion within the Boundaries*. I am grateful to Clifford Orwin for helping to persuade me that it would be wrong to omit Kant from the dialogue assembled in this book.

[61] The fundamental distinction is encapsulated on p. 164 as religion sought "within us" versus religion sought "from the outside." This emphasis on moral autonomy also contributes crucially to the very strong anticlericalism expressed by Kant in Part 4 of *Religion within the Boundaries* – to the extent that Kant refers to "the spiritual despotism [*geistlichen Despotismus*] found in all ecclesiastical forms" (p. 170, note; cf. p. 173, note, and p. 174).

[62] Kant's main account of Judaism is presented on pp. 130–132 and 162–163 of *Religion within the Boundaries*, as well as the note on pp. 139–140.

Christianity in its most mature form is the pure type of a religion of autonomy. It is possible to see this rhetoric of autonomy (which brilliantly encapsulates what is at stake in the Enlightenment as a whole) as launching an intellectual and cultural trajectory that has its eventual endpoint in Freud's view of religion. Freud famously depicted religion as a form of infantile neurosis – that is, a syndrome of arrested development having its basis in individual and collective neurosis (analyzed according to characteristic Freudian narratives of primordial trauma and so on). Obviously, there is a huge difference between Kant's view of religion and Freud's view of religion. Nonetheless, it is not hard to perceive the logic whereby the Kantian trope of casting off the limitations of childhood and rising to maturity leads directly to the Freudian conception of religion in general as a neurotic inability to achieve maturity.[63] Following Rousseau's lead, Kant pursues the idea that if true religion has its source in conscience, then in our own highest moral and rational capacities, human beings can evolve ways of being religious that do not involve reliance upon revelation.[64] In that sense,

[63] Cf. John Forrester, Introduction to Sigmund Freud, *Interpreting Dreams*, trans. S. A. Underwood (London: Penguin, 2006), p. xxiv.

[64] Consider Kant's distinction, in the Preface to the first edition (*Religion within the Boundaries*, pp. 37–39), between theologians who are guardians of "biblical theology" and philosophers who are exponents of "philosophical theology." This already implies some kind of opposition between revealed religion as the concern of theologians and natural religion as the concern of philosophers. On p. 39, Kant points out that "the pure *philosophical* doctrine of religion" can "avail itself of everything, the Bible included"; but leaving theologians in charge of "biblical theology" certainly implies that the Bible is not central to the philosophical version of theology. Steven B. Smith, in *Spinoza, Liberalism, and the Question of Jewish Identity* (New Haven: Yale University Press, 1997), p. 183, writes that "the *Religion* amounts to an attack on or critique of revelation as such." Nonetheless, one would hardly expect Kant to present his philosophical theology as a critique of, let alone an attack on, revelation. In the Preface to the second edition (*Religion within the Boundaries*, p. 40), he suggests that the appropriate image for capturing the relation between revelation and philosophy is not "two circles external to one another" but two concentric circles, with philosophy corresponding to the inner circle (limited to a priori reason and not experience) and revelation corresponding to the outer circle (encompassing reason and experience). This image of their relation allows one to postulate "not only compatibility but also unity [between reason and Scripture]." Admittedly, Kant wrote this knowing (as he flagged at the start of the paragraph I have quoted) that the title he gave to his book had aroused the same kind of suspicions provoked by the titles given by Locke and Toland to their books. It should be pointed out, however, that there is at least one direct subversion of Scripture in *Religion within the Boundaries* (and indeed a subversion of potentially enormous proportions). At the end of Part 2, Kant writes that if God is presented as acting in a way that is "directly in conflict with morality," what Scripture presents as a divine miracle (namely the appearance of God commanding immorality) absolutely cannot be one. His example is the story of Abraham and Isaac in chapter 22 of *Genesis* (*Religion within the Boundaries*, p. 100; cf. p. 180, as well as Immanuel Kant, *The Conflict of the Faculties*, trans. Mary Gregor, Lincoln: University of Nebraska, 1992, p. 115, note). If the veracity of *this* presentation of God in Scripture is to be challenged on the basis of an independent appeal to practical reason, clearly the door is wide open to a broad set of such challenges to biblical presentations of God. (Furthermore, one can well ask this: *How is the required martyrdom of Jesus different in principle from the commanded sacrifice of Isaac?*) Although Kierkegaard never cites Kant in his book, it is tempting to interpret *Fear and Trembling* as a book-length reply, on behalf of biblical religion,

it is not at all implausible to picture Lessing's *The Education of the Human Race* as constituting a bridge between Spinoza and Kant: Lessing's schema of a third dispensation that transcends the Christian revelation just as the Christian revelation transcended the Jewish one is not only an encapsulation of Spinoza's project but also an anticipation of Kant's project.[65]

"[M]orality is ... in need neither of the idea of another being above [the moral agent] in order that he recognize his duty, nor, that he observe it, of an incentive other than the law itself. ... Hence on its own behalf morality in no way needs religion ... but is rather self-sufficient by virtue of pure practical reason."[66] Thus there is, right from the opening sentences of *Religion within the Boundaries*, a certain throwing down of the gauntlet. Religion enters the scene, not with respect to what motivates human beings to be moral but with respect to the outcomes that attach to their moral performances. Once again, we immediately see Kant's reliance on Rousseau's "Profession of Faith." The Vicar had highlighted the issue of whether virtue receives its proper reward; he had argued that this is not to be expected without the conception of a just divinity who takes responsibility for rebalancing the scales of virtue and reward, vice and punishment.[67] Kant introduces the relevance of religion to morality in exactly the same terms: "[W]e must assume a higher, moral, most holy, and omnipotent being" to secure "the idea of a highest good in the

---

to Kant's account of Abraham and Isaac on pp. 100 and 180 of *Religion within the Boundaries*. The note on p. 118 of *Religion within the Boundaries* provides some other examples of apparent immorality in the Bible, but pp. 118–120 suggest that we are obliged to interpret Scripture in ways that allow us to square it with what we know morality to require, even if this involves forced interpretations. Cf. p. 127: "[T]he moral predisposition in us [is] the interpreter of all religion" (which one can easily construe as a suggestion that philosophers are more reliable interpreters of Scripture than theologians are).

[65] Lessing radicalized Spinoza by presenting both the Old and New Testaments as "primers" on the road to Enlightenment. Kant's contribution to the famous pantheism controversy conducted by Jacobi and Mendelssohn was his 1786 text, "What Does It Mean to Orient Oneself in Think-ing?" (*Religion within the Boundaries*, pp. 3–14). In that text, Kant forcefully rejects Spinoza's metaphysics (p. 11, note) while siding with the rationalism of Mendelssohn, the defender of the alleged Spinozist Lessing. What, however, is Kant's stance toward the *Theological–Political Treatise*? The notion of Kant's *Religion within the Boundaries* being influenced by Spinoza may seem surprising, but consider Steven B. Smith, "How to Commemorate the 350th Anniversary of Spinoza's Expulsion," *Hebraic Political Studies*, Vol. 3, No. 2 (Spring 2008): 160: "[Hermann] Cohen claimed that Spinoza had created negative stereotypes about Judaism and biblical religion that were later to influence Kant, who depended upon Spinoza's research." See also Smith, *Spinoza, Liberalism, and the Question of Jewish Identity*, pp. 255–256, n. 88; on p. 181, Smith states that "*Religion Within the Limits of Reason Alone* ... reads like a sum-mary of the [*Theological-Political Treatise*]." According to Jürgen Habermas (*The Future of Human Nature*, Cambridge: Polity, 2003, p. 110), Kant offered "the first great example ... of a secularizing, but at the same time salvaging, deconstruction of religious truths." It does not seem credible that Kant's enterprise was as novel as Habermas suggests; rather, as we have seen from previous chapters, this business of simultaneously salvaging and deconstructing revealed religion had been underway for more than a century before Kant picked up the baton.

[66] *Religion within the Boundaries*, p. 33.

[67] See note 18 (including the citation of the "Letter to Franquières").

world," which in turn requires "happiness proportioned to [the observance of duty]."[68] Human beings ought to act dutifully because that is what the moral law commands, not because it is what (a heteronomous) God demands. However, will they be rewarded for doing what the moral law commands? This *cannot* be something to which moral agents are indifferent; caring whether they inhabit a just or unjust universe is inscribed in the very structure of moral agency.[69] Furthermore, would morality survive the thought that virtuous or dutiful action earns no reward, just as vicious action earns no punishment? This was a key issue for Rousseau's moral theology, and it is no less central for Kant. Hence morality requires religion, not because morality is founded on anything other than rational autonomy, but because virtue needs assurance that it is not being played for a fool by a universe where cosmic injustice reigns.[70] Therefore morality requires the idea of a just God ("a mighty moral lawgiver").[71]

Applying Rousseau's "Profession of Faith" as a template by which to measure Kant's version of the same enterprise,[72] we see that Kant commences his rational theology with a meditation on what I referred to as the Vicar's third dogma, namely the postulate of human moral freedom. That is, Kant does not base his natural theology on a deist account of the providential ordering of nature; instead he proceeds straight to a discussion of the metaphysical presuppositions of morality. Expressed in Kantian vocabulary, the idea is this: Our actions reflect our maxims, and our maxims are not reducible to natural impulses but instead are traceable to an ultimate (and inscrutable) "first ground" (this is the key notion in Kant's account).[73] We can either choose fidelity to the moral law (good) or rejection of the moral law

---

68 *Religion within the Boundaries*, p. 34. Cf. the note on p. 36, on the possibility that "happiness and desert perhaps never converge" because there is no afterlife. As he puts it later in the same note, the essential issue for Kant (as for Rousseau) is the proportionality between happiness and worthiness to be happy. Because this proportionality cannot be guaranteed without a divine "ruler of the world," it follows that "morality leads inevitably to religion." One could say that both Rousseau and Kant are haunted by Plato's ring of Gyges problem, and both of them despair of solving the problem without – literally – a *deus ex machina*.

69 Twice on p. 34, Kant uses the phrase "it cannot possibly be a matter of indifference."

70 Kant's formulation is that the idea of the highest good "rises out of morality and is not its foundation" (ibid.)

71 Ibid., p. 35.

72 One of the first quotations in Part 1 of *Religion within the Boundaries* is a motto from Seneca lifted from the title page of Rousseau's *Emile* (see *Religion within the Boundaries*, p. 46, note *h*), which signals pretty clearly that Kant composed his rational theology with *Emile* very much in mind.

73 As Kant puts it on p. 59 of *Religion within the Boundaries*, a supreme maxim presumed to be corrupt "corrupts the ground of all maxims." On pp. 64 and 67 he calls it the "supreme ground of all our maxims"; on p. 68 he calls it the "universal root" of individual vices; on p. 78, he calls it "the first and inmost ground." For Kant, there are only two ultimate moral possibilities: Either the moral law as such is "the supreme ground of all our maxims," or evil is the supreme ground. No allowance is made for a third possibility, and the absence of a third possibility is the very foundation of Kant's entire moral theology.

(evil) – ultimately, human beings per se are moved either by a "good heart" or an "evil heart"[74] – and Kant thinks that such a judgment of innate goodness or evil can be rendered not just with respect to individuals but with respect to the human species as a whole.[75] As Robert Merrihew Adams discusses in his Introduction to *Religion within the Boundaries*, Kant's central aim in Part 1 of the book is to offer a secularized account of the doctrine of human sinfulness. Part of what is involved in offering a secularized account is that one no longer calls it "sin" (Kant calls it "radical evil" or the "evil heart").[76] Whether one calls it sin or something else, however, the basic point is that what draws the moral philosopher into the domain of religion is the sinfulness of human beings in general.

Kant says that "we can spare ourselves [a] formal proof" of his thesis because the evidence of the natural depravity of the human will is, to his mind, overwhelming.[77] Kant is fully aware of how paradoxical it is for him to speak of a "natural propensity to evil," given his uncompromising nature–freedom dualism.[78] Accordingly, Kant exerts himself to develop a quite complex and intricate account of how the "naturalness" or "innateness" of human evil can be squared with his dualism. Particular practical maxims are the expression of a "supreme maxim"[79] that governs the moral life of human beings so pervasively that it is legitimate to speak of evil being "somehow entwined with humanity itself and, as it were, rooted in it."[80] Nevertheless, adoption of this "supreme maxim" is absolutely our own responsibility, the product of the pure freedom exercised in our "moral faculty of choice."[81] The most striking

---

[74] Ibid., p. 53.

[75] Ibid.

[76] The term "*Sünde*" occurs in various places (e.g., pp. 54 and 61) because Kant is either quoting or commenting on texts from the New Testament; therefore, strictly speaking, *Sünde* is not part of Kant's own philosophical vocabulary. On p. 62, Kant makes explicit his rejection of the Christian doctrine of original sin, on the grounds that it renders impossible the agent's own responsibility for evil. On p. 63 he makes explicit that the vocabulary of sin is associated with "transgression of the moral law as *divine command*" (Kant's italics), as opposed to the transgression of a rationally autonomous moral law; cf. p. 89.

[77] Kant's indictment of human nature is powerfully encapsulated on pp. 56–57. With Rousseau's account of the state of nature in mind, Kant insists that moral corruption is just as present in savage societies as in civilized societies (p. 56). Kant clearly regards Rousseau's account of evil as a superficial one: The problem is not the corruptions of social life but rather "the human heart" per se. In this sense, Kant's account of evil (despite its secularized character, its being a transposition of Christian insights into philosophy) is far closer to the Christian account than Rousseau's. However, at the start of Part 3 (p. 105), Kant gives an account of "the causes and the circumstances that draw" the human being into a morally perilous state that appears virtually identical to Rousseau's.

[78] Cf. Robert Merrihew Adams, Introduction to *Religion within the Boundaries*, pp. xi–xv. As Kant puts it on p. 54, his thesis is that "the propensity to evil among human beings is universal . . . that it is woven into human nature."

[79] *Religion within the Boundaries*, p. 55.

[80] Ibid., p. 56.

[81] Ibid., p. 54. As I have already intimated, Kant's concept of the "supreme maxim" (characterized on p. 55 as "intelligible" rather than "empirical") is precisely his secularized counterpart to

and characteristic aspect of Kant's account is what he says under the rubric of "the impurity of the human heart"; his doctrine here is that human beings show themselves to be evil *even when they are acting well* because "actions conforming to duty are not done purely from duty."[82] The claim that radical evil is inscribed in human nature per se follows directly from Kant's moral theory, for Kantian practical philosophy sets the standard of dutiful moral existence so transcendently high that it is indeed highly improbable that even the most virtuous human being meets that standard.[83]

A doctrine of innate evil requires doctrines of grace and redemption (the next stage in Kant's enterprise of secularizing Christianity), and this is the set of issues that Kant takes up starting in the General Remark that concludes Part 1. The notion of being able to redeem evil strikes Kant as counterintuitive; as he puts it, "how can an evil tree bear good fruit?"[84] Nonetheless, much as Kant rejects Scripture's presentation of our primordial corruption in the form of a historical narrative,[85] Kant does agree with Scripture that there was a primordial "fall" from good into evil. Hence it should in principle be possible for there to be an "ascent from evil back to the good."[86] For this possibility to be realized, there must be "supernatural cooperation," "a higher assistance inscrutable to us,"[87] and this assistance must be earned through a radical "change of heart."[88] However corrupted we may be in our failure to maintain moral purity, there remains in us, for Kant, "a germ of goodness"

the idea of original sin. Kant's core argument is that "the deep roots the propensity [to evil] has in the power of choice, on account of which we must say that it is found in the human being by nature" in no way qualifies our absolute responsibility as "freely acting beings" (p. 58). Freedom and evil (our incapacity to prove ourselves equal to the unyielding stringency of the moral law) are *both* essential attributes of the human being.

[82] Ibid., pp. 53–54.

[83] Hence Kant's insistence that "even the best" human being participates in what he presents as a *universal* propensity to evil (p. 54; cf. p. 59). Rousseau's view is that Jesus is morally superior to Socrates (*Collected Writings*, Vol. 8, pp. 269–270), but Socrates and Cato are at least in the vicinity, morally speaking, of Jesus (p. 266). Rousseau sets a very high standard for virtue, but unlike Kant he is not committed to a moral doctrine that in effect guarantees that all human beings will as a matter of course fall short. Morality, for Kant, is a test that all human beings fail.

[84] *Religion within the Boundaries*, p. 66; cf. pp. xv–xxv (Adams's Introduction).

[85] *Religion within the Boundaries*, p. 65.

[86] Ibid., p. 66.

[87] Ibid., pp. 65, 66; cf. p. 71: "cooperation from above." According to Adams, "Kant has an uneasy relation to [grace as a] central concept of Christian theology. He fears the concept of grace for the potential he sees in it for a corrupt relaxation of the stern demands of morality" (*Religion within the Boundaries*, p. xxi, citing pp. 71–72); cf. p. xxii: "The very idea of [grace] is problematic for Kant... because of his insistence that anything by virtue of which our lives are to have moral worth must be the work of our own freedom." Kant's reference on p. 77 to "the lazy and timid cast of mind [that] waits for external help" nicely encapsulates his reservations about the idea of grace.

[88] *Religion within the Boundaries*, p. 68. This aspect of Kant's version of philosophical Christianity is highly reminiscent of Locke's doctrine of repentance, which I discussed in Chapter 13.

that is forever uncorrupted,[89] and this residue of our original goodness offers the promise of, if not holiness, at least an *aspiration toward* holiness.[90] This is the philosophical core of Christianity, which has itself been corrupted by false conceptions such as the notion that God's commands are governed by "the principle of happiness."[91] Human beings can never be innocent, but they can exert themselves never endingly to render themselves less corrupt, and it is through this endless struggle to work a revolution upon themselves that they are able to make themselves "pleasing to God."[92]

Kant's theology in *Religion within the Boundaries*, like that of Rousseau in *Emile*, is focused overwhelmingly on the experience of morality – indeed, more so than in *Emile* because Rousseau did have things to say about God's providence, God's justice, and so on.[93] God seems almost tangential to Kant's account of religion (certainly at this stage of the argument): Religion, for Kant, is primarily a function of humankind's relation to its own moral law, rather than the relation to God. As Adams notes in his Introduction, the notion of making oneself "pleasing to God" through one's efforts at inner moral revolution is virtually a symbolic representation of (a stand-in for?) that to which one more immediately aspires in Kant's depiction of the revolutionary change

---

[89] *Religion within the Boundaries*, p. 66.

[90] Ibid., p. 67.

[91] On p. 71, Kant refers to this "false imputation" as an example of "impure religious ideas." In this text, Kant asserts (implausibly) that Christianity is the only religion "so far known" that is in the full sense a "moral religion" elevated above impure incentives. In other words, he asserts (again implausibly) that actual Christianity already coincides with the purified moral religion he is attempting to articulate. On p. 69, Kant states that it is an object of "the highest wonder" that reason is able to command us compellingly "without however either promising or threatening anything thereby." It seems to follow pretty directly from this claim that images of God associating Him with promises and threats are less impressive than moral reason as depicted by Kant. It follows just as directly that traditional biblical Christianity is less sublime as a religion than Kant's philosophical version of Christianity. Kant's challenge to false conceptions of God is reinforced by his affirmation (p. 77, note) of the Stoic idea of reason as "the sole legislator." (On p. 113, Kant writes that "all religion consists in this, that in all our duties we look upon God as the lawgiver." According to this definition of religion, though, if reason is the sole legislator, then one might infer that Kant's challenge is not just to revealed religion but to religion per se.)

[92] Ibid., p. 68; on the notion that this Sisyphean "moral labor" stretches to "infinity" and can never permit itself to relax, cf. pp. 70–71. See also p. 105: "[H]is freedom [being] constantly under attack, he must henceforth remain forever armed for battle." The struggle to return from evil to goodness *may* be conceived as extending into an afterlife, but Kant is wary of the transgression of the limitations of reason involved in asserting the doctrine of an afterlife as a positive dogma (pp. 86–87).

[93] This is not to say that conceptions of God's justice or providence are absent in Kant (consider, for instance, the reference to "the profound wisdom of divine creation" on p. 188, or to "God's love for humankind" on p. 126). But Rousseau develops his natural theology in a way that builds on such conceptions; in Kant, by contrast, these attributes of God seem to be add-ons rather than foundational. Indeed, it would not make sense for Kant to base his natural religion on an account of God's attributes, for as he lays out very clearly in the note on p. 153, God is not an object of theoretical cognition but rather an "idea" postulated according to the needs of our practical reason.

of heart – making oneself pleasing to one's own inward conscience.[94] God is somewhat more of a presence in Part 2 of *Religion within the Boundaries* than He was in Part 1. The cosmic struggle of human beings to extirpate an evil supreme maxim from their disposition is a spectacle producing either divine pleasure (secularized grace) or divine displeasure (punishment in accordance with divine justice).[95] The dominant function served by God in Part 2 of *Religion within the Boundaries* is as Judge sitting at "the heavenly tribunal."[96] Curiously, though, we self-deluding humans can more readily pacify our conscience in thinking of *that* judge than in conjuring up "the accuser within us"[97]: "Address [the] question [of the fitting verdict to be applied to an individual's moral life] to the judge within him, and the human being will pronounce a stern judgment upon himself, *for he cannot bribe his reason.*"[98] By contrast, God, according to standard images of him, *can* be bribed – for instance, "by mollifying him with prayers and entreaties."[99]

How does Jesus figure in Kant's account? We can only be pleasing to God through our struggle to move in the direction of moral duty, and for this purpose we need a "prototype" of the purely good human being. The Son of God is this prototype.[100] Nonetheless, the historical person of Jesus is, so to speak, incidental to this prototype, for "there is no need... of any example from experience to make the idea of a human being morally pleasing to God a model to us; the idea is present as model already in our reason."[101] Indeed, if this were merely a *historically* based faith, such as a faith in miracles supposedly performed by the empirical Jesus,[102] then we would be confessing to our "lack of faith in virtue": "[O]nly faith in the practical validity of the idea that lies in our reason has moral worth."[103] "[T]he required prototype always resides only in reason."[104] That is, as between an intelligible prototype of moral purity and an empirical prototype, the intelligible prototype is of infinitely greater significance, yet the historical Jesus is an empirical prototype. Kant goes further: To the extent that we emphasize the divinity or superhumanity of Christ, we

---

94 *Religion within the Boundaries*, p. xvi, citing p. 93.

95 Ibid., pp. 89–90.

96 Ibid., p. 92.

97 Ibid.

98 Ibid., p. 93; emphasis added.

99 Ibid.

100 Ibid., pp. 80–84; cf. Kant's discussion on pp. 125–126. *Das Urbild*, which di Giovanni translates as "prototype," is translated as "archetype" by T. M. Greene and H. H. Hudson. To my ear, at least, "archetype" has a somewhat better ring.

101 Ibid., p. 81.

102 For a fuller account of how belief in miracles stands in relation to a properly "moral religion," see pp. 98–102. The thrust of Kant's argument is that reckoning with miracles leads both to a paralysis of theoretical reason and a confounding of practical reason. Because true religion is entirely oriented toward morality, and because we have far more reliable access to the moral law than we do to any miracles, it does not make any sense to bring miracles into religion.

103 Ibid., p. 81.

104 Ibid.; cf. p. 82.

in effect negate his relevance to us as an example to be emulated, for we are neither divine nor superhuman.[105] Moreover, Kant makes clear that the notion of Jesus as Redeemer is philosophically unacceptable, for it suggests a morally illegitimate conception of the innocent assuming responsibility for the "debt of sins" that only the culprit himself or herself can discharge.[106] Overall, it is not hard to discern in these texts rather bold suggestions with regard to the ultimate redundancy of both the Father and the Son.[107]

The notion of God "as the supreme lawgiver of an ethical commonwealth" and "as a moral ruler of the world"[108] is the theme pursued in Part 3. One may question how all of this is consistent with the autonomy of practical reason. As I noted earlier, Kant both refers to reason as "the sole legislator" (which is a bit reminiscent of Locke's line about reason as the "only Star and compass"),[109] and points out that *all* religion entails looking upon "God as the lawgiver."[110] Again, one may wonder how one can square these two seemingly opposed points of view. Nonetheless, Kant makes a number of theoretical moves that serve to reassert the primacy of the moral law. First, Kant offers a distinction between "merely statutory [religious] laws," which are associated with the historical content of revealed religions, and "purely moral laws," which Kant associates with the one true religion.[111] "[T]he concept of the Divinity actually originates *solely* from the consciousness of these [purely moral] laws and from reason's need to assume a power capable of procuring for them the full effect possible in this world in conformity with the moral final end."[112] Moreover, in Part 4 Kant offers a distinction between revealed religion and natural religion that crucially distinguishes between two opposing ways of recognizing duties as divine commands.[113] According to revealed religion, something is recognized as a duty because it is antecedently recognized as a divine command; according

---

[105] Ibid., pp. 82–83. As he puts it on p. 82, "the elevation of such a Holy One above every frailty of human nature would . . . stand in the way of the practical adoption of the idea of such a being for our imitation." In effect, we can only imitate those who share our nature; we cannot imitate a "God-like human being" (p. 80). In Part 2, Section 2, Kant turns to the historical-mythical account of Jesus in the New Testament – as distinct from the philosophical account of Jesus as a prototypical representation of a moral ideal in Part 2, Section 1 – hence Kant there speaks of Jesus "as an example for everyone to follow" (p. 97). However, the context is a commentary on *Luke* 4:5–7 that Kant eventually encapsulates with the Spinozistic trope that it is a "vivid mode of representing things . . . *suited to the common people*" (ibid.). This Spinozist trope is also implicit on p. 120: "[T]he people [*das Volk*] . . . demand a divine revelation" (intimating that more philosophical individuals can draw their religion directly from reason).

[106] Ibid., p. 89. The phrase "debt of sins" really does not belong in Kant's vocabulary, for as he again highlights in the same passage, "sin" corresponds to an idea of "divine command" that stands outside Kant's philosophical religion.

[107] Cf. Adams, Introduction, p. xvi.

[108] *Religion within the Boundaries*, p. 110.

[109] Ibid., p. 77, note; Locke, *First Treatise*, § 58.

[110] *Religion within the Boundaries*, p. 113; cf. p. 118.

[111] Ibid. p. 113.

[112] Ibid.; emphasis added.

[113] Ibid., pp. 153–154.

to natural religion, something is recognized as a divine command because it is antecedently recognized as a duty. (This issue, of course, actually goes back to Plato's *Euthyphro*.) There is no question which of these two forms of religion is the one with which Kant aligns himself. The net effect of these theoretical operations is to present God as a lawgiver who legislates what has already been legislated by the moral law.

For Kant there are three unavoidable problems with revelation-based religion as compared with reason-based religion – problems that apply to Christianity as much as they apply to any other historical faith. First, a Scripture-based religion relies on ancient narratives that cannot be verified; the source of a reason-based religion, by contrast, is unmediated.[114] Second, a historical faith is also an ecclesiastical faith in the sense that it necessarily invites a class of priests to assert a privileged authority in interpreting the holy texts that define the religion, which in turn fundamentally violates Kant's idea of moral autonomy. The Reformation partly addressed this but did not fully solve the problem.[115] Third, a historical faith can aspire to win over the whole of humanity, but relying as it does on particular scriptures and particular narratives, it cannot fulfill this aspiration; reason can. All three problems matter to Kant, but the third matters most.

Kant treads an unmistakably Spinozist path when he asserts that there is a broad diversity of faiths, but only *one* true religion – namely "a purely moral religion."[116] This is in fact an important part of Kant's view as sketched in Part 3: "The concept of a divine will, determined merely according to purely moral laws, allows us to think of only *one* religion which is purely moral."[117] The ethical commonwealth that occupies Kant in Part 3 is defined by a moral law having universal validity.[118] By contrast, "historical faith . . . has only particular validity, namely for those in contact with the history on which the faith rests."[119] Only moral practice in fidelity to the moral law (by contrast to the particularistic "statutory laws" specified by particular churches or particular faiths) constitutes true service to God. It follows that the ethical community for which God is conceived as the lawgiver is a *single* ethical community (a single church). A universal religion may be expressed in particular faiths,[120] but it cannot be strictly coterminous with particular scriptures, particular narratives, particular traditions. Only a "religion of reason" can therefore satisfy

---

[114] This problem is spelled out on pp. 162–163.
[115] This issue is very forcefully addressed on p. 174. That the Reformation did not solve the problem is implicit in Kant's point that the question of whether the church has a "monarchical or aristocratic or democratic" constitution does nothing to change the intrinsically "despotic" character of priestly authority.
[116] Ibid., pp. 116, 113.
[117] Ibid., p. 113.
[118] Ibid., p. 122.
[119] Ibid.
[120] This is Kant's suggestion on pp. 118–119.

the conditions of religion in the strictest sense.[121] Hence there is at least one clear sense in which Kant's *Religion within the Boundaries* stands in a direct lineage from Spinoza's *Theological–Political Treatise*. In chapter 7 of the *Treatise*, Spinoza adduces Euclid's geometry as the ultimate standard of rational intelligibility: Euclid's proofs admit of clear conceptions and an absolutely secure confidence as to his intended meaning, "and what we here say of Euclid can be said of all who have written on matters which of their very nature are capable of intellectual apprehension." Spinoza's point is that the sayings of the prophets in Scripture manifestly fail to meet this standard. Kant's objection to biblical theology (implicit in the fact that he sees a need for philosophical theology in the first place) makes a similar point. As Spinoza and Kant both highlight, Scripture is composed of *historical* narratives that (even if they could be reliably verified) unfold in the (merely) empirical domain. By contrast, philosophical theology deals with – to put it in Kantian vocabulary – that which is "intelligible" (noumenal) rather than empirical (phenomenal).[122] Kant may try to insist that his intellectual enterprise in the *Religion within the Boundaries* is intended to complement rather than displace biblical theology, but his philosophical affirmation, throughout his work, of the plain superiority of the intelligible realm to the empirical realm aligns him in this respect with Spinoza. Kant was neither the first nor the last Western philosopher to suggest that religion is more safely deposited in the hands of philosophers than in those of priests and theologians; we see from Kant, just as we saw with Spinoza, Locke, and Bayle before him, that this Spinozistic (Platonic?) tradition contributes in a very important way to the history of liberalism.

The issue of Kant's implicit Spinozism finds expression in his treatment of the Spinozistic theme of whether the move from Judaism to Christianity fulfills philosophy's need for universality. Christianity may *appear* to offer a universal faith relative to (what Spinoza and Kant see as) the parochialism of Judaism,[123] but is it fully universal? Kant quite clearly gives a negative answer. Christianity, like Judaism and Islam, is a "historical faith," that is, a faith "based upon revelation as experience" and therefore having "only particular validity."[124] A particular revelation, whether intended for one privileged nation or intended to be propagated more widely, necessarily defines a particular faith and a particular (nonuniversal, therefore nontrue) church. "Only the pure faith of religion, based entirely on reason, can be recognized as necessary and hence as the one which exclusively marks out the *true* church."[125] That is, the

---

[121] Ibid., p. 119; cf. p. 120: "[T]o have universality a religion must always be based on reason." See also p. 121: The religion of reason "alone is *authentic* and valid for the whole world."

[122] See *Religion within the Boundaries*, p. 99, where Kant is emphatic that only morality, not faith in "historical reports," can make us well pleasing to God.

[123] Ibid., pp. 131, 132.

[124] Ibid., p. 122. On p. 119, Kant declares that the historical element in the holy books of the world religions (including Christianity) "is something in itself quite indifferent."

[125] Ibid., p. 122. The phrase "based entirely on reason" can only be interpreted as a very severe challenge to revelation-based religion. At the start of this discussion, I questioned whether

Christian church, based on Christian revelation, is not the true church. For the time being, we can satisfy ourselves with a merely historical faith as the "vehicle" [*Leitmittel*] of "pure religion,"[126] and we can even treat it as if it were the true religion, but the Kingdom of God will not fully arrive until, by asymptotic approach to "pure religious faith," "finally we can dispense [with] that vehicle [*um jenes Leitmittel endlich entbehren zu können*]."[127] This pretty clearly puts on the agenda (as was previously put on the agenda by Lessing's *The Education of the Human Race*) the eventual supersession of Christianity, and its replacement by something more enlightened (more mature).[128] Kant's crucial statement is that "one need only allow *the seed* [*der Keim*] *of the true religious faith now being sown in Christianity* . . . to grow unhindered, to expect from it a continuous approximation to that church, ever uniting all human beings, which constitutes the visible representation (the schema) of an invisible Kingdom of God on earth."[129] If currently existing Christianity is merely the "seed" of a more universal faith yet to come, then Christianity as it currently exists is clearly not "the true religious faith" that Kant associates with the earthly manifestation of the Kingdom of God. The fundamental schema is the same as Lessing's: a first childhood (Judaism); a second childhood (Christianity); and then, finally, maturity.[130]

Before it is safe for politics, religion must undergo a process of massive liberalization.[131] The thinkers canvassed in Chapter 13 and then in this chapter, following in the footsteps of Spinoza, represent key moments in the great liberal

---

Kant would acknowledge *Religion within the Boundaries* as what Steven Smith claimed it to be: a critique of revelation. On p. 136, Kant urges that one avoid "useless or malicious attacks" on Scripture, implying that that is the effect of full-blown Spinozism (and that his own stance toward revelation is more tolerant, leaving it more or less in peace out of consideration for those who need it). However, notwithstanding the image of the two concentric circles in the Preface to the second edition (see note 64), there is arguably more Spinozism in Kant than he would want to avow.

[126] Cf. *Religion within the Boundaries*, pp. 123, 125, and 128, note.

[127] Ibid., p. 122; cf. p. xxxi (Adams's Introduction). See also p. 127: "[I]n the end religion will gradually be freed of all empirical grounds of determination, of all statutes that rest on history. . . . The leading-string[s] of holy tradition . . . become bit by bit dispensable, yea . . . turn into a fetter." Furthermore see p. 152, where he discusses "eventually being able to dispense with ecclesiastical faith," and p. 170, where he thinks "at some future time [we could] . . . be able to dispense with statutory articles altogether."

[128] Cf. Kant's reference (p. 128, note) to "a true enlightenment" [*wahren Aufklärung*]. Perhaps the strongest statement of Kant's thesis of an eventual supersession of Christianity as a historical faith (that it will "cease and pass over into" a pure religion of reason) is in the first note on p. 138.

[129] *Religion within the Boundaries*, p. 135; emphasis added. The imagery of bearing and propagating seeds also occurs on p. 128; also see p. 130 (Christianity as the "germ" [*der Keim*] of the true religion). On p. 127, Kant employs the imagery of the shedding of the embryo's integuments that accompanies the developed human being's emergence from the womb. In the first note on p. 138, the image used is that of a "shell" [*Hülle*] that is not yet ready to be cast off.

[130] Cf. the text from *I Corinthians* 13:11 cited by Kant on p. 127.

[131] For further discussion of this theme, see Chapter 23.

tradition that took responsibility for this process of liberalization. However, the project to subordinate religion to philosophical reason is not limited to revelation-based religions. Arguably, such a project was first initiated by Plato when he demanded an "apologia" from poets like Homer prior to admission to citizenship in a polis whose terms were to be set by philosophy (*Republic*, 606e–608b).[132] What this tells us is that the enterprise shared by Spinoza, Locke, Rousseau, Kant, and Hegel, to issue a similar demand that revealed religion meet philosophical criteria for admission to the civic sphere, is not an enterprise of modern political philosophy alone; it is coeval with the history of political philosophy from its very origin.

---

[132] In *Collected Writings*, Vol. 9, p. 84, Rousseau conjures up the same analogy, namely excluding theologians from his republic with the same severity with which Plato excluded poets from his. When Locke writes that "Arguments . . . [are] the only right Method of propagating Truth [including religious truth]" (*A Letter Concerning Toleration*, ed. James Tully, Indianapolis: Hackett, 1983, p. 33), it is possible to read this as a modern version of Plato's demand that the poets supply an apologia that meets philosophical standards. The same idea is implicit in Kant's insistence that disputes between the theologian and the philosopher must be conducted on the terrain of reason: See Kant, *Philosophical Correspondence 1759–99*, ed. Arnulf Zweig (Chicago: University of Chicago Press, 1967), p. 205 (letter to C. F. Stäudlin of May 4, 1793).

18

Hume as a Successor to Bayle

The fanatical spirit, let loose, confounded all regards to ease, safety, interest, and dissolved every moral and civil obligation. The great courage and conduct, displayed by many of the popular leaders, have commonly inclined men to do them, in one respect, more honor than they deserve, and to suppose, that, like able politicians, they employed pretexts, which they secretly despised, in order to serve their selfish purposes. 'Tis however probable, if not certain, that they were, generally speaking, the dupes of their own zeal.... So congenial to the human mind are religious sentiments, that, where the temper is not guarded by a philosophical skepticism, the most cool and determined, it is impossible to counterfeit long these holy fervors, without feeling some share of the assumed warmth.

– David Hume[1]

[P]hilosophers, who cultivate reason and reflection, stand less in need of [religious] motives to keep them under the restraint of morals; and ... the vulgar, who alone may need them, are utterly incapable of so pure a religion, as represents the Deity to be pleased with nothing but virtue in human behaviour.

– David Hume[2]

[A folly] derivd from Religion [is one that has] flowed from a Source, which has, from uniform Prescription, acquird a Right to impose Nonsense on all Nations & all Ages.

– David Hume[3]

No good comes in the end of untrue beliefs.

– Iris Murdoch[4]

[1] David Hume, *The History of Great Britain: The Reigns of James I and Charles I*, ed. Duncan Forbes (Harmondsworth: Penguin, 1970), pp. 502–503.
[2] David Hume, "Dialogues Concerning Natural Religion," in *Writings on Religion*, ed. Anthony Flew (La Salle, IL: Open Court, 1992) [hereafter, Flew], p. 285.
[3] *The Letters of David Hume*, ed. J. Y. T. Greig (Oxford: Clarendon Press, 1932), Vol. II, p. 197 (Letter to the Rev. Hugh Blair, March 28, 1769).
[4] Iris Murdoch, *The Bell* (London: Vintage, 2004), p. 186.

Hume presents "superstition" and "enthusiasm" as two aberrational "corruptions of true religion."[5] Nonetheless, no alert reader could fail to suspect that Hume in fact believes that these two ideal–typical extremes describe a continuum of religious possibilities that comprehends the totality of religions known throughout history. The "superstitious" give power to priests in the hope of compensating for their own unworthiness to communicate with God; the "enthusiastic" whip themselves up into a state of unshakeable conviction of their religious competence to interact directly with God, without reliance on the higher competence of priests. All known religions fall somewhere between the poles of this continuum.[6] Even if one were persuaded that in Hume's view there is the hypothetical possibility of a "philosophical religion" elevated above this continuum of false religions,[7] Hume makes very clear that such a philosophical religion is morally, politically, culturally, and historically irrelevant: Religion just *is* (one variety or another of) false religion.[8] (Hume would have found it unimaginable that fully secular societies were on the horizon, historically speaking; he writes that although "it will probably become difficult to persuade [nations in a future age] that any human, two-legged creature could ever embrace [principles as absurd as the doctrine of Transubstantiation], it is a thousand to one, but these nations themselves shall have something full as absurd in their own creed."[9])

---

[5] "Of Superstition and Enthusiasm," Flew, p. 3. For a somewhat different version of the same distinction, see Kant, *Religion within the Boundaries of Mere Reason*, ed. Allen Wood (Cambridge: Cambridge University Press, 1998), pp. 169–170.

[6] I believe that Ernest Gellner (in *Plough, Sword and Book: The Structure of Human History*, London: Collins Harvill, 1988, p. 114), although he is correct in identifying "enthusiasm" with "zealous egalitarian scripturalism," is mistaken in identifying "superstition" with "an indulgent pluralistic pantheon." In my view, this is a misinterpretation explained by the fact that Hume's discussion of pagan superstitions in *The Natural History of Religions* is not what concerns Hume in "Of Superstition and Enthusiasm." In the latter text, "superstition" refers to Catholicism (hence the emphasis on rule by priests), whereas "enthusiasm" (i.e., zealotry) refers to radical Protestant sects. The distinction is clearly drawn from Hume's analysis of religious conflict in seventeenth-century England: See, for instance, *The History of Great Britain*, pp. 71–72, 96–99. In this context, Anglicanism is assumed to be closer to the superstition end of the spectrum (which is why, for the Puritans, adherence to episcopy was tantamount to papism).

[7] See "Of Superstition and Enthusiasm," Flew, p. 5, where Hume states that "there [is] nothing but philosophy able entirely to conquer [the] unaccountable terrors" that are at the source of religious superstition. Cf. "Dialogues Concerning Natural Religion," Flew, p. 287.

[8] It is true that Hume cites the Quakers, originally a sect of enthusiasts, as having become "nearly the only regular body of *Deists* in the universe," and he refers at the same time to *literati* adherents of Confucianism ("Of Superstition and Enthusiasm," Flew, p. 8). However, these are perhaps the exceptions that prove the rule. (As regards the Quakers, d'Holbach and Paine were of the same view: See Baron d'Holbach, *Christianity Unveiled*, trans. W. M. Johnson, New York: Gordon Press, 1974, p. 91, note; and Thomas Paine, *The Age of Reason*, ed. M. D. Conway, Mineola, NY: Dover, 2004, pp. 185 and 204.) Cf. *Natural History of Religion*, Flew, p. 143: "The vulgar, that is, indeed, all mankind, a few excepted." Also see *Natural History*, Flew, p. 157: "[U]nfortunately the bystanders are few."

[9] *Natural History of Religion*, Flew, pp. 155–156. In addition, Hume's conclusion in *Natural History* that popular religion is one of the "natural infirmities" whose "root . . . springs from the

Hume directly challenges the idea of a civil religion. (Admittedly, nothing is ever entirely "direct" in Hume, for he adopts a whole range of ingenious literary devices to mask the directness of his challenge.[10]) In the *Enquiry concerning Human Understanding*, Section XI, the question is posed in terms of whether the atheist inquiries of a philosopher like Epicurus can proceed "in great harmony" with the society in which such philosophers live.[11] Hume states, in his own voice, the question, namely whether Epicurean subversion of civic beliefs ("the established superstition")[12] "loosen[s], in a great measure, the ties of morality, and may be supposed, for that reason, pernicious to the peace of civil society."[13] Hume puts the answer to this challenge in the mouth of "a friend who loves skeptical paradoxes."[14] The so-called friend aims to demonstrate that "when, in my philosophical disquisitions, I deny a providence and a future state, I undermine not the foundations of society."[15]

Here is a short encapsulation of the friend's argument: "The religious hypothesis," that is, the hypothesis of a theistic creator of nature, even if granted, allows one to postulate a cause sufficient to account for nature *exactly as it is* ("the present scene of things, which is so full of ill and disorder"[16]; "that evil and disorder, with which the world so much abounds"[17]). What the religious hypothesis does not warrant, however, is the postulation of superworldly phenomena, such as a better world, beyond the appearances of this one, where the virtuous obtain extra rewards, the vicious obtain extra punishments, and the injustices of this world are made good in a higher justice. The core of the argument is that if a creating God *qua* ultimate cause is an inference from the created world as the effect of that cause, it would be an epistemic extravagance to speculate about better worlds that that Creator-God would *also* fashion for other unknown and unknowable purposes. "When we infer any particular cause from an effect... [t]he cause must be proportioned to the effect; and if we exactly and precisely proportion it [namely by postulating a God sufficient to cause the natural world we actually have], we shall never find in it any qualities, that point farther, or afford an inference concerning any other design or performance."[18]

---

essential and universal properties of human nature" (Flew, p. 179) implies as well that this is not a condition that human beings are likely ever to outgrow.

[10] In the case of the text I am about to discuss – *An Enquiry concerning Human Understanding*, Section XI – there are two major "artifices," as Anthony Flew calls them (Flew, p. 53): First, Hume puts his own view in the mouth of a "friend" (and goes so far as to put objections to the friend's argument in his own mouth!); second, the friend presents his argument as a speech by Epicurus to the Athenians, which has the effect of casting the whole debate in a pre-Christian context.

[11] Flew, p. 90.

[12] Ibid.

[13] Flew, p. 91.

[14] Flew, p. 89.

[15] Flew, p. 92.

[16] Flew, p. 94.

[17] Flew, p. 95.

[18] Flew, p. 93.

A form of theism stripped of doctrines of providence and rewards and punishments in an afterlife will obviously offer little in support of morality and political life. Indeed, Hume (that is, the "friend") insists that these appeals to providence and extraworldly rewards and punishments are superfluous in vindicating common virtue. Secular considerations are perfectly sufficient:

[T]he course itself of events . . . lies open to every one's inquiry and examination. . . . [I]n the present order of things, virtue is attended with more peace of mind than vice, and meets with a more favourable reception from the world. . . . [F]riendship is the chief joy of human life, and moderation the only source of tranquility and happiness. . . . [T]o a well-disposed mind, [between the virtuous and the vicious course of life] every advantage is on the side of the former.[19]

Again, the hypothesis that there is a moral order of things "proceed[ing] from intelligence and design" is morally superfluous: "[T]he disposition itself, on which depends our happiness or misery, and consequently our conduct and deportment in life is still the same."[20] "All the philosophy . . . in the world, and all the religion, which is nothing but a species of philosophy, will never be able to carry us beyond the usual course of experience, or give us measures of conduct and behaviour different from those which are furnished by reflections on common life."[21]

Hume never really explains why the friend's demonstration of the epistemic illegitimacy of notions of otherworldly rewards and punishments vindicates the morality of the Epicurean as equal to that of the believer. The missing premise is that fallacious reasoning can never supply a helpful support for morality. Because the religionist draws inferences that are not philosophically respectable ("No new fact can ever be inferred from the religious hypothesis; no event foreseen or foretold [*and therefore*] no reward or punishment expected or dreaded beyond what is already known by practice and observation"),[22] the religionist's morality must be similarly suspect, and this somehow offers negative vindication for the Epicurean's morality. However, Hume himself, in his own voice, in his final rejoinder to the friend[23] presents a decisive objection to this premise. It presumes that what is *intellectually* unsound cannot have

---

[19] Flew, p. 96.

[20] Ibid. Assuming that the friend speaks here for Hume himself, this is the clearest statement of Hume's commitment to the Baylean thesis that morality can sustain itself without any extraneous support from religion.

[21] Flew, pp. 101–102. The suggestion that "religion . . . is nothing but a species of philosophy" is startling. It is surely a way of restricting religion to philosophically legitimate conceptions and banishing notions that do not meet philosophical standards. (Once religion is rendered subject to *philosophical* judgment, though, do any religious conceptions, in Hume's view, survive fully rational scrutiny?) On the important notion of a morality founded on "common life," in contrast to a morality depending on appeal to considerations transcending common life (where we "are like foreigners in a strange country"), cf. "Dialogues Concerning Natural Religion," Flew, p. 194.

[22] Flew, p. 102.

[23] Flew, pp. 102–103.

practical efficacy. But why think that? Hume rightly protests that the friend concludes

that religious doctrines and reasonings *can* have no influence on life, because they *ought* to have no influence; never considering, that men reason not in the same manner you do, but draw many consequences from the belief of a divine Existence, and suppose that the Deity will inflict punishments on vice, and bestow rewards on virtue, beyond what appear in the ordinary course of nature. Whether this reasoning of theirs be just or not, is no matter. Its influence on their life and conduct must still be the same.[24]

"Good reasoners" may not be "good citizens and politicians" because "they free men from one restraint upon their passions, and make the infringement of the laws of society, in one respect more easy and secure."[25] In short, the argument for the salutariness of civil religion has yet to be refuted!

Hume in his own voice has a more modest argument for why "the state ought to tolerate every principle of philosophy."[26] One could call this the argument from harmlessness: "There is no enthusiasm among philosophers; their doctrines are not very alluring to the people."[27] Ultimately, who cares what philosophers are up to in the seclusion of their studies (or in the case of Epicurus, in the privacy of their "gardens"),[28] and in the idleness of their intellectual inquiries? Zealots are indeed dangerous, but true philosophers are *antizealots*.[29] As Hume says, he and his friend agree on the "general conclusion in favour of liberty"[30] (including, in this case, the liberty of philosophers to subvert religious beliefs) – the friend says, "nor have the political interest of society any connexion with the philosophical disputes concerning metaphysics and religion" and Hume says, "nor is there any instance, that any government has suffered in its political interests by such indulgence [of philosophers and their intellectual liberty]."[31] But if the intellectual pursuits of philosophers like Hume and his friend subvert what Hume himself concedes is quite possibly a

---

[24] Flew, p. 102.

[25] Ibid. Hume makes a similar suggestion (about the vulgar multitude requiring the discipline of religious beliefs) in the second epigraph to this chapter. Incidentally, Hume's characteristic references to the vulgar multitude are a good tip-off with respect to Hume's "Platonism." It would be a gross mistake to see the political philosophies of Hume and Plato as far removed from each other. In their philosophizing on political life, Hume and Plato strike a similar note in their deep pessimism, their gentle cynicism, their ironical detachment, and their utter conviction that reason and philosophy can have very little purchase on the passions that grip the souls of nonphilosophers. Both are committed rationalists who, though they write philosophical dialogues, despair of the efficacy of reason. It may well be that most thinkers in the tradition of Western political philosophy are in that sense Platonists.

[26] Flew, p. 102.

[27] Ibid.

[28] Flew, p. 96.

[29] The true peril for states and citizens is "persecution and oppression" (Flew, p. 102), and this menace is hardly likely to emanate from the efforts of skeptical, free-thinking intellectuals of the Epicurean variety.

[30] Flew, p. 102.

[31] Ibid.

necessary restraint on the passions of human beings (namely the doctrine of invisible rewards and punishments, and of an ultimate cosmic justice), how can philosophizing be either idle or harmless?

The debate on whether religion is or is not helpful in sustaining morality within a society seems, then, inconclusive. The friend believes he has demonstrated that beliefs in providence and future rewards and punishments, because philosophically unsound, do not make for superior morality. Hume, though, in his final reply to the friend, raises a powerful objection: Beliefs that are intellectually unsound can nonetheless be practically efficacious. Where, then, does this leave civil religion? Should one resort to religion in the interests of civic morality?

In the final analysis, the only place from which an answer can be drawn is Hume's actual intellectual praxis: Whether in his own voice or in the guise of characters in his philosophical dialogues, Hume fearlessly explodes unsound philosophical–theological views – blasting away at the intellectual underpinning of forms of superstition and enthusiasm by which human beings are bewitched and enslaved.[32] Therefore he surely cannot be finally of the view that we need to rely on intellectually discredited religious beliefs to restrain human passions. If so, he also agrees with the friend that good morality can be upheld without appeal to civil religion. We can draw the same conclusion from Hume's forthright affirmation in a letter to Gilbert Elliot of March 10, 1751:

---

[32] In *The Natural History of Religion* (Flew, p. 120), Hume uses the wonderful phrase "thrown on their knees" ("men are much oftener thrown on their knees by the melancholy than by the agreeable passions") to sum up the human tendency to subordinate itself to religious authority. Hume's *Natural History of Religion* is far less radical than his *Dialogues Concerning Natural Religion*, which presumably explains why *Natural History* was published during Hume's lifetime whereas the *Dialogues* were published only posthumously. Throughout *Natural History*, on one hand, it is presumed that "pure theism" (i.e., deism) constitutes a rational standard by which to measure "idolatry" (paganism) and impure theisms (Judaism, Islam, and Catholicism) as varieties of superstition. In the *Dialogues*, on the other hand, Hume's mouthpiece, Philo, offers a devastating set of challenges precisely to any deistic or rationalizing theology. In the *Dialogues*, the whole project of reconciling religion with reason is presented not as a means of combating residues of idolatry and superstition, but rather as a colossal and hopeless mistake. The whole rhetoric of *Natural History* is shaped by the appeal to the argument from design as a genuinely "philosophical" religion in relation to which the "popular religions" (especially pagan popular religions) can be ridiculed; that is certainly not Hume's view in the *Dialogues*. Consequently, *The Natural History of Religion* (where most of Hume's ammunition is directed against the relatively safe target of pagan superstition, and his intellectual challenge to theism as such is kept quite muted) can easily have the effect of masking the radicalism of Hume's views. Leon Wieseltier's review of a book by Daniel Dennett published in the *International Herald Tribune* (February 18–19, 2006) offers a nice case in point. Rejecting claims by Dennett to be an heir of Hume, Wieseltier quotes a deist passage from Hume's *Natural History* and concludes from it that Hume's "God was a very wan god [but] still a god." However, this merely shows Hume's impressive capacity to throw credulous readers off the scent of his antitheism; for as I have already noted, the deism avowed in *Natural History* is itself thoroughly debunked in the *Dialogues*.

"The worst speculative Sceptic ever I knew, was a much better Man than the best superstitious Devotee & Bigot."[33]

The problem, of course, is that religion does not simply provide a "restraint upon [the] passions" with effects that are morally positive. It also enflames the passions, and very destructive ones at that. Damnation, for instance (including, from the best that human beings are able to judge such matters, damnation of the innocent), is an evil doctrine.[34]

It is certain, that, in every religion, however sublime the verbal definition which it gives of its divinity, many of the votaries, perhaps the greatest number, will still seek the divine favour, not by virtue and good morals, which alone can be acceptable to a perfect being, but either by frivolous observances, by intemperate zeal, by rapturous extasies, or by the belief of mysterious and absurd opinions.[35]

For Hume, it is a real puzzle why "virtue and good morals" is not taken to be what defines "all religion, or the chief part of it"; for "there is no *man* so stupid, as that, judging by his natural reason, he would not esteem virtue and honesty the most valuable qualities, which any person could possess."[36] Citing the Islamic practice of fasting during Ramadan, as well as various penances and austerities associated with Hinduism, Buddhism, Russian Orthodoxy, and Catholicism, Hume notes that human beings are able to perform superstitious rituals "more severe than the practice of any moral duty." Why? Paradoxically, human beings will sooner perform "odious and burdensome" superstitious practices than perform "agreeable" practices of virtue.[37]

Hume proposes the following solution to the riddle. Precisely on account of the naturalness of moral life, morality appears to the pious person as religiously useless. The "superstitious man . . . considers not, that the most genuine method of serving the divinity is by promoting the happiness of his creatures," and instead looks for something *unnatural* "which can peculiarly recommend him to the divine favour and protection."[38] "In restoring a loan, or paying a debt, his divinity is nowise beholden to him; because these acts of justice are what he was bound to perform, *and what many would have performed, were there no god in the universe.* But if he fast a day, or give himself a sound whipping," he imagines that such austerities represent "distinguished marks of devotion," and as such, proofs of "the divine favour."[39] Hume's conclusion is that it is

---

33 Flew, p. 22. Cf. the crucial exchange between Cleanthes and Philo on whether "[r]eligion, however corrupted, is still better than no religion at all": "Dialogues Concerning Natural Religion," Flew, p. 283. What follows from Philo (Hume) is an unremittingly harsh indictment of religion's contribution to human misery throughout history.

34 See the harsh indictment that Hume quotes from Andrew Michael Ramsey: *Natural History*, Flew, pp. 171–173.

35 Flew, p. 175.

36 Flew, p. 176.

37 Flew, pp. 176–177.

38 Flew, p. 177.

39 Ibid.; emphasis added.

"unsafe to draw any certain inference in favour of a man's morals, from the fervour or strictness of his religious exercises," and in fact "the greatest crimes have been found, in many instances, compatible with a superstitious piety and devotion" (including "enormities of the blackest dye").[40] Hume insists that we are better off with "a manly, steady virtue," which produces "calm sunshine of the mind," than with forms of religion that more typically divert human beings from their moral duties than guarantee their performance.[41] In short, Hume is at one with Bayle: Not only is it the case that atheists can be virtuous and reliable citizens, it is also the case that religionists can be (generally are?) cruel and ignorant ones.[42]

[40] Flew, p. 178.

[41] In a famous conversation with Boswell shortly before his death, Hume affirmed that "when he heard a man was religious, he concluded he was a rascal": See James Boswell, "An Account of My Last Interview with David Hume," in Early Responses to Hume, ed. James Fieser (Bristol: Thoemmes Continuum, 2005), Vol. 9, p. 288. Hume did allow that he had encountered some exceptions to this rule.

[42] That the subversion of religion was, according to Hume's own self-conception, at the center of his intellectual purposes is made explicit in Hume's invented conversation with Charon modeled on Lucian's Dialogues of the Dead; the joke was told to Adam Smith as Hume approached death and was recounted in Smith's famous letter to William Strahan of November 9, 1776. Hume seeks to postpone his voyage to the land of the dead and comes up with the following excuse why he should be allowed to linger a little longer in the land of the living: "I have been endeavouring to open the eyes of the Public. If I live a few years longer, I may have the satisfaction of seeing the downfal of some of the prevailing systems of superstition." Charon's reply: "You loitering rogue, that will not happen these many hundred years. Do you fancy I will grant you a lease for so long a term? Get into the boat this instant, you lazy loitering rogue." According to Ian Simpson Ross, The Life of Adam Smith (Oxford: Clarendon Press, 1995), p. 303, the phrase "seeing the downfal of some of the prevailing systems of superstition" represented a wholly ineffectual attempt by Smith to cushion the blow of Hume's anticlericalism. As reported in Smith's letter to Alexander Wedderburn of August 14, 1776, Hume's actual phrase was "seeing the churches shut up, and the Clergy sent about their business." For the two versions of the story, see The Correspondence of Adam Smith, ed. E. C. Mossner and I. S. Ross (Oxford: Clarendon Press, 1987), 2nd ed., p. 219 and pp. 203–204. For discussion of Hume's debt to Bayle, see Alasdair MacIntyre, Whose Justice? Which Rationality? (Notre Dame, IN: University of Notre Dame Press, 1988), pp. 288–290. MacIntyre also cites (on p. 282) a reported deathbed statement by Hume according to which he expressed regret that his death would prevent him from completing "the great work" of liberating Scotland from "the Christian superstition."

19

Adam Smith's Sequel to Hume (and Hobbes)

Science is the great antidote to the poison of enthusiasm and superstition.
        – Adam Smith[1]

[In contrast to] those great sects, whose tenets being supported by the civil magistrate, are held in veneration by almost all the inhabitants of extensive kingdoms and empires, [the propagation of a large number of small sects] might in time probably reduce the doctrine of the greater part of them to that pure and rational religion, free from every mixture of absurdity, imposture, or fanaticism, such as wise men have in all ages of the world wished to see established.
        – Adam Smith[2]

As we saw in Chapter 18, Hume bracketed religion in general under the rubric of "superstition and enthusiasm" (he called them "corruptions of true religion," but they exhaust the phenomena of religious experience as he conceived them to the point where it is hard to know where to look for "true religion"). Smith provides a subtle (or perhaps not so subtle) indication of the Humean lineage of his own analysis of religion by referring, immediately before an acute discussion of religion in Book 5 of *The Wealth of Nations*, to "the delusions of enthusiasm and superstition."[3] (If, according to Hume's formula, superstition is code for Catholicism and enthusiasm is code for the Reformation, then any reference to the corruptions of superstition and enthusiasm is necessarily a loaded reference.) However, as was the case for Hume, the conjunction is less important, analytically speaking, than what distinguishes superstition and enthusiasm as separate categories. As we will see, Smith's analysis hinges no less on this distinction than was true in the case of Hume.

[1] Adam Smith, *An Inquiry into the Nature and Causes of the Wealth of Nations*, ed. R. H. Campbell and A. S. Skinner (Indianapolis: Liberty Classics, 1981), Vol. 2, p. 796.
[2] Ibid., p. 793.
[3] Ibid., p. 788. Superstition and enthusiasm are also paired once on p. 793 and twice on p. 796 (one of these texts being the first epigraph quoted at the beginning of this chapter).

The bulk of Book 5, chapter 1, Part 3, Article 3 of *The Wealth of Nations* is devoted to a historical narrative of the relations between church and state with respect to the shifting balance of wealth and power. The hardheadedness about the realities of wealth and power displayed by Smith in this narrative is entirely in the spirit of great figures in the tradition of anticlerical thought such as Hobbes and Hume.[4] In effect, Smith provides a history of the power dynamics within pre-Reformation and post-Reformation Christendom. Much of the story up until the Reformation is one of increasing centralization of power and authority. Originally, there was provision for joint election of bishops by the clergy and the people. The people's right of election soon gave way to what was for the clergy an "easier" arrangement – election solely within the clergy.[5] Having been elected, the bishop in turn controlled all lesser ecclesiastical benefices. "All church preferments were in this manner in the disposal of the church," leaving the sovereign with "no direct or sufficient means of managing the clergy. The ambition of every clergyman naturally led him to pay court, not so much to his sovereign, as to his own order, from which only he could expect preferment."[6] However, the process of consolidation of clerical power did not end there. The power of the bishops was then largely appropriated by the papacy, not only disempowering the bishops but leaving "the condition of the sovereign . . . still worse than it had been before."[7] The papal regime constituted "a sort of spiritual army," dispersed across Europe, "directed by one head, and conducted upon one uniform plan." Thus, the Pope amounted to "a foreign sovereign" with "arms" that were "the most formidable that can well be imagined." The clergy with all their wealth were like "the great barons" lording it over their feudal vassals.[8] Like the barons, the clergy controlled great landed estates that had both political and economic aspects. In its political aspect, it provided the clergy with independent jurisdictions that "were equally independent, and equally exclusive of the authority of the king's courts, as those of the great temporal lords."[9] In its economic aspect, it provided the clergy with "a very large portion of the rents of all the other estates in every kingdom of Europe," yielding an "immense surplus" – the source of charity for the poor and hospitality for itinerant knights.[10] The effect was to erect a parallel feudalism in which clerical power and authority exceeded that of the

---

[4] A good example of Smith's hardheaded insight into the dynamics of wealth is his very sharp analysis on pp. 810–812 of how the professions of "eminent men of letters" are a function of whether the church in a given country provides modest (e.g., Scotland) or lavish (e.g., France) positions. In countries with a poor church, such as Scotland, the universities flourish, whereas in countries with "opulent and well-endowed churches" like France and England, the universities are "drained" of great intellectuals. (In other words, in England, Smith would be not a university professor but a bishop!)

[5] Ibid., p. 799.

[6] Ibid., p. 800.

[7] Ibid.

[8] Ibid.

[9] Ibid., p. 801.

[10] Ibid.

king, resulting in the clergy's "total exemption from the secular jurisdiction."[11] Smith characterizes the Church during this epoch, spanning the tenth to thirteenth centuries, as "the most formidable combination that ever was formed against the authority and security of civil government, as well as against the liberty, reason, and happiness of mankind, which can flourish only where civil government is able to protect them."[12]

How did this "immense and well-built fabric" begin to unravel? – for "the feeble efforts of human reason" would never have been sufficient to dislodge it.[13] With the development of "arts, manufactures, and commerce," the clergy were exposed to greater temptation to spend "their whole revenues upon their own persons" and indeed succumbed to these temptations. As Smith takes his narrative into the fourteenth and fifteenth centuries, the clergy increasingly become a typical corrupt oligarchy, more concerned with squeezing additional profits out of their estates but less interested in spending the immense surplus, as before, on charity and hospitality, and more interested in spending it on "the gratification of their own private vanity and folly." As the "inferior ranks of people" saw the clergy lose interest in their traditional function as "comforters of their distress" and "relievers of their indigence," retainers drifted away and the people's deference to the clergy declined.[14] This in turn weakened both the spiritual authority of the clergy and their temporal power. Various European sovereigns were keen to exploit the new situation by trying to reestablish their former influence over the election of bishops. In particular, the Gallican church asserted its independence vis-à-vis the court of Rome, thereby setting in motion the process by which the power of the pope began to retreat (with a corresponding rebound in the power of the state).[15] This "declension" in the authority of the Church set the background for the full-scale rebellion unleashed in the Reformation.[16]

The Reformation, of course, changed the whole power balance. The popular appeal of the doctrines of the Reformation allowed various European princes to gain once more the upper hand in their quarrels with the Church. The corruption of the clergy had already begun the process of shifting power back to the princes, and the de facto revolt against the Church's authority represented by the Reformation gave a huge further impetus to this rebalancing. "Establishing the reformation in their own dominions" was a means by which "the princes who happened to be on bad terms with the court of Rome" could "revenge themselves" on the papacy.[17] In various ways, this was what happened in northern Germany, in Sweden, in Denmark, and in Switzerland. Variations on

---

[11] Ibid., p. 802.
[12] Ibid., pp. 802–803.
[13] Ibid., p. 803
[14] Ibid., pp. 803–804.
[15] Ibid., pp. 804–805.
[16] Ibid., p. 805.
[17] Ibid., p. 806.

this story also occurred in England and Scotland.[18] Because there was, in those states where the Reformation prevailed, no centralized enforcer of orthodoxy equivalent to the papacy, different regimes of church–state power came into being. In those states where Lutheranism prevailed as well as in England under the Church of England, a system of church government was established that favored "submission to the civil sovereign": episcopal government, a system of subordination among the clergy, and a grant to the sovereign of more or less "disposal of all the bishopricks." This Lutheran–Anglican regime "rendered [the sovereign] the real head of the church."[19] In the case of England, this was a system generating "peace and good order" because it was by "recommend[ing] themselves to the sovereign, to the court, and to the nobility and gentry of the country" that the clergy "chiefly expect[ed] to obtain preferment."[20] Such a hierarchical clergy excels in "pay[ing] court... to the higher ranks of life," but it makes a less favorable impression on the lower ranks, and their "sober and moderate doctrines" are vulnerable to attack from the "ignorant enthusiast."[21]

Smith casts a far more adverse judgment on the much more democratic order that prevailed in Calvinist states. Its principle of "the most perfect equality among the clergy" was innocent in its effects, but the norm of giving congregations the right to elect their own pastor was a source of "nothing but disorder and confusion" wherever it was tried – causing both religious schism and political faction and constantly spurring fanaticism both in the clergy and in the congregations that elected them.[22] It is not that Smith sees in the Lutheran–Anglican system only virtues and no vices, for he points out, for instance, that paying court to patrons (an essential part of how this ecclesiastical politics works) sometimes involves "the vilest flattery."[23] Still, it is clear that the vices of the Calvinist system are (certainly from a civil-secular perspective) much worse: never-ending factionalism, and the setting in motion of a contest of fanaticism where the highest prize goes to "the most factious and fanatical."[24] This is followed by a discussion of the restoration of "the rights of patronage" in Scotland, and of how it led to a church system governed "by nobler and

---

[18] Ibid., pp. 806–807.

[19] Ibid., p. 807.

[20] Ibid., pp. 807–808.

[21] Ibid, p. 808. One can almost hear an anticipation of Nietzsche's bitter polemic against the Reformation in Smith's discussion of how the Reformers excelled in "all the arts of popularity," driven by "coarse and rustick eloquence" (p. 806; cf. p. 809 in the Presbyterian context). However, Smith's strong contrast between the Lutheran and Calvinist branches of the Reformation suggests that he associates these "popular [i.e., vulgar] arts" primarily with the Calvinists and Presbyterians. Lutheranism, in his view, despite the democratizing thrust of the Reformation in general, retains a more aristocratic bias.

[22] Cf. the discussion on p. 809 of "the old fanatical spirit" in Scotland.

[23] Ibid., p. 808; cf. p. 809. Smith's discussion on p. 810 of the virtues associated with "mediocrity of benefice" in the Presbyterian system (the clergy's "exemplary morals," modest and unaffected "plan of life") also implies large vices associated with a more hierarchical clerical system: "vanity," "contemptuous and arrogant airs."

[24] Ibid., p. 808.

better arts."[25] This discussion leads to the surprisingly sympathetic judgment that "[t]here is scarce perhaps to be found any where in Europe a more learned, decent, independent, and respectable set of men, than the greater part of the presbyterian clergy of Holland, Geneva, Switzerland, and Scotland."[26] It may be that in Smith's view (though he does not spell it out), Presbyterianism offers a unique combination of virtues insofar as it rests its foundation on "the common people" yet is an established church and makes essential allowance for "benefices" (clerical office) based on patronage.[27]

The funding of churches reflects what is in effect a regime of distribution of public expenditure ("expence"), for "the revenue of every established church [is a branch] of the general revenue of the state, which is thus diverted to" one particular purpose rather than another.[28] (In that sense, the funding of churches is analogous to the funding of schools; as is suggested by the titles of Article 2 and Article 3, respectively, just as schools provide "Institutions for the Education of Youth," so churches provide "Institutions for the Instruction of People of all Ages.")

The tythe...is a real land-tax, which puts it out of the power of the proprietors of land to contribute [to other public purposes]....The more of this fund that is given to the church, the less, it is evident, can be spared to the state.... [A]ll other things being supposed equal, the richer the church, the poorer must necessarily be, either the sovereign on the one hand, or the people on the other.[29]

It follows that the status of churches within a particular society is a direct topic of political economy, and by no means the least significant one.

Smith directly addresses the central issue posed by the problem of civil religion in the history of political philosophy (addresses it more directly, really, than Hume does). There is at the heart of the state a head-on contest of authority between "the sovereign" and "the clergy." The sovereign naturally has important instruments of power by which to "influence" the doctrines propagated by an established church – namely manipulation of feared "deprivation" or hoped-for "preferment"[30] – but in decisive respects, these instruments are unequal to the powers of the church if the church chooses to exert its authority

---

[25] Ibid., p. 809.
[26] Ibid, p. 810. Cf. the discussion on p. 813 of "[a]ll the good effects, both civil and religious," secured by the Presbyterian clergy: "uniformity of faith, the fervour of devotion, the spirit of order, regularity, and austere morals in the great body of the people." "[T]he protestant churches of Switzerland...produce those effects in a still higher degree."
[27] Smith's overall analysis tends to suggest that established churches will generally err on the side of overcompensating their clergy, resulting in "negligence," "idleness," "vanity," and "dissipiation," all of which will cause these corrupted clergymen to be discredited "in the eyes of the common people" (pp. 813–814). The Scottish church, although an established church, offers a counterinstance. The key to its success, as Smith sees it, would seem to reside in its poverty: Its lack of resources prevented it from compensating its clergy enough to corrupt them.
[28] Ibid., p. 812.
[29] Ibid.
[30] Ibid., p. 798.

to the utmost (as was the case with "[t]he revolutions which the turbulence of the Greek clergy was continually occasioning at Constantinople" as well as "the convulsions which, during the course of several centuries, the turbulence of the Roman clergy was continually occasioning in every part of Europe").[31] Even if the sovereign decides to resort to force in reasserting his ultimate authority, this "cannot . . . give him any lasting security" because the soldiers upon whom he relies are themselves subject to being "corrupted by those very [church] doctrines" that are the source of the problem.[32]

In reflecting on this crucial problem of ultimate state authority, Smith applies a Hobbesian analysis. The core of the problem is that the latent contest of authority between church and state, if pushed to the limit, favors the church because its sources of authority trump those of the state: "[T]he authority of religion is superior to every other authority. The fears which it suggests conquer all other fears."[33] If "the authorized teachers of religion" are determined to "propagate through the great body of the people doctrines subversive of the authority of the sovereign,"[34] they will win and the sovereign will lose. Hobbes put the same point this way: "For Christ hath said . . . that 'we should not fear them who slay the body, but cannot kill the soul; but rather fear him, who can cast both soul and body into hell' (*Matth.* x.28). Neither is any man so mad, as not to choose to yield obedience rather to them who can remit and retain their sins, than to the powerfulest kings."[35]

The sovereign, as Smith presents him, is in an uncomfortable bind. Smith speaks of "the benefices of [Christian] clergy" as "a sort of freeholds which they enjoy, not during pleasure, but during life, or good behaviour."[36] However, if the sovereign endeavors to render the tenure that they hold "more precarious," for instance by depriving them by violence of their freeholds whenever a "disobligation" is committed, this does not solve his problem but instead makes it even worse: "[H]e would only render by such persecution, both them and their doctrines ten times more popular, and therefore ten times more troublesome and dangerous than they had been before."[37] "Fear is in almost all cases a wretched instrument of government," whereas "management and persuasion are always the easiest and the safest instruments of government," and this principle applies with particular force to relations between the sovereign and the clergy: "[T]here is no order of men . . . upon whom it is so dangerous, or rather so perfectly ruinous, to employ force and violence, as upon the respected clergy

[31] Ibid.
[32] Ibid.
[33] Ibid., p. 797.
[34] Ibid., pp. 797–798.
[35] Thomas Hobbes, *Man and Citizen*, ed. Bernard Gert (Garden City, NY: Anchor Books, 1972), p. 357. For evidence that Smith gave careful reflection to Hobbes's analysis of the problem, see Adam Smith, *The Theory of the Moral Sentiments*, ed. D. D. Raphael and A. L. Macfie (Indianapolis: Liberty Fund, 1982), p. 318.
[36] *Wealth of Nations*, Vol. 2, p. 798.
[37] Ibid.

of any established church."[38] In principle, the clerical order can be "managed" by the sovereign's manipulation of "the preferment which he has to bestow upon them," and whether or not he can succeed in so managing them constitutes a crucial test of the skill of the sovereign.[39]

Yes, the established clergy can be "managed" if the sovereign is sufficiently skillful, but for Smith the true solution is to have a clerical order that is not an "order" at all because it is one not dominated by an established church. Radical proliferation of sects will solve the problem. Here Smith takes issue with what he takes to be Hume's position. Smith refers to Hume as "by far the most illustrious philosopher and historian of the present age" and then quotes a long passage from his *History of England*,[40] the purpose of which is to argue that although the state generally profits from industriousness and competitiveness on the part of its citizenry, this principle *does not* apply to religion. A free market in religious sects, where the sellers of various doctrines exert themselves with full energy and industry, will run counter to peace and good order in civil society. "Each ghostly practitioner" will do his utmost to stoke up religious enthusiasm to recruit a larger crowd. "Customers" will be attracted to this or that creed by "practicing on [their] passions and credulity." Hence, "this interested diligence of the clergy is what every wise legislator will study to prevent." An established church, Hume concludes, is a much better investment on the part of the state:

[I]n the end, the civil magistrate will find, that he has dearly paid for his pretended frugality, in saving a fixed establishment for the priests; and that in reality the most decent and advantageous composition, which he can make with the most spiritual guides, is to bribe their indolence, by assigning stated salaries to their profession, and rendering it superfluous for them to be farther active, than merely to prevent their flock from straying in quest of new pastures.

This salaried and therefore less industrious, more neglectful clergy is, in Hume's judgment, the best way to reconcile "ecclesiastical establishments" with "the political interests of society."[41]

---

[38] Ibid., pp. 798, 799.

[39] Ibid., p. 799.

[40] Quoted on pp. 790–791. For the original text, see David Hume, *The History of England* (Indianapolis: Liberty Classics, 1983), Vol. 3, pp. 134–137; the text quoted by Smith is on pp. 135–136.

[41] See also Voltaire's reference to Anglicanism as "the real religion [in England], the one by which one makes one's fortune": *Philosophical Letters: Or, Letters Regarding the English Nation*, ed. John Leigh, trans. Prudence L. Steiner (Indianapolis: Hackett, 2007), p. 15. What Hume meant by "bribing the indolence" of the clergy is well captured, I think, in the following newspaper commentary: "There was a time when the country vicar was a staple of the English dramatis personae. This tea-drinking, gentle eccentric, with his polished shoes and kindly manners, represented a type of religion that didn't make non-religious people uncomfortable. He wouldn't break into an existential sweat or press you against a wall to ask if you were saved, still less launch crusades from the pulpit or plant roadside bombs in

As we saw earlier, important elements of Smith's own subsequent analysis point in a similar direction. At this point in the text, though, he rejects Hume's argument. In fact, he adopts a line sharply opposed to the one he quotes from Hume. Smith regards state intervention in people's choice of religion as illegitimate and corrupting. In particular, state enforcement of one privileged sect (i.e., establishment) must be avoided. Smith concedes to Hume that "interested and active zeal can be dangerous and troublesome," but he argues that this is so only where only "one sect [is] tolerated," or where there are "two or three great sects."[42] The solution is the breaking up of such religious monopolies or near monopolies into precisely a free market of countless small entrepreneurs[43]:

[T]hat zeal must be altogether innocent where the society is divided into two or three hundred, or perhaps into as many as many thousand small sects, of which no one could be considerable enough to disturb the publick tranquility. The teachers of each sect, seeing themselves surrounded on all sides with more adversaries than friends, would be obliged to learn that candour and moderation which is so seldom to be found among the teachers of those great sects, whose tenets being supported by the civil magistrate, [one has no choice but to hold] in veneration.[44]

the name of some higher power. Safe though he was, the nice country vicar in effect inoculated vast swaths of the English against Christianity. A religion of hospital visiting and flower arranging, with a side offering of heritage conservation, replaced the risk-all faith of a man who asked his adherents to take up their cross and follow him.... In a country exhausted by wars of religion, the creation of the nonreligious priest was a masterstroke of English inventiveness.... The same genius at containing the power of religion was at work in the establishment of the Church of England. Secularists think this arrangement gives the church too much influence over the state, but it's the other way round: it secularises the church. When Puritan settlers in America set up a firewall between church and state, it wasn't to protect the state from the church, but to protect their church from the state.... Establishment domesticates the potentially dangerous enthusiasm of religion" (Giles Fraser, "Resurgent religion has done away with the country vicar," *The Guardian*, Thursday, April 13, 2006, p. 33). For Hume, though, there are limits to the idea of bribing indolence. After the text quoted by Smith, Hume goes on to discuss how his principle applies to the Catholic religion. The logic of Hume's argument would seem to justify the Catholic hierarchy centered in Rome no less than the Anglican hierarchy. Thus Hume proceeds to explain why the evils of Catholicism are such that its "advantages" are far outweighed by its "inconveniencies." In particular, in the Catholic case the priests were so greedy for revenues that receipt of an ecclesiastic salary *did not* succeed in purchasing their indolence (*History of England*, Vol. 3, p. 137).

[42] *Wealth of Nations*, Vol. 2, pp. 792–793.

[43] One can credit L. Ron Hubbard with having given to the idea of an entrepreneurship of religion its most pithy formulation: "I'd like to start a religion. That's where the money is" (*The Sunday Times Magazine*, April 16, 2006, p. 21). For an interesting attempt to apply a Smithian analysis in trying to understand the success of Korean Pentecostalism, see "In God's Name: A Special Report on Religion and Public Life," *The Economist*, November 3, 2007, pp. 6–11. The lesson drawn by *The Economist* is that religions like Pentecostalism that encourage entrepreneurial hustle expand exponentially whereas religions that do not (e.g., Buddhism) see their "market share" decline. Eliza Griswold, "God's Country: Muslims and Christians in Nigeria," *The Atlantic*, March 2008, pp. 40–55, offers a similar argument. See also the discussion of "market-savvy sects" in Clifford Orwin, "Onward Christian Salesmen," *The American Interest*, September/October 2009, pp. 91–95.

[44] *Wealth of Nations*, Vol. 2, p. 793.

Given a policy of laissez-faire, one could trust that the sects would "of their own accord subdivide themselves fast enough, so as soon to become sufficiently numerous," and therefore harmless.[45] Although he does not endorse their fanaticism, Smith thinks the English Puritans were right in rejecting anything associated with church establishment and says that these views, "though of a very unphilosophical origin," should in principle supply a foundation for "the most philosophical good temper and moderation with regard to every sort of religious principle."[46] Smith's model is Pennsylvania, where, although of course there is a numerically predominant sect (namely the Quakers), "the law in reality favours no one sect more than another."[47]

All of this gives the impression of a ready solution to the problem of church and state. However, when one compares this normative analysis with the lessons suggested in Smith's historical narrative in the rest of the text, the latter has the effect of largely canceling out the former. The contrast of Calvinist and Lutheran forms of church regime teaches that a more democratic, less hierarchical ordering of the church is likely to pose far greater threats of subversion. A Church-of-England-style bestowing of "preferments" from the top yields "peace and good order" and establishes the sovereign as "the real head of the church" (or rather, achieves the former *because* it situates ultimate ecclesiastical power in the hands of the civil sovereign). As I said, the rejection of church establishment and the approval of a maximum proliferation of sects contained in Smith's normative analysis cancel out all these decisive advantages of an established, hierarchical, church–state regime.[48] If Smith really believed that the proliferation of "many thousand sects" would solve the problem, how does this square with his subsequent analysis that the more democratic order

---

[45] Ibid., p. 794; cf. *Federalist 51*'s appeal to "multiplicity of sects" as a guarantee of rights for religious minorities. See also Voltaire, *Philosophical Letters*, p. 20: "Were there only one religion in England, despotism would be a threat; were there two, they would be at each other's throats; but there are thirty, and they live happily and at peace with one another." Rebecca E. Kingston, in "Montesquieu on Religion and on the Question of Toleration," in *Montesquieu's Science of Politics*, ed. D. W. Carrithers, M. A. Mosher, and Paul A. Rahe (Lanham, MD: Rowman & Littlefield, 2001), p. 394, draws attention to the fact that there is also an argument for the civic advantages of having a "multiplicité des religions" in Letter 85 of Montesquieu's *Persian Letters*, which may well have influenced these later arguments. Steven B. Smith, *Spinoza, Liberalism, and the Question of Jewish Identity* (New Haven: Yale University Press, 1997), p. 3, cites Voltaire and Madison as promoting the idea of "creation of a competitive market in religious sects" but does not mention Smith.

[46] *Wealth of Nations*, Vol. 2, p. 793.

[47] Ibid. Voltaire, too, had a high opinion of Pennsylvania under Quaker laws, as did Montesquieu (*Spirit of the Laws*, Book 4, chapter 6: "Mr. Penn is a true Lycurgus"). See also Thomas Paine, *The Age of Reason*, ed. M. D. Conway (Mineola, NY: Dover, 2004), p. 185: "The only sect that has not persecuted are the Quakers; and the only reason that can be given for it is, that they are rather Deists than Christians"; and p. 204: "Every sectary, except the quakers, has been a persecutor."

[48] See, as I have already discussed, the strongly proestablishment account of Scottish Presbyterianism on pp. 809–810. Cf. p. 813's reference to "[a]ll the good effects, both civil and religious, which an established church can be supposed to produce."

embodied in Calvinist (and Presbyterian)[49] congregations produced nothing but anarchy? We are left with a puzzle of not small proportions concerning precisely how Smith thinks the problem can really be solved.

It is in Smith's debate with Hume concerning the advantages of a salaried and quiescent clergy (established religion) versus those of an active and "entrepreneurial" clergy (free market of religion) that we come back to Hume's formula of "superstition and enthusiasm" and the theoretical importance of the distinction between them. One naturally associates "superstition" in Hume's sense with an established church and its entrenched and privileged clergy, and one associates "enthusiasm" with the entrepreneurs of a more open free market of sects. The proestablishment argument that Smith quotes from *The History of England* (stressing the civil advantages of an established church, and expressing a desire to do anything necessary to avoid the kind of dissenting sects that ran riot at the time of the English Civil War) is actually in important respects in tension with the argument Hume made in his essay, "Of Superstition and Enthusiasm." In that text, Hume had argued that enthusiastic religions are in the long term more favorable to liberty, and that the cause of English liberty owed a considerable debt to the zealots who stood for religious enthusiasm during the Civil War. "[S]uperstition is an enemy to civil liberty, and enthusiasm a friend to it.... [S]uperstition groans under the dominion of priests, [whereas] enthusiasm is destructive of all ecclesiastical power." It seems reasonable to conclude that *both* Smith and Hume have complex and ambivalent thoughts about the relative advantages of superstition and enthusiasm.[50]

In any case, the dialogue with Hume highlights an essential issue: Do we want an active and energetic clergy, exerting themselves to win adherents, or do we want an indolent and somewhat corrupt clergy who will help to foster an orderly society? This question is easy to answer for Hume, but Smith's position is more complicated. He admires the conscientious Scottish clergy, with their low salaries and austere morals. In other departments of life, it is more or less assumed that greater industry on the part of practitioners of a particular profession is preferable to lesser industry. Nevertheless, in light of Hume's argument that in the case of clergy, greater industry breeds greater zeal, which in turn breeds greater civil conflict, the general preference for industry over indolence is put in question.[51]

---

[49] However, as we saw earlier, the initial adverse judgment on Presbyterianism as a mode of Calvinism gets radically modified once the Scottish church becomes an established church and reembraces a system of appointment to office by patronage rather than by popular election.

[50] See Ernest Gellner, *Postmodernism, Reason and Religion* (London: Routledge, 1992), pp. 92–93 for an interesting discussion of paradoxes in Hume's analysis of superstition and enthusiasm – the main paradox being the one just presented, namely that Hume, as a champion of moderation and social order, has good reason to prefer superstitious religions to enthusiastic religions, yet (at least in this one significant text) he defends hyperenthusiastic seventeenth-century Puritan sects because he sees them as being in the long term "freedom-friendly." (As I pointed out in Chapter 18, note 6, Gellner misinterprets Hume's concept of superstition.)

[51] The treatment of religion in *The Wealth of Nations*, Vol. 2 (Book 5, chapter 1, Part 3, Article 3) follows a parallel analysis of education (Book 5, chapter 1, Part 3, Article 2), so it is natural to

The same question (industry or indolence) comes up, more obliquely, early in the section on religion. Smith cites the important Machiavellian discussion of St. Francis and St. Dominic in Book 3, chapter 1 of the *Discourses on Livy* that figured so prominently in my own interpretation of Machiavelli in Part I of this book.

> The establishment of the two great mendicant orders of St. Dominick and St. Francis, it is observed by Machiavel, revived, in the thirteenth and fourteenth centuries, the languishing faith and devotion of the catholic church.[52]

To be sure, those who founded these new religious institutions put new life back into Christianity – reanimated something that was "languishing." But does Machiavelli *want* Christianity to be revitalized, and does he therefore genuinely have a reason to celebrate the founders of monastic orders who are responsible for revitalizing it? Does Smith?[53] A vibrant church governed by devout and virtuous clergy is only desirable if Christianity is in fact the most

compare the discussion of clergy with that of teachers. The general principle is that a guaranteed income dampens down the zeal with which one practices one's profession. Because it is obvious that we want educators who elicit the educational interest of their charges with as much zeal and enthusiasm as possible, Smith is in no doubt that education, particularly university education, is corrupted insofar as teachers know that their salary is guaranteed rather than keyed to the quality of their performance (p. 796: "giving salaries to teachers [will] make them negligent and idle"). If one takes Hume's argument into consideration, however, it is not nearly so clear that maximum industry on the part of the clergy is similarly good for society.

52 Ibid., p. 790. Hume also highlights Machiavelli's critique of Christian asceticism (in *The Natural History of Religion*, end of Section 10): In *Writings on Religion*, ed. Anthony Flew (La Salle, IL: Open Court, 1992), p. 150, Hume makes explicit reference to *Discourses* II.2, but his discussion of St. Dominic and St. Francis (as well as St. Anthony and St. Benedict) on the previous page is a tacit reference to Machiavelli's account in *Discourses* III.1 of how the founding of the monastic orders put new life into Christianity. There is also a striking echo of *Discourses* II.2 in the passage from *The Theory of Moral Sentiments* cited in the next note.

53 Relevant here are Smith's consistent expressions of disdain concerning Christian asceticism, particularly the asceticism associated with the monastic life. Consider, for instance, his reference to the Anglican clergy's admirable "contempt of those absurd and hypocritical austerities which fanatics inculcate and pretend to practice" (p. 808); his reference to the philosophical conception according to which "heaven was to be earned only by penance and mortification, by the austerities and abasement of a monk; not by the liberal, generous, and spirited conduct of a man" (p. 771); and his complaint that European universities came to be geared toward "the education of ecclesiasticks," and therefore inculcated an ascetic morality that "certainly did not render it more proper for the education of gentlemen or men of the world, or more likely either to improve the understanding, or to mend the heart" (p. 772). On p. 771, n. 22, the editors refer us to *The Theory of Moral Sentiments*, p. 134, where Smith reacts very indignantly to the suggestion that the self-abnegation of "monks and friars" ("the futile mortifications of a monastery") should be privileged over various worldly virtues. This passage in turn is plausibly traced by the editors of the latter volume to Hume's *Enquiry Concerning the Principles of Morals* (*Theory of Moral Sentiments*, p. 133, n. 15; cf. Appendix II, p. 401). One should also relate this antimonastic theme in Smith to several other important texts in the liberal tradition. See, for instance, Montesquieu, *Spirit of the Laws*, Book 23, chapter 29; Hume, *History of England*, Vol. 3, chapter 31 (pp. 255–256) and Vol. 3, chapter 29 (p. 136: "monasteries.... those receptacles of sloth and ignorance"); and Kant, *Religion within the Boundaries of Mere Reason*, ed. Allen Wood and George di Giovanni (Cambridge: Cambridge University Press, 1998),

attractive vision of life, as well as a sound foundation for well-ordered civil life. Once again, the most relevant question is the one posed by Hume when he asks whether the best interests of society are not served by a form of church regime that is willing to "bribe [the] indolence" of the clergy.

One should not go so far as to identify Smith with Hume,[54] but he clearly shared Hume's preoccupation with civil disorders associated with religion, and he even saw, in ways that were reminiscent of Hobbes, that a powerful clergy is capable of threatening to subvert the very foundations of a secular political order per se.

pp. 134 and 168. Cf. Kingston, "Montesquieu on Religion and on the Question of Toleration," in *Montesquieu's Science of Politics*, p. 390. Both Hume and Montesquieu anticipate James Joyce's dictum that "the priest spells poverty" (*Ulysses*, Harmondsworth: Penguin, 1986, p. 526). As we saw in Chapters 2–4, Machiavelli presents Christian monastic orders as in effect the *model* of republican virtue. As I have discussed elsewhere in this book, Montesquieu, in his analogy between republican virtue and monastic virtue (with respect to the *extremity* of both types of virtue) in *Spirit of the Laws*, Book 5, chapter 2, in effect accepts Machiavelli's suggestion, but he turns it *against* republicanism as a political vision. Needless to say, all of this heightens the broader theoretical significance of the liberal critique of monasticism. Cf. Stephen Holmes, *The Anatomy of Antiliberalism* (Cambridge, MA: Harvard University Press, 1993), pp. 220–221, on how rejection of "the hair-shirt ethics of the monastery" helps to define the liberal tradition.

[54] D. D. Raphael offers a fascinating discussion of how Smith was always shadowed by a cloud of suspicion by virtue of his relationship with Hume: See *The Theory of Moral Sentiments*, Appendix II (pp. 383–401). Smith "was temperamentally averse from public controversy on matters of religion" (p. 400; cf. the Introduction, p. 27, where the editors quote a contemporary reviewer of *The Theory of Moral Sentiments* who is particularly approving of the fact that "there is the strictest regard preserved, throughout, to the principles of religion, so that the serious reader will find nothing that can give him any just ground of offense"). Nonetheless, there are some intriguing Humean gestures in his work. Most significantly, in the sixth edition of *The Theory of Moral Sentiments*, Smith deleted a long statement of "Christian doctrine about expiation and atonement" and replaced it with "a sentence so Humean in tone that it might almost be called a libation to Hume's ghost" (p. 400; see pp. 91–92 for the actual texts). Notwithstanding his friendship with Hume, Smith maintained a public stance of piety – yet that did not prevent him from concluding an important discussion of religion in *The Theory of Moral Sentiments* by citing a highly impious verse from Voltaire (p. 134; on Smith's high opinion of Voltaire, see *Wealth of Nations*, Vol. 2, p. 811, n. 30). On pp. 19–20 of their Introduction to *The Theory of Moral Sentiments*, the editors conclude that Smith never embraced Hume's religious skepticism (cf. Appendix II, p. 400). Still, there is more than a trace of the spirit of Hume in the letter from Smith to Alexander Wedderburn (August 14, 1776) quoted by the editors: "Poor David Hume is dying very fast, but with great chearfulness and good humour and with more real resignation to the necessary course of things, than any Whining Christian ever dyed with pretended resignation to the will of God" (Introduction, p. 19). It is interesting to compare Smith's vindication of Hume after his death with Shaftesbury's vindication of Pierre Bayle after *his* death. See Stanley Green, *Shaftesbury's Philosophy of Religion and Ethics* (Athens, OH: Ohio University Press, 1967), p.16: "[Bayle] had undeniably such qualities and virtues as might grace the character of the most orthodox of our age."

20

Christianity as a Civil Religion

Tocqueville's Response to Rousseau

> From the beginning, politics and religion were in accord, and they have not ceased to be so since.
>
> – Alexis de Tocqueville[1]

Various contemporary theorists have looked to Tocqueville as the theoretical source of a distinctively American solution to Rousseau's problem of the political need for a civil religion.[2] Indeed, Tocqueville's classic work, *Democracy in America*, does seem to show how an actual society can square the circle of a Christian republicanism that Rousseau declares to be an impossibility. Nevertheless, a closer inspection of the tensions at work in Tocqueville's thought reveals that he gets readily drawn into the very same perplexities that grip Rousseau, and the apparent solution furnished by the political religiosity of the Americans proves to be in some ways no less elusive than the civil religion that appears like a mirage at the end of the *Social Contract*.

---

[1] Alexis de Tocqueville, *Democracy in America*, trans. Harvey C. Mansfield and Delba Winthrop (Chicago: University of Chicago Press, 2000), p. 275. All following citations are from this edition.

[2] See the following works for some examples: Robert N. Bellah, "Civil Religion in America," *Daedalus*, Vol. 96, No. 1 (Winter 1967): 1–21; Robert N. Bellah, Richard Madsen, William M. Sullivan, Ann Swidler, and Steven M. Tipton, *Habits of the Heart: Individualism and Commitment in American Life* (Berkeley: University of California Press, 1985), pp. 219–249; Wilson Carey McWilliams, "Democracy and the Citizen," in *How Democratic Is the Constitution?*, ed. Robert A. Goldwin and William A. Schambra (Washington, DC: American Enterprise Institute, 1980), pp. 79–101; William A. Galston, "Liberalism and Public Morality," in *Liberals on Liberalism*, ed. Alfonso J. Damico (Totowa, NJ: Rowman & Littlefield, 1986), pp. 129–147; Thomas L. Pangle, "The Liberal Paradox," *Crisis*, Vol. 10, No. 5 (May 1992): 18–25; Stephen G. Salkever, "The Crisis of Liberal Democracy: Liberality and Democratic Citizenship," in *The Crisis of Liberal Democracy: A Straussian Perspective*, ed. Kenneth L. Deutsch and Walter Soffer (Albany, NY: SUNY Press, 1987), pp. 245–268; Stephen Salkever, *Finding the Mean: Theory and Practice in Aristotelian Political Philosophy* (Princeton, NJ: Princeton University Press, 1990), pp. 245–262.

Let us begin by sketching Tocqueville's critique of Rousseau.³ Rousseau's fundamental argument in *Social Contract* IV.8 is, of course, that there is an essential incompatibility between the cultic requirements of a healthy republican politics and the basic impulse of Christian religiosity. Tocqueville's critique consists in showing that American religion satisfies all the conditions of the vision of a liberal republicanism with which Rousseau concludes his book, while also showing that this civil religion of the American republic is fully and indeed emphatically Christian. Consider the following passage from the final chapter of Volume 1 of *Democracy in America*:

In the United States, even the religion of the greatest number is itself republican; it submits the truths of the other world to individual reason, as politics abandons to the good sense of all the care of their interests, and it grants that each man freely take the way that will lead him to Heaven, in the same manner that the law recognizes in each citizen the right to choose his government.⁴

Thus the democratic citizens of the American republic have put into practice the religious liberalism upon which Rousseau insists in the closing paragraphs of the *Social Contract*. Moreover, the religious life of the American citizens described by Tocqueville does exactly what Rousseau says a civil religion should do: It fosters good citizenship, attaches the citizenry to the laws and institutions of the political community, and serves a thoroughly patriotic purpose.⁵ American religious life *is* a civil religion in precisely the sense according to which Rousseau defines a civil religion. Nevertheless, this civil religion of the Americans is, Tocqueville insists, through and through Christian, undeniably so. "In the United States, Christian sects vary infinitely and are constantly modified, but Christianity itself is an established and irresistible fact that no one undertakes either to attack or defend."⁶ According to Tocqueville, the first Americans "brought to the New World a Christianity that I cannot depict better than to call it democratic and republican."⁷ Thus what Rousseau declares to be a flat impossibility, a Christian republicanism, is demonstrated by Tocqueville to be not only a conceptual possibility but indeed a historical reality in Protestant America.

A further dimension of the Tocquevillean critique of Rousseau is Tocqueville's more consistent Lockeanism, which highlights, at least implicitly,

---

³ We have it on Tocqueville's own authority that he considered himself to be in a lifelong dialogue with Rousseau: "Il y a trois hommes avec lesquels je vis tous les jours un peu c'est Pascal, Montesquieu et Rousseau." Alexis de Tocqueville, *Oeuvres Complètes*, ed. J.-P. Mayer, Tome XIII: *Correspondance d'Alexis de Tocqueville et de Louis de Kergorlay* (Paris: Gallimard, 1977), p. 418.

⁴ *Democracy in America*, p. 381.

⁵ Ibid., p. 277: "One can say … that in the United States there is no single religious doctrine that shows itself hostile to democratic and republican institutions. All the clergy there hold to the same language; opinions are in accord with the laws, and there reigns so to speak only a single current in the human mind."

⁶ Ibid., p. 406.

⁷ Ibid., p. 275.

the tensions inherent in Rousseau's only partial embrace of Locke at the end of the *Social Contract*. In effect, Tocqueville is arguing against Rousseau (though he never mentions Rousseau in this context) that if what he desires is the deistic, Lockean religion of liberal toleration upheld at the end of the book, he is wrong to encourage the vague quasi-theocratic longings that run through much of the civil-religion chapter. Rather than plumping for Hobbes over Locke on the question of theocracy, Rousseau would be better off wholeheartedly affirming a Lockean separation of church and state and expunging any trace of theocratic aspirations for the sake of religious liberalism. As Tocqueville correctly perceives, you cannot have both – theocratic politics and liberal religion, Hobbesian unity of church and state and Lockean toleration – and so Rousseau ends up in a contradiction. Tocqueville's position avoids the tension by opting more thoroughgoingly for a Lockean conception of the relation between religion and politics. Whereas Rousseau equivocates between Hobbes and Locke, Tocqueville clearly sides with Locke against Hobbes and thus secures a politics that is both liberal and republican.[8]

However, this is not to suggest that Tocqueville, in defining his stance toward the American civil religion, is free of tensions of his own. The liberal religion celebrated in *Democracy in America* is of course overwhelmingly Protestant. Nonetheless, Tocqueville, both in practice and in theory, is firmly committed to Catholicism.[9] Thus it emerges that Tocqueville's efforts to navigate the

---

[8] Tocqueville's implicit response to Rousseau's civil-religion teaching consists in an attempt to show that one can have a political religion that is both Christian and moderately this worldly, both tolerant in spirit and yet politically useful in securing the required ethos of a democratic state. To this modest Tocquevillean civil religion, Rousseau would no doubt reply that what it offers is a very watered-down version of Christianity in the service of a very watered-down version of republicanism.

[9] In speaking of Tocqueville's commitment "in practice and in theory" to Catholicism, I do not mean to imply that he believed in the dogmas of the Catholic faith. As Tocqueville himself puts it (*Democracy in America*, p. 280), "I do not know if all Americans have faith in their religion – for who can read to the bottom of hearts?" [*qui peut lire au fond des cœurs?*]. In fact, the discussions of religion in *Democracy in America* offer ample hints that he was a man plagued by inner doubts (see esp. his description of the regretful unbeliever on pp. 286–287). See also his letter to Gobineau of January 14, 1857: "Alas!... many who are sincerely searching for [absolute conviction in regard to Christianity] did not yet have the good fortune of finding it" (Alexis de Tocqueville, *The European Revolution and Correspondence with Gobineau*, ed. John Lukacs, Garden City, NY: Doubleday Anchor Books, 1959, p. 306). All I mean is that he attended the Catholic mass, whatever his private doubts, that he gave no outward display of these doubts, and that he defended in theory the political superiority of Catholicism. For biographical evidence of Tocqueville's troubled relationship to his own Catholicism, see André Jardin, *Tocqueville: A Biography* (New York: Farrar, Straus & Giroux, 1988), pp. 61–64, 384–385, 512, 528–532. Melvin Richter writes, in regard to Montesquieu, that as "[Montesquieu] lay dying, he asked for a confessor so that he might be given the final sacrament of the church. His choice was a Jesuit who had helped him publish the *Considerations*. Something of a contest resulted between the Society of Jesus and this noted author. Montesquieu, who denied ever having been in a state of disbelief, was made to consent to various conditions, such as permitting his last words to be made public.... [I]t remains unknown to what degree [Montesquieu] believed in the dogmas of his church. To the end he resisted the Society's attempts to gain control over his manuscripts.

curious relationship in his thought between liberalism and Catholicism are no less tension ridden than Rousseau's efforts to square Hobbesian theocracy with Lockean toleration.

There are three main strands to Tocqueville's argument in regard to religion in *Democracy in America*. The first strand is to argue, counter to Rousseau, that Christianity can be politically useful, that, despite the account given by Rousseau of the otherworldly "spirit of Christianity," it is capable of supporting and furthering worldly concerns,[10] and that therefore any civil religion should have a specifically Christian character. The second strand is to argue, also counter to Rousseau, in favor of a strict separation of church and state.[11] The third strand argues for the political superiority of Catholicism to Protestantism and other Christian or quasi-Christian alternatives, insofar as Catholicism offers a more reliable counterweight to the vices of democracy while it possesses greater affinities with democracy than is generally appreciated, which is, once again, an anti-Rousseauian argument. It should be evident that all three strands of the argument show Tocqueville to be as much concerned with French politics in the wake of the anticlerical French Revolution as he is with American democracy.

The following pertains to the first strand: As Robert N. Bellah rightly points out, the French Revolutionaries "attempted to set up an anti-Christian civil religion"[12] (surely in fealty to what they took to be Rousseau's encouragement of such a contrivance). Tocqueville would no doubt view this as one among many misguided impulses of the French Revolution, and in this respect his description of a republican Christianity in America serves to show that even political actors who are attracted to and wish to embrace a civil religion need not follow Rousseau's counsel in this regard.

The following pertains to the second strand: Tocqueville's case for a separation of church and state is, oddly enough, motivated by civil-religion considerations. Religious support for citizenship is beneficial. To serve this salutary function, religion must avoid any unnecessary entanglements that impugn its own integrity or that sully its reputation among the citizens it hopes to shape and influence.[13] More specifically, religion must strenuously avoid the kind

---

Much of the same story was to be repeated on the deathbed of Alexis de Tocqueville." Melvin Richter, *The Political Theory of Montesquieu* (Cambridge: Cambridge University Press, 1977), pp. 16–17.

[10] Tocqueville seems to anticipate Max Weber's thesis of the paradoxical worldliness of Puritanism. See *Democracy in America*, pp. 43, 423, 429–430, 505–506. Given this "innerworldly asceticism" of certain Protestant sects, Rousseau's case for the necessarily otherworldly character of Christianity as such is shown to be mistaken.

[11] A fairly obvious sign of this quarrel with Rousseau is Tocqueville's rejection of Islam; ibid., pp. 419–420. Tocqueville rejects Islam for the very reason that Rousseau approves of it. Cf. *The European Revolution and Correspondence with Gobineau*, ed. Lukacs, p. 212.

[12] Bellah, "Civil Religion in America," p. 13. Bellah's article offers valuable historical evidence in support of Tocqueville's argument that a "Christian republicanism" is more feasible than Machiavelli and Rousseau suggest.

[13] For similar arguments, as articulated in the American constitutional tradition, see Michael J. Sandel, *Democracy's Discontent* (Cambridge, MA: Belknap Press, 1996), p. 61.

of mistakes committed by the Catholic Church in France in casting its lot so conspicuously with the losing side in politics, namely the pre-Revolutionary ancien régime. There is no surer way for a religion to discredit itself than to back the wrong horse in the political arena. The French Catholic hierarchy was thus its own worst enemy, and the American segregation of church and state offers the most secure means of precluding this political catastrophe of French Catholicism. For a civil religion to work, it must keep itself unsullied in the eyes of its followers, and to do this it must keep its hands impeccably clean, politically speaking. Hence the imperative that religion remain aloof from the offices and institutions of the state. The hearty religiosity of the Americans proves the efficacy of this policy (whereas the crisis of European Catholicism proves the perils of the policy adopted by the Catholic Church in resisting the egalitarian revolution that erupted in 1789).[14]

Finally, the following pertains to the third strand: In arguing that Catholicism has a better opportunity to win support in democratic America than it appears at first glance to have, Tocqueville at the same time wants to argue that Catholicism can (and should) reconcile itself to democracy, for it can do so without being untrue to itself. Tocqueville's purpose, then, is two-sided: to argue that it is in the best interests of American democracy to opt for Catholicism rather than remaining Protestant, and to argue that it is in the best interests of French Catholicism to opt for liberal democracy rather than remaining hierarchical and authoritarian. From both angles, the American–democratic one and the French–Catholic one, Tocqueville is urging the entry into an unlikely alliance of democracy and Catholicism. Tocqueville clearly wants to employ the American example to teach French Catholics to embrace the democratic movement, rather than to continue to sink their fortunes in a losing cause.[15] It

[14] This argument is laid out in *Democracy in America*, pp. 275–288. Cf. Alexis de Tocqueville, *The Old Régime and the French Revolution*, trans. Stuart Gilbert (Garden City, NY: Doubleday Anchor Books, 1955), pp. 5–7. For a forceful contemporary reassertion of Tocqueville's argument, see John Rawls, "The Idea of Public Reason Revisited," in *Collected Papers*, ed. Samuel Freeman (Cambridge, MA: Harvard University Press, 1999), p. 604, n. 76, as well as "*Commonweal* Interview with John Rawls," *Collected Papers*, p. 621.

[15] On Tocqueville's desire for a union of Catholicism and "the new society," see Jardin, *Tocqueville*, pp. 364–365, 476–477. On pp. 10–13 of *Democracy in America*, Tocqueville states explicitly that he presents his analysis of democratic America with the object of mediating the conflict between clericalism and liberalism in France. From some perspectives (say, that of Sheldon Wolin), Tocqueville appears as being far short of a fully committed democrat. However, seeing Tocqueville from the vantage point of nineteenth-century ultraconservatives helps one appreciate how anxious Tocqueville was to meet democracy halfway. Gobineau, for instance, wrote the following: "[S]ome future day, when you despair of this century, you will be tempted to agree a little with me" – to which Tocqueville made this response: "Yes, I sometimes despair of mankind. Who doesn't, even when he lives as isolated from it as I do? But I do not despair of this century" (*The European Revolution and Correspondence with Gobineau*, ed. Lukacs, pp. 249, 252). In the same volume, a statement quoted from F. X. Kraus (p. 27) provides in effect a nice gloss on what Gobineau was getting at: "For long I haven't agreed with Tocqueville; he seems to have made his peace with Democracy too cheaply and too soon." For an excellent statement of Tocqueville's democratic commitment, see his letter to Gobineau of January 24, 1857 (ibid., pp. 308–310). Incidentally, the editor's suggested parallel (*The European*

is in this third strand of his argument that the tensions in Tocqueville's point
of view come most visibly to the fore.

How does Tocqueville justify the project of a Catholic America? Consider
the contrast between his account of the Puritan origins of America in Volume 1,
Part 1, chapter 2, and his depiction of the promise of Catholicism in Volume 2,
Part 1, chapters 5 and 6. As Volume 1, Part 1, chapter 2 makes clear, the Americans were the people that they were by virtue of the democratic-republican
Protestantism of their Puritan founders.[16] As he puts it in that chapter, "the
character of Anglo-American civilization" is to be primarily accounted for by
its unique combination of the spirit of religion and the spirit of freedom,[17] and
the spirit of American religion was entirely Puritan. "Puritanism . . . was almost
as much a political theory [*une théorie politique*] as a religious doctrine," and
the kind of politics that English Puritanism impressed upon the American way
of life "blended at several points with the most absolute democratic and republican theories."[18] Given the special character of its religiosity, it was no accident
that the Americans were passionate republicans. As Tocqueville insists in Volume 1, Part 2, chapter 9, "[n]ext to each religion is a political opinion that
is joined to it by affinity,"[19] and in America, this religious–political outlook
can only be defined in terms of militant Protestantism: Those who peopled
America shook off the authority of the Pope and "brought to the New World
a Christianity that I cannot depict better than to call it democratic and republican: this singularly favors the establishment of a republic and of democracy
in affairs. From the beginning, politics and religion were in accord, and they
have not ceased to be so since."[20] If anything serves to define the Americans as
a people, it is the curious paradox by which a fairly narrow and rigid religious
sectarianism can nonetheless be the ground of a very open and free politics.[21]
Is America minus the Puritan ethos still America? Moreover, as Tocqueville is
surely aware, the democratic egalitarianism of America is distinctively Protestant; as he acknowledges at the beginning of Volume 1, "*Protestantism* asserts
that all men are equally in a state to find the path to Heaven."[22]

Nevertheless, Tocqueville goes to great pains, in both volumes of *Democracy in America*, to try to show that Catholicism is not necessarily antithetical
to the American sensibility, nor is America necessarily antithetical to a Catholic
experience of religious faith, and that in some respects they may be even *more*

Revolution, pp. 16, 19–20) between the Tocqueville–Gobineau dialogue and the Nietzsche–
Burckhardt dialogue in the same century – as well as the Machiavelli–Guicciardini dialogue
several centuries earlier – is an interesting one.

[16] *Democracy in America*, pp. 32–39; cf. pp. 429–430.

[17] Ibid., p. 43.

[18] Ibid., pp. 35, 32. Was the concept of political theory coined by Tocqueville? I am not aware of
any prior use of the term by any other figure in the political theory canon.

[19] Ibid., p. 275.

[20] Ibid.

[21] Ibid., pp. 43–44.

[22] Ibid., p. 6; emphasis added.

suited to each other than the current alignments: democracy and Protestantism; Catholicism and antirepublicanism. In Volume 2, Part 1, chapter 6, Tocqueville suggests that Catholics need merely let go of the crippling burden of clericalist politics to liberate the tremendous potential appeal of Catholicism for a democratic culture: "I hardly doubt that this same spirit of the century that seems so contrary to it would become very favorable to it, and that all at once it would make great conquests."[23] However, as Volume 2, Part 1, chapter 5 makes clear, the "Catholicism" here recommended by Tocqueville is a curiously Protestantized Catholicism, with a dilution of ritual elements, and a relinquishing of saint worship (which he characterizes as neopagan!).[24] The analysis in these two chapters is somewhat contradictory: A successful Catholicism in America must limit external observances as much as possible to conform itself to a democratic people's religious preference for simplicity and generality, yet Tocqueville also insists that Catholicism has for them the potential appeal that it does on account of "a secret admiration for its government [*son gouvenement*]."[25] In other words, Catholicism must be Protestantized to cater to a democratic people's natural preference for Protestant simplicity, yet we are told at the same time that Catholicism holds special cultural advantages over the Protestant sects in precisely those respects in which Catholic Christianity is *non*-Protestant.

In Volume 1, Part 2, chapter 9, Tocqueville is committed to the same pro-Catholic analysis. It is surely striking that Tocqueville's most powerful example of how a civil religion functions in America is a *Catholic* example (a priest's address to a gathering of Polish Catholics),[26] which shows tellingly that Catholicism can serve not only as a European civil religion, but even as an American civil religion. Again, Tocqueville highlights the democratic appeal of Catholicism to a surprising degree. Amazingly, we are told that Catholicism is, among the various Christian sects, "one of the most favorable to equality of conditions."[27] Provided that the priests forgo the political ambitions that disfigure Catholicism in Europe, "there are no men more disposed by their beliefs than Catholics to carry the idea of equality of conditions into the political world."[28] In addition, Tocqueville makes the extraordinary statement that Protestantism breeds inequality because it "generally brings men much less to equality than to independence," as if one could reasonably draw from Catholicism a more egalitarian view of the world than is offered by Protestant Christianity.[29] However, as I have already suggested, these strange assertions probably have as much to do with Tocqueville's desire to see the

---

[23] Ibid., p. 425.
[24] Ibid., pp. 421–423.
[25] Ibid., p. 424. The sentence continues, "its great unity attracts them."
[26] Ibid., p. 277.
[27] Ibid., p. 276.
[28] Ibid.
[29] Ibid.

democratization of Catholicism in France as they have to do with any descriptive claims about America.[30]

The tensions in Tocqueville's account of religion show themselves with a much greater intensity when we peer behind his public pronouncements on the subject, and we see that in private, he was much more equivocal about the attractions of Catholicism, as is disclosed in his remarkable letter of June 29, 1831 to Louis de Kergorlay.[31] As the same private correspondence also reveals (but *Democracy in America* does not, except by very guarded insinuations), Tocqueville was in possession of a deeper analysis of why the Americans, supposedly secure in their attachment to Christianity, might require the more full-bodied discipline of Catholicism.[32] The relevant portion of Tocqueville's letter begins with the suggestion that Protestantism of whatever complexion is really just watered-down Catholicism, and the more Protestantism evolves, the more watered down it gets: "The Catholic faith is the immobile point from which each new sect distances itself a little more, while drawing nearer to pure

[30] As I have already noted, Tocqueville makes no secret of his wish to make a didactic use of the American experience, for the instruction of a European audience. Volume I, Part I, chapter 9 is full of references back to the European situation, particularly the struggle between clericalism and secularism in France. In Tocqueville's view, America proves that *both* sides in this French *kulturkampf* are in error: The clerical side is wrong in identifying democracy as such with unbelief, and the secular side is wrong in thinking that republicanism can survive and flourish in the absence of a religiously sustained ethos. Realigning Christianity with liberalism and democracy was a concern that Tocqueville shared with his political-intellectual predecessors, such as Constant, Madame de Staël, and Guizot: For an account of the relevant historical background, see Larry Siedentop, *Tocqueville* (Oxford: Oxford University Press, 1994), pp. 27–28, 31–33, 49–51, 97–100. For a particularly strong statement of Tocqueville's commitment to the view that religion is socially indispensable, see *Oeuvres Complètes*, ed. J.-P. Mayer, Tome IX, p. 68: "Je croirais plutôt à la venue d'une nouvelle religion qu'à la grandeur et à la prosperité croissante de nos sociétés modernes sans religion. Si le christianisme doit en effet disparaître comme tant de gens se hâtent de le dire, il nous arrivera ce qui est déjà arrivé aux anciens avant sa venue, une longue décrépitude morale, une viellesse vicieuse et troublée qui finira par amener je ne sais d'ou ni comment une rénovation nouvelle." ["I would sooner believe in the coming of a new religion than believe in the greatness and growing prosperity of our modern societies in the absence of religion. If Christianity must in effect disappear, as so many people hasten to pronounce, the result will be what already happened to the ancients before the coming of Christianity – a long moral decrepitude, a vicious and troubled dotage, concerning which one can discern neither its destination nor the source of a fresh renewal."] (*The European Revolution and Correspondence with Gobineau*, ed. Lukacs, offers a truncated version of this letter – perhaps because in the letter Tocqueville contemplates a post-Christian epoch, thus disrupting Lukacs's agenda of presenting Tocqueville in his correspondence with Gobineau as writing strictly within the horizon of a confident and firmly committed Catholicism.)

[31] Alexis de Tocqueville, *Selected Letters on Politics and Society*, ed. Roger Boesche (Berkeley: University of California Press, 1985), pp. 45–59.

[32] Although in *Democracy in America* Tocqueville's formulation of the problem is guarded, the veiled analysis is easiest to glimpse in his compact discussion of pantheism in Vol. 2, Part I, chapter 7, as well as the crucial final sentence of Vol. 2, Part I, chapter 6 ("I am brought to believe that... our descendants will tend more and more to be divided into only two parts, those leaving Christianity entirely and others entering into the bosom of the Roman Church").

deism."[33] What follows from this logic is that left to itself, American Protestantism will eventually lead to the self-exhaustion of Christianity.[34] This is in all likelihood what prompts Tocqueville in *Democracy in America* to emphasize the potential of a fresh burst of American Catholicism and to highlight its unsuspected affinities with a democratic way of life. The implicit message is that America *needs* Catholicism to save Christianity as a religion that still means something within that kind of society. "Protestants of all persuasions," he writes, "live and die in compromises, without ever concerning themselves with reaching the depths of things."[35] Protestant ministers, by contrast to Catholic priests, are merely "businessmen of religion."[36] Whereas Catholicism "seizes the senses and the soul deeply," the Protestant denominations leave one reeling with uncertainties.[37] Protestantism, he asserts, is merely a transitional religion, a stopgap compromise, that is "approaching its end."[38] The contest between Protestantism and Catholicism presented in *Democracy in America* – a contest that this letter to Kergorlay suggests cannot in any way be won by Protestantism – discloses a hidden predicament that the work itself merely hints at, but that is analyzed quite candidly in the letter, namely the prospect of the death of Christianity at the hands of American democracy. The ostensible celebration of American religiosity in *Democracy in America* obscures this dark prospect, whereas Tocqueville's quixotic obsession with the hope of building Catholicism in America allows us to glimpse his underlying desperation about how Christianity might be rescued from a democratic ethos that renders people indifferent to "the depths of things." Thus American Christians are destined to become either more Christian or less Christian. Protestantism leads Americans to a fork in the road: Which way will they go? Will they opt for a return to full-bodied Christianity (Catholicism), or will they opt for a complete dilution of religious authority (quasi-deist Unitarianism)? "Here I am absolutely lost in uncertainty," Tocqueville confesses.[39] This is the stupendous drama looming behind the highly compressed chapters 6 and 7 of *Democracy in America*, Volume 2, Part 1.

---

[33] *Selected Letters*, ed. Boesche, p. 49.

[34] This aspect of Tocqueville's thought concerning Christianity is anticipated by Edward Gibbon in the eighteenth century, according to whom there is the distinct possibility that the long-term effect of the Protestant Reformation will be for popular devotion to "insensibly subside in languor and indifference." Gibbon, *The History of the Decline and Fall of the Roman Empire*, ed. David Womersley (London: Allen Lane, 1994), Vol. 3, p. 437. (I owe this reference to Gabriel Bartlett.) Cf. Gibbon's reference on p. 439 to the "sigh [of] the modern clergy."

[35] *Selected Letters*, ed. Boesche, p. 50.

[36] Ibid.

[37] Ibid., p. 51.

[38] Ibid., pp. 49–50. This stark prospect is echoed in *Democracy in America*, in the conclusion of Vol. 2, Part 1, chapter 6 that I quoted in note 32 of this chapter. Despite the seeming vitality of American Protestantism, Protestantism really has no future in America. American Christianity will either have to become more Christian (the Catholic option) or it will evaporate into a mere shadow of Christianity ("pantheism").

[39] *Selected Letters*, ed. Boesche, p. 52.

In the end, Tocqueville comes up against the same contradictions of the human condition that stymie Rousseau:

But do you not wonder at the misery of our nature? One religion works powerfully on the will, it dominates the imagination, it gives rise to real and profound beliefs; but it divides the human race into the fortunate and the damned, creates divisions on earth that should exist only in the other life, the child of intolerance and fanaticism. The other preaches tolerance, attaches itself to reason, in effect its symbol; it obtains no power, it is an inert work, without strength and almost without life. That is enough on that subject, to which my imagination is constantly dragging me back and which in the end would drive me mad if I often examined it deeply.[40]

In the contest between deism and Catholicism, Tocqueville would seem to opt clearly for Catholicism; and yet, as this passage unmistakably reveals, the prospect of a Catholic America is, for Tocqueville, a both attractive and unattractive prospect. Put otherwise, America is what it is by virtue of being Christian. However, to *stay* Christian, it must become Catholic, and in becoming Catholic it will become more European and less American, thus losing the innocence and liberal spirit that render Protestant America so attractive to a Catholic European like Tocqueville. In short, you can't win.

Although the liberalized American civil religion praised by Tocqueville in *Democracy in America* seems to offer a solution to Rousseau's problem, the admission made here that Protestantism is an unworkable compromise between deism and Catholicism whose tensions will drive it toward either zealotry or banality, discloses that – for Tocqueville as for Rousseau – there is no ultimate solution.

---

[40] Ibid., p. 53. In reading this passage, one naturally thinks of the condemnation of Catholicism with which Rousseau closes the civil-religion chapter, according to which Catholicism is defined by its rigorous division of humanity into those who are saved and those who are damned. (Tocqueville had better reason than Rousseau to single out Catholicism in this respect, for although the Protestant sects Tocqueville encountered in America were no doubt milder and less intolerant – although by no means consistently so – it seems unlikely that the Calvinism of Rousseau's native Geneva was any less worthy of condemnation on this score than was Catholicism.)

21

John Stuart Mill's Project to Turn Atheism into a Religion

The kinds of unbelief with which we are most familiar today are respectful indifference and such a nostalgia for lost faith as goes with an inability to distinguish between theological truth and myth. Are not these kinds of unbelief much more insulting to belief than is an unbelief like Machiavelli's which takes seriously the claim to truth of revealed religion by regarding the question of its truth as all-important and therefore is not, at any rate, a lukewarm unbelief?

– Leo Strauss[1]

If we secular humanists have our way, the liberal democracies will eventually mutate into societies whose most sacred texts were written by John Stuart Mill.

– Richard Rorty[2]

If the purpose of the civil-religion project is to domesticate religion in the light of political requirements, then the liberal tradition as a whole is in some sense closely allied with that project. If the project of domesticating religion per se is what defined civil religion, then one would even be justified in saying that the liberal tradition is coterminous with the civil-religion project. However, in order for the domestication of religion to count as specifically a civil-religion project, it must be animated by the idea of using *religion itself* to domesticate religion. Somewhat surprisingly, as we have seen in earlier chapters of Part II, there *are* some liberal political philosophers who cross into civil-religion theorizing in this sense.[3] Reading John Stuart Mill's proposal for a Religion of

---

[1] Leo Strauss, *Thoughts on Machiavelli* (Glencoe, IL: The Free Press, 1958), p. 51.
[2] "Religion in the Public Square: A Reconsideration," *Journal of Religious Ethics*, Vol. 31, No. 1 (2003): 144.
[3] Montesquieu appears to us as coming closest to this image of a civil-religion liberal. There are undoubtedly strong elements of civil-religion theorizing in Tocqueville, but for Tocqueville, unlike other liberals, the domestication of religion is not what motivates this civil-religion theorizing. On the contrary, Tocqueville's concern is that democratic society will promote an *atrophy* of religion that will in turn undermine civic virtue. Hence the problem for Tocqueville

Humanity in his essay "Utility of Religion,"[4] one is at first tempted to add him to this list of "civil-religion liberals." On closer examination, though, it becomes clear that his Religion of Humanity is *not* a civil religion as we have just defined it. Mill wants to give believers *something* that they can embrace in place of the "old religions" that he is urging them to relinquish, and calling this something a religion should, he thinks, ease the transition to this new more radically humanist dispensation. Whatever existential needs were satisfied by the old religions – for consolation in the face of loss and death, for a sense of absolute foundation for human purposes, for giving support to our intuitions that there is grandeur and meaning to human doings rather than unrelieved insignificance – can therefore continue to be met when those old religions fall into eclipse. Ultimately, though, what he means by a Religion of Humanity is an *ungrounded* faith in the meaning of human purposes – that is, a faith ungrounded in anything beyond itself – and a "religion" that could achieve this, rather than being in meaningful continuity with the history of religions throughout human experience, would break this continuity and show that human beings had safely arrived at a stage of their development where they could deal with their world without religion.

Mill takes it as given that the old religions (including Christianity) have been historically superseded,[5] mainly because modern science has demonstrated that

is not how to rein in forms of religion that are overpowerful, but rather how to sustain the civic advantages of religion in an age of (potentially) waning faith.

[4] John Stuart Mill, *Three Essays on Religion*, 3rd ed. (London: Longmans, Green and Co., 1923), pp. 109–122. All subsequent references to the three essays ("Nature," "Utility of Religion," and "Theism") will refer to this edition. For a rich and illuminating discussion of the essays on religion, see Borys M. Kowalsky, *Hellenism and Hebraism: The Moral and Social Implications of the Quarrel between Science and Religion in the Thought of John Stuart Mill*, PhD dissertation, University of Toronto (2000). As is noted by James Fitzjames Stephen, Mill borrows the term "Religion of Humanity," though not its content, from Auguste Comte: Stephen, *Liberty, Equality, Fraternity*, ed. Stuart D. Warner (Indianapolis: Liberty Fund, 1993), p. 3; cf. editor's Foreword, pp. xix–xx, and Richard Vernon, *The Career of Toleration* (Montreal: McGill-Queen's University Press, 1997), pp. 99–100. See also *Liberty, Equality, Fraternity*, pp. 167–168, 170, 175–176, 179, and 182–184; as this discussion in chapter 6 of Stephen's book makes clear, the idea of a Religion of Humanity is already implicit, and to some extent explicit, in Mill's essay on *Utilitarianism*. In an interesting argument, Allan D. Megill discusses how Mill not only rejects Comte's version of the Religion of Humanity but also has severe worries about possibly antiliberal implications of *his own* version: see "J. S. Mill's Religion of Humanity and the Second Justification for the Writing of *On Liberty*," in *Mill and the Moral Character of Liberalism*, ed. Eldon J. Eisenach (University Park: Pennsylvania State University Press, 1998), pp. 301–316. On p. 313 and p. 314 n. 31, Megill praises Stephen for appreciating this problem in Mill. The Millian texts most relevant to Megill's interpretation are Mill, *Utilitarianism, On Liberty, and Considerations on Representative Government*, ed. H. B. Acton (London: Dent, 1972), p. 31; and Mill, *Autobiography* (London: Oxford University Press, 1924), pp. 139–141 and 215–216.

[5] "Theism," p. 126: The fully enlightened view of the place of religion within the history of humankind is to regard "Christianity or Theism [as] things once of great value but which can now be done without."

key pillars of that older belief structure are no longer credible. Religion and science are inescapably in conflict, and where the two contradict each other, science necessarily prevails.[6] What then is Mill's Religion of Humanity? It is the capacity of human beings to feel a quasi-transcendent sense of their species-destiny and of their moral mission in the world *in the absence of* supernatural beliefs that supply transhuman guarantees of this elevated sense of mission and destiny.

In "Utility of Religion," Mill points out that the ancient Romans had managed to attain "a certain greatness of soul" even though their civic religion contributed little to their sense of human purpose.[7] That is, they demonstrated, through their way of life, that it is possible to realize a sense of absolutely intense human purpose through intrahuman means alone; and here, I think, the fundamental riddle of Mill's Religion of Humanity opens itself to a solution. Mill never mentions Tocqueville in his essays on religion, but the question of *why* Mill feels driven to construct his social–moral ideal as a "new religion" becomes intelligible, I believe, as soon as one thinks of it in relation to Tocqueville's analysis. Tocqueville writes the following:

I do not know ... whether this great utility of religions is not still more visible among peoples where conditions are equal than among all others. One must recognize that equality, which introduces great goods into the world, nevertheless suggests to men very dangerous instincts ... it tends to isolate them from one another and to bring each of them to be occupied with himself alone. It opens their souls excessively to the love of material enjoyments. The greatest advantage of religions is to inspire wholly contrary instincts. There is no religion that does not place man's desires beyond and above earthly goods and that does not naturally raise his soul toward regions much superior to those of the senses. Nor is there any that does not thus draw him, from time to time, away from contemplation of himself. This one meets even in the most false and dangerous religions.[8]

If one accepts the reading of Tocqueville that I offered in Chapter 20, Tocqueville is preoccupied by the place of religion in a liberal-democratic regime not because he himself has a stable solution to the problem of civil religion, but rather because he is powerfully gripped by *anxieties* about the moral and intellectual health of a society that jettisons concern with religion. The fundamental lesson taught by John Stuart Mill's musings about a Religion of Humanity is

---

[6] Ibid., p. 129.

[7] "Utility of Religion," p. 107.

[8] Alexis de Tocqueville, *Democracy in America*, trans. Harvey C. Mansfield and Delba Winthrop (Chicago: University of Chicago Press, 2000), p. 419. Tocqueville's view can in turn be traced back to Rousseau: "Irreligion ... causes attachment to life, makes souls effeminate and degraded, concentrates all the passions in the baseness of private interest, in the abjectness of the human *I*, and thus quietly saps the true foundations of every society" (*Emile*, trans. Allan Bloom, New York: Basic Books, 1979, p. 312, note).

that Mill, although he is less persuaded than Tocqueville is of the civic virtues of supernatural religion, is gripped by the very same anxieties.

There is also a striking Tocquevillean echo in another important passage toward the end of "Theism." The context here is the question why a religious skeptic – that is, one who, to be sure, does not rule out the possibility of a God but regards the evidence for His existence as "amounting only to one of the lower degrees of probability"[9] – would, having moved beyond "belief," continue to invest *hope* in notions of a caring and active (interventionist) God. Here is Mill's answer to the question:

> To me it seems that human life, small and confined as it is, and as, considered merely in the present, it is likely to remain even when the progress of material and moral improvement may have freed it from the greater part of its calamities, stands greatly in need of any wider range and greater height of aspiration for itself and its destination, which the exercise of imagination can yield to it without running counter to the evidence of fact; and that it is a part of wisdom to make the most of any, even small, probabilities on this subject, which furnish imagination with any footing to support itself upon.[10]

In short, human beings, to fulfill their full humanity, need to be inspired by a "height of aspiration"[11] that one associates with the various world religions. The context here is the continued longing for the traditional "domain of the supernatural,"[12] so it is not even clear that the Religion of Humanity presented in the "Utility of Religion" essay would adequately suffice for this purpose. This furnishes more evidence that Mill was haunted by Tocqueville's suggestion that a fully secularized liberal society would be in some fundamental sense humanly demeaning or "banalizing." (As we shall see in Part IV of this work, Nietzsche had his own more radicalized version of this same preoccupation.)

Mill, one could say, turns Tocqueville's argument in the opposite direction. Rather than saying that only religion can confer upon human beings an absolutely exalted sense of purpose ("greatness of soul"), let us say instead that anything that does in fact confer this exalted sense of purpose, gives individuals greatness of soul, we shall *call* a religion. By this trick of redefinition, Mill disarms Tocqueville's colossal challenge to the existential adequacy of a modern, liberal, skeptical, mass-democratic civilization. If only religion redeems the banality of a modern civilization and elevates it to the plane of grand questions of higher destiny, then let us think of the highest moral and social purposes available to us within the horizon of what is strictly human, strictly this worldly, and call that a religion.

[9] "Theism," p. 242.
[10] Ibid., p. 245.
[11] Cf. p. 250, where he speaks of "the loftier aspirations."
[12] Ibid., p. 244.

It would be difficult to regard Mill's Religion of Humanity as a civil religion.[13] Mill himself insists that it is "entitled to be called a religion"[14] – it is "a real religion"[15] – but his argument is far from fully persuasive. Mill's new religion (contrasted comprehensively with "the old religions")[16] shares virtually nothing with the historical world religions. Everything "supernatural," to use Mill's all-encompassing term, has been banished. There is no God who issues transcendent commands. There is no otherworldly vocation for human beings; our only ultimate vocation is to make the world more habitable and more geared to a comfortable and happy existence for sentient creatures like ourselves. Mill's Religion of Humanity leaves us with very little sense of "createdness" – of being in the care of benevolent higher powers. What remain as the only objects of faith are the ever-accumulating powers (including moral powers) of our own species. It is a faith in progress, in science, and in the eventual goodness of our moral nature. Ultimately, it is a faith in liberalism. Nature is not providential.[17] There is no loving God or gods who make special provisions for the needs of their creatures, or take an interest in their welfare.[18]

---

[13] In an important sense, the fact that Mill is not a civil-religion theorist is already implicit in Mill's privileging of natural religion over supernatural religion throughout the three essays on religion. Consider what Eldon Eisenach writes concerning Hobbes: "Hobbes denies all efficacy in the world to a religion based on what unaided reason can tell us [viz., natural religion]. As Hobbes makes plain, even as early as chapters 11 and 12 [of *Leviathan*], no civil or moral philosophy in the past has made its way in the world without the aid of supernatural gods, real or imagined; in all of man's past, prophets and not philosophers have given intellectual birth to the opinions creating power among men." Eldon J. Eisenach, *Two Worlds of Liberalism: Religion and Politics in Hobbes, Locke, and Mill* (Chicago: University of Chicago Press, 1981), p. 14. This explains why Hobbes is a civil-religion theorist and Mill is not.

[14] "Utility of Religion," p. 110.

[15] Ibid., p. 109; cf. "Theism," pp. 255–256, where Mill discusses "that real, though purely human religion, which . . . calls itself the Religion of Humanity."

[16] See, e.g., "Utility of Religion," pp. 89, 111.

[17] The whole of the essay on "Nature" is devoted to developing this argument. In his concluding paragraph he writes that the "scheme of Nature regarded in its whole extent, cannot have had, for its sole or even principal object, the good of human or other sentient beings" (p. 65). For the same argument in "Utility of Religion," see esp. *Three Essays on Religion*, p. 112: "[I]t is impossible that any one who habitually thinks, and who is unable to blunt his inquiring intellect by sophistry, should be able without misgiving to go on ascribing absolute perfection to the author and ruler of so clumsily made and capriciously governed a creation as this planet and the life of its inhabitants. . . . [B]lind partiality, atrocious cruelty, and reckless injustice . . . all . . . abound to excess in the commonest phenomena of Nature." However, as suggested in the next note, this hard-line antiprovidentialist doctrine gets quite significantly relaxed in the essay on "Theism."

[18] However, Mill makes significantly greater allowance for a more providentialist conception of God in the "Theism" essay. The idea in "Theism" is that it is reasonable to postulate an Intelligent Mind who *would* promote the welfare of His creatures *if* He had the powers sufficient to do so; alas, His powers do not quite rise to this level. See, for instance, "Theism," p. 243: Given what we are able to deduce about this postulated deity (especially with respect to limits on his omnipotence), the present order of the universe reflects a Creator "whose love for his creatures was not his sole actuating inducement, but who nevertheless desired their good"; "it

Nature in some respects provides impressively for the beings encompassed by its laws, but there are unlimited respects in which it is a scene of horror and catastrophe. Animals prey on each other, and most of them (including humans) die horrendous deaths.[19] Nature crashes down on them with floods, plagues, and earthquakes, destroying the virtuous and vicious alike.[20] There is certainly no just and omnipotent God, for an omnipotent God would have created a less cruel universe.[21] To understand and master our circumstances, we rely on natural science and nothing else. We use natural science to "amend" nature so it

remains a simple possibility, which those may dwell on to whom it yields comfort to suppose that blessings which ordinary human power is inadequate to attain, may come...from the bounty of an intelligence beyond the human, and which continuously cares for man." Mill does not exactly affirm a faith of this kind in his own name (that is, faith in a less-than-omnipotent but caring God), but he certainly legitimizes such a quasi-providentialist faith from the standpoint of agnostic reason. On pp. 247–248 of the "Theism" essay, Mill offers some account (albeit implicit) of why there is such a striking discrepancy between that essay and the emphatic antiprovidentialism expressed in the "Nature" essay. (Cf. John Morley, *Nineteenth Century Essays*, ed. Peter Stansky, Chicago: University of Chicago Press, 1970, pp. 214–215: Mill's project to uncover evidence for "a partial measure of Benevolence" on the part of the deity has the result that "most of the tremendous indictment against Nature [in] the first essay, must assuredly be considered as cancelled and abandoned.") Mill writes, "[t]o what purpose, indeed, should we feed our imagination with the unlovely aspect of persons and things?" (p. 247). If we focus on "degrading instead of elevating associations," then the "imagination and feelings become tuned to a lower pitch" (p. 248). Knowing that we must die does not require "that we should be always brooding over death" (p. 247). We have to ensure that "the poetry is [not] taken out of the things fullest of it" (p. 248). Implicit in all of this is the suggestion that dwelling on a mercilessly cold-eyed view of nature will leave human beings utterly dispirited and despairing. The antidote is to prop up human hopes – including, if necessary to achieve the intended purpose, theistic hopes. (One sees a clear parallel here with Kant: One should allow intellectual space for theism not because one *knows* that theism is true, but because without it, the hopes that moral life requires may be hard to sustain.) As I will discuss in the next chapter in the context of John Morley's critique of Mill, conventional believers would not be wrong to welcome this qualified green light to providentialism as a net gain.

19 Cf. David Hume, "Dialogues Concerning Natural Religion" (in *Writings on Religion*, ed. Anthony Flew, La Salle, IL: Open Court, 1992, p. 257): "The whole earth, believe me, PHILO, is cursed and polluted. A perpetual war is kindled amongst all living creatures [cf. p. 274].... Weakness, impotence, distress, attend each stage of [human] life: and 'tis at last finished in agony and horror." There are similar reflections in the seventh dialogue of Maistre's *St. Petersburg Dialogues*, but for Maistre this is somehow consistent with a providentialist view of the world, whereas for Hume and Mill it stands as the refutation of all providentialism. Compare also J. M. Coetzee, *Slow Man* (London: Secker & Warburg, 2005), pp. 96–97: "This tranquil-seeming world we inhabit contains horrors, Paul, such as you could not dream up for yourself in a month of Sundays. The ocean depths, for instance, the floor of the sea – what goes on there exceeds all imagining."

20 Cf. Voltaire's challenge to Rousseau's providentialism referred to in Chapter 17, note 17.

21 Cf. Hume, "Dialogues Concerning Natural Religion" (ed. Flew), pp. 261–262, 264–265. Cleanthes, in the "Dialogues," eventually concedes the nonomnipotence of God (p. 266), but this is hardly enough to satisfy Hume in the character of Philo, for Philo argues unflinchingly in Part XI of the "Dialogues" that a world as "botched and bungled" (p. 228) as the one we know reflects only ill will or incompetence in the divine architect.

comes closer to what a just and omnipotent God *would* have created.[22] When atheism is turned into a religion, we can be assured that the Enlightenment trajectory has reached its end point.

But *was* Mill (in the end) an atheist? In his late essay on "Theism" (written at least ten years after the other two essays included in *Three Essays on Religion*), he presents himself as what one might call a "minimalist theist." ("[T]he order of nature affords some evidence of the reality of a Creator, . . . [but] all the evidence of his existence is evidence also that he is not all-powerful."[23]) This yields a rather bizarre discrepancy between the argument of "Utility of Religion" and the argument of "Theism." The purpose of the former is to affirm a "religion" that is resolutely not supernatural. The purpose of the latter is to establish, on the basis of "natural religion" (theological considerations that do not appeal to revelation), the notional plausibility of a "minimalist" conception of God (good, powerful, but not all-beneficent and certainly not omnipotent).[24] Having established (or at least not ruled out) this God grounded on indications "by the phenomena of Nature,"[25] even the God of revealed religion is to some extent vindicated – or at least shown to be less implausible. (Natural religion gives us some reason not to dismiss "the sender of the message," i.e., God as disclosed by revelation, as "a sheer invention."[26]) Thus "supernatural religion" is in that sense put back in contention, although Mill obviously remains highly skeptical of any particular claim offered by any particular revealed religion. Near the end of the "Theism" essay, Mill offers the following summary of his view: "[T]he rational attitude of a thinking mind towards the supernatural, whether in natural or in revealed religion, is that of skepticism as distinguished from belief on the one hand, and from atheism on the other."[27] Unlike the essay on "Utility of Religion," in "Theism" the domain of the supernatural is not dispensed with but rather "removed from the region of Belief into that of simple Hope."[28] The shift in Mill's conception of a Religion of Humanity is made most explicit in the final sentence of "Theism": "[S]upernatural hopes . . . may

---

[22] Cf. Rorty, "Religion in the Public Square," p. 142: "[L]eftist politics – the sort whose sacred texts are *On Liberty* and *Utilitarianism* – is strengthened just insofar as belief in a providential deity who will provide pie in the sky is weakened."

[23] "Theism," p. 240.

[24] The essay on "Nature" offers some anticipations of this doctrine of the limited power of the Creator (*if* there is a Creator). See, for instance, p. 58: "If we are not obliged to believe the animal creation to be the work of a demon, it is because we need not suppose it to have been made by a Being of infinite power"; and p. 65: "Whatsoever, in nature, gives indication of beneficent design, proves this beneficence to be armed only with limited power." Interestingly, James Fitzjames Stephen, on pp. 198–199 of *Liberty, Equality, Fraternity*, takes the opposite tack: God as all-powerful but not necessarily benevolent.

[25] "Theism," p. 213.

[26] Ibid.

[27] Ibid., p. 242.

[28] Ibid., p. 244. John Morley captures this view in a nice (and rather cutting phrase): In Mill's version of rational theism, the cardinal propositions of religion are "reduce[d] from the august rank of certainties to the humbler place of holy possibilities" (*Nineteenth Century Essays*, p. 165). In the same vein, Morley refers to Mill's "twilight hopes and tepid possibilities" (p. 167),

still contribute not a little to give to this religion [the religion of the Future, that is, Religion of Humanity] its due ascendancy over the human mind."[29] In his presentation of the Religion of Humanity in "Utility of Religion," Mill had assumed that human beings are ready for this new religion[30] when they can leave supernatural conceptions behind.

Eldon Eisenach offers an illuminating argument according to which, for Mill no less than for Hobbes and Locke, human beings are not only creatures of reason and interest but also creatures of duty; not only "born for liberty" but also "born for servitude" (that is, "servitude" to sacred texts and a sacred history that are antecedently binding for their adherents). In other words, to use terms later introduced by Michael Sandel, liberal political philosophy (contrary to what is usually assumed about it) must address itself not to unencumbered selves but precisely to encumbered selves – and religion is necessarily a key dimension of what keeps these encumbered selves from being unencumbered.[31] But the problem with Eisenach's argument, at least as applied to Mill, is that the rhetoric of Mill's three essays on religion, including "Utility of Religion," is overwhelmingly that of ahistorical reason.[32] What Mill ultimately offers is not any positive account of how religion might serve as the bulwark of a liberal society (à la Tocqueville), but merely Tocquevillean *anxieties* about whether a thoroughgoingly secular liberal society would be able to sustain the highest human purposes – this is so on Eisenach's reading of Mill as well as my own. When Eisenach writes that "a new religion of humanity reintroduces 'traditional stories' and new prophecies to redeem men from spiritual enslavement to a world created in the image of Benthamism,"[33] this is quite misleading. Supernatural elements have been purged from Millian religion, so stories and prophecies are precisely what Mill's Religion of Humanity does *not* offer.

J. S. Mill's political thought is fundamentally synthetic; not unlike Hegel, he takes opposing perspectives and tries to forge them into an encompassing whole. Most explicitly, Mill presents himself as a synthesis of Bentham and

---

and also speaks of "Mr. Mill's creed of low probabilities and faintly cheering potentialities" (p. 168). Morley's formulation on p. 187 is quite a bit sharper: "the virtual elevation of naked and arbitrary possibilities into the place of reasonable probabilities." I will offer more discussion of Morley's critique of Mill in Chapter 22.

[29] "Theism," p. 257. Morley is right that "the third essay, strange to say, is on its most important side a qualified rehabilitation of supernatural hypotheses" (*Nineteenth Century Essays*, p. 201).

[30] Cf. "Theism," p. 255, where he speaks of "purely human religion."

[31] Eisenach's book is cited earlier in note 13.

[32] Cf. Morley, *Nineteenth Century Essays*, p. 169: Mill's "training, which was marked by the characteristic spirit of the eighteenth century, prevented him from putting the history of ideas before an inquiry into the ideas themselves." As Morley rightly emphasizes, Mill "had plenty of that historic sense, which he noticed as deficient in Bentham" (ibid.), but it did not lead to the kind of historicism that would diminish the intellectual priority of the question, Is this true or is it not true? There is, as Morley puts it, "a duty of definite judgment" (p. 170), and this intellectual duty was necessarily privileged by Mill in how he approached the problem of religion.

[33] Eisenach, *Two Worlds of Liberalism*, p. 213.

Coleridge, or Bentham and Comte. I, however, prefer to see Mill's reflection on religion's (dispensable–indispensable) role in human life as a cross between Hume and Tocqueville. The Humean side of Mill sees religion as a residue of superstition that must finally be displaced by a more scientific view of the world. The Tocquevillean side of Mill worries that a view of the world robustly purged of religion will also entail a shallower and less ennobling experience of life. The Religion of Humanity is Mill's solution to the Hume–Tocqueville conundrum, for it will retain the ennobling function of religion while banishing all supernaturalism. Nonetheless the solution is not so much unstable as useless, for as Hume saw especially clearly, a religion that is appealing to philosophers will for just that reason have no purchase on the sentiments of humanity at large.[34]

[34] Cf. Karl W. Britton, "John Stuart Mill on Christianity," in *James and John Stuart Mill: Papers of the Centenary Conference*, ed. John M. Robson and Michael Laine (Toronto: University of Toronto Press, 1976), p. 33: Mill "lacked the language and lacked the *Spielraum* to give an account of a possible God who would command reverence and love. And for the existence of this possible God there is said to be some but not enough evidence. Could anything be less satisfactory?"

22

Mill's Critics

> When priests, of whatever creed, claim to hold the keys of heaven and hell and to work invisible miracles, it will practically become necessary for many purposes to decide whether they really are the representatives of God upon earth, or whether consciously or not they are impostors, for there is no way of avoiding the question.
>
> – James Fitzjames Stephen[1]

> We are brought back, then, to the question, Are these doctrines true?
>
> – James Fitzjames Stephen[2]

Mill died in 1873; the *Three Essays on Religion* was published the following year. This same period (the end of 1872 to the beginning of 1875) saw the publication, from two opposing sides, of stringent intellectual challenges to Mill's views about religion. It may help to clarify Mill's attempt to fashion a compromise between religion and humanism through a discussion of how Mill's work gets caught in the crossfire between a tough-minded liberal humanist like John Morley and an equally tough-minded political defender of religion like James Fitzjames Stephen.[3]

Let us start with John Morley's sharp and witty commentary on the *Three Essays*.[4] Morley was an intellectual and later a prominent politician who was personally close to Mill, who clearly looked up to Mill as a true exemplar of both intellectual and political life at their best, and who owed his own loss of

---

[1] James Fitzjames Stephen, *Liberty, Equality, Fraternity*, ed. Stuart D. Warner (Indianapolis: Liberty Fund, 1993), p. 41.

[2] Ibid., p. 50.

[3] My interest in John Morley was sparked by Daniel S. Malachuk, *Perfection, the State, and Victorian Liberalism* (New York: Palgrave Macmillan, 2005); see in particular pp. 154–155. I owe my appreciation of the importance of James Fitzjames Stephen to the work of Eldon Eisenach.

[4] John Morley, "Mr. Mill's Three Essays on Religion," in Morley, *Nineteenth Century Essays*, ed. Peter Stansky (Chicago: University of Chicago Press, 1970), pp. 164–223.

faith, apparently, "in part at least [to] having read *On Liberty*."[5] In the light of Morley's self-conception as "a follower" of Mill,[6] there is no question that the essays on religion (especially the third) were a deep disappointment.[7] It would perhaps be overstating the point to say that Morley received the *Three Essays* as an act of intellectual betrayal, but his response to the essays clearly leans in that direction.[8]

Even in his preliminary remarks, it is already clear that Morley cannot help perceiving the book as a case of serious backsliding from Mill's rationalistic agnosticism. Believers "will nourish a certain private thankfulness for the buckler with which Mr. Mill has furnished them against the fiery darts of the dogmatic unbeliever."[9] "Theologians who know their trade . . . will certainly be able to construct a far more respectable kind of defence than they had any reason to hope, out of Mr. Mill's concluding admissions."[10] Mill's scruples about not going too far in ruling out the possibility of a rational theism open the door to "positions which are not at all unlikely to be the springs of a new and mischievous reaction towards supernaturalism."[11] "I for one cannot help regarding the most remarkable part of the book as an aberration not less grave than the aberrations with which he rightly charged Comte."[12] And, most damningly, this: Believers "will [gleefully] contrast the iron unfaith of James Mill . . . with the eagerness of his son and most important disciple to restore the domain of the supernatural."[13] Crucially, Mill concedes that the existence of a caring even if not omnipotent Creator-God is a real possibility, from which it follows that those who seek consolation and validation of their worldly purposes from such a God have not sinned against secular rationality, which provides for a legitimate claim to their beliefs. Admittedly, this demotes tenets of faith from matters of assured conviction to mere articles of hope, but this is enough to put the supernaturalist enterprise back in business. Whether

---

5 "Editor's Introduction," in *Nineteenth Century Essays*, ed. Stansky, p. xiii. Stansky points out that the year in which Morley parted company with Christianity – 1859 – was (not coincidentally) the same year in which *On Liberty* was published.

6 Morley, p. 188. Stephen, too, characterizes himself as a disciple of Mill "up to a certain point": See Stephen, *Liberty, Equality, Fraternity*, p. 4, as well as Warner's Foreword, pp. xxi–xxii. Nonetheless, the rhetoric of *Liberty, Equality, Fraternity* is that of a full-blown opponent, not that of a disappointed follower.

7 One has to be impressed with the delicacy with which Morley phrases this disappointment: "To us both the conclusions at which Mr. Mill arrives, and . . . the spirit of the conclusions, are a rather keen surprise" (Morley, p. 187).

8 Malachuk's formulation is that Morley thought that Mill's idea of meeting the theists halfway would "backfire" because it would be received as a sign of a loss of nerve on the progressivist side, and therefore would simply boost the morale of social and religious conservatives (*Perfection, the State, and Victorian Liberalism*, p. 155). Stansky's formulation is that Morley saw the *Three Essays* as a "soft-minded" cave-in to Christianity ("Editor's Introduction," p. xvi).

9 Morley, p. 167.

10 Ibid., p. 165.

11 Ibid., p. 168.

12 Ibid.

13 Ibid., p. 167.

consciously or not, Mill has thereby, according to Morley's judgment, foolishly handed the keys to the fortress of agnostic rationalism to the enemy.

Morley is fully in sympathy with the purpose of the "Nature" essay, and it is hardly surprising that he offers no real criticisms of it.[14] The central issue in "Utility of Religion" is the Baylean one of whether morality can be disassociated from religion. Morley acknowledges that there are intelligible historical reasons why European intellectuals have worried about the stability of morality that jettisons its religious foundations. He cites the experience of the French Revolution, which aroused "apprehension of the social perilousness of truth" (assuming truth to be aligned with the eclipse of religious belief). Burke and Maistre, it is implied, were not unique in their anxiety that "disclosure of the truth [again assuming that truth equals disbelief] will inflict irreparable moral injury both on human nature and on organized society."[15] Morley, like Mill, presumes that there is a process of moral evolution that entrenches the habits of morality in ways that render morality increasingly less dependent on religious conditioning and religious sanctions.[16] However, even assuming that there are real advantages for moral life accruing from a commitment to various forms of religious belief, Mill raises the issue of whether "these benefits of religion may be attained without traveling beyond the boundaries of human existence."[17] Here, of course, is where the Religion of Humanity gets put on the Millian agenda, and Morley poses good challenges on this score. He confesses himself to be "unable to derive . . . a clear and firm idea of what [Mill] took to be the essence of religion."[18] "Mr. Mill considers religion to be the expression of the same cravings as those which inspire Poetry: the cravings for 'ideal conceptions grander and more beautiful than we see realized in the prose of human life.'"[19] A Religion of Humanity, if we could be motivated to embrace it, would supply "a poetry . . . equally fitted to exalt the feelings and still better calculated to ennoble the conduct."[20]

Are we then given to understand that there is nothing that marks religion as a distinctive apprehension of life beyond its capacity to spawn an uplifting poetry of moral experience? Can one speak of a rigorously this-worldly religion, or

---

[14] The only "criticism" that Morley pursues is that the essay on "Nature" offers no response to the challenges arising from Darwinism to Mill's vision of morality and society. Given the date of composition of Mill's essay, however, this is not a real criticism. Morley returns on pp. 216–217 to the issue of how Darwinian theory transforms our views about nature, and in particular whether Mill's speculations about intelligent design in "Theism" can survive validation of that theory; cf. p. 218. For Mill's own acknowledgment that his arguments in "Theism" might not survive eventual validation of Darwinist theory, see *Three Essays*, p. 174.

[15] Morley, p. 188. Morley cites James Fitzjames Stephen as one of "those who urge that by tampering with religion you are knocking away the only props of the morality that was first practiced in association with it" (p. 194).

[16] Ibid., pp. 193–194.

[17] Ibid., p. 194.

[18] Ibid., p. 195.

[19] Ibid., p. 195, quoting *Three Essays*, p. 103.

[20] Morley, p. 195, quoting (with minor editing) *Three Essays*, p. 105.

is it the case that a notion like this cannot help but be oxymoronic? Morley rightly presses these questions and concludes that Mill's Religion of Humanity "cannot be regarded as more than a highly poetized morality."[21] Assimilating religion to poetry allows Mill to fudge the all-important question of whether there is a defining aspect of religion per se that cannot be fully cashed out in terms of its relevance for moral life.[22] Morley nicely traces the inconsistencies in Mill's account with respect to whether the essence of religion is or is not defined by what lies "beyond the boundaries of human existence." Contrary to what Mill suggests, "morality is not of the essence of religion; is not its vital or constitutive element; does not give the secret of its deep attachments in the human heart.... [Religion] is at its root wholly unconnected with principles of conduct."[23] Mill's determination to view religion strictly from the perspective of the moralist thereby skews his perception of the meaning and human appeal of religion, and it allows him to pursue the dubious experiment of envisioning nonsupernaturalist versions of religion.

At the end of his account of "Utility of Religion," Morley comes back again to the question of the relationship between truth and utility. Naturally, Mill is generally committed to the view that there is a natural harmony between truth and utility. As Morley highlights with much force, however, Mill goes out of his way to exempt religion from this principle. Religion moves in a zone where "the only truth ascertainable is that nothing can be known"; therefore one does not necessarily gain anything from causing believers to be disabused of trust in religious "guide-marks" that, "though fallacious," may point "more conspicuously and legibly" in the right (moral) direction.[24] The idea here is that what is at stake in the sphere of religion is merely "negative truth" (the debunking of fallacies), not the establishment of "positive truth" (because positive truths of theology are in principle inaccessible). The deeper issue, as Morley sees clearly, is whether Mill's distinction provides a ground for relaxing the link between truth and utility. Morley concedes that a mere withdrawal of trust does not assert a positive truth, but he vigorously contests the suggestion by Mill that there is not something positive at stake in challenging theological fallacies: "To become 'disabused of our trust in some former guide-mark' is the first condition of curiosity and energy in seeking guide-marks which shall be more worthy of trust."[25]

Morley finds it "truly remarkable" that a committed rationalist like Mill would be prepared to grant that a religion "may be morally useful without being intellectually sustainable."[26] Even though Mill himself favors a non-supernatural form of "religion" over the standard supernaturalist versions, he

---

[21] Morley, p. 196.
[22] Ibid.
[23] Ibid., p. 197.
[24] Ibid., p. 198, quoting *Three Essays*, p. 73.
[25] Ibid.
[26] Morley, p. 199, quoting *Three Essays*, pp. 73–74.

is willing to "go easy" on religion with respect to its intellectual foundations provided it can offer assistance to the moral life. In response, Morley lets fly a whole volley of tough challenges. Let us suppose Mill is right that religion sometimes promotes "charity, humility, brotherly love"; but what if it secures these moral benefits by relying on motives that are in various ways "debilitating, retarding, distorting"?[27] Is there an overall gain in utility if morality is bolstered at the price of "weakening rational habits of thinking"?[28] Mill's tolerance for supernatural beliefs provided they contribute to moral utility only makes sense if critics of religion are wrong in attributing to religion "the effect of enervating the reasoning faculties, of engendering vicious habits of spiritual self-indulgence, of encouraging intellectual and moral [sophistry]."[29] If morality draws support from dubious theological beliefs, "in proportion as the theological beliefs become untenable, there is a risk of the useful truth being involved in the same ruin."[30] Above all, morality is owed "the strong defence of reality instead of the weak defense of superstition."[31] In short, Morley is more firmly committed than Mill is to the maxim cited from Iris Murdoch's *The Bell* in Chapter 18: "No good comes in the end of untrue beliefs."[32]

Although Morley is somewhat perturbed by the concessions to religion in the second of the three essays, he clearly sees the third essay as a much more radical cave-in. Morley calls Mill's account a "remarkable scheme of probabilities and potentialities"; admittedly, he says it constitutes only "a very modest and unsubstantial fabric," but even as such, he says it supplies principles "capable of supporting much more elaborate structures."[33] As we have already seen, herein lies the source of what Morley previously described as the "private thankfulness" that believers should rightfully nourish toward Mill.[34] In his discussion of the "Theism" essay, Morley zeroes in on three key articles of Christian faith that are readmitted as credible possibilities by Mill. First, as we saw at the end of Chapter 21, the notion of a caring (albeit not omnipotent)

---

[27] Morley, p. 199.

[28] Ibid.

[29] Ibid., p. 198.

[30] Ibid., p. 199.

[31] Ibid.

[32] There is a similar line in *The Treatise of the Three Impostors*: "The truth, of whatever nature it may be, can never harm, whereas error, however innocent & even useful it may appear, must necessarily in the long run have most disastrous effects." Abraham Anderson, *The Treatise of the Three Impostors and the Problem of Enlightenment* (Lanham, MD: Rowman & Littlefield, 1997), p. 14. Malachuk claims that the issue between Mill and Morley concerning the social–moral role of religion is a purely "strategic" one (*Perfection, the State, and Victorian Liberalism*, p. 155). However, if I am right that Morley ultimately adheres more radically than Mill does to the idea that *truth* should be the only appropriate consideration, then there is nothing strategic about Morley's approach to the problem of religion.

[33] Morley, pp. 202, 201.

[34] Ibid., p. 167.

Creator-God is back in the picture.[35] Second, we have allowance made for a conception of Christ's mission, not merely as that of a "moral reformer" alongside Socrates and Confucius but one infused with "a special, express and unique commission from God."[36] This in itself would upset the view of nature as a "general system of government" ordered by rationally intelligible processes of "natural development," and thereby resorts back to – or at least reopens the door to – conceptions of miraculous intervention ("a deviation from the general system of the government of the world").[37] This is a line in the sand for Morley, and Mill, even merely countenancing a unique divine mission for Christ as a coherent possibility, has placed himself on the wrong side of this line. "I am unable to conceive how such a person [namely the author of *On the Logic of the Moral Sciences*] can admit the possibility of Christ's mission being special or express, any more readily than the possibility of the sun having stood still at the command of Joshua in the valley of Ajalon."[38] As Morley put it at the outset of his discussion of Mill's third essay, the whole thrust of Mill's account is toward "a qualified rehabilitation of supernatural hypotheses,"[39] which has the unavoidable effect of voiding Mill's whole enterprise of resting the understanding of nature and history on firmly naturalist foundations.

In any case, "Theism"'s presentation of the morality of the Gospels as an unsurpassable morality[40] entails a significant modification of Mill's own views and prompts Mill to exaggerate the perfection of Christ's own moral exemplarity (Morley speaks of Mill's "excessive panegyric" to the life of Christ).[41] As Morley is keen to remind readers of the *Three Essays*, insofar as "even the Christ of the Gospels holds out the promise of reward from heaven as a primary inducement to" morality, Mill had been committed to the view that Christian morality evidences "a radical inferiority... compared with the Religion of Humanity."[42] The point here is that the Religion of Humanity was intended by Mill to improve upon existing religions by purging the latter of

---

[35] Ibid., pp. 201–202. As Morley points out, this is not really a Creator-God but rather a "Demiurgic" God: p. 212. Cf. the passage from p. 191 of *Three Essays* quoted in Morley, p. 215, where Mill refers to his hypothetical deity as "a contriver" rather than a "Creator."

[36] Morley, p. 203; p. 202, quoting *Three Essays*, p. 255.

[37] Morley, p. 203, quoting *Three Essays*, p. 236.

[38] Morley, p. 204.

[39] Ibid., p. 201.

[40] Cf. Mill's account of Christianity as a religion "of the progressive portion of mankind," as opposed to, for instance, Islam and Hinduism as religions "of the stationary portions," in Mill, "The Subjection of Women," in *Essays on Sex Equality*, ed. Alice S. Rossi (Chicago: University of Chicago Press, 1970), pp. 176–177. Nonetheless, Morley's point is that, however Christianity fares morally in relation to other historical religions, Mill's view in "Utility of Religion" was that one ought to conceive a *humanist* religion that in various ways would be morally superior to Christianity.

[41] Morley, p. 207.

[42] Ibid., pp. 208–209; *Three Essays*, p. 111. This echoes an important theme in my discussion of Spinoza given earlier in Chapters 9–11.

supernatural supports[43]; by backtracking to the position that Christianity is morally unsurpassable, Mill simultaneously relinquishes the ambition to envision a religion substitute that would be both cognitively *and morally* superior to the historical religions. The third article of faith to which Mill gives renewed encouragement is the doctrine of the immortality of the soul, and Morley has no problem in showing that Mill's questioning of "the relation of thought to a material brain" flies in the face of everything that modern science has to teach about "the relations between soul and body."[44]

Morley's view is that something has clearly gone seriously awry with Mill's whole intellectual project if he finds himself drawn into the business of providing a theodicy.[45] Nevertheless, there is a broader objection to the kind of quasi-theologizing unfolded in the "Theism" essay. Ultimately, Morley's critique comes to this: For Mill to enter into the enterprise of weighing more plausible or less plausible theological "hypotheses" is to muddle up the distinction between science and what is in principle incapable of being submitted to the disciplines of scientific judgment. Can one apply hypotheses to theology in the way that one can in the realm of science – weighing up "evidence" that supports or challenges this or that hypothesis? What Morley had expected of Mill was "a warning to people to remember how arbitrary all such hypotheses must be, and a clear-voiced counsel to abandon them."[46] Treating theology as if it were amenable to the procedures of science necessarily draws one back into the swamp of asserting a kind of pseudo-knowledge regarding the ultimate origins of the universe – something that is in principle unknowable ("each of these hypotheses is as arbitrary as the rest").[47] That is, by trying to locate a sphere of rational inquiry where theology and science can speak to each other, Mill

[43] Cf. Allan D. Megill, "J. S. Mill's Religion of Humanity and the Second Justification for the Writing of *On Liberty*," in *Mill and the Moral Character of Liberalism*, ed. Eldon J. Eisenach (University Park: Pennsylvania State University Press, 1998), pp. 304–305 and 308.

[44] Morley, pp. 220–222. As Morley puts it, if it were reasonable to detach thoughts and feelings from a cerebral organ, one would be on the road to a situation in which "all human knowledge" would be just as easily "nullified" (p. 222).

[45] Consider the statement Morley cites from Book 2 of Plato's *Republic*: "[F]ar fewer are the goods of human life than its evils" (p. 211). This is one version of the familiar problem of evil, and the only way to salvage God's benevolence in the face of this problem is to place constraints on His power (which shows that Mill is exerting himself intellectually precisely on behalf of the needs of theodicy). However, Morley complains, for Mill (unlike conventional believers or real theologians) to gear his argument toward such considerations of theodicy is to bow to "a sentiment which is out of place in an inquiry that pretends to be scientific" (p. 212). On pp. 215–216, Morley does a good job of highlighting the stark contradictions between the forceful antiprovidentialism of the "Nature" essay and the hypothetical providentialism of the "Theism" essay. Morley's verdict concerning the latter is well captured in his response to Mill's suggestion that "pleasure is agreeable to the Creator," who tolerates pain only when it is impossible to contrive otherwise (p. 215, quoting *Three Essays*, p. 191); this construction, Morley concludes, "is tainted with arbitrariness and anthropomorphism from beginning to end" (Morley, p. 216).

[46] Morley, p. 213.

[47] Ibid.

has merely given rise to a kind of pseudo-science (approximating that of the cosmological speculations of the pre-Socratic philosophers).[48] Mill's project, like Kant's, is to reorient theology from "Belief" to "Hope,"[49] conceiving that he can exploit religious resources to bolster the sense of high purpose needed to sustain very high moral ideals; but Morley makes an effective case that in offering merely "a very modest and unsubstantial fabric" of hypotheses and speculations, what Mill actually does is to compromise the integrity of his commitment to science, without necessarily doing much for morality. What Mill offers in his *Three Essays on Religion*, and especially in his "Theism" essay, is clearly a compromise position. One can say that the primary thrust of Morley's challenge is to argue that the problem of religion and secular culture really does not admit of compromise: One cannot split the difference between theism and humanism and hope that that will yield something coherent.

We encounter a diametrically opposite set of challenges to Mill in James Fitzjames Stephen's conservative classic, *Liberty, Equality, Fraternity*.[50] For Stephen, the problem is not Mill's loss of nerve in standing up for his secularism-promoting liberalism; the problem is the liberalism itself. In Stephen's view, a liberalism like Mill's seeks to excise religion from its necessary place in a well-governed social order. It is doubtful that one can address this problem, as Stephen depicts it, without thereby raising deep challenges to liberalism per se.

Stephen begins the book with a striking anticipation of the Religion of Humanity idea that was soon to be published in the *Three Essays*. The slogan "Liberty, Equality, Fraternity," Stephen says, encapsulates a secular religion ("it is the creed of a religion") that partly absorbs Christianity, partly replaces it, and is partly at war with it. Stephen's great fear is that it will entail the ultimate transformation of Christianity "into a system of optimism."[51] He in fact calls this a "Religion of Humanity,"[52] directly anticipating Mill's idea, and

---

[48] Ibid., p. 214.

[49] Mill, *Three Essays*, p. 244; cf. Morley, p. 205. Karl W. Britton offers a reasonable challenge to Mill's attempt to sever hope from belief: "How . . . can we hope for something that altogether transcends experience, unless we have some beliefs that altogether transcend experience?" For instance, to say that one has insufficient grounds for believing in an afterlife, but that one nonetheless hopes for one, hardly seems a credible basis for a religion, or even a religion substitute. See Britton, "John Stuart Mill on Christianity," in *James and John Stuart Mill: Papers of the Centenary Conference*, ed. John M. Robson and Michael Laine (Toronto: University of Toronto Press, 1976), pp. 32–34.

[50] Morley is also a key interlocutor in the second edition of Stephen's book, for Stephen repeatedly responds to defenses of Mill offered in Morley's essay, "Mr. Mill's Doctrine of Liberty" (also reprinted in *Nineteenth Century Essays*). For helpful discussions of how Stephen relates to later conservative critics of Mill, see Megill, "J. S. Mill's Religion of Humanity," pp. 313–315; and Richard Vernon, *Friends, Citizens, Strangers: Essays on Where We Belong* (Toronto: University of Toronto Press, 2005), pp. 144–145. For an interesting account of parallels between the Mill–Stephen debate and the Locke–Proast debate two centuries earlier, see Richard Vernon, *The Career of Toleration* (Montreal: McGill-Queen's University Press, 1997), chapter 5.

[51] Stephen, p. 3.

[52] Stephen defines this Religion of Humanity as the view "that the human race collectively has before it splendid destinies of various kinds, and that the road to them is to be found in the

if he had had access to the *Three Essays* when he wrote these lines, there is no doubt whatsoever that he would condemn the essays for promoting precisely the dilution and effeminization of Christian doctrine to which Mill was in fact (from Stephen's point of view) committed. What is the more muscular version of Christianity that Stephen opposes to this progressivist creed?

Right from the start, Stephen associates the kind of religion of which he approves with the coercive sanctions that he thinks a well-ordered society requires: "[A]ll existing religions in so far as they aim at affecting human conduct [involve] an appeal either to hope or fear, and to fear far more commonly and far more emphatically than to hope."[53] In the first instance, religion is to be thought of as a device for rendering the sanctions of morality far more difficult to shrug off. As we saw earlier, Morley highlights the fact that Mill's Religion of Humanity is intended to be superior to actual religions in its resolute rejection of doctrines of otherworldly punishment. Stephen, by contrast, has no qualms about embracing a doctrine of "fear of punishment in a future state of existence" as religion's first and most essential contribution to morality.[54] Stephen hints[55] that he himself does not believe in this doctrine, or at least considers it open to doubt ("I do not say that this doctrine is true"),[56] but this in no way inhibits his commitment to fear of an afterlife as an essential backstop for moral life. Stephen returns to the issue of otherworldly sanctions in chapter 6 (the chapter devoted to the critique of "the religion of fraternity"[57]). Again, Stephen maintains that religion, especially of the punitive and coercive kind, is

---

removal of all restraints on human conduct, in the recognition of a substantial equality between all human creatures, and in fraternity or general love.... [This,] in the most general terms, is the religion of which I take 'Liberty, Equality, Fraternity' to be the creed" (ibid., pp. 3–4). Cf. p. 5: Mill's doctrine turns liberty into a "religious dogma." See also p. 48, p. 203, and the sarcastic reference on p. 243 to "the beauties of a religion of which this impalpable cloud [namely 'Humanity'] is the God."

53 Ibid., p. 8; cf. p. 47: "[A]ll experience shows that almost all men require at times both the spur of hope and the bridle of fear, and that religious hope and fear are an effective spur and bridle." Mill, as we saw earlier, wanted to retain the "spur" but eliminate the "bridle."

54 Ibid., pp. 8–9. On p. 14 he writes that "power derived from threats as to a future state ... is the commonest and most distinctive form of religious power of which we have practical experience." According to Stephen, "Mr. Mill does not draw [the inference that a doctrine of otherworldly punishment of the sinful is morally unacceptable], but I think his theory involves it" (p. 9). As Morley underscores (see my note 40, this chapter), this implication of Mill's thought is indeed made explicit in the "Utility of Religion" essay.

55 These are hints in the first edition; in the Preface to the second edition, Stephen makes his views fully explicit – see the discussion later in this chapter.

56 Stephen, p. 9; cf. "Whether or not there will ever be a day of judgment is not the question" (ibid.). Consider also the phrase "if they are real" in the penultimate sentence of the top paragraph on p. 71. On p. 193 he refers to "those who believe in a definite literal heaven and hell," implying unmistakably that he does not share these beliefs. At the same time, Stephen strongly questions the viability of doctrines of a noble lie: "A man who wishes to persuade his neighbours [on the basis of lies] must lie to himself in the first instance, or he will not have the heart to go on with his lie" (ibid., p. 50).

57 Ibid., p. 183.

an indispensable pillar of morality.[58] Remove doctrines of otherworldly reward and punishment, and morality will collapse or become severely attenuated. No mere religion of mutual love or of commitment to reciprocal benefit will be able to sustain morality in the way that "the old ones"[59] did.

The second edition of Stephen's book is a running debate not only with John Morley but also with a contemporary Comtean, Frederic Harrison. Harrison labels Stephen's political philosophy "the Religion of Inhumanity" and plays up Stephen's reliance on the terrors of damnation.[60] In the Preface to the second edition, Stephen explicitly acknowledges that he rejects the doctrine of hell ("In fact, I do not hold that doctrine, for I see no sufficient evidence of it")[61] while retaining a more open-ended commitment to a doctrine of the afterlife.[62] Nonetheless, the main purpose of his debate with Harrison is to blast away at what Stephen sees as the wrong-headedly sentimentalized religion substitute associated with the creed of fraternity that Mill and Harrison share.

Stephen's views about religion and morality, as robust as they are, are not free of significant tensions. Stephen's basic view is that we must believe in religion because we must believe in a future state, and we must believe in a future state because morality would not likely survive the extinction of this belief. Hence, "[i]f there is a God, but no future state, God is nothing to us."[63] Stephen insists that it is an utter delusion "[t]o suppose that Christian morals can ever survive the downfall of the great Christian doctrine of a future state of rewards and punishments."[64] All of this would seem necessarily to suggest that he himself is strongly committed to a view of otherworldly rewards and (especially) punishments that would be effective as "a real sanction for morals."[65] But *is* he committed to such a view, and what defines the content of that view? Chapter 6 contains a fairly lengthy disquisition on "the permanent element in men" and "the doctrine of a future state,"[66] but Stephen's reflections on this topic seem far too nebulous to supply the morally required sanctions he is hoping for. Stephen feels strongly that Harrison's critique is grossly unfair to him, but it *does* seem to be the case, as Harrison suggests, that Stephen is trying to appeal to otherworldly rewards and punishments as "a real sanction

[58] Ibid., pp. 175–176.

[59] Ibid., p. 165.

[60] See esp. p. 176, note; p. 193, note; and pp. 235–244.

[61] Ibid., p. 236.

[62] Ibid., p. 238. For a good statement of Stephen's view, see pp. 238–239: "[I]t is natural to suppose that that which survives death will be that which is most permanent in life.... [namely] mind, self-consciousness, conscience or our opinion of ourselves." This means that an afterlife will *not* feature bodily torments or bodily bliss because the "body has been dispersed to the elements." If an afterlife involves torment, it will be limited to torments of conscience.

[63] Ibid., p. 204; cf. p. 194: "Take away the belief in a future state, and belief in God ceases to be of any practical importance."

[64] Ibid., p. 227; cf. p. 241.

[65] Ibid., p. 193.

[66] See ibid., pp. 188ff.

for morals" while remaining "reticent about the form of future torment"[67] –
that is, reticent because he does not actually believe in these doctrines in the
robust but naïve version accepted by those credulous souls for whom they *are*
a real sanction for morals. Virtue has no foundation without a Divine Enforcer
because "Where there is no lawgiver there can be no law; where there is no
law there can be no duty."[68] However, if God's laws are laws insofar as they
are accompanied by direct sanctions, how is Stephen able to reconcile this view
with his concession that he himself rejects "the common doctrines about heaven
and hell"?[69] Harrison seems basically right that Stephen wants to draw from
Christianity the most fearful sanctions of morality that it is capable of supplying
but without a corresponding conviction in the truth of these doctrines. One
could say that the core of Stephen's view is that moral life lacks the resources
within itself to sustain itself: If life is limited to earthly existence, the spurs to
virtue look pitifully weak.[70] One could also say, though, that Stephen holds
this view about morality's need for religion with far more confidence than he
holds the religious dogmas that would actually supply what is needed.[71]

Perhaps a deeper tension pertains to the consistency or lack of consistency
between Stephen's endorsement of Christianity and his ferocious critique of the
creed of fraternity.[72] Stephen has no patience for "humanitarians" like Mill
and Harrison, yet he wants to make Christianity (with *its* teaching of universal
brotherhood) a central pillar of morality. One can ask the following question:
Is not the creed of universal fraternity and love for humanity that Stephen
polemicizes against in chapter 6 in large measure what defines Christianity as
a religion?[73] In fact, Stephen himself poses the relevant challenge: "What is the
relation of all this [viz., the rejection of universal brotherhood] to Christianity?
Has not the humanitarianism of which you think so ill a close connection,

---

[67] Ibid., p. 193, note.

[68] Ibid., p. 194; cf. the very emphatic view at the end of the same paragraph: *No* justification for
the practice of virtue exists "except that God is a legislator and virtue a law in the proper sense
of the word" (meaning, in part, that punishments await those who violate the law).

[69] Ibid., pp. 238, 236.

[70] Ibid., pp. 195–196: "[O]bvious immediate self-interest, in its narrowest shape, is constantly
eating away the edges of morality, and would destroy it if it had not something deeper for its
support." Stephen's formula for the solution to the problem is as follows: "Christianity,... in
relation to morals, is a means whereby morality may be made transcendental."

[71] Chapter 7 of *Liberty, Equality, Fraternity* is a reflection on the necessary lack of certainty
regarding the ultimate questions. Alexander Bain was certainly in the right when he wrote that
Stephen "insists on the vital connexion between a belief in God and in Immortality and our
existing ethical code; yet he himself has endeavoured to show the insufficiency of the evidences of
Christianity, which is our present embodiment of Theism." Bain, *John Stuart Mill: A Criticism*
(London: Longmans, Green, and Co., 1882), p. 112.

[72] Related to this is Harrison's complaint (p. 195, note) that the harsh view of life that Stephen
associates with Christianity is in fact very far removed from anything recognizably Christian.

[73] Arguably, this is implicit in Stephen's allusion on p. 180 to the famous line by Milton: "New
Presbyter is but old Priest writ large." The new "religion of fraternity" to which Stephen is so
hostile is in fact merely a secularized version of Christian ideals. What the new priests preach
is not very different from what the old priests preached.

both historically and theoretically, with the Sermon on the Mount and the Parables?"[74] Because the answer to this question is obviously yes, Stephen, to his credit, makes clear that he would sooner jettison the Sermon on the Mount than drop his objections to the ideal of fraternity:

[I]f Christianity really is what much of the language which we often hear used implies, it is false and mischievous.... When, for instance, we are told that it is dreadful to think that a nation pretending to believe the sermon on the Mount should employ so many millions sterling per annum on military expenditure, the answer is that no sane nation ever did or ever will pretend to believe the Sermon on the Mount in any sense which is inconsistent with the maintenance to the very utmost by force of arms of the national independence, honour, and interest. If the Sermon on the Mount really means to forbid this, it ought to be disregarded.[75]

Stephen is clearly aware that there are aspects of Christianity that lend them-selves to appropriation by contemporary liberal humanitarianism, but he thinks that those aspects must be firmly downplayed and much greater emphasis given to the aspects of religion that have formed the English nation into "an anvil which has worn out a good many hammers."[76] "[T]hough Christian-ity expresses the tender and charitable sentiments with passionate ardour, it has also a terrible side.... [H]ell is an essential part of the whole Christian scheme.... [T]he tenderness and the terrors mutually imply each other."[77] One is tempted to say that this is civil religion with a vengeance.

Contrary to Mill's "liberty as a religious dogma," Stephen's bedrock con-viction is that in order for moral life to be sustained, coercion is required; and religion supplies one of the prime instrumentalities for this moral coercion. Mill clearly wants to bring about a radical rebalancing of the scale between liberty and coercion. Stephen's counterargument is focused on the point that coercion is central, not just to moral life but also to religious life in its rele-vance for moral life. Law without coercion obviously makes no sense – but can there be a morality without coercion? Indeed, can there be a religion without coercion? Stephen argues forcefully that although the modalities of coercion in morals and religion operate very differently than those of a legal system, they too are emphatically geared toward the *enforcement* of specific forms of human conduct: If they restrained behavior only insofar as it threatened harm to others and otherwise gave free rein to human volition, they would fail to ful-fill the purposes we standardly associate with a morality or a religion. ("[B]oth

---

74 Stephen, p. 200.
75 Ibid., pp. 202–203.
76 Ibid., p. 195.
77 Ibid., p. 201; so does one abide the tenderness and charity of Christianity in order to obtain the terrors? On p. 67 Stephen denies that his principles are consistent with Maistreanism (he wants to think of himself as a stern, morally old-fashioned liberal rather than as a Maistrean); but it seems undeniable that Maistre was an important intellectual influence (cf. Warner's note, p. 67, n. 11). See also Richard A. Lebrun, "Joseph de Maistre in the Anglophone World," in *Joseph de Maistre's Life, Thought, and Influence*, ed. Lebrun (Montreal: McGill-Queen's University Press, 2001), pp. 277–278.

religion and morality are and always must be essentially coercive systems."[78])
Stephen says the following in regard to religion: "If Mr. Mill's view of liberty had always been adopted and acted upon to its full extent – if it had
been the view of the first Christians or of the first Mahomedans – everyone
can see that there would have been no such thing as organized Christianity or
Mahommedanism in the world."[79] "[T]he agents by which in fact men have
been improved have been mostly coercive."[80] The question for Stephen is what
it takes for "a vigorous creed"[81] to establish itself; those creeds that are nonvig-
orous obviously make zero impression on human history. "Religions [*including
Christianity*] are not founded on mildness and benevolence" but on terror and
intimidation.[82] "[T]he principle is universally true that the growth of religions
is in the nature of a conquest made by a small number of ardent believers over
the lukewarmness, the indifference, and the conscious ignorance of the mass
of mankind."[83] The capacity of religion to regulate human life is analogous
to the funneling of water through a drainage system: Its fundamental mode
of operation is by restraint, not liberty.[84] The idea that religion would have
any effect upon the lives of human beings without exerting very considerable
pressure on "their principles and even their tastes and feelings"[85] is for Stephen
pure fantasy.

Above all, Stephen does a brilliant job of conveying how remote Mill is in
his own experience of these things from how religious controversies "go to the
very core and root of life."[86] Mill's account of religion illustrates "the manner
in which the most acute intellect may be deceived by generalizing upon its own
peculiar experience."[87] Mill is an intellectual, and therefore he assumes that
all human beings relate to issues of religious commitment as intellectuals do –
by weighing reasons for and against.[88] He assumes that questions of religious

[78] Stephen, p. 13; cf. Vernon, *The Career of Toleration*, p. 95.
[79] Stephen, p. 13.
[80] Ibid., p. 13, note.
[81] Ibid., p. 14.
[82] Ibid., p. 15, note. In this note, Stephen endorses a passage in Gibbon according to which
Christianity succeeded in prevailing over pagan polytheism thanks to its deployment of "the
menace of eternal tortures" (p. 14, note). See also p. 67: Christianity flatters itself as "peculiarly
humane" yet at the same time it "recognizes and *is founded on* hell" (emphasis added). The
discussion on pp. 80–81 implies that no organized religion can hope to establish itself as a
religion without a doctrine of hell. As we saw in Chapter 17, Rousseau, in the important
Poul-Serrho note responding to Bayle, states the same view (notwithstanding all the theological
liberalism in his "Profession of Faith").
[83] Stephen, p. 14.
[84] Ibid., pp. 14–15. Stephen uses similar imagery on pp. 23, 118, and 119.
[85] Ibid., p. 14.
[86] Ibid., p. 54.
[87] Ibid., p. 55.
[88] On p. 22, Stephen puts the question as follows: Do millions of devout Muslims embrace
Mohammed in the same way that individual scholars embrace Adam Smith? Would merely intellectual assent account for the decision to base one's whole existence on worship of Mohammed?

belief acquire their vitality when they are matters of lively intellectual debate and grow stale when they are not being freely debated. However, this intellectualizing account is wholly off the mark: "If the Protestants and Catholics or the Christians and the Pagans had confined themselves to argument, they might have argued forever, and the world at large would not have cared."[89] The real test of religious vitality is not argument but persistence "in the face of the wheel, the stake, and the gallows."[90] Contrary to what Mill imagines, "the discussion became free just in proportion as the subjects discussed lost their interest."[91] If, on one hand, Mill is right that it is possible "to retain the morality which [modern liberals] like, after getting rid of the religion which they disbelieve,"[92] then nothing is lost in conceiving religion merely as a matter of intellectual debate – a matter of mere "curiosity," in Stephen's cutting phrase.[93] If, on the other hand, Stephen is right that the whole of morality and the whole of political order hang on the truth of religious conceptions, then far too much is at stake in the outcome of religious conflicts for it to be cast merely in the image of intellectual contests.[94]

It seems clear that both Morley and Stephen would agree (against Mill) that Mill's synthesis of liberal progressivism and (watered-down) Christianity is a very uneasy synthesis. Both these critics of Mill, from opposing sides, identified intellectual and political perils in the Millian enterprise that arise specifically from trying to put post-Christian or Christian-derived religiosity in the service

---

Cf. *Collected Writings of Rousseau*, Vol. 7, ed. John T. Scott (Lebanon, NH: University Press of New England, 1998), p. 317. See also the following passage from Rousseau's "Moral Letters": "Listen to a mullah speechify in Persia, a bonze in China, a lama in Tartary, a Brahman in the Indies, a Quaker in England, a rabbi in Holland, you will be astonished by the force of persuasion that each of them can give to his absurd doctrine. How many people as sensible as you has each of them convinced? If you hardly deign to listen to them, if you laugh at their vain arguments, if you refuse to believe them, what resists their prejudices in you is not reason, it is your prejudices. Life would have flowed away ten times before one might have discussed a single one of these opinions to the bottom." *Collected Writings of Rousseau*, Vol. 12, ed. Christopher Kelly (Lebanon, NH: University Press of New England, 2006), p. 183.

[89] Stephen, p. 56.
[90] Ibid.
[91] Ibid.
[92] Ibid., p. 48.
[93] Ibid., p. 53.
[94] Indeed, the stakes are so high with respect to the inextricability of religious and political order that Stephen, on the basis of this perspective, even goes so far as to express sympathy for Pontius Pilate's policy of crucifying Christ: The argument is that exercise of the weightiest judicial–political responsibilities does not allow the luxury of tolerating new cults that might upset the existing order. His "defence" of Pilate is developed on pp. 58–64. Stephen does nothing to disguise the fact that his analysis of Pilate and Christ is really a commentary on the challenges faced by the British Empire in maintaining religious and political peace in India. In fact, the stern demands of imperial order in British India are a pervasive theme in the book. Cf. the discussion on p. 28 of how Henry VIII and Elizabeth I had to "muzzle" warring religious disputants, and the parallel discussion of British policy toward Islam and Hinduism in India on pp. 38–39.

of liberal ends.[95] This is not to say that Stephen's particularly harsh version of Christian political theology is necessarily the most persuasive version of Christianity; nor is it to say that all liberals are obliged to be Morley-style agnostics. It does suggest to us, however, that we should not be surprised if Mill's project of drawing believers and unbelievers happily together under the liberal banner turns out to be a trickier enterprise than Mill probably hoped it would be.

---

[95] One can say that *both* critiques come down to the charge of sentimentalization on the part of Mill: Morley charges Mill with sentimentalizing the role of religion in social life, and Stephen charges him with sentimentalizing the character of liberal principles. Although the two critiques move in opposing directions, both critics aim at being more tough-minded thinkers than Mill.

23

John Rawls's Genealogy of Liberalism

[I]n spirit [Rawls's conception of the political offers] a Rousseauian regime of public virtue and of a civil religion with reasonableness as its dogma.

– Sheldon Wolin[1]

[P]ublic reason sees the office of citizen with its duty of civility as analogous to that of judge with its duty of deciding cases. Just as judges are to decide cases by legal grounds of precedent, recognized canons of statutory interpretation, and other relevant grounds, so citizens are to reason by public reason [rather than by invoking their privately-held comprehensive doctrines] and to be guided by the criterion of reciprocity, whenever constitutional essentials and matters of basic justice are at stake.

– John Rawls[2]

[I]t is impossible to avoid commitment in political theory. If we try too hard to be non-sectarian, we will end up saying nothing.

– Jeremy Waldron[3]

Contrary to what is suggested in the first epigraph by Wolin, there is certainly no civil-religion project in John Rawls. There is, however, a project to

---

[1] Sheldon S. Wolin, *Politics and Vision: Continuity and Innovation in Western Political Thought*, Expanded Edition (Princeton, NJ: Princeton University Press, 2004), p. 540; cf. p. 548: "Rawls constructs the equivalent of a civil cult."

[2] John Rawls, "The Idea of Public Reason Revisited," in Rawls, *Collected Papers*, ed. Samuel Freeman (Cambridge, MA: Harvard University Press, 1999), p. 605. It follows from this view of citizenship that when Barack Obama told religious leaders in Iowa in October 2007 that "his commitment to protecting the environment was shaped by his relationship with Jesus Christ" (http://www.thestar.com/article/268433), he was betraying his office as citizen. To be sure, Rawls limits the application of public reason to "constitutional essentials and questions of basic justice," but he does not really spell out how to draw the line between "constitutional essentials" and the rest of politics, nor is it terribly clear how one *could* draw this line. Cf. Mark S. Cladis, "Nothing special about religion": http://www.ssrc.org/blogs/immanent_frame/2008/06/25/nothing-special-about-religion), p. 3.

[3] Jeremy Waldron, *God, Locke, and Equality* (Cambridge: Cambridge University Press, 2002), p. 239.

domesticate religion, and this project is central to the defining purposes of
Rawls's liberalism. Arguably, just as it may be true that John Locke's real greatness as a philosopher of liberalism rests not with his views concerning property
or individual rights but rather with his theoretical response to religion, so the
same may be no less true of John Rawls. The whole intellectual trajectory
sketched in Part II of this book finds its consummation in the Introduction to
Rawls's *Political Liberalism*. Liberalism is really defined by religion, and by
the challenges that illiberal religions pose to a secular civic order (an association of citizens ordered for the sake of citizenship). There is a wide consensus
today that Rawls's political philosophy represents the crowning expression of
the liberal tradition, at least up until the end of the twentieth century. (Who
knows what further articulations of liberalism lie in the future?) It therefore
seems fitting to conclude Part II's survey of liberalism with some reflections
on Rawls's views about citizenship and religion. My response to Wolin is that
Rawls might actually have come up with a more viable account of his philosophy of liberalism if he had allowed himself to articulate *more* of a "civic cult"
in his liberalism than he does. My thesis in this chapter, to put it very briefly,
is that Rawls is so averse to religious theocracies that he goes excessively out
of his way to avoid legislating (what he sees as) a kind of "liberal theocracy" –
and thereby weakens his liberalism.

   Political Liberalism has generated an astonishing set of debates within contemporary liberalism.[4] This is perfectly understandable, for the post-Rawlsian
debates raise issues of profound significance for contemporary society (i.e., the
current situation of radical ethnic, cultural, and religious pluralism). I do not
doubt that the questions raised by Rawls about liberal citizenship and how
it ought to accommodate illiberal forms of religion are entirely worthy of the
attention they have received from political philosophers. However, I do think
there is one striking text in *Political Liberalism* that has received less attention
in the Rawls literature than it merits – namely Rawls's effort to define liberalism, notably in his Introduction,[5] in relation to the Wars of Religion in the
sixteenth and seventeenth centuries. Of course, it is hardly a novel idea to trace
liberalism back to this historical context; on the contrary, it is virtually a cliché
to say that liberalism arose out of the Wars of Religion (which of course does

---

[4] John Rawls, *Political Liberalism* (New York: Columbia University Press, 1996), henceforth cited
as *Political Liberalism*.

[5] *Political Liberalism*, pp. xxiii–xxx. There are also brief discussions in *Political Liberalism*,
pp. 148–149, 159, and 303–304, as well as the important statement on p. 154: "Were justice
as fairness to make an overlapping consensus possible it would *complete and extend* the movement of thought that began three centuries ago with the gradual acceptance of the principle
of toleration and led to the nonconfessional state and equal liberty of conscience" (emphasis
added). See also the posthumously published *Lectures on the History of Political Philosophy*, ed.
Samuel Freeman (Cambridge, MA: Harvard University Press, 2007), p. 11, where Rawls lists the
response to the Reformation and the Wars of Religion it set off as constituting the first of "three
main historical origins" of modern liberalism, the other two being constitutional government
and universal suffrage.

not mean that this isn't true). Thus it is interesting that Rawls chooses to introduce his crowning articulation of his own version of liberalism with a story of this kind. It is especially interesting exactly how Rawls crafts this story – so to speak, how he chooses to flesh out (however compactly or telegraphically) this old cliché or truism. It may even pay dividends for our understanding of the other debates that *Political Liberalism* has aroused.

Are the Wars of Religion still relevant to contemporary liberals? What I propose to do in this discussion of Rawls is to look at his highly compressed account of the genesis of liberalism in the Introduction of *Political Liberalism*, and to explore how this genealogical narrative possibly shapes the larger theoretical agenda in late Rawls – which turns out to be highly problematical (for reasons I will try to explain). Rawls's genealogy of liberalism in the Introduction to *Political Liberalism* is amazingly concentrated, but I think it is of decisive importance for grasping both the nature of the philosophical structure laid out in *Political Liberalism* and its animating principle.

Before turning to Rawls's genealogy, let us briefly sketch Rawls's view that founding the liberal state on "comprehensive doctrines" (including *liberal* comprehensive doctrines) is not just dispensable but illegitimate – which is unquestionably the core idea of *Political Liberalism*. In an important sense, Rawls, in *Political Liberalism*, sets himself apart from the history of liberalism, whereas in *A Theory of Justice* he aligned himself with the history of liberalism (or at least aligned himself with one version of liberalism engendered in that history). To be a liberal, Rawls now insists, it is not necessary to formulate some grand conception of what it is to be human – or what purposes are distinctively human purposes – according to which being a liberal serves the human vocation. Both Kant and J. S. Mill in their different ways embraced this view. This defines their shared commitment to "liberalism as a comprehensive doctrine" – hence Rawls's famous distinction between "comprehensive" versions of liberalism and (merely) "political" versions of liberalism. In Rawls's view (formulated in *Political Liberalism*), not only is it not *necessary* to have a grand view of this kind, but one can in fact be a better liberal by not asserting such a view – because one can display respect for a wider array of fellow citizens.

Nevertheless, there is a deep puzzle about why Rawls is so averse to justifying liberalism by appeal to comprehensive doctrines. His official line is that if the state privileges, for instance, liberal autonomy as a comprehensive view of life, then the state thereby treats unfairly those who do not share this particular view of life. Let us call this "grand liberalism." What Rawls in effect presents as the implicit injustice of requiring grand liberalism for all members of the liberal state prompts him to opt instead for what we can call, by contrast, "modest liberalism." Modest liberalism limits itself to minimum conditions of shared citizenship: a liberalism of (mere) citizenship rather than a liberalism of existential world views.

Here is where the puzzle kicks in. Rawls's later philosophy of liberalism perhaps does not assert individual autonomy as a civically privileged view of life. It does, however, privilege the view that citizenship is important – sufficiently important that religious commitments should not trump a commitment to ecumenical citizenship. In what sense does this privileging of citizenship not entail a view of life?[6] In what sense is a view of life not entailed in the notion that shared multidenominational coexistence should be normatively affirmed and theocracy (or theocratic ambitions) should be normatively repudiated? Indeed, in what sense is there not a (liberal) view of life expressed in the ideal of mutual respect between citizens *qua* citizens? It starts to look as if, in Rawls's modest liberalism, although grand liberalism has been barred from the front door, key aspects of it have been slipped in the back door.[7]

I am already starting to get more drawn into the standard debates about Rawls's formulation of political liberalism than I want to be[8] (though I will come back to some of these challenges later in this chapter), so let me hasten to my discussion of the genealogy. The question raised by the genealogy is whether, in Rawls's view, liberalism is fundamentally an ahistorical system of ideas – a system of ideas that is morally and intellectually compelling because it can be laid out in a way that exhibits its philosophical coherence (which is what is suggested by Rawls's two main works of political philosophy), or whether the compellingness of liberalism follows from our grasp of a particular set of historical experiences; and if the latter, how religion figures in this history. The place where Rawls most directly addresses this question is the Introduction to *Political Liberalism*, and the answer he gives there is far more oriented toward history (verging on a philosophy of history) than his main works of political philosophy would lead one to expect.[9] In what follows, I am especially interested in why Rawls feels impelled to insert a potted history of the genesis of

6 Just to spell it out, my suggestion is that "civicism" rather than individual autonomy is the "comprehensive doctrine" to which Rawls should commit himself to render his liberalism fully coherent. However, it goes without saying that recasting Rawls's liberalism in this way entails a radical attenuation of the firm distinction between civic republicanism and civic humanism that Rawls develops in *Political Liberalism*, pp. 205–206. A further point: Rawls's standard line is that carrying one's comprehensive views into the public realm rather than leaving them at the doorstop undermines civic unity. However, if the comprehensive view that one is carrying into the public realm is a commitment to shared civic life, then it makes no sense to say that *this* comprehensive doctrine is a solvent of civic unity.

7 At the end of Rawls's genealogy (*Political Liberalism*, p. xxx), he writes this: "The general problems of moral philosophy are not the concern of political liberalism, *except insofar as they affect how the background culture and its comprehensive doctrines tend to support a constitutional regime*" (emphasis added). This seems precisely an invitation to sweep "grand liberalism" in through the back door.

8 Patrick Neal, "Is Political Liberalism Hostile to Religion?," in *Reflections on Rawls*, ed. Shaun P. Young (Farnham, UK: Ashgate, 2009), pp. 153–175, offers a very helpful summing-up of these "standard debates" insofar as they bear on religion. Neal makes a persuasive case that at the end of the day, Rawls's civic exclusion of religionists is nowhere near robust enough to have justified the kind of fuss it provoked among his critics. However, then one can ask this: If Rawls is willing *in practice* to allow considerable latitude for the expression of religious comprehensive doctrines in political debate, what was the point of making such a big issue of the need to subordinate comprehensive doctrines to public reason?

9 Putting the point in this way suggests that the Introduction to *Political Liberalism* is *external* to *Political Liberalism* rather than a stage-setting aspect of the argument of *Political Liberalism*.

liberalism, and in how this genealogical story possibly skews core conceptions in Rawls's fully developed account of his liberalism.

Rawls introduces the genealogy by claiming that his conception of political liberalism is not a philosophical invention but rather the theoretical expression of the specificity of modern democratic political culture as shaped by the unfolding of a particular history – a history that opens up a decisive chasm between ancients and moderns. Rawls emphasizes that his own version of the narrative has only the status of a "conjecture" (*Political Liberalism*, p. xxiii), but he clearly believes that some such account shapes the agenda of modern politics in a crucial way. What is Rawls's genealogical story? The story begins with the ancient Greeks. He claims that the Greeks offered the true model of a "civic religion" – a religion centered on integration into the basic practices of the society and performance of central civic duties rather than doctrinal commitment or adherence to the precepts of a sacred text. It did not dispense salvation presided over by a class of priests but rather told citizens how to be citizens.[10] Insofar as the world of the Greeks expressed a conception of the highest good identified with "success and honor, power and wealth, social standing and prestige" (*Political Liberalism*, p. xxiv), Homeric religion did not challenge the supremacy of these ideals but instead reinforced them: The Homeric gods basically replicated this conception of the highest good for human beings, albeit embodied in immortal rather than mortal beings. Thus the challenge to this vision of life (expressing the ethic of an ancient warrior class) came not from religion but from Socratic and post-Socratic moral philosophy (*Political Liberalism*, pp. xxiii–xxiv). Rawls conceives the Socratic tradition not as *challenging* the reigning civic religion but simply addressing a different set of questions than the civic religion sought to address, and appealing more directly to reason in attempting to address that different set of questions.[11]

Rawls then very quickly leaps ahead to modernity, focusing on three key developments: the Reformation, the consolidation of a centralized state, and the emergence of modern science. Of these three key developments, the one that clearly interests Rawls the most is the Reformation, both with respect to how it transformed medieval Christianity and with respect to how it served as the ultimate source of the astounding religious, cultural, and social pluralism in the post-eighteenth-century world. What is laid out in Rawls's genealogy is therefore not a two-stage history (ancients and moderns) but really a three-stage history (civic religion, pre-Reformation Christianity, and the post-Reformation

---

I realize that this is a bit paradoxical, but I think the point I am making is nonetheless clear enough.

10 For some sharp criticisms of Rawls's account of Greek religion, see Daniel A. Dombrowski, *Rawls and Religion: The Case for Political Liberalism* (Albany, NY: SUNY Press, 2001), pp. 3–4. The thesis of Dombrowski's book is that the engagement with religion is not unique to *Political Liberalism* but rather extends through the entirety of Rawls's oeuvre, to an extent insufficiently appreciated in the Rawls literature.

11 The explicit challenges to Homer posed by Plato in *The Republic* force one to ask whether there was not more direct rivalry between the Homeric and Socratic traditions than Rawls suggests.

situation, including liberalism as a response to the warfare between Stage 2 and Stage 3). How does Stage 2 relate to Stage 1? Rawls articulates a number of important differences: Medieval Christianity is authoritarian in a way that Greek civic religion was not; it offers a "religion of salvation," promising eternal life for those who are saved; it is a doctrinal religion, requiring embrace of a specific compulsory creed; it is, as Hobbes and Rousseau highlighted, "a religion of priests"; and it is, finally and crucially, an imperialist religion making universal claims that far exceed those asserted by the civic religion of particular ancient city-states (*Political Liberalism*, p. xxv). These various aspects of medieval Christianity form an integrated package, and although Rawls does not cite Rousseau, all of these features of Christianity figure prominently in Rousseau's analysis in his civil-religion chapter. However, what crucially defines the Reformation's relationship to this hegemonic religion is that it emphatically did not dissolve these authoritarian, illiberal, and imperialist features of its civilizational predecessor. On the contrary, Reformation religion spawned a kind of *replicant twin* of medieval Christianity: equally dogmatic, equally intolerant (*Political Liberalism*, p. xxv).[12] With these two salvationist, doctrinal, and imperialist religions confronting each other, it is no surprise that the result was centuries of horrific religious warfare.[13]

The Reformation did not just confront a dogmatic and intolerant authoritarian church with a set of dogmatic and intolerant sects; it also gave rise to a tremendous pluralism of worldviews that eventually set the stage for political liberalism as the object of an overlapping consensus among those worldviews

---

[12] For another important discussion of the theme of how medieval Catholicism and Reformation Protestantism mirror each other with respect to religious intolerance, see Rawls, *A Theory of Justice* (Oxford: Oxford University Press, 1973), pp. 215–216. See also Rawls, "The Idea of Public Reason Revisited," p. 603, n. 75: "A persecuting zeal has been the great curse of the Christian religion. It was shared by Luther and Calvin and the Protestant Reformers, and it was not radically changed in the Catholic Church until Vatican II." Cf. Kant's notion of "arch-catholic protestants": Immanuel Kant, *Religion within the Boundaries of Mere Reason*, ed. Allen Wood and George di Giovanni (Cambridge: Cambridge University Press, 1998), p. 117, as well as Thomas Paine's skepticism that the Reformation represented a significant improvement on Catholic Christianity (*The Age of Reason*, ed. M. D. Conway, Mineola, NY: Dover, 2004, p. 62). Gibbon offers a very nice encapsulation of the affinities between Catholic zeal and Protestant zeal: "The nature of the tyger was the same"; Edward Gibbon, *The History of the Decline and Fall of the Roman Empire*, ed. David Womersley (London: Allen Lane, 1994), Vol. 3, p. 438. On the issue of whether Protestant theology was less despotic than Catholic theology, Gibbon comments, quite cuttingly, that "many a sober Christian would rather admit that a wafer is God, than that God is a cruel and capricious tyrant" (p. 437).

[13] *Political Liberalism*, pp. xxvii–xxviii: "[T]he clash between salvationist, creedal, and expansionist religions . . . introduces into people's conceptions of their good a transcendent element not admitting of compromise. . . . Political liberalism starts by taking to heart the absolute depth of that irreconcilable latent conflict." That is, if one had been insistent on adjudicating this war of worldviews on the plane of conceptions of the good, the Wars of Religion would have lasted forever. Liberal societies succeeded in extricating themselves from this mess by starting to articulate an independent conception of *political* justice (or civic justice) that abstracted from these warring conceptions of the good.

that met the standard of reasonableness. Although it was far from what was intended by Luther and Calvin (who remained entirely oriented toward the notion of a unique and binding theological truth), the ultimate consequence of the Reformation was the possibility of pluralism – a pluralism only possible on the basis of "the division of Christendom" – which in turn allowed for religious liberty.[14] Considering the wars that were its immediate result, it is easy to see the fracturing of Christendom as an unmitigated "disaster," but this is trumped by its long-term meaning: reasonable pluralism founded on the natural "exercise of reason under the conditions of freedom" (*Political Liberalism*, p. xxvi). Political liberalism "assumes the fact of reasonable pluralism as a pluralism of comprehensive doctrines, including both religious and nonreligious doctrines" (ibid.), and in this way it has the Reformation to thank for its own possibility. Rawls concedes that prior to the historical experience of a functioning pluralist society, it was not unreasonable or unnatural to assume "that social unity and concord requires agreement on a general and comprehensive religious, philosophical, or moral doctrine" (*Political Liberalism*, p. xxvii) – that is, some kind of theocracy, or at least civil religion. It was only "the successful and peaceful practice of toleration in societies with liberal institutions" that proved that stability need not be founded on intolerance (ibid.). Even if religion encourages us to believe in the damnation of those who are not coreligionists, the practice of ecumenical cooperation "with trust and confidence, long and fruitfully . . . in maintaining a just society" (ibid.) persuades us otherwise. Even though the Reformers still believed that stability requires theocracy, the long historical experience of trying to cope with the pluralism generated by the Reformation has taught liberal societies that *true* stability in a radically pluralistic situation requires the opposite (toleration and respect for freedom of conscience).

Solution of the problem consists in separating political justice from "the highest good" (*Political Liberalism*, p. xxvii).[15] The ancients did not have to wrestle with this problem of political justice because "the clash between salvationist, creedal, and expansionist religions" (ibid.) is something they never experienced. Nor was it experienced within medieval Christianity because the Church then held a theological monopoly. In this sense, the Reformation introduced something utterly unique: the problem of joining in a mode of civic cooperation those who *do not* share a comprehensive doctrine. Shared citizenship among those "divided by profound doctrinal conflict" (ibid.) seems impossible until one hits on the idea of separating justice and "the good." According to Rawls, "the good" was defined for moderns by their religion (ibid.), and therefore modern liberalism's solution to the problem posed by the

---

[14] Rawls (*Political Liberalism*, p. xxvi) aptly cites Hegel's view that it was through the very division of the Christian Church "that the state has been able to fulfil its destiny [*Bestimmung*; T. M. Knox's translation is 'appointed end'] as self-conscious rationality and ethical life."

[15] There are echoes of Hobbes in this formulation. I will come back to this toward the end of this chapter.

Reformation only became possible when one succeeded in placing questions of the good (comprehensive doctrines) outside the sphere of justice. That is precisely the historical shift that political liberalism claims to conceptualize at the level of theory.

In the last section of the genealogy (*Political Liberalism*, pp. xxviii–xxix), Rawls gives a brief but incisive account of the intellectual movement (spearheaded by the heroic intellectual labors of Hume and Kant) whereby "moral knowledge" was detheologized and declericalized. Apprehensions of moral order came to be seen as coming from within rather than from an external source, and as universally accessible rather than confined to a clerical elite. Moreover, the great thinkers of the Enlightenment brought about a moral revolution in suggesting that it was possible for human beings to do what is morally right without being prompted to do so by divine sanctions. So does Rawls align himself with this great liberalizing movement in moral philosophy? No, because although these thinkers would have been right had they taken these positions as something required by "a political conception of justice for a constitutional democratic regime" (*Political Liberalism*, p. xxix), they in fact delivered an overreaching version of liberalism by seeking "to establish *a basis of moral knowledge* independent of ecclesiastical authority and available to the ordinary reasonable and conscientious person" (*Political Liberalism*, p. xxviii; emphasis added) – that is, the establishment of a new set of moral *truths* that would answer on the plane of philosophical analysis the questions that the warring salvationist doctrines were also presuming to answer. As long as these questions are to be settled in the register of ultimate truth, we are still in principle stuck in the sixteenth-century sinkhole we are trying to escape. By contrast, political liberalism "maintain[s] impartiality between comprehensive doctrines" (*Political Liberalism*, p. xxx) by not presuming to judge between, say, the view that moral order is immanent in human nature and the view that it is the product of divine command.[16]

What the genealogy traces (albeit with amazing concision) is the historical process whereby comprehensive doctrines that insist on a political monopoly and reject all compromise turn into *reasonable* comprehensive doctrines. What is a reasonable comprehensive doctrine? A reasonable comprehensive doctrine is one that does not assert truth (Rawls would be naturally inclined to say *its* truth) sufficiently forcefully as to exclude shared citizenship with other comprehensive doctrines.[17] This harks back to the conclusion of Rousseau's civil-religion chapter: In Rousseau's view, if we think of those committed to other

---

[16] This is the Rawlsian trade-off: Religions that refuse to join the overlapping consensus will be politically delegitimized, whereas those that do join it will be spared any moral or philosophical challenges. One set of critics will attack the first side of this trade-off; another set of critics will attack the other side of it. Rawls's compromise will satisfy neither those most committed to religion nor those most hostile to it.

[17] Cf. *Political Liberalism*, p. 151: "[E]qual liberty of conscience . . . takes the truths of religion off the political agenda."

doctrines of salvation as slated for damnation, we obviously cannot share citizenship with them.[18] The purpose of Rawls's genealogy is to lay out a history of preliberal religions (including Catholic Christianity and Protestant Christianity) that are not reasonable in this sense. To be reasonable (i.e., to become ecumenical-citizenship enabling), these religions must undergo a process of liberalization. The Wars of Religion were of course wonderfully educational with respect to the need for this liberalization vis-à-vis other religions in equal need of the same kind of liberalization. Political liberalism only becomes *possible* once this process of liberalization (this genealogy) has already unfolded itself.[19] It would therefore be reasonable to speak of Rawls's political liberalism as an "owl of Minerva" doctrine – it can only be articulated philosophically when the work of liberalization has already been done via a particular historical process. What the genealogy discloses is that Rawls's liberalism is a mode of "Hegelian" liberalism insofar as it is not intellectually freestanding (i.e., ahistorical) but, rather, dependent on a required (antecedent) history of liberalization.[20] In other words, it is part of the philosophical structure of Rawls's political philosophy,

[18] Jean-Jacques Rousseau, *On the Social Contract*, ed. R. D. Masters, trans. J. R. Masters (New York: St. Martin's Press, 1978), pp. 131–132: "[W]hoever dares to say *there is no salvation outside of the church* should be chased out of the State" (Book IV, chapter 8). There is a brief commentary on this passage from Rousseau's civil-religion chapter in Rawls, *A Theory of Justice*, pp. 215–216, but Rawls's focus in this discussion is on Rousseau's own intolerance – criticizing Rousseau for denying toleration to Catholics. One can also attempt to interpret Rawls's key idea of "overlapping consensus" in relation to Rousseau's formulation of the general will in Book II, chapter 3: "[T]ake away from [private wills] the pluses and minuses that cancel each other out, and the remaining sum of the differences is the general will" (*On the Social Contract*, ed. Masters, p. 61). This juxtaposition of Rousseau and Rawls suggests the interesting thought that, in both cases, political consensus is arrived at less by founding it on something positive than by politically subtracting commitments that will set citizens apart from one another. More generally, see the interesting suggestion by Brian Barry about Rawls as standing within a Rousseauian tradition of reflection on social order: Barry, "John Rawls and the Search for Stability," *Ethics*, Vol. 105 (July 1995): 880.

[19] Cf. Brendan O'Leary, "Liberalism, Multiculturalism, Danish Cartoons, Islamist Fraud, and the Rights of the Ungodly," *International Migration*, Vol. 44, No. 5 (2006): 24: Current liberalized versions of monotheistic religion "are, of course, no longer, at least for now, the religions they were. Many exponents of Christianity and Judaism have tempered or modified the historic cores of their beliefs precisely because of scientific falsification, textual criticism, and ridicule in the heartlands of the West." In this context, O'Leary refers to "John Rawls's risible claim of an 'overlapping pluralist consensus' among all religions, which he believed to be compatible with liberalism"; one can add that Rawls seems to make the tacit assumption that these religions have already undergone a prior process of liberalization. See also O'Leary, p. 32: "[L]iberal principles taken seriously are an affront to all seriously held historic versions of monotheism." The phrase "at least for now" in the first quotation from O'Leary is very ominous.

[20] Cf. "*Commonweal* Interview with John Rawls," in Rawls, *Collected Papers*, ed. Freeman, p. 621: "I give a historical answer, I don't give a theoretical answer." This helps explain why Richard Rorty aligns Rawls with Hegel and Dewey rather than with Kant: See "The Priority of Democracy to Philosophy," in Rorty, *Objectivity, Relativism, and Truth* (Cambridge: Cambridge University Press, 1991), pp. 180–181, 184–185. There are also suggestive remarks about Hegelian aspects of Rawls's enterprise in Duncan Ivison, *Postcolonial Liberalism* (Cambridge: Cambridge University Press, 2002), pp. 7–8.

as it is for Hegel's, that it offers a retrospective or backward-looking liberalism rather than a forward-looking liberalism (as did the liberalisms of Spinoza, Locke, Montesquieu, and so on).

But then one can ask this: What does such an "owl of Minerva" philosophy add to what history has already accomplished? One could say it is not *trying* to do anything; it merely acknowledges the history of liberalization that has already been unfolded. Presented with religions that have not participated in this history of liberalization, it cannot supply "true" arguments or "normative foundations" that will encourage them to liberalize. It can merely remind them genealogically of the story that the history of illiberal religions already teaches: that unreasonable religions shed rivers of blood to no purpose whereas reasonable religions reap the benefits of ecumenical citizenship.

Having said all this, it still must be conceded that it is far from obvious why the Wars of Religion are directly relevant to the concerns of contemporary liberals. Rawls himself acknowledges this in a few places. Right after he completes his presentation of the genealogy in the Introduction to *Political Liberalism*, he writes this (p. xxx):

It may seem that my emphasis on the Reformation and the long controversy about toleration as the origin of liberalism is dated in terms of the problems of contemporary political life. Among our most basic problems are those of race, ethnicity, and gender [whereas those of religion have been largely solved, he seems to be saying – R. B.].

Furthermore, in a discussion of J. S. Mill in relation to Locke's doctrine of toleration, in his *Lectures on the History of Political Philosophy*, Rawls writes this:

During the wars of religion it was taken for granted that the content of belief was above all important. One must believe the truth, the true doctrine, otherwise one put one's salvation in jeopardy. Religious error was feared as a terrible thing; and those who spread error aroused dread. By Mill's time, however, the view of the question has obviously changed. The struggle over the principle of toleration has long since been settled.[21]

If Rawls thinks the problem of toleration "has long since been settled,"[22] why does he make a point of reactivating it by putting the Wars of Religion back on the liberal agenda?

On one hand, it is not obvious that the Wars of Religion are relevant to the problem of how to theorize contemporary liberalism. On the other hand,

---

[21] Rawls, *Lectures on the History of Political Philosophy*, p. 309. Interestingly, Steven B. Smith, in a review of this book, criticizes Rawls for failing to incorporate what he knows about the sixteenth- to seventeenth-century context in his readings of canonical liberal thinkers: See Smith, "The Philosopher of Our Times," *The New York Sun*, May 11, 2007 (http://www.nysun.com/article/54265, p. 3).

[22] In addition, when Rawls writes that "equal liberty of conscience . . . takes religious truths off the political agenda" (*Political Liberalism*, p. 151), one could interpret this as the summary of a historical accomplishment: Because the seventeenth-century fight for liberty of conscience was successful, religious truths have been taken off the political agenda.

neither is it obvious that the Wars of Religion are *not* still relevant (or becoming relevant once again). Consider what Mark Lilla writes in a recent book:

For over two centuries, from the American and French revolutions to the collapse of Soviet Communism, political life in the West revolved around eminently political questions. We argued about war and revolution, class and social justice, race and national identity. Today we have progressed to the point where we are again fighting the battles of the sixteenth century – over revelation and reason, dogmatic purity and toleration, inspiration and consent, divine duty and common decency. We are disturbed and confused. We find it incomprehensible that theological ideas still inflame the minds of men, stirring up messianic passions that leave societies in ruin. We assumed that this was no longer possible, that human beings had learned to separate religious questions from political ones, that fanaticism was dead. We were wrong.[23]

This may be in some respects a persuasive view of our situation as seen from a post-9/11 vantage point. (After all, a world offering the prospect of theocratic states armed with nuclear weapons – our world! – cannot plausibly be considered to be a world safely nested in the hands of secularism.[24]) It is unlikely, however, that it was in this spirit that Rawls offered his narrative about the Wars of Religion. So what else presents itself as a plausible interpretation of the relevance of the sixteenth century for Rawls's philosophical project?

Here I can attempt to provide several possible answers to this question while I also try to reconstruct how the genealogy sets the larger agenda for *Political Liberalism*. Our general thesis is that Rawls excavates the origins of liberalism *qua* reaction to the devastation wrought by the Wars of Religion because it conveys in an especially dramatic way why it is necessary for political liberalism to detach itself from any and all comprehensive views (insofar as this is possible). Put somewhat polemically, one could say that the Wars of Religion are a kind of rhetorical sledgehammer that can be brought to bear whenever citizens of a liberal polity feel tempted to make their comprehensive doctrines (especially religious comprehensive doctrines) the topic of public exchange. What the Wars of Religion scenario highlighted in the Introduction to *Political Liberalism* teaches us is that what it means to bring one's comprehensive doctrine into the political domain is to aspire to *impose* this comprehensive doctrine by means of state power precisely in the manner of sixteenth-century theocracies. I would describe this as a skewing of the Rawlsian agenda, but Rawlsians will obviously see the matter quite differently.

---

[23] Mark Lilla, *The Stillborn God: Religion, Politics, and the Modern West* (New York: Knopf, 2007), p. 3. Lilla, in an encapsulated version of his argument ("The Politics of God," *The New York Times Magazine*, August 19, 2007, p. 30), rightly highlights Iranian President Ahmadinejad's Open Letter to George W. Bush (May 8, 2006) as a remarkable testament to the continued (or resumed) salience of theocratic politics in the contemporary world.

[24] "Theocracies with nuclear weapons" can come about *either* through Iran acquiring nuclear arms *or* through Pakistan becoming more of a theocratic state than it currently is. Neither possibility can be ruled out.

Rawls again refers back to the Wars of Religion in his *Commonweal* interview, and we can see from that discussion as well that the continuing relevance of sixteenth-century rival theocracies (Catholic and Protestant) connects directly with Rawls's conception of public reason versus comprehensive views. Presented with the standard kind of objection to the core argument of *Political Liberalism* (namely that there is a "veiled argument for secularism" in Rawls's appeal to public reason), Rawls gives this response: "How many religions are there in the United States? How are they going to get on together? One way, which has been the usual way historically, is to fight it out, as in France in the sixteenth century. That's a possibility. But how do you avoid that?.... I can't see any other solution [apart from public reason]."[25] Again, there is an aspect of rhetorical arm-twisting here: No one ought to be unwilling to relinquish his or her comprehensive commitments in the political domain if failure to do so means a return to the sixteenth-century situation where one has to "fight it out" (by implication, the unavoidable outcome once comprehensive doctrines enter the realm of state authority).

The cure for preliberal Wars of Religion is to prohibit Catholics from requiring a Catholic view of life as a condition of citizenship; to prohibit Protestants from requiring a Protestant view of life as a condition of citizenship; and so on. Nonetheless, I think this suggested to Rawls a far-reaching theoretical predicament: If Catholics cannot insist on a Catholic view of life, and Protestants cannot insist on a Protestant view of life, can liberals insist on a liberal view of life? If we allow ourselves to think of liberalism as a kind of secular religion, should a "liberal theocracy," so to speak, be permitted while Catholic and Protestant theocracies are prohibited?[26] All comprehensive doctrines, whether religious or philosophical, are in principle "sectarian" and therefore cannot be appealed to in underwriting a properly liberal regime. Hence (despite the paradox), it is illegitimate to appeal to a liberal philosophy of life in founding a liberal polity.

One can certainly see the line of thinking here, but it raises the very large question of whether one can be, for civic purposes, agnostic about the ends of life while decidedly privileging the needs of citizenship over the demands of faith

---

[25] "*Commonweal* Interview with John Rawls," pp. 619, 620.

[26] One can relate this back to the analysis in Chapters 21 and 22 of Mill's attempt to present liberalism as a new universal creed. Cf. Richard Vernon, *Friends, Citizens, Strangers: Essays on Where We Belong* (Toronto: University of Toronto Press, 2005), p. 144: "If liberalism is a kind of religion, how can it claim to impose obligations on those who do not even subscribe to it?" Also relevant here, of course, is Stanley Fish's emphatic argument that liberalism is in no way exempt from the Lockean principle that every church is orthodox to itself: "Mission Impossible: Settling the Just Bounds between Church and State," *Columbia Law Review*, Vol. 97, No. 8 (December 1997): 2255–2333. Rawls came to develop the argument of *Political Liberalism* as he did precisely because he came to *agree* with Fish that all comprehensive doctrines (including liberalism) are in principle sectarian; nevertheless, it hardly seems likely that Fish is convinced by the argument of *Political Liberalism* that Rawlsian liberalism has ceased to be a church orthodox to itself.

(at least in cases in which faith is anticivic). In the Introduction to *Political Liberalism*, Rawls writes that to "maintain impartiality between comprehensive doctrines, [political liberalism] does not specifically address the moral topics on which those doctrines divide" (p. xxx). He similarly writes that "a zeal for the whole truth" represents a temptation to found liberal society on a more ambitious set of philosophical ideals than is appropriate for a constitutional regime, and political liberalism succeeds in resisting this temptation (*Political Liberalism*, pp. 42–43). However, can a view of society that is robustly egalitarian, "civicist" (committed to a strong doctrine of shared citizenship), and basically secular be "impartial between comprehensive doctrines" in the way that Rawls suggests?

Why is Rawls so averse to casting his liberalism as founded upon a comprehensive view? In many ways, doing so would render his philosophical enterprise a much simpler one. Not least, it would absolve him of charges by his critics (which are not unreasonable) that he is hiding his more robust philosophical commitments behind a façade of neutrality.[27] It is as if Rawls has somehow convinced himself that anyone committed to a comprehensive doctrine – including those committed to comprehensive versions of *liberalism* – latently harbors the ambition to impose this doctrine by force on all members of society. On p. 37 of *Political Liberalism*, he makes this statement:

[A] continuing shared understanding on one comprehensive religious, philosophical, or moral doctrine can be maintained only by the oppressive use of state power. If we think of political society as a community united in affirming one and the same comprehensive doctrine, then the oppressive use of state power is necessary for political community.... [T]he Inquisition was not an accident; its suppression of heresy was needed to preserve that shared religious belief. The same holds, I believe, for any reasonable comprehensive philosophical and moral doctrine, whether religious or nonreligious. A society united on a reasonable form of utilitarianism, or on the reasonable liberalisms of Kant or Mill, would likewise require the sanctions of state power to remain so.

In an accompanying note (pp. 37–38, n. 39), Rawls acknowledges that all of this (that is, the notion of Kantian or Millian tyranny) seems paradoxical; yet he again reasserts that the idea of a whole society joined in one particular philosophy, including a liberal philosophy, requires the coercive imposition of that philosophy upon the whole society (with Kantian or Millian Inquisitors, etc.), in principle no different from the political enforcement of medieval Catholicism. Again, it is as if what it meant to hold a comprehensive doctrine, whether a religion or a philosophy, was to aspire to coerce the whole society to accept that doctrine – to impose the true philosophy by means of

---

[27] Cf. George Klosko, "Rawls's Public Reason and American Society," in *Reflections on Rawls*, ed. Young, p. 32: "[I]n the guise of protecting citizens from one another's comprehensive views, neutralists use their position to insure that their own views win"; Klosko is presenting the views of Michael McConnell, but Klosko clearly is persuaded that this critique has quite a lot of force. Needless to say, similar challenges are mounted by a hefty battalion of critics of Rawls.

"autocratic use of state power" (*Political Liberalism*, p. 304).[28] The thought experiment being laid out here is indeed a very strange one. Those engaged in the enterprise of philosophy are typically committed to reflection on the plane of comprehensive doctrines (i.e., as a purely intellectual activity) without any desire (latent or expressed) to see those doctrines enforced politically. Leaving aside Plato's image of philosopher-kings, why would one even conceive the notion of philosophies like those of Kant or Mill being coercively imposed as state religions on whole societies?

There is a related text in *Political Liberalism*, pp. 134–135: Rawls states that he is providing an alternative to "the dominant tradition," from Plato and Aristotle all the way up to Sidgwick and (in our day) Raz and Dworkin, which sought to identify the one true conception of the good. The intellectual breakthrough associated with political liberalism consists in realizing that "the question the dominant tradition has tried to answer has no answer: no comprehensive doctrine is appropriate as a political conception for a constitutional regime" (p. 135). Again, this suggests that what the dominant tradition was aiming at was provision of an official theology for a state-imposed orthodoxy. Why can't one be animated by "a zeal for the whole truth" (pp. 42–43) without at the same time being driven by a zeal for political enforcement of this truth?[29]

It is important to add that one can also raise problems with Rawls's comprehensive doctrine–political doctrine distinction that have nothing to do with religion. Suppose one is a Marxist, say, or an environmentalist. Can one separate these political commitments from grander views of the ends of life? The issue is not whether these "sectarian" views should be allowed to impose their philosophy on the whole society (on the model of theocracy), but whether these views can even be given a legitimate hearing in ways that express their intended scope. What we wind up with, it seems, is a general contraction or flattening of the domain of political reflection and debate.[30] If most nonliberal political views – not just those held by religionists – engage grander views

---

[28] Cf. the important statement in "Justice as Fairness: Political not Metaphysical," in *Collected Papers*, ed. Freeman, pp. 394–395: "The only alternative to a principle of toleration is the autocratic use of state power. Thus, justice as fairness deliberately stays on the surface, philosophically speaking.... Philosophy as the search for truth about an independent metaphysical and moral order cannot, I believe, provide a workable and shared basis for a political conception of justice in a democratic society." Similar views are presented in Richard Rorty, "The Priority of Democracy to Philosophy," pp. 175–196.

[29] There is a striking parallel between Rawls's view (as well as Rorty's) on this issue and Hannah Arendt's conception of the relation between politics and truth. For a commentary on Arendt's version of these ideas, see Ronald Beiner, "Rereading 'Truth and Politics,'" *Philosophy and Social Criticism*, Vol. 34, Nos. 1–2 (January–February 2008): 123–136. It is certainly *not* the case that all philosophers have the hidden ambition to be philosopher-kings.

[30] Dombrowski, *Rawls and Religion*, p. 116: Rawlsians ought to make clear why we need "the *lingua franca* provided by public reason" by pointing out "the disrespect involved in politics if one speaks to others strictly in the terms idiosyncratic to one's own comprehensive doctrine." Does a Green Party activist show disrespect for fellow citizens by trying to expand the existing terms of political discussion by means of a far-reaching engagement with alternative philosophies of life? Do we risk Wars of Religion by allowing politics to be a mutual contest of such philosophies?

of what is at stake in politics, the only citizens who will not have their political commitments delegitimized will be Rawlsian political liberals. In fact, the same challenge applies in the case of *liberals* (like Christopher Hitchens) who are committed to challenging religionists in politically charged ways that Rawlsian strictures would not permit. Daniel Dombrowski is concerned to respond to worries on the part of Rawls's critics that "Rawls's strategy of avoidance robs political philosophy of its excitement and importance."[31] Well, the more serious worry is that this theoretical strategy will rob *politics* of its excitement and importance. Rawls's "reasonable pluralism" is an attempt to pacify pluralism on the assumption that an unpacified pluralism, expressed politically, will all too easily lead to the resumption of a sixteenth-century-style politics of the sword (whose twentieth-century equivalent is Lebanon, and whose twenty-first-century equivalent is Iraq).

The incoherence in Rawls's doctrine of public reason seems to flow from trying to be inclusive and exclusionary at the same time: It is a big tent that welcomes all "reasonable" comprehensive doctrines but must bar those that are unreasonable. Nonetheless, if the boundary between reasonable and unreasonable is defined by whether one wishes to bring a not-yet-shared set of comprehensive commitments to bear on political life, it is hard to see how this will not entail an illiberal contraction of the scope of political deliberation by predefining many political possibilities as unreasonable before they have even been given a chance to make their case. If (again) Marxists had to adhere to the same strictures applied to fundamentalist Christians, they would be barred from making the political arguments they make on the basis of the philosophic commitments that define them as Marxists. Being required to cast their views only in terms that would be antecedently accessible to all citizens, Marxism would thereby be banished as a political possibility; it could survive only as a form of private faith. The paradox is that although Rawls's political liberalism set out to avoid coercing people into a liberal philosophy of life, exclusion by normative fiat of those outside the liberal mainstream is precisely what is achieved with respect to existential commitments that straddle politics and worldview.[32]

Political liberalism does not exist – it is a phantom of the Rawlsian imagination.[33] As I discuss in a little greater length in Chapter 24, a liberal regime always reflects and embodies a liberal view of life, even if it is not cashed out in terms of Kantian or Millian autonomy. If liberals prize ecumenical citizenship above commitment to some more parochial but more overarching vision of things, that is *itself* a liberal view of life. The more Rawls emphasizes the need to subordinate comprehensive doctrines to the needs of

[31] Ibid., p. 112.

[32] Cf. Stanley Fish's typically spirited argument along similar lines in "Mutual Respect as a Device of Exclusion," in *Deliberative Politics: Essays on Democracy and Disagreement*, ed. Stephen Macedo (New York: Oxford University Press, 1999), pp. 88–102. Fish's target is Gutmann and Thompson, but his challenges also apply well enough to Rawls.

[33] Cf. Robert Audi and Nicholas Wolterstorff, *Religion in the Public Square* (Lanham, MD: Rowman & Littlefield, 1997), pp. 97–98.

what one can call "pan-civic citizenship," the more he asserts, willy-nilly, his *own* (fairly attractive) comprehensive doctrine – which ought to be defended as such. Calling this "political liberalism" merely obscures what should instead be acknowledged as a foundationalist principle.[34]

There remains one other way of interpreting why Rawls goes out of his way to highlight the continuing relevance of the Wars of Religion. As is intimated in Rawls's nod to Judith Shklar in the Introduction to *Political Liberalism* (p. xxvi, n. 10), Rawls agrees with many liberals in thinking that the compellingness of liberalism is best founded not as the articulation of a positive philosophy of life, but rather as the imperative to avoid a *"summum malum"* (in this view, the most compelling reasons for being a liberal are negative, not positive). The Wars of Religion serve supremely well (as they did for Hobbes!) as the concretization of the *summum malum*. This relates back to Rawls's fundamental strategy of steering clear of liberalism as a comprehensive doctrine, and it raises anew the question of whether this is the best strategy for grounding liberalism in the face of challenges from nonliberal comprehensive doctrines.

It seems to me that there is still an easy challenge to Rawls's foundational distinction between comprehensive doctrines and a political doctrine that is virtually impossible to banish. Why should devotees of an "unreasonable" comprehensive doctrine allow a need for common citizenship to trump this all-encompassing commitment (which is precisely what the adjective "comprehensive" is meant to conjure up)?[35] If the answer is that we are obliged to be fair to co-citizens who hold divergent commitments, we can again ask why this sense of fairness should have trumping power over an all-encompassing interpretation of what gives purpose to life. In other words, why would an adherent of a nonliberal comprehensive doctrine defer to an understanding of shared citizenship that did not even claim for itself the moral and philosophical authority of a comprehensive doctrine?[36] It is as if Rawls, in conceiving the idea

---

[34] Political liberalism, with its idea of "apply[ing] the principle of toleration to philosophy itself," of keeping liberalism philosophically shallow, and so on (*Political Liberalism*, pp. 10, 152, 154, 242) – i.e., basing politics on notions that are supposed to be in some sense philosophically uncontroversial, as if such a thing were possible – is merely a more radical version of the neutralism asserted by Rawls in *A Theory of Justice* with his doctrine of "the priority of the right to the good." (Conceptions of the good, in both cases, refer to that sphere of religious and philosophical controversy above which Rawlsian liberalism seeks to elevate itself.) The neutralism advanced by early Rawls was not philosophically plausible, and the neutralism advanced by late Rawls is no more plausible. (In my view, one encounters similar problems in Habermas's presumption that political philosophy today must be practiced in a "post-metaphysical" mode.)

[35] Cf. *Collected Papers*, ed. Freeman, p. 617: "A comprehensive doctrine, either religious or secular, aspires to cover all of life.... It aims to cover everything."

[36] To be sure, one can say, "Forget about those committed to anti-civic comprehensive doctrines; rather, put your civic energy into cultivating citizenship with those capable of citizenship." Still, it does not seem very satisfying theoretically to abstain from giving a comprehensive account of citizenship as a human good if one might have, on a different understanding of liberalism, given such an account.

of a political doctrine that is not a comprehensive doctrine, puts a self-willed moral–philosophical vacuum at the center of his philosophy of citizenship. Why should that be thought to be a practical–political *advantage*? These questions of "why should citizenship trump X?"[37] therefore lead us toward the idea that only citizenship formulated as *itself* a comprehensive doctrine can answer these challenges. If being a citizen among citizens is an important part of living a full, flourishing life, then we can begin to respond to questions about why merely political commitments can trump (what are by definition more metaphysically and more existentially ambitious) comprehensive commitments.[38] However, moving in this direction would require Rawls not only to drop his political–comprehensive distinction but also to embrace liberal perfectionism – and therewith, Rawlsian liberalism, admitting that its core conceptions fail to achieve their purpose, would be forced back to the drawing board. Acknowledging that commitment to citizenship stands within the sphere of reflection on the ends of life will not turn liberalism into a form of secular theocracy.

In any case, John Rawls certainly offers no Rousseauian civic cult of the kind suggested by Sheldon Wolin.[39] There is, however, at least one sense in

---

[37] When one thinks about the possible contents of this "X," Rawls's assimilation of religions and philosophies as comprehensive doctrines starts to look much less persuasive. For a utilitarian or a Kantian to subordinate their philosophies of life to imperatives of shared citizenship does not appear very difficult. For the member of an Amish community or for an Islamist to do so is an entirely different proposition. Nonliberal *religions* pose challenges to Rawls's philosophy of citizenship that philosophical comprehensive doctrines do not.

[38] A similar challenge is put to Rawls (drawing on Rawls's own acknowledgment of the problem) in William A. Galston, "Realism and Moralism in Political Theory," in *Reflections on Rawls*, ed. Young, p. 116, n. 20. Cf. "Civic Resources in a Liberal Society: 'Thick' and 'Thin' Versions of Liberalism," in Ronald Beiner, *Liberalism, Nationalism, Citizenship: Essays on the Problem of Political Community* (Vancouver: University of British Columbia Press, 2003), pp. 58–59. My argument in that essay is that Stephen Macedo is able to formulate a more robustly civicist version of liberalism than Rawls's because, although Macedo interprets himself to be faithful to Rawlsian political liberalism, he does not allow himself to be hobbled by Rawls's doctrinal distinctions to the extent that Rawls himself is.

[39] It is hard to make sense of why Wolin is so bitterly critical of Rawls in the expanded edition of *Politics and Vision*, for Rawls's idea that members of a liberal society should embrace a "political conception of themselves" that defines a more encompassing identity as a citizen – i.e., more encompassing than their nonpublic identities – ought to be very appealing to Wolin. Interpreted according to its most attractive aspect (from my point of view and also that of early Wolin), the fundamental meaning of Rawlsian public reason is that, civically speaking, citizens (and even more so, judges and public officials) are in some ultimate sense obliged to address fellow citizens on a basis of citizen to citizen and not sectarian to fellow sectarian or sectarian to possible convert. Part of what this entails is that all citizens *qua* citizens have a civic identity that, within the specifically political realm, takes priority over their other nonpolitical identities. This is precisely the set of ideas that seems quite close to Wolin's own conception, at least in the original edition of *Politics and Vision*. It is true that I too have been fairly critical of Rawls in this chapter. Let me make my own position clear: I think there are sound and unsound aspects of the doctrine of public reason. The idea of giving special weight to the civic exertion by which one assumes the identity of a citizen among citizens seems perfectly sound (and again, it is puzzling that Wolin did not find this aspect of Rawls more appealing). However, where the Rawlsian conception of public reason goes badly off the rails is in its implausible suggestion that

which Rawls does offer civil religion – as all liberals do – namely a religion that has been *made civil* (as opposed to all the varieties of religion that are uncivil and sometimes actively anticivic), that respects and ultimately defers to civil authority. This helps us to appreciate Rawls's endeavor to join with leading predecessors in the history of liberalism in the enterprise of responding to the perennial political challenges of religion: Seen in this light, Rawls secures his place in the history of liberalism interpreted as an intellectual tradition decisively defined by the project of a philosophical containment of religion.

conceptions of what is valuable in life should be excluded from legitimate public discourse in the interests of maximizing shared ground among citizens. Cf. "*Commonweal* Interview with John Rawls," p. 622: "[T]his form of regime . . . has its own public form of discourse." On p. 242 of *Political Liberalism*, Rawls speaks of "the duty to adopt a certain form of public discourse." He concedes that excluding comprehensive doctrines may lend a certain "shallowness" to the tenor of public discourse, but he nonetheless insists that this shallowness is an acceptable price to pay to be faithful to "our duty of civility to other citizens." Also see the important formulation on p. 152: "[B]y avoiding comprehensive doctrines we try to bypass religion and philosophy's profoundest controversies so as to have some hope of uncovering a basis of a stable overlapping consensus." I grant that assuming a strong civic identity must emphasize what citizens share, but why must we be *that* focused on what we share? (Cf. Audi and Wolterstorff, *Religion in the Public Square*, p. 109.) Again, it seems an overreaction to the Rawls-constructed Wars of Religion scenario.

24

Prosaic Liberalism

Montesquieu versus Machiavelli, Rousseau, and Nietzsche

> Nietzsche himself had a Christian view of history, seeing the present moment always as some crisis, some fall from classical greatness, some corruption or evil to be saved from. I call that Christian.
>
> – Saul Bellow[1]

> I do in fact think that the organization of social life on this earth turns out, in the end, to be rather prosaic.
>
> – Raymond Aron[2]

What is there in common between thinkers as different as Machiavelli, Rousseau, and Nietzsche? Framing the contours of a liberal subtradition within the tradition of modern political philosophy helps to answer this question. Relative to the tradition of liberal political philosophy, we can say that all three are agreed that a bourgeois-commercial vision of life appears as cowardly and effeminate – as lacking in grandeur, or in the moral heroism that renders human beings fully human.[3] In Chapter 1, I discussed Montesquieu's comparison of

---

[1] Saul Bellow, *Herzog* (New York: Penguin, 2003), p. 61.

[2] Raymond Aron, *Memoirs: Fifty Years of Political Reflection*, trans. George Holoch (New York: Holmes & Meier, 1990), p. 224.

[3] Cf. Rousseau's reference to patriotism as "the most heroic of all the passions": "Discourse on Political Economy," in *On the Social Contract*, ed. R. D. Masters, trans. J. R. Masters (New York: St. Martin's Press, 1978), p. 219; and *Collected Writings of Rousseau*, Vol. 9, ed. Christopher Kelly and Eve Grace (Lebanon, NH: University Press of New England, 2001), p. 68: "[J]ust as people in Lapland would be mistaken to establish four feet as the natural stature of man, we ourselves would be no less mistaken to establish the size of human souls on the basis of the people we see around us." Another key text with respect to the argument of this chapter is Rousseau, *The Government of Poland*, trans. Willmoore Kendall (Indianapolis: Hackett, 1985), p. 7: The laws of Lycurgus "transformed [the Spartans] into beings more than merely human" [*des êtres au-dessus de l'humanité*]. As regards the yearning for a heroic approach to life in Nietzsche, one can say that what most impugns Nietzsche's philosophy is its astonishing *innocence* – being able to write in a cavalier way about the coming century of ideological wars without conveying the slightest sense of how ghastly and horrific these wars would be. (Relevant texts are cited in Kurt Rudolf Fischer, "Nazism as a Nietzschean 'Experiment,'" *Nietzsche-Studien*, Band 6,

republican virtue and monkish "austerity" in *Spirit of the Laws*, Book 5, chapter 2. Montesquieu's formulation is that in the case of the virtue of the ancient republican citizen, as in the case of the austerities of the self-abnegating monk, "their regimen deprives them of everything upon which ordinary passions [*les passions ordinaires*] rest." The notion of "ordinariness" suggested in this text merits further reflection, for in fact it goes to the heart of the liberal conception of social life. In this respect, Montesquieu presents himself as an exemplar of the liberal tradition, in juxtaposition to whom we can consider Machiavelli, Rousseau, and Nietzsche as virtual "allies."

There is no question that the work of Montesquieu enacts an ongoing critical dialogue with the theoretical challenge of Machiavelli – just as there is in Rousseau a continuous critical dialogue with Montesquieu. (Interestingly, one finds no discussion of Montesquieu in the work of Nietzsche; there is only a single passing reference to Montesquieu in the entire published work of Nietzsche.[4]) For one very striking vindication of this subterranean philosophical dialogue, consider the terms in which Montesquieu offers his decisive articulation of the idea of *moeurs douces*: "[O]ne should not be surprised if our mores are less fierce [*féroces*] than they were formerly" (*Spirit of the Laws*, Book 20, chapter 1). The reference to ferocity in this text cannot help but make one think that Montesquieu's intention is to respond to Machiavelli's critique of Christianity in *Discourses on Livy*, II.2 (with its invocation of the impressive bloodletting of Roman spectacles). Machiavelli and Montesquieu share a fascination with the larger-than-life grandeur of ancient politics, but Montesquieu's ultimate commitment is to the judgment of ancient politics according to the standards of modern, liberal, post-Christian notions of "soft mores," moderation, respect for each other's humanity, and devotion to law,[5] and there is no corresponding commitment to any of this in Machiavelli.

1977: 116–122.) As if there could be anything properly *heroic* in a war like the First World War! Would the actual experience of those ideological wars have turned even Nietzsche into a liberal? One has to wonder. (Evidently, Nietzsche's brief service in the Franco-Prussian War did not help to liberalize his view of war. Nor is it the case that Heidegger was turned into a liberal by his experience of war in the twentieth century; but an important difference between Nietzsche and Heidegger is that unlike Heidegger, Nietzsche was impervious to the seductions of nationalism.)

[4] The single reference, of no real consequence, is in *The Gay Science*, § 101. There are also a couple of references to Montesquieu in Nietzsche's *Nachlass*, one of which is a quite suggestive quotation copied from Montesquieu: "Pour qu'un homme soit au-dessus de l'humanité, il en coûte trop cher à tous les autres." ("In order for one man to be placed beyond humanity, a price must be paid for this which is too expensive for all the others.") *Kritische Studienausgabe*, ed. Giorgio Colli and Mazzino Montinari (Berlin: de Gruyter, 1988), Band 12: *Nachgelassene Fragmente, 1885–1887*, p. 222; see also Band 11, p. 527 (a flattering reference to Montesquieu). The latter volume also contains a flattering reference to Tocqueville (p. 442).

[5] It is possible to interpret the entirety of Montesquieu's theoretical enterprise as a thoroughgoing reversal of Machiavelli's famous dictum (*The Prince*, chapter 12) that one can dispense with "reasoning on laws" and instead focus on "arms" because "there cannot be good laws where there are not good arms, and where there are good arms there must be good laws." For Montesquieu, arms (and everything else in the human experience of politics) must always be subordinated to a concern with law as the defining emblem of our humanity. Of course, in

Why was Machiavelli unsatisfied with a vision of politics that was through-and-through secular? The answer, I think, has to do with the special character of the kind of civic republicanism inaugurated by Machiavelli, relative to the civic republicanism of, say, Aristotle. For the older civic republicanism whose canonical version is laid out in *The Politics*, becoming a citizen means fulfilling one's inborn human nature. For the more radical civic republicanism formulated by Machiavelli, by contrast, being a citizen in the highest sense means denaturing and "renaturing" one's human nature. This Machiavellian position is restated by Montesquieu and Rousseau with tremendous force. Hence Montesquieu speaks of squelching the "ordinary passions" by the exercise of monkish austerity, and Rousseau, in *Government of Poland*, chapter 6, speaks of *"passions qu'il faudroit étouffer"*: passions that must be "stifled" or "suffocated."[6] What are the "ordinary" passions that civic-republican citizenship, according to this Machiavelli–Montesquieu–Rousseau consensus, must trump? Living a comfortable life; having access to various pleasures and enjoyments; having a home that is one's own home, a space that is one's own space; not being constantly mobilized for "existential" action, where one's entire existence is on the line. In sum, not being required to live a life that is a heroic life – a life responsible for securing the supreme meaning of a human existence.[7] What Machiavelli yearns for is not just a crafty prince but a Mosaic "redeemer" (*Prince*, chapter 26),[8] and it seems not unreasonable to say that he anticipates the nineteenth- and twentieth-century tendency of seeking in secular nationalism a religion substitute that is in some respects more religion than politics. Above all, Machiavelli cannot be satisfied with a strictly secular vision of political life precisely because

insisting upon the essential role of law in fashioning political order, Montesquieu was responding to Machiavelli not just on his own behalf but also on behalf of the entire modern liberal tradition (and perhaps also on behalf of *ancient* political philosophy with respect to what is shared between Platonic–Aristotelian political philosophy and modern liberalism).

6 Rousseau, *The Government of Poland*, p. 30; cf. p. 23, "tear out of its bosom those passions that elude the laws." Kendall's translation of the text in chapter 6 ("passions that would have to be hauled out by the roots") is a rather free one but helpful nonetheless. It is not clear that any other translation (even if more literally accurate) could capture as powerfully the radicalness of what Rousseau is suggesting in this text, although "strangling the passions" perhaps comes close.

7 This formulation of Machiavelli's ideal is perhaps influenced by the political philosophy of Hannah Arendt. Conversely, one could say that her thinking about civic life in these terms demonstrates her essential debt to Machiavelli. There is unquestionably a quite strong dose of romanticism in Arendt's ideal of politics for its own sake (i.e., for the sheer pleasure of being seen and talked about by one's fellow citizens, of being at the center of the action). Is it, however, a question of romanticism and nothing more? If that were so, one would have to draw the conclusion that there is nothing normatively attractive about Machiavelli's vision of life, and that conclusion, in my view, would not be fully fair to Machiavelli or Arendt.

8 This is one of many ways in which Nietzsche presents himself as Machiavelli's direct intellectual successor – namely this-worldly power politics conceived as a vehicle of "redemption." In *The Antichrist*, Nietzsche lists "redeemer" as one of the words that "should be used as terms of abuse, to signify criminals" (see *The Anti-Christ, Ecce Homo, Twilight of the Idols, and Other Writings*, ed. Aaron Ridley and Judith Norman, Cambridge: Cambridge University Press, 2005, p. 67). However, in the *Genealogy of Morals*, Second Essay, last paragraph of § 24, Nietzsche awaits his own version of "the *redeeming* man" (*der erlösende Mensch*).

one cannot forgo the special disciplines that religion makes available if one is fully to live up to this exalted conception of civic life (as Montesquieu's analogy between republican virtue and monastic self-abnegation serves to express).

Returning to the two epigraphs to this chapter, we can say that in Bellow's sense, Machiavelli, Rousseau, and Nietzsche are *all* Christian. Montesquieu, however, is *not* Christian. Machiavelli, Rousseau, and Nietzsche are poets of our political condition, whereas Montesquieu, for all of his acute sensitivity to the attractions of political poetry, is ultimately a champion of what Aron calls "the prose of reality."[9] Arguably, the deepest human objection to liberalism as a way of life is its deliberately nonheroic or antiheroic attitude to life, its banalization of the problem of human existence – a concern powerfully thematized even by defenders of liberalism such as Tocqueville, to say nothing of radical critics of liberalism such as Rousseau, Nietzsche, and Sorel.[10] Liberal society takes care of the necessities of life (health, physical security, material comfort, the domestication of nature, civil peace), but it does not attempt to address the needs of the soul or the extremities of the human spirit (the sort of existential imperatives that might motivate someone to become a real artist, or a nun, or, say, an expert in defusing explosives[11]). Nonetheless, one should never forget that there *was* a heroic aspect to liberalism in its struggle against

---

[9] Aron, *Memoirs*, p. 221. The theme of poetry versus "modern prose" also figures in Leo Strauss's reading of Montesquieu: See *What is Political Philosophy?* (Chicago: University of Chicago Press, 1988), p. 50. Cf. Ridolfi's characterization of Guicciardini's relationship to Machiavelli: "[Guicciardini] never took pleasure in poets, and in politics they seemed to him dangerous." Roberto Ridolfi, *The Life of Niccolò Machiavelli*, trans. Cecil Grayson (London: Routledge & Kegan Paul, 1963), p. 188; cf. p. 241: Guicciardini vs. Machiavelli corresponds to prose vs. poetry. What Guicciardini had in mind in conceiving Machiavelli as a romanticizing poet of political life is nicely encapsulated in his suggestion in one of his *ricordi* that Machiavelli allowed himself to imagine that the citizens of Florence, who were in fact jackasses, could be conjured into Roman chariot horses. See Francesco Guicciardini, *Maxims and Reflections*, trans. Mario Domandi (Philadelphia: University of Pennsylvania Press, 1965), p. 69, Series C, n. 110. One must therefore be careful about taking at face value Machiavelli's broadside against "imaginary republics and principalities" in *Prince*, chapter 15. From Guicciardini's perspective, Machiavelli himself is still a philosophical dreamer. For Guicciardini's full critique of Machiavelli's "idealism," see Francesco Guicciardini, "Considerations of the *Discourses* of Niccolò Machiavelli," in *The Sweetness of Power: Machiavelli's Discourses and Guicciardini's Considerations*, trans. James B. Atkinson and David Sices (DeKalb, IL: Northern Illinois University Press, 2002), particularly the implied association of Machiavelli with "a city that seeks to live according to philosophy" on p. 388 (cf. p. 402) – as if Machiavelli is more closely aligned with Platonic utopianism than Machiavelli himself wants to acknowledge. As noted elsewhere in this book, there is a striking parallel between Guicciardini's relation to Machiavelli and Burckhardt's relation to Nietzsche. One can say that those who were most intellectually akin to Machiavelli and Nietzsche could see with greatest clarity the folly of their politics: Just as Burckhardt was right to see Nietzsche as a reckless revolutionary, so Guicciardini was right to see Machiavelli as a hopeless romantic.

[10] Cf. Richard Rorty's forthright judgment that liberalism means embracing the notion of human beings as "bland, calculating, petty and unheroic" in order to secure a society that cherishes individual liberty. Rorty, *Philosophical Papers, Volume 1: Objectivity, Relativism, and Truth* (Cambridge: Cambridge University Press, 1991), p. 190.

[11] This existential option was explored in the film *The Hurt Locker*.

theocratic religion – a struggle that has not yet reached a final conclusion (and perhaps never will).[12] Evoking at least something similar to Nietzsche's imagery of the tension in the bow, can liberalism's continuing struggle to fend off the challenges of religion help liberalism vindicate itself against charges of banalization?

[12] For an interesting appeal to resummon this sense of liberal heroism, see Brendan O'Leary, "Liberalism, Multiculturalism, Danish Cartoons, Islamist Fraud, and the Rights of the Ungodly," *International Migration*, Vol. 44, No. 5 (2006): 22–24: "The late Ernest Gellner argued that liberalism is a 'miracle,' by which he meant both that its emergence is not easy to explain, and that it is not the 'natural' condition of humanity.... He described our natural (or default) condition as the 'tyranny of the cousins' [clan rule], or 'the tyranny of the 'ideo-crats' [theocrats or ideological monopolists], and celebrated the exit from these mentally repressive equilibria.... Many liberals in Canada, the coastal United States, and urban London breathe liberal air, i.e., they live in an atmosphere which has been liberal (and libertarian) for a while, but not that long.... Contemporary liberals, I find, have too easily accepted the fall of Communism and the quiet retreat of those who claimed 'Asian values,' and there is nowhere nicer to be complacent than Canada [this is a jab at one of my colleagues – R. B.]. Such liberals have not won their faith in any hard trials.... In consequence, they do not understand why those who have just emerged from illiberal environs, or who have lived or worked in deeply illiberal places, are much more concerned than they are to draw liberal 'red lines' on certain matters, especially in the homelands of liberalism. One of these red lines is the right to criticize all religions."

PART III

THEOCRATIC RESPONSES TO LIBERALISM

25

Joseph de Maistre

The Theocratic Paradigm

[Man] grovels painfully like a reptile whose back has been broken.
– Joseph de Maistre[1]

We shall keep our priests within the confines of their temples in the same way as we shall keep our professional army within the confines of their barracks.
– Theodor Herzl[2]

True theocracy is not a civil religion. In the light of Hobbes, one could even say that theocracy is the *opposite* of civil religion, for civil religion seeks to instrumentalize religion on behalf of *political* purposes, whereas true theocracy subordinates politics to *religious* ends. Civil religion must therefore oppose itself to secularist regimes on the one side and to theocratic regimes on the other side; and in this sense civil religion represents, in relation to the spectrum of religious–political possibilities, a kind of unstable middle position between real theocracy at one pole of the spectrum and secular liberalism at the opposite pole.

Why study Joseph de Maistre today? Maistre is such a renegade figure within the history of political thought that one feels compelled to ask this question. One answer is that if we are really going to measure up to the challenges of contemporary theocracy, we probably need to start doing a better job of thinking outside liberal horizons. There is certainly no question that when we enter Maistre's intellectual world, we have left the liberal universe far behind. As we see theocracies or potential theocracies springing up in various parts of the world, the realization dawns that we need to start thinking this through

---

[1] Joseph de Maistre, *Against Rousseau*, ed. Richard A, Lebrun (Montreal: McGill-Queen's University Press, 1996), p. 38.
[2] Theodor Herzl, *The Jewish State*, 6th ed., trans. Sylvie D'Avigdor (London: H. Pordes, 1972), p. 71.

philosophically. Liberal philosophers like Rawls do not permit sufficient penetration into the illiberal mind (none at all, really) to be of any help here.[3]
The parallel with nationalism suggests itself: Both in the case of nationalism
and in the case of theocracy, liberals cherished pious hopes that these political
phenomena would fade away and become politically irrelevant, that they were
capable of being privatized or defanged. If we are to be properly equipped to
face these challenges, we need (at least as an exercise in the enlargement of
political imagination) to try to enter an intellectual horizon from within which
liberalism's expulsion of religion from the public domain looks like madness –
not sane and rational, as it necessarily appears to any liberal, but, as it were, a
violation of nature's dictate.

To take up the theocratic challenge, we need to start by acknowledging that
our (liberal) world is not an open horizon (though it typically represents itself
as such); it is circumscribed. This theme has been powerfully ventilated in the
work of Stanley Fish.[4] Fish's argument is that there *is* no expulsion of religion
from the public domain; in effect, all politics (not excluding liberal politics)
is theocratic politics ("every Church is orthodox to itself," a Lockean dictum
that Fish regards as applying with equal force to "liberal orthodoxy"). This
is in basic harmony with the Maistrean claim that there is no such thing as
religious neutrality; one is either a defender of the faith or an enemy of the
faith. Either way, one's politics are a kind of theocratic politics.[5] This is a
serious argument, not easily dismissed. Fish shows how neutrality in relation

---

[3] I do not want to suggest that Maistre has been entirely neglected by contemporary liberal
thinkers. Two notable examples are Isaiah Berlin's interpretation of Maistre in "Joseph de
Maistre and the Origins of Fascism," in Berlin, *The Crooked Timber of Humanity* (New York:
Vintage, 1990), pp. 91–174; and Stephen Holmes, *The Anatomy of Antiliberalism* (Cambridge,
MA: Harvard University Press, 1993), chapter 1. The contrast between what motivates Berlin
to enter Maistre's world and what motivates Holmes is striking. In Holmes's case, it is just a
method for tarring, by guilt by association, communitarians he dislikes. (This purpose is made
perfectly clear in Holmes's epigraphs in Part I of *The Anatomy of Antiliberalism*; the epigraphs
suggest that the whole crowd of communitarians and critics of liberalism are really weak-kneed,
and unknowing, Maistreans.) In Berlin's case, there is a more intellectually serious purpose: It is
a way of highlighting the inadequacies of Enlightenment rationalism and universalism – not, of
course, conceding any fatal flaws of liberalism as such, but rather surveying these inadequacies to
make a case for a broader, more complex liberalism – one less tied to the premises of eighteenth-
century rationalism/universalism. This is Charles Taylor's project as well, but Taylor never goes
so far as to confront Maistre as a way of expanding his liberal horizons by trying to enter
sympathetically into illiberalism; one has to give Berlin credit for trying to do this.

[4] See esp. "Mission Impossible: Settling the Just Bounds between Church and State," *Columbia
Law Review*, Vol. 97, No. 8 (December 1997): 2255–2333. I appreciate the force of Fish's
challenge to liberal neutralism, but I certainly do not in any way endorse what I see as his perverse
polemics against reason and universalism. Fish's philosophy is submitted to good challenges in
J. Judd Owen, *Religion and the Demise of Liberal Rationalism* (Chicago: University of Chicago
Press, 2001).

[5] John Rawls, as we saw in Chapter 23, interprets versions of liberalism other than his own as
implicitly sectarian or theocratic; in that sense, there is a surprisingly broad overlap between
Fish and Rawls. The crucial difference, of course, is that Rawls thinks that this does not apply
to his own version of liberalism.

to religion is absolutely central to the liberal self-image, and he also exposes this neutrality as bogus. Nevertheless, there are defenders of liberalism (often the best) who are quite forthright about liberalism's nonneutrality vis-à-vis religion.

For instance, Stephen Holmes, in his defense of liberalism, offers several fundamental acknowledgments of this nonneutrality. First, in listing the basic principles common to all liberals, the *first* item cited by Holmes is the following: "They all believed that society can be held together without the fear of God . . . on the basis of secular norms and a shared interest in the fruits of cooperation."[6] Second, Holmes describes the liberal image of the state of nature as "a deft piece of anti-Christian mythology, an alternative to biblical versions of the origins of society and government."[7] Third, he makes this statement: "To assert that the central aim of government is the protection of property, first of all, is to deny that the central aim of government is to save souls. To make property essential is to help secularize politics and disentangle authority and obedience from religious life."[8] Fourth, according to Holmes, liberalism's embrace of self-interest is to be understood in opposition to "religious self-disgust and self-effacing obedience to God's inscrutable will."[9] In short, there is nothing religiously or theologically neutral about any of these central aspects of liberalism. I think Holmes would say that he has no particular quarrel with Fish's debunking of liberal pretensions to neutrality. So one might say that the first step in the direction of pursuing a liberal–illiberal dialogue, or a liberal–theocratic dialogue, consists in an acknowledgment of the bogusness of liberal claims to neutrality vis-à-vis religion.[10] Again, this is already a significant concession to Maistre.

If such a thing as political philosophy is possible, then in principle one should be able to stage a theoretical dialogue between, say, John Rawls and Joseph de Maistre (or between Rawls and Nietzsche). Those who practice political philosophy from within a Rawlsian horizon are likely to see this as pointless or farfetched: Someone like de Maistre is just too far beyond the pale to count as a legitimate philosophical interlocutor.[11] Nonetheless, it can be suggested that the very idea of philosophy requires that we make the effort

---

[6] Holmes, *The Anatomy of Antiliberalism*, p. 188.

[7] Ibid., p. 299, n. 7; cf. Bernard Yack's discussion of Montesquieu's strategy of reanimating interest in classical republicanism to serve a similar purpose: Yack, *The Longing for Total Revolution* (Princeton, NJ: Princeton University Press, 1986), p. 39.

[8] Holmes, *The Anatomy of Antiliberalism*, p. 213; cf. pp. 218 and 221.

[9] Ibid., p. 255.

[10] J. Judd Owen rightly points this out: "Contemporary liberals who suppose that liberalism requires treating all opinions with strict neutrality . . . have the benefit of working with opinions that have already been somehow transformed by the Enlightenment. Contemporary liberalism can think itself neutral in this way because the horizon of popular opinion has already been significantly liberalized." Owen, "The Tolerant Leviathan," *Polity*, Vol. 37, No. 1 (January 2005): 141–142.

[11] Cf. Richard Rorty, *Objectivity, Relativism, and Truth* (Cambridge: Cambridge University Press, 1991), pp. 187–188.

to get beyond the pale of our own horizon. In this sense, one might say that what is at stake in this understanding is the possibility of philosophy itself. The basic idea here is to go off in exploration of a foreign territory.[12] The idea of a dialogue between Rawls (or Locke) on the one hand and a theocrat like Maistre on the other is a way of prying open the most fundamental dimensions of what it means to be committed to a liberal vision of the social universe. To understand ourselves, we have to look at ourselves from a considerable distance away; simply reading Rawls or reading Locke does not do the trick. This engagement with theocracy can be especially helpful once we recognize (happily or unhappily) that liberalism is not and likely never will be a universal dispensation. Moreover, if the purpose is to be properly met, one has to travel pretty far; it is not easy (for us at least) to reach the borders of our liberal landscape. This is the same reason as the reason for reading Nietzsche (though many read him today as if they can do so without stepping outside the liberal world – a view that is totally mistaken!). As intimated elsewhere in this book, theocracy is back on the political agenda. Therefore we can only profit from engagement with a thinker like Maistre, who not only defends theocracy but finds himself unable to conceive of forms of politics that are nontheocratic: Just as Hobbes sees absolutism and anarchy as the only alternatives, so Maistre sees theocracy and anarchy as the only alternatives.

The best way of entering this alien territory is by a careful reading of Maistre's magisterial work, the *St. Petersburg Dialogues*.[13] The first thing one is struck by in reading Maistre is the gracefulness and eloquence of his writing. Going by his reputation, one fully expects to be ushered into, so to speak, a dark, grim, ugly dungeon with blood on the floor and bats and cobwebs on the ceiling.[14] His writing is not like that at all! The *style* of Maistre's writing is as lively and playful as that of Montesquieu or Rousseau, although the *content*,

---

[12] This is also a way of taking up Holmes's challenge to contemporary critics of liberalism, which is that they are afraid to look at the ugliest incarnations of the antiliberal tradition. Fine! Let's look at them.

[13] Joseph de Maistre, *St. Petersburg Dialogues: Or Conversations on the Temporal Government of Providence*, trans. Richard A. Lebrun (Montreal: McGill-Queen's University Press, 1993).

[14] Consider Maistre's self-declared disciple, Carl Schmitt, whose political vision is as brutal as Maistre's but whose lugubrious prose is closer to one what might have expected of Maistre. (For a critical examination of Schmitt's claim to being a Maistrean, see Graeme Garrard, "Joseph de Maistre and Carl Schmitt," in *Joseph de Maistre's Life, Thought, and Influence*, ed. Richard A. Lebrun, Montreal: McGill-Queen's University Press, 2001, pp. 220–238; and for a more generous assessment of the literary qualities of Schmitt's work, see Mark Lilla, *The Reckless Mind*, New York: New York Review Books, 2001, pp. 61-62.) Maistre's own judgment of the importance of literary style is expressed in his sixth dialogue when he deems Locke's *Essay Concerning Human Understanding* to be "as boring as anything an absolute lack of genius and style could create" (p. 190) and states that the book delivers its rational philosophy "with the eloquence of an almanac" (p. 192). Bacon's philosophy is equally suspect, but he merits a much more favorable rating as a literary stylist (p. 190), as is also true of Hume (p. 180). Of course, similar judgments about the relation between philosophy and style abound in Nietzsche.

of course, is radically different. (Nietzsche is another case in which one cannot let the levity of the style mislead one about the gravity of the content.[15])

The dialogue consists of three characters: (1) the Count – narrator of the dialogue and, one presumes, a self-depiction of Maistre himself[16]; (2) the Senator – a Russian politician; and (3) the Chevalier – a young French exile. In accordance with Maistre's famous dictum that there is no generic humanity,[17] the three characters represent three different nationalities.[18] The conversations are hosted by the Count. What we have here, basically, are two old fogeys – politicians with a bent for metaphysical disquisitions. The Chevalier is much younger – a man of action, less of an intellectual.[19] This has the basic structure of a Platonic dialogue: The Chevalier is somewhat attracted to the religious philosophizing of the two others, but he is also somewhat skeptical.[20] In short, the Chevalier needs to be won over. Thus the dialogue is a test of Maistre's Socratic art – letting himself be seen by someone who clearly finds him fairly impressive but is not fully won over, who is not fully sure the Count is not just an old fart with some self-important ideas about the role of religion and the decline of modern morality and culture. The Count really is not concerned with winning over the Senator, who is already old enough to be settled in his views; rather, the key pedagogical relationship is between the Count and the Chevalier.[21] Hence there is a Socratic tension here, without which we really *would* be in the company of just a bunch of diehard reactionaries cursing a world they are unhappy with.

A couple of things to notice before the dialogue itself begins: First, it is striking that Maistre refers to the French Revolution in the very first sentence

---

[15] Why do contemporary readers love Nietzsche but not Maistre? Nietzsche found the kind of poetry to make Maistre's politics palatable, and indeed extraordinarily seductive. Maybe Nietzsche's secret was something like this: One needs the cover of radical atheism – a kind of Trojan horse, to borrow Hobbes's metaphor – to render theocratic politics attractive. (One could say that just as Hobbes offered divine right without the divine, to recall Clifford Orwin's formulation, so Nietzsche offered theocracy without theism.) In any case, it is not beside the point to ask this question: What is the actual difference between Nietzsche's politics and Maistre's politics? (I suppose it might be possible to make the same point about *Plato*; one can write in a playful and artistically gifted way and yet be committed to a grim vision of politics.) The connection between Nietzsche and Maistre is also noted by Corey Robin in "Garbage and Gravitas" (http://www.thenation.com/article/garbage-and-gravitas).

[16] Maistre in effect avows this on p. 67, n. 68. Maistre was of course a count, so identifying him with "the Count" does not require subtle discernment. On pp. 264ff., we encounter the strange literary device of Maistre's making his appearance in the guise of an anonymous author admiringly quoted by the Count!

[17] Joseph de Maistre, *Considerations on France*, ed. Richard A. Lebrun (Cambridge: Cambridge University Press, 1994), p. 53.

[18] Cf. p. 197, emphasizing that the Count is not French by nationality, even if French is his mother tongue.

[19] Cf. p. 164, where he confesses he has not read Locke.

[20] See p. 197, where the Chevalier says explicitly that he finds the Count's reasoning less than overwhelming; he says he tends to find the Senator more persuasive.

[21] Cf. p. 310, on the issue of intergenerational transmission of culture.

of the book. It is also noteworthy how Maistre invokes "the presence of the
sovereign" (viz., the Russian Czar) on the first page of the book.[22] Another part
of the stage setting is the statue of Peter the Great that the three friends sail past
on their way to the Count's residence: "Looking at him, one does not know
whether this bronze hand protects or threatens."[23] These are the two dramatic
poles of the dialogue – the awesome seat of sovereignty in St. Petersburg on
the one side, and, on the other side, the brazen overturning of sovereignty in
revolutionary Paris. The war between these two principles – sovereignty and
antisovereignty – has yet to be decided. They cannot coexist. Either the Revolution will prevail and destroy Europe, or the Counter-Revolution will reassert
itself and the enemies of Christianity will be routed. The drama of the dialogue
remains incomplete until this larger historical drama plays itself out (hence
the fragmentary "Sketch of a Final Dialogue," which anticipates the consummation of the Counter-Revolution). As Maistre writes in the *Considerations
on France*, the "present generation is witnessing one of the greatest spectacles
ever beheld by human eyes; it is the fight to the death between Christianity
and philosophism.... As in Homer, *the father of gods and men* is holding the
balance in which these two great causes are being weighed; one of the scales
will soon descend."[24] There is Maistre in a nutshell!

The dialogue starts with the same problem as Book 1 of Plato's *Republic*:
the problem of justice. Can the wicked be happy? Does good flow only to
the good? This is also (or primarily) a problem of *divine* justice: the problem
of providence. Does *God* reward the good, punish the wicked? The problem
of justice is aligned with the problem of providence, which is simultaneously
aligned with the problem of punishment. That Plato is Maistre's model is
made more explicit when he presents their conversation as a renewal of the
ancient tradition of philosophical *symposia*.[25] The topic of their philosophical
symposium is "the happiness of the wicked and the misfortune of the just."[26]
"This is the great scandal to human reason," says the Senator.[27] Right at the
start of the dialogue, the Count says, "perverse hearts never have beautiful
nights or beautiful days."[28] But is this true?

Just before the Senator calls the misfortune of the just "the great scandal
to human reason," the Count talks about his own happiness and unhappiness.
Referring to his own misfortune of being "struck twice by lightening" (having his fortunes turned upside down by the French Revolution and suffering
quasi-exile in Russia), he says, "I no longer have the right to what is vulgarly
called *happiness*."[29] Is *he* a victim of divine injustice? Or is he, too, guilty, and

---

[22] Ibid., p. 3.
[23] Ibid., p. 5.
[24] Maistre, *Considerations on France*, p. 45.
[25] Maistre, *St. Petersburg Dialogues*, p. 6.
[26] Ibid., p. 7.
[27] Ibid.
[28] Ibid., p. 5.
[29] Ibid., p. 7.

therefore rightly inflicted with misfortune and unhappiness? (The idea of unde-
served unhappiness simply does not have a place in Maistre's universe.) According to the Count, the issue is "the temporal government of Providence"[30] –
that is, the idea that God does not simply reward the good and punish evil
in an afterlife but rather orders *this* world according to justice. The Chevalier
assumes that the Count's theodicy must rely on an idea of eternal life – and
rightly points out that this would be insufficient: How would we *know* that
the just are rewarded and the wicked punished unless we could see this happen
in our world, the temporal world, or unless there were at least some worldly
evidence of this other-worldly outcome? The Count, however, had specifically
referred to the *temporal* government of Providence – the divine rulership of
this world.

The Senator puts the same worry this way: Rewards and punishments in
an afterlife are fine, but they will not do much to scare unbelievers. Therefore
appeals only to an afterlife as the site of providential justice are "extremely
dangerous": To really be effective, unbelievers need to be convinced that divine
justice has a this-worldly application; hence he agrees with the Chevalier that
the real issue is whether "a truly moral government exists *in this world*."[31] The
Count, in reply, says "the distribution of blessings and misfortunes is a kind of
lottery."[32] This, however, rather than answering the challenge to divine justice,
obviously merely restates the problem. To be sure, the wicked are not free of
misfortunes, and the good are not utterly deprived of blessings. But why do the
good suffer at all? Why do the wicked enjoy any happiness?

The Count gives the following answer to the charge of providential injustice:
It would be a case of injustice only if the good suffered *because* they were good
and the wicked prospered because they were wicked – but this is not the case.
Rather, "good and evil are distributed indifferently to all men."[33] It is a matter
of fortune and misfortune, not of justice and injustice. The Chevalier objects
that what is at issue is not just the distribution of external misfortunes. "The
impunity of crimes . . . is the great scandal."[34] The Count concedes that he has
yet to win the point; in fact, it is not even clear that external misfortunes
are randomly distributed. "The world is governed by general laws."[35] One
cannot expect God to intervene every time the good suffer misfortune, every
time criminals prosper. If, as the Chevalier already conceded, the distribution
of good and evil is beyond moral judgment, then one loses the basis upon
which to complain about "the impunity of scoundrels."[36] To be human is to
be subject to various misfortunes. No individual as such (however virtuous)
can claim exemption from this fate.

[30] Ibid., p. 8.
[31] Ibid., p. 9.
[32] Ibid., p. 10.
[33] Ibid., pp. 12–13.
[34] Ibid., p. 14.
[35] Ibid., p. 15.
[36] Ibid.

At this point, the argument seems surprisingly similar to the deistic cosmology of Maistre's Enlightenment enemies. God sets the world in motion but does not intervene to ensure just outcomes in particular instances. However, it is hard to see how the Count can stick with this position; a deistic view of nonintervention would be intolerable for someone trying to vindicate the providential character of human history! So, as he should, the Count retreats somewhat with a more subtle version of his argument: Of course, there has to be *some* relation between virtue and reward. Nonetheless, if there were too close an association between deed and reward or punishment, people would stop acting for the sake of virtue itself and act only for the reward. "The moral order would disappear entirely."[37] This does not mean that there is not some correspondence between deed and reward, but it must not be too obvious, too proximate (not a one-to-one relation) – otherwise, people would be moved only by instrumental, not moral, considerations.

We next move to what is clearly Maistre's favorite theme: not rewards for virtue but punishments for sin. "The whole race of men is kept in order by punishment; for a guiltless man is hard to find."[38] Punishment, he says, is the "divine and terrible prerogative of sovereigns."[39] This is perhaps the Count's ultimate answer to the challenges that have been put to him: If all are guilty, no one can claim to suffer divine injustice. If the supposed distinction between the virtuous and the guilty dissolves in universal guilt, then indeed we are all subject to a common fate. On p. 16, the Count says his appeal to "general and necessary laws" that presume a basic equality of the human condition – an equality of being subject to more or less random misfortunes – was assumed for the sake of argument, but is in fact a false premise. Nonetheless, if all are sinners, as Maistre repeatedly asserts, then we are back to some kind of basic human equality. This leads into Maistre's famous passage describing the executioner: "[H]e is both the horror and the bond of association. Remove this incomprehensible agent from the world, and in a moment order gives way to chaos, thrones fall, and society disappears. God, who is the author of sovereignty, is therefore also the author of punishment."[40] God has suspended our earth on these two poles: sovereignty and punishment.

One is struck by a colossal paradox here. Maistre in this passage certainly appears to be offering a celebration of the scaffold. However, when one thinks of the French Revolution, which defines everything that Maistre hated, then one thinks first of all of the scaffold, of the orgy of executions. It is almost as if Maistre was obsessed by the French Revolution precisely because he and the French revolutionaries shared a fascination with the executioner. In fact, there is no question that Maistre, while he abhorred the manner in which the revolutionaries exercised their sovereignty, at the same time admired them for

---

[37] Ibid., p. 16.
[38] Ibid., p. 18.
[39] Ibid.
[40] Ibid., p. 20.

their ruthless upholding of the principle of sovereignty. As long as someone retains the authority to perform executions, sovereignty remains intact, and the revolutionaries, however much damage they did to church and throne, at least knew how to keep the more basic principle of sovereignty alive. When one reads the *Considerations on France*, it is clear that Maistre did not hesitate to give them credit for *that* (which is no small matter).

In the Count's last major speech of the first dialogue, he challenges the distinction between punishment (ordained by sin) and illness (supposedly a function of mere misfortune). In fact, illness, too, is often punishment for sin: It is the physical consequence of our moral failings. If we were free of moral disorders, we might also be free of illnesses. The basic message is this: Sin explains everything. One of the things I find interesting in this first dialogue is the challenge it poses to the political philosophy of Nietzsche (by anticipation, of course, because Maistre wrote at the beginning, and Nietzsche wrote at the end, of the nineteenth century). Nietzsche, one might say, wanted the sense of *authority* and *hierarchy* – and also, one could say, the sense of the seriousness of the human vocation, the sense of how high the stakes are in how the human destiny turns out – of the theocratic tradition.[41] Thus there is clearly a strong "theocratic" element in Nietzsche's thought. Nietzsche, however, wanted all this without the preoccupation with sin and guilt of Christian theocracy. Nietzsche, it seems, never refers to Maistre. *Why not?* Why does he not use Maistre to bash the Enlightenment, to bash the optimism and shallowness of liberal-egalitarian culture?

The answer, it seems obvious, is that he would not have been able to abide all the emphasis on sin, evil, and punishment. What Nietzsche seems to have wanted is theocracy without loss of innocence.[42] There is no innocence in Maistre, however – only guilt and submission. Therefore, strangely enough, Nietzsche is completely at one with Maistre in the war against liberalism, but

[41] By the way, a strong link between Maistre and Nietzsche in this first dialogue is the Count's appeal, on pp. 17–18, to the laws of Manu as a model of a theocratic morality – one gets exactly the same thing in Nietzsche's *Antichrist* (as I will discuss in Part IV). It strikes me that Maistre appeals to the laws of Manu in exactly the same spirit as Nietzsche does: as an assertion of absolute moral authority. It is hard to believe this is just a coincidence; cf. Maistre's citation of the law of Manu in the "Elucidation on Sacrifices," *St Petersburg Dialogues*, pp. 369–370. Like Nietzsche in § 56 of *The Antichrist*, Maistre refers to how the law of Manu defines the moral governance of women. However, Maistre offers a vastly more plausible account: Unlike Nietzsche, he sees in a clear-sighted way that this ancient morality, in common with all other ancient moralities, is based on the "mistreatment" and "degradation" of women. By contrast, Nietzsche in *The Antichrist* (*The Portable Nietzsche*, ed. Walter Kaufmann, New York: Viking Press, 1954, p. 643) asserts (totally implausibly) that the law of Manu embodies a view of women full of tenderness, gracefulness, and unsurpassed courteousness.

[42] Hence there is a striking contrast between what Maistre emphasizes in the Book of Manu and what Nietzsche emphasizes. Maistre, as one would expect, emphasizes sin and punishment; Nietzsche, in contrast, offers the following description, which is intended as a countermodel to Christian morality: "a feeling of perfection, an affirmation of life, a triumphant delight in oneself and in life – the *sun* shines on the whole book." *The Portable Nietzsche*, ed. Kaufmann, p. 642.

Nietzsche is at the same time obliged to wage uncompromising war against Christianity. In interesting ways, Maistre's position is more consistent and free of tensions (although, of course, much of the magic of Nietzsche's writings resides precisely in all the tensions and inconsistencies). Maistre is saying that what you have here is a package deal: order and authority on the one side, sin and guilt on the other. Maistre would say to Nietzsche that if you want one side of this equation, you need to have the other as well. What holds the two sides together is *punishment* and *sovereignty*. Theocratically sanctioned punishment is the mark of sovereignty (by this criterion, the Jacobins were legitimate sovereigns!). The sovereign is the instrument of God's wrath for human sinfulness – hence the overwhelming emphasis in the first dialogue on the executioner. This is not just a gruesome whim or a function of Maistre's warped personality; it is in fact the centerpiece of the Maistrean system of political (theocratic) order.

How would Nietzsche respond to Maistre? I think we get an implicit response in the preface to *Beyond Good and Evil*. There, Jesuitism and the Enlightenment are presented as actually being *on the same side*. From Nietzsche's point of view, *both* Christians and *philosophes* are "unbending the bow" – undoing the creative tension in Western experience. Both are conspiring against a more radically new dispensation. Here, perhaps, is the basis for responding to Berlin's charge against Maistre of protofascism. No, Maistre does not want anything radically new. In fact, in the face of twentieth-century fascism, he might say this: See, give up Christianity and anything can happen! Maistre, in contrast to Nietzsche, merely wants to return to the old order that the French Revolution destroyed: executioners representing the sovereignty of church-sanctioned monarchs rather than executioners acting on behalf of priest-hating and nobility-hating atheists. Nietzsche, by contrast, is aiming for something far more ambitious – something unprecedented.[43] (When Nietzsche, in *Twilight of the Idols*, "whispers to the conservatives" that it is impossible to "walk backwards,"[44] this has to be taken with deadly seriousness.)

The second dialogue starts with the question of whether or not to have a second cup of tea, and it takes only about two seconds for the three interlocutors to be drawn into a discussion about the nature of Providence and the relation between the visible and invisible worlds! The Senator asserts, "Nothing happens by chance in the world"[45] (everything is providential), and he says that if there is only one world, that world is the invisible world, "since matter is nothing." This is in agreement with the Count's views. "[E]very evil is a

---

[43] There is some concession of this point when Berlin writes the following: "Like Nietzsche he detested equality, and thought the notion of universal liberty an absurd and dangerous chimera, but he did not revolt against the historical process, or wish to break the frame within which humanity had thus far made its painful way" ("Joseph de Maistre and the Origins of Fascism," p. 173).

[44] *The Portable Nietzsche*, pp. 546–547.

[45] Maistre, *St. Petersburg Dialogues*, p. 32.

punishment."[46] Because this is so, every evil is avoidable by spiritual means: either by spiritual reform, or by prayer. The Chevalier, however, is more skeptical. He raises the issue of the justice of the transmission of sinfulness (of culpability, and therefore accountability) by original sin. He says, in effect, that it is bad enough we have to carry the sins of Adam and Eve – do we also have to carry the sins of our grandparents and great-grandparents? The Count takes up this challenge and defends the idea of the transmissibility of crime: "[D]egradation is transmissible."[47] A whole race can be "tainted."[48] In this context, the Count refers to Rousseau (because of his enthusiastic attitude toward savages) as "one of the most dangerous sophists of our century."[49] The Chevalier, rather than pursuing the question of original sin, challenges the Count on his account of savage languages.

The Count's view is that *all* creatures of nature (beavers, swallows, bees) are degraded; human beings are simply distinguished by their *self-consciousness* of degradation.[50] This is a bizarre admission, for it seems to put in radical question the goodness of creation. Previously he had attributed sin to human free will (although this appears to be in tension with the doctrine of original sin); but if even swallows and bees are degraded, then the misery of existence *is not* a function of human freedom. This really seems to put the whole providential cosmology of Maistre's "Christianity" in a very puzzling light. "*The whole of man is only a disease.*"[51] If things are really this bad, how can God bring himself to bestow grace on such an abomination? Doesn't there have to be something in the human being that is other than disease for God's grace to be intelligible? Again, there seems to be something suspect in the idea that Maistre's vision is a fully *Christian* vision.

The Count asserts that these facts of nature (the degradation of human existence, man's unmitigated responsibility for this degradation) are so evident that the doctrine of original sin can be traced back to pagan philosophy (including Plato and Aristotle): "*we are in this world to expiate certain crimes in another.*"[52] The Count attributes to Cicero the famous Kantian image of nature not as maternal but as "stepmotherly" in its poor provision for human good. Again, though, doesn't all of this attenuate the idea of evil as rooted in the perverse exercise of human freedom? If nature is "stepmotherly" rather than beneficent, why should all the blame be loaded onto human beings? We get a brilliant summary of the argument in the following syllogism: "[S]ince all degradation can only be a punishment, and all punishment presupposes a crime, reason alone [presumably secular reason, not reason instructed by

[46] Ibid., p. 33.
[47] Ibid., p. 35.
[48] Ibid., p. 34.
[49] Ibid.
[50] Ibid., p. 36.
[51] Ibid.
[52] Ibid., p. 37.

Christian faith] finds itself led forcefully to original sin."⁵³ All evil is punishment; all punishment implies guilt; hence we carry original sin.

"Wherever you find an altar, there civilization is to be found."⁵⁴ The Count totally rejects Rousseau's state of nature thesis. We do not start off with an innocent state of nature (savage man) and work our way toward a degraded civilization. Rather, we start off with civilization (defined by immediate intuition of religious truth) and work our way toward degraded barbarism. "Contemporary philosophy ... used these savages to prop up its vain and culpable declamations against the social order."⁵⁵ This leads into a long discussion of the origin of languages – a central preoccupation of eighteenth-century thought. Maistre utterly rejects the Condillacian account of language as a human invention. (He acknowledges, grudgingly, that this puts him much closer to a Rousseauian understanding of language⁵⁶ – grudgingly, of course, because he hates Rousseau, no less than he hates the other leading thinkers of the eighteenth-century Enlightenment.) Language is not an invention but a gift.⁵⁷ This, in turn, leads into a polemic against seventeenth- to eighteenth-century empiricism.⁵⁸

The main development in this dialogue is the emergence of a certain philosophical tension between the Count and the Chevalier. The Chevalier is clearly more disposed to grant philosophical respectability to empiricism, whereas the Count is utterly unyielding in his antiempiricism. (This philosophical tension is expressed dramatically in the Count's insinuation that the Chevalier served in a Napoleonic army.⁵⁹ The Chevalier heatedly denies this. It seems mysterious why the Chevalier would have served in a Napoleonic campaign if he is an exile from the French Revolution. Perhaps the Count's intention here is subtly to impugn the Chevalier's anti-Enlightenment credentials.)

The third dialogue again begins with the question of the justice of original sin and whether all suffering can be a matter of merited punishment. Although the question is put by the Senator, it is the Chevalier who challenges the Count's unyielding position on these questions. We get more intimations of the existential tension between the Chevalier and the Count. The Count and the Senator are old moralists; the Chevalier, by contrast, is a young man of action, inclined toward "society" and the world of social pleasures,⁶⁰ not gloomy reflections about sin and guilt. The Chevalier refers to the Count and the Senator as "accomplices" in urging upon him pious authors he is resistant to reading (hence the Chevalier says to the Senator, "you want to seduce me and get me involved in your favourite reading").⁶¹

⁵³ Ibid., p. 38.
⁵⁴ Ibid., p. 44.
⁵⁵ Ibid., p. 45.
⁵⁶ Ibid., p. 47.
⁵⁷ Ibid., p. 55.
⁵⁸ Ibid., p. 59.
⁵⁹ Ibid., p. 54.
⁶⁰ Cf. pp. 27–28.
⁶¹ Ibid., p. 93.

Throughout most of the third dialogue, the Senator and the Count had been arguing, Platonically, that virtue is its own reward, and so if it appears that the unjust prosper in relation to the just, this appearance is based on a false understanding of real happiness, of the real goods of life. Right at the end of the dialogue, however, the Count switches direction and starts to argue that one cannot impugn the justice of Providence because *no one is innocent*; therefore no one can claim that Providence treats them unfairly relative to their merit.[62] Obviously, one cannot use the suffering of the just as an argument against Providence if everyone is guilty. (We have heard this argument before.) However the Count himself concludes this dialogue with the story of a young girl stricken with a horrible cancer that seems very dramatically to contradict his own doctrine that "all evil is a punishment."[63]

As the fourth dialogue begins, the three interlocutors turn to the problem of prayer. This follows from the idea that all evil is punishment. One is punished for deeds that could have been otherwise. This implies free will. Prayer is a matter of supplications intended to disarm the sovereign. God is a sovereign who punishes the guilty. Those who have erred must seek God's grace to mitigate His punishment.

The fourth dialogue reaches a defining moment when the Chevalier quotes Voltaire.[64] The Count will not stand for this; it confirms his worst suspicions about the Chevalier. It is hard not to think here of the argument in *Considerations on France* that those defeated by the French revolutionaries deserved their defeat; it constituted punishment for moral weakness. The Chevalier, even though he is (like the Count) a victim of the Revolution, presents himself to the Count's eyes as a soul corrupted (at least to some extent) by the Enlightenment. In the Chevalier's description of Voltaire as "a brilliant French possession," Maistre is in effect explaining why the French ruling class was doomed. The Count's response is to defend the Index: Writers like Voltaire deserve to be censored.[65] The Chevalier then compounds his sin by quoting Rousseau.[66] More evidence of his corruption! After the Count's long rant against Voltaire, the Senator takes up the Chevalier's challenge to the idea of prayer. The central issue is the Chevalier's appeal to the notion of "invariable laws of nature."[67] If one accepts this idea, then the Enlightenment triumphs and piety is defeated. The Chevalier is right that prayer makes no sense if the laws of nature are invariable. So the Senator takes up this challenge. The crux of the Senator's argument is that it is reasonable to believe in the efficacy of prayer because

---

[62] Ibid., p. 98.

[63] Ibid., p. 101.

[64] Ibid., p. 108.

[65] Ibid., p. 109. The following text nicely encapsulates Maistre's view of the extent of Voltaire's intellectual culpability: "Voltaire's corrosive writings gnawed for sixty years at the very Christian cement of this superb structure whose fall has startled Europe" (*Against Rousseau*, ed. Lebrun, p. 106). That is, allow Christianity to be subverted by the likes of Voltaire, and the French Revolution is a natural consequence.

[66] *St. Petersburg Dialogues*, p. 111.

[67] Ibid.

people everywhere have always believed in it – which would seem to beg the question. (One implication of the emphasis on the question of prayer is that it excludes deism from the theistic domain: No one prays to a deistic God. Without prayer there is no religion. Even *Voltaire* says, *"no religion without prayer."*[68] Hence, deism amounts to atheism.)

The theme of the indispensable role of prayer may be a bit misleading because it might suggest an emphasis on private faith, whereas in fact Maistre is more oriented toward theocratically organized worship (similar to Hobbes's emphasis on public worship). "[I]f the *public cult* did not offer some little opposition to the universal degradation (we need no other proof of its indispensable necessity), I honestly believe that we would finally be reduced to veritable brutes."[69] (Presumably, "public cult" here means the Russian Orthodox Church, because the Senator is the one speaking here.) The efficacy of prayer, the Senator says, can be inferred "from the innate belief of all men."[70] If all men *believe* that God responds to prayer, then it is so – or as the Count formulates the same point, "the general feelings of all men form, so to speak, verities of intuition before which all the sophisms of reasoning disappear."[71] Nevertheless, prayer is in need of defense because, obviously, *not* "all men" presume its efficacy: Subsequent to the Enlightenment (to say nothing of premodern skeptics going back to the ancient atomists and Epicureans, and so on), the meaningfulness of prayer is entirely open to contestation; hence, again, appealing to a universal consensus of mankind begs the question.

The Count then returns to the question of invariable natural laws: He asserts that modern philosophers postulate invariable laws of nature to "prevent men from praying."[72] That is, modern science does not represent a bona fide claim to truth; rather it is merely a (moral, not cognitive) weapon in a conspiracy to subvert religion. Next, the Count goes head to head against the most influential challenge to theodicy ever written: namely Voltaire's famous poem on the Lisbon earthquake. Herder was wrong to respond to Voltaire by asserting that God was not responsible on account of invariable natural laws.[73] Rather,

---

[68] Ibid., p. 112.

[69] Ibid. (emphasis added); cf. p. 128, n. v, on Kant's repugnance for public prayer. For Kant's contrast between "temples" (associated with public worship) and "churches" ("places of assembly for instruction and inspiration in moral dispositions"), see Immanuel Kant, *Religion within the Boundaries of Mere Reason*, ed. Allen Wood and George di Giovanni (Cambridge: Cambridge University Press, 1998), p. 115. Although Maistre sometimes suggests that all that matters is a commitment to religion as such, not so much the content of this or that religion, clearly this is not his true position: The superiority of *public* religions (such as the civic cults of antiquity, with their temples) to *private* religions like Kant's pietism is presupposed. The contrast between Kant and Pythagoras in this note virtually suggests the superiority of ancient paganism to Protestant versions of Christianity!

[70] *St. Petersburg Dialogues*, p. 116. Interestingly, what the Senator suggests his interlocutors pray for is "the grace of returning [to France]" – that is, the Restoration.

[71] Ibid.

[72] Ibid., p. 117.

[73] Significantly, Maistre associates this Herderian view with "Spinozism": See p. 117, n. 16.

Voltaire is right: God is free, and can inflict or prevent earthquakes as he pleases. To Voltaire's question *"Why do we suffer under a just master?"* there is a more straightforward answer: "BECAUSE WE DESERVE IT."[74] Just as a human sovereign, in punishing an unruly population, brings his fist down upon adults and children alike, so the divine sovereign must do the same, and no injustice is involved. (But why *is* it not unjust for a human sovereign to let his wrath fall on innocent children?) The Chevalier clearly finds this whole line of argument pretty hard to swallow.[75]

Voltaire asks, Why Lisbon and not Paris? Are the Parisians less sinful than the Portuguese? The Count's answer: Look at the French Revolution! God *did* give the sinners the punishment they deserve.[76] This is, once again, in effect a restatement of the argument of *Considerations on France*: The good thing about the French Revolution is that it proves that sinners do not go unpunished. The Chevalier listens silently to all of this and does not attempt to pose any more challenges to the Count's case for theodicy.[77] It is worthwhile considering Maistre's relation to Leibniz in the context of this discussion of theodicy: On the one hand, he praises Leibniz for his commitment to the intellectual enterprise of theodicy[78]; on the other hand, he rebukes Leibniz sharply for his rejection of the efficacy of prayer.[79] One treads a tightrope here; one wants to vindicate the ways of God by arguing that the world is as it should be, but one does not want to go so far in arguing for a perfectly law-governed natural order that prayer becomes redundant.

Most of the dramatic tension in the book focuses on subtle tensions between the Chevalier on the one hand and the Senator and the Count on the other hand. However, we should not forget that the Senator and the Count do not represent a seamless alliance. Consider the exchange between the Senator and the Count on Latin versus Greek versions of Christianity[80]: This is a reminder that the Count and the Senator are not so much as one as the dialogue has hitherto suggested. In fact, they bear allegiance to rival wings of Christianity.[81] The Count refuses to accept this division; he thinks Christianity needs to be reunited as a unitary religion. He would not hesitate to sign a peace treaty with

---

74 Ibid., p. 118.
75 Ibid., p. 119. One obvious irony of this discussion is that it places Maistre and Rousseau in a tacit alliance against Voltaire (although Rousseau's providentialism, such as it is, is nowhere near as emphatic as Maistre's is).
76 *St. Petersburg Dialogues*, p. 121.
77 Cf. the intervention by the Senator on p. 122, which seems intended to shut him up: Pride "misleads us by inspiring in us an unfortunate spirit of contention that makes us seek difficulties to have the pleasure of arguing instead of referring them to a proven principle." It is hard not to interpret this as an attempt to reproach and intimidate the Chevalier.
78 Ibid., p. 92, n. 15.
79 Ibid., p. 124, n. 28
80 Ibid., p. 123.
81 Cf. p. 224, where the Count draws attention to the fact that he and the Senator belong to different churches; and the Senator's reference on p. 237 to "your church"/"our church."

the Orthodox Church, he avows.[82] (But would he sign a peace treaty with the Protestants? The possibility of peace between Roman Catholicism and Eastern Orthodoxy merely underscores the much deeper rift between Catholicism and Protestantism – really, a cultural war that cannot be settled merely by liberal-style toleration – and not *just* a "cultural" war, conducted with merely intellectual weapons.[83])

Before moving on, let me just pause to reemphasize the key point in the fourth dialogue: Not just any religion or putative religion will do in serving the political (theocratic) purposes that Maistre wants a religion to serve. For Maistre, deism is tantamount to atheism. (Protestantism is not much better!) This follows directly from the all-important claim that without prayer, there is no religion. What one needs is precisely a *providential* god who cares about human destiny and is prepared to exercise His will in guiding historical outcomes. It is hard not to be struck by the extent to which this is an Old Testament form of religiosity, that is, theocratic religiosity – God as watching over His people at every moment, and striking them with His wrath every time they step out of line. It is hard to see any "theocracy" in the New Testament, but the Old Testament, of course, is full of it. It was for the same reason that Nietzsche so profoundly preferred the Old Testament to the New Testament, and it can be taken as a tangible indication that Nietzsche, too, is fundamentally "theocratic" in his thinking. Without *this* kind of god (a theocratic god), religion is dead and, Maistre thinks, the prospect of achieving a politics of good social order is hopeless.

The fifth dialogue begins by resuming the argument against Lockean empiricism that had been pursued in the second dialogue. The argument is jointly advanced by the Senator and the Count, and the key argument turns on the question of animal instinct, which cannot be accounted for on empiricist grounds. It is striking that the Senator chooses the example of what a dog would be able to make of an execution! Of the countless examples Maistre could have picked, execution is the one that comes most readily to his mind, which certainly tells us a lot about the character of Maistrean thought.

The Senator and the Count then broaden their critique to natural science in general as a science of material causes. The Senator states, "I have read millions of witticisms about the ignorance of the ancients *who saw spirits everywhere*: it seems to me that we are much more foolish in never seeing them anywhere."[84] Again, it is the Chevalier who intervenes to defend the honor of natural science and of the eighteenth-century Enlightenment. As before, the Chevalier is more or less bludgeoned into silence, but one naturally suspects

---

[82] Ibid., p. 124.

[83] Cf. p. 327, where Maistre reacts to the liberal-Protestant doctrine of toleration pretty much the way Ulster Loyalists used to react to truces with the I.R.A.: Toleration merely provides a cover behind which one's enemies can continue to arm themselves to pursue their war with you all the more effectively.

[84] Ibid., p. 133.

that he fails to be convinced by the Count's arguments. Next, the target of the Count's polemic switches from Locke to Bacon. Bacon, he says, was full of an unthinking rancor against all spiritual ideas; he used all his abilities to promote the physical sciences to the point of leading men to dislike all the rest. "Bacon spared nothing to turn us away from the philosophy of Plato, which is the human preface of the Gospel."[85] What the philosophy of the Enlightenment produced was "a veritable system of practical atheism."[86] In Maistre's view, what is driving eighteenth-century philosophy is "theophobia" ("this strange malady").[87]

Running throughout this dialogue, connecting it to the argument of the preceding dialogue, is the theme of the Enlightenment's challenge to the idea of prayer. This is what is really at stake in this whole discussion: that the materialism of Enlightenment philosophy impugns the very notion of the meaningfulness of prayer. However, note carefully here the kind of God to which one prays, according to Maistre's conception – not a God who bestows blessings and Christian love on humankind; rather, a punishing God whose grace must be sought in order to avert a deserved punishment. According to Enlightenment philosophy, it does not make sense to conceive of a God who "revenges himself on you, you are too small"; "celestial punishments" seem unworthy of the deistic god of the Enlightenment.[88] Prayer falls into oblivion because the wrathful God whose forgiveness must be sought has also fallen into oblivion. Again, it is hard not to observe how Old Testament all of this is; the loving god of the New Testament seems barely present.

Maistre's objection to deism is that it postulates a God who never punishes, and who likewise cannot be supplicated in order that He may absolve warranted punishment. Maistre, at the end of the dialogue, spells out very clearly that for him the paradigm of divine action is the Old Testament God's infliction of the Flood. An easy way of summarizing the Maistrean theology is to say that, for Maistre, God is inseparably bound up with the issue of crime and punishment.[89] Any theology that abstracts from this identity of God and punishment amounts to atheism. All of the *political* crimes of the generation of the French Revolution are to be explained by the fact that Enlightenment *philosophy* has rendered incredible the notion of a God who punishes human deviance.

In the sixth dialogue we get a continuation of the discussion concerning the nature of prayer. This time it is the Senator who gets chastised by the Count for

---

[85] Ibid., p. 142. This bears comparison with Voegelin's view of Plato. It is interesting that some of the most vociferous *critics* of Christianity (I have in mind D'Holbach and Nietzsche) had the same view: See Baron d'Holbach, *Christianity Unveiled*, trans. W. M. Johnson (New York: Gordon Press, 1974), p. 18 (especially the first footnote), and p. 41, first footnote.

[86] *St. Petersburg Dialogues*, p. 148.

[87] Ibid.

[88] Ibid.

[89] See p. 149: The philosophical writers of the eighteenth century "declare themselves as *defenders of revelation*; but of *God*, of *crime*, of *punishment*, not a word."

citing an Enlightenment philosopher, namely Locke.[90] Why is prayer suspect from an Enlightenment perspective? In war, for instance, Side A prays that they win; Side B prays that *they* win. The prayers of both sides cannot be answered, nor is it clear whether prayer contributes anything to who wins and who gets defeated.[91] According to the Count, we first need to ask, what constitutes genuine prayer? Does it suffice, to constitute prayer, that one merely desires this or that? No, what defines prayer is true faith. However, one would need to see into the recesses of the heart to determine who, in their prayers, really has this faith.[92] Most worshippers who appear to be praying are not really doing so. The Chevalier cracks that in any case the *Count* is not praying because he is preoccupied with philosophical reflections on the nature of prayer![93] The Count makes the observation that "[a]s soon as man bases himself on his reason, he ceases to pray"[94]; but as the Chevalier had noticed, this critique of reason can be applied to the Count himself *qua* philosopher as opposed to the pure believer. (Pure believers just pray; they do not philosophize about the meaning of prayer.) In any case, the real question does not concern prayers by individuals, and whether they are heard or not, but prayer by nations, and whether they have the right to be heard by God.[95] In other words, prayer is a *political* question, not just a matter of individual faith. What seems implied here is that what is really driving Maistre in all these discussions is the following question: Why hasn't God answered the prayers of the European aristocracy for the restoration of the French throne? The true representatives of the French nation have been praying since 1789, and God seems deaf to their entreaties. Maistre needs to offer an answer to this – namely the fact that *atheists* (who *certainly* do not pray) seem to have won. Vindicating the meaningfulness of prayer consists in demonstrating why one should not succumb to despair and give up the fight against the Jacobins and their Napoleonic successors.

On p. 163, the Chevalier finally puts himself forward as a partisan of Locke. The rest of the sixth dialogue is devoted to polemics against Locke. The real source of Maistre's animus against Locke comes to light on p. 171: It is not (just) his empiricism, not (just) his influence on the French Enlightenment, but his Protestantism. Or rather, all of these things go together! (It does not seem to be going too far to say that, from Maistre's point of view, empiricism and Enlightenment thinking are just spin-offs from the Protestant schism. So, philosophical problems with empiricism, for instance, are inextricably tied to what is theologically objectionable about Protestantism. Furthermore, Maistre's philosophical quarrel with thinkers such as Bacon and Locke can never abstract from his inability to accept their Protestant commitments.) As Maistre puts it on

---

[90] Ibid., p. 157.
[91] Ibid., p. 155.
[92] Ibid., p. 159.
[93] Ibid., pp. 159–160.
[94] Ibid., p. 161.
[95] Ibid., p. 162.

p. 186, Locke was "*deceived* by the sectarian spirit." In other words, what was really driving him was not a particular set of philosophical beliefs but a gut-level hostility to Catholicism. Therefore, in linking up philosophical arguments with theological battles, Maistre is simply taking the philosophical issues back to the religious–theological stakes that actually provoked them in the first place. "Above all, [Locke] wanted to oppose his church, which I have more reason than he to hate, and which I nevertheless venerate in a certain sense as the most reasonable among the unreasonable."[96] What Maistre seems to be saying here is that if he were forced to choose among the various Protestant sects, he would prefer Anglicanism to the others, because there is still some kind of theocratic residue. Locke is not just Protestant but hyper-Protestant: "Enemy of all moral authority, he wanted to oppose received ideas." Here is Maistre's description of the moral–intellectual context for Locke's reception: "Sufficiently prepared by Protestantism, the human mind was beginning to shake off its own timidity, and preparing boldly to draw out all the consequences of the principles that had been posed in the sixteenth century. A dreadful sect was beginning to organize itself."[97]

Maistre finds Locke's politics no less dangerous than his epistemology. Here we may note an interesting discrepancy between Maistre and Burke. Burke drew a firm distinction between the "Old Whiggism" of Locke (to which he claimed to bear allegiance) and the "New Whiggism" of the English fellow travelers of the French Jacobins (this argument is famously spelled out in his *Appeal from New to Old Whigs*). Maistre, in sharp contrast, sees an inexorable continuity between the empiricism and Protestantism of Locke and the materialism and quasi-atheism of the French Enlightenment. It is also worth mentioning in this context that Burke, in his early philosophical works (such as the *Philosophical Enquiry into the Origin of our Ideas of the Sublime and Beautiful*) presents himself as a committed empiricist; Maistre never (as far as I know) addresses Burke's Lockeanism and his empiricism and whether it impugns his authority as an intellectual source of the Counter-Revolution.[98] (One suspects that Maistre would see it as a symptom of Burke's having failed to plumb with sufficient depth the roots of the Jacobin disease – traceable, via French anglophiles like Voltaire, back to English thinkers such as Bacon and Locke.[99]) Locke's *Essay Concerning Human Understanding* "can be considered as the preface of all eighteenth-century philosophy, which is totally negative

---

96 Ibid., p. 187.
97 Ibid., p. 189. Note that for Maistre, Protestantism (as well as its less pious offshoots) is never more than a mere "sect."
98 Cf. Richard A. Lebrun, "Joseph de Maistre and Edmund Burke," in *Joseph de Maistre's Life, Thought, and Influence*, ed. Lebrun, p. 169.
99 It is striking that Bacon and Locke, rather than any Continental philosophers, are the two primary intellectual targets of the *St. Petersburg Dialogues*. The worst political effects of modernity seem to have erupted in France, but philosophically speaking the roots of the problem appear to lie in English empiricism.

and in consequence null."[100] "Locke only wrote to contradict received ideas, and especially to humiliate an authority that shocked him immeasurably"[101] – namely the papacy. In other words, anti-Catholicism is the secret driving force behind the whole Lockean philosophy. "Locke was always led by his dominant prejudice; loyal to the principle that rejects all authority" – that is, his anti-Catholicism.[102] The refutation of innate ideas is intended to liberate "use of their own reason and judgment."[103] Maistre emphasizes that this is a deliberately Protestant – that is, anti-Catholic – rhetoric. In trying to refute innate ideas, Locke "wanted to direct his attacks more particularly against Catholic teaching."[104] Nonetheless, Anglican bishops, too, had reason to fear Locke, for "he attacked *all* spiritual authority."[105] All of these texts make clear that Maistre sees the philosophy of the eighteenth century as merely bringing to fruition the seeds planted by Lockean philosophy.

It is not hard to see why the need to refute – or discredit – Lockean empiricism would be a major priority of Maistre's philosophical project. Consider the following text from Locke's *Essay Concerning Human Understanding* (IV.18.2):

Reason therefore here, as contradistinguished to faith, I take to be the discovery of the certainty or probability of such propositions or truths which the mind arrives at by deduction made from such ideas which it got by the use of its natural faculties, viz., by sensation or reflection. Faith, on the other side, is the assent to any proposition, not thus made out of the deductions of reason, but upon the credit of the proposer, as coming from God in some extraordinary way of communication. This way of discovering truths to men we call "revelation."

It is very easy to see how a passage like this would suggest to Maistre that the empiricist concept of reason is a dagger aimed at the heart of revelation. It is no wonder that a generation of thinkers steeped in such doctrines would turn into skeptics and atheists.[106] The alternative is therefore clear: Either allow this

---

[100] *St. Petersburg Dialogues*, p. 193.
[101] Ibid.
[102] Ibid., p. 201, n. xi.
[103] Ibid., p. 203, n. xxxi.
[104] Ibid., p. 204, n. xxxii.
[105] Ibid. (emphasis added).
[106] Cf. Jonathan Israel, *Radical Enlightenment* (Oxford: Oxford University Press, 2001), p. 8, citing the views of Paolo Mattia Doria: "[A]ll they [the *Lochisti*, i.e., the followers of Locke] would accomplish... would be to further split the middle ground.... [T]hey were simply opening the door, albeit inadvertently, to the awesome fifth column, the radicals or *Epicurei-Spinosisti*." The same issue is raised in Israel's rigorous distinction between the "moderate mainstream" Enlightenment and the Radical Enlightenment in *Enlightenment Contested* (Oxford: Oxford University Press, 2006), p. 808: "[T]he conservative moral and social theories of Locke, Voltaire, Montesquieu, Hume, and Kant were all expressly intended to avoid forging moral philosophy systematically on the basis of philosophical reason and nature, in the interest of salvaging major elements of tradition, custom, and theology. All of these moral philosophers are by definition and by design... wholly at odds with the consistent naturalism sought by Spinoza, Bayle, Boulainvilliers, Diderot, and d'Holbach.... [T]he moral theories of the hard-core French High Enlightenment, Du Marsais, Diderot, d'Argens, Helvétius, d'Holbach,

concept of reason to utterly discredit revelation, *or* utterly discredit empiricism to safeguard revelation.

The seventh dialogue addresses the puzzle of war. Why would human beings ever be moved to fight wars? The Chevalier's answer, that they do so because they are ordered to do so by the sovereign, is rejected as superficial by the Senator. There are many things that a sovereign would not dare command (the Senator cites the example of the reform of an inaccurate calendar), whereas war is easy to command. Another possible answer to the puzzle is the human love for glory. However, two problems present themselves here: First, the average soldier obtains little glory – glory goes to the generals. Second, it is not clear *why* wars confer glory, which merely restates the original puzzle. Soldiers are more honored than executioners. But why? Soldiers murder the innocent; executioners murder the guilty. The executioner ("this sublime being"!) "is the cornerstone of society.... [I]f you deprive the world of the executioner all order will disappear with him."[107] The question being raised here is that of the inscrutability of nobility. (This question – What is noble? – is of course also the question posed in the last chapter of Nietzsche's *Beyond Good and Evil*.) The soldier is noble and the executioner is ignoble, yet this bears no relation at all to justice or to objective social purpose.

What is at issue here is what the Chevalier calls "the indefinable aura of honour."[108] The Senator again poses the central question: How is it that the right to shed innocent blood innocently has always been the most honorable thing in the world, according to the judgment of all of humanity, without exception?[109] According to contractarian thinkers like Rousseau, individuals were able to exit from a presocial state of nature into a state of society, yet nations are still in their original state of nature vis-à-vis each other. What is the explanation for this mystery? Here the Senator can offer no explanation other than what he calls "an occult and terrible law demanding human blood."[110]

This dialogue expresses the profound complexity in Maistre's stance toward war: on the one hand, utter disgust, and on the other hand, the perception of a working of divine providence, punishment for human sinfulness. As the Senator says on p. 215, "the functions of the soldier are terrible, but of necessity they belong to a great law of the spiritual world, and we must not be astonished

and Condorcet,... follow Spinoza and Bayle in adopting a fully secular and universalist ethic based exclusively on the 'common good,' equity, and equality." Israel in this passage does not mention Rousseau, but Rousseau's declared aim, which I discussed in Chapter 17, of mediating between orthodoxy and atheism, piety and impiety, would align him fairly clearly with the first (moderate mainstream) group; this project of mediation was (at least in Israel's account) in some sense the aim of all of them. Obviously, the Maistrean view is that such a project of mediation is in principle impossible. Insofar as one can distinguish between two Enlightenments, as Israel does, the moderate mainstream Enlightenment necessarily propels itself down a slippery slope toward the Radical Enlightenment.

[107] *St. Petersburg Dialogues*, p. 207.
[108] Ibid., p. 208.
[109] Ibid., p. 210.
[110] Ibid., p. 211.

that all the nations of the world have agreed in seeing in this scourge something more particularly divine than others ... it is not without a great and profound reason that the title GOD OF HOSTS shines forth from all the pages of Holy Scripture." (It is striking, and rather astonishing, that he says here "*all* the pages," not just the Old Testament. One might well ask where the God of the New Testament presents Himself as a God of Hosts.) Maistre adds in an accompanying note a quotation that ends: "Is not the most august title that God has given to himself that of GOD OF HOSTS?"[111] Consider, also, this text: "We must always ask God for success and always thank him for it, since nothing in the world is more immediately dependent on God than war. Since here he restricts man's natural power, and since he loves to be called *the God of war*, there are all sorts of reasons for us to redouble our entreaties when we are struck by this terrible scourge."[112] Here, as elsewhere in the *St. Petersburg Dialogues*, one is left with the strong impression that Maistre's religiosity owes a lot more to the Old Testament than to the New Testament. (Can one possibly imagine that the New Testament God "loves to be called the God of war"?[113])

There is no question in Maistre's mind about the horribleness of war; it is an atrocious confirmation of human evil. Nevertheless, the more horrible war is, the more profoundly it expresses the stern demands of God's justice. This dual assessment is captured nicely in the following statement by the Senator: "If you look closely at war, never will Christianity appear more sublime, more worthy of divinity, and better suited for men."[114] How should we interpret this statement? According to one plausible interpretation of Christianity, one can assume that the religion of the New Testament, as a profoundly pacific and otherworldly faith, highlights just how awful human violence and cruelty are. To be sure, this is part of what the Senator's statement says, but it certainly does not exhaust Maistre's much darker vision of Christian truth. First of all, the idea of Christianity as an entirely pacific religion is hard to reconcile with the Senator's argument on pp. 212–213 concerning the compatibility not only between the military vocation and virtue but also between military service and *piety*: "[N]othing in this world agrees better than the religious spirit and the military spirit."[115] Here he cites Voltaire that "an army ready to die in obedience to God would be invincible."[116] This resumes the earlier argument against Rousseau's thesis that Christians cannot be soldiers or good citizens. There certainly may be religions of which it would be true to assert the compatibility of the religious spirit and the military spirit (it is hard not to think of the origins of Islam as a conquering and imperial creed), but it seems bizarre to include the religion of the Gospel as a religion that lends itself to

---

[111] Ibid., p. 240, n. vii.
[112] Ibid., p. 224.
[113] Cf. the view of E. M. Cioran cited in Garrard, "Joseph de Maistre and Carl Schmitt," p. 236.
[114] *St. Petersburg Dialogues*, p. 215.
[115] Ibid., p. 213.
[116] Ibid.

use as an inspiration to military service. This, however, is not the whole story. Another important part of the complexity in Maistre's view of the relation between war and religion is that the bloodiness of war nicely complements the centrality of blood sacrifice to Maistre's view of the Christian Gospel. (I will come back to this when I conclude with a short discussion of the "Elucidation on Sacrifices.") This vision is beautifully encapsulated by this statement on p. 217: "The entire earth, perpetually steeped in blood, is nothing but an immense altar."[117]

True religion is a sacrifice of the innocent for the atonement of sin, and war in that sense (i.e., as providing the "altar" where these sacrifices are performed) is the very core of Maistre's religious vision. As the Count says on p. 225, the "words *crime* and *criminal* are found in all languages, but *sin* and *sinner* belong to Christian language" (Nietzsche would agree!). If sinners failed to be punished, then one could make a good case that there is no divine justice; therefore the existence of war as punishment for sin constitutes the "divinity" of war. This makes sense of the statement on p. 215 already quoted, that "all the nations of the world have agreed in seeing in this scourge [war] something more particularly divine than others." The Senator summarizes his view on p. 218: "War is...divine in itself, since it is a law of the world."[118] War is both a "scourge" and something "divine in itself" – *more* divine than any of the other curses that attach themselves to the human condition.[119]

A crucial question arises in trying to interpret this dialogue: Why is this whole "celebration" of war in the seventh dialogue put in the mouth of the Senator? Why not the Count? In fact, when the conversation in this dialogue shifts from the Senator to the Count, the topic shifts from war back to prayer. What we then get is a discussion of prayer as a window into the different characteristics of the various historical cultures: "[E]ach nation's prayer is a kind of indicator that shows us with mathematical precision the nation's moral standing."[120] For instance, the inadequacy of the ancient conception of prayer discloses the limits of pagan experience, for "none in antiquity knew how to express repentance in their prayers.... They never knew how to ask pardon in their prayers."[121] In the context of this discussion of prayer, the Count defends the Old Testament against Enlightenment critics. One gets a much better appreciation of just how sympathetic Maistre is to Judaism (and even Islam!)[122] when one considers how consistently and viciously hostile he is to any form of Protestant Christianity – for example, his reference to the Reformation as "one of the greatest crimes men have ever committed against

---

[117] Cf. p. 290: "The scaffold is an *altar*"!

[118] Cf. p. 217: The violent destruction of living things is a "universal law."

[119] Cf. p. 240, n. viii, quoting Euripides: The purpose of war is "to purify the earth, defiled by the overflowing of all their crimes." Maistre also quotes Mohammed ("it is right to learn from a foe"): "If God did not raise nation against nation, the earth would be completely corrupted."

[120] Ibid., p. 224.

[121] Ibid., p. 225.

[122] See p. 240, n. viii.

God."[123] Like Nietzsche, if Maistre had to choose between Moses and Luther, there is no question about which of the two he would favor.[124]

An exchange between the Chevalier and the Count discloses more about Maistre's attitude toward the Old Testament. The exchange begins with a confession by the Chevalier that he admires David (as poet of the Psalms) a bit as he admires Pindar, on hearsay.[125] The Count objects to putting David and Pindar on the same level – the latter is irrecoverable and belongs to a world we have left behind. "David, on the other hand, defies time and place because he accorded nothing to place and circumstance; he sang only of God and his immortal truths. Jerusalem has not disappeared for us; *it is everywhere we are.*"[126] *Greek* religiosity is time bound, but *biblical* religiosity (whether Judaic or Christian) is eternal. The proof offered by the Count concerning the continuity between the Old and New Testaments centers on the doctrine of original sin. David "knew well the terrible law of our defiled nature; he knew that men *are conceived in iniquity.*"[127] Maistre offers the following proto-Christian quotes from the Psalms: "In guilt was I born, and in sin my mother conceived me." "From the womb the wicked are perverted."[128] In answer to the question of why the Chevalier fails to discern the beauty of the Psalms, the Count reaffirms the Platonic doctrine of truth as recollection and the doctrine of innate ideas, namely the notion that it is impossible for people to grasp ideas that are not already innate within them, embodied in "intellectual temperament."[129] If one follows through this doctrine to its logical conclusion, it is hard to see what point can be served by the kind of conversation taking place between the Count, the Senator, and the Chevalier. Perhaps the Count can nudge the Chevalier toward insights consistent with his "intellectual temperament," but this same innate spiritual equipment sets immovable limits to what a conversation like this can accomplish. (For Maistre it goes without saying that a conversation between men and women on these topics would be

---

[123] Ibid., p. 311. The key Maistrean text on this theme is his "Reflections on Protestantism in its Relations with Sovereignty" (1798): See *Œuvres*, ed. Pierre Glaudes (Paris: Robert Laffont, 2007), pp. 311–330.

[124] Cf. the Count's defense of Judaism on pp. 277–280. On p. 280, he refers to Judaism as "this noble cult." For more on Maistre's view of Moses, see Garrard, "Joseph de Maistre and Carl Schmitt," pp. 235–236. The parallels with Nietzsche (especially the bitter hostility to the Reformation) are striking and might help to render somewhat less surprising my reference in note 15 of this chapter to Nietzsche as a quasi-theocrat. (I will pursue these themes at greater length in Part IV of the book.) This, of course, constitutes another reason for studying Joseph de Maistre: Appreciating "quasi"-theocratic aspects of Nietzsche's thought requires that we first acquaint ourselves with the real thing.

[125] *St. Petersburg Dialogues*, p. 226.

[126] Ibid., p. 227.

[127] Ibid., p. 230. Maistre's emphasis on men being "conceived" in iniquity (they "*rebel against the divine law from their mother's womb*") has the effect of transposing a stringent Catholic doctrine of original sin back into the Old Testament.

[128] Ibid., p. 230, n. 41. The Scriptural texts are Psalm 51:5 and Psalm 58:3.

[129] *St. Petersburg Dialogues*, p. 234.

pointless, because the gulf between their respective intellectual temperaments is too wide to be bridged.[130])

As I already intimated, the great puzzle of this dialogue is why the Count shifts the topic from war to prayer. It is striking that this is the first dialogue where the course of the conversation is not principally led by the Count. Is this Maistre's way of suggesting that the Count and the Senator are playing a kind of good cop–bad cop routine? It turns out that the Senator's vision of the world is much grimmer than the Count's.[131]

Near the start of the eighth dialogue, the Chevalier offers a summary of the entire course of the conversation thus far. According to the Chevalier, *"there is no such thing as a just man.* Thus it is by a special act of kindness that God chastises in this world instead of chastising more severely in the next."[132] This could come straight out of the mouth of the Count. The Chevalier also affirms that "there is nothing I believe in more firmly than purgatory."[133]

In the second half of the dialogue, we get a lengthy statement of the core of the Count's theology: Apparent disorder presupposes a notion of ultimate cosmic order (because one cannot make a judgment about disorder without invoking a standard of order that allows us to make sense of the idea of disorder), which in turn presupposes an ultimate supreme intelligence who is the *source* of that order. Claims about God's injustice make no sense because they presume the possibility of elevating ourselves *above* God, applying a higher standard to which we have access and by which God is bound and to which He is answerable. All of this, for Maistre, is completely incoherent.

The concluding discussion of the eighth dialogue concerns the atheism of the eighteenth-century Enlightenment. The regime associated with the Enlightenment involved rule by savants, and it is insanity to confer moral and spiritual judgment upon intellectuals: "It belongs to prelates, to noblemen, to great officers of the state to be the depositories and guardians of saving truths."[134] "As for the one who speaks or writes to deprive people of a national dogma, he

---

[130] Ibid.

[131] See the bottom of p. 235 and the top of p. 236, where the Senator rebukes the Count for being too optimistic about "the reign of prayer"! The Count is not the true hardliner in this set of dialogues.

[132] Ibid., p. 248.

[133] Ibid.; cf. pp. 260–261, notes i and ii, on the relation between Catholicism and Protestantism. In particular, the Protestant rejection of purgatory is an unnatural sectarian prejudice. (Catholicism is the "natural" religious sentiment; Protestantism is "the prejudice of sect and education.") Pagan thinkers are open to purgatory; so too are certain Protestants, but it goes against the grain of their Protestantism. Note that even the more liberal-minded Chevalier, who (at least relative to the Senator and the Count) verges on being an Enlightenment fellow traveler, remains firmly wedded to these ghastly doctrines.

[134] Ibid., p. 260; cf. the discussion, on p. 282, n. iii, of Christianity vs. philosophy (the context is an attack on Voltaire for putting Stoicism on a par with Christianity): "It is not a question of *talking* about [the love of God]. It is a question of having it, and of inspiring it by virtue of a general institution reaching all minds. . . . [T]his is what Christianity did, and this is what philosophy never did, and will never be able to do. . . . [P]hilosophy does nothing for man's heart. . . . It plays around the heart; it never enters it." Philosophy can never make good what

must be hung like a housebreaker. Rousseau himself agreed with this without dreaming of what he was asking for himself."[135] That is, whereas Rousseau, in *Social Contract* IV.8, was pretending to be safeguarding religion (and even seemed to countenance capital punishment for those who betray the state dogmas[136]), he was actually doing the opposite: He should be counted among the social-order-destroying atheists of the Enlightenment rather than among their opponents.

In the ninth dialogue, the Count once again reassumes leadership of the conversation. The discussion briefly turns more directly political. Hereditary monarchy is said to be the best regime that can be imagined, and it is claimed that we know this from experience (notwithstanding all the merely theoretical arguments against it). Arguments for popular sovereignty "all amount to nothing."[137] "The best constituted people is the one that has the fewest written constitutional laws, and every written constitution is worthless."[138] Nevertheless, within a couple of pages we are plunged back into the deep waters of theology. In particular, the discussion centers on the problem of self-sacrifice (a dogma "which is perfectly natural to man although appearing difficult to arrive at by reason"). The Count refers to "these terrible austerities... practised by certain religious orders" (presumably he has in mind the harsher forms of monastic discipline) and then adds the observation that Christianity "rests entirely on an enlargement of this same dogma *of innocence paying for crime.*"[139] If the dogma of self-sacrifice makes no sense, then Christianity makes no sense. (After all, Christianity first proved itself as a historical force through demonstrating its power to inspire martyrdom!)

This leads us into the part of the conversation that corresponds to the "Elucidation on Sacrifices" that forms an appendix to the book. "[T]here is an expiatory power in blood."[140] Maistre also invokes his "theory of sacrifices" in commenting on "the inexplicable custom of circumcision."[141] What circumcision means is this: "Anathema on human generation, and SALVATION BY BLOOD."[142] The sacrifice of Christ is simply the extension of this universal dogma ("everywhere one finds *a painful and bloody operation* carried

---

will be destroyed when Christianity succumbs to the attacks of the intellectuals. Christianity has an institution-sustaining power that mere philosophy can never equal.

[135] Ibid., p. 260.

[136] *On the Social Contract*, ed. R. D. Masters (New York: St. Martin's Press, 1978), p. 131. See also Masters's editorial note, p. 154, n. 140.

[137] *St. Petersburg Dialogues*, p. 263.

[138] Ibid.

[139] Ibid., p. 267. This page features quotations from the "anonymously-authored" *Considerations on France* (so the Count is in effect quoting himself without revealing that that is what he is doing).

[140] Ibid., p. 268; cf. p. 270: "this world is a military expedition, an eternal combat.... [T]he greatest glory goes to the one who returns wounded."

[141] Ibid., p. 268.

[142] Ibid., p. 269.

out on the organs of reproduction"). Man "has always sought his regeneration through blood."[143] "[T]his whole doctrine of antiquity [namely the idea of theocide – for instance, in Aeschylus's *Prometheus Bound*] was only the prophetic cry of humanity announcing salvation by blood.... Christianity has come to justify this prophecy by putting the reality in place of the type."[144] The Count refers to this dogma as "a bright light amidst all the shadows of paganism" (including Plato[145]). This is the core of Christianity, namely the power of expiatory sacrifice. If blood is not shed, then human evil goes unredeemed.

The tenth dialogue begins with the Senator's elaboration of a highly extravagant quasi-pantheistic metaphysics. ("Our mutual unity results from our unity in God.... The pantheism of the Stoics, and that of Spinoza, is a corruption of this great idea."[146]) There seems to be implicit in this metaphysics of all-encompassing spiritual unity a wholesale rejection of secular science. The Senator in this context quotes St. Paul on the vanities of knowledge: "Knowledge puffs up, but charity edifies." "Knowledge left to itself divides rather than unites."[147] The Senator also deploys the Augustinian argument that humanity is a unity because human evil originates in a unitary act of evil by Adam. Evil is "the hereditary consequence of a fundamental transgression, and which has the support of the mass of human traditions."[148] "The fall of man can thus be numbered among the proofs of human unity ... *[S]alvation likewise came from a single man*."[149] Rather surprisingly, the Count dismisses the Senator's reflections on the sources of human unity as "vain speculations."[150] Why is the Count so resistant to (or nervous about) the Senator's metaphysics?

In urging greater humility and religious conformity upon the Senator, the Count is insistent: "We must subordinate all our learning to religion.... [W]e study by praying.... [E]very metaphysical proposition that does not issue from a Christian dogma is and can only be nothing but a culpable extravagance."[151] Nevertheless, the Count's own philosophizing has hardly demonstrated a shortage of metaphysics. Why does he clamp down *now* on excessive metaphysics? (Of course, it is quite possible that all of this is a subtle skirmish at the level of opposing *theological* commitments; maybe from the Count's Catholic perspective, Russian Orthodoxy too easily lends itself to an overly metaphysical version of Christianity.) It is hard to be sure what is really going on, but (leaving the theology aside) let me suggest one other possibility. Looking carefully

---

143 Ibid.
144 Ibid.
145 See p. 267, n. 6. This association of Plato with the doctrine of salvation by blood sacrifice recalls Maistre's earlier reference to Plato's philosophy (p. 142) as "the human preface of the Gospel."
146 Ibid., p. 291.
147 Ibid., pp. 293–294.
148 Ibid., p. 294.
149 Ibid.
150 Ibid., p. 295.
151 Ibid., p. 301.

at the passage on p. 291 concerning the Senator's doctrine that the spiritual union of human beings comes about through "material unions," one can see that what the Senator is actually discussing is *kissing*,[152] but it would be easy to extend this line of argument to apply the same conception to sexual intercourse itself. This is as close as Maistre ever comes in this book to considering the spirituality (and not just sinfulness) of sex, and therefore, seen in this context, it is not at all surprising that the Count, while acknowledging the piety that animates the Senator's intentions, nonetheless rebukes the Senator for going a little too far with his metaphysical speculations. What the Count is saying (according to this reading) is that the Senator, despite his pious intentions, is wandering onto dangerous territory. The Chevalier basically sides with the Count in this argument: "It seems to me, Senator, that you have given a little too much latitude to your religious ideas."[153]

The Senator interprets the Count's challenge as based on an opposition between science and religion (although it seems bizarre that the Count, of all people, would side with science *against* religion). In reply, the Count insists that there is no disagreement between them concerning the relation between religion and science. They both agree that religion is the mother of science. Europe is a great scientific civilization precisely because it is simultaneously a Christian civilization.[154] However, if science liberates itself from its theological origins, it will lead us down into the abyss. Science needs to be disciplined by theology and religion. (Berlin, in his commentary on Maistre, presents him as straightforwardly opposed to science as such.[155] But as this passage illustrates – and there are other such passages in the *St. Petersburg Dialogues* – Maistre's attitude toward science is a lot more complex than Berlin suggests.[156]) The Count states that science will be a great evil unless it is kept under control by the necessary religious preparations: "Teach young people physics and chemistry before they have been imbued with religion and morals, or send a new nation academicians before sending missionaries, and you will see the result."[157] Again, there is a big difference between saying that science requires religious discipline and saying that science as such is to be stifled and opposed. He also says that he is opposed "to all curious research that goes beyond man's temporal sphere,"[158] which implies that science that keeps within its proper limitations and does not

---

[152] Cf. p. 314, n. i.
[153] Ibid., p. 303; cf. p. 304 (Chevalier to Senator): "[Y]our taste for explanations of an extraordinary kind could perhaps lead you and others into very grave dangers.... I think that you have gone a bit too far."
[154] Ibid., p. 300: "The scepter of science belongs to Europe only because it is Christian."
[155] See, e.g., *The Crooked Timber of Humanity*, p. 142: Maistre "was not interested in the methods of natural science: he was interested in the visionary Swedenborg and mystical explanations of natural phenomena; and would have agreed no less readily than his contemporary William Blake that more recondite wisdom was to be found in the occult sciences than in manuals of modern chemistry or physics."
[156] Cf. *Against Rousseau*, ed. Lebrun, p. 109 and p. 110, n. 1.
[157] *St. Petersburg Dialogues*, p. 300.
[158] Ibid., p. 302.

trespass on the jurisdiction of religion is acceptable. The Count quotes Bacon's maxim, "Religion is the spice that prevents science from becoming tainted," and endorses it, saying that his only objection is that Bacon's own practice as an ideologist for science betrayed his own maxim.[159] This again implies the possibility of a form of science that is *not* tainted.

Nonetheless, there are some other statements in the same speech that suggest a more straightforward opposition to the scientific enterprise. On p. 302 he says that the "more intelligence knows, the guiltier it can be"; on p. 303 he states, "I thank God for my ignorance even more than for my knowledge, for my knowledge is my own... and in consequence I cannot be sure it is good, while my ignorance... is from him [God], and so I have all possible confidence in it." Finally, on p. 300 he says that science, "if it is not *entirely* subordinated [emphasis added] to the national dogmas," degrades man and corrupts his citizenship. (Rousseau, he says, came halfway, but only halfway, toward grasping this truth.) It is hard to see how science "subordinated to the national dogmas" can still be science: If Galileo must defer to the priests, for instance, then it is pointless to talk about science at all.

This same speech also includes some very important statements about the relation between religion and politics. Scholars as such are bad statesmen and inept administrators, declares the Count.[160] Far superior are priests: The sacerdotal order produces proportionately more statesmen than all other orders of society. Bishops make monarchies like bees make a hive![161] This is the core of Maistre's theocratic politics: To the extent that priests are at the center of political life, politics is sound; to the extent that scientists and intellectuals are at the center of political life, politics is corrupt. All of Maistre's judgments about political affairs flow from this central set of alternatives.

In this dialogue, the Count, strangely enough, presents himself as a metaphysical skeptic, trying to restrain the speculative excesses of his two interlocutors. This is certainly a profound reversal in relation to the preceding dialogues. The empiricism of the eighteenth century tries to expunge all metaphysics, and clearly the Count hates empiricism for this reason; but here the Count emphasizes that it is possible to err in the opposite direction as well – to be carried by speculative enthusiasm beyond the strict tenets of religious orthodoxy. As the Senator admits on p. 291, his metaphysics of all-embracing unity in God verges on pantheism, which is hardly consistent with Christian orthodoxy. It is possible, of course, that the purpose here is a self-criticism of Maistre's own earlier dabblings in mystical and Masonic heresies, but let me suggest another

---

[159] Ibid., p. 302.

[160] Ibid., p. 301.

[161] Ibid. Maistre's principle that priests are to monarchy as bees are to the beehive might be helpful in explaining why thinkers such as Harrington who are committed to republicanism are equally committed to banishing clericalism. Of course, this does not explain Hobbes's anticlericalism, but it does explain why republican thinkers are powerfully drawn to Hobbes. For a comprehensive treatment of this theme, see Paul A. Rahe, *Against Throne and Altar* (Cambridge: Cambridge University Press, 2008).

possibility. A less biographical way of reading this whole dialogue is to see it as expressing the success of the Count's pedagogical project. The Count occupies the same pedagogical role that Socrates enacts in a Platonic dialogue. As Socrates tries to inoculate his young interlocutors against sophism, so the Count seeks to inoculate the young Chevalier against empiricism and atheistic materialism. (As the Count says to the Chevalier, "you will pass on to [a later generation] the culture you have gained from us."[162]) The Count is so successful in this endeavor that, by the end of the book, he is obliged to reintroduce a skeptical note in order to restrain the metaphysical extravagance of his two companions. If the danger is now "over-indulgence" in metaphysics[163] rather than repudiation of it, this proves that the Count's pedagogy has been an overwhelming success.

In the eleventh and last dialogue, the Count again presents himself as a religious moderate, restraining the mystical and prophetic enthusiasms of the Senator. Here the great danger is the seductions of "illuminism," which from the Count's point of view approximates a kind of Protestant heresy. He even goes so far as to write this: "Read without notes and without explanation, Holy Scripture is a poison"; *private interpretation* constitutes "the foolish and yet fundamental dogma of Protestantism."[164] The spread of the Protestant Reformation is coterminous with the radical destruction of Christianity.[165] Illuminism, to the extent that it liberates the interpretive capacities of human beings from regulation by the Church, points in the same direction; it represents, the Count says, an "aversion for all authority and sacerdotal hierarchy."[166] Hence illuminism "totally annihilates authority, which is still the base of our system."[167] Again, Maistre here may simply be offering a public repudiation of doctrines with which he flirted in his less orthodox youth. The Count agrees with the Senator that they are on the brink of "a great event"[168] – and the "Sketch of a Final Dialogue" on pp. 348–349 seems to announce the consummation of this great reversal in European destiny – but he rejects the Senator's recourse to prophetism and extravagant augury-seeking in second-guessing Providence. One must cleave to Catholic orthodoxy, and *any* departure from orthodoxy, even one motivated by religious enthusiasm, must be resisted. Any attempt to offer interpretations not sanctioned by the Catholic hierarchy amounts to joining the Reformation, which in turn makes one complicit in the destruction of all authority.

There is one last thing worth mentioning in connection with the eleventh dialogue. On p. 325, we finally get an explanation for a small puzzle that runs throughout the whole book, namely why Maistre refers consistently to

---

[162] *St. Petersburg Dialogues*, p. 310.
[163] Ibid.
[164] Ibid., p. 335.
[165] Ibid., p. 327.
[166] Ibid., p. 331.
[167] Ibid., p. 333.
[168] Ibid., p. 334.

the eighteenth century as "our century," even though the book was actually written in the nineteenth century. He writes, "the eighteenth century... still endures today, for intellectual centuries do not conform to the calendar like *centuries* properly speaking." It is as if Maistre refuses to acknowledge the start of the nineteenth century until the success of the Counter-Revolution (achieved after Maistre started writing the *St. Petersburg Dialogues*)[169] has put an official end to the century of intellectual and spiritual disaster; the eighteenth century can only be declared over once a new epoch has buried the doctrines of eighteenth-century philosophers/atheists.

Let us turn finally to the "Elucidation on Sacrifices," which spells out in more detail the core doctrine of expiation by blood sacrifice developed by Maistre in the ninth dialogue.[170] "[H]eaven... could only be appeased by blood.... [There is] an expiatory power in the shedding of blood."[171] For Maistre, the central doctrine here is what he calls *the dogma of substitution*: "[T]he innocent can pay for the guilty.... [L]ife being guilty, a less valuable life can be offered and accepted for another." For instance, consider the Law of Moses: In every *other* respect, Mosaic law goes out of its way to distinguish itself from pagan rites – *but not with respect to sacrifices*. In fact, not only did Moses conform to "the fundamental rite of the nations," "he reinforced it at the risk of giving the national character a harshness it did not need." "There is not one of the ceremonies prescribed by this famous legislator, and especially, there is not a purification, that does not require blood."[172]

Sacrifices, Maistre insists, are not a matter of a mere offering, a gift to the gods. "It is a question of *blood*, it is a question of *immolation*, properly

---

[169] The book straddles the Napoleonic and post-Napoleonic eras since Maistre began to write it in 1809, and the book was left unfinished when he died in 1821.

[170] For an interesting discussion of this text, see Owen Bradley, "Maistre's Theory of Sacrifice," in *Joseph de Maistre's Life, Thought and Influence*, ed. Lebrun, pp. 65–83. According to Laurence Lampert, Nietzsche has his own version of this Maistrean doctrine: "[A] profound force in the human soul demands sacrifice.... [§ 55 of *Beyond Good and Evil*] describes the three most important rungs on the ladder of religious cruelty: first is the premoral sacrifice of human beings; second, the moral sacrifice of 'one's instincts, one's "nature"' to antinatural, supernatural gods. The final cruelty sacrifices those gods themselves [which is nihilistic sacrifice] because it sacrifices the very things for the sake of which humanity's other sacrifices were made." Lampert, *Nietzsche's Task* (New Haven: Yale University Press, 2001), p. 115; see also *Genealogy of Morals*, Second Essay, § 21.

[171] *St. Petersburg Dialogues*, p. 358.

[172] Ibid., p. 359. For a vivid depiction of the spilling of blood as a cultural symbol (specifically in Jewish kosher rituals, but also more generally), see Philip Roth, *Indignation* (Toronto: Viking Press, 2008), esp. pp. 157–161. Admittedly, the slaughter of animals seems a very modest version of this theme compared with the Christian variant of blood-splattering "theocide." Nonetheless, Bradley in "Maistre's Theory of Sacrifice" argues that, in Maistre's view, both the sacrifice of animals and the sacrifice of Christ share the same logic of "substitution and reversibility" – namely the hope that God will accept the shedding of the blood of the innocent in lieu of the blood of the guilty. (This obsessive theme in Maistre prompts one to ask whether a Maistrean analysis is not of some help in fathoming the choice of grisly decapitation as a favored technique of execution among Islamist fanatics in the present day.)

speaking."[173] What is crucial is not the offering of flesh but the shedding of blood as expiation. As Maistre had emphasized in the ninth dialogue, this is a universal feature of human religions.[174] What is unique about Christianity is not the emphasis on the expiatory properties of blood but instead the placing of the full sacrificial burden upon Christ alone, thereby liberating humanity from the otherwise universal practice of human sacrifice. On p. 367, Maistre claims that only Christianity has ever succeeded in putting an end to the practice of human sacrifices. What applies to all pre-Christian religions would apply as well to post-Christian existence if the atheistic philosophers of the Enlightenment were to succeed in destroying Christianity. Hence he claims that Christianity alone keeps human beings from reverting to cannibalism, and he cites the French Revolution as proof for the truth of this claim.[175]

Maistre says it was a corruption of the doctrine of substitution that "gave birth to the horrible superstition of human sacrifices."[176] Apart from Christianity, this "horrible superstition" is quasi-universal. One would have thought that the universality or near-universality of such an awful expression of human religiosity would serve to impugn most religions, if not religion in general. Maistre takes up this challenge in the context of a debate with Lucretius. As a kind of ancient anticipation of the Enlightenment, Lucretius blames all these abuses (cannibalism, human sacrifice, and so on) on religion. "He was unaware that the abuse of human sacrifices, however outrageous it was, would fade in comparison to the evils produced by absolute impiety."[177] Better to have human sacrifice inspired by genuine religiosity than to have human sacrifice inspired by the atheism of the Jacobins! The easy route for Maistre to take would be to draw a strong contrast between true religion and the false religions of antiquity, and therefore make no admission of a need to justify the horrors generated by non-Christian religions. Maistre, however, refuses to take this cowardly way out. On the contrary, Lucretius is criticized because he failed to see "that there is not and cannot be a completely false religion."[178] *All* religions, however horrific some of their practices may be, anticipate the truth of Christianity. The sins of religion are always minor in comparison with the sins of impiety. So, for instance, Maistre dismisses the excesses of the Portuguese Inquisition as "some drops of very guilty blood shed *legally* from time to time."[179]

---

[173] *St. Petersburg Dialogues*, p. 372.

[174] See p. 354: "[T]here is no Christian dogma that does not have its root in man's inner nature and in a tradition as old as humanity"; p. 359, n. 2: "[S]acrifice was always the foundation of every kind of religion, without distinction of place, time, opinions, or circumstances"; p. 359: The "idea of spiritual rebirth through blood" is common to the pagan and biblical religions.

[175] Ibid., p. 371. No doubt, a contemporary Maistrean could cite the Nazis to make the same point.

[176] Ibid., p. 364.

[177] Ibid., p. 371.

[178] Ibid.

[179] Ibid., p. 376, n. 28; cf. p. 374. As Tracy B. Strong highlights in his Foreword to Carl Schmitt, *The Leviathan in the State Theory of Thomas Hobbes* (Chicago: University of Chicago Press, 2008), p. xxiv, this is clearly one respect in which Schmitt proves himself to be a loyal Maistrean.

Hence Maistre's purpose is not just to vindicate Christianity but to vindicate all religions as politically indispensable. It is true not only of Christian (i.e., Catholic) nations but all well-governed nations (including those of pagan antiquity) that religion constituted "the cement of the political structure."[180] Maistre points out that Epicurean dogmas contributed to the onset of Roman tyranny by undermining religion.[181] It is impossible to miss the implied parallel with the contemporary French situation: Enlightenment dogmas, by undermining religion, contribute to Napoleonic tyranny. Wherever religion is weakened, the outcome is either anarchy or despotism or some combination of both. However, if all religion is based on the idea of blood sacrifice, the "idea of spiritual rebirth through blood," then one has a clearer idea of what it means to sustain religion. To secure the political benefits of religion one needs either the real thing (real shedding of blood) or, preferably, the vicarious Christian version (symbolic participation in Christ's sacrifice). Religion that does not reach this deeply into the mysteries of divinity will accordingly fail to achieve political efficacy. Maistre puts it this way at the end of chapter 1 of the "Elucidation": "The roots of so extraordinary and so general a belief must go very deep. If there was nothing real or mysterious about it, why would God himself have retained it in the Mosaic law? Where could the ancients have found this idea of spiritual rebirth through blood? Moreover, why, *always* and *everywhere*, have men chosen to honour the Divinity, to obtain its favours, and to turn away its wrath by means of a ceremony that reason in no way suggests and that feeling rejects?"[182]

In the last chapter of the "Elucidation on Sacrifices," we get an astonishing account of just how far the dominion of sinfulness extends. On pp. 382–383, Maistre writes that according to Catholic doctrine, redemption by Christ not only redeems mankind but it redeems the whole universe. Maistre quotes Origen: "[T]he lamb alone could take upon himself the sins of the whole world"; "The altar was in Jerusalem, but the blood of the victim bathed the universe." He also quotes the Passion Sunday hymn: "And the earth, the sea, the stars themselves; / All creatures, finally, are washed by this blood." This seems an extraordinary outcome for a philosophy that sought to furnish a providential account of the world. Why would a providential Creator-God create a world so steeped in sinfulness that "the earth, the sea, the stars themselves, all creatures" would need to be cleansed by a sacrificial blood? Does this not undermine Maistre's suggestion elsewhere that it is human evil alone that requires a providential order to inflict punishment on the sinful? If the whole world is in need of redemption, does this not create doubt concerning the providential character of God's creation?[183]

---

[180] *St. Petersburg Dialogues*, p. 371.

[181] Ibid., pp. 371–372.

[182] Ibid., p. 359.

[183] Cf. p. 267, where the Count quotes the following passage from Maistre's own *Considerations on France*: "There is nothing but violence in the universe...we are spoiled by a modern philosophy that tells us that *all is good*, whereas evil has tainted everything, and in a very real sense, *all is evil*." Needless to say, it seems very strange to get a passage like this in the context

I began my account of the *St. Petersburg Dialogues* with a comparison between Maistre and Nietzsche; let me close with a summary of (my reconstruction of) the Maistre–Nietzsche debate. Maistre and Nietzsche entirely agree on the nature of Christianity – for both of them, it is a religion steeped in sin, blood, and guilt. Quite telling is the last sentence of the "Elucidation on Sacrifices," in which Maistre writes that the need for God to sacrifice himself as Christ to atone for the radical evil in human beings demonstrates the truth of the doctrine of the human race's "radical degradation" and of "the substitution of the merits of the innocent paying for the guilty and SALVATION BY BLOOD" (in Maistre's view, the *core* of Christian dogma).[184] "[T]his *theandric* blood [of Holy Communion; theandric is the uniting of divine and human elements in Christ] penetrates *the guilty entrails* to devour the defilements within them."[185] Man wallows in sin, and therefore blood must flow to expiate man's guilt: This is the essence of Christianity. But for Nietzsche, this is an utterly perverse view of the human condition that renders any experience of innocence or good will toward oneself strictly impossible; it *poisons* one's relation to oneself and to the world more generally. For Maistre, in contrast, it is a condition of human nobility, and any *other* experience of life amounts to pure degradation.

of an argument intended to vindicate a "providential" vision of the world. It obviously seems more like the expression of an antitheodicy than a theodicy.

[184] Ibid., p. 385.
[185] Ibid.

26

Maistrean Politics

Political authority is not mysterious, nor is it to be sanctified by symbols and rituals citizens cannot understand in terms of their common purposes.

– John Rawls[1]

[Good politics requires] the absolute and general rule of national dogmas.... [I]f each man makes himself the judge of the principles of government you will see immediately the rise of civil anarchy or the annihilation of political sovereignty. Government is a true religion; it has its dogmas, its mysteries, its priests; to submit it to individual discussion is to destroy it.

– Joseph de Maistre[2]

All the most interesting thinkers are uncompromising radicals, prepared to follow their respective thought-paths as far as it takes them. There is no question that this applies to Maistre. Consider Isaiah Berlin's description of Maistre's radicalism: "[Maistre] resembled Rousseau. Just as Rousseau imposed a kind of Calvinist logical strait-jacket upon what was really a kind of burning private lunacy, so Maistre imposes an official legitimist Catholic framework upon what is really a deeply violent, deeply revolutionary inner passion."[3] There may be reason to consider this a very unjust slander of Rousseau, and it may or may not do justice to Maistre, but Berlin's statement does nicely capture the utter radicalism of Maistre's thought.

To carry a bit further our brief tour of Maistre's intellectual world, let us take a look at the *Considerations on France*. Maistre begins the book with a *defense* of the providential character of the French Revolution. This is absolutely extraordinary for someone who hated the French Revolution with every fiber of his soul! Maistre writes, "never has the Divinity shown itself so clearly

---

[1] John Rawls, *Political Liberalism* (New York: Columbia University Press, 1996), p. 431.
[2] *The Works of Joseph de Maistre*, ed. Jack Lively (New York: Macmillan, 1965), pp. 108–109.
[3] "Introduction" to Joseph de Maistre, *Considerations on France*, ed. Richard A. Lebrun (Cambridge: Cambridge University Press, 1994), p. xxxiii.

in any human event. If the vilest instruments are employed, punishment is for the sake of regeneration"[4]; and "we should not be surprised if [France] is brought back to her mission by terrible means. It has been a long time since we have seen such frightful punishment inflicted on such a large number of guilty people."[5] This is far from what one would expect – not that the Revolution was inflicted by a small band of madmen and criminals upon the innocent, but rather that the Revolution was a justified punishment for a nation that was guilty. Maistre loves the Reign of Terror – because it punishes the guilty (i.e., everyone is guilty). Again, this is utterly extraordinary coming from someone who hated the Revolution with his whole being. Politics, for Maistre, is a realm of submission to divine authority and, in the case of revolt, of the inflicting of divine punishment. Punishment is central to politics, and all punishment is divinely ordained.

How can Maistre bring himself to justify the Reign of Terror? His argument is that if the regicide had been immediately followed by counterrevolution, there would have been no way to avoid pardon of most of the criminals.[6] By allowing the Revolution to punish its own (through the Reign of Terror), providential justice was satisfied. He refers, in this context, to genocidal punishment in the Old Testament: "There have been nations literally condemned to death like guilty individuals."[7] The Jacobins are *both* regicidal villains *and* agents of Providence: "The revolutionary government hardened the soul of France by tempering it in blood. . . . The horror of the scaffolds . . . nourished external force . . . this monstrous power, drunk with blood and success, the most frightful phenomenon that has ever been seen and the like of which will never be seen again, was both a horrible chastisement for the French and the sole means of saving France."[8] The regicides were in fact saving France for the next monarchy![9] A triumph of the counterrevolution would bring kindness, clemency, justice, and all the gentle and peaceful virtues. Opposed to all this is "the sombre rigour of the revolutionary regime."[10] Maistre turns Montesquieu precisely on his head: Better to have bloodthirsty republicans than to have a reinstated monarch who "would have only *humane* means at his disposal."[11]

---

[4] *Considerations*, p. 8; cf. Rousseau's suggestion that Christians are unable to resist tyranny because it is natural for them to interpret the tyrant as "the rod with which God punishes His children"; *Social Contract*, Book IV, chapter 8.

[5] *Considerations*, p. 9.

[6] Ibid., p. 14.

[7] Ibid.

[8] Ibid., p. 16.

[9] Ibid., pp. 16–17: "All the monsters born of the Revolution have, apparently, laboured only for the monarchy. . . . [T]he king will reascend his throne with all his pomp and power, perhaps even with an increase of power. . . . [E]verything is happening for the advantage of the French monarchy. . . . These horrors [were] very useful to the future king." (*Considerations on France* was published in 1797, i.e., seventeen years before the Restoration.)

[10] Ibid., p. 17.

[11] Ibid.

What defines politics, for Maistre, is a world-historical battle for the survival of religion: Rome and Geneva on the one hand; on the other hand, "the power that wants no religions"[12] (viz., republican France). France, Maistre says, is the citadel of Christianity; therefore it is the natural place for the enemies of Christianity to attack it.[13] Rome and Geneva, however, are only to a very limited degree on the same side in this great battle. Protestant churches are described by him as parasitic plants, "sterile mistletoes that live only from the substance of the tree which supports them and which they impoverish."[14] In chapter 3 he writes, "it is from the shadow of a cloister [i.e., Luther, Calvin] that there emerges one of mankind's very greatest scourges ... and finally, in our day, from the same source, the French Revolution."[15] (Is *Protestantism* ultimately to blame for the French Revolution?[16]) The basic axiom of Maistre's political philosophy is that politics has to be interpreted theocratically; one might say that from Maistre's point of view, politics is necessarily "epiphenomenal" in relation to the more basic theocratic drama that is always dictating political events. He writes, "one would be tempted to believe that the political revolution is only a secondary object in the great plan unrolling before us with such terrible majesty."[17] He refers to a case in which the Dutch Reformed Church was politically disestablished and then makes this remark: "If Providence *erases*, it is no doubt in order to *write*."[18] In other words, any political setbacks for religion must be interpreted as part of a larger theocratic design. The French Revolution, he says at the end of chapter 2, "is a means as much as a punishment"[19] – that is, a means toward the establishment of a more well-grounded theocracy.

There are only two real possibilities: reinforcement of the religious spirit or utter dissolution of the social bond.[20] From this point of view "the French Revolution is a great epoch,"[21] for it represents the ultimate test of whether history points toward a reconsolidation of theocratic politics or toward the triumph of destructive secularism. "Pay attention when the Lord punishes you."[22] It is as if all the blood and destruction associated with the Revolution were simply a way of highlighting the historical importance of this apocalyptic moment in the cosmic drama over the fate of religion; *everything*, for Maistre, hangs in the balance. Christianity's fate is being decided, and if the revolutionary upheaval

---

[12] Ibid., p. 20.
[13] Ibid., p. 21.
[14] Ibid.
[15] Ibid., p. 27.
[16] Hence Maistre's characterization of Protestantism as "le *sans-cullottisme* de la religion": Joseph de Maistre, *Œuvres*, ed. Pierre Glaudes (Paris: Robert Laffont, 2007), p. 330. Cf. the editor's note in *Considerations on France*, p. 27, n. 35.
[17] *Considerations*, p. 20.
[18] Ibid.
[19] Ibid., p. 22.
[20] Ibid., p. 21.
[21] Ibid.
[22] Ibid., p. 21, n. 27, citing the Old Testament.

of the 1790s *does not* lead to a rejuvenated theocratic politics, then Europe is finished as the site of a Christian civilization.

In chapter 5 Maistre presents the argument that the French Revolution, with its deliberate political exclusion of religion ("the nation will support no form of worship"), is "historically unique."[23] That is, it is unprecedented for a state to go out of its way to deny itself resources of religious sanction that have always seemed to political actors throughout history as indispensable. "Either every imaginable institution is founded on a religious concept or it is only a passing phenomenon. Institutions are strong and durable to the degree that they are, so to speak, *deified*." Human reason is "incapable of supplying these foundations."[24] Again, "true or false, [religious ideas] nevertheless form the unique basis of all durable institutions. Rousseau, perhaps the most self-deceived man who ever lived, nevertheless hit on this observation without wishing to draw the consequences from it."[25] Maistre quotes Book II, chapter 7 of the *Social Contract*, on great legislators like Moses and Mohammed, and comments that Rousseau "had only to draw the logical conclusion from this."[26] What *is* the logical conclusion that Rousseau missed? Obviously, that this political fact must be interpreted "theocratically," or providentially, rather than taking political theology and *secularizing* it, or treating it as a department of mere political science. Maistre from time to time cites Machiavelli favorably (the Senator in the *St. Petersburg Dialogues* refers to Machiavelli as "this pious writer"!),[27] but it is clear that Rousseau is merely following Machiavelli in this respect: namely in absolutely privileging the political side of the politics and religion equation. Maistre's point is that what Moses and Mohammed teach us is not the formidable capabilities of political legislators (à la Machiavelli), but rather the political intentions of *God* (namely that human beings are intended to be ruled theocratically). Although Rousseau refers appreciatively to various theocratic regimes, including Geneva, he certainly never considers going this far. Rousseau, like Machiavelli and all his successors within the tradition of modern political philosophy, shifts attention to the human legislator, whereas Maistre insists on the *Divine* Legislator as the foundation of all social order. Rousseau himself probably sees his civil-religion teachings as a rebuke to the Enlightenment, whereas Maistre (not without reason) sees Rousseau's *affinities* to the Enlightenment![28] Immediately after the initial discussion of Rousseau,

[23] Ibid., p. 41.
[24] Ibid.
[25] Ibid., p. 42.
[26] Ibid.
[27] Joseph de Maistre, *St. Petersburg Dialogues*, trans. Richard A. Lebrun (Montreal: McGill-Queen's University Press, 1993), p. 325.
[28] Cf. *Considerations*, p. 57, n. 8, where Maistre asserts that Rousseau, in Book II, chapter 7 of the *Social Contract*, "absent-mindedly lets the truth slip out" concerning the dependence of this-worldly legislators upon heavenly sanctions and otherworldly symbolism. That is, Rousseau acknowledges this truth *in spite of himself* – contrary to his own natural inclination to embrace a more radically secularist political vision.

Maistre takes up the Rousseauian question of whether Christians can be soldiers. Rousseau, of course, in Book IV, chapter 8 of the *Social Contract*, had asserted that the martial virtues essential for republican liberty are beyond the capacity of Christians: "True Christians are made to be slaves.... [T]his brief life is of too little worth in their view [to invest great energies in defending liberty]."[29] Maistre refers to the crusading orders, "this strange amalgam of monk and soldier," and also to the Jesuits as a quasi-army. The Jesuits, in particular, Maistre thinks, refute Rousseau's idea that secular political leadership suffices to establish social institutions: "[A]ll the sovereigns in the world would never succeed" in creating what is fashioned by a St. Ignatius.[30] "[T]he humble missionary," he writes, "will succeed [where great political leaders fail] and be obeyed two thousand years after his death."[31]

The reference to the Christian crusading orders is especially significant because it tacitly picks up on Rousseau's challenge to Christianity. Rousseau wrote, "I don't know of any Christian troops. The crusades will be cited. Without arguing over the valor of the crusaders, I shall note that very far from being Christians, they were soldiers of the priest, they were citizens of the Church; they were fighting for its spiritual country, which the church had made temporal in some unknown way. Properly understood, this amounts to paganism. Since the Gospel does not establish a national religion, a holy war is impossible among Christians."[32] How does Maistre reply to this challenge? Rousseau has opened an enormous question here, namely the dubious relationship between the authentic Christianity of the Gospels and what goes under the name of organized Christianity, and Maistre, as far as I know, never adequately addresses this challenge. Maistre never sees a tension between the temporal structures of churchly authority and the anarchism of the Gospel, and he passes up Rousseau's invitation to address this problem. Maistre's claim is that "European institutions...are all *Christianized*.... [R]eligion mingles in everything, animates and sustains everything,"[33] and that this is evidence of a principle of divine inspiration. However, he never spells out what it means for institutions to be "Christianized," and the fact that, for instance, the Knights of Malta have endured for centuries does not by itself demonstrate a divine efficacy.

Another indication of Maistre's failure to engage Rousseau's challenge is his reference to Christianity as "the old national religion."[34] This can be read as a direct rebuke to Rousseau's statement that "the Gospel does not establish

---

[29] *On the Social Contract*, ed. R. D. Masters, trans. J. R. Masters (New York: St. Martin's Press, 1978), p. 130.

[30] *Considerations*, p. 43.

[31] Ibid., p. 44.

[32] *On the Social Contract*, p. 130.

[33] *Considerations*, p. 42.

[34] Ibid., p. 48; cf. p. 48, n. 15: Christianity is what *defines* French nationhood; and p. 101, n. 22, on Vico on "the national religion." It may be observed that the strong appeal to "*national* dogmas" in this and other texts seems in tension with Maistre's militant anti-Gallicanism.

a national religion." Nonetheless, how can a religion as otherworldly as that expressed in the Christian Gospel be reconciled with the temporal structures of a theocratic political order (with priests as political agents, as it were, and often, as Maistre himself repeatedly emphasizes, as political agents in the most literal sense)? This is Rousseau's challenge, and I do not know of anywhere in Maistre's work that the challenge is directly addressed. (One can also read Tocqueville as striving to answer this same Rousseauian challenge, as I discussed earlier in Chapter 20.)

The crucial question is whether it is possible to have a nontheocratic regime, and whether the very notion of attempting such a thing is an unnatural monstrosity. In this sense, the fate of a restored Christian theocratic regime is a secondary question; the primary question is political theocracy (whether Christian or non-Christian) versus political secularism. Maistre makes this statement: "All true philosophy must opt between these two hypotheses: either a new religion is going to come into existence or Christianity will be rejuvenated in some extraordinary way."[35] That is to say, political secularism is not an option. Theocracy is unavoidable. Either one will have a rejuvenated *Christian* theocracy, or the eclipse of Christianity will give way to some new post-Christian religion. Obviously, Maistre himself puts his money on the first of these two possibilities.

We are now at the core of Maistre's theocratic idea – what he refers to as the truth that Rousseau "absent-mindedly lets slip out" – namely the idea that all social order is a product of religious order. Maistre would surely say that Rousseau offers a formal acknowledgment of this truth, but fails utterly to follow through on it by reshaping his social vision in a theocratic direction. Rather, Rousseau merely makes use of this notion at the margins of his political thought, but the core of his political thinking is still merely liberal-secular-Enlightenment inspired. I think Maistre is right to characterize Rousseau's political philosophy in this way, for whatever Rousseau's polemical intentions in his civil-religion chapter, his thought is certainly closer to Enlightenment horizons than it is to any serious theocratic purpose. Now I offer some texts that spell out Maistre's basic theocratic idea:

1. On p. 51, he writes that the "polity and the religion are founded together; the legislator is scarcely distinguishable from the priest." Legislators "only combine preexisting elements in the customs and character of a people; and this gathering together . . . is accomplished only in the name of the Divinity."
2. On the next page, against Rousseau as well as every other modern political philosopher from Machiavelli onward (the accompanying note cites Machiavelli), he makes this assertion: "No mere assembly of men can form a nation."

[35] Ibid., p. 45.

3. On p. 63, Maistre argues that priestly participation in civil government was central to what defined the old French constitutional order: "This monarchy possesses a certain theocratic element that is peculiarly its own and that has given it a lifespan of fourteen hundred years. There is nothing so national as this element." The same is true of England: "If England ever banished the words *Church and State* from its political vocabulary, its government would perish just like that of its rival."

4. In chapter 10, Maistre writes that "religion, lending its authority to politics, will give the strength that can be drawn *only* [emphasis added] from this august sister.... Look at history and you will not see any institution of any strength or duration that does not rest on a divine idea. It does not matter what kind of idea, for there is no entirely false religious system."[36]

5. In an important note on Vico (p. 101, n. 22), Maistre argues that the adherence of the nobility to the national religion is the key to social order. "If the nobility renounces the national dogmas, the state is lost."[37] What is required for durable social order is a unity of the nobility and the priesthood; this is what the Enlightenment rendered no longer possible. It inflicted upon the Christian–European social order "philosophism" – "the universal solvent" – whose pivotal effect was to cause *the nobility* to lose its faith. Following Vico, Maistre maintains that no society can survive such a catastrophe. Maistre puts it this way near the end of chapter 5: "Philosophy having corroded the cement that united men, there are no longer any moral bonds."[38]

6. In a note at the beginning of chapter 6, Maistre quotes Algernon Sidney: "It would take a fool to ask who gave liberty to the cities of Sparta, Rome, etc. These republics did not receive their charters from men. God and nature gave them to them."[39] That is, constitutions are not *human* contrivances; they are always a gift of "God and nature." Maistre's own dictum here is the following: "No constitution is the result of deliberation."[40] That is, the Americans could not really have

---

[36] Ibid., pp. 84–85.

[37] Ibid., p. 101. On Maistre's debt to Vico, see Mark Lilla, *G. B. Vico: The Making of an Anti-Modern* (Cambridge, MA: Harvard University Press, 1993), p. 13.

[38] *Considerations*, p. 47.

[39] Ibid., p. 49, n. 1.

[40] Ibid., p. 49. Graeme Garrard points out that "Maistre granted just one 'magnificent' exception" to this principle, namely the Mosaic constitution of ancient Israel. See "Joseph de Maistre and Carl Schmitt," in *Joseph de Maistre's Life, Thought, and Influence*, ed. Richard A. Lebrun (Montreal: McGill-Queen's University Press, 2001), pp. 235–236. The text where Maistre spells this out is *On God and Society: Essay on the Generative Principle of Political Constitutions and Other Human Institutions*, ed. Elisha Greifer (Chicago: Henry Regnery, 1959), pp. 41–42. If, however, one rejects the assumption on the part of the civil-religion tradition that the Mosaic laws were the work of Moses *qua* lawgiver and instead maintains that these laws were God given (as Maistre emphatically does), then of course the example of the Mosaic constitution is *not* an exception to Maistre's dismissal of man-made constitutions.

done what they thought they were doing: designing a political constitution for themselves. So Maistre's view must be that the putative American Constitution is really a bogus Constitution and can be expected to collapse sooner or later. In fact, this is basically what Maistre says at the end of chapter 7: "[T]here is too much deliberation, too much *humanity* in this business [of designing Washington as the American capital], and one could bet a thousand to one that the city will not be built, that it will not be called *Washington*, and that the Congress will not meet there."[41] It goes without saying that this absurd prediction has dire consequences for the plausibility of Maistre's social theory in general. Like Marx, Maistre offers promises of providential victory for his cause.[42] If history fails to vindicate his promises, then he is refuted.[43] It is hard to avoid the conclusion that Maistre would be forced to accept that the survival of secular regimes like the United States and France for over two centuries *refutes* his theocratic claims, even if theocracy itself has not been banished from the modern world.

I do not want to suggest that there is a complete absence of liberal aspects to the kind of political thought presented in Maistre's *Considerations on France*. On the contrary, chapter 8 of the book offers a striking celebration of the *liberalism* of the ancien régime. Maistre goes out of his way to highlight the king's subordination to the rule of law. The monarchy that Maistre defends in this book is constitutional monarchy, not absolutist monarchy.[44] In the section "Of Vengeance" at the end of chapter 10, Maistre presents himself as a moderate royalist: He encourages pardon and amnesty, rather than being bent on vengeance. He insists that the revolutionaries will be protected by the rule of law and monarchical forgiveness. "France is ready to forsake convulsions and horrors; it wants no more blood."[45] "Even crime and usurpation will be treated with a measured severity, with a calm justice that belongs to legitimate power only. The king will bind up the wounds of the state with a gentle and paternal hand."[46] Maistre (at least in this work), like Burke, is a liberal reactionary: To be sure, he wants a restoration of the old order, but he has a fairly liberal understanding of what defined the old order.

---

[41] *Considerations*, p. 61.
[42] Cf. the "Sketch of a final Dialogue" at the end of the *St. Petersburg Dialogues*.
[43] Cf. *Considerations*, p. 48, where Maistre says in effect that if atheism wins, he will concede defeat. Only one side or the other can emerge triumphant, and if the "philosophers," the intellectual foes of Christianity, can hold the fort, one will have to face up in a clear-sighted way to the fact that Christianity has been definitively conquered.
[44] What amounts to constitutional monarchy is also a theme in Maistre, *Against Rousseau*, ed. Richard A. Lebrun (Montreal: McGill-Queen's University Press, 1996), pp. 69–73 and 85–86.
[45] *Considerations*, p. 103.
[46] Ibid., p. 105. This relates back to the theme of the King's *humane* means ("kindness, clemency, justice, all the gentle and peaceful virtues") discussed previously (ibid., p. 17). The bloodletting that the revolutionaries (and the nation as a whole) truly deserve is conveniently left to Divine Providence, God's just wrath.

Maistre's "liberalism" in the *Considerations on France* is confirmed by his reliance on Hume in the last chapter of the book. How can a theocrat like Maistre cite as an authority *Hume* of all people? How can one deny Hume's relation to the Enlightenment for which Maistre blames all of France's troubles?[47] The purpose of chapter 11 is to show that Hume's critical analysis of Cromwell's revolution anticipates the pathologies of the French Revolution. Somewhat surprisingly, Cromwell's revolution is presented not as a theocratic regime but as an attack on religion comparable to that of the French Revolution.[48] What this seems to suggest is that radical Protestantism is on a par with atheism, and the political consequences in the two cases are identical.[49] Another interesting aspect of the chapter is how Hume's discussion of Cromwell seems full of premonitions of Napoleon.[50] It is as if Maistre can see the Empire coming. The choice *is not* between monarchy and republic, but between (legitimate) monarchy and (usurped) Empire! This has the effect of casting Maistre, again, as the real constitutionalist, the real liberal. The alternative is Cromwellian–Napoleonic dictatorship.[51]

Finally, I want to raise a question about where the *Considerations on France* leaves Maistre in relation to other leading political philosophers of the modern tradition. How far out of line is he? To be sure, he goes out of his way to debunk modern political theory in general. Real constitutions cannot be founded on theory, so the idea of founding a political order on Bacon, Locke, Hume, or Montesquieu is an insane idea: "There is the same difference between political theory and constitutional laws as there is between poetics and poetry. The illustrious Montesquieu is to Lycurgus, in the intellectual hierarchy, what Batteux [an obscure literary scholar] is to Homer or Racine. [So it is no surprise that Locke] fumbled badly when he presumed to give laws to the Americans."[52] One does not have to be a theocrat, however, to have this view of the relation between theory and practice. There is nothing here that one would not get from Burke – and, in fact, it is a reasonable position: Despite Montesquieu's

---

47 On p. 50, n. 2, Maistre refers to "the wise Hume." For a view of Hume closer to what one would expect from Maistre, see the "Elucidation on Sacrifices," in *St. Petersburg Dialogues*, p. 373, referring to Hume's "odious" *Natural History of Religion*, and p. 378, n. 39, referring to Hume's "impiety." See also *St. Petersburg Dialogues*, p. 180, where Hume is referred to as "the most dangerous, perhaps, and the most guilty of those deadly writers who will never cease to accuse the last century in the eyes of posterity, the one who employed the most talent in the most cold-blooded way to do the most harm."

48 See *Considerations*, pp. 111–112. For a twentieth-century counterpart to this argument, see the bitter polemic against the Cromwellian Revolution (and the Reformation more generally) in Eric Voegelin, *The New Science of Politics* (Chicago: University of Chicago Press, 1952), chapter 5.

49 Voegelin's analysis seems to point in the same direction.

50 *Considerations*, pp. 115–116.

51 Chapter 11 is full of paradoxes: On p. 108, Maistre's quotes Hume's tribute to religion (even the most famous atheist of the eighteenth century is capable of appreciating the political benefits of religion!). Even more paradoxical still, the whole chapter is a radical critique of one of the notable cases of bona fide theocratic politics in modern Europe. Basically, what Maistre the theocrat does in this chapter is to plagiarize a religious skeptic criticizing a theocracy!

52 Ibid., p. 52.

suggestion to the contrary at the end of Book 29 of the *Spirit of the Laws*, philosophers are not legislators. (In fact, even Montesquieu in this text cites philosophers as exemplary legislators only to show what bad legislators they are!)

So what sets Maistre apart from his fellow modern political philosophers? As Maistre himself acknowledges at various points throughout the book, theorists like Machiavelli and Rousseau made big concessions to the political importance of religion. This is an even more conspicuous theme in Montesquieu, and – although he wrote after Maistre – Tocqueville goes even further still in this direction. So what is unique about Maistre? The crucial issue, it seems to me, is whether one is writing as a secular political scientist analyzing the advantages for a temporal political order of otherworldly beliefs, rites, and customs (without question, this is how Machiavelli, Montesquieu, Rousseau, and Tocqueville treat the relation between politics and religion) or whether one writes as a genuine theocrat for whom it would be unthinkable to reduce the political significance of religion to a merely instrumentalist dimension. Does Maistre want religion for the sake of the monarchy, or monarchy for the sake of religion? No doubt, Maistre himself would see this as a false dichotomy; to instrumentalize the relation between a given political order and the kind of religiosity that sustains it is already to kill both religion and his preferred political regime. As Maistre expresses most clearly in a key passage of the *Considerations*, what is really at stake in the political battles of the day is a life-and-death struggle between two spiritual orders: Christianity and "philosophism."[53] It is "one of the greatest spectacles ever beheld by human eyes."[54] (Nietzsche would agree.) To reduce the stakes to merely a contest between alternative regimes would appear to Maistre as a fatal misunderstanding of what the politics of the late eighteenth to early nineteenth centuries is really about. This, more than anything else from Maistre's point of view, condemns the tradition of modern political theory from Machiavelli to Tocqueville – however much it may have appreciated the political utility of religion.

---

[53] *Considerations*, p. 45. For very powerful elaborations of the theme that the key political problem is that the reigning regime in Europe is in effect a regime ruled by *philosophers*, see *Against Rousseau*, pp. 76–77, 102–107, and 109–112; cf. p. 105: "What is philosophy in the modern sense? *It is the substitution of individual reason for national dogmas*"; and p. 103, where he states that "individual reason . . . is like an impure insect. . . . Swollen with pride, it is only venom." If philosophy is a venomous spider that "works only to destroy," religion, by contrast, is the "innocent and peaceful" silkworm that forms "the cloak of kings." On pp. 110–111, referring to Spinoza, Rousseau, Voltaire, and the *philosophes*, Maistre writes that the crimes of the French Revolution "are their work, since the criminals are their disciples."

[54] *Considerations*, p. 45.

27

Maistre and Rousseau

Theocracy versus Civil Religion

"Gods would be needed to give laws to men." Not at all, it only takes one.

– Joseph de Maistre[1]

So this is how they reason when they separate man from the Divinity.... [I]t would cost them little to turn their eyes toward the source of being, but such a simple, sure, and consoling way of philosophizing is not to the taste of the writers of this unfortunate century.

– Joseph de Maistre[2]

If Rousseau insists that "a State has never been founded without religion serving as its base," is there not crucial common ground between Rousseau's account of civil religion and Maistrean theocracy?[3] Indeed, as I cited in Chapter 26, Maistre, in *Considerations on France*, acknowledged that Rousseau was *right* that religious ideas "form the unique basis of all durable institutions."[4] He reaffirmed Rousseau's teaching, in Book II, chapter 7 of the *Social Contract*, that among the great legislators of history, one ought to privilege theocratic

---

[1] Joseph de Maistre, *Against Rousseau: "On the State of Nature" and "On the Sovereignty of the People,"* ed. Richard A. Lebrun (Montreal: McGill-Queen's University Press, 1996), p. 63.

[2] Ibid., p. 51. "On the Sovereignty of the People" was composed in the mid-1790s, so "this unfortunate century" obviously refers to the eighteenth century.

[3] Cf. *Against Rousseau*, pp. xviii–xix (Lebrun's Introduction).

[4] Joseph de Maistre, *Considerations on France*, ed. Richard A. Lebrun (Cambridge: Cambridge University Press, 1994), p. 42. Lebrun notes that "of six specific references to Rousseau [in the *Considerations on France*], all but one involve citing Rousseau with approval in support of Maistre's own argument" (*Against Rousseau*, p. xx). (Cf. Jack Lively in *The Works of Joseph de Maistre*, ed. Lively, New York: Macmillan, 1965, p. 44: "Although [Maistre] quotes [Rousseau] several times with approval, he does this with surprise that so much good sense should have come from the man who, more than any other, symbolized the self-will and pride of his age.") Lebrun also highlights the fact that Maistre's assertions that "religious ideas form 'the unique basis of all durable institutions'" and that *"no institution whatsoever can endure if it is not founded on religion"* can be read as generalizations of Rousseau's claim about the state (*Against Rousseau*, p. xx). Lebrun speaks of this as the "development of a shared idea."

lawgivers such as Moses and Mohammed. (Maistre is obviously less enthusiastic about Calvin!)[5] Rousseau "had only to draw the logical conclusion
from this."[6] The logical conclusion, of course, is that politics is *intrinsically*
theocratic – to which one must add that it was not a simple oversight on
Rousseau's part to have failed to draw this conclusion, but rather the consequence of a principled opposition between Rousseauian politics and Maistrean
politics.

Maistre's unfinished essay, "On the Sovereignty of the People," does not
directly address Book IV, chapter 8 of the *Social Contract*.[7] It does, however,
offer an extended discussion of Book II, chapter 7, which is the section of the
Social Contract most closely linked to the chapter on civil religion. What light
does that discussion shed on the Rousseau–Maistre relationship with respect to
theocracy and civil religion? First of all, for Maistre it is somewhat misleading
to speak of human legislators per se, for the ultimate legislator in any society is
always God. God is the source of sovereignty, and because sovereignty issues
in laws, the authority to make laws is fundamentally traceable back to God.
"[S]ince [God] *willed* society, he also *willed* sovereignty and the laws without
which there is no society. Therefore laws come from God in the sense that he
wills that there be laws and that they be obeyed."[8] "[S]ociety is not the work of
man, but the immediate result of the will of the Creator."[9] Maistre, of course,

---

[5] "Le détestable Calvin," Maistre calls him. Joseph de Maistre, *Œuvres*, ed. Pierre Glaudes (Paris:
Robert Laffont, 2007), p. 314. On p. 60 of *Against Rousseau*, Maistre makes explicit his
annoyance at Rousseau's having elevated Calvin to the class of exemplary legislators.

[6] *Considerations on France*, ed. Lebrun, p. 42.

[7] Cf. Lebrun: "Maistre does not challenge Rousseau" with respect to Rousseau's political critique
of Christianity (*Against Rousseau*, p. xviii).

[8] *Against Rousseau*, p. 46; cf. p. 54: "[T]he establishment of society and sovereignty... is the
immediate work of nature, or to put it better, of its author." Not just sovereignty in general
but "[e]ach form of sovereignty [for discrete societies] is the immediate result of the will of the
Creator" (p. 57). See also p. 58, where he states that "the divinity has intervened directly in
the establishment of [the] particular sovereignties [of particular nations]," and p. 84: "Every
particular form of government is a divine work, just like sovereignty in general. A constitution
in the philosophical sense is... only the mode of political existence attributed to each nation
by a higher power." This Maistrean view helps explain why he felt compelled to come up
with a providentialist interpretation of the French Revolution in *Considerations on France*.
If sovereignty in every society is willed by the Creator, then presumably the Jacobin regime is
equally a product of divine will. Why would God create such a despicable sovereign? The answer
is: to punish the impious French for their sins. On pp. 75–76, Maistre quite indignantly rejects
Jacobin notions that their Declaration of the Rights of Man and the Citizen has the blessing of
the Supreme Being: "God does not choose a turbulent multitude, agitated by vile and frenzied
passions, to be the instrument of his wishes in the exercise of the greatest act of his power on
earth: the political organization of nations." At the same time, one can say – and Maistre more
or less says this – that the Jacobins themselves thereby offer a kind of perverse confirmation of
the principle that all laws must present themselves as possessing the sanction of the divinity.

[9] *Against Rousseau*, p. 49. This Maistrean doctrine is more fully elaborated in *On God and Society:
Essay on the Generative Principle of Political Constitutions and Other Human Institutions*,
ed. Elisha Greifer (Chicago: Henry Regnery, 1959).

does not deny that this divine legislation is necessarily mediated by human legislators. Nonetheless, to focus on the human legislators in abstraction from sovereignty as something willed by God is for him a colossal error that stands in the way of a proper understanding of social order. This is a breach between Maistre and Rousseau that can never be bridged.

This difference of views shapes Maistre's treatment of Rousseau's doctrine of the legislator. For Maistre, Moses and Mohammed are not (as they are for Rousseau) primarily *human legislators* whose claim to prophetic status renders their work of legislation more efficacious and more durable. Rather, Maistre sees the prophetic status of these preeminent legislators[10] as testimony to the essentially theocratic character of politics. As we have seen in *Considerations on France*, this is the "logical conclusion" that Maistre says Rousseau had failed to draw. For Maistre, the biblical account of the coronation of King Saul – "consecrated by an immediate intervention of the divinity" – serves as an archetype for the establishment of political authority in *all* societies:

[T]he annals of every nation in the world assign the same origin to their particular governments.... All show us the cradle of sovereignty surrounded by miracles; always divinity intervenes in the foundation of empires; always the first sovereign, at least, is a favourite of heaven: he receives the scepter from the hands of the divinity. Divinity communicates with him, it inspires him; it engraves on his forehead the sign of its power; and the laws that he dictates to his fellows are only the fruit of his celestial communications.[11]

Rousseau is capable of writing in the same vein, but he makes clear that these stories are for him, no less than for Machiavelli or Hobbes, civic myths employed for the consolidation of political order.[12] For Maistre, in contrast, they represent in a fully literal sense the most authentic emblem of God's direct hand in creating sovereignty. To comprehend the true foundations of political order, we must go back to "those mythological times whose true history would instruct us much better than all the others."[13] It is a mistake to dismiss these as mere fables, for "the fables of all peoples... cover many realities."[14] "[E]very universal idea is natural"; hence the "universal dogma of the divine origin of sovereignty" proves its truth.[15] Nor is this a case of pious frauds: "It is truly folly to imagine that this universal prejudice [namely the conception of

---

[10] Maistre calls them "the two most famous legislators in the world": *Against Rousseau*, p. 69. For a powerful vindication of the Mosaic and Mohammedan civilizations that provides, one might say, a point of intersection between Rousseau and Nietzsche, see pp. 88–89.

[11] Ibid., p. 58.

[12] Cf. Mark Lilla, *The Stillborn God* (New York: Knopf, 2007), p. 41. Nietzsche's keen interest in the same phenomenon – ancient law codes that invoke the authority of "divine origin" – in *The Antichrist*, § 57, betrays the civil-religion aspect of Nietzsche's thought that I will explore in Part IV.

[13] *Against Rousseau*, p. 58.

[14] Ibid.

[15] Ibid., p. 59.

sovereignty as divine in its essence] is the work of sovereigns." To be sure, the general belief in the divine origin of sovereignty is sometimes abused by unscrupulous princes, but if these images of sovereignty were not "founded on the inner consent of peoples, [then] the sovereigns could not have imagined such a fraud."[16] For Rousseau, *but not for Maistre*, the fables concerning God's involvement in the origins of nations are a matter of civil religion.

In Book I, chapter 6 of "On the Sovereignty of the People," Maistre zeroes in on the critical difference between himself and Rousseau – between the political appeal to divine favor as a theocratic conception and as a mode of civil religion. In Book II, chapter 7 of the *Social Contract*, Rousseau's argument is that the real legislator must present himself as divinely inspired because the task of founding a virtuous political community is of such heroic proportions that restricting oneself to resources available within the human sphere will not suffice. Of course, any human being can claim to act on the basis of divine sanction, but only the rarest human being can make good on this claim, thereby exhibiting his or her *superhuman* qualities.[17] The world is full of charlatans, but that does not mean anyone can be a legislator. "Any man can engrave stone tablets," but that does not make him Moses. "[P]retending to have a secret relationship with some divinity [or] train[ing] a bird to talk in his ear" does not make one a potential founder of an empire. "The Legislator's great soul is the true miracle that should prove his mission." Maistre supports all of this ("Rousseau . . . shows perfectly how and why all legislators have had to speak in the name of the divinity"),[18] yet he still insists that Rousseau's ultimate position is completely wrong. Why is that? Answering this question serves as an essential elaboration of Maistre's suggestion in *Considerations on France* that there are genuine insights in Rousseau concerning the relationship between politics and religion, but that Rousseau fails to draw the correct conclusions

---

[16] Ibid. Maistre does not explain how "the inner consent of peoples" proves that these are not frauds. Maistre again acknowledges the problem of pious fraud or pseudo-religious deceit on pp. 80–82, but Maistre is emphatic on p. 82 that "[abuses of religion] mean nothing": The union of religion and politics is so essential that one must not be deterred by the possibility of religion being manipulated for deceitful purposes.

[17] Maistre points out that Rousseau borrows the notion of the legislator as a quasi-god from Plutarch's life of Lycurgus ("a god rather than a man"): Ibid., p. 64; cf. p. 68, on the "powers [confided by God] to rare men, to the true elect. Scattered at long intervals through the centuries, they rise like obelisks on the route of time."

[18] Ibid., p. 64. Maistre refers to the passage about what distinguishes true legislators from "those who train a bird to talk in his ear" as "brilliant and even profound." Cf. p. 68, where Maistre again endorses Rousseau's argument that the charisma of the greatest founders cannot be reduced to trickery or charlatanry. Rousseau's critical response to the idea of Moses and Mohammed as "lucky impostors" (*heureux imposteurs*) can be read as an allusion to *The Treatise of the Three Impostors* (and Maistre, in the text on p. 68, seems to have the *Treatise* in mind as well); cf. Voltaire's reference to "the palace of imposture" quoted on p. 106. However, as is not lost on Maistre, the fact that Rousseau immediately goes on to cap his argument with the assertion that religion is instrumental to politics in these great acts of founding puts Rousseau back in the vicinity of the views he is supposedly rebutting.

from these insights. The all-important conclusion of Book II, chapter 7 reads as follows:

> One must not conclude from all this, as Warburton does, that politics and religion have a common object for us, but rather that at the origin of nations, one serves as an instrument of the other [*l'une sert d'instrument à l'autre*].

Civil religion consists in an *instrumentalization* of religion for political purposes, and this is precisely the conception that is formulated in Rousseau's rejection of Warburton. In Maistre's view, if Rousseau were true to his distinction between charlatans who merely dissemble divine favor and "real McCoy" legislators like Moses and Mohammed who have gifts that cannot be simulated, he ought to have agreed with Warburton's notion of a reciprocity of religion and politics.[19] The fact that Rousseau spells out his rejection of Warburton in the precise way that he does provides the clearest articulation of the gulf separating a civil religion like Rousseau's and a theocratic politics like Maistre's.

In Book 1, chapter 8 of "On the Sovereignty of the People," Maistre offers what amounts to his own corrected version of the key passage in Rousseau's doctrine of the legislator. The broader issue is what Maistre refers to as "the weakness of human power" when it tries to found its enterprises on unaided reason: This is the conception that Maistre thinks Rousseau had glimpsed but in relation to which he fell short.

> True legislators have all sensed that human reason could not stand alone, and that no purely human institution could last. This is why they interlaced, if it may be put this way, politics and religion, so that human weakness, strengthened by a supernatural support, could be sustained by it.[20]

The true politics is one in which "politics is divinized, and human reason, crushed by the religious ascendancy, cannot insinuate its isolating and corrosive poison into the mechanisms of government." This is why Moses and Mohammed were able to achieve the greatness that they did only by becoming "at the same time pontiffs and legislators."[21] The most fundamental political reality is "the absolute nullity of human reason reduced to its own resources."[22] Hence one requires citizens who are at the same time "believers whose loyalty is

---

[19] Quoting Horace, Maistre says that Rousseau's argument "ends up as a fish" (p. 65, n. 8) – that is, like a mermaid, beautiful on top and "black and ugly" where it ends. As Maistre stresses, the point is not whether politics and religion share a common object but rather whether politics' reliance on religion can be reduced to an instrumental relation.

[20] Ibid., p. 78.

[21] Ibid.

[22] Ibid., p. 77; cf. p. 87: "Human reason reduced to its own resources is perfectly worthless. . . . [T]o conduct himself well, man needs not problems but beliefs. His cradle should be surrounded by dogmas."

exalted to faith, and obedience to enthusiasm and fanaticism."²³ Rewriting the
fatal conclusion of Book II, chapter 7, of the *Social Contract*, Maistre affirms
that "[g]reat political institutions achieve perfection and durability proportion-
ate to the closeness of the union of politics and religion within them."²⁴

There is actually a text, rightly highlighted by Richard Lebrun in his
Introduction to *Against Rousseau*, in which Maistre directly appropriates
Rousseau's term "civil religion" for his own purposes. It is from Maistre's 1798
essay, "Reflections on Protestantism in its Relations with Sovereignty" (penned,
therefore, just a couple of years after the two Rousseau essays). Maistre makes
this statement:

> Christianity is the religion of Europe: this soil suits it better even than its native land; it
> has sunk deep roots there; it is mingled with all our institutions: for all the nations of
> northern Europe, and for all those that, in the centre of this part of the world, supplanted
> the Romans, Christianity is as ancient as civilization itself. These new nations were
> fashioned by the hand of this religion; the cross is on all the crowns; all the codes begin
> with its symbol; the kings are *anointed*; the priests are *magistrates*; the priesthood is
> an *order*; the empire is *sacred*, the religion is *civil*; the two powers are merged; each
> lends the other part of its strength, and, despite the quarrels that have divided these two
> sisters, they cannot live separated.²⁵

This is indeed one obvious way of solving Rousseau's problem of reunifying
the two heads of the eagle, but it is a solution with which Rousseau, and most
of the thinkers surveyed in this book, would have no sympathy.

---

²³ Ibid., p. 78. Recall Rousseau's response to Bayle in the epigraph to Chapter 1 of this book.
   This was a case of Rousseau's gesturing in a Maistrean direction, but Maistre shows us what is
   involved in actually following through on Rousseau's gesture.
²⁴ *Against Rousseau*, p. 79. In the balance of Book 1, chapter 8, Maistre reprises themes that are
   familiar from Machiavelli's account of civil religion: reliance on oracles in Lycurgus's Sparta,
   the reliance on the oath and on auspices in Numa's Rome, and so on. Maistre never mentions
   Machiavelli, but by implication he contrasts the piety of Livy to Machiavelli's impiety (ibid.).
   Maistre also offers an implicit reply to Hobbes (or to what Rousseau draws from Hobbes) in
   the important manuscript passage reproduced in n. 24 on pp. 81–82.
²⁵ *Against Rousseau*, p. xix. I have used most of Lebrun's translation but have supplemented it
   to make good his elisions. For the full text, see *Œuvres*, ed. Glaudes, p. 312. Part of what
   Maistre intends by calling Christianity a civil religion is captured by the converse claim that
   Protestantism is not only a religious heresy but equally a civil heresy (ibid.). That is, religion and
   politics are inseparable, so what is religiously sound is ipso facto politically sound, and what
   is religiously unsound, politically unsound. Jack Lively has written that "[Maistre's] thought is
   not strictly theological, nor, in spite of his deference to the Papacy, theocratic.... [I]n only one
   work did he make anything like an approach to demanding control of secular government by
   the Church" (*Works of Joseph de Maistre*, ed. Lively, p. 40). However, to this one can reply
   that if a vision of politics sees no distinction between political order and sacerdotal order, and
   conceives political officials in the image of priests, then it fully deserves to qualify as theocratic.

28

Carl Schmitt's "Theocratic" Critique of Hobbes

> Like the serpent that slithered onto the scene after the bucolic description of
> Adam and Eve in the garden, Hobbes's *Leviathan* slithered and seemed to choke
> off Christianity.
>
> – A. P. Martinich[1]

The intellectual dialogue between Carl Schmitt and Thomas Hobbes in
Schmitt's 1938 Hobbes book[2] is one of the most bizarre episodes in the
history of political philosophy, and raises questions that are central to the
three-way debate (civil religion, liberalism, and theocracy) laid out in this
book. Schmitt rightly sees a moment of liberalism in Hobbes's civil religion,
and according to Schmitt's perverse reading, Hobbes is taxed with responsibility for what Schmitt sees as a "Jewish" intellectual–political legacy of
cosmopolitanism, liberalism, and Enlightenment. One could say that Schmitt's
Hobbes-interpretation, for all of its perversity, fits nicely with the view of civil
religion I am developing in this book – namely that civil religion and liberalism
ultimately have more in common with each other than either has with real
theocracy, because both civil religion and liberalism aim at a domestication of
religion on behalf of the political state (or what Schmitt calls "public reason").[3]
A fully theocratic civil religion would leave no space for anything other than

---

[1] A. P. Martinich, *Hobbes: A Biography* (Cambridge: Cambridge University Press, 1999), p. 236.
There are liberal versions of Hobbes, including those of Michael Oakeshott and Richard Flath-
man; what Carl Schmitt gives us is a Nazified version of the *Leviathan*. It is unclear whether
Schmitt wants to devour Christianity, but Schmitt's version of Hobbesian theory is indeed a
slithering snake.

[2] Carl Schmitt, *The Leviathan in the State Theory of Thomas Hobbes: Meaning and Failure of
a Political Symbol*, trans. George Schwab and Erna Hilfstein (Westport, CT: Greenwood Press,
1996); republished by University of Chicago Press in 2008. For an illuminating general sketch
of Schmitt and his influence, see Mark Lilla, *The Reckless Mind* (New York: New York Review
Books, 2001), chapter 2.

[3] Schmitt, p. 55.

unreserved deference to the civil-religious unity embodied in the state's absolute sovereignty. The core of Schmitt's interpretation is that Hobbes *betrayed* his own theocratic political philosophy and contaminated it with the virus of liberalism that was to unfold fully in the eighteenth and nineteenth centuries. Schmitt calls it "the seed of death that destroyed the mighty leviathan from within"![4]

How is this quirky reading of Hobbes related to Schmitt's own political philosophy? In what follows, I have tried to answer this question. Nevertheless, in trying to draw a core political philosophy from the Hobbes book, it is quite possible that I have attributed more coherence to Schmitt's political thought than it actually possesses. Schwab, the coeditor, cites the view of Helmut Rumpf that the Hobbes book is hobbled by a fundamental incoherence: "[B]ecause Schmitt's formulations can be interpreted as a critique of the totalitarian system as well as 'a totalitarian critique of Hobbes,' it is difficult to conclude where Schmitt actually stood."[5] It is indeed true that the antiliberal spirit of the book comes out most clearly in the hateful outbursts, whereas the actual philosophical standpoint is highly blurred, to say the least. One is tempted to say that it was only when he was ranting that Schmitt was able to achieve intellectual clarity.

Decisionism is what defines Schmitt's political philosophy, and therefore Hobbes, whom he refers to as "the great decisionist,"[6] must count as one of his intellectual heroes. However, there are both decisionism and liberalism in Hobbes's political thought, and Schmitt must therefore divide the wheat from the chaff. It may be that Schmitt wrote the Hobbes book to answer Leo Strauss's challenge to him: that as a Hobbesian, Schmitt was still fundamentally a liberal.[7] By distinguishing what was genuinely decisionistic ("political") in Hobbes, and what constituted a "seed" of liberalism, Schmitt could affirm Hobbes's decisionism while disavowing (fairly violently) the latent liberalism.[8]

---

[4] Ibid., p. 57.

[5] George Schwab, "Introduction," p. xxi.

[6] Schmitt, p. 55. Schmitt adds the gloss: "*Auctoritas, non Veritas.* Nothing here is true: everything here is command."

[7] Leo Strauss, "Comments on Carl Schmitt's *Der Begriff des Politischen*," in Carl Schmitt, *The Concept of the Political*, trans. George Schwab (New Brunswick, NJ: Rutgers University Press, 1976).

[8] There are clear intimations of another, more personal agenda in the book. What are telling are the recurrent discussions of how "his own people" had turned their backs on Hobbes's radical conceptualization of the state (e.g., pp. 79–81). In his final tribute to Hobbes as his "great teacher," Schmitt refers to him as "lonely as every pioneer; misunderstood as is everyone whose political thought does not gain acceptance among his own people" (p. 86). Transparently evident in these passages is Schmitt's projection onto Hobbes of his own self-perceived situation in relation to the Nazi regime – or conversely, Schmitt's image of himself as a heroic and unjustly rejected and marginalized Hobbes-figure in 1930s Germany. (Although he joined the Nazi Party in 1933, the Nazis remained highly suspicious of him; for a helpful discussion see Tracy B. Strong's Foreword to the 2008 edition, pp. xx–xxi.) Like Hobbes, Schmitt conceived a grand image of the state that "his own people" refused to embrace in place of the prevailing ideology. Clearly, Heidegger was not the only philosopher of that epoch with an insanely hubristic view of his possible relation to this evil regime!

Stephen Holmes describes the Hobbes book as "simultaneously spellbinding and repulsive."[9] "Spellbinding" may be overgenerous to Schmitt, but "repulsive" is an epithet that is fully earned. The fundamental narrative of the book is that Hobbes saw no less clearly than did Machiavelli and Vico, Nietzsche and Georges Sorel, that the deepest medium of political life is *myth*, and therefore he drew upon the biblical imagery of the terrifying leviathan (whale or dragon) to establish the symbolic authority of his distinctive vision of a state commanding decision-making authority of unlimited proportions.[10] Tragically, this vision found no resonance in England, and ultimately in Europe as a whole it succumbed to the pluralistic political vision of liberalism. In particular, it was subverted by a chain of Jewish thinkers starting with Spinoza but also including Moses Mendelssohn and the nineteenth-century jurisprudential thinker, Friedrich Julius Stahl-Jolson – an intellectual trajectory that Schmitt leaves little doubt amounted to a Jewish conspiracy stretching over centuries to "castrate" the leviathan.[11] However, Hobbes himself contributed to the subversion of his own theory of the state by qualifying the rightful jurisdiction of his civil religion (as Rousseau was to do as well in his own civil religion), namely requiring that the sovereign restrict itself to enforcing outward profession of the civil creed, not attempting to peer into the souls of his subjects. This liberal distinction between outer conduct and inward belief was the downfall of Hobbes's project to achieve unqualified unity in the seat of sovereignty, and it provided a kind of Trojan horse whereby Hobbesian decisionism could actually promote the eventual triumph of liberal pluralism.[12]

Decisionism is a political philosophy of absolute sovereignty, and sovereignty in the strict sense implies utter *unity* in the authority that makes decisions concerning life and death. This is the great aspiration embodied in Hobbes's conception of the state, with its necessity for a civil religion that would unify

---

[9] Stephen Holmes, "Introduction," in Thomas Hobbes, *Behemoth, or The Long Parliament*, ed. Ferdinand Tönnies (Chicago: University of Chicago Press, 1990), p. xlv, n. 87.

[10] See Schmitt, p. 11; and in more detail, the discussion of Machiavelli and Vico on pp. 84–85.

[11] Schmitt, p. 70: "[I]n the great historical continuum that leads from Spinoza by way of Moses Mendelssohn into the century of 'constitutionalism,' Stahl-Jolson did his work as a Jewish thinker – that is, he did his part in castrating a leviathan that had been full of vitality." Cf. pp. 81–82: Hobbes's theory of the state cast in the image of the leviathan "could have been a grand signal of restoration of . . . vital energy and political unity. . . . That image . . . perished as a result of its encounter with the forces arrayed behind the traditional Jewish interpretation of the leviathan. . . . They [the 'indirect powers' that succeeded in draining away the absolute sovereignty of the state] have killed and eviscerated him."

[12] For an interesting discussion of this theme of Hobbes as anticipating the emphasis on freedom of thought in later liberals, starting with Spinoza, see Alan Ryan, "Hobbes, Toleration, and the Inner Life," in *The Nature of Political Theory*, ed. David Miller and Larry Siedentop (Oxford: Clarendon Press, 1983), pp. 197–218. Ryan's discussion is nicely attuned to the difficulties of pinning down Hobbes's position in a conclusive way, but he is at least open to the possibility that there is more liberalism in Hobbes than is generally assumed (thus providing support for Schmitt's account of Hobbes's incipient liberalism). Needless to say, what Ryan sees as an aspect of Hobbes's thought that partly redeems his political philosophy is for Schmitt a basis for violent criticism.

civil and ecclesiastical authority. From a Schmittian perspective, one can say that it is what constitutes the grandeur of the Hobbesian project. The project is nicely encapsulated near the beginning of the book where Schmitt summarizes the fundamental alternatives as viewed by Hobbes. He starts by citing Leo Strauss's view according to which "Hobbes regarded Jews as the originators of the revolutionary state-destroying distinction between religion and politics."[13] It turns out, however, that this is not exactly Schmitt's view.

Hobbes opposed the typically Judeo-Christian division of the original political unity. [In this respect, Schmitt agrees with Strauss's interpretation.] The distinction between the secular and the spiritual power was, according to Hobbes, alien to the heathens because religion was to them a part of politics; the Jews brought about unity from the side of religion. Only the Roman papal church and the power-thirsty Presbyterian churches or sects [i.e., the two main wings of post-Reformation Christianity!] thrive on the state-destroying separation of the spiritual and the secular power. Superstition and misuse of alien beliefs in spirits arising from fear and illusion have destroyed the original and natural heathen unity of politics and religion. The struggle to overcome the Roman papal church's division between a 'Kingdom of Light' and a 'Kingdom of Darkness' – that is, the restoration of the original unity – is . . . the actual meaning of Hobbes' political theory [again, in agreement with Strauss].[14]

In other words, we have three fundamental possibilities: (1) civil religion – the "natural," "heathen" (pagan) unity of religion and politics; (2) Jewish theocracy, where the unity is brought about "from the side of religion"; and (3) the fundamentally Christian-theocratic rejection of state–religion unity. That is, Christianity is far more subversive of Hobbes's idea of sovereignty than either paganism or Jewish theocracy (and in the light of our readings of Hobbes in Part I, this is surely a correct rendering of his view). One cannot mistake the strong resemblance of this analysis to Rousseau's civil-religion analysis. Schmitt does not pursue the suggestion here that Hobbes, according to his own analysis of the alternatives, ought to have preferred paganism to monotheistic religions, à la Machiavelli and Rousseau; nor does he pursue the suggestion that Jewish theocracy, although inferior to the pagan solution, is politically superior to Christianity; nor does he pursue the suggestion that Christianity as such is fundamentally irreconcilable with the whole Hobbesian project. Instead, Schmitt goes on to explore how Hobbes, in an extremely subtle aspect of his civil-religion doctrine, subverts his own enterprise (and opens the door to a more far-reachingly subversive liberalism).

Schmitt rightly sees that civil religion is the very heart of Hobbes's project to unify political sovereignty. However, according to Schmitt, this project has a fatal Achilles heel: It resides in Hobbes's anxiety that the sovereign's justified demand for outward tokens of absolute obedience not trump the freedom of thought of intellectuals like himself. (Here Hobbes of course anticipates what

---

[13] Schmitt, p. 10.
[14] Ibid., pp. 10–11.

becomes, a century later, the Enlightenment's full rebellion against religion.) For instance, if the sovereign claims to heal his subjects by performing miracles on their behalf, Hobbes *qua* citizen must concede the miracle but *qua* intellectual must reserve a private space of intellectually free judgment where he can exercise skepticism.[15] The most urgent problem for Schmitt is why Hobbes's decisionism ultimately gives way to his liberalism, or how it comes about that the former is betrayed by the latter. Partly it is a case of self-subversion emanating from Hobbes's own (incipient) liberalism, and partly it is a case of subversion by opportunistic later liberals. This is where Schmitt's intellectual conspiracy theory takes flight.

Schmitt's slogan "indirect powers"[16] is his name for a liberal–pluralistic regime that rejected a state with authoritarian pretensions, and his *primary* purpose in the Hobbes book is to identify a group of culpable intellectual figures (starting with Spinoza) who have contributed to discrediting state authoritarianism and legitimizing liberal pluralism. It is no accident that virtually all of the thinkers grouped together in this gallery of intellectual culprits are Jewish and are constantly highlighted by Schmitt as being Jewish.[17] However, what

---

[15] Schmitt discusses this interesting example (e.g., the 23,000 cases of royal miracle healing claimed by Charles II) on p. 54. Cf. p. 53: "The sovereign state power alone, on the basis of its sovereignty, determines what subjects of the state have to believe to be a miracle"; and p. 55: "A miracle is what the sovereign state authority commands its subjects to believe to be a miracle." Hobbes's recoil from outright theocracy and his corresponding betrayal of his own concept of sovereignty are traced by Schmitt to Hobbes's unexpungeable urge to retain a space of intellectual judgment where he could say a private no to such assertions of the miraculous. As Schmitt says on p. 53, "the question of faith and miracle" is the crucial one, and from a Schmittian perspective, it "became [the] misfortune" (i.e., the decisive downfall) of the entire Hobbesian enterprise. Cf. the discussion of "the healing power" of the sovereign in Joseph de Maistre, *Against Rousseau*, ed. Richard A. Lebrun (Montreal: McGill-Queen's University Press, 1996), p. 58.

[16] See, e.g., p. 86: The most important lesson that Hobbes, as "an incomparable teacher," has to teach in the present age consists in his "struggle against indirect powers"; his greatness as a "champion" of fearless thought resides in his having "destroyed the murky distinctions of indirect powers." Hobbes's purpose was to "confront medieval pluralism with the rational unity of a rational centralized state" ("Appendix: The State as Mechanism in Hobbes and Descartes," p. 96), and Schmitt's consistent theme is that modern liberal pluralism represents the final undoing of Hobbes's project.

[17] The cotranslator of the Hobbes book, George Schwab, claims that "the charge of anti-Semitism cannot be sustained. Schmitt's relapse into a narrow, exclusionary theology, although it overlapped with Nazi anti-Semitism and, as such, added to the poisoned atmosphere, lacked the cornerstone of Nazi ideology, a hodge-podge theory of race. What remains of Schmitt's state theory is not totalitarian in nature but authoritarian in form and content" ("Introduction," p. xxii). This is a remarkable attempted defense of Schmitt. Schwab's agenda is to argue that by the time he wrote the Hobbes book, Schmitt (as a Catholic) was a target of the Nazi regime, and hence his thought could not have been consistent with Nazi ideology. However, nothing in this exculpates Schmitt of the charge of anti-Semitism – especially because the whole rhetoric of chapters 5–7 of the Hobbes book is through-and-through anti-Semitic. Schwab gestures at a disgusting whitewash of Schmitt's anti-Semitism – cf. the claim on p. xx that "in 1938 [Schmitt] neutralized the venom that he had reserved for Jews [in 1936]." Nonetheless, it is a pathetically ineffective whitewash: The exculpation of Schmitt asserted in Schwab's first sentence quoted in

gives narrative drama to Schmitt's account is his interpretation of how Hobbes himself, despite himself, gives crucial impetus to these nefarious liberals. In Schmitt's account, Hobbes inserts a crucial wedge in the unity of the theocratic state, and this wedge is exploited by Jews like Spinoza and Moses Mendelssohn until it becomes a full "rupture" between politics and religion that for Schmitt is associated with the evils of liberalism.[18] Hobbes's mistake was to open up the very *possibility* of this rupture – in other words, liberalizing his political philosophy in a way that lent itself to exploitation by Jewish liberals like Spinoza and Mendelssohn.[19]

How does latent liberalism in Hobbes turn into full-blown liberalism in Spinoza? According to Schmitt, Spinoza's corruption of Hobbes consists in the following "inversion": Whereas Hobbes put the primary emphasis on "public peace and the right of sovereign power," with a "proviso" for freedom of thought, Spinoza made freedom of thought the primary concern and reduced "the necessities of public peace [and] the right of the sovereign power" to "mere

---

this note is directly contradicted in the very next sentence! As regards Schmitt's Catholicism, it is a major puzzle of the book that Schmitt nowhere blanches in the face of Hobbes's aggressive anti-Catholicism. Cf. Graeme Garrard, "Joseph de Maistre and Carl Schmitt," in *Joseph de Maistre's Life, Thought, and Influence*, ed. Richard A. Lebrun (Montreal: McGill-Queen's University Press, 2001), pp. 233–234. See, for instance, Schmitt, p. 83, where Hobbes is hailed for his brave leadership in "the struggle that the English nation waged against the papal church's and the Jesuits' claims to world hegemony"; cf. "Appendix: The State as Mechanism in Hobbes and Descartes," p. 94. Schmitt also nowhere responds on behalf of Catholicism to the problem that is obviously central for Hobbes: If the *unity* of political sovereignty is the paramount concern, how can the political claims of the Catholic Church be anything other than utterly illegitimate? See p. 10: "[T]he Roman papal church [thrives] on the state-destroying separation of the spiritual and the secular power." How Schmitt reconciles his commitment to Hobbesian hypersovereignty with his Catholicism is a complete mystery. Particularly striking in this regard is Schmitt's assertion (pp. 14–15, n. 12) that Hobbes was right to combat "power-hungry priests," and that his "heathen-Christian-Erastian arguments" served the cause of a genuine "*civitas Christiana*, in which the sovereign does not touch the sole essential dogma that *Jesus is the Christ*." A parallel case is that of Eric Voegelin – another Christian-theocratic thinker who is also nonetheless sympathetic (at least to some extent) with Hobbes's project to put Christianity to work as a *theologia civilis* to regulate the political chaos generated by Christianity itself: See Voegelin's *The New Science of Politics* (Chicago: University of Chicago Press, 1952), chapter 5. The various complicated tensions in Schmitt's political theology are captured well in Tracy Strong's Foreword to the most recent edition (2008) of the Hobbes book. Strong presents Schmitt as being *both* as suspicious of Christianity as Hobbes was *and* as committed to the Papist church as Maistre was. Admittedly, it requires a thinker of uncommon vigor to hold onto both of these positions simultaneously.

[18] In the light of these passages, it is not farfetched to think that Schmitt's antiliberalism has its closest political counterpart today in Islamist theocracy. In *Terror and Liberalism* (New York: Norton, 2003), p. 87, Paul Berman writes that "[notwithstanding Sayyid Qutb's manifest anti-Semitism,] what agitated him most of all was the split between the sacred and the secular in modern liberalism, and this was not a Jewish creation." Interestingly, it was precisely Schmitt's view in the Hobbes book that this split *was* a Jewish creation.

[19] The core of this critique of Hobbes is on pp. 55–57. The term "rupture" occurs on p. 55. Stephen Holmes offers a similar reading of Schmitt's intention in *The Anatomy of Antiliberalism* (Cambridge, MA: Harvard University Press, 1993), pp. 50–53.

provisos."[20] In short, Hobbes's decisionism was conjured into liberalism by a "Jewish" sleight of hand:

A small intellectual switch emanating from the nature of Jewish life accomplished, with the most simple logic and in the span of a few years, the decisive turn in the fate of the leviathan.[21]

Liberalism, one could say, is from Schmitt's perspective a Jewish conspiracy to "drain the life out of" leviathan,[22] prompted by the *völkisch* interests of a people with a special stake in liberalism.[23] Spinoza allows

the sovereign state power [to] regulate the public religious cult and [maintains] that every citizen must accommodate himself to this regulation.... The state's power, however, determines *only* the external cult [emphasis added]. Hobbes laid the groundwork for separating the internal from the external in the sections of the *Leviathan* that deal with a belief in miracles and confession. The Jewish philosopher pushed this incipient form to the limit of its development until the opposite was reached and the leviathan's vitality was sapped from within and life began to drain out of him.[24]

The absolute state can demand everything but only outwardly. The *cujus regio ejus religio* [he who commands the territory also commands the religion] has been realized, but the *religio* has in the meantime landed in an entirely different, unexpectedly new realm – namely, the private sphere of freedom of the free thinking, free feeling, and, in his disposition, absolutely free individual.[25]

This new regime of "inner reservations" was advanced by "all kinds of sectarians" (Rosicrucians, freemasons, illuminates, mystics, and pietists), but

above all [by] the restless spirit of the Jew who knew how to exploit the situation best until the relation of public and private, deportment and disposition was turned upside down. In the eighteenth century it was Moses Mendelssohn who... validated

---

[20] Schmitt, p. 58.

[21] Ibid.

[22] Nietzsche's imagery of vampirism in *The Antichrist* comes to mind. I discuss this in my reading of Nietzsche in Part IV. See also the theme of vampirism in *Ecce Homo*: Nietzsche, *The Anti-Christ, Ecce Homo, Twilight of the Idols, and Other Writings*, ed. Aaron Ridley and Judith Norman, trans. Judith Norman (Cambridge: Cambridge University Press, 2005), p. 150.

[23] The essential difference between Hobbes and Spinoza is that "the Englishman did not endeavour... to appear out of context of the beliefs of his people but, on the contrary, to remain within it, whereas the Jewish philosopher, on the other hand, who approached the religion of the state as an outsider, naturally provided a proviso [recognizing the rights of sovereign power] that emanated from the outside" (pp. 57–58). Cf. what Schmitt says on p. 8 concerning "the unique, totally abnormal condition and attitude of the Jewish people towards all other peoples."

[24] Schmitt, p. 57; cf. p. 59 on the "relegation of the state to an outward cult, as proposed by Spinoza," and its appropriation by Goethe. It is noteworthy that Rousseau does not figure at all in Schmitt's narrative, but of course this is Rousseau's view as well. In fact, it defines the core of his civil-religion doctrine – which is why the tacit liberalism that Rousseau's critics fail to detect in his civil religion becomes more visible once we appreciate his debt to Hobbes. Ironically, Schmitt can help us better discern this liberalism in Rousseau.

[25] Schmitt, pp. 59–60.

the distinction between inner and outer, morality and right, inner disposition and outer performance and demanded from the state freedom of thought.... [What was expressed here was] the unerring instinct for the undermining of state power that served to paralyze the alien and to emancipate his own Jewish folk.[26]

In other words, there was just enough liberalism in Hobbes's political philosophy for it to be possible for "Jewish" thinkers to take this trace of liberalism in Hobbes and turn it into the dominant philosophy, thereby transforming Hobbes's apotheosis of the state into a doctrine effectually subversive of the state's authority. Spinoza's great sin was to have "expanded this thought [viz., Hobbes's distinction between inner and outer] into a universal principle of freedom of thought, perception, and expression,"[27] and therein consists his liberal corruption of Hobbes. Schmitt consistently claims that Hobbes's Leviathan state is not totalitarian, but rather has its foundations in a healthy individualism. Nevertheless, he condemns Hobbes for having failed to make good on the promise of "unity" – typified in the breach between inner and outer (viz., inner conviction and outward conduct).[28] What Schmitt seems to be suggesting is that the very discrimination between inner and outer, morality and politics, leads inexorably to Kant's liberalism (mediated by Spinoza's liberalism).[29]

The intellectual parameters within which one moves in the creepy world of Schmitt's political thought become somewhat clearer in the last chapter of the book, chapter 7. Although one naturally connects the image of leviathan to the "monarchical absolutism" of the Stuarts, strangely enough, the "brief historical moment" when the English state might genuinely have become a Leviathan state was during Cromwell's dictatorship.[30] Instead, what developed politically was a liberal (Lockean) anti-absolutist state based on sea power and a commercial (cosmopolitan) way of life. Hobbes's vision was betrayed by his own people, and the idea of state absolutism was left to be developed by continental states, notably France and Prussia. "The English Isle and its world-conquering seafaring needed no absolute monarchy, no standing army, no state bureaucracy, no legal system of a law state [_Gesetzesstaat_] such as became characteristic of continental states."[31] In short, England evolved into a Montesquieuian state rather than a Hobbesian state: a state that was "open" rather than "closed," commercial rather than autarchic,[32] and "mixed" rather than "absolutist."

[26] Ibid., p. 60.

[27] Ibid., p. 57.

[28] This seeming contradiction between, on the one hand, defending the individualism of Hobbes and, on the other hand, denouncing Hobbes for opening up "the barely visible crack" that was later expanded into a full "rupture" in the theocratic unity of the state (pp. 55, 57) is the essential point made by Helmut Rumpf as cited in note 5.

[29] See Schmitt, p. 59, on "the separation of right and morality" in Kant.

[30] Ibid., p. 79.

[31] Ibid., p. 80.

[32] Note Schmitt's enthusiastic citation of a 1938 article on "Der Begriff des autarchischen Staates": p. 76, n. 7.

The decisionism of absolutist thinking is foreign to the English spirit. The concept of the sovereignty of the absolute state in a conceptually "clean" form, that is, one that shuns mixing and balancing with other state forms, has found no echo in the public power of England.[33]

The ultimate test of whether the regime is Hobbesian or not is what concept of enemy it implies: England's rejection of decisionism is expressed, therefore, in its deviation from "cabinet- and combat-determined notions of land warfare waged by absolute states on the continent."[34]

What is most clear in this bizarre narrative is that Schmitt regards the Hobbesian vision of the state – captured in the mythicized image of the state as leviathan – as a fundamentally noble political vision, and he regards it as having been displaced by less noble conceptions of the state. In the twentieth century, the image of the Leviathan state is no longer relevant because we live fundamentally in a world of "total technology," as highlighted by Ernst Jünger[35] – a world insensitive to the nobility of exercising unqualified state responsibility: "command and the assumption of emergency action, power and responsibility."[36] Instead what we get is rule by "indirect powers" – "distinctions and pseudo-concepts of a *potestas indirecta* that demands obedience without being able to protect, that wants to command without assuming responsibility for the possibility of political peril"[37] – a form of "rule" that is in essence ignoble. In chapter 6, Schmitt associates these "indirect powers" with, for instance, "modern political powers, trade unions, social organizations" (he also refers to churches in this context), all of which he insists were profoundly antistatist and determined to "place the leviathan in harness."[38] That is, the Leviathan state was pushed aside by the world of social and political pluralism – the world of liberalism. He describes the eclipse of Hobbes's leviathan vision (or leviathan myth) as a "tragedy" – a tragedy paralleled by the fact that Hobbes's "piety" was unappreciated and his resolve to "stand bravely at the head of his people" – "a Christian people" – went for naught.[39] The "tragedy," as Schmitt perceives it, is that the nobility of the absolute-responsibility decisionist state gives way to the ignobility of the liberal–pluralist state, and that the "seed" of liberalism in Hobbes's political vision gets exploited by "Jewish" thinkers on behalf of precisely this ignoble liberal pluralism. One is drawn to the conclusion that Schmitt's political thought is a case of a hyperexaggerated version of Max Weber's notion of the ethics of responsibility concentrated in officials of the state that goes so far in fetishizing unlimited political responsibility that it turns into a kind of self-parody. It is as if Schmitt is unable to see any form of

---

33 Ibid., p. 80.
34 Ibid.
35 Ibid., p. 82.
36 Ibid., p. 83.
37 Ibid.
38 Ibid., p. 73.
39 Ibid., pp. 82–83.

political action short of declaring war as morally serious,[40] or to see any form of state authority short of dictatorship as possessing existential nobility.

Schmitt's political philosophy is an intellectual disgrace, but it is nonetheless helpful in prompting us to appreciate Hobbes's civil religion as an unlikely source of liberalism. (One could say that the liberalism in Rousseau's civil religion follows directly from the liberalism in Hobbes's civil religion. Schmitt himself might have noted this, had he not been so violently fixated on tracing liberalism to a Jewish conspiracy.)[41] The correct and far-reaching Schmittian insight here (explored in this book) is that civil religion as such, as the attempt to put religion to use for *civic* purposes, is ultimately more liberalizing than antiliberal. This is perhaps the fundamental reason why Hobbes is partly embraced, but *only* partly embraced, by this radical theocrat.[42]

---

[40] The core of Schmitt's theorizing is expressed in what Schmitt says about Norbert Gürke on p. 102, n. 14.

[41] The only reference to Rousseau is in a quotation from Ferdinand Tönnies on p. 68 that presents his political philosophy (reasonably enough) as mediating between Hobbes and the French Revolution.

[42] Is Schmitt really a theocrat? If one defines theocracy as rule by priests, then Schmitt's endorsement of Hobbes's policy toward "power-hungry priests" would suggest that he is as antitheocratic as Hobbes is. However, if one takes theocracy in a broader sense as an absolute antithesis to liberalism – along a continuum with Locke at one extremity, Maistre at the other – then even Nietzsche, for all his hatred of priests, can be interpreted as a theocrat. At the Locke end of the continuum, individuals are given quite substantial space to work out the meaning of existence according to their own lights, whereas at the Maistre end of the continuum, there is little or no space because the requirements of social order demand that members of society interpret their existence according to an obligatory script that is collectively imposed. According to this broader meaning of theocracy, Schmitt is clearly very close to Maistre, whereas Hobbes, as a good civil religionist, is somewhere in the middle.

PART IV

POSTMODERN "THEISM"

Nietzsche and Heidegger's Continuing Revolt against Liberalism

29

Nietzsche, Weber, Freud

The Twentieth Century Confronts the Death of God

Jehovah, collector of prepuces, is no more.

– James Joyce[1]

In this final part of the book, my main purpose is to present Nietzsche as a resumption (and terminus?) of the civil-religion tradition. Before I begin that presentation of Nietzsche, though, it might be helpful to situate him briefly in relation to two of his most important successors – namely Sigmund Freud and Max Weber. Both Freud and Weber take Nietzsche, in a sense, as their starting point. Both accept the Nietzschean axiom that we now live in a godless, or god-divested, world – that is, a radically post-Christian, post-Judaic moral universe. Nevertheless, they offer philosophical responses to this Nietzschean universe that diverge radically from Nietzsche's own position. Of the three thinkers, Freud adheres most closely to the classical Enlightenment view. In Freud's *Future of an Illusion*, his position is basically this: We now live in a world where God is dead, where we have killed Him with our modern, scientific ways of thought. Great! Good riddance to all that. Religious ideas of a great providential Divine Benefactor were really just a lot of infantile neurosis, the product of a cowardice to face up to the terrors of an adult world.[2] We are grown up now, and we can finally (with the aid of science) face up to

---

[1] James Joyce, *Ulysses* (Harmondsworth: Penguin, 1986), p. 165.

[2] The view of religion as "neurosis" is first suggested by Nietzsche: see *Beyond Good and Evil*, § 47. As Laurence Lampert rightly points out in a valuable commentary on chapter 3 of *Beyond Good and Evil* that complements the interpretation offered in the next chapter, for Nietzsche (in sharp contrast to Freud), "the religious instinct . . . can take healthy as well as neurotic forms." Lampert, *Nietzsche's Task* (New Haven: Yale University Press, 2001), p. 112. Hence Nietzsche is as much a defender of religions as he is a destroyer of religions. Because Lampert presents Nietzsche as a philosopher who has thought through his problems with absolute comprehensiveness, how does he think Nietzsche can escape what I called, in Chapter 10, the civil-religion paradox? The problem here is how it is possible to bring religion back *qua* civil religion after it has been ruthlessly exposed *qua* religion; or how it is possible to embrace religion for its utility in the absence of a conviction of its truth. Lampert's answer, I think, is that Nietzsche's new

our responsibilities as adults. Our major challenge as individuals is to put the Oedipal Complex behind us, and the same is true of ourselves as a civilization or as a species – namely, to outgrow our collective Oedipal Complex in relation to the Divine Father, and this is precisely what the death of God represents: long-delayed adulthood.[3] Needless to say, this is not Nietzsche's position. To be sure, he anticipates some of this celebratory rhetoric, or "Promethean" rhetoric, but he thinks the legacy of God's death is much more culturally ambiguous, and much more fraught with peril, and he certainly cannot bring himself to celebrate the Enlightenment in the way that Freud so cheerfully does.[4] Freud ends *The Future of an Illusion* with paeans to the god of Logos. This, however, is certainly not Nietzsche's god!

Weber's position is again much more complex. He too accepts the axiom of a Nietzschean disenchanted universe, but, like Nietzsche, he portrays this fate of modern disenchantment in much grimmer colors than Freud's exuberant faith in the Enlightenment. The relevant text here is Weber's *Science as a Vocation*. The scientific exposé of what had formerly invested people's lives with a sense of secure meaningfulness is not an unambiguous liberation; it has more the aspect of a moral catastrophe (and again, this is closer to the Nietzschean pathos). Weber nonetheless differs crucially from Nietzsche. According to Weber, in agreement with Freud, science teaches us that religious belief demands a "sacrifice of the intellect" (that is, a renunciation of reason). Weber, however, insists that it would be preferable to sacrifice one's reason according to the established canons of the older (albeit discredited) religions than to look to philosophers as sources of *new* prophecies, *new* religions.[5]

---

religion, the religion of the eternal return, involves the introduction of new myths (or the revival of old myths) but does not involve religious beliefs per se. Still, Nietzsche's heavy emphasis in the later sections of *Beyond Good and Evil*, chapter 3, on the instrumentalization of religion (religion as a *tool* in the hands of a philosophical ruling class) suggests that a version of the civil-religion paradox continues to apply to Nietzsche.

[3] The uncompromising character of Freud's rationalism is captured in a story narrated in Michael Ignatieff's biography of Isaiah Berlin. Berlin was paying a visit to the Freud household in 1938. Frau Freud mentioned a relative who was known to Berlin and referred to his being an observant Jew. "She went on, 'Every Jewish woman wants to light the Sabbath candles on Friday night, but this monster,' and here she pointed at her husband, 'forbids it. Says it is a superstition.' Freud nodded with mock-gravity and said, 'Religion is a superstition.' This was obviously a joke sewn into the very fabric of their marriage." Ignatieff, *Isaiah Berlin: A Life* (Toronto: Viking Press, 1998), p. 91.

[4] It is interesting that in Leo Strauss's polemic against Freud, the nastiest put-down he is able to fling against Freud is to suggest that Nietzsche's depiction of the last man is lost on Freud. The implication is that, for Nietzsche, religion is still a worthy cosmic adversary, that in combating it one is raising oneself to a higher existential level, whereas the banality of Freud's existential stance is revealed in the fact that for him religion is just a neurosis to be analyzed. See "Freud on Moses and Monotheism," in Strauss, *Jewish Philosophy and the Crisis of Modernity*, ed. Kenneth Hart Green (Albany, NY: SUNY Press, 1997), pp. 305–306.

[5] Max Weber, *The Vocation Lectures*, ed. David Owen and Tracy B. Strong (Indianapolis: Hackett, 2004), pp. 30–31. "Sacrifice of the intellect" possibly refers back to Nietzsche's characterization of Pascal in *Beyond Good and Evil*, § 229.

This, clearly, is a direct response to Nietzsche, who encourages the idea of new prophets (or "postmodern" versions of *old* prophets: Zarathustra!) as a way of coping with the eclipse of the old religions. (One might think of Weber's argument also as an anticipation of Heidegger, who also invites the prophecy of new gods.) Weber clearly sees Nietzsche as committed to the project of reenchanting the world, and of conferring upon *philosophers* or modern intellectuals the responsibility for guiding and orchestrating this project of reenchantment. Weber's response to this project is to say that we would be better off remaining bound to ancient superstitions than to invest our contemporary philosophers with the authority to invent modern, post-Christian superstitions. So, clearly, we have here three quite different responses to our modern post-Christian situation. Notwithstanding their radical differences, each of these thinkers agrees in regarding the question of how to respond to this cultural crisis as a major challenge of our civilization; one way or another, theoretical reflection cannot evade the task of addressing the problem of how to deal with this collapse of religious foundations.

Part of what it means to understand a philosophy is to grasp what is for that philosophy its defining metaphor. In Nietzsche's philosophy, as we will see in the next chapter, the pivotal metaphor is "tensing the bow." Although Nietzsche welcomes the defeat of *Christianity*, his stance toward a more general defeat of religion and theism by modern Western secularization is much more ambivalent because he associates liberal secularity and the Enlightenment precisely with relaxation of the bow (that is, relaxation of cultural–spiritual tension within the West as a whole). The primary object of this book is a dialogue between liberals and antiliberals on one of the topics that crucially defines that debate, namely religion. What defines liberalism, generally speaking, is a nervousness about religion and a desire to contain it. The antiliberal argument, roughly speaking, is that the consequences of this liberal impulse are worse than the thing it is trying to combat. Nietzsche is an unqualified antiliberal, and his antiliberalism is so militant that it might not be entirely surprising if we discover that he gets drawn into a defense of religion against liberal secularity. When we look closely at some relevant writings of his, we see that this is indeed the case.

30

Nietzsche's Civil Religion

[T]he idea of the eternal recurrence [bars the evasion] into the blind secularization of man.

— Karl Löwith[1]

I will say it again: what seems to be essential "in heaven and on earth" is that there be *obedience* in one direction for a long time. In the long term, this always brings and has brought about something that makes life on earth worth living – for instance: virtue, art, music, dance, reason, intellect – something that transfigures, something refined, fantastic, and divine. The long un-freedom of spirit, the mistrustful constraint in the communicability of thought, the discipline that thinkers imposed on themselves, thinking within certain guidelines imposed by the church or court or Aristotelian presuppositions, the long, spiritual will to interpret every event according to a Christian scheme and to rediscover and justify the Christian God in every chance event, – all this violence, arbitrariness, harshness, terror, and anti-reason has shown itself to be the means through which strength, reckless curiosity, and subtle agility have been bred into the European spirit.

— Friedrich Nietzsche[2]

It is easy to view Nietzsche and Heidegger as heroic atheists. This is a radically incomplete view; in fact, their mortal opposition to liberalism and to everything associated with a liberal philosophy of life forces them to embrace what amounts to a radicalized version of antiliberal theocracy. One can understand why a reader of Nietzsche like George Grant can conceive Nietzsche as "the first great explicit right-wing atheist."[3] This view, however, does not capture

---

[1] Karl Löwith, *Nietzsche's Philosophy of the Eternal Recurrence of the Same*, trans. J. Harvey Lomax (Berkeley: University of California Press, 1997), p. 86.

[2] Friedrich Nietzsche, *Beyond Good and Evil*, ed. Rolf-Peter Horstmann and Judith Norman (Cambridge: Cambridge University Press, 2002), § 188, p. 78.

[3] George Grant, 1974/75 Nietzsche Lectures, 1st Half: Book I, typescript, p. 13. Grant goes on to note that prior to Nietzsche, the right wing had been defined by devotion to "the throne and the altar." If the point is that Nietzsche is not de Maistre, one can hardly disagree. Still,

the whole story of Nietzsche's complicated stance toward theism in general or even Christian theism in particular.

If we want to think about Nietzsche in the context of civil-religion theorizing, here is a good puzzle to start with: Why does Nietzsche loathe the Protestant Reformation to the extent that he does ("spiritually unclean and boring," "spiritually stale," "lazy," "a homoeopathy of Christianity," "a recrudescence of Christian barbarism")?[4] Furthermore, Nietzsche is hardly in the business of "saving" Christianity by identifying more effete and less effete versions of it; so why does he see the move from Catholic Christianity to Protestant Christianity as a kind of inner corruption of Christian theism ("[a]ctual superiority of Catholicism")?[5] The short answer is that Nietzsche, like Max Weber after him, sees a decisive connection between Protestantism and modernity, and his hatred of modernity is such that he cannot restrain himself from hating Protestantism as a correlate of modernity – *even if* Protestantism helps to hurry along the decrepitude of Christianity itself.[6] The purpose of this chapter is to offer a more detailed account of this intriguing, paradox-ridden Nietzschean view of religion.

---

the description "right-wing atheist" misses the "Maistrean" aspects of Nietzsche's political philosophy. I am grateful to Arthur Davis for giving me access to various unpublished texts on Nietzsche by George Grant cited in this chapter. Selections from Grant's Nietzsche lectures have recently been published in *Collected Works of George Grant*, Vol. 4, ed. Arthur Davis and Henry Roper (Toronto: University of Toronto Press, 2009), pp. 962–1018.

4 Friedrich Nietzsche, *The Will to Power*, ed. Walter Kaufmann, trans. Walter Kaufmann and R. J. Hollingdale (New York: Random House, 1967), pp. 54–55. It is worth highlighting that Machiavelli, given his strenuous views on papal corruption, as we saw in Part I, would radically disagree with Nietzsche's position (e.g., *Genealogy of Morals* I.16) that the Reformation destroyed Renaissance virtue; cf. Guicciardini: *The Sweetness of Power: Machiavelli's Discourses and Guicciardini's Considerations*, trans. James B. Atkinson and David Sices (DeKalb, IL: Northern Illinois University Press, 2002), p. 404 and p. 405 n. 1. Both Machiavelli implicitly and Guicciardini explicitly are in sympathy with Luther; the reason, no doubt, is that both Machiavelli and Guicciardini were close enough to Renaissance papacies to see with their own eyes just how corrupt these papacies were. However, in *Genealogy* I.16, Nietzsche writes that what most condemns the Reformation is that it brought about "the restoration of the church" – which suggests a possible reconciliation between Nietzsche's view and Machiavelli's.

5 *The Will to Power*, p. 54.

6 As Ernest Gellner argues in *Plough, Sword and Book: The Structure of Human History* (London: Collins Harvill, 1988), pp. 100–112, an important "nexus between generic Protestantism and modernity" (p. 105) is easily visible even if one does not accept Weber's specific thesis concerning the nature of the connection. For instance, a "modern society is inherently one in which a high culture becomes *the* culture of the entire community: dependence on literacy and formal education, the standardization of procedures and measures (in a broad as well as a literal sense), all require it. A style of production which is simultaneously innovative *and* involves the cooperation of countless, anonymous agents cannot function without shared, standardized measures and norms. Protestantism points humanity in the direction of such a social order, well in advance of the actual arrival of modernity" (Gellner, p. 107). In short, modernity is Protestant, and therefore Nietzsche is obliged, by virtue of his root-and-branch rejection of modernity, to direct the full force of his polemical powers against the revolution in social consciousness that he, in common with Weber and Gellner, traces ultimately to the Reformation.

We can take George Grant as the encapsulation of a (on the face of it, plausible) view of Nietzsche as straightforwardly atheist and hypermodern. In his Nietzsche lectures of 1974–1975, Grant states that nobody ever ridiculed with greater acuteness than Nietzsche the modern ideologies (liberalism and socialism) that arose from the secularization of Christianity, although "he did not do so in the service of a pious way of thought – but in the name of an even greater [that is, more radical] modernity." In particular, Grant remarks, Nietzsche radicalizes rather than challenges the West's turn toward atheism. Hence the language of values, the language that typifies Nietzsche's thought, "is unequivocally an atheistic language."[7] In Grant's view Nietzsche's (successful) championing of the language of values suffices to establish him as the spearhead of radical modernity – as the spearhead of radical modernity, moreover, defined in terms of the civilizational triumph of atheism. There is an important measure of truth in this view, but again, it is not the complete truth about Nietzsche's stance toward modernity or theism. To begin with, there are three major challenges to its hermeneutical adequacy. First, Nietzsche states – quite unequivocally – that theism is practically and politically superior to atheism. Second, Nietzsche affirms – with equal unequivocacy – the practical–political superiority of Catholicism to Protestantism. Finally, Nietzsche's general standard for evaluating Christianity is not post-Christian modernity but rather a range of *premodern* religions: Hinduism, paganism, Judaism, and Islam. (Clearly, modernity is not the standard precisely because it *is* post-Christian – that is, thoroughly infiltrated by Christian value-perspectives.) Nietzsche judges each of the premodern alternatives to be practically–politically superior to Christianity, whether in its more modern Protestant version or its less modern Catholic version. It is hard to see how anyone who is committed to the three propositions just mentioned can be a radical proponent of modernity, or how Nietzsche can be conceived as a wholehearted champion of modern atheism. Again, though, Nietzsche does clearly endorse all of the three propositions.

To appreciate the overpowering appeal for Nietzsche of religions that are not just premodern but archaic and radically illiberal, we must first clarify in a more general sense what freedom and exercise of the will mean for Nietzsche, because he often uses a modern-sounding creative-voluntaristic vocabulary that makes him sound hyperliberal, whereas his deepest underlying cultural–political aims tend to be illiberal in the extreme. The hypermodernity of Nietzsche's thought is expressed more than anything in Nietzsche's elevation of the human will to a status unprecedented in Western thought: He takes his bearings neither from nature nor from history but rather from the sheer creativity of the will in emancipating itself from natural and historical constraints. It hardly seems necessary to refer to a great many texts. Consider, for instance, *The Will to Power*, § 1011: "[W]e have to realize to what degree we are the *creators* of our value feelings – and thus capable of projecting 'meaning' into history"; § 495: "The joy in shaping and reshaping – a primeval joy! We can comprehend only

[7] Grant, 1974/75 Nietzsche Lectures, p. 4.

a world that we ourselves have made"; or § 605: "The ascertaining of 'truth' and 'untruth,' the ascertaining of facts in general is fundamentally different from creative positing, from forming, shaping, overcoming, willing, such as is of the essence of philosophy. To introduce a meaning – this task still remains to be done.... On a yet higher level is to *posit a goal* and mold facts according to it."[8] Reading such passages, one could easily get the impression that Nietzsche's ideal is the absolute sovereignty of the willing individual, as though Nietzsche were committed to a wildly exaggerated version of liberalism.[9] One would be radically mistaken, for in fact Nietzsche's intention is at the furthest extremity from the liberal freedom that encourages individuals to choose their own purposes. As Nietzsche rightly insists, "[m]y philosophy aims at an ordering of rank: not at an individualistic morality" (*The Will to Power*, § 287). Although there is certainly a great quantity of hyperindividualistic rhetoric in Nietzsche, his ultimate project is the cultivation or "breeding" of entire cultures. What is required for this purpose is the very opposite of freedom as liberal modernity understands it.

The Nietzschean emphasis on radical willing has the effect not of opening horizons so that we may will what we choose, but the very opposite: of *closing* horizons so that whole societies regain the sense of cultural purpose that modernity inexorably disrupts. Thus he writes in *Beyond Good and Evil*, § 188, that "there should be *obedience* over a long period of time and in a *single* direction." He goes on to say, "'You shall obey – someone and for a long time: – *else* you will perish and lose the last respect for yourself' – this appears to me to be the moral imperative of nature." In the same context he bitterly condemns the anarchists for demanding *laisser aller*; any "natural" morality (as opposed to the "unnatural" morality of Christian-derived modernity) "teaches hatred of the *laisser aller*, of any all-too-great freedom, and implants the need for limited horizons." This paradoxical consequence – that the Nietzschean liberation of the will requires a severe constraining of freedom[10] – comes out very well in a crucial text, *The Will to Power*, § 144: "Moralities and religions are the principal means by which one can make whatever one wishes out of man, provided one possesses a superfluity of creative forces and can assert one's will over long periods of time – in the form of legislation, religions, and customs." In Nietzsche's view, modernity is the name for precisely that form

---

8 Cf. George Grant, *Time as History* (Toronto: CBC, 1969): "We must live in the knowledge that our purposes are simply creations of the human will and not ingrained in the nature of things. But what a burden falls upon the will when the horizons of definition are gone" (p. 30); "Most men, when they face that their purposes are not cosmically sustained, find that a darkness falls upon their wills. This is the crisis of the modern world to Nietzsche" (p. 31).

9 Something like this notion is implied in the connection that Grant draws between Nietzsche and Kant: "Now Nietzsche's will to power is the opposite of Plato's eros, and it comes from Kant's will, with its lack of need.... For Kant the sovereignty of the human individual presupposes the absence of poverty or need." George Grant, Notebook K: Kant 1977–78, typescript, p. 3.

10 At least a severe constraining of freedom *as moderns understand it*: See *Twilight of the Idols*, "Skirmishes of an Untimely Man," §§ 38 and 41.

of social organization (or social disorganization!) that is utterly incapable of such legislation. Thus he makes this statement in *Twilight of the Idols*: "The whole of the West no longer possesses the instincts out of which institutions grow, out of which a *future* grows: perhaps nothing antagonizes its "modern spirit" so much. One lives for the day, one lives very fast, one lives very irresponsibly: precisely this is called 'freedom'" ("Skirmishes of an Untimely Man," § 39). He adds that "we moderns, with our anxious self-solicitude and neighbor-love, with our virtues of work, modesty, legality, and scientism – accumulating, economic, machinelike – appear as a *weak* age" ("Skirmishes of an Untimely Man," § 37).[11] Are these sentences that could have been written by a celebrator of modernity? Admittedly, the Nietzschean emphasis on *willing* the civilizational possibility of premodern institutions is radically modern: One might formulate the paradox by saying that Nietzsche offers a stridently modern vocabulary in defense of a rabidly antimodern way of life. Nonetheless, it remains the case that no one who reads §§ 37–39 of "Skirmishes of an Untimely Man" could conceive of Nietzsche as being in any sense a defender of modernity.

The core of Nietzsche's way of thinking concerning the will (that is, the Nietzschean dialectic of freedom and constraint) is given decisive expression in *Beyond Good and Evil*, § 262: Modern freedom *relaxes* the bow, whereas Nietzsche wants urgently to *tighten* the bow.[12] *The Will to Power*, § 961, makes the same point: "The significance of protracted despotic moralities: they tense the bow." "Freedom" as defined in accordance with the Nietzschean conception of the will is the antithesis of liberal freedom, and therefore the antithesis of freedom as modernity conceives it.

Let us now turn to the question of religion proper. For my purposes, the crucial Nietzschean text is *The Will to Power*, § 151: "[R]eligions are destroyed by belief in morality. The Christian moral God is not tenable: hence 'atheism' – as if there could be no other kinds of god." What is implied in this text? Atheism is not the inevitable product of the maturation of the species, as imagined, for instance, in some Enlightenment scenario of a liberation from ignorance or a leap into truth; rather, atheism is caused by Christianity, that is, by the wrong kind of theism. Moreover, if, as Nietzsche thinks, certain decisive features of Christian theism have been responsible for the outcome of atheism in the West, this is not something for which Christianity deserves to be congratulated; on

---

[11] *The Portable Nietzsche*, ed. Walter Kaufmann (New York: Viking Press, 1968), pp. 543, 540; cf. p. 544, where Nietzsche distinguishes between modern and premodern institutions (e.g., marriage and the family) according to whether society can or cannot "affirm itself as a whole, down to the most distant generations." Cf. also p. 543: "In order that there may be institutions, there must be a kind of will, instinct, or imperative, which is anti-liberal to the point of malice: the will to tradition, to authority, to responsibility for centuries to come, to the solidarity of chains of generations, forward and backward, *ad infinitum*."

[12] It should be noted that in both *Beyond Good and Evil*, § 262, and *Twilight of the Idols*, "Skirmishes of an Untimely Man," § 38, Nietzsche refers to "aristocratic commonwealths" such as Venice or the cities of Greek and Roman antiquity as exemplary in this regard.

the contrary, it obliges us to render a damning judgment against Christianity. According to Nietzsche's view (as I interpret the text), Christian theism makes inevitable a *descent* (not an *ascent*) into atheism – a descent from which it is necessary to rise to new theistic possibilities. Christianity is, because of its moralism, a religion destroyer, a force destructive of our "God-inventing spirit" (as Nietzsche refers to religion in *The Will to Power*, § 1062). To recover the "god-forming instinct" (§ 1038), Christianity must be abolished. If we could but pry ourselves away from the assumption that our god must be a *moral* god, we could liberate our human creativity for the spawning of new forms of theism. "[H]ow many new gods are still possible!" Nietzsche twice exclaims in § 1038. The creative well that is the source of culture-nourishing divinities has dried up, thanks to the Christian drought, and needs to be replenished.[13]

It is important to be aware that Nietzsche does not simply condemn Christianity as such; he is also concerned to rank competing versions of Christianity. If one conceives of Nietzsche as a prophet of radical modernity, it comes as an astonishing surprise that he ranks Catholicism as decidedly superior to Protestantism. However, the more one reflects on Nietzsche's actual judgments on modernity, the more this makes sense. The decisive texts here are §§ 87–89 of *The Will to Power*. In § 87 Nietzsche writes the following: "Decline of *Protestantism*: understood as a halfway house [*als Halbheit*] both theoretically and historically. Actual superiority of Catholicism.... Protestantism simply doesn't exist any more." In § 88 he again refers to Protestantism as a "halfway house" [*etwas Halbes*].[14] In § 89, he asks the question: "Can one even imagine a spiritually staler, lazier, more comfortably relaxed form of the Christian faith than that of the average Protestant in Germany?" That Nietzsche criticizes Protestantism as spiritually stale, lazy, and relaxed would seem to imply that he would approve of a version of Christianity that would be less relaxed, less lazy, more spiritually robust. His reference, in § 87, to the "actual superiority

---

[13] Heidegger has made sure that we cannot fail to recall *The Antichrist*, § 19, in this context: "Almost two thousand years – and not a single new god!" This, in turn, makes one think of Machiavelli, *Discourses* II.5, according to which the passage of two millennia makes it reasonable to expect a change of religion.

[14] On Protestantism as a *Halbheit*, cf. *The Portable Nietzsche*, pp. 654–656. For a similar judgment concerning Protestantism as a compromise with modernity, see Martin Heidegger, *Nietzsche, Volume Four: Nihilism*, ed. D. F. Krell, trans. F. A. Capuzzi (San Francisco: Harper & Row, 1982), p. 99. However, it is not typical for Heidegger to condemn the Protestant Reformation, let alone to do so with the consistent venom that Nietzsche expresses on this question. Indeed, the young Heidegger, as we know from Heidegger's pupils, was intellectually infatuated with the young Luther: See Karl Löwith, "The Political Implications of Heidegger's Existentialism," in *The Heidegger Controversy*, ed. R. Wolin (Cambridge, MA: MIT Press, 1993), pp. 172–173; Hans-Georg Gadamer, "Erinnerungen an Heideggers Anfänge," *Dilthey-Jahrbuch für Philosophie und Geschichte der Geisteswissenschaften*, Vol. 4 (1986–1987): 22. However, it would be relevant to observe that for Heidegger, who struggled to break free of his Catholic upbringing, Luther would have been liberating in a way that he obviously would not have been for Nietzsche, who was brought up as a Lutheran. I shall return to these questions, and to the rhetoric of *Halbheit*, in the next chapter.

of Catholicism" [*Tatsächliches Übergewicht des Katholizismus*] may carry the same implication. If Nietzsche thinks that Christianity is a bad thing, should he not *welcome* a version of the Christian faith that is stale and spiritually exhausted?[15]

For Nietzsche there is no going back; one must thrust forward. Certainly, going back from Protestantism to Catholicism is, from Nietzsche's standpoint, no solution at all to our predicament. In going forward, though, one can learn from past possibilities, and Nietzsche's utmost aim is to derive maximum instruction from what the religions of antiquity have to teach us. Indeed, the further one retreats from late-Christian modernity, the more valuable becomes the instruction one hopes to gather from the various religious traditions. (This is not to say that Nietzsche does not think we have much to learn from Christian experience; his sometimes hysterical outbursts against Christianity often fail to do full justice to the complexity of his relationship to the Christian legacy.) Nietzsche is therefore committed not only to a hierarchical ranking of different varieties of Christianity relative to each other but also to a hierarchical ranking of Christian theism in general relative to non-Christian and anti-Christian (including pre-Christian) theisms. The most obvious alternative to Christianity is, of course, paganism, and Nietzsche gives us plenty of reasons to think his ultimate goal is a recuperation of pagan possibilities. His later writings contain repeated invocations of the Greek god Dionysus. In *The Will to Power*, for example, he addresses his preferred readers as "we pagans" (§ 1034), and he says that his task is to "demonstrate to what extent the Greek religion was higher than the Judaeo-Christian" (§ 1042). As we will soon see, however, Nietzsche's ambitions as a theorist of civil religion are not exhausted by the project of recovering pagan horizons.[16]

There is ample evidence of Nietzsche's favorable attitude toward Jewish theism (or at least a version of it) relative to Christianity.[17] His determination to side with the ancient Jews against the ancient Christians is very sharply expressed in *Genealogy of Morals*, Third Essay, § 22, where he exclaims, "I do

[15] Cf. *The Antichrist*, § 10: "Definition of Protestantism: the partial paralysis of Christianity." At the end of § 61 of *The Antichrist*, Nietzsche refers to German Protestantism as "the most unclean kind of Christianity that there is." If Protestantism is the most unclean kind of Christianity, then again it follows that Nietzsche regards Catholicism as theoretically superior.

[16] Karl Löwith, in a very illuminating article on "Nietzsche's Revival of the Doctrine of Eternal Recurrence," highlights the pagan antecedents of that doctrine but also shows why Nietzsche's version necessarily stands, owing to its Judeo-Christian aspect, outside the pagan horizon. As Löwith presents him, Nietzsche is a thinker who desperately wants to resuscitate paganism, but – *malgré lui* – is precluded from doing so by his involuntary debt to the biblical tradition. Karl Löwith, *Meaning in History* (Chicago: University of Chicago Press, 1949), pp. 214–222 (especially pp. 220–222); note also that the title of the book seems to refer back to *The Will to Power*, § 1011.

[17] Perhaps the most dramatic illustration of Nietzsche's overwhelming partiality for the Old Testament is the fact that it is only by detecting an affinity between Luther and the Jewish prophets that he can bring himself to say something positive about the Reformation: *The Portable Nietzsche*, p. 668 (*Nietzsche contra Wagner*).

not like the 'New Testament,' that should be plain. . . . The *Old* Testament –
that is something else again: all honor to the Old Testament! I find in it great
human beings, a heroic landscape, and something of the very rarest quality in
the world, the incomparable naïveté of the *strong heart*." Nietzsche's rejection
of the Christian appropriation of the Old Testament is expressed even more
sharply in *The Antichrist*, § 45: "*Impertinent* rabble! They compare themselves with the prophets, no less."[18] Christianity is also deeply impugned by
Nietzsche's analysis, in §§ 16–17 of *The Antichrist*, of the distinction between
national gods (gods who embody a people's pride, its sense of thankfulness, its
belief in itself) and cosmopolitan gods (gods who, having lost their organic link
to a particular people, are consigned to a condition of rootlessness, a sort of
divine tourism). Nietzsche is wholly and uncompromisingly on the side of the
former, and therefore he praises the Old Testament God who adheres to His
chosen people and he condemns the New Testament God whose cosmopolitanism is the mark of His decadence. Cosmopolitanism is a *Christian* legacy,[19]
and Nietzsche means to deliver the most severe reproach to Christianity when
he declares that "Christianity was not 'national.'"[20] It is according to the same
"national" standard that Nietzsche proclaims his overwhelming partiality for
the Old Testament: "I find a people" [*ich finde ein Volk*] (*Genealogy of Morals*,
Third Essay, § 22). "A people that still believes in itself retains its own god"
(*The Antichrist*, § 16); hence the God of Israel, as the god of a people, is far
superior to the Christian God, which is a cosmopolitan, and therefore unnatural and unhealthy, god.[21]

Nietzsche's ranking of religions is summarized in *The Will to Power*, § 145,
where religions are categorized primarily on the basis of a class analysis. The
religions unfolded in the lawbook of Manu, in the lawbook of Mohammed, and
in the older parts of the Old Testament are said to be affirmative [*ja-sagende*]
religions; those unfolded in the New Testament and in Buddhist texts are said
to be negative [*nein-sagende*] religions. The reference to "the older parts of
the Old Testament" indicates a crucial complexity in Nietzsche's evaluation
of the Hebrew Bible. Notwithstanding Nietzsche's very generous statements in

---

[18] Cf. *Beyond Good and Evil*, § 52.

[19] Cf. Rousseau: "[I]t was only Christianity that generalized [cosmopolitan ideas] sufficiently."
Geneva Manuscript, in *On the Social Contract*, ed. R. D. Masters, trans. J. R. Masters (New
York: St. Martin's Press, 1978), p. 162.

[20] *The Antichrist*, § 51: "Das Christentum war nicht 'national,' nicht rassebedingt." The context
is Nietzsche's rejection of the thesis that Christianity arose out of "the decline of race" (i.e.,
as a product of the national decline of the Romans): "Sie drückt *nicht* den Niedergang einer
Rasse aus." The point here is that Christianity gathers together the weak of all nations, rather
than expressing the decadence of one particular nation. In Nietzsche's judgment, cosmopolitan
decadence is far more calamitous than mere national decadence.

[21] Viewed more strictly, Judaism both is and is not a "national religion" in Rousseau's sense.
Freud remarks aptly on this peculiarity of Judaism: See *Moses and Monotheism* (New York:
Vintage, 1958), p. 55: "[One is astonished by] the conception of a god suddenly 'choosing' a
people, making it 'his' people and himself its own god. I believe it is the only case in the history
of human religions. In other cases the people and their god belong inseparably together; they
are one from the beginning."

appreciation of the Old Testament relative to the New, there are, of course, many passages in *The Antichrist* and elsewhere in which Nietzsche's judgments on the Jewish contribution to Western theism seem just as harsh as his judgments on the Christian legacy. As § 145 of *The Will to Power* clearly implies, there is a simple solution to this puzzle, for Nietzsche makes a sharp distinction between the "heroic" books of the Old Testament, which for him express an aristocratic warrior creed comparable to Hinduism and Islam, and the later books of the Old Testament, which for him reflect the hegemony acquired by the priests. The story of this crucial transformation in Jewish history is told in *The Antichrist*, § 26, where Nietzsche writes that "in the hands of the Jewish priests the great age in the history of Israel became an age of decay; the Exile, the long misfortune, was transformed into an eternal punishment for the great age – an age in which the priest was still a nobody.... *From now on* all things in life are so ordered that the priest is indispensable everywhere."[22] It is this "hijacking" of Judaism by the priests that turns the Hebrew religion into a proto-Christian phenomenon. This, then, explains the tension in *The Antichrist* between those passages in which Nietzsche strongly endorses the Hebrew Bible and those in which he harshly condemns it.[23]

Where all this is leading, clearly, is toward legislating a post-Christian regime, and everything in *The Antichrist*, as well as in his other writings that analyze the various religions, is intended as preparatory to such a post-Christian regime. As Nietzsche puts it in *The Will to Power*, § 361, "I have declared war on the anaemic Christian ideal ... not with the aim of destroying it but only of putting an end to its tyranny and clearing the way for new ideals, for *more robust* ideals." (In § 1051, however, the tone is less conciliatory, as he seeks "to *overcome* everything Christian through something supra-Christian, and not merely to put it aside.") In §§ 20–23 of *The Antichrist*, Nietzsche offers a distinction between two kinds of nihilistic religion: Buddhism, which represents the end point of a civilization that has exhausted its energies, and whose nihilism (a kind of tranquillizer for old age) is excusable; and Christianity, which serves to domesticate youthful Europe's barbarian energies and whose nihilism is therefore not excusable. Weary civilizations are permitted to drug themselves to sleep, but Christianity lacks this excuse. Nonetheless, at the end of § 22, Nietzsche concludes this analysis of Buddhism with the

---

[22] *The Portable Nietzsche*, pp. 596–597; emphasis added. Nietzsche has a similar story to tell about Hinduism. In *The Will to Power*, § 145, he distinguishes between a good stage of the religion, when power belonged to the warrior caste, and a bad stage, when power shifted to the priests. Exactly parallel to his account of the Old Testament, this thesis accounts for Nietzsche's similarly ambivalent judgments in regard to the lawbook of Manu.

[23] Freud's theory of the double origin of Judaism (as a fusion of an Aton religion of Egyptian origin and a Jahve religion of Midianite origin) bears some affinity with Nietzsche's account in *The Antichrist* of two Old Testaments – namely a religion of noble warriors (corresponding to Jahve) and a religion of ignoble priests (corresponding to Aton). Had Nietzsche been given an opportunity to acquaint himself with Freud's theory, Nietzsche might have seen its key relevance for his own account in the fact that, in Freud's view, the prior (but ultimately prevailing) Aton religion was rooted in an experience of slavery that was not shared by the adherents of the Jahve religion. See esp. *Moses and Monotheism*, pp. 64–65.

following astounding claim: "Christianity finds no civilization as yet – under certain circumstances it might lay the foundation for one [*es begründet sie unter Umständen*]." He surely does not mean that Christianity furnishes an adequate basis for a substantial civilization. What he means, what he must mean, is that a resolutely anti-Christian thinker such as himself can survey the rubble left by Christianity, with a view to erecting on this inert base a radically different post-Christian civilization.

The Antichrist does not itself present a civil religion but rather supplies the standards of evaluation that a suitably post-Christian civil religion (*Thus Spoke Zarathustra*?)[24] would have to satisfy. In §§ 16–17, *The Antichrist* teaches us that national deities are superior to cosmopolitan deities. In §§ 59–60 it teaches us that unabashedly masculine warrior religions are superior to religions of feminine love and benevolence.[25] In §§ 20–23 it teaches us that even among the nihilistic religions, a ranking is necessary: Forms of nihilism, such as Buddhism, that express the twilight of a great civilization are superior to a form of nihilism (Christianity) that opposes itself to still-vibrant civilizations and drains them of all vitality. (Related to this is the vampire theme of §§ 49, 58, 59, and 62.)[26] Further important clues to Nietzsche's theocratic or civil-religion teaching are offered in §§ 56–57 of *The Antichrist*. In § 55 Nietzsche states that what is common to all religions, healthy as well as decadent, is lying: Whether one looks at paganism, Confucianism, the religion expressed in the law of Manu, Islam, or Christianity, the universal law is that the priest lies. Platonic theology is the same, but it distinguishes itself from the others in claiming explicitly the right to lie; indeed, in asserting the necessity of a "philosophic-priestly rule" based on lying. However, at the beginning of § 56, Nietzsche emphasizes that he has no objection to lying as such: "[I]t is a matter of the *end* to which one lies."[27]

Here, Nietzsche's preferred model of a well-functioning civil religion seems to be found in the Hindu lawbook of Manu. It hardly seems likely that Nietzsche's choice of the Hindu caste system as his privileged alternative to Christianity is merely coincidental. Nevertheless, in a parallel discussion in

---

[24] This is what is suggested by Nietzsche's reference to the eternal recurrence in *The Will to Power*, § 462, as a substitute religion. Cf. George Grant, 1974/75 Nietzsche Lectures, 2nd Half: Lectures on *Beyond Good and Evil*, typescript, p. 22: "Zarathustra a founder of a new religion beyond Christianity. A new Bible – a new ironic bible parodies the Bible while overcoming it or claiming to overcome it." Also see Löwith, *Nietzsche's Philosophy of the Eternal Recurrence of the Same*, pp. 61–62: *Zarathustra* as a "fifth Gospel" (quoted from a letter to Franz Overbeck); p. 83: eternal recurrence "as an *atheistic religion* and as a *physical metaphysics*"; and p. 86: "an atheistic gospel."

[25] The most forceful statement of Nietzsche's standard of judgment is offered in the last sentence of *Antichrist*, § 59: "Islam is a thousand times right in despising Christianity: Islam presupposes *men*." Cf. *The Will to Power*, § 145.

[26] Hence the relevance of Nietzsche's argument in *The Antichrist*, § 51, that Roman antiquity was not a spent force, undone by its own decadence ("the scholarly idiocy which upholds such ideas even today cannot be contradicted harshly enough"). Rather, it was "vampirized" and subverted by Christianity – as Nietzsche puts it in § 59, "[n]ot vanquished – merely drained."

[27] The italics are Nietzsche's, although they are omitted by Kaufmann.

the section entitled "The 'Improvers' of Mankind" in *Twilight of the Idols*, Nietzsche appears to be far more critical of the Hindu laws; and in several sections of *The Will to Power* (notably §§ 142–143), he is more critical still (although in other sections, such as § 145, he seems less critical). We seem to get a solution to this puzzle in *The Will to Power*, § 116: The lawbook of Manu made no mistake in dividing society into castes; its mistake was to place the *priests* at the apex of the social pyramid, giving *them* the power to rule all. In this respect, as Nietzsche insists in §§ 142–143, it had a disastrous influence on other religions, for it established the universally imitated model of a priestly regime.[28] Nietzsche's prescription, as announced in § 116, is to retain the Hindu caste structure but to invert its content, with *priests* as the new chandala class (outcasts, untouchables),[29] and "*blasphemers, immoralists, free-floating individuals of every description, artiste-performers, Jews, street minstrels*" at the very top.[30] This text suggests a way of achieving a perfect

---

[28] The most ambitious statement of this thesis occurs in a letter to Peter Gast (May 31, 1888) in which Nietzsche relates that he has been reading the lawbook of Manu in a French translation and describes its impact on him:

> This absolutely *Aryan* work, a priestly codex of morality based on the Vedas, on the idea of caste and very ancient tradition – *not* pessimistic, albeit very sacerdotal – supplements my views on religion in the most remarkable way. I confess to having the impression that everything else that we have by way of moral lawgiving seems to me an imitation and even a caricature of it – preeminently, Egypticism does; but even Plato seems to me in all the main points simply to have been well instructed by a Brahmin. It makes the Jews look like a Chandala race which learns from its *masters* the principles of making a *priestly caste* the master which organizes a people.... The Chinese also seem to have produced their Confucius and Lao-tse under the influence of this *ancient classic of laws*. The medieval organization looks like a wondrous groping for a restoration of all the ideas which formed the basis of primordial Indian-Aryan society.

See the *Selected Letters of Friedrich Nietzsche*, ed. Christopher Middleton (Chicago: University of Chicago Press, 1969), pp. 297–298.

[29] The chandalas are outcasts or untouchables by virtue of being of mixed caste. Strictly speaking, the chandalas are not a caste but a subcaste, that is, beneath or outside of the fourfold caste system of priests, warriors, farmers, and servants. See Louis Dumont, *Homo Hierarchicus* (Chicago: University of Chicago Press, 1970), pp. 52–53, 66–71, 284 n. 32f. For regulations concerning relations between the castes, see *The Laws of Manu*, trans. G. Bühler (Delhi: Motilar Banarsidass, 1964), pp. 13–14, 24–28, 399–430. For regulations concerning the chandalas, see pp. 92, 119, 141, 183, 192, 343, 404–405, 407–409, 414–415, 425, 466–467, 496. Nietzsche's quotations in *The Antichrist*, § 56, correspond very roughly to V:130, V:133, and V:132 on p. 192 of the Bühler edition; presumably he is quoting from memory. In any case, Nietzsche is conspicuously overgenerous in praising the "tenderness" of Manu's teaching concerning women (see the Bühler edition, pp. 195–197, 327–332). Nietzsche frequently uses the term "chandala" to characterize Judeo-Christian religion. This appropriation of Hindu vocabulary is obviously a deliberate strategy within his Machiavellian project of a "revaluation of values." It is difficult not to feel a chill going up one's spine when one considers that in the 1930s, the Nazis, too, appropriated Hindu vocabulary to pursue *their* revaluation of values.

[30] The German reads as "die *Gottesläster*, die *Immoralisten*, die Freizügigen jeder Art, die Artisten, die Juden, die Spielleute." I have revised Kaufmann's translation; the context stresses disreputableness, which Kaufmann's rendering does not fully convey. Needless to say, a society ruled by circus performers and street minstrels would constitute a very peculiar regime!

reconciliation between the apparent praise of the lawbook of Manu in *The Antichrist* and its apparent condemnation in *Twilight of the Idols*. On one hand, insofar as it entrenches the rule of priests, the Hindu lawbook serves as a dreadful precedent in the history of religion, one duly followed by every other religion. On the other hand, as the most radical example of a set of laws giving religious sanction to the idea of a caste-structured society, it offers the most impressive alternative to Christian egalitarianism.[31] What appear to be contradictory judgments concerning the Hindu laws can, in fact, be rendered fully consistent. Strangely enough, there is no analogous tension in Nietzsche's judgments concerning Plato's *Republic*, for although he notes in many passages the similarities between the Hindu rule by Brahmins and the Platonic rule by philosophers (in fact, he claims repeatedly that Plato – via Asian or Egyptian sources – *borrows* his basic conception from the Hindu laws),[32] he never *credits* Plato with having legislated a caste-based politics. Rather, Nietzsche consistently focuses on one sole aspect of Plato, namely Plato's having sown the seeds of everything Nietzsche hates about Christianity.[33] This yields a very striking irony that Nietzsche has no inclination to acknowledge: Although the philosophy of Plato's *Republic* is radically antithetical to Nietzsche's, its politics are surprisingly similar to Nietzsche's own politics.[34] The clearest illustration of this similarity is in fact Nietzsche's account in §§ 56–57 of *The Antichrist* of what he admires in the lawbook of Manu.

---

[31] How far from egalitarianism does Nietzsche intend to take us? The following description of ancient Hindu norms provides a bracing standard: "Death was the sentence to an untouchable who wanted an education. The Laws of Manu, followed by orthodox Hindus, prescribed the method of execution. If an untouchable even overheard Sanskrit, the language of the scriptures, he was to be killed by having molten lead poured into his ears." See Gita Mehta, *Snakes and Ladders: Glimpses of Modern India* (New York: Anchor Books, 1997), p. 120.

[32] In addition to the letter cited in note 28 above, see *The Will to Power*, § 143.

[33] See, for instance, *The Portable Nietzsche*, pp. 557–558: "[Plato is] so pre-existently Christian.... [Plato] made it possible for the nobler spirits of antiquity... to set foot on the bridge leading to the cross." See also *The Will to Power*, § 427: "preparation of the soil for Christianity."

[34] One place where Nietzsche does acknowledge how much he shares with the politics of Plato's *Republic* is at the end of his early essay, "The Greek State": Friedrich Nietzsche, *On the Genealogy of Morals*, ed. Keith Ansell-Pearson, trans. Carol Diethe (Cambridge: Cambridge University Press, 1994), pp. 185–186. Consider also *The Gay Science*, § 18, where Nietzsche encapsulates the politics of the ancient philosophers as a broadening of the slave class to encompass as a slave everyone who is not a philosopher. Is this not a way of characterizing Nietzsche's own politics? A crucial way of illuminating this aspect of Nietzsche's political thought, one has to say, is by tracing its alarming affinities with nineteenth-century protofascists like Gobineau (to whom Nietzsche was linked through the dubious shared company of Wagner). Consider, for instance, Gobineau's idea of human beings as decadent sheep in need of ruthless shepherds. As Tocqueville nicely puts it, Gobineau thinks people need to be ruled by the whip, yet he does not volunteer to present his own bare back for flogging; see Alexis de Tocqueville, *The European Revolution and Correspondence with Gobineau*, ed. John Lukacs (Garden City, NY: Doubleday Anchor Books, 1959), p. 309. One cannot perceive Nietzsche's political thought in its true light without appreciating how horrendous is the idea of "nobility" in the hands of nineteenth-century ultrareactionary enemies of democracy like Gobineau and Nietzsche.

Nietzsche finds it impossible to discuss these questions without bringing Plato into the center of the discussion. When Nietzsche says, "[n]either
Manu nor Plato nor Confucius nor the Jewish and Christian teachers have
ever doubted their right to lie" (*Twilight of the Idols*, "The 'Improvers' of
Mankind," § 5), he implies that Plato's *Republic* offers a civil religion. Moreover, Nietzsche is committed to the view that Plato's civil religion is, *despite
appearances*, closer in spirit to Christian egalitarianism than to Hindu hierarchy. If we go back to the text with which we started, namely *The Will to Power*,
§ 151, we can begin to see more clearly why Plato looms so large within Nietzsche's civil-religion argument. We may recall that according to Nietzsche's
suggestion in § 151, what killed Judeo-Christian theism was the incredibility
of the notion of the biblical God as a supposedly *moral* god. Conversely, if it
were possible for there to be a post-Christian theism, it would be preferable,
perhaps indispensable, for the post-Christian gods to be decidedly *immoral*
gods.[35] This is clearly intended as a direct inversion of Plato. In the Platonic
theology at the end of Book 2 and the beginning of Book 3 of *The Republic*,
Plato rejects Homer's gods on the grounds of their immorality – thus anticipating the Christian God, who is irreproachably moral. It is arguable that the
God of the Hebrews is rather more like the Homeric gods in this respect, which
is obviously why Nietzsche so ardently prefers the God of the Old Testament
to the God of the New Testament.[36] In this sense, the Christian culpability for
Western atheism, as Nietzsche understands it, is ultimately traceable back to
Plato, insofar as Christianity gave Plato the kind of theism he wanted, namely
a theism purged of gods capable of immoral conduct.[37] It is precisely this
Platonic–Christian (that is to say, anti-Homeric) theism that, in Nietzsche's
view, drives the West in the direction of atheism.

Nietzsche plays a more elaborate version of the same tune in § 16 of *The
Antichrist*. This section, although it appears to be addressed strictly to Christianity and its "revaluation" of the Old Testament, is actually an implicit
dialogue with Plato's *Republic* 377d–391e. When Socrates says to Adeiman-
tus, "[a]bove all, it mustn't be said that gods make war on gods, and plot
against them and have battles with them,"[38] Nietzsche gives this response:
"What would be the point of a god who knew nothing of wrath, revenge, envy,

---

[35] For further elaboration of this thought, see *The Will to Power*, §§ 1034–1038, as well as § 1011.
In § 1034 Nietzsche makes it perfectly clear that his own preference would be for pagan gods.
Insofar as one must have something like the biblical God, Nietzsche argues in § 1037 that such
a god should at least be defined, not surprisingly, in terms of His power rather than of His
goodness or wisdom. Cf. Hobbes, *Leviathan*, chapter 31.

[36] This is what Nietzsche implies when he writes the following: "A great moralist is, among other
things, necessarily a great actor.... And indeed, it is said that the moralist imitates in that no
less a model than God himself: God, the greatest of all immoralists in practice" (*The Will to
Power*, § 304). The context suggests that what Nietzsche is referring to here is Machiavelli's
description of God as the "tutor" [*precettore*] of Moses in chapter 6 of *The Prince*.

[37] Cf. *The Will to Power*, § 438: "Moral fanaticism (in short: Plato) destroyed paganism." See
also Nietzsche's comments on the Homeric gods in *Genealogy of Morals*, Second Essay, § 23.

[38] *The Republic of Plato*, trans. Allan Bloom (New York: Basic Books, 1968), p. 56.

scorn, cunning, and violence? who had perhaps never experienced the delightful *ardeurs* of victory and annihilation? No one would understand such a god: why have him then?" When Plato insists, against Homer, that "the god, since he's good, wouldn't be the cause of everything, and that, "of the bad things, some other causes must be sought and not the god,"[39] Nietzsche makes this reply on behalf of Homer:

[R]eligion is a form of thankfulness. Being thankful for himself, man needs a god. Such a god must be able to help and to harm, to be friend and enemy – he is admired whether good or destructive. The *anti-natural* castration of a god, to make him a god of the good alone, would here be contrary to everything desirable. The evil god is needed no less than the good god.

The national god of the Hebrews is superior to the god of the New Testament for the same reason that Homer's gods are superior to Plato's god, namely that a god who knows nothing of "wrath, revenge, envy, scorn, cunning, and violence" is humanly unintelligible, and therefore eventually discredits theism.[40]

One could say a great deal more about Nietzsche's preoccupation with evaluating religions by analyzing their cultural–political implications. For our purposes here it suffices to quote *The Will to Power*, § 144: "Moralities and religions are the principal means by which one can make whatever one wishes out of man, provided one possesses a superfluity of creative forces and can assert one's will over long periods of time – in the form of legislation, religions, and customs." The spirit in which one embarks on this awesome enterprise is clearly stated in *The Will to Power*, § 1051: "To wait and to prepare oneself; to await the emergence of new sources... to wash one's soul ever cleaner from the marketplace dust and noise of this age; to *overcome* everything Christian through something supra-Christian, and not merely to put it aside." One way in which all of this can be summed up is by remarking that Heidegger's famous pronouncement, "[o]nly a god can save us," echoes a recognizably Nietzschean mode of response ("waiting and preparing") to our current dispensation – except that in Nietzsche's thought this recourse to awaited gods finds a more directly political expression.

At the risk of oversimplifying Nietzsche's theocratic or quasi-theocratic teaching in all its elusive complexity, let me try to summarize the theistic dimension of Nietzsche's theorizing. I start with the idea of a hierarchy or ranking of theistic possibilities, with Christianity at the bottom: "The Christian conception of god... is one of the most corrupt conceptions of the divine ever attained

---

[39] Ibid., p. 57; cf. p. 58.
[40] As we saw in Chapter 9, the anthropomorphism of the Old Testament God is a big issue for Spinoza. In an interesting discussion, Harold Bloom traces the "human-all-too-human" traits of Yahweh to the personality and literary genius of "J," or the Yahwist; he also discusses the unease with which "normative Judaism" received this often startling depiction of God. See "The Author J," in *The Book of J*, trans. David Rosenberg (New York: Vintage, 1991), pp. 1–55.

on earth. It may even represent the low-water mark in the descending development of divine types."[41] Concerning the criteria that define this hierarchy, Nietzsche argues, first, that national gods are better than cosmopolitan gods; second, that immoral gods are better than moral gods; and third, that gods that are more masculine are better than gods that are more feminine. This analysis obviously presupposes the idea of constituting, first philosophically and then in practice, a post-Christian civilization. As I noted earlier, this is surely what Nietzsche has in mind with his bizarre formulation in *The Antichrist*, § 22, that "Christianity finds no civilization as yet – under certain circumstances it might lay the foundation for one" [*das Christentum findet sie noch nicht einmals vor – es begründet sie unter Umständen*].[42] Nietzsche's suggestion here is incredible – as if we are still awaiting the emergence of a civilization founded on Christianity! The meaning of this strange utterance is that for Nietzsche, "Christian civilization" is a contradiction in terms (just as, for him, "liberal civilization" and "democratic civilization" are oxymorons). His aim, therefore, is to turn the whole inheritance of Christianity into a mere foundation stone upon which to erect a new civilization that is not only post-Christian but anti-Christian. Finally, Nietzsche's civil-religion argument teaches us, as *The Antichrist*, § 19 suggests, that what most condemns Christianity is that it deactivates the "god-creating power" of human beings. Europe has put up with the Christian God for 2,000 years and has made no attempt to dispose of Him (although it has not lacked opportunities to do so). We await the enchanting variety of new post-Christian gods that will arise with the reawakening of the "*creator spiritus*" that Christianity put to sleep.[43]

Why is Nietzsche so obsessed with the question of how an ancient Hindu law code managed to fashion one particular galaxy of human life? Why do two of his last books give such concentrated attention to what appears, surely, as an obsolete possibility? The answer, clearly, is that *Nietzsche* was not convinced that religions had, for all time, relinquished the capacity to steer human beings in specific directions. On the contrary, it seems evident that this was still, for him, a live option; and *only* on the presumption that Nietzsche thought civil religion could be resurrected in the West can we make sense of this dimension of his theorizing. It confers a unique energy on his efforts to render comparative judgments on the spectrum of human religions, and, having done so,

---

[41] *The Antichrist*, § 18. Cf., for instance, *The Will to Power*, § 200: "Christianity as the most fatal seductive lie that has yet existed. . . . the most disgusting degeneration culture has yet exhibited"; and *Beyond Good and Evil*, § 62: "Christianity has been the most calamitous kind of arrogance yet."

[42] The phrasing is not fully unambiguous, but the basic meaning seems to be: Whereas Buddhism was associated with the end point of a grand civilization, Christianity was at the outset *and continues to be* "pre-civilizational." Under the right circumstances, however, it is not too late for it to contribute to a real civilization.

[43] See, for instance, *The Will to Power*, § 1038 and the end of § 1005. In *Beyond Good and Evil*, § 53, Nietzsche distinguishes between "the religious instinct" and the theistic manner of satisfying this instinct, but it is not entirely clear what this means.

to arrange those religions in a philosophically grounded rank order. Having ranked religions, one then legislates them: "The philosopher as *we* understand him ... as the man of the most comprehensive responsibility who has the conscience for the over-all development of man ... will make use of religions for his project of cultivation and education, just as he will make use of whatever political and economic states are at hand."[44] At the same time, "one always pays dearly and terribly when religions do *not* want to be a means of education and cultivation in the philosopher's hand but insist on having their own *sovereign* way, when they themselves want to be ultimate ends and not means among other means."[45] As Leo Strauss rightly points out, the "fundamental alternative is that of the rule of philosophy over religion or the rule of religion over philosophy."[46]

Notwithstanding Nietzsche's statement in *The Will to Power*, § 116, that "[w]e are proud of no longer having to be liars," if Nietzsche is committed to the view (as he states it in *The Antichrist*, both at the beginning of § 56 and at the beginning of § 58) that what matters is not lying but the *end* to which one lies, then (by his own account) he accepts in principle the whole project of a civil religion. He intends to modify religions as historically given in two key respects: First, one will be lying for life-affirming rather than life-negating ends; second, one will ensure that responsibility for these lies will not be in the hands of a class of priests. However, in this respect Nietzsche is entirely faithful to the modern tradition of civil religion set forth, as we saw in Part I, by Machiavelli, Hobbes, and Rousseau. For each of these authors it is possible to embrace a politics that is both "theocratic" and radically anticlerical. In the words of Leszek Kolakowski, modern theorists of civil religion opt for theocracy (what Hobbes labeled "the Priesthood of Kings") but not for clerocracy (what Hobbes labeled "the Kingdom of Priests").[47]

That Nietzsche is such an unremitting opponent of priestly rule should, one might think, make him quite sympathetic to the aspirations of the Enlightenment.[48] Of course, Nietzsche is perfectly well aware that his own

---

44 *Beyond Good and Evil*, § 61.

45 Ibid., § 62.

46 Leo Strauss, "Note on the Plan of Nietzsche's *Beyond Good and Evil*," in *Studies in Platonic Political Philosophy* (Chicago: University of Chicago Press, 1983), p. 176. A similar battle of authority is intimated in a celebrated text by Kant (one of my epigraphs to Chapter 17): Religion wants to wrap itself in an aura of sanctity, but the imperatives of legitimacy in an age of *Kritik* do not permit this – at the end of the day, religion must "submit" (*sich unterwerfen muss*) to the judgment of critical reason. See *Critique of Pure Reason*, Axi, note.

47 Leszek Kolakowski, *Modernity on Endless Trial* (Chicago: University of Chicago Press, 1990), p. 179. For Hobbes's version of the distinction between theocracy and clerocracy, see *Leviathan*, chapter 35; cf. DeCive, chapter 16.

48 For a helpful account of the evolution in Nietzsche's stance toward the Enlightenment – from Enlightenment sympathizer in his middle period to firm Counter-Enlightenment theorist in his mature work – see Graeme Garrard, *Counter-Enlightenments: From the Eighteenth Century to the Present* (London: Routledge, 2006), chapter 5. As Garrard highlights, the key to this transformation in Nietzsche's thinking lies in the *Beyond Good and Evil* Preface's reference

project of combating Christianity presupposes the contribution of the Enlightenment in loosening the grip of Christianity on our civilization. Nonetheless, the fact that Nietzsche is an enemy of clerocracy does not make him a friend of the Enlightenment. Although Nietzsche is prepared to forgive the lunacies of past millennia ("I am careful not to hold mankind responsible for its mental disorders"), what he finds utterly intolerable is "modern times, *our* time. Our time *knows better*" (*The Antichrist*, § 38).[49] For Nietzsche, not unreasonably, one cannot separate modernity from the political legacy of liberalism, egalitarianism, democracy, humanitarianism, and so on. Furthermore, all these political fruits of the rationalist Enlightenment are inseparable from the legacy of Christianity. In that sense, being radically anti-Christian entails being radically antimodern.

The clearest statement of Nietzsche's position concerning the Enlightenment is in the Preface to *Beyond Good and Evil*:

[T]wice already attempts have been made in the grand style to unbend the bow – once by means of Jesuitism, the second time by means of the democratic enlightenment which, with the aid of freedom of the press and newspaper-reading, might indeed bring it about that the spirit would no longer experience itself so easily as a "need."[50]

to the "*democratic* Enlightenment." As long as Nietzsche could conceive of the Enlightenment as aristocratic (centered on the figure of Voltaire), he could and did embrace it. As soon as Nietzsche's conception of the Enlightenment gravitated more toward the democratizing influence of Rousseau, he was obliged to reject it.

The view of Nietzsche offered by Laurence Lampert in "Strauss's Recovery of Esotericism," in *The Cambridge Companion to Leo Strauss*, ed. Steven B. Smith (Cambridge: Cambridge University Press, 2009), p. 91 – that Nietzsche in his early works "counseled...esotericism to facilitate healthy if false horizons within which alone humanity could flourish," whereas in his later works he became a radical Enlightener – is a surprising one, and is not borne out by the texts. As Lampert surely knows, the theme of legislating false but life-enhancing horizons does not drop away in Nietzsche's late philosophy; Nietzsche's view, in his later works even more than in his earlier ones, is that the Enlightenment, although it perhaps deserves some appreciation for discrediting Christianity, is to be thoroughly repudiated for its promotion of rationalism and democracy.

[49] Cf. *The Anti-Christ, Ecce Homo, Twilight of the Idols, and Other Writings*, ed. Aaron Ridley and Judith Norman, trans. Judith Norman (Cambridge: Cambridge University Press, 2005), p. 67: "One should be harsher with Protestants than with Catholics, harsher with liberal Protestants than with orthodox ones. The criminality of being Christian increases with your proximity to science." As Aaron Ridley notes in the Introduction to this volume and in the section on Further Reading, Nietzsche's works of 1888 have tended to be unfairly slighted by Nietzsche scholars. There are, however, important exceptions. See, for instance, Gary Shapiro, in "The Writing on the Wall: *The Antichrist* and the Semiotics of History," in *Reading Nietzsche*, ed. Robert C. Solomon and Kathleen M. Higgins (New York: Oxford University Press, 1988), which offers an attempt to take *The Antichrist* seriously as a philosophic text. As such, it sheds much light on various dimensions of the work, such as Nietzsche's relationship to nineteenth-century theological philology. For another significant reading of *The Antichrist*, see Peter Berkowitz, *Nietzsche: The Ethics of an Immoralist* (Cambridge, MA: Harvard University Press, 1995), chapter 4.

[50] For other passages in which Nietzsche invokes the same metaphor, see *Beyond Good and Evil*, §§ 206 and 262; *Genealogy of Morals*, First Essay, § 12; and *The Will to Power*, § 961.

According to Nietzsche, what bent the bow of the European spirit in so magnificent a fashion was "the fight against the Christian-ecclesiastical pressure of millennia." However, rather than *crediting* the Enlightenment with having participated in this epic anti-Christian struggle, he does the opposite: He accuses the Enlightenment of trying to see to it that the fight against Christianity has only the most feeble and mediocre outcome – mere democracy. The fact that Nietzsche is so critical of the Enlightenment means at the same time that he is less than happy with the cultural price we pay for all the science, rationalization, and technological progress that define our modernity (however much he may nonetheless appeal to the authority of science in denouncing Christianity). If Nietzsche had to choose between living in a disenchanted world that had been thoroughly rationalized by science and living in a world where religious myth and mystery continued to furnish durable horizons within which human beings could have a meaningful existence defined for them, there seems little doubt that he would choose the latter. To repeat what was quoted earlier, "it is a matter of the *end* to which one lies."

In Nietzsche, we are presented with an atheist who passionately longs to found a new religion.[51] How is this paradoxical enterprise possible, if not for Nietzsche's profound abhorrence toward the form of social and political order willed into existence by the liberal tradition?[52] From a liberal point of view, the basic institutions of liberal society are fully reasonable, and therefore Nietzsche's uncompromising rejection of it looks like a hysterical reaction against a fundamentally reasonable organization of social and political life. For those more sympathetic to Nietzsche's dimension of theorizing, his doubts and anxieties about a liberal mode of life are themselves worthy of articulation, and even for those who ultimately opt for a liberal vision of society and politics, it is possible to believe that Nietzsche should nonetheless be honored for his contribution to a necessary effort at self-reflection, and a tremendous deepening of that self-reflection, on the part of those inhabiting a liberal order of life. I think a reasonable argument can be made on behalf of this second response to Nietzsche's vehemently counterliberal political philosophy, and in the reading of Nietzsche I have offered it has been presupposed that even committed

---

[51] In *Ecce Homo*, Nietzsche writes that "there is nothing in me of a founder of a religion" (*Basic Writings of Nietzsche*, trans. and ed. Walter Kaufmann, New York: Modern Library, 1968, p. 782). Nietzsche says this, but his work says otherwise. Cf. Löwith's discussion of the "biblical" character of Nietzsche's Zarathustra in *Nietzsche's Philosophy of the Eternal Recurrence of the Same*, e.g., p. 103: "Zarathustra's noon resembles more the doomsday of the prophets and apostles than the noon at which isolated existence sinks back into the total life of nature."

[52] Nietzsche's Burckhardtian distaste for the kind of commercial–technological frenzy he would clearly associate with this social–political order is nicely encapsulated in *The Will to Power*, § 33. Here are some of the "causes" of European nihilism, as he sees it: "that diminution, sensitivity to pain, restlessness, haste, and hustling grow continually – that it becomes easier and easier to recognize this whole commotion, this so-called 'civilization,' and that the individual, faced with this tremendous machinery, loses courage and submits." Cf. *The Will to Power*, § 1051: "to wash one's soul ever cleaner from the marketplace dust and noise of this age."

liberals can profit from reflection on Nietzsche's root-and-branch challenge to liberalism.

We can appreciate the depth of the challenge that Nietzsche poses to a liberal social order and be grateful to him for the effort of self-questioning that this provokes, but this does not mean that there are not important theoretical challenges that Nietzsche himself ought to be obliged to answer. In pursuing his civil-religion project, Nietzsche might be charged with violating his own strictures against decadent modernity. In section 7 of *The Case of Wagner* Nietzsche tells us that the decadent is one whose style approximates "the anarchy of atoms," where the part triumphs over the whole: "The whole no longer lives at all: it is composite, calculated, artificial, artifact." This passage is bound to make us think of contemporary postmodernism, with its cut-and-splice approach to inherited cultural traditions. However, isn't Nietzsche's project of a new post-Christian synthesis, which appropriates elements of paganism, Hinduism, atheism, and even Christianity, proto-postmodern in just this sense? Indeed, the same accusation might be leveled against the ersatz scripture that Nietzsche attempts to construct in *Thus Spoke Zarathustra*. It is not too hard to see why Nietzsche admits in the preface to *The Case of Wagner* that "I am, no less than Wagner, a child of this time; that is, a decadent." Nonetheless, he also tells us that as a philosopher he comprehended his own decadence and resisted it; what he wished for more than anything was to fashion something that was *more* than a composite, calculated, and artificial artifact made up of bits and pieces of old religions.

Needless to say, there is a real paradox underlying the whole project of a Nietzschean civil religion (and perhaps in this sense the whole modern idea of a civil religion comes to a final terminus in Nietzsche). The more remote a particular religion is from modern horizonlessness, the more attractive Nietzsche finds it – hence his preference for the lawbook of Manu over the Gospels, for Islam over the New Testament, for Catholic Christianity over Protestant Christianity. Most critics of modernity (including Heidegger) view modernity as a frenzied engine of willing; Nietzsche, by contrast, sees modernity, shaped by Christian humanitarianism and Enlightenment rationalism, as defined by a woeful incapacity to will something truly grand, or at least nonephemeral. (Nietzsche's judgment is not easy to refute. Can one imagine any *modern* society producing anything remotely comparable to medieval cathedrals or ancient Indian temples?)[53] Indeed, from Nietzsche's point of view, modernity is unable to will anything at all: Judged by the standard of power, modernity stands for

---

[53] I can think of only one modern counterexample: Antoni Gaudí's Sagrada Familia. However, even if Gaudí shows that *modernity* is capable of producing the equivalent of medieval cathedrals, this certainly does not show that *secular* modernity is capable of producing such a thing. Cf. Leo Strauss, "An Introduction to Heideggerian Existentialism," in Strauss, *The Rebirth of Classical Political Rationalism*, ed. Thomas Pangle (Chicago: University of Chicago Press, 1989), p. 42 (in the context of a presentation of Heidegger's thought as Strauss understands it): "[T]here has never been a high culture without a religious basis."

impotence, not omnipotence. Therefore, as Nietzsche sees it, to genuinely liberate the human capacity for willing, one must transcend modernity, that is, create a *transmodern* civilization that might well restore some of the defining characteristics (hierarchy, reverence for the ancestral, rootedness in centuries-long tradition) of the *premodern* civilizations that Nietzsche admired. Nevertheless, the very fact that we are in a position to survey the totality of world religions and to judge them from an independent philosophic standpoint – which implies detachment from any particular religious tradition – seems radically modern. It is as if we could legislate a new religious dispensation by a sheer act of will, which is precisely what lends to Nietzsche's "theism" its aspect of hypermodernity. This is the distinguishing mark of Nietzsche's paradoxical modernism–antimodernism: One must embrace modern voluntarism in its most radical version to will something radically antimodern![54]

Of course, a more straightforward repudiator of modernity could insist that a Grantian view of Nietzsche as the spearhead of radical atheistic modernism remains perfectly valid unless Nietzsche actually *believes* in the theism he propounds, rather than simply proposing it as an object of political invention, or as a vehicle for the will to power of post-Christian founder-princes. Consider here Nietzsche's view, expressed in *The Will to Power*, § 972, that Mohammed's only mistake was to believe in the theism he so successfully established as the basis for a new regime. All the better if one can do what founder-princes such as Numa or Mohammed did without belief. Once again, though, if Nietzsche's "theism" is such that theism gets reduced to the limitless creativity of *Übermenschen*, or of prophets of new religions, one can object that this is what *defines* Nietzsche's radical modernism rather than helps to supply him with antimodern credentials.[55] This is an important point, yet it does not suffice to establish the vision of Nietzsche as an uncompromising modernizer, for there are equally good grounds for seeing Nietzsche as conducting, in alliance with Burckhardt, a kind of cultural war against modernity.[56] It is in

---

[54] To Nietzsche's paradoxical modernism–antimodernism corresponds his paradoxical atheism–theism. Cf. Strauss, *Studies in Platonic Political Philosophy*, p. 179.

[55] As we see from the powerful example of Machiavelli, one does not have to be a philosopher of late modernity to believe that religions are this-worldly products of the political creativity of founder-princes. We can recall here our discussion in Part I of *Discourses* II.5's doctrine that the revolutionary introduction of new religions is "from men," not "from heaven." This, too, does not prove that Nietzsche is not a radical modernist, because one can argue, as Strauss does, that Nietzsche simply completes a trajectory set in motion by Machiavelli – and this is precisely what defines intellectual modernity.

[56] See Richard Sigurdson, *Jacob Burckhardt's Social and Political Thought* (Toronto: University of Toronto Press, 2004), for a very helpful discussion of Nietzsche's debt to Burckhardt (hardly a defender of untrammeled modernity). Of particular relevance here is Sigurdson's observation that Burckhardt's "attack on the spirit of the Reformation" anticipates Nietzsche (p. 223). Burckhardt's critical analysis of the Protestant Reformation is presented in Sigurdson's doctoral dissertation, "Jacob Burckhardt as Political Thinker" (University of Toronto, 1991), pp. 303–315.

Nietzsche's Burckhardtian hostility to modernity that we can locate the deepest meaning of his statements – which otherwise appear highly perplexing, perhaps incomprehensible – that theism is superior to atheism, that Catholicism is superior to Protestantism, that Judaism and Islam are superior to Christianity, and that theocracy is superior to Enlightenment.

31

Heidegger's Sequel to Nietzsche

The Longing for New Gods

There's no lack of void.

— Samuel Beckett[1]

To develop a case that Heidegger marks a continuation of some of the concerns and themes expressed in Nietzschean civil religion, let me restate what I associate with the problem of civil religion in relation to Nietzsche. One rendering of the civil-religion idea is nicely encapsulated in Nietzsche's statement in *The Antichrist* that "[a] people that still believes in itself retains its own god."[2] This corresponds to what Rousseau at the end of the *Social Contract* labels "the national religions," which he seems to invoke in order to elaborate his own conception of a civil religion but which (as we saw in Part I) he ultimately repudiates. Nietzsche's central purpose, of course, is to show why Christianity cannot possibly be a "national religion" in this sense, and here again his analysis comes into close proximity with Rousseau's. For Nietzsche, the great enormity perpetrated by Christianity is not that it itself fails to offer a national religion of this kind, but that it sets in motion a tendency in Western civilization that renders it impossible for there to *be* national religions at all.[3] Thus it precipitates a tremendous spiritual crisis in the historical destiny of the West. This is expressed very powerfully in a crucial aphorism in *The Will to Power*: "Religions are destroyed by belief in morality. The Christian moral God is not tenable: hence 'atheism' – as if there could be no other kinds of god."[4] Far from celebrating the end of Western theism, Nietzsche blames Christianity for

---

[1] Samuel Beckett, *Waiting for Godot: A Tragicomedy in Two Acts* (London: Faber & Faber, 1956), p. 66.

[2] *The Portable Nietzsche*, ed. Walter Kaufmann (New York: Viking Press, 1968), p. 582.

[3] Because Nietzsche presents himself as a severe critic of nationalism, it seems strange that he puts such emphasis here on religion as the self-expression of "a people" (*Ein Volk, das noch an sich selbst glaubt*). Of course, this is only one of many paradoxes in Nietzsche's political philosophy.

[4] Friedrich Nietzsche, *The Will to Power*, ed. Walter Kaufmann, trans. W. Kaufmann and R. J. Hollingdale (New York: Vintage, 1968), § 151, p. 95.

having driven us into the dead end of atheism! According to Nietzsche, it is the greatest argument against Christianity that it has undermined our capacity as a civilization to "retain our own gods."

There are two signal texts in the oeuvre of Martin Heidegger that indicate to us that Heidegger moves in the orbit of the same concerns. One is his famous utterance in the posthumous *Der Spiegel* interview that "only a god can save us."[5] The second is the motto that prefaces Heidegger's two-volume commentary on Nietzsche, and that Heidegger draws from Nietzsche's *The Antichrist*: "Well-nigh two thousand years and not a single new god!"[6] These two key texts indicate very clearly that Heidegger fully shares Nietzsche's conviction that the awakening of the West from its present spiritual coma will be marked by its finding the confidence, the sense of its own destiny – Nietzsche would say, the *will* – to summon up new (post-Christian) gods.[7]

As Hans-Georg Gadamer rightly observes, judging from the image of Heidegger popularized by people like Jean-Paul Sartre, one would never have guessed that there is this "theistic" side to Heidegger's thought: "In his admiration for Heidegger, [Sartre] presented him outright, alongside Nietzsche, as one of the representative atheistic thinkers of our time. . . . [S]uch an understanding of Heidegger can only derive from an appropriation of his philosophy which remains superficial."[8] Quite so; but as I shall try to show in this chapter,

---

[5] The full text reads as follows: "Nur noch ein Gott kann uns retten. Uns bleibt die einzige Möglichkeit, im Denken und im Dichten ein Bereitschaft vorzubereiten für die Erscheinung des Gotts oder für die Abwesenheit des Gottes im Untergang; dass wir im Angesicht des abwesenden Gottes untergehen." William J. Richardson, in *Heidegger: The Man and the Thinker*, ed. Thomas Sheehan (Chicago: Precedent Publishing, 1981), p. 57, translates *Untergang* in this passage as "decline." To be sure, this translation offers a quite appropriate echo of Oswald Spengler's *Der Untergang des Abendlandes*, but I am not sure it captures the full force of *Untergang*: downfall, ruin, the sinking into sunkenness. A more forceful translation is offered by Maria P. Alter and John D. Caputo in *The Heidegger Controversy: A Critical Reader*, ed. Richard Wolin (Cambridge, MA: MIT Press, 1993), p. 107: "The sole possibility that is left for us is to prepare a sort of readiness, through thinking and poetizing, for the appearance of the god or for the absence of the god in the time of foundering; for in the face of the god who is absent, we founder."

[6] Martin Heidegger, *Nietzsche, Volume One: The Will to Power as Art*, ed. David Farrell Krell (San Francisco: Harper & Row, 1979), p. 1; *The Portable Nietzsche*, p. 586.

[7] Cf. Catherine H. Zuckert, *Postmodern Platos: Nietzsche, Heidegger, Gadamer, Strauss, Derrida* (Chicago: University of Chicago Press, 1996), p. 268: "Modern philosophers . . . undermined the most effective, popular basis of human self-restraint (or self-government) when they waged an unremitting attack on revelation. . . . [Nietzsche] and Heidegger both indicated the unsatisfactory character of that solution when toward the end of their careers they both looked forward to the revelation of a new god."

[8] Hans-Georg Gadamer, "The Religious Dimension in Heidegger," in *Transcendence and the Sacred*, ed. Alan M. Olson and Leroy S. Rouner (Notre Dame, IN: University of Notre Dame Press, 1981), p. 193. To be sure, there is nothing Christian about Heidegger's quasi-theism. Although Heidegger in the early 1920s still thought of himself (as Löwith and Gadamer testify) as a "Christian theologian," by the late 1920s he had decisively broken with Christianity. Instead, his theism, shaped by the influence of Hölderlin, has neopagan overtones (as Nietzsche's

the atheistic Heidegger preferred by Sartre is far off the mark for reasons rather different than those adduced by Gadamer (reasons that align Heidegger much more closely with Nietzsche than Gadamer is willing to countenance).

Nietzsche and Heidegger share the same framework of analysis. What they share can, I think, be summed up in this formula: "despiritualization of the West."[9] This implies the need for "respiritualization," which in turn implies a call for new gods (hence the writings of both of them contain sometimes desperate prayers for the appearance of new civilization-creating divinities). Part of the underlying structure of argument here is the notion that poetic *ethos* is more profound than rational *logos*, and therefore that no civilization can claim to touch the deepest depths without issuing in an intimate relation to its own gods. For Nietzsche and Heidegger, what Weber called "the disenchantment of the world" goes all the way back to Plato. In Heidegger, this is expressed in terms of a forgetfulness of the mystery of Being. Even Christianity is implicated in this process of disenchantment, insofar as it is thoroughly entangled in the history of Western metaphysics. This explains why modern Western god-killing rationalism is such a catastrophe, for it condemns us to an incorrigible

---

"theism" does as well). Cf. Otto Pöggeler, "Heidegger's Political Self-Understanding," in *The Heidegger Controversy* (MIT Press edition), p. 243, n. 21: The divinities that Heidegger sought to draw from Hölderlin "appeared as gods of the people or the homeland" (i.e., what Heidegger wants are *German* gods). For a critique of the idea of "national gods" from the universalistic standpoint of post-Platonic philosophy, as if in anticipation of Heidegger, see Edmund Husserl, *Phenomenology and the Crisis of Philosophy*, trans. Quentin Lauer (New York: Harper & Row, 1965), pp. 173, 176–177. On Husserl's account, the conception of national gods is necessarily *prephilosophic*; Heidegger's concern is, one might say, to resurrect national gods as a *postphilosophic* possibility.

9 According to Derrida, in Heidegger's prominent use of the term *geistig*, particularly in his writings of the 1930s, Heidegger betrays his own "deconstruction," in earlier and later writings, of metaphysical categories (including the term *Geist*). See Jacques Derrida, *Of Spirit: Heidegger and the Question*, trans. Geoffrey Bennington and Rachel Bowlby (Chicago: University of Chicago Press, 1989); and Derrida, "Philosophers' Hell: An Interview," in *The Heidegger Controversy*, ed. Richard Wolin (New York: Columbia University Press, 1991), pp. 264–273. I would read this the other way around: I would say that Derrida overlooks the political–cultural concerns that drive Heidegger's critique of metaphysics, namely his perception of the *ungeistig* character of our cultural situation in the present. For a good critique of Derrida's "interpretive strategy," see Richard Wolin, "French Heidegger Wars" and "Preface to the MIT Press edition: Note on a Missing Text," in *The Heidegger Controversy* (MIT Press edition), pp. 272–300 and ix–xx. As Wolin suggests, Derrida is completely mistaken in assimilating the discourse of spirit in Husserl to the discourse of spirit in Heidegger. When Husserl writes, for instance, that "the spirit alone is immortal" (*Phenomenology and the Crisis of Philosophy*, p. 192), he means the spirit of reason, or reason as spirit; whereas when Heidegger writes, for instance, that the "gathering of the spiritual forces [*geistigen Kräfte*] . . . grows ever more urgent" (letter to Carl Schmitt, *Telos*, No. 72, 1987: 132), what *he* means is the spiritual forces that reason can never command. For a good survey of how the rhetoric of "despiritualization" figures in a wide range of antiliberal and antimodernist ideologies, see Ian Buruma and Avishai Margalit, *Occidentalism: A Short History of Anti-Westernism* (London: Atlantic Books, 2005).

shallowness in experiencing the abyss of Being.[10] Nietzsche and Heidegger are agreed in tracing this ontological shallowness of Western rationalism back to Greek philosophy – hence Heidegger's remark in the "Letter on Humanism" that the *ethos* is preserved more primordially in Sophocles's tragic sagas than it is in Aristotle.[11]

Nietzsche's slogan, "the death of God," may be thought of as offering a kind of sociological hypothesis: We are pro forma committed to a set of beliefs, moral practices, and cultural symbols in which we, as a civilization, no longer believe. If this is true, it represents a civilizational catastrophe of the largest magnitude. A sociocultural void opens that requires a "political" response. Politics (*"grosse Politik"*) must fill the emptiness disguised by the façade of a continuing allegiance to Judeo-Christian religious–cultural horizons. Nietzschean politics presumes to shape new horizons in response to this sociological reality. This is more or less what I take Heidegger to be saying when he writes in *The Will to Power as Art* that the "phrase 'God is dead' is not an atheistic proclamation: it is a formula for the fundamental experience of an event in Occidental history."[12]

Another way of formulating this analysis would be to say that our narrative resources have dried up, or are in the process of drying up. A civilization cannot survive in the absence of such a capacity for telling itself stories that give that civilization its destiny, its raison d'être, its sense of itself. Again, the all-important mark of a civilization's ability to explain itself to itself is its capacity to give itself gods.[13] The last men who "blink" do so because they have no awareness that they have lost possession of the cultural resources by which to give meaning to their own existence.[14] An *Übermensch* may be defined as one capable of restoring narrative resources to our civilization. Nietzsche writes *Zarathustra* to prove that in a case where shared narrative capacities have dried up, new ones can be invented by sheer creative willpower. Again, Heidegger, translating this analysis into his own vocabulary, nicely sums it up

---

[10] Cf. Martin Heidegger, *An Introduction to Metaphysics*, trans. Ralph Manheim (New Haven: Yale University Press, 1959), p. 46: "The lives of men began to slide into a world which lacked that depth from out of which the essential always comes to man."

[11] Martin Heidegger, *Basic Writings*, ed. David Farrell Krell (New York: Harper & Row, 1977), pp. 232–233.

[12] Heidegger, *The Will to Power as Art*, p. 156.

[13] Cf. the account that Heidegger gives of poetry in "Hölderlin and the Essence of Poetry," in Martin Heidegger, *Existence and Being* (Chicago: Henry Regnery, 1949), pp. 270–291. According to this account, poetry is the foundation of history (p. 283). This is so precisely because the poet mediates between peoples and gods (p. 288). Poetry founds a new historical epoch because when the old gods flee, it is the poet who anticipates the gods that are to come (pp. 289–290).

[14] In *What is Called Thinking?*, trans. J. Glenn Gray (New York: Harper & Row, 1968), pp. 82–85, Heidegger gives a rather more metaphysical interpretation to this "blinking" of the last men.

in his restatement of Nietzsche's fundamental thesis at the very end of *The Will to Power as Art*:

[C]reation itself is to be estimated according to the originality with which it penetrates to Being.... Being able to estimate, to esteem, that is, to act in accordance with the standard of Being [i.e., the *Nietzschean* standard of Being – R. B.], is itself creation of the highest order. For it is preparation of readiness for the gods; it is the Yes to Being. "Overman" is the man who grounds Being anew – in the rigor of knowledge and in the grand style of creation.[15]

Notice how Heidegger emphasizes, in the penultimate sentence of the book, that Nietzschean creativity is inseparable from "preparation of readiness for the gods." (The book thus begins and ends with the dream of new gods.[16])

As soon as one begins to consider the thought of Nietzsche and Heidegger in its "religious" or god-seeking dimension, one cannot fail to be struck by a sense of overwhelming paradox: Nietzsche, coming from a family of Lutheran pastors, is so vehement in his denunciation of the Protestant Reformation, and of Luther in particular, that one is tempted to think of him as a kind of "backhanded Catholic" in the depth of his anti-Protestantism. (Indeed, as we have seen, in *The Will to Power*, § 87, Nietzsche explicitly affirms the superiority of Catholicism.) Heidegger, by contrast, was brought up as a pious Catholic and was trained in Catholic theology (Heidegger for a while was actually a novice at a Jesuit seminary), yet his first major philosophical work resonates with such an intensity of Protestant sensibility – Kierkegaardian angst, Augustinian fallenness, the call of conscience, the authenticity of the individual face-to-face with his or her own mortality – that one readily thinks of it as elevating to philosophical expression a kind of "hyper-Protestantism" (or one might say, "Protestantism with a vengeance").[17] Add to this the further paradox that both Nietzsche and Heidegger, notwithstanding their intense preoccupation with the Christian legacy, cannot resist pagan categories in thinking about possibilities of redivinization. (When Heidegger echoes Nietzsche's cry of "[t]wo thousand years without a single new god!" he indicates his sympathy for Nietzsche's verdict that Christianity leads into a metaphysical dead end, and therefore the new gods that are needed seem to herald a rebirth of paganism.)

[15] Heidegger, *The Will to Power as Art*, p. 220.
[16] Ibid. To be sure, *The Will to Power as Art* is a "book" only in the four-volume English version; in the German original, it is merely the first half of Band I of *Nietzsche*.
[17] See Karl Löwith, "The Political Implications of Heidegger's Existentialism," in *The Heidegger Controversy* (MIT Press edition), pp. 172–173: "It was above all the young Luther...to whom Heidegger was attracted." On Heidegger's "Lutheranism," cf. Hans-Georg Gadamer, "Erinnerungen an Heideggers Anfänge," *Dilthey-Jahrbuch für Philosophie und Geschichte des Geisteswissenschaften*, Vol. 4 (1986–1987): 22. Another important part of the story is Karl Barth's revitalization of eschatological Protestant theology and the broader impact it had on German culture in the 1920s. For a helpful account, see Mark Lilla, *The Stillborn God* (New York: Knopf, 2007), chapter 6.

The voice of Martin Heidegger as a civil-religion theorist can be heard most clearly in Section 15 of his lectures on European nihilism, entitled "The Dominance of the Subject in the Modern Age":

That Christianity continues to exist in the development of modern history; has in the form of Protestantism abetted [mitfördert] the development; has asserted itself success-fully in the metaphysics of German Idealism and romanticism; was in its correspond-ing transformations [Abwandlungen], adaptations [Angleichungen], and compromises [Ausgleichen] in every instance reconciled [versöhnt] with the spirit of the times, and consistently availed itself of modern accomplishments for ecclesiastical ends – all of that proves more forcefully than anything else how decisively Christianity is bereft of the power it had during the Middle Ages to shape history. Its historical significance no longer lies in what it is able to fashion for itself.[18]

This is Heidegger's most compact statement of the essential meaning of Chris-tianity in the modern age. The meaning of modern Christianity is compro-mise (Ausgleich, or evening things out, splitting the difference). Rather than remaining true to its own mission in the world, Christianity, certainly since the Reformation, has accommodated itself to the metaphysics of modernity. Here Heidegger echoes Nietzsche's fundamental thesis (The Will to Power, §§ 87–88): Protestantism is "a half-way house" (etwas Halbes) between the original Christian vocation and secular modernity.[19] As Heidegger puts it, Protestantism not only adapted itself to the development of modern history but it in fact "abetted the development."[20] In consequence, Christianity has forfeited its claim to "shape history" on the basis of its own spiritual impulses. On the contrary, it yields to more momentous historical forces rather than con-tinuing to attempt to assert its own vision of the world as a counterprinciple to modernity.

---

[18] Martin Heidegger, Nietzsche, Volume Four: Nihilism, ed. David Farrell Krell, trans. F. A. Capuzzi (San Francisco: Harper & Row, 1982), p. 99.

[19] Cf. The Portable Nietzsche, p. 324: "Break, break this word ["contract"] of the softhearted and half-and-half!" [solch Wort der Weich-Herzen und Halb- und Halben!] (Thus Spoke Zarathus-tra, Third Part: "On Old and New Tablets," § 25). In addition, see Nietzsche's description of modernity as a "cowardly compromise" (The Portable Nietzsche, p. 569), as well as his reference to the "half-heartedness – three-eighths-heartedness" [alle Halbheiten – Drei-Achtelsheiten!] that most ails Europe (The Antichrist, § 61). See also "Gadamer on Gadamer," in Gadamer and Hermeneutics, ed. Hugh I. Silverman (New York: Routledge, 1991), p. 15: "[T]he young Heidegger, driven by religious doubts and questions of existence," was inspired by Kierkegaard's "vehement critique of the lukewarm Christianity of his native Denmark."

[20] It might be argued that Nietzsche, in his paradoxical "embrace" of Catholicism, is consistent with his efforts to make as radical a break as possible with his own Protestant heritage, whereas Heidegger, by contrast, in the criticisms of Protestantism in the quoted passage from Nihilism, is inconsistent with his parallel effort (e.g., in the "hyper-Protestant" themes of Being and Time) to make as radical a break as possible with his own Catholic heritage. Heidegger might reply to this that the actual historical record of Protestantism does not in any way measure up to the existential radicalness of a figure like Luther. In that sense, Heidegger could claim that the existential impulse lying behind the Protestant Reformation was much more radical than what actually issued from it; this seems to me a consistent position.

To be sure, Heidegger vehemently rejects Nietzsche's own solution, which Heidegger sees as incorporating, and indeed as radicalizing and giving further impetus to, the dominant metaphysical tendencies of the West – notwithstanding Nietzsche's own presumption that he is countering or overcoming Western metaphysics: Nietzsche too, in his metaphysics of will to power, rides the crest of modernity rather than providing a genuine counterprinciple. (Thus, for instance, Heidegger links up Nietzsche's idea of a post-Christian equivalent to the Jesuits as a spiritual army with modernity's quest for "absolute dominion over the entire earth.")[21] The essential point here, however, is that Heidegger and Nietzsche entirely agree that modern Christianity has irreversibly compromised itself and thereby relinquished its right to shape meaning and purpose in the West. The corollary is inescapable: If Christianity no longer exercises this history-shaping capacity, it should move aside and allow *another* world-civilizational force to take over and fill the vacuum. (It is self-evident to Nietzsche and Heidegger that the liberal, secular, humanistic rationalism of the Enlightenment is certainly not up to the task!) This leaves us pretty much where Heidegger says we now stand: in a forsaken lot, abandoned by the old gods, waiting for the new gods to arrive.

As a challenge to my reading of Heidegger, it may be worth pausing to consider Hans-Georg Gadamer's alternative view concerning Heidegger's "new gods." Although Gadamer elsewhere acknowledges Heidegger's regrettable tendency to play prophet, he downplays this aspect of Heidegger's thought in the specific context of Heidegger's talk of new gods; Gadamer maintains that Heidegger's intention in these oracular utterances is really much more modest than it might appear to be. In an interview, Gadamer makes this remark:

This idea of the god or gods who are to save us? That is entirely vague. Didn't Heidegger just mean that the planners cannot save us?[22]

In another interview, Gadamer says something quite similar:

When [Heidegger] first started coming out with his mysterious allusions to the return of the gods, we were really shocked. I contacted him again and saw that that was not what he had in mind. It was a *façon de parler*. Even his famous statement, *Nur ein Gott kann uns retten*, means only that calculating politics is not what will save us from the impending catastrophe.[23]

---

[21] Heidegger, *Nihilism*, pp. 100, 99. See Nietzsche, *The Will to Power*, § 757, p. 398; § 783, p. 411; § 796, p. 419; § 1057, p. 545.

[22] Hans-Georg Gadamer, "The 1920s, the 1930s, and the Present," in *Hans-Georg Gadamer on Education, Poetry, and History: Applied Hermeneutics*, ed. Dieter Misgeld and Graeme Nicholson, trans. L. Schmidt and M. Reuss (Albany, NY: SUNY Press, 1992), p. 152.

[23] "Gadamer on Strauss: An Interview," *Interpretation*, Vol. 12 (1984): 11. Cf. Hans-Georg Gadamer, *Heidegger's Ways*, trans. John W. Stanley (Albany, NY: SUNY Press, 1994), p. 134. In contrast, see Gadamer's reference to Heidegger's "dream of a 'national religion'": *Martin Heidegger and National Socialism: Questions and Answers*, ed. Günther Heske and Emil Kettering (New York: Paragon House, 1990), pp. 142–143.

Gadamer thereby tries to distance Heidegger from Nietzsche, who, Gadamer assumes, *is* being serious in presuming to deliver prophetic anticipations of new gods. A *façon de parler* it may well be, but our argument is that Heidegger's references to "readiness for the gods" are too frequent and too deliberate to be *merely* a *façon de parler*. Heidegger is more of a Nietzschean than Gadamer is willing to concede.

Heidegger seems to go out of his way to insist that the concerns of philosophy cannot be religiously motivated. Thus he writes in *The Will to Power as Art* that "Christian philosophy" is a contradiction in terms because "There is no true philosophy that could be determined anywhere else than from within itself."[24] So, to the extent that what concerns philosophy overlaps with what concerns religion, philosophy's way of treating these topics is entirely determined "from within itself." This means that the question of the gods is drawn from within a strictly *philosophical* horizon of concerns; that is, for Heidegger as for Nietzsche, religion is radically subordinated to philosophy. As Nietzsche suggests in Part 3 of *Beyond Good and Evil* (see § 61), religion is merely one among a variety of tools in the hands of the philosophical legislator. This is another aspect of the Nietzschean rendering of the civil-religion idea: namely that religion is instrumental to the larger (political) project of culturally regenerating a civilization that Christianity has rendered impotent.[25] (If one defines civil religion as the instrumentalization of religion for political purposes, it may not be stretching the term too far to classify Martin Heidegger alongside Nietzsche as a civil-religion theorist in this sense.) In any case, the basic point here is that what Heidegger has in common with Nietzsche is that Heidegger's talk of new divinities and of saving gods, like corresponding passages in Nietzsche, has *zero* religious import; it is strictly metaphysical–political, in a sense that remains to be clarified.

One way of formulating Heidegger's profound intellectual affinity with Nietzsche is to say that both thinkers converge on a dimension of philosophical preoccupations that can with equal warrant be qualified as either "political" or "metaphysical." (Interestingly, and perhaps surprisingly, both Nietzsche and Heidegger in this respect practice a mode of theorizing that is strikingly similar to that of Plato.)[26] When Nietzsche declares that nihilism, the most uncanny of

---

[24] Heidegger, *The Will to Power as Art*, p. 5. Cf. *An Introduction to Metaphysics*, p. 7: "A 'Christian philosophy' is a round circle"; *Nihilism*, p. 88: "[A] 'Christian philosophy' is even more contradictory than a round circle." Also note the following: "Within thought, nothing can be accomplished which could prepare or contribute to the determination of what happens in faith and grace. If faith were to call me in this way, I should shut up shop." J. Greisch, *Heidegger et la question de Dieu* (Paris: Grasset, 1980), p. 335; cited in Derrida, *Of Spirit*, p. 115, n. 3.

[25] Cf. Heidegger's explicit reference to the "impotence" [*die Ohnmacht*] of the Christian God: *Nihilism*, p. 8.

[26] What I mean by this claim is the thought that the close proximity between metaphysical judgments and political judgments in, for instance, Books 6–8 of *The Republic* or in the

all guests, stands at the door,[27] is this a metaphysical claim or a political claim? Clearly, it is both at once. When Heidegger speaks of the final exhaustion of spiritual energy, "darkening of the world," "flight of the gods," destruction of the earth, massification of human beings, and so on,[28] are these metaphysical claims or political claims? Again, these pronouncements inhabit a space of reflection that is indistinguishably political and metaphysical. As the text from Heidegger just cited suggests, the question of the gods is located at the very crux of this intersection of politics and metaphysics typical of Nietzschean and Heideggerian theorizing.

This is why it makes no sense to consider Heidegger's preoccupation with the history of Western ontology in abstraction from politics. For Heidegger, metaphysics *is* politics. He claims that "Being" has been reduced from "the spiritual destiny of the Western world" to a meaningless word; he then immediately goes on to draw from this a political conclusion: "From a metaphysical point of view, Russia and America are the same: the same dreary technological frenzy, the same unrestricted organization of the average man."[29] This is precisely what "spiritual decline of the earth" and "flight of the gods" *mean*. Obviously, Heidegger is here using the term "metaphysical" in a way that is quite different from the way that other philosophers might use it. My point is that it is not at all different from what metaphysics means for Nietzsche (nor, as I already suggested, is it necessarily very different from what it might have meant for Plato). Nietzsche and Heidegger invoke images of the deicide of old gods or the awaiting of new gods because this is a dramatic way of calling forth that dimension of "metaphysical" (i.e., political–spiritual) theorizing that is of greatest concern to them.

What does Heidegger mean when he declares that Russia and America are "metaphysically" the same – and, by implication, that the national self-assertion of the German *Volk* offers at least the possibility of a mode of being that is "metaphysically" different? Clearly, he is employing the term "metaphysics" in a way that encompasses, or subsumes, the historical–political. This is again brought out sharply in the various passages in the *Nietzsche* volumes in which Heidegger speaks of a need for metaphysical decisions that do not admit of compromises (*Ausgleichen*) or half-measures (*Halbheiten*).[30] Are the "half-measures" to be avoided metaphysical or political? (Heidegger

Gorgias is strikingly similar to the close proximity between metaphysical judgments and political judgments in, for instance, *An Introduction to Metaphysics* or in *What is Called Thinking?*

[27] Nietzsche, *The Will to Power*, § 1, p. 7.

[28] Heidegger, *An Introduction to Metaphysics*, pp. 38, 45.

[29] Ibid., p. 37.

[30] See, for instance, Martin Heidegger, *Nietzsche, Volume Three: The Will to Power as Knowledge and as Metaphysics*, ed. David Farrell Krell (San Francisco: Harper & Row, 1987), pp. 6, 204, 207; Martin Heidegger, *Nietzsche, Volume Two: The Eternal Recurrence of the Same*, trans. David Farrell Krell (San Francisco: Harper & Row, 1984), p. 179; cf. "Only a God Can Save Us," in *The Heidegger Controversy*, ed. Wolin (MIT Press edition), pp. 104–105; and Heidegger, *What is Called Thinking?*, p. 67.

refers in this context to "Reason, Progress, political and economic 'Socialism,' or mere Democracy" as ways of trying to deflect nihilism rather than facing up to it squarely to overcome it; he refers to them, disparagingly, as "rescue operations": *Rettungsversuche*.[31]) I do not think any attentive reader of these texts can fail to perceive that these pronouncements are inextricably metaphysical and political. As always, what Heidegger suggests is that because we are screwed up metaphysically (or screwed up ontologically), therefore we are screwed up politically ("Europe, in its ruinous blindness forever on the point of cutting its own throat,"[32] and so on). Without question, Heidegger has the tremendous rhetorical impact that he does because he shares with Nietzsche a mode of discourse that *straddles* the metaphysical and the political. (Peter Strawson was obviously right when he offered the judgment that Heidegger is for those "who like their sermons long and their visions dark,"[33] but one would have to be spiritually tone deaf not to experience at least in some measure the power of this Heideggerian rhetoric.)

The fact that, for Heidegger, the question of the presence or absence of the gods transcends mere religiosity, or mere theology, comes out very clearly in the following passage:

Whether the god lives or remains dead is not decided by the religiosity of men and even less by the theological aspirations of philosophy and natural science. Whether or not God is God comes disclosingly to pass from out of and within the constellation of Being.[34]

---

[31] In the *Der Spiegel* interview, Heidegger challenges his interviewer to tell him where he had spoken of democracy as a half-measure. The answer is *Eternal Recurrence of the Same*, p. 179. Also see *What is Called Thinking?*, p. 67, citing the passage in *Twilight of the Idols* where Nietzsche refers to the German *Reich* as one of the *Halbheiten* of modern democracy. In reading these Heideggerian texts, one naturally thinks of the Nietzschean texts cited in note 19 of this chapter – namely Nietzsche's references to Protestantism as a halfway house (*The Will to Power*, § 87: *als Halbheit*; *The Will to Power*, § 88: *etwas Halbes*), his denunciation of the half-heartedness of contemporary Europe in *The Antichrist*, § 61, and his dismissal of the liberal discourse of contractarianism as a notion for the *Halb- und Halben* (*Thus Spoke Zarathustra*, Third Part: "On Old and New Tablets," § 25). This Nietzschean–Heideggerian rhetoric of the need to avoid "half-measures" can arguably be traced all the way back to Machiavelli's final sentence in *Discourses on Livy*, I.26.

[32] Heidegger, *An Introduction to Metaphysics*, p. 37.

[33] P. F. Strawson, "Take the B Train," *New York Review of Books*, April 19, 1979, p. 36. Cf. Jürgen Habermas, *The Future of Human Nature* (Cambridge: Polity, 2003), p. 113: A self-disclaiming reason "is easily tempted to merely borrow the authority, and the air, of a sacred that has been deprived of its core and become anonymous." That is, a philosophy such as Heidegger's, because it has lost confidence in its commitment to reason, abuses religion by itself masquerading as a pseudo-religion. Habermas calls it a kind of "religious kitsch," and he applies the same criticism to Adorno and Derrida. Habermas also makes the further point that his own brand of theorizing, precisely because it maintains an unbroken ("nondefeatist") commitment to reason, can better respect the autonomy of religion.

[34] Martin Heidegger, "The Turning," in *The Question Concerning Technology and Other Essays*, ed. William Lovitt (New York: Harper & Row, 1977), p. 49.

God is not the source of Being; rather, Being is the source of God (hence Heidegger's reference to "the god of Being".)[35] What is meant by "Being" here is the following: that dispensation by which it is given to us to be able to experience this or that in a given historical epoch; or that horizon of disclosure that allows us to experience our destiny in one fashion or another. To say that the presence or absence of god is a "metaphysical" rather than religious dispensation suggests a conception of the metaphysical that encompasses both "spiritual" (spiritual–cultural) and political possibilities.

The gods have fled; we await new gods.[36] For Heidegger, this is again a metaphysical proposition, not a religious one; and it is metaphysical in a sense that encompasses what is available to us or given to us or opened up to us within a horizon of possibilities both spiritually and politically. Whether the gods are present or absent, departing or arriving, is of interest to Heidegger not with respect to the gods themselves, or as a matter of religious concern, but "metaphysically," on account of what it tells us about the spiritual possibilities of a political–historical community within a particular epoch. Being is never understood by Heidegger apart from this question of the coming forth of spiritual–political possibilities within the historical destiny of various epochs; it is in this sense that *Sein* and *Zeit* are inseparable.

This conception of metaphysics is stated with clarity in the opening sentences of Heidegger's essay, "The Age of the World Picture":

In metaphysics reflection is accomplished concerning the essence of what is, and a decision takes place regarding the essence of truth. *Metaphysics grounds an age*, in that through a specific interpretation of what is and through a specific comprehension of truth it gives to that age the basis upon which it is essentially formed. This basis holds complete dominion over all the phenomena that distinguish the age.[37]

It is in precisely this sense of the metaphysical that one must speak of our having lost the gods (the modern destiny) or of regaining gods (the prospect of transcending modernity?) as requiring a metaphysical decision. This is brought out clearly in two other passages in the same essay. In the first of these passages, Heidegger says that one of the defining phenomena of the modern age is the loss of the gods (*Entgötterung* – more literally, the dedivinizing of the world).

This expression does not mean the mere doing away with the gods, gross atheism. The loss of the gods is a twofold process. On the one hand, the world picture is Christianized inasmuch as the cause of the world is posited as infinite, absolute. On the other hand, Christendom transforms Christian doctrine into a world view (the Christian world view), and in that way makes itself modern and up to date. The loss of the gods is the situation of indecision regarding God and the gods. Christendom has

---

35 Heidegger, *The Will to Power as Knowledge*, p. 182.

36 Obviously, Heidegger was deaf to Weber's warnings about the intellectual invention of "new religions," "academic prophecy," and those who "tarry for new prophets and saviors": *From Max Weber: Essays in Sociology*, ed. H. H. Gerth and C. Wright Mills (New York: Oxford University Press, 1958), pp. 155–156.

37 *The Question Concerning Technology*, ed. Lovitt, p. 115; emphasis added.

the greatest share in bringing it about. But the loss of the gods is so far from excluding religiosity that rather only through that loss is the relation to the gods changed into mere "religious experience." [That is, this does to experience of the gods what the category of "aesthetic experience" does to the experience of the work of art, namely reducing a mode of ontological disclosure to a mere function of the subject, a mere aspect of subjectivity. – R. B.] When this occurs, then the gods have fled. The resultant void is compensated for by means of historiographical and psychological investigation of myth. [That is, experience of the gods is no longer anything more than a cultural relic left to the curiosity of anthropologists. – R. B.][38]

In the second passage, Heidegger turns from loss of the gods to the question of a possible resurgence of gods.

For now the melting down of the self-consummating essence of the modern age into the self-evident is being accomplished. Only when this is assured through world views will the possibility arise of there being fertile soil for Being to be in question in an original way – a questionableness of Being that will open ample space for *the decision as to whether Being will once again become capable of a god*, as to whether the essence of the truth of being will lay claim more primally to the essence of man. Only there where the consummation of the modern age attains the heedlessness that is its peculiar greatness is future history being prepared.[39]

With the dawning of the modern age, the gods withdraw. When we once again find ourselves capable of harboring gods, that will, perhaps, be the sign of our having crossed beyond modernity. (In this sense, "postmodernism" has not yet arrived!) Metaphysics is the realm within which we test our epoch to see whether it is or is not capable of harboring gods. Modernity is a destiny that emanates from the history of Being; until modernity recedes, we wait. "[Man's] essence is to be the one who waits."[40]

For Heidegger, the term "secularization" offers barely a hint of that constriction of ontological possibilities that characterizes the modern West.[41] Heidegger is drawn to Nietzsche because Nietzsche says the same thing: hence, in Nietzsche's parable of the madman, the God murderers are so cut off from

---

[38] Ibid., pp. 116–117.

[39] Ibid., p. 153; emphasis added.

[40] Heidegger, "The Turning," p. 42. Let me hasten to add that the conception of Heidegger as a pure antimodernist needs qualification. Certainly, one is familiar with, for instance, his denunciations of modern art in the *Der Spiegel* interview. Nevertheless, the image of Heidegger as a conservative critic of modernity cannot begin to do justice to the breadth of his cultural appeal. Heidegger's own philosophy is itself a consummate expression of intellectual modernism; thus it is no surprise at all to see, for instance, a contemporary hero of pop rebellion like the character played by Ethan Hawke in the 1994 film *Reality Bites* reading a copy of *Being and Time* in a café. Of course it is also impossible to forget that Heidegger is at the root of just about every contemporary intellectual movement, modern as well as hypermodern, from Sartre to Derrida to Foucault. It is just this characteristically dual aspect of Heidegger's genius, both radically modern and radically antimodern, that accounts for his incomparable impact upon contemporary culture. To express this in a diagram, one might draw one line leading from Oswald Spengler and another line leading up to Samuel Beckett, and then imagine the parallelogram of Heidegger's cultural force as located at the intersection of these two vectors.

[41] Cf. Heidegger, *Nihilism*, p. 100.

their own ontological situation that they are oblivious to the enormity of their deeds; they do not even know that God is dead, let alone that His blood is dripping from their very own deicidal hands.[42] Of course, Heidegger and Nietzsche have no interest in assessing this from a religious point of view, or in relation to religious concerns. Rather, they share a horror of modern secularization from a political–spiritual or political–metaphysical perspective: What this means is that the West loses touch with its own depth, or, one might say, loses the very *possibility* of experiencing that depth.[43] This is, to use Heideggerian terminology, what is meant by "the forgetfulness of Being." It is, to employ Nietzschean vocabulary, the epoch of the last man, in which modern Western societies come to be inhabited by blinking idiots who live according to the delusion that it is possible to live a satisfying life in the absence of grand goals, grand passions, grand horizons. (To translate Nietzsche's "last man" into contemporary terms, one could say that it is a society in which everyone, or nearly everyone, is on Prozac. Is this very different from the society in which we now live?)[44]

As Heidegger points out, Nietzsche's madman who announces the death of God bursts upon the marketplace with the cry that he *seeks* God; hence Nietzsche's diagnosis of the eclipse of the divine is located in the context of a search for gods.[45] Those to whom the madman addresses himself, by contrast, are unaware that God has been killed precisely because they are indifferent to this quest for gods. Heidegger shares Nietzsche's longing for gods (preferably new gods) because only in the dread of awareness that the gods are absent can we hope to reach the depths of genuine thinking, as opposed to the calculative reason that amounts to a "dread in the face of dread."[46] For

---

[42] Friedrich Nietzsche, *The Gay Science*, trans. Walter Kaufmann (New York: Vintage, 1974), § 125, pp. 181–182.

[43] See note 10.

[44] It would be irresponsible, however, not to make clear the nature of the alternative to liberal banality being proposed by Nietzsche. The Nietzschean alternative is one where the collective purposes of the society are *so* grand, *so* impressive, that the happiness and welfare of most individuals count for virtually nothing. In other words, if the ultimate alternatives are liberalism (the society of the last men) and fascism (the society of the *Übermensch*), it is hard to see how any sane and decent person could choose the latter. There is some analogy here with bin Ladenist ideology, characterized by Christopher Hitchens as "Islamo-fascism," particularly when one sees the similarities between Nietzsche's critique of the decadence of the West and bin Laden's critique of the decadence of the West. For a full elaboration of the idea of contemporary jihadist Islamism as a successor to the totalitarian movements of the twentieth century, see Paul Berman, *Terror and Liberalism* (New York: Norton, 2003); Berman presents Islamism as the latest in a series of "apocalyptic rebellions against liberalism" (p. 154). See also in the same vein Bernard-Henri Lévy, *Left in Dark Times*, trans. Benjamin Moser (New York: Random House, 2008), p. 184. It is a jarring experience to read pp. 317–319 of Walzer's *The Revolution of the Saints* (a book originally published in the mid-1960s) with 9/11 in mind: Walzer's model of "radicalism as a general historical phenomen[on]" (p. 317), summarized on those pages, applies directly to contemporary jihadist Islamism.

[45] Martin Heidegger, "The Word of Nietzsche: 'God is Dead,'" in *The Question Concerning Technology*, ed. Lovitt, pp. 111–112.

[46] Ibid., p. 112; cf. Martin Heidegger, *Early Greek Thinking*, trans. D. F. Krell and F. A. Capuzzi (New York: Harper & Row, 1975), p. 78: "the narcotization of anxiety in the face of thinking."

Heidegger, metaphysics is identical with politics, and politics is identical with Hölderlinian "theism." Liberalism, democracy, Christianity cannot rescue us; rescue can only come from gods that are summoned by the poets and serve to express a people's reawakened grasp of its own destiny – "gods of the people or the homeland" (Pöggeler) – gods that encapsulate a newly recharged, respiritualized experience of being that refuses to make "compromises," refuses to abide "half-measures." (Whether these are Nazi half-measures or liberal-democratic half-measures is, for Heidegger, a matter of indifference; hence, World War II, for him, "decided nothing."[47])

Let me conclude by summarizing my argument. As we saw in *The Will to Power*, § 151, Nietzsche condemns Christianity not for its theism but precisely because it discredits theism. According to my interpretation, Heidegger is thoroughly inspired by this "theistic" dimension in Nietzsche, and so Heidegger's appropriation of Nietzschean "theism" is not a mere *façon de parler*, as Gadamer would have it. Of course, Nietzsche's talk of the death of old gods and Heidegger's notion that only new gods can save us are not theological claims; rather, they are to be construed in what one might call a "sociological" mode. Heidegger and Nietzsche are after the same thing – and for the same reasons. "De-spiritualization of the West" requires a "political" response. Only religions (or quasi-religions) secure meaningful horizons. Without such horizons, people live empty, purposeless lives. Christianity has exhausted its cultural energies.[48] The West needs a new religion (or religions) to respiritualize it, to invest it with new cultural energies. Nietzsche and Heidegger's "readiness for the gods" has the intensity that it does because they take "cultural politics" with a seriousness that is perhaps unrivalled in the history of Western consciousness.[49]

---

[47] Heidegger, *What is Called Thinking?*, p. 66. What is most striking in this passage is the fact that for Heidegger, the only political event that deserves consideration as possibly lending "metaphysical" significance to the outcome of the war is the renting asunder (*Riss durch seine Mitte*) of *unter Vaterland* into two Germanies – namely an Americanized Germany of the West and a Soviet-Russianized Germany of the East. Caught in the pincers of East and West, the spiritual heart of Europe is cut in two, one side claimed by despiritualized Americanism and the other side claimed by despiritualized Russian Sovietism. For Pöggeler's discussion of this passage, see "Heidegger's Political Self-Understanding," p. 207.

[48] See Heidegger's reference to "the historical bankruptcy of Christianity": Pöggeler, "Heidegger's Political Self-Understanding," p. 206. The text cited by Pöggeler can be found in *Gesamtausgabe*, Bd. 55: *Heraklit* (Frankfurt am Main: Vittorio Klostermann, 1979), p. 209.

[49] Certainly, for Nietzsche the idea of a politics distinct from culture was inconceivable; cf. Sheldon S. Wolin, *Politics and Vision*, expanded ed. (Princeton, NJ: Princeton University Press, 2004), pp. xix and 472–473. In a letter to Carl von Gersdorff dated June 21, 1871 (*Selected Letters of Friedrich Nietzsche*, ed. Christopher Middleton, Chicago: University of Chicago Press, 1969, p. 81), Nietzsche described how he was "for several days annihilated" after receiving the (in fact false) rumor that the Paris Commune had torched the Louvre. This experience of being traumatized by what he perceived to be the cultural barbarism of the masses pretty much encapsulates what was for Nietzsche centrally at stake in modern politics (and why extreme measures were necessary to reverse direction).

Conclusion

There is something nice about being in the dark, he discovers, something thrilling about not knowing what is going to happen next. It keeps you alert, he thinks, and there's no harm in that, is there? Wide awake and on your toes, taking it all in, ready for anything.

– Paul Auster[1]

The readers should be alone with the books, and if anyone dared to say anything about them, they would be shot or imprisoned right on the spot. Yes, shot.... You should let people fight with the books on their own and rediscover what they are and what they are not.

– Philip Roth[2]

My primary aim in this book has been to take a large group of leading thinkers from the last half-millennium of Western political philosophy, and try to unpack some of the complexities, riddles, ironies, tensions, and paradoxes in their views about religion. The spirit in which I have tried to read the texts analyzed in the preceding chapters is captured in the two epigraphs here. That spirit involves, first, not presuming that one knows in advance where the texts are going to go, and being radically open to all the unexpected twists and turns in the texts – that is, accepting that one is always inescapably "in the dark," not only about the deepest intentions of the authors of the texts but also about the philosophical issues that they (and we) are most concerned to address. Advancing one's understanding is always a matter of plunging fearlessly into the unknown. Second, my conception of the theoretical enterprise involves striving for a *direct*, largely unmediated relationship to the texts. This

---

[1] Paul Auster, *The New York Trilogy* (London: Faber & Faber, 2004), pp. 154–155.

[2] Martin Krasnik, "'It no longer feels a great injustice that I have to die,'" (Interview with Philip Roth), *The Guardian*, December 14, 2005, g2, p. 16. The context is a rant against book reviews and literary criticism.

may seem, according to many understandings of scholarly practice, unscholarly, but according to my understanding of the essential practice of political philosophy, existing scholarly traditions can be distracting as well as helpful.[3] By necessity the texts are primary, and the conversation that composes a work in political philosophy is in the first instance a conversation *with* (not merely about) the texts themselves.

Above all, in this study I have wanted to think about master-thinkers in the tradition of political philosophy by analogy with the immediacy of dialogue that often occurs between great artists – dialogue pursued as if anything else intervening in this dialogue could be filtered out as irrelevant. I have in mind, for instance, the intensity with which Eric Fischl puts his own artistic concerns in dialogue with those of Matisse.[4] Admittedly, no real dialogue between artists or thinkers can completely fulfill this conception of pure immediacy; but attempting to present the relationship between political philosophers *as if* this conception were capable of fulfillment opens up a dimension of intellectual possibility that is absent in other ways of doing political philosophy (and that the greatest practitioners of political philosophy themselves almost certainly intended at least in part to live up to).[5]

The third principle that has guided these studies in the history of political philosophy is to be especially on the lookout for tensions and paradoxes in any system of ideas, for it is at these points of tension and paradox that a thinker's deepest thoughts will most tellingly disclose themselves. If we are to be alert, wide awake, on our toes, this is where our alertness will be most required. The fourth principle is to let the texts speak for themselves (in dialogue with each other) – to chart the logic of the texts and try to penetrate the rhythms of their rhetoric without interposing my own substantive views. This does not

---

[3] The standard readings of Rousseau's civil-religion chapter that I sought to challenge in Part I provide a good example. They take an enormously rich set of philosophical *questions* and turn them into pedestrian political *answers*.

[4] "Looking at Matisse," in Robert Enright, *Peregrinations: Conversations with Contemporary Artists* (Winnipeg: Bain & Cox, 1997), pp. 340–344. Another very good example is "A Late-Night Conversation with Lucian Freud," in *Freud at Work* (New York: Knopf, 2006), pp. 11–42, which makes clear that Freud's reaction to the particular artists he loves and hates (Henry Moore, Munch, Klimt, Schiele, and Matisse) connects directly with his own self-consciousness as an artist.

[5] Again, as intimated in our Preface, Machiavelli's famous letter to Vettori of December 10, 1513, remains the exemplary image of this conception (as well as the deathbed dream of conversing with Plato in hell also cited in the Preface). In a book review of a biography of Alfred Kazin, Brian Morton discusses the biographer's criticism of Kazin to the effect that he "insists on being alone with his writers – one-on-one, writer to writer," and thereby slights the contribution of fellow critics. "Coming upon this passage, the reader may be tempted to deface the margin with a comment like 'What the hell should he be doing?' Being alone with writers is what any good critic does, what any good reader does." Morton also cites Kazin himself: "Above all, the writer does not work with anyone; he is not a collaborator, he is not cooperative." *New York Times Book Review*, Sunday, January 27, 2008, p. 16. This one on oneness, or writer to writerness, as practiced by Kazin, is not the only way of reading and doing criticism, but it should be obvious that I agree with Morton in finding it exemplary rather than deficient.

mean an airy neutrality, for of course the selection of particular authors and the highlighting of particular themes are a positive act.

The fifth principle is not to allow the intellectual agenda with respect to canonical texts to be overly dominated by questions of practical relevance or practical applicability. If we allow our philosophical inquiry to be "leashed" to the immediate preoccupations of practice, our theoretical reflections may be less intellectually productive than they ought to be. There has to be a willingness to abstract from our most urgent practical concerns (which are absolutely obvious in the case of the problem of politics and religion) if the tradition of theory is to yield its full fruit. We need to, in effect, "suspend" (not cancel out) the practical preoccupations of the moment and take a longer view, for taking the longer view is precisely the point of reflection on a tradition of political philosophy that has sustained itself for many centuries.[6] Related to this is the idea that the chief contribution of works of the canon may not necessarily consist in providing answers; a larger contribution may consist in simply raising questions, and hence promoting the intellectual liberation associated with the raising of (the right) questions. The sixth principle is always to be aware of how dangerous it was for most of these thinkers to communicate their honest thoughts on this topic, and to maintain an unbroken intellectual solidarity with them in their determination to think freely.

Let me say a bit more about the sixth principle. Books like Hobbes's *Behemoth*, Spinoza's *Theological–Political Treatise*, and Hume's *Dialogues Concerning Natural Religion* were written on the basis of the knowledge that religion is not innocent, that Christianity and the other world religions had centuries of blood on their hands – and, we can add, this culpability extends right up to our own day. Thinkers like Hobbes, Spinoza, and Hume were determined to do something about this – determined to change (through intellectual struggle) the fundamental nature of the relationship between religion and the political domain. My own view is that our first duty as intellectuals is to honor that struggle and to affirm moral and intellectual solidarity with those great enlighteners in our own thinking about religion and politics.[7] As I suggested

---

[6] I could put this point just a little more strongly. I think it undercuts what draws people into becoming political theorists if one thinks that the *only* reason for immersing oneself in the texts of the canon is to gain insights or guidance with respect to contemporary predicaments. For a good discussion, see Jeremy Waldron, "What Plato Would Allow," in *NOMOS XXXVII: Theory and Practice*, ed. Ian Shapiro and Judith Wagner DeCew (New York: New York University Press, 1995), pp. 138–178.

[7] Cf. Laurence Lampert's vindication of the Enlightenment (against Strauss) in "Strauss's Recovery of Esotericism," in *The Cambridge Companion to Leo Strauss*, ed. Steven B. Smith (Cambridge: Cambridge University Press, 2009), p. 92. George Kateb criticizes the canon of Western theory for being "for the most part . . . pious toward religious piety" – that is, for being intellectually cowardly. "The canonical theorists are all themselves heterodox in belief or unbelievers, but few until the Enlightenment admitted as much." See "The Adequacy of the Canon," in Kateb, *Patriotism and Other Mistakes* (New Haven: Yale University Press, 2006), p. 395; cf. p. 403. This is a serious accusation, but even if it is well grounded, it should perhaps heighten our admiration of those Enlightenment thinkers who set new standards for intellectual courage. One

at the end of Part II, the Number 1 objection to liberalism, humanly speaking, is its banality, its pedestrian character as a view of life. (It is very telling that Nietzsche and Marx could *agree* that liberalism offers a philosophy for shop-keepers!) However, the more one considers liberalism in relation to religion, the more one comes to appreciate the *heroic* side of liberalism: Hence it may well be that this heroic aspect of the liberal tradition in its long struggle against religious orthodoxy and clerical power represents the most powerful rejoinder to such challenges.

What should define the relationship between politics and religion? The history of political philosophy has made available three possibilities: (1) the idea that politics and religion should be kept separate (liberalism)[8]; (2) the idea that politics and religion should be joined together but governed by the supremacy of religion (theocracy); and (3) the idea that politics and religion should be joined together but governed by the supremacy of politics (civil religion).[9] At first glance, it may seem obvious that the second and third possibilities stand closer to each other than either does to the first. It has been the argument of this book, however, that on deeper examination, there is in fact a latent alliance between the third and first possibilities.[10] Needless to say, there are all kinds of complexities in this argument. For instance, according to this classification, Nietzsche (as we interpret him) deserves to be classified as a civil-religion theorist, yet there is surely no trace of liberalism in his political philosophy.[11] In any case, the attempt to uncover subterranean affinities between civil religion and liberalism – and trying to do justice to the complexities in this relationship – has, I hope, kept this enterprise interesting, and given it intellectual impetus.

What can we learn from the thinkers canvassed in our survey of modern political philosophy?[12] First, we can learn from the three civil-religion

---

can add that it is easy for Kateb to speak about the cowardice of pre-Enlightenment thinkers of the canon, but Strauss is surely right that the persecution of philosophers is not something that has been merely imagined. See *Persecution and the Art of Writing* (Chicago: University of Chicago Press, 1988), p. 33. (No less than seven of the thinkers interpreted in this book are on Strauss's list of persecuted philosophers!)

[8] Cf. Richard Vernon's account of "the typical liberal model" in *Friends, Citizens, Strangers: Essays on Where We Belong* (Toronto: University of Toronto Press, 2005), pp. 143–144.

[9] Cf. Montesquieu's encapsulation of Roman civil religion in "Dissertation sur la politique des Romains dans la religion" (*Œuvres complètes*, ed. Daniel Oster, Paris: Du Seuil, 1964, p. 39): The legislative genius of the Romans consisted in "putting the gods in submission to politics," and "fashioning religion for the sake of the state" rather than "the state for the sake of religion."

[10] Consider the striking illustration of Erastianism in practice offered by Bertrand Russell in *Why I Am Not a Christian* (New York: Simon & Schuster, 1957), p. 5: In England, belief in eternal hellfire "ceased to be an essential item because of a decision of the Privy Council, and from that decision the Archbishop of Canterbury and the Archbishop of York dissented; but in this country our religion is settled by Act of Parliament, and therefore the Privy Council was able to override their Graces and hell was no longer necessary to a Christian."

[11] Why did Nietzsche hate the Reformation much more than he hated pre-Reformation Christianity? Clue: It was not because he objected to theocratic aspects of the Reformation (for instance, in Calvinism). This tells one a lot about Nietzsche's relationship to theocracy and liberalism.

[12] Mark Lilla's good response to Charles Taylor's critique of *The Stillborn God* offers a very helpful account of how to engage these texts in a way that allows them to speak beyond their

theorists – Machiavelli, Hobbes, and Rousseau – that the state as a locus of political authority must beware of claims to authority emanating from religion. Hobbes gave the problem its most concentrated formulation when he made this statement: "Men cannot serve two Masters."[13] As Hobbes again powerfully highlights, if it comes to a supreme contest for ultimate authority, state authority is more or less guaranteed to be trumpable simply because, in principle, for believers the stakes are so much higher in the sphere of religious authority.[14] So this problem of conflicting authority must be taken very seriously indeed. It does not follow, of course, that one should therefore go the civil-religion route – that is, go so far as to *appropriate* religion, to make it a direct tool of political power (an *instrumentum regni*, in Ridolfi's phrase[15]). Religion is a perilous device in the realm of politics, and putting it to work for directly political purposes seems an extreme response to the predicament jointly identified by the three civil-religion theorists.[16] One can take seriously the civil-religion statement of the problem without embracing the civil-religion solution.

Spinoza clearly represents an important step on the road to liberalism. Nevertheless, civil religion remains sufficiently present in his theorizing that he captures very nicely the tension-ridden character of the civil-religion project. Spinoza holds to the view that politics and morality need religion – this is the

<hr />

immediate historical context. See Lilla "The rules of the game" (http://www.ssrc.org/blogs/immanent_frame/2008/02/14/the-rules-of-the-game), replying to Taylor, "Two books, oddly yoked together" (http://www.ssrc.org/blogs/immanent_frame/2008/02/two-books-oddly-yoked-together).

13 Thomas Hobbes, *Leviathan*, ed. C. B. Macpherson (London: Penguin, 1985), p. 600.

14 Thomas Hobbes, *Man and Citizen*, ed. Bernard Gert (Garden City, NY: Anchor Books, 1972), p. 357: "Neither is any man so mad, as not to choose to yield obedience rather to them who can remit and retain their sins, than to the powerfulest kings." Hobbes's formulation of the same idea in *The Elements of Law* is even more forceful: "If... kings should command one thing upon pain of death, and priests another upon pain of damnation, it would be impossible that peace and religion should stand together." Thomas Hobbes, *Human Nature and De Corpore Politico*, ed. J. C. A. Gaskin (Oxford: Oxford University Press, 1994), p. 162. David Johnston, in *The Rhetoric of Leviathan* (Princeton, NJ: Princeton University Press, 1986), p. 149, calls this "the ultimate root of Hobbes's argument." See also Pierre Bayle, *Political Writings*, ed. Sally L. Jenkinson (Cambridge: Cambridge University Press, 2000), pp. 87–88; and Montesquieu, *Spirit of the Laws*, Book 24, chapter 14: "Men who believe in the certainty of rewards in the next life are beyond the power of the legislator; they will have too much scorn for death." As I pointed out in the chapter on Adam Smith in Part II, the same line of thought is expressed by Smith: "[T]he authority of religion is superior to every other authority. The fears which it suggests conquer all other fears." See Adam Smith, *An Inquiry into the Nature and Causes of the Wealth of Nations*, ed. R. H. Campbell and A. S. Skinner (Indianapolis: Liberty Classics, 1981), Volume 2, p. 797.

15 Roberto Ridolfi, *The Life of Niccolò Machiavelli*, trans. Cecil Grayson (London: Routledge & Kegan Paul, 1963), p. 253.

16 Salman Rushdie, in an interview with Eleanor Wachtel originally aired on CBC Radio on December 14, 2008 (see http://www.cbc.ca/wordsatlarge/blog/2008/12/ salman_rushdie_speaks_with_ele.html), offers a particularly helpful example of how civil religion is a matter of playing with fire. During the Arab struggle against colonialism, secular nationalists in Egypt and North Africa embraced Islam as an instrument of liberation. This eventually boomeranged against them in the form of the Muslim Brotherhood and other theocratic movements for which Islam emphatically was not merely a political tool serving secular ends.

civil-religion side of his thought. However, he also believes that politics needs to be liberated from religion – this is the liberal side of his thought. Surely there is an evident contradiction between these two views; hence Spinoza, in his political theory, fluctuates back and forth between the civil-religion position and the liberal position. In fact, however, this same tension is present in *all* the civil-religion thinkers – Machiavelli, Hobbes, Rousseau, and even Nietzsche insofar as we identify him with a mode of civil-religion theorizing. Each of them sought to use religion for civic-moral purposes but also sought to liberate human beings from the yoke of religion. One can draw from this the negative judgment that civil religion is therefore an inherently unstable and contradictory mode of political thought, or one can cast the same idea in a much more positive light: that precisely its tension-ridden character accounts for what is so deep and intriguing in civil religion as a mode of theorizing.

Again, what can we learn from this whole extended dialogue in the history of political philosophy? The idea that any one of the thinkers covered in our study could trump all the others in intellectual authority and comprehensiveness of insight is unrealistic and intellectually irresponsible. We have to learn from all of them in different ways. We can draw insights about the political dangers of clericalism from the Hobbesian–Rousseauian teaching that clerics per se always pose a threat to civil authority.[17] Hobbes, especially, can teach us (and Hume can teach it too) that "private zeal" (*De Cive*, chapter 16)[18] is an ever-present danger in all societies subject to the political ambitions of religion. Spinoza can teach us that *nothing* can ever force conformity upon the inward freedom of the mind. Tocqueville can teach us that it *is* possible to combine liberalism and civil religion (and to some extent Montesquieu can teach this as well),

---

[17] Cf. Immanuel Kant, *Religion within the Boundaries of Mere Reason*, ed. Allen Wood and George di Giovanni (Cambridge: Cambridge University Press, 1998), p. 134, on the perennial temptation on the part of priests "to transgress into [the station] of ruler"; and p. 153, note, on "ambitious clerics." As we saw in Chapter 28, this is (rather surprisingly) a theme in Schmitt as well. What the examples of Nietzsche and Schmitt show, I guess, is that anticlericalism is not a theme unique to liberal thinkers and that one can also encounter radical anticlericalism in radically illiberal thinkers. Emile Perreau-Saussine sent me a characteristically thoughtful critical response to this book shortly before his very untimely death. In it, he made the point that whether appeal to the city of God as a higher authority is a good or bad thing depends crucially on the extent of justice or injustice in the earthly city. If we are dealing with an evil regime like Hitler's, or with racist politics in the pre-civil-rights United States, then it would be wrong not to *welcome* clerical interventions that challenge the existing political authority. This seems a perfectly fair point, and it highlights an aspect of the relation between politics and religion that perhaps is given insufficient attention in this book. At the same time, Perreau-Saussine's Augustinian argument leaves me with a lingering worry, for if these clerical interventions in the political sphere presume to represent a higher authority than merely political authority, do they not pose a challenge not just to *unjust* political authority but to political authority per se? Thus the question then becomes this: How do we avail ourselves of the sometimes salutary effects of religion in the public sphere without opening a door to theocratic politics?

[18] The illegitimacy of "Private Zeal" is also a notable theme in *Leviathan*, ed. Macpherson, pp. 723–725. In this text Hobbes champions the rule of law over "that pretence of *Jus Zelotarum*" ("a Right of Zeal").

but the combination is (for reasons elaborated throughout this book) a highly unstable one. We can learn from John Stuart Mill that providential concern for human beings can come only from the exertions of human beings and not from supernatural gods. A tough-minded conservative like James Fitzjames Stephen can help us to reflect on the extent to which religions are sustained by coercion rather than liberty. We can learn from Nietzsche that even the death of God will not put an end to the longing for grandeur and more sublime civilizational projects than any merely secular society can hope to supply. We can also learn from him that even if the currently dominant religions do not seem that humanly impressive judged by the highest cultural–political standards, it does not follow that a secular, god-emptied civilization will appear any more impressive judged by the same standards. Indeed, Nietzsche seems to assume that such a secularized civilization (achieved by watering down religion until there is nothing left) is likely to be far *less* impressive. More generally, we can learn from theocratic thinkers that there is no once-and-for-all triumph over theocracy on the part of liberal society.[19] We can learn both from "real" theocrats like Maistre and from postmodern theocrats like Nietzsche why a retheocratization of politics continues to look attractive from certain theoretically extreme points of view, and we can also learn from thinkers like Bayle that it is possible to dispense with all forms of civil religion as human beings have become capable of organizing their moral and civic life in ways that are (at least in some societies) completely independent of religion (on this, Bayle is right and Rousseau is wrong). Above all, we can learn from Montesquieu and other Enlightenment liberals not to allow even the most illuminating criticisms of liberalism to lure us into forgetting the virtues of a society that is impervious to any version of the theocratic temptation. The liberal tradition as a whole teaches us that we must not only be resolute in resisting theocratic politics but must also fend off the quasi-theocratic temptation, expressed in the civil-religion tradition from Machiavelli to Nietzsche, to found politics on a cult of Moses or a cult of Mohammed.[20]

There are two ways of interpreting the civil-religion idea in its relationship to liberalism. The first interpretation is to see it as a way of rendering politics permanently bound to religion, or as fusing the two. Seen in this way, civil religion can be construed as an intrinsically illiberal idea, because most

---

[19] Although he discusses neither Maistre nor Nietzsche and Heidegger, Mark Lilla develops essentially the same argument in *The Stillborn God: Religion, Politics, and the Modern West* (New York: Knopf, 2007); see esp. chapter 7. For some interesting (though somewhat dated) reflections on this theme of cultural backsliding, see Conor Cruise O'Brien, "Enlightenment under Threat," in *History and the Idea of Progress*, ed. A. M. Melzer, J. Weinberger, and M. R. Zinman (Ithaca, NY: Cornell University Press, 1995), pp. 155–166.

[20] Bayle's harsh rejection of Islam can be interpreted in this light: See Pierre Bayle, *Various Thoughts on the Occasion of a Comet*, § 72. This is not to say that there are not, even within the liberal tradition, considerable hesitations about relinquishing the perceived advantages of civil religion – as we saw in my discussion in Part II of Spinoza, Montesquieu, Tocqueville, and even to some extent J. S. Mill.

versions of liberalism aim to keep politics and religion separate. This is the interpretation reflected in conventional readings of Rousseau's civil religion.[21] According to the second interpretation, civil religion is intended to make religion *serviceable to* politics or citizenship – to put the former at the disposal of the latter. It is striking that in Rousseau's own account of his conversion back to Protestantism, the conversion was not religiously motivated but civically motivated, which reinforces the point that religion can serve (not dictate) citizenship.[22] Hence one can also see this second interpretation, from the civic point of view, as a *domestication* of religion, and therefore as pointing in the direction of liberalism. Liberalism merely pursues the same goal by different means (by segregating religion and politics rather than subordinating one to the other). Even if one sees Rousseau's account as straddling these two opposing ways of thinking about civil religion, it confers an open-endedness upon his civil-religion theorizing that is radically different from what is conventionally assumed about it. My approach in this work has been to see Rousseau's civil religion not as a definite solution to the problems of political life as Rousseau saw them, but rather, and more modestly, as a way of opening up a grand dialogue with Machiavelli, Hobbes, and Bayle (the three theorists Rousseau

[21] The conventional reading is expressed, for instance, in the following formulation: Rousseau rejected "the Enlightenment idea of a secular, rational state. Rousseau wished to tear down the wall between church and state that the *philosophes* had sought to erect, defending a civil religion and arguing against religious diversity modelled on ancient Sparta and Calvinist Geneva" (Graeme Garrard, *Counter-Enlightenments: From the Eighteen Century to the Present*, London: Routledge, 2006, p. 27). For another encapsulation of the conventional interpretation, see Peter Gay, "Introduction" to Jean-Jacques Rousseau, *The Basic Political Writings*, ed. and trans. Donald A. Cress (Indianapolis: Hackett, 1987), p. xvii: The "harsh set of propositions [comprising Rousseau's civil-religion doctrine] is not a casual or accidental addition to Rousseau's political thinking: it lies squarely at the heart of his earnest Calvinist commitment to virtue." For a full catalogue of versions of the conventional reading, see Terence Ball, *Reappraising Political Theory: Revisionist Studies in the History of Political Thought* (Oxford: Clarendon Press, 1995), chapter 5. Admittedly, one has to concede to the conventional reading that the idea that one should apply capital punishment to those who profess the civil faith and then do not practice it (*Basic Political Writings*, ed. Cress, p. 226) is neither an attractive nor a liberal view. Ronald Ian Boss presents this aspect of Rousseau's civil creed as the central paradox of the civil-religion chapter: Rousseau wants toleration and respect for the sanctity of conscience yet simultaneously proposes to execute those who commit themselves to the civil creed but then fall into unbelief. See Boss, "Rousseau's Civil Religion and the Meaning of Belief: An Answer to Bayle's Paradox," *Studies on Voltaire and the Eighteenth Century*, Vol. 84 (1971): 152; cf. p. 181. This most acute tension in Rousseau's theory contributes decisively to Boss's overall judgment on the philosophical failure of Rousseau's civil religion: "Unsuccessful in resolving the tension within social religion caused by combining toleration with Erastianism, he vacillated between the two" (Boss, p. 180).

[22] See Jean-Jacques Rousseau, *Confessions: The Collected Writings of Rousseau*, Volume 5, ed. C. Kelly, R. D. Masters, and P. Stillman (Lebanon, NH: University Press of New England, 1995), p. 329: Because "everything that is form and discipline in each country fell within the competence of the laws.... it followed that, *wanting to be a Citizen*, I ought to be a Protestant and return into the worship established in my country" (emphasis added).

himself explicitly addresses in his discussion of civil religion), as well as all the other theorists in the modern political philosophy tradition.

Going back to the start of our story, we saw that, in Rousseau's own view, civil religion is a hopeless project. If civil religion is a hopeless project, then it may well be that civic republicanism is a hopeless project – for, as is insisted upon within the Machiavelli-inspired republican tradition, full-bodied civic republicanism requires a civil religion. What are the other alternatives?

Locke and Maistre represent the two extremities in the problem of politics and religion – the liberal extremity and the theocratic extremity. Most other thinkers represent middle positions, that is, civil-religion positions. Consider that even Hume, in the light of Smith's debate with Hume, appears almost as a kind of civil-religion theorist insofar as he sees the attractions for social order of a hierarchical, established church. One could add that Burke too represents a middle (incoherent?) position between liberalism and theocracy. He was in strong sympathy with the moderate liberalism of Montesquieu but panicked when it looked like Enlightenment liberalism was spinning out of control – hence he tried to *resacralize* the ancien regime.[23] Tocqueville, with his superior sociological understanding, returned to the liberalism of Montesquieu.

The history of liberal responses to civil religion in this book is intended also to encompass a history of liberal responses to the civic-republican tradition. Here again Montesquieu is a key figure in this double narrative, for he was the first liberal to confront the civic-republican vision on its own terms, conceding its genuine human attractiveness as a vision of life but *not* yielding to it. (Constant, perhaps, is a successor to Montesquieu in this endeavor.) Locke never engages in a philosophical debate with civic republicanism (he has other fish to fry), and Hobbes was simply contemptuous of what he saw as civic-republican romanticism.[24]

---

[23] That there is an implicitly theocratic dimension to Burke's political philosophy becomes apparent when one notices that Burke's famous passage about "the great primaeval contract of eternal society" not only binds together past and future generations but also connects "the visible and invisible world." It would be a mistake, however, to see theocratic politics as the exclusive property of the conservative tradition. For a provocative example of contemporary leftist theocratic politics, see George Shulman, "Civil Religion, Prophecy, and Obama" (http://blogs.ssrc.org/tif/2009/06/11/civil-religion-prophecy-and-obama/), which appeals to the prophetic tradition in America to defend the politics of Rev. Jeremiah Wright. When Thomas Paine, speaking as the voice of the liberal tradition, describes theocratic politics as a "mule-animal" that illegitimately combines church and state, this can be seen as *simultaneously* a criticism of Burke and of Rousseau; see Christopher Hitchens, *Thomas Paine's Rights of Man: A Biography* (Vancouver: Douglas McIntyre, 2006), pp. 99–100. (Cf. Part I, chapter 1 of *The Age of Reason*, where Paine refers to "the adulterous connection of church and state.")

[24] Hence Hobbes's famous scorn for the civic liberty on which the citizens of Lucca prided themselves: *Leviathan*, chapter 21. In the same chapter he also blames Aristotle and Cicero for the false seductions of civic republicanism. Although he does not refer explicitly to Machiavelli, Hobbes would surely deem Machiavelli at least equally guilty of irresponsible sentimentalizing. (As Thomas Hueglin points out in *Classical Debates for the 21st Century: Rethinking Political Thought*, Peterborough, Ontario: Broadview Press, 2008, p. 99, the conception of

Although Montesquieu is on the Tocqueville side of the Rousseau–Tocqueville debate about whether Christianity can be a civil religion, Montesquieu is (to a greater extent than Tocqueville) part of the civil-religion tradition on account of his emphasis that religion is to be judged not by religious standards but by political standards. Reading Montesquieu – and to some extent also reading Tocqueville – gives one a better appreciation of the fact that civil religion and liberalism are not entirely distinct intellectual traditions: There *is* such a thing as liberal civil religion, although its existence as an intellectual possibility seems at first glance paradoxical. Nevertheless, there is an important difference of emphasis between Montesquieu and Tocqueville. Montesquieu is far closer to the core civil-religion tradition in seeking the domestication of religion, its submission to strictly civil purposes. (Tocqueville seems more concerned about revivifying religion than domesticating it.) In particular, it is by reflecting on the Montesquieu–Rousseau relationship (and grasping the extent to which Montesquieu may even have been an inspirer of Rousseau's civil-religion concerns, on a par with Machiavelli and Hobbes) that one garners the most acute appreciation of liberalism's decisive proximity to civil religion – namely in the shared aim to domesticate religion. Civil religion as a political project was certainly a misguided endeavor, but the theorists of civil religion (Machiavelli, Hobbes, and Rousseau) were far from mistaken in what *motivated* their civil-religion theorizing: deep anxiety about the radicalness of the threat that religion poses to the integrity of civic life.

Let us return once more to Rousseau: If Rousseau really does go all the way with a civic-republican vision of political community, he should be willing to embrace the "national religion" idea that Machiavelli affirms and Rousseau rejects. Rousseau wants to present himself as uncompromisingly anticosmopolitan, but he rejects civil religion because it ultimately means a people's self-affirmation as the "chosen people" of its civic gods to the exclusion of the rest of humankind. Does even Rousseau, the most strongly committed civic republican since Machiavelli, pass the civil-religion test? No.[25] Rousseau's acknowledgment of the truth of Christian universalism is also a tacit acknowledgment of the untruth, or limited truth, of his own civic-republican doctrine, and therefore it constitutes an opening wedge inserted in Rousseau's political philosophy that, if pushed sufficiently far, would explode his own civic republicanism and push him, grudgingly or ungrudgingly, into liberalism. Although Rousseau appears unreservedly to side with Machiavelli in the Machiavelli–Montesquieu debate, the problem that civil religion poses for Rousseau is, again, the philosophical wedge that, if thought through with sufficient rigor,

---

liberty attacked by Hobbes in *Leviathan*, chapter 21, on the grounds that it leads to a perverse "favouring [of] tumults" could well be read as a tacit reference to Machiavelli.)

[25] The great paradox that we encountered in our reading of Nietzsche in Part IV is that Nietzsche (although he was no civic republican), in his celebration of the "national" god of the Old Testament in *The Antichrist*, *does* pass this test! In that sense at least, Nietzsche was a more faithful Machiavellian than Rousseau was.

would eventually force Rousseau to let go of his commitment to Machiavelli and sign on to Montesquieu's affirmation of modernity.

Ultimately, Hume is the one who represents a version of liberalism at the furthest extremity from both theocracy and civil religion, because Hume is the one who believes most strongly that, in the words of Iris Murdoch, "no good comes in the end of untrue beliefs."[26] Whereas Hobbes, for instance, hates priests and thinks religion can be truly dangerous to civic life, he also thinks religion can nonetheless be domesticated for civic purposes and that civic order is perhaps impossible without this domestication and instrumentalization of religion. Hume, too, believes that banishing superstitious religion from human life is highly unlikely,[27] yet Hume is far from reconciling himself to religion sufficiently to put it to work for this-worldly purposes. Here we encounter a root-and-branch clash between liberalism and civil religion, with Hobbes on the civil-religion side and Hume on the liberal side. If Hume is right that "no good comes in the end of untrue beliefs," then civil religion is a misguided civic project. According to our interpretation in this book, civil religion means the civilizing/civicizing of religion – the domestication of religion for political purposes. If one really wants to domesticate religion, though, it seems to make more sense to go the liberal route: to more or less expel religion from the public sphere.[28]

Nonetheless, this intellectual enterprise is sustained not by the imperative to side with one thinker or set of thinkers against the others, but rather by respect bordering on reverence for this tradition of philosophical dialogue as a whole – that is, the tradition of dialogue associated with the history of political philosophy as a whole. Hobbes wrote, "if it bee well considered, the praise of

---

[26] As we saw in Chapter 22, this is a question that went to the heart of John Morley's quarrel with John Stuart Mill. In his speculations about the possible contribution to utility accruing from dubious beliefs, Mill, very much out of character, was essentially flirting with the idea of compromising one's commitment to the pursuit of truth for the sake of utility. Morley's firm position was that this was not a path any committed liberal should consider treading.

[27] One could of course say the same about Spinoza. For a good encapsulation of the pessimism of intellectual secularizers such as Hobbes, Spinoza, and Hume, see Montesquieu, *Œuvres complètes*, ed. Oster, p. 1074 (*Mes pensées*, No. 2110): "What for me proves the necessity of a revelation is the insufficiency of natural religion, considering the fear and superstition of men: because, if you were to place men today in a pure state of natural religion, tomorrow they would fall back into some manner of gross superstition." Hobbes says the same thing in *Leviathan*, chapter 12: "Powers invisible, and supernaturall . . . can never be so abolished out of humane nature, but that new Religions may againe be made to spring out of them." As David Johnston comments in *The Rhetoric of Leviathan*, p. 206, Hobbes "had little in common with the naïve optimism of the later historical Enlightenment. Even if the struggle between enlightenment and superstition were won by the forces of reason, their victory would never be so secure that their enemies could be forgotten."

[28] One could say that civil religion is what Nietzsche and Heidegger call a "half-measure" (*Halbheit*). If one really intends to domesticate religion, one should go all the way and embrace liberalism (although, as we have seen in this book, various liberals – Montesquieu, Tocqueville, even J. S. Mill, to say nothing of countless contemporary liberals – are tempted to keep religion morally and politically in play).

Ancient Authors, proceeds not from the reverence of the Dead, but from the competition, and mutuall envy of the Living."[29] If the *only* purpose achieved by this study is to persuade some readers that it is possible to participate in a dialogue with the tradition of political philosophy that proceeds "from reverence" rather than "from competition and envy," then I will be well satisfied.[30]

[29] *Leviathan*, ed. Macpherson, p. 727.
[30] Cf. *Collected Works of John Stuart Mill, Vol. 18: Essays on Politics and Society*, ed. J. M. Robson (Toronto: University of Toronto Press, 1977), p. 7.

Index